Make the Grade.
Your Atomic Dog Online Edition.

The Atomic Dog Online Edition includes proven study tools that expand and enhance your text. Reinforce and review the information you absolutely 'need to know' with features like:

- **Review Quizzes**
- Key term Assessments
- Interactive Animations and Simulations
- Notes and Information from Your Instructor
- Pop-up Glossary Terms
- A Full Text Search Engine

Ensure that you 'make the grade'. Follow your lectures, complete assignments, and take advantage of all your available study resources like the Atomic Dog Online Edition.

How to Access Your Online Edition

If you purchased this text directly from Atomic Dog ....
Visit atomicdog.com and enter your email address and password in the login box at the top-right corner of the page.

If you purchased this text NEW from another source....
Visit our Students' Page on atomicdog.com and enter the **activation key located below** to register and access your Online Edition.

If you purchased this text USED from another source....
Using the Book Activation key below you can access the Online Edition at a discounted rate. Visit our Students' Page on atomicdog.com and enter the **Book Activation Key in** the field provided to register and gain access to the Online Edition.

Be sure to download our *How to Use Your Online Edition* guide located on atomicdog.com to learn about additional features!

This key activates your online edition. Visit atomicdog.com to enter your Book Activation Key and start accessing your online resources. For more information, give us a call at (800) 310-5661 or send us an email at support@atomicdog.com

196KYPRK5

PKG

*Some online Editions do not contain all features.

CENGAGE Learning™

Criminal Justice

Criminal Justice

Eighth Edition

Sue Titus Reid, J.D., Ph.D.
Florida State University

CENGAGE
Learning™

Australia • Brazil • Japan • Korea • Mexico • Singapore • Spain • United Kingdom • United States

Criminal Justice, 8e

Sue Titus Reid

V.P. Product Development: Dreis Van Landuyt

Developmental Editor: Sarah Blasco

Custom Production Editor: Kim Fry

Technology Projec t Manager: Angela Makowski

Permissions Specialist: Todd Osborne

Marketing Specialist: Lindsay Shapiro

Manufacturing Manager: Donna M. Brown

Sr. Production Coordinator: Robin Richie

Library of Congress Control Number: 2007902466

BOOK ISBN-13: 978-1-426-62635-7
BOOK ISBN-10: 1-426-62635-5

PACKAGE ISBN-13: 978-1-426-62727-9
PACKAGE ISBN-10: 1-426-62727-0

Cengage Learning
5191 Natorp Blvd.
Mason, OH 45040
USA

Cengage Learning products are represented in Canada by Nelson Education, Ltd.

For your course and learning solutions, visit **academic.cengage.com**

Purchase any of our products at your local college store or at our preferred online store **www.ichapters.com**

Printed in the United States of America

Brief Contents

Contents

the most serious domestic problems in the United States is crime. U.S. incarceration rates are among the highest in the world, and the country faces intense problems associated with criminal activity. The concern for crime extends beyond the nature and frequency of occurrence to include official and unofficial reactions to crimes. Criminal justice systems appear inadequate to prevent crime and are questionable systems for coping with crimes that do occur.

Some react with bitter criticism of U.S. criminal justice systems but with no meaningful suggestions for improvement. Others take the law into their own hands, fight back, wounding, and in some cases, killing those who attempt to victimize them. Still others take a close look at the systems with the hope of retaining the best parts and changing those that need improvement.

The latter view is taken in this text, which also considers the interrelationships of the various parts of the system, for it is important to understand that a change in one area of a criminal justice system may and usually does have a significant impact on other areas of that system.

Significant changes were made in previous editions of this text, with the number of chapters being reduced from 18 to 14 and then to 12. These changes were made after the author used an edition with 18 chapters and discussed with adopters the difficulties she experienced in covering that much material in a traditional semester. The cost of texts was another consideration.

With the increase in size and production costs (resulting from more color and greater photography), the student's cost for purchasing criminal justice texts has escalated. Secondhand copies are expensive, too, with students receiving only a small portion of the original price for resale. In addition to the cost of the text, students have the cost of a Study Guide, should they choose to utilize one.

The publishers and author of this text decided that it is possible to write and produce a book that contains sufficient and up-to-date coverage of criminal justice issues, along with an inclusion of charts, graphs, and other study aids, while keeping the price within a more reasonable range for the average student budget. We believe that the format and coverage of this text provides an excellent alternative to the more expensive, four-color, hardbound texts.

The text retains the author's reputation for including the most recent information on topics discussed. All topics have been checked for the latest information available at the time of publication. All legal citations, including cases and statutes, have been checked to determine whether they have been altered or overruled by subsequent legislation or court decisions. Where possible, issues are illustrated with recent cases, although some older cases are presented because they are *classic* statements on the law and are still in effect or because they represent the latest U.S. Supreme Court decisions on these issues.

Along with recent scholarly research in the social sciences, this eighth edition retains the practice of using recent current events from popular sources to illustrate what is happening in criminal justice. These events are updated to the latest point in the book's publication.

Chapter Format

Each chapter begins with an overview, an outline of the chapter's content, and a list of learning objectives, which are designed to suggest to students what they should be learning during their progression through the chapter. Combined with the end-of-chapter "Apply It" questions and the "Chapter Wrap-Up," these objectives provide an excellent study guide for each chapter. Key terms are boldfaced within each chapter and defined in the margin as well as in the Glossary at the end of the text. Key terms are listed alphabetically at the end of each chapter, along with the pages on which they occur. Material within each chapter is illustrated and emphasized further by tables, figures, graphs, and "Spotlight" boxes. Each chapter also includes a "Professions" box, which will enlighten those students who are seeking a career in the criminal justice field. As mentioned earlier, each chapter closes with a detailed "Chapter Wrap-Up," followed by "Apply It" essay questions that will assist students to analyze the subjects covered in that chapter.

Organization of the Text and Important Content Changes

The text is divided into five parts. Part 1, "Introduction to Criminal Justice Systems," contains two chapters. The first, "Criminal Justice: An Overview," covers issues regarding punishment, criminal law, the concept of crime, and the purposes of criminal law. The chapter's topics are illustrated with references to the crimes of Timothy McVeigh, Dennis Rader, and the international child pornography ring. Recent U.S. Supreme Court cases are referenced, including: *Lawrence v. Texas* (concerning sodomy), *Ashcroft v. Free Speech Coalition* (concerning virtual child pornography), *Ashcroft v. American Civil Liberties Union* (concerning the Child Online Protection Act), *Reno v. American Civil Liberties Union* (concerning the Communications Decency Act of 1996), and *Gonzales v. Raich* (concerning the use of marijuana for medicinal purposes).

The recent approach of treating rather than punishing first and second nonviolent drug offenders is discussed in light of the Idaho and California statutes. The chapter contains an updated and expanded discussion of date rape and club drugs. More information on substance abuse is included. The section on fetal abuse, new in the last edition, is also updated.

Chapter 2 contains the latest official data on crime and victimization, emphasizing crimes, offenders, and victims, along with the interrelationships between the latter two. More information on the National Incident-Based Reporting System (NIBRS) is featured. This chapter's topics are illustrated by such recent cases as those of basketball player, Kobe Bryant (against whom criminal charges ultimately were dropped) and the tortuous death of Imette St. Guillen, a John Jay School of Criminal Justice graduate student.

Part 2, "Entry into Criminal Justice Systems: Policing," contains three chapters. Chapter 3, "The Emergence and Structure of Police Systems," covers the history of policing, noting some of the problems of policing at the local, state, and federal levels. Professions 3-1, concerning U.S. Marshals, is updated with a discussion of 2006 Operation FALCON II. It contains a new section on problem-oriented policing and an expanded and updated discussion of the federal COPS program, including the proposed 2008 budget. The renewal of the USA Patriot Act is noted, along with recent problems and evaluations of the Federal Bureau of Investigation (FBI). Information on the Department of Homeland Security (DHS) and the changes that resulted in other federal departments as a result of the establishment of the DHS are also discussed. The chapter closes with a new section entitled, "Police Strategies and Crime Reduction," which introduces recent programs, such as COMPSTAT, that are alleged to have been responsible for significant reductions in crime.

Chapter 4, "Policing in a Modern Society," explores the structure and function of policing, featuring additional information on the recruitment, training, and education of police. Prominently featured is a May 2006 publication of the Bureau of Justice

Statistics (BJS) concerning information on policing and police departments. Recent data on police salaries are included, while information on racial profiling is expanded.

Chapter 4 also contains discussions of several recent U.S. Supreme Court cases, such as *United States v. Grubbs* (2006, upholding anticipatory warrants) and *Georgia v. Randolph* (2006, holding that when one co-occupant refuses to permit a home search, the search is illegal even though the other occupant consented).

In Chapter 5, "Problems and Issues in Policing," the discussion of intimate partner violence, new to the previous edition, is updated and contains a graph published in 2006. A new Spotlight box explores highlights of family violence data, while the text updates the discussions of police stress and suicides. The discussion of police corruption features the New York City Police Department (NYPD), including the results of the Mayor's Commission to Combat Police Corruption and the highly publicized and controversial cases involving two former detectives, who were convicted and sentenced to life without parole, only to get a reversal of both, and then face other charges. This chapter also features new information on women and minorities in policing.

The three chapters in Part 3, "Processing a Criminal Case: Criminal Court Systems," explore the procedures and issues that arise from arrest through sentencing and appeals. Chapter 6, "Criminal Court Systems," sets the stage for this discussion with an overview of court systems. It contains numerous updates and features a new Spotlight box on the code of conduct for U.S. judges and a new figure on federal criminal case processing. A 2005 survey by the American Bar Association is also discussed.

Chapter 7, "Prosecution, Defense, and Pretrial Procedures," begins with an analysis of the role of lawyers in criminal court systems and proceeds through the pretrial procedures. It examines the roles of prosecutors and defense attorneys historically and currently, paying close attention to the modern problems of providing an adequate defense for indigent defendants. The chapter discussion of the prosecutor's role has been significantly revised, with the addition of seven subheads and inclusion of a new topic, *community prosecution*, an approach similar to that of *community policing*.

The potential for the abuse of prosecutorial discretion is illustrated with a discussion of the rape charges against three Duke University lacrosse players in the spring of 2006. The right to counsel is discussed in light of a 2006 case in which the U.S. Supreme Court faced the issue of whether the trial court can exclude admitting an out-of-state attorney chosen by the defendant (*United States v. Gonzalez-Lopez*). Spotlight 7-4 now features the American Bar Association's recent findings about the status of indigent defense services in the United States. Bail is discussed in light of the case of Mary Winkler, convicted of voluntary manslaughter in the shooting death of her husband, a Tennessee pastor. The chapter closes with updates on the treatment of enemy combatants, featuring the 2006 U.S. Supreme Court case, *Hamden v. Rumsfeld*.

Chapter 8, "Trial, Sentencing, and Appeal," describes the basic procedures involved in the trial, sentencing, and appeal phases of criminal cases. Current issues discussed in the chapter include accusations against the Duke University lacrosse players (which were subsequently dropped), the issue of the right to a speedy trial, the dropping of rape charges against basketball star Kobe Bryant when the complainant no longer wished to press charges, and the change of venue issue in the case of John Couey, convicted of raping and murdering Jessica Lunsford.

Chapter 8 also features three recent U.S. Supreme Court cases on capital punishment: *Hill v. McDonough* (regarding the use of lethal injection as a method of execution), *Kansas v. Marsh* (concerning an automatic death penalty in a capital case in which the jury finds that aggravating and mitigating circumstances are equal), and *House v. Bell* (concerning the defendant's access to a review of a capital case after all appeals have been exhausted). Figure 8-1 is a new graph on the exoneration of death row inmates by state. The chapter includes expanded and updated discussions on such topics as three strikes legislation, efforts to control sentencing, and gender and race issues in sentencing. Data on capital punishment are updated through April 2007.

Part 4, "Confinement and Corrections," consists of three chapters that examine the methods of confining offenders in total institutions or of placing them in the community under supervision. The discussion begins in Chapter 9, "The History and Structure of Confinement," with a look at the history of prisons and jails and a discussion of the federal and state prison systems. Attention is given to the problems of local jails, and the discussion of privatization of prisons and jails has been updated with a look at the impact that increased border security is having on private detention centers. The discussion of boot camps is enlarged significantly, with attention given to the boot camp closings in some states, such as Florida (and that state's new statute, the Martin Lee Anderson Act of 2006, named for an inmate who died in a boot camp), and in the federal system. A new topic discussed in this chapter is the work ethic camp. All topics and data are checked and updated through the spring of 2007.

Chapter 10, "Life in Prison," discusses inmates and correctional officers and the interaction between them. Particular attention is given to the methods of social control that involve inmates and officers. The chapter examines how inmates cope with the pains of imprisonment, and also distinguishes between the adjustments of female and male inmates. Special attention is given to AIDS and other medical issues in prisons, along with the growing problems of dealing with elderly, and physically and mentally challenged inmates. The chapter also notes the special problems of female inmates as well as of female correctional officers.

New to this edition's Chapter 10 are the following: a discussion of two recent U.S. Supreme Court cases on prison law: *Beard v. Banks*, concerning the prohibition of newspapers and other items in the most restrictive part of a prison, and *Overton v. Bazzetta*, regarding visitation privileges; recent examples of significant problems between correctional officers and prison administrators; a discussion of the Florida Department of Corrections with regard to investigations of criminal involvement of some staff; a 2006 settlement with inmates in New York City; findings and recommendations from the Commission on Safety and Abuse in America's Prisons; expanded coverage of prison gangs, including the 2006 trial of Aryan Brotherhood inmates for murder; updated data on AIDS in prison; significant new information on the care of elderly inmates, prison education programs, women in prison, children of inmates, and prison suicide. The chapter also discusses the deadly shootout in a Tallahassee, Florida, prison in June 2006.

Part 4 closes with Chapter 11, "Community Corrections, Probation, and Parole," which examines the preparation of inmates for release, problems they face upon release, and the supervision of offenders in the community. The chapter contains a section on the diversion of nonviolent drug offenders, which expands and updates information on drug courts and includes information on the California community treatment approach to nonviolent drug offenders. A look at the National Institute of Corrections' new program, Transition from Prison to the Community Initiative, underscores the importance of preparing inmates for their return to society. All data are updated, and data on recidivism are included. The discussion of electronic monitoring and global positioning systems is updated. The 2006 U.S. Supreme Court case of *People v. Sampson* highlights the issue of searching and seizing parolees. The chapter concludes with a discussion of the Adam Walsh Child Protection and Safety Act of 2006, which is expected to increase the effectiveness of law enforcement attempts to apprehend sexual pedophiles.

The final part of the text, Part 5, "Juvenile Justice: A Special Case," contains one chapter on juvenile justice systems, a special approach that was developed for the processing of juveniles who get into trouble with the law or who are in need of supervision or care because of neglectful parents or other guardians. Chapter 12, entitled "Juvenile Justice Systems," explains juvenile justice systems, contrasts those systems with adult criminal court systems, and considers the changes in juvenile justice systems that have resulted from decisions of the U.S. Supreme Court, as well as those of lower courts.

In this chapter, the information on gangs is expanded, including a new section on female gang members. More information on status offenders and how to process them is featured. The requirement of registration of juvenile sex offenders includes a discussion of the failed attempt in Illinois to relax that rule. Considerable new information on juvenile correctional facilities is included, along with U.S. Department of Justice settlements that occurred in 2006, with two state juvenile systems accused of violating the civil rights of juveniles.

Two appendices assist the reader with legal issues. Appendix A reprints selected amendments to the U.S. Constitution that are cited throughout the text. Appendix B explains the abbreviations and references that are used in legal case citations. Individual indexes assist the reader who desires quick access to names, subjects, and legal cases cited in the text.

Online and in Print

This eighth edition of *Criminal Justice* is available online as well as in print. The online version demonstrates how the interactive media components of the text enhance presentation and understanding. For example,

- Animated illustrations help clarify concepts and bring them to life.
- Clickable glossary terms provide immediate definitions of key concepts.
- References and footnotes "pop up" with a click.
- Highlighting capabilities allow students to emphasize main ideas. They can also add personal notes in the margin.
- The search function allows students to quickly locate discussions of specific topics throughout the text.
- An interactive study guide at the end of each chapter provides tools for learning, such as interactive key-term matching and the ability to review customized content in one place.

Students may choose to use just the online version of the text or both the online and print versions together. This gives them the flexibility to choose which combination of resources works best for them. To assist those who use the online and print version together, the primary heads and subheads in each chapter are numbered the same. For example, the first primary head in Chapter 1 is labeled 1-1, the second primary head in this chapter is labeled 1-2, and so on. The subheads build from the designation of their corresponding primary head: 1-1a, 1-1b, etc. This numbering system is designed to make moving between the online and print versions as seamless as possible.

Finally, next to a number of figures in the print version of the text, you will see an icon similar to the one in the margin. This icon indicates that this figure in the Online Edition is interactive in a way that applies, illustrates, or reinforces the concept.

Supplements

Atomic Dog is pleased to offer a robust suite of supplemental materials for instructors using its textbooks. These ancillaries include a Test Bank, PowerPoint® slides, and an Instructor's Manual.

The Test Bank for this book has over 800 questions, including true/false, multiple-choice, completion, and short-answer questions in a wide range of difficulty levels for each chapter. The Test Bank offers not only the correct answer for each question, but also a rationale or explanation for the correct answer and a reference—the location in the chapter where materials addressing the question content can be found.

A full set of over 200 PowerPoint slides is available for this text. This is designed to provide instructors with comprehensive visual aids for each chapter in the book. These slides include outlines of each chapter, highlighting important terms, concepts, and discussion points.

The Instructor's Manual for this book offers chapter outlines and notes, key terms and definitions, learning objectives, additional web resources, and answers to and rationales for the online Practice Quiz.

About Atomic Dog

Atomic Dog is faithfully dedicated to meeting the needs of today's faculty and students, offering a unique and clear alternative to the traditional textbook. Breaking down textbooks and study tools into their basic "atomic parts," we then recombine them and utilize rich digital media to create a "new breed" of textbook.

This blend of online content, interactive multimedia, and print creates unprecedented adaptability to meet different educational settings and individual learning styles. As part of *Cengage Learning*, we offer even greater flexibility and resources in creating a learning solution tailor-fit to your course.

Atomic Dog is loyally dedicated to our customers and our environment, adhering to three key tenets:

Focus on essential and quality content: We are proud to work with our authors to deliver a high-quality textbook at a lower cost. We focus on the essential information and resources students need and present them in an efficient but student-friendly format.

Value and choice for students: Our products are a great value and provide students with more choices in "what and how" they buy—often at savings of 30 to 40 percent less than traditional textbooks. Students who choose the Online Edition may see even greater savings compared to a print textbook. Faculty members play an important and willing role—working with us to keep costs low for their students by evaluating texts and supplementary materials online.

Reducing our environmental "paw-print": Atomic Dog is working to reduce its impact on our environment in several ways. Our textbooks and marketing materials are all printed on recycled paper. We encourage faculty to review text materials online instead of requesting a print review copy. Students who buy the Online Edition do their part by going "paperless" and eliminating the need for additional packaging or shipping. Atomic Dog will continue to explore new ways that we can reduce our "paw-print" in the environment and hope you will join us in these efforts.

Atomic Dog is dedicated to faithfully serving the needs of faculty and students—providing a learning tool that helps make the connection. We hope that after you try our texts, Atomic Dog—like other great dogs—will become your faithful companion.

Acknowledgments

Throughout my writing career, special friends and colleagues have been supportive and encouraging, and to them I give my unconditional thanks. In particular, I would like to thank David Fabianic, Professor, University of Central Florida. Dave has taught sociology and criminal justice since the 1960s, when we first became acquainted during our teaching days in Iowa. Dave is one of the two most dedicated teachers I have known; he never seems to stop preparing a new lecture or even a new course. I fully expect that when Dave is on his deathbed he will be reading another source to check for updating one of his lectures.

Also a friend and colleague since the 1960s in Iowa is Marlyn Mather, who taught with me at Cornell College. Marlyn, the other most dedicated teacher I have known, has remained a friend through all these years and has supported my writing as well as encouraged and counseled me during every important event I have experienced during almost all of the years of my teaching and writing career.

To the management and staff of our new publisher, Cengage Learning, a big thanks for your patience, kindness, efficiency, and assistance during the revision and production of the book. Editor Sarah Blasco, production manager Victoria Putman, and copy editor Mary Monner all worked tirelessly and with enthusiasm to transform my original words into a finished product.

I am deeply indebted to my friends who assist me with the logistics of traveling weekly between Portland, Maine, and Tallahassee, Florida. My beloved twin cats, "Kristina" and "Ashley," were well cared for by their nanny, Sandy Louis, who stopped by daily to provide food, water, and most of all, loving attention. Mike Wescott cared for my car as if it were a child and transported me to and from the Portland Jetport from his business. My car was always returned to me clean, warm, and without snow. Thanks, Mike, for easing one of the most difficult parts of my journey.

Finally, I want to express my appreciation to the men and women of Delta Airlines and Atlantic Southeast Airlines, who planned, executed, and navigated my way between two distant cities and got me to my destinations safely. The frustration of frequent schedule changes was eased by Donald Day, Customer Services, Atlantic Southeast Airlines. The Portland, Maine, and Tallahassee, Florida, agents handled schedule changes with efficiency and concern, even in the face of insurmountable odds of pleasing all passengers. The long hours I spent in the Atlanta airport were made enjoyable by the Delta Crown Room agents. In particular, I am grateful to Jeffrey Penzkowski, who always knew how to handle a problem, no matter how complicated it appeared to the rest of us. Jeff performed his magic in diverse, complex, and, at times, tense situations, leading me to conclude that he is a master at public relations and customer service. Many of his colleagues also assisted me in my travel, and to these special agents, a big thanks: Libby Hunt, Bruce Moniz, Michele Patrick, Norm Pawloski, and Barbara Reeves.

Almost daily emails from my college roommate, Heidi Trept van Hulst, and my friend, Chris Morales, both of whom supplied humor just when I needed it, gave me energy and determination, even on the most difficult days. The police in my New

Hampshire village provided me with a source of information and reaction to ideas. Thanks, Chief Karl F. Myers and Officer Sean Cowland, for dedicating your professional lives to policing and for sharing some of your experiences with me. Thanks also to Jerry Jacobson, general manager, and the entire staff of the Eagle Mountain House, who provided me with excellent food and service at Sunday champagne brunches, during which this manuscript was often proofread. Finally, I could not produce a book without frequent and extensive technical computer assistance. Thanks to Robin Reid for always being there to answer questions and solve problems.

Sue Titus Reid, J.D., Ph.D.
Professor and Director of the Undergraduate Program
Reubin O'Donovan Askew School of Public Administration and Policy
Florida State University

This book is dedicated to the men and women in all phases of our criminal justice systems, And to the students who aspire to joining them in dedicating their professional lives to the cause of justice.

About the Author

Sue Titus Reid, professor and director of the Undergraduate Program in the Reubin O'Donovan Askew School of Public Administration and Policy at Florida State University, Tallahassee, has taught law students, graduate students, and undergraduate students in many states. In 2000, she received a university teaching award at Florida State University. She has served on the board of the Midwest Sociological Society and the executive staff of the American Sociological Association. She has served as chairperson, associate dean, and dean. In 1985, she held the prestigious George Beto Chair in criminal justice at the Criminal Justice Center, Sam Houston State University, Huntsville, Texas.

Dr. Reid was influenced in her choice of career by her family background and early experiences in a small East Texas community. She graduated with honors from Texas Woman's University in 1960 and received graduate degrees in sociology (M.A. in 1962 and Ph.D. in 1965) from the University of Missouri–Columbia. In 1972, she graduated with distinction from the University of Iowa College of Law. She was admitted to the Iowa Bar that year and later to the District of Columbia Court of Appeals. She has been admitted to practice before the U.S. Supreme Court as well.

Dr. Reid is unique among authors in the criminal justice field because of her distinguished qualifications in both law and the social sciences. Her first major publication, *Crime and Criminology,* 1976, now in its eleventh edition, has been widely adopted throughout the United States and in foreign countries. Dr. Reid's other titles include *The Correctional System: An Introduction,* and *Criminal Law,* seventh edition. She has contributed a chapter to the *Encyclopedia of Crime and Justice,* as well as to other books, in addition to publishing scholarly articles in both law and sociology. Dr. Reid's contributions to her profession have been widely recognized nationally and abroad. In 1982, the American Society of Criminology elected her a fellow "for outstanding contributions to the field of Criminology." Other national honors include the following: Who's Who among Women; Who's Who in Criminal Law; Who's Who in American Education; 2,000 Notable Women (Hall of Fame for Outstanding Contributions to Criminal Law, 1990); Personalities of America; and Most Admired Woman of the Decade, 1992. Her international honors include International Woman of the Year, 1991–1992; International Who's Who of Intellectuals; International Order of Merit, 1993; Distinguished Alumna Award, 1979, Texas Woman's University; Who's Who in American Law; The World's Who's Who of Women; Who's Who of American Women; Who's Who in American Education; and Research Board of Advisors, American Bio. Institute, Inc. In 2002, Dr. Reid received a university teaching award from Florida State University.

Dr. Reid has traveled extensively to widen her knowledge of criminal justice systems in the United States and in other countries. In 1982, she was a member of the People-to-People Crime Prevention delegation to the People's Republic of China. Her several trips to Europe included a three-month study and lecture tour of ten countries in 1985.

Introduction to Criminal Justice Systems

Criminal justice systems throughout the world vary considerably; even within the United States, there are differences among the various state systems. The federal system has unique features, too. All criminal justice systems, however, face common issues, such as a punishment philosophy, definitions of the conduct to be included in criminal law, definitions of the elements of crimes, and crime data collection. Criminal justice professionals must decide how to respond to crime victims and how to process the accused and sanction the convicted.

Part 1 of this text features U.S. criminal justice systems. The first chapter presents an overview of the punishment philosophies on which these systems are based and explores the reality of how they work. Chapter 1 also contains an overview of criminal law, beginning with the nature and philosophical bases of punishment. It mentions the components of criminal justice systems and discusses the meaning of criminal law as compared with civil law, the sources of criminal law within the context of the adversary system, and the constitutional limits of criminal law. The concept of crime is explored in greater detail, with consideration given to the elements of crimes. The final section analyzes the reach of criminal law, looking in particular at crimes against public morality, such as sexual behavior, child pornography, and substance abuse; considering the legal use of marijuana for medicinal purposes; and finally, looking at the changing nature of criminal law that today, in some jurisdictions, characterizes as murder the killing of a fetus.

Chapter 2 discusses the methods for securing and analyzing crime and victimization data. It includes an analysis of the characteristics of offenders and of victims.

The chapters in Part 1 set the stage for the subsequent and more extensive analyses of the basic parts of criminal justice systems—police, prosecution and defense, courts, and corrections—that constitute the remainder of the text.

Criminal Justice: An Overview

The largest mass murder scene in U.S. history stunned the campus of Virginia Tech University and the nation when, on Monday morning, 16 April 2007, a lone gunman and student killed 32 students on the university's campus in Blacksburg, Virginia. Cho Seung-Hui, a quiet young man who rarely spoke to anyone, killed two people in a dormitory at approximately 7:15 A.M. and then mailed a package to NBC News. He then entered a classroom building, chained the doors, and murdered another 30 people before killing himself. He left a bitter manifesto, as well as videos in which he appeared with guns and other weapons, angry, and blaming others for his behavior.

The peace and tranquility of Oklahoma City and the nation were shattered on 19 April 1995, when a bomb ripped through the federal building, resulting in the deaths of 168 people, including children and infants. Timothy McVeigh was found guilty of those crimes and executed in June 2001. In a federal trial, Terry L. Nichols was found guilty of conspiracy and of manslaughter, but not of murder, and was sentenced to life in prison.

At the time, the Oklahoma City bombing was the most atrocious terrorist act on American soil in history, but the number of deaths and property damage were exceeded on 11 September 2001 in a series of terrorist acts. On that day, terrorists overpowered the crew of four U.S. commercial aircraft, flying two of them into the Twin Towers of the World Trade Center in New York City; another into the Pentagon in Washington, D.C.; and a fourth into a field in Shanksville, Pennsylvania. This plane was probably flying toward another target in Washington, D.C., perhaps the U.S. Capitol or the White House, but crashed after passengers attempted to stop the hijackers. Approximately 3,000 people lost their lives, the World Trade Center was demolished, the Pentagon was damaged, and untold numbers of persons lost money or jobs as a result of the economic effects of these unbelievable terrorist acts.

Numerous other shocking violent crimes have been committed in the United States in recent years. In March 2005, a shooting rampage on an Indian reservation in Red Lake, Minnesota, left 10 people dead and others injured. This was the deadliest school rampage since 15 people were killed at Columbine High School in Littleton, Colorado, in April 1999. The Red

LEARNING
OBJECTIVES

After reading this chapter, you should be able to do the following:

* **List, define, and illustrate the major punishment philosophies.**
* **Discuss the importance and impact of discretion in criminal justice systems.**
* **List and describe briefly the major components of criminal justice systems.**
* **Explain the difference between *civil law* and *criminal law*.**
* **Contrast the *inquisitory* and the *adversary* systems.**
* **Explain what is meant by constitutional limits on criminal law.**
* **List and analyze the sources of criminal law.**
* **Define *crime*, explain how crimes are classified, and discuss the meaning of the general elements of a crime.**
* **Explain criminal *defenses*.**
* **Explain the pros and cons of including sexual behavior, child pornography, and substance abuse within the reach of criminal law.**
* **Analyze the issues involved in the legal use of marijuana for medicinal purposes.**
* **Consider the legal issues involved in legislation encompassing a fetus as a person.**

Lake shootings were attributed to a loner, Jeff Weise, who killed himself in the rampage. Among the victims were Weise's grandfather and his companion.

Also in March 2005, the nation's judicial system was the focus of two violent attacks. Inside an Atlanta, Georgia, courtroom, Superior Court Judge Rowland W. Barnes and his court reporter, Julie Ann Brandau, were fatally shot. Outside the courtroom, Sergeant Hoyt Teasley was shot and killed; Cynthia Hall, a guard, was overpowered, shot, and wounded. After the suspect, Brian Nichols, 33, escaped the courthouse, he allegedly shot and killed David Wilhelm, an off-duty federal customs agent, and committed other crimes, including his final one: the kidnapping of Ashley Smith, who became a heroine when she convinced Nichols to turn himself in to authorities. Nichols was scheduled to go on trial in September 2007 at the Fulton County Courthouse in Atlanta, where the first killings occurred.

Prior to the Atlanta shootings, Judge Joan Humphrey Lefkow of the United States District Court in Chicago, found her mother, Donna Humphrey, 89, and her husband, Michael F. Lefkow, 64, dead in the Lefkow home. Both were victims of gunshot wounds. Bart A. Ross, 57, who killed himself after police stopped his car, stated in a suicide note that he was responsible for these killings.

In February 2005, law enforcement authorities arrested Dennis L. Rader, 59, in Wichita, Kansas. Rader was charged with multiple counts of first-degree murder, as evidence was said to link him with the serial killings that terrorized that city off and on for three decades. Rader, who selected for himself the initials B.T.K. (bind, torture, and kill), was an unlikely suspect. The husband, father of two, active church member, and long-time member of the community aroused no suspicion with regard to his criminal life. He was finally linked to the killings through information on a computer disk that he sent to a local television station. According to the pastor of a local church, that disk was traced to a computer in his church. The pastor recalled showing Rader, the president of the church, how to use the computer to print information concerning a church meeting over which Rader presided. Rader eventually pleaded guilty and was sentenced to 10 life prison terms. He will not be eligible for parole until he serves 175 years in prison.

Professions 1-1

Criminal Justice Careers

Most of the chapters in this text include "Professions" boxes that focus on careers. Although it is not possible to discuss all of the careers available in criminal justice or to prepare students for applying for specific jobs, exposure to job possibilities is always beneficial. This "Professions" box presents a brief overview of criminal justice careers.

Careers in criminal justice encompass a wide range of activities, from custodial services to high levels of administrative and professional positions, such as that of a U.S. Supreme Court justice. They include professions in law, psychology, criminology, sociology and other social sciences, architecture, accounting, physical sciences, and many other fields. Persons in criminal justice may be investigating criminal activities on the streets or in the labs, engaging in administrative activities in a wide variety of settings, counsel-ing adult or juvenile offenders, designing prisons or jails, supervising persons on parole or probation, training correctional officers or other personnel, supervising shop or other job assignments or training in correctional facilities, teaching college students in criminal justice, or engaging in many more kinds of activities. These and other positions require training and education ranging from a high school education and on-the-job training to a Ph.D. or a law degree, perhaps with experience.

This text will introduce you to criminal justice systems and their functions. Not all of you will become employed in the field, but even for those who do not, the information should be of general usefulness in related professions.

Enjoy your excursion through one of the most important and challenging areas of employment.

All crimes are of concern, and this text will focus on many of them. The lasting impact of the 9/11 terrorists attacks, however, will be noted where applicable, as these acts affected U.S. criminal justice systems in particular and American life in general in significant ways.

This chapter analyzes some of the issues in a **criminal justice system** regarding the imposition of punishment in criminal courts before looking briefly at the systems that impose that punishment and the criminal law on which punishment is based. Emphasis on careers is included, too, as noted in Professions 1-1.

The chapter begins with a look at the nature and meaning of punishment, along with the historical and current acceptable philosophies underlying punishment. But in reality, societies punish for other reasons, some of which are illegal. It is important to understand the reality of any criminal justice system, and this chapter looks at the wide discretion of decision making in criminal justice systems.

The chapter describes the basic components of criminal justice systems—police, prosecution, courts, and corrections. An overview of criminal law follows, with an examination of the distinction between criminal and civil law, an exploration of the adversary system, and a brief explanation of the constitutional limitations on criminal law. The sources of criminal law are mentioned briefly. The concept of crime is analyzed in terms of the ways in which crimes are classified and the basic elements of a crime. Brief attention is given to defenses to criminal allegations. The chapter contains a discussion of how far criminal law should reach in its efforts to control behavior, looking closely at the areas of sexual behavior, child pornography, and substance abuse, which some would argue constitute crimes against morality. Two relatively new areas of legal concern conclude the chapter. The first is a discussion of legalizing the use of marijuana for medicinal purposes. The second is the topic of fetal abuse, which focuses on criminalizing the use of illegal drugs by pregnant women, as well as on defining a fetus as a *person* for purposes of murder statutes.

> **Criminal justice system**
> The entire system of criminal prevention, detection, apprehension, trial, sentencing, punishment, parole, probation, or other forms of supervision within the community.

1-1 The Nature and Philosophical Bases of Punishment

A criminal justice system is designed to prevent people from violating its rules and to **sanction**, or impose legal punishments on, those who do. Issues arise, however, regarding

> **Sanction** A penalty or punishment that is imposed on a person in order to enforce the law.

Spotlight 1-1   Two Cases of Murder?

One element of all U.S. criminal justice systems is intent, but the presence of that element does not ensure a conviction in all cases that could be considered murder. Consider the following cases, both of which apparently involved an intent to kill. Do you think the crimes should be treated alike? Would the death penalty be an appropriate punishment for either or both cases?

In the first case, a young woman driving a Chevrolet Caprice along Interstate 57 in southern Cook County, Illinois, on the night of 3 June 1973 was forced off the highway by a car occupied by four men. With one of the men pointing a gun at her, she was ordered to remove her clothing and climb through a barbed-wire fence at the side of the road. Henry Brisbon Jr. responded to her pleas for her life by thrusting a shotgun into her vagina and firing. She was in agony for several minutes before her assailant fired the fatal shot at her throat.

In less than an hour, Brisbon had committed two more murders. Brisbon's next victims, also riding in their car along Interstate 57, were planning to be married in six months. When they pleaded that their lives be spared, Brisbon told them to lie on the ground and "kiss your last kiss," after which he shot each in the back. Brisbon took $54 in cash, two watches, an engagement ring, and a wedding band from his victims. He was arrested and convicted of these crimes, but because the death penalty in Illinois had been invalidated, he was given a term of 1,000 to 3,000 years. While serving that term, he killed an inmate and was sentenced to death under the state's new death penalty statute.

During an earlier incarceration, Brisbon had been involved in 15 attacks on guards and inmates and responsible for beginning at least one prison riot. He had hit a warden with a broom handle and crashed a courtroom during a trial. Despite these acts of violence, Brisbon said, "I'm no bad dude…just an antisocial individual." He blamed his problems on the strict upbringing by his Muslim father, who taught him to dislike white people—the result: "I didn't like nobody." How did he feel about his victims? "All this talk about victims' rights and restitution gets me. What about my family? I'm a victim of a crooked criminal system. Isn't my family entitled to something?"[1]

How should Illinois have reacted to the crimes of Henry Brisbon? At the trial that resulted in his death sentence, the prosecutor described Brisbon as "a very, very terrible human being, a walking testimonial for the death penalty." The attorney who prosecuted him for the Interstate 57 murders said, "On the day he dies…I plan to be there to see that it's done. Nobody I've heard of deserves the death penalty more than Henry Brisbon."[2]

Brisbon remains on death row in Illinois. In February 2003, noted lawyer and best-selling novelist Scott Turow was interviewed on National Public Radio (NPR) about the death penalty and specifically about Brisbon. Turow had just published *Reversible Errors*, his novel about a lawyer who was trying to free a man facing imminent execution. Turow had visited Brisbon in the supermax prison in Thames, Illinois. According to Turow,

> Henry Brisbon tends to be the poster child for capital punishment in Illinois….in addition to having been convicted twice of murder,…he's got an atrocious disciplinary record, over 250 disciplinary incidents, many of them involving…serious acts of alleged violence.[3]

Turow pointed out that such dangerous persons as Brisbon evoke little if any sympathy but that it is the most atrocious cases that are most likely to produce mistakes in prosecution, leading to the conviction of the innocent. This is because of the enormous public pressure on law enforcement officials to obtain convictions in these cases. In Turow's judgment, the supermax prisons, such as the one in which Brisbon is incarcerated, are sufficiently secure to mitigate the possibility that he will kill again.[4]

In contrast to the case of Brisbon is that of Hans Florian. In March 1983, Florian, age 79, went to the hospital to visit his wife of 51 years, who was suffering from a disease that eventually would make her senile and helpless. Florian had placed his wife in a nursing home because he was unable to care for her, but when she became too ill for that facility, she was hospitalized. Florian visited his ailing wife daily. On each visit, he placed her in a wheelchair and pushed her around the floor of the hospital to give her a change of scenery. On the day in question, he wheeled her into a stairwell and shot her in the head, ending her life quickly. Friends claimed that Florian was not a murderer. He killed his wife because he loved her so much that he wanted her to be free of her suffering.[5]

Florian was charged with first-degree murder. Should he have been convicted of that charge? Apparently, his act was premeditated and without legal justification. If convicted, should he have been sentenced to death?

1. "An Eye for an Eye," *Time* (24 January 1983), p. 30.
2. Ibid.
3. "Scott Turow Discusses the Death Penalty," Show: *Fresh Air* (National Public Radio, 18 February 2003), 12 noon.
4. Ibid.
5. "When Is Killing Not a Crime?" *Washington Post* (14 April 1983), p. 23.

---

the behavior that should be covered by **criminal** punishments, who should be sanctioned, and which sanctions should be applied. These issues are discussed in various chapters throughout the text, but at this point, we look at the philosophical bases for punishment.

Consider the two cases described in Spotlight 1-1. Most people have no difficulty contrasting the cases of Henry Brisbon and Hans Florian, in view of the number and

▶ **Criminal** A person found guilty of an act that violates criminal law.

nature of the killings Brisbon committed. But a case can be made that the legal elements of first-degree murder were present in both cases. Brisbon remains on death row in Illinois and may never be executed, due to the moratorium on executions announced by Illinois Governor George Ryan in 2000 and continued in 2003 by his successor.

In the second case mentioned in Spotlight 1-1, that of Hans Florian, the grand jury refused to indict. Similar cases have, however, resulted in indictments, trials, convictions, and incarcerations. For example, consider another case that received national media attention. In 1990, Florida officials approved the release from prison of Roswell Gilbert, age 81, who was incarcerated for murdering his ailing wife in what he called a mercy killing. Gilbert was convicted of first-degree murder and sentenced to 25 years to life in prison. He served several years before his release for health reasons. Should Gilbert have been convicted of first-degree murder on facts similar to those of Florian and others? All these persons claimed that they acted out of love when they killed their terminally ill spouses, who begged to be relieved of their suffering. If Gilbert deserved to serve time in prison, why should he have been released for medical reasons?[1] Gilbert died in 1994.

These cases may be analyzed in terms of four objectives recognized historically as bases for punishment: **incapacitation**, **retribution**, **rehabilitation**, and **deterrence**. These objectives are defined and analyzed in historical perspective in Spotlight 1-2, which also mentions other factors that might be considered in punishment. The debate over which of these objectives ought to be the basis for punishment continues. The main punishment philosophies in vogue in the past century were rehabilitation and deterrence, with the former dominating the scene until recently and the latter the dominant philosophy today. Both continue to influence legislation and court decisions.

Rehabilitation has been described as the rehabilitative ideal, which is based on the premise that human behavior is the result of antecedent causes that may be known by objective analysis and permit scientific control. The assumption is that the offender should be treated, not punished. In the mid-1900s, social scientists endorsed the rehabilitative ideal and began developing treatment programs for institutionalized inmates. The ideal was incorporated into some statutes, proclaimed by courts, and supported by presidential crime commissions.

The demise of the rehabilitative ideal was emphasized in a 1982 magazine headline: "What Are Prisons For? No Longer Rehabilitation, but to Punish and to Lock the Worst Away." The article referred briefly to the original purpose of U.S. prisons: not only to punish but also to transform criminals "from idlers and hooligans into good, industrious citizens." It concluded, however, that

> no other country was so seduced for so long by that ambitious charter. The language, ever malleable, conformed to the ideal: when a monkish salvation was expected of inmates, prisons became penitentiaries, then reformatories, correctional centers and rehabilitation facilities.[2]

The simple fact is that prisons did not work as intended. The result was a movement toward more severe and definite sentences. California, a state that used the rehabilitation philosophy, led the way in returning to a punitive philosophy by declaring in its statutory changes in 1976 (to become effective the following year) that "the purpose of imprisonment for crime is punishment."[3] Likewise, the U.S. Congress eliminated rehabilitation as a goal in the federal system.[4]

Recent evidence, however, suggests a movement back to rehabilitation. Since 2001, California law has provided for treatment rather than incarceration for nonviolent drug offenders convicted of first or second offenses, and Idaho provides for treatment rather than criminal prosecution for some cases of substance abuse in order that those persons "may lead normal lives as productive members of society."[5]

The second and more recognized punishment philosophy in vogue today is *deterrence*. Deterrence is based on the assumption that, if punishments are unpleasant or severe enough, people will not engage in criminal behavior. This philosophy is one of

Incapacitation
A punishment theory usually implemented by imprisoning an offender to prevent the commission of any other crimes by that person. In some countries (and in earlier days in the United States), incapacitation involved mutilation, such as removing the hands of thieves and castrating sex offenders.

Retribution *See* **Just deserts**.

Rehabilitation
A punishment philosophy based on the belief that the offender can and will change into a law-abiding citizen through treatment programs and facilities. Rehabilitation may be most likely to occur in community-based programs rather than during incarceration in penal institutions. The *rehabilitative ideal* is embodied in probation, parole, the indeterminate sentence, and the juvenile court.

Deterrence A punishment philosophy based on the assumption that the acts of potential offenders can be prevented. *Individual deterrence* refers to the prevention of additional criminal acts by the specific individual being punished. *General deterrence* refers to the presumed effect that punishing one offender will have on other potential offenders.

Spotlight 1-2 Punishment Philosophies

1. *Incapacitation of the offender.* In the past, corporal punishment involved incapacitating the offender by making it impossible for him or her to commit further offenses of a like nature. The hands of a thief were cut off; the eyes of a spy were gouged; rapists were castrated; prostitutes were disfigured to make them unattractive. Another form of incapacitation in earlier days was to brand the offender with a letter symbolizing the crime; thus, an adulteress was branded with the letter *A*. The assumption was that, if people knew the nature of this person's criminal activity, they would avoid him or her. In modern times, incapacitation has been accomplished primarily through incarceration.

2. *Retribution.* Historically, revenge has been one of the most important justifications for punishment. The philosophy of revenge, or retribution, is the eye-for-an-eye doctrine, which can be traced back for centuries.

   Not only was revenge acceptable, but it was expected. The victim (or the victim's family) was expected to avenge the offender. Private revenge was replaced by official government punishment, and today the philosophy of revenge has been replaced by that of retribution, which is widely recognized as an appropriate reason for punishment. The earlier eye-for-an-eye approach is not recognized legally today, but the U.S. Supreme Court has approved retribution as a basis for punishment.[1]

3. *Rehabilitation.* For years the rehabilitation philosophy dominated U.S. criminal justice policies. It is based on the belief that offenders can be changed through proper treatment and care. Some can be rehabilitated outside institutions; others may require confinement for this goal to be accomplished. Rehabilitation through treatment is seeing a comeback in some jurisdictions today, as subsequent discussions of drug abuse will show.

4. *Protection of society: deterrence theory.* Deterrence implies that punishment is imposed to keep people from victimizing others. *Individual deterrence* refers to preventing the apprehended offender from committing criminal acts. *General deterrence* assumes that punishing that offender will keep others from engaging in criminal acts because potential offenders will refrain from criminal behavior after seeing the punishment imposed on actual offenders.

5. *Preservation of social solidarity.* It has been suggested that the only justification for punishment is that it upholds society's norms and prevents private revenge. According to sociologist Émile Durkheim, the true function of punishment "is to maintain social cohesion intact."[2] Thus, punishment may reinforce the morals of society and bind its members closer together in their fight against offenders.

6. *Reparation or restitution.* The reparation or restitution approach to punishment assumes that the victim should be returned to his or her former position. This approach has been used mainly in civil cases but recently has become more acceptable in criminal cases. Although injured persons (or the family of a deceased individual) may not be restored to their former positions by money, a financial contribution from offenders (or from society) eases the burdens caused by the crime. This type of punishment is more workable when victims have suffered crimes against property.

1. See *Gregg v. Georgia*, 428 U.S. 153 (1976).
2. Émile Durkheim, *The Division of Labor in Society* (New York: Free Press, 1984), p. 108.

the main justifications for punishment in U.S. criminal justice systems. There are two types of deterrence: individual (or specific) and general. **Individual deterrence** refers to the effect of punishment in preventing a particular individual from committing additional crimes. In the past, this form of deterrence often involved incapacitation, or taking actions to make it impossible for a particular offender to repeat the crime for which he or she had been convicted. Today, incapacitation usually takes the form of incarceration (or milder forms of restraint, such as house arrest) or capital punishment. In recent years, however, attempts have been made to use more traditional methods of incapacitation, such as the **castration** of sex offenders.

In Texas, for example, there has been a movement to castrate inmate Larry Don McQuay, a convicted pedophile, but legal and other problems have prevented that, even though McQuay has asked to be castrated. In California, however, a statute that took effect in 1997 was the first to provide for chemical castration for repeat child sexual offenders. Under this statute, persons who are convicted of a second offense against a child under the age of 13 must undergo weekly injections of Depo-Provera, a drug that reduces sexual desire. It is doubtful that a statute providing for involuntary surgical

▶ **Individual deterrence** *See* **Deterrence**.

▶ **Castration** Removal of the testes in the male or the ovaries in the female. In earlier times, castration was used as a punishment for male rape offenders. In recent times, some courts have ordered chemical castration of sex offenders. This process involves using female hormones to alter the male's chemical balance to reduce his sex drive and potency.

General deterrence *See* **deterrence**.

Just deserts The belief that those who commit crimes should suffer for those crimes. Also, the amount or type of punishment a particular offender deserves to receive.

castration of sex offenders would survive constitutional challenges, although the California statute provides that those offenders for whom the law prescribes mandatory chemical castration may *choose* surgical castration instead.[6]

The second type of deterrence, **general deterrence**, is based on the assumption that punishing individuals convicted of crimes will set an example for potential violators, who, being rational people and wishing to avoid such pain, will not violate the law. Pro and con opinions as to whether this is the case may be based on conjecture, faith, or emotion, with little significant empirical data. This approach leads to dogmatic statements, which cloud the issues and should be examined carefully.

A third punishment philosophy in vogue today is the justice approach, or the **just deserts** model. It is based on two philosophies, deterrence and retribution, and constitutes a reaction against the perceived ineffectiveness of rehabilitation.[7] The retribution basis assumes that offenders will be assessed the punishment they deserve in light of the crimes they have committed. It presumes that appropriate punishments will deter those criminals from engaging in further criminal acts and deter others from committing crimes.

Under the justice model, an incarcerated person should be allowed to choose whether to participate in rehabilitation programs. The only purpose of incarceration is to confine for a specified period of time, not to rehabilitate the criminal. The offender receives only the sentence he or she deserves, and that sentence is implemented according to fair principles.

The justice model sounds good. People should be punished in accordance with what they deserve. But try applying it to the cases discussed in Spotlight 1-1 and the accompanying text. Which, if any, of the offenders *deserve* to be executed? If Brisbon is not executed, will more people commit atrocious murders such as those he committed? If he is executed, will people who contemplate such murders refrain from them? How about mercy killing? Did incarcerating a Florida mercy killer deter others from such acts? Would incarceration have deterred Florian from committing that offense again, or was imprisonment unnecessary for specific deterrence in his case? Or is it possible that, regardless of the stated underlying punishment philosophies accepted by a society, the reality is that particular decisions are sometimes made for other reasons? Is it also possible that reactions to crime are due to other reasons, such as politics?

1-2 The Role of Discretion in Punishment

It is characteristic of criminal justice systems throughout the world that decisions may be made for political reasons that have little, if anything, to do with the issues. A large body of scholarship has developed in an attempt to explain criminal justice systems as an area where critical decisions are made by those in power for the purpose of maintaining control over those not in power. It is alleged, for example, that in the United States women, minorities, and the poor can expect the blunt end of justice, whereas white men make most of the important decisions legislatively, administratively, and judicially.

Others disagree with this position, and the conflict may be expected to continue. But as long as **discretion** is possible, decisions may be made for political reasons. *Discretion* means that individuals may use their own judgment to make decisions. The text discussion of Spotlight 1-1 provides examples of the exercise of discretion. Hans Florian was not tried for the murder of his wife, but Roswell Gilbert, who took his wife's life under similar circumstances, was convicted and served prison time. The jury could have chosen not to convict him, as has been the case in other so-called mercy killings. Thus, the jury had considerable discretion. In Gilbert's case, the governor exercised his discretion in releasing Gilbert before the completion of his sentence.

Various persons within criminal justice systems, including police, prosecutors, judges or justices, correctional officials, and paroling authorities, may exercise discretion. In addition, defense attorneys exercise discretion in determining which defenses to advance at trial. Defense attorneys and prosecutors exercise discretion in plea bargaining.

Discretion In the criminal justice system, authority to make decisions based on one's own judgment rather than on specified rules. The result may be inconsistent handling of offenders, as well as positive actions tailored to individual circumstances.

Discretion is inevitable within criminal justice systems, although the degree to which it is permitted varies. Discretion may be abused, but it is not necessarily a negative aspect of the system. It is possible to establish guidelines for the exercise of discretion, but it is not possible to eliminate all discretion. In addition, attempts to abolish discretion in one area of the system may increase it in others. Thus, for example, if longer sentences are instituted to control crime but juries perceive these sentences as being too harsh, juries might acquit rather than convict persons believed to be guilty. In such cases, the system would have no alternative but to free the accused. On the other hand, conviction of more offenders with longer sentences has clogged courts and prisons, creating serious overcrowding problems in both areas.

1-3 Components of Criminal Justice Systems

Criminal justice systems are composed of several components and processes, and they differ throughout the world. Figure 1-1 diagrams the most common model in the United States, although states organize and operate their systems in different ways. The federal system also has some unique features. The various criminal justice systems have many common features, which are emphasized throughout this text.

In the United States, the most common organization of criminal justice systems consists of four institutions: police, prosecution, courts, and corrections (noted at the top of Figure 1-1). The different stages are discussed in more detail where appropriate throughout the text.

A case may enter the system when a crime is reported to the police or when police observe behavior that appears to be criminal. After a crime has been reported, police may conduct a preliminary investigation to determine whether there is sufficient evidence that a crime was committed. If so and the suspect is a juvenile, he or she may be processed through the juvenile rather than the adult division of the system.

Not all arrested suspects proceed to the end of the criminal justice system. In fact, most cases do not go that far for a number of reasons. Police may decide that no crime has been committed or that a crime has been committed but that there is not enough evidence on which to arrest a suspect. A suspect may be arrested but released quickly for lack of evidence. Persons who remain suspects through booking, the initial appearance, and the preliminary hearing may be dismissed, or the charges may be dropped at any of those stages. These decisions may be made for lack of evidence or other reasons, some of them highly controversial, such as political pressures. Even after formal charges have been made against the accused, they may be dropped or reduced.

Suspects who proceed to trial may not be convicted. Despite strong evidence against them, they may be acquitted. They may be convicted but placed on probation, fined, or sentenced to work in the community in place of being sent to prison. Those sent to prison may not serve their full terms.

Criminal justice systems are a process as well as a set of stages, and many factors affect how a suspect experiences the system. Those factors are considered throughout the text, but first, we look at the basis of criminal justice systems—criminal law.

1-4 Criminal Law: An Overview

This overview of criminal law begins with the differences between civil and criminal law. Criminal and civil law, however, are not always distinguishable; in some instances, they overlap.

1-4a Criminal and Civil Law Distinguished

Criminal law may be defined by contrasting it with **civil law**, which pertains to private rights. Criminal laws provide the basis for the actions that take place in criminal justice systems. They define acts that are so threatening to society (not just to the individual

▶ **Criminal law** Statutes defining acts so offensive that they threaten the well-being of society and require that the government prosecute the accused. Criminal laws prescribe punishments that may be imposed on offenders.

▶ **Civil law** Distinguished from criminal law as that law pertaining to private rights.

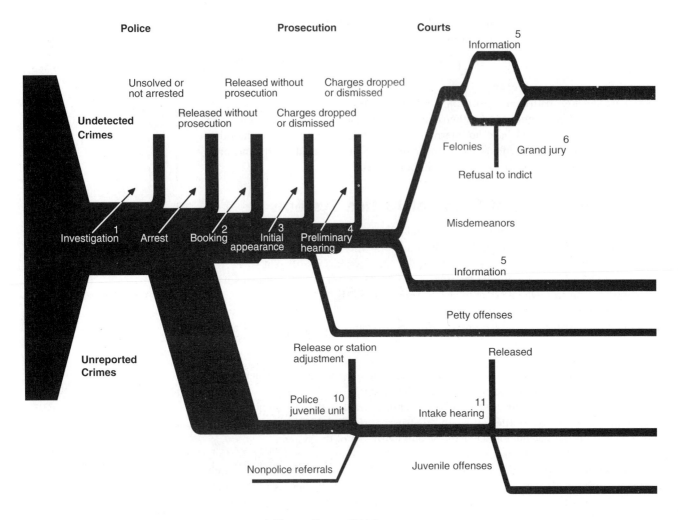

1. May continue until trial.
2. Administrative record of arrest. First step at which temporary release on bail may be available.
3. Before magistrate, commissioner, and justice of the peace. Formal notice of charge, advice of rights. Bail set. Summary trials for petty offenses usually conducted here without further processing.
4. Preliminary testing of evidence against defendant. Charge may be reduced. No separate preliminary hearing for misdemeanors in some systems.
5. Charge filed by prosecutor on basis of information submitted by police or citizens. Alternative to grand jury indictment; often used in felonies, almost always in misdemeanors.
6. Review whether government evidence sufficient to justify trial. Some states have no grand jury system; others seldom use it.

Figure 1-1

Institutions and Stages in American Criminal Justice Systems

Source: President's Commission on Law Enforcement and Administration of Justice, *The Challenge of Crime in a Free Society* (Washington, D.C.: U.S. Government Printing Office, 1967), pp. 8–9.

victim) that they require that the government prosecute offenders. They define punishments that may be imposed on offenders.

Civil laws provide a vehicle for legal redress for those who are harmed by others. They are used to uphold certain institutions, such as the family. Civil laws regulate marriage and divorce or dissolution, the handling of dependent and neglected children, and the inheritance of property. They protect legal and political systems, organize power relationships, and establish who is superordinate and who is subordinate in given situations.

Civil and criminal cases are governed by different procedural rules; there are differences in the evidence that may be presented and in the extent of proof needed to win the case. Whether the action is civil or criminal may determine the type of court in

7. Appearance for plea; defendant elects trial by judge or jury (if available); counsel for indigent usually appointed here in felonies. Often not at all in other cases.
8. Charge may be reduced at any time prior to trial in return for plea of guilty or for other reasons.
9. Challenge on constitutional grounds to legality of detention. May be sought at any point in process.
10. Police often hold informal hearings, dismiss or adjust many cases without further processing.
11. Probation officer decides desirability of further court action.
12. Welfare agency, social services, counseling, medical care, etc. for cases where adjudicatory handling not needed.

which the trial is held. In some cases, the act may not be considered a crime the first time it occurs. For example, a first offense for driving while intoxicated is considered a traffic violation and not a crime in some jurisdictions, but a second or third offense may be a crime. And the first offense might be considered a crime if it results in a death.

The distinction between a civil and a criminal violation is important. The repercussions of being accused of violating a criminal law are more serious than those of violating a civil law. In addition to the possibility of a prison sentence, persons accused of a crime may expect social repercussions, even if they are acquitted. Some people lose their jobs as soon as they are charged with a crime, particularly when it involves sexual offenses. Criminal law should not be taken lightly, and the term *criminal* should be used only in referring to people who have been convicted of a *criminal* offense.

Because of the serious impact of a criminal conviction, the law provides greater safeguards for those accused of crimes than for those facing civil suits. The most important safeguards are embodied in the concept of the adversary system.

1-4b   The Adversary System

U.S. criminal justice systems are **adversary systems**, in contrast to the **inquisitory system** characteristic of some other countries. The two approaches may be distinguished in several ways. The adversary approach presumes that the accused are innocent. They do not have to prove their innocence; that burden lies with the state (or the federal government if it is a federal trial). In contrast, the inquisitory system presumes guilt, and the accused must prove that they are innocent. This difference between the two approaches is related to another basic contrast: the inquisitory approach places a greater emphasis on conviction than on the *process* by which that conviction is secured.

The adversary approach requires following proper procedures designed to protect the rights of the accused. Those procedures are guided by two important principles: **due process** and **equal protection**, concepts considered necessary to create a system in which the accused has a fair chance against the tremendous powers of the prosecutor and the resources of the state. Theoretically, the protections prevent the prosecutor from obtaining a guilty verdict for an innocent defendant. In reality, justice does not always prevail.

The impossibility of explaining exactly what is meant by the concept of due process is illustrated by the comment of a former U.S. Supreme Court justice, who said that due process "cannot be imprisoned within the treacherous limits of any formula. 'Due process' is not a mechanical instrument. It is not a yardstick. It is a process."[8]

The basis for the right to due process and equal protection comes from the Fourteenth Amendment to the Constitution (see Appendix A), which guarantees that we shall not be deprived "of life, liberty, or property, without due process of law." Nor can we be denied "the equal protection of the laws." The U.S. Supreme Court has decided numerous cases in which it has been argued that the due process or equal protection rights of individuals have been violated. It would take an extensive course in constitutional law to explore these concepts adequately, but we can look at them briefly. They are explained in more detail where relevant in subsequent chapters.

The concept of due process means that those who are accused of crimes and who are processed through a criminal justice system must be given the basic rights guaranteed by the U.S. Constitution. For example, defendants may not be subjected to unreasonable searches and seizures. When questioned by police about acts that, upon conviction, may involve a jail or prison term, they do not have to answer until they have an attorney. If they do not wish to talk then, they may remain silent. If they cannot afford an attorney, the state must provide one for them. They do not have to testify against themselves at trial. Certain rules of evidence must be followed during the trial.

Defendants may not be tried twice for the same offense; once a judge or jury has decided that the defendant is not guilty, the state (or federal government) may not bring the same charges again in an effort to wear down the accused. In short, the state must conduct the criminal trial and the processes preceding, during, and following that trial by the rules embodied in the U.S. Constitution, as interpreted by the U.S. Supreme Court, and according to the established procedural statutes of the relevant jurisdiction. State trials must also follow the procedural safeguards established by their respective state constitutions and legislatures, as interpreted by their state courts.

The equal protection clause of the Fourteenth Amendment is also the focus of frequent lawsuits. That clause means that, in general, the government may not infringe on the rights of persons solely because of characteristics such as race, age, national origin,

▶ **Adversary systems**   One of two primary systems for settling disputes in court. The accused is presumed to be innocent. A defense attorney and a prosecuting attorney attempt to convince a judge or a jury of their versions of the case. *See also* **Inquisitory system**.

▶ **Inquisitory system**   One of two primary systems for settling disputes in court, in which defendants must prove their innocence, in contrast to the adversary system, which has a presumption of innocence, requiring the state (or federal prosecutors in federal cases) to prove a defendant's guilt beyond a reasonable doubt.

▶ **Due process**   The constitutional principle that a person should not be deprived of life, liberty, or property without reasonable and lawful procedures that must be made available in any criminal proceeding, including postconviction procedures, such as prison disciplinary hearings or parole revocations.

▶ **Equal protection**   All persons under like circumstances must receive essentially the same treatment in the criminal justice system; they may not be discriminated against because of race or ethnicity, gender, minority status, disability, or religion.

ethnicity, religion, or gender. Some jurisdictions have added disability and sexual orientation by statute, constitutional amendment, or judicial decision.

1-4c Constitutional Limitations on Criminal Law

The adversary model comes under attack frequently. Critics assert that it hinders law enforcement and, consequently, crime prevention and control. There is no question that observation of defendants' due process and equal protection rights creates obstacles for law enforcement. If authorities could accuse anyone of a crime regardless of available evidence, search and seize at will, interrogate suspects for unlimited periods of time when those suspects do not have an attorney, coerce confessions physically and psychologically, and so on, there could be more convictions, but the resulting loss of individual freedom and liberty would not be tolerable in U.S. criminal justice systems.

In addition to the constitutional limits of due process and equal protection, state legislatures and Congress are limited by the federal Constitution (and interpretations of that document by lower federal courts and the U.S. Supreme Court) in how they may define criminal law. They are also limited in criminal procedures. Throughout the text, these limitations are discussed wherever relevant, but a few that are of importance to a general understanding of criminal law are noted here.

Criminal laws cannot be vague or too broad. Laws may not specify everything that is prohibited; they must be flexible. However, to avoid being held unconstitutional due to vagueness, laws must meet three criteria: (1) they must give notice or warning to all who are subject to them; (2) they must protect against arbitrary and discriminatory enforcement; and (3) they must not unreasonably deny other rights, such as the First Amendment rights to free speech, religion, and so on (see Appendix A). With regard to breadth, a statute should not "sweep within its ambit other activities that constitute an exercise" of other constitutional rights.[9]

Another constitutional limitation of particular importance in criminal justice is that of the Eighth Amendment's prohibition against **cruel and unusual punishment** (see Appendix A). The issue arises frequently in capital punishment cases, and although the U.S. Supreme Court has ruled that capital punishment per se is not unconstitutional, it may be so if applied arbitrarily and capriciously.

The conflict between the legitimate concern of governments to maintain peace and control and the rights of citizens to be free of unreasonable governmental interference may be expected to continue.

1-5 Sources of Criminal Law

Although many people think of law as those provisions written in the statute books after passage by legislatures, laws come from three sources: constitutions, statutes, and court decisions. State legislatures enact statutes that apply to actions in their respective states. Congress enacts statutes that apply to the federal government as well as to the District of Columbia. These statutes are called **statutory law**. They apply only to the **jurisdiction** in which they are passed, with the exception that no state may enforce statutes conflicting with the rights guaranteed by the U.S. Constitution. That document and state constitutions are also sources of law.

Some statutes define the procedures that are appropriate for law enforcement. These are called *procedural laws*. Others define the elements that are necessary for an act to constitute a violation of the civil or criminal law. They are called *substantive laws*. For example, a statute may define *murder* as the killing by one human being of another with malice aforethought. Convicting a person under that statute requires proof of these elements: that a person was killed, that the person was killed by the accused, and that the killing involved malice aforethought.

What does *malice aforethought* mean? It refers to the requirement of an intent to kill and the absence of any legal justification for that killing. But if the statute does not

---

Cruel and unusual punishment The punishments prohibited by the Eighth Amendment to the U.S. Constitution, as interpreted by the courts. Some examples are torture, prison conditions that "shock the conscience," excessively long sentences, and the death penalty for rape but not murder of an adult woman.

Statutory law Law that the legislature has originated and passed by a written enactment.

Jurisdiction The lawful exercise of authority. The area within which authority may be exercised, such as the geographical area within which a particular police force has authority. Courts may have *original jurisdiction* to hear a case. If more than one court has authority to hear the same case, those courts have *concurrent jurisdiction*. *Exclusive jurisdiction* means that only one court may hear the case. *Appellate jurisdiction* is the power of a court to hear a case on appeal.

▶ **Case law**   Legally binding court interpretations of written laws or rules made by the courts. *See also* **Common law**.

▶ **Common law**   Broadly defined, the legal theory and law that originated in England and is also common in the United States. More specifically, common law consists of the guidelines, customs, traditions, and judicial decisions that courts use in decision making. It is contrasted with *constitutions* and *written laws*.

▶ **Administrative law**   Rules and regulations made by agencies to which power has been delegated by a state legislature or by the U.S. Congress. Administrative agencies investigate and decide cases concerning potential violations of these rules.

▶ **Crime**   An illegal act of omission or commission that is punishable by criminal law.

▶ **Misdemeanor**   A less serious offense, punishable by a fine, probation, or a short jail term, in contrast to a felony, a more serious crime.

▶ **Felony**   A serious offense, such as murder, armed robbery, or rape. Punishment ranges from execution to imprisonment in a state or federal institution but also includes probation, community work service, fines, and other less punitive sanctions, as well as a combination of these measures.

define that element, then court decisions, another source of law, may be used for a definition. Law that comes from court decisions is called **case law**. Much U.S. case law is derived from or influenced by **common law**, which consists of those customs, traditions, judicial decisions, and other materials that guide courts in decision making but that have not been enacted by legislatures into statutes or embodied in the U.S. Constitution.

The common law developed in England after the Norman Conquest in 1066. Previously, there had been no distinction among law, custom, religion, and morality. Decisions could vary in different communities. The Normans wanted to establish some unity, so the king employed representatives to travel to the various jurisdictions. These representatives kept the king informed about the various decisions and carried news to each jurisdiction of what was happening in the others. "The result of all this was that the legal principles being applied began to be similar, or common, in all parts of England. Thus, the terms 'Common Law of England,' and 'Common Law.'"[10] English common law has had a significant impact in the United States.

Another source that is important to an understanding of criminal law is **administrative law**. State legislatures and Congress delegate rule-making power to state and federal agencies. For example, prison officials are given authority to make rules that regulate the daily operations of their institutions; the Federal Bureau of Investigation (FBI) is granted power to make rules governing the enforcement of laws under its jurisdiction. Such rules must be made according to specific procedures and guidelines. These rules are very important, but normally, the violation of administrative rules is not viewed as criminal.

Violation of administrative rules may become criminal under some circumstances. Suppose that an administrative agency with the power to enforce rules concerning pure food discovers that a restaurant is serving spoiled food. Although this is not a criminal action (assuming it is not intentional), the agency may issue an order to the restaurant to stop the practice. If the practice is not stopped, the administrative agency may get a court order for enforcement; if that order is violated, the restaurant officials may be cited for a criminal offense. Even in those cases, however, persons who do not comply with the court order are not viewed in the same way as those who violate criminal law, and data on violations of administrative rules and regulations are not a part of official crime data.

1-6   The Concept of Crime

A **crime** may be defined as an "act or omission prohibited by law for the protection of the public, the violation of which is prosecuted by the state in its own name and punishable by incarceration."[11] Some jurisdictions define certain acts as *violations* or *infractions*. Those acts may be subject to fines or other minor penalties in criminal law or to civil penalties, but the commission of those acts is not considered criminal. When an act is not defined or processed as a crime, it should not be labeled as a crime.

1-6a   Classification of Crimes

Crimes are classified according to the seriousness of the offense into two main categories. **Misdemeanors** are the less serious offenses, whereas **felonies** are the more serious ones. Generally, misdemeanors are punishable by a short jail term, fine, probation, or a combination of these or other penalties that do not involve incarceration in a secure facility. Felonies are normally punishable by more than a year in jail, incarceration in a prison, or capital punishment, although in some cases they, too, involve alternative punishments, such as community service or even a fine or probation.

Crimes may also be classified as ***mala in se*** and ***mala prohibita***. *Mala in se* refers to acts that are considered criminal in nature, such as murder and rape. *Mala prohibita* refers to acts that are not universally regarded as criminal; they are criminal because the legislature has designated them as crimes. Violations of laws regulating the private, consensual sexual conduct of adults, the use of some drugs, and the use of alcohol by certain age groups are examples of *mala prohibita* crimes.

1-6b   Elements of a Crime

Certain elements must be proved before a person can be convicted of a crime. These vary from crime to crime and from jurisdiction to jurisdiction, but some common elements distinguish crime from noncrime.

An Act

In U.S. criminal justice systems, a person may not be punished for his or her thoughts; an act, or the omission of an act, must be committed, although some crimes do not require an act in the traditional definition of the term. For example, in the crime of conspiracy, which involves an agreement between two or more people to commit an illegal act, the agreement constitutes the act. Two parties may be convicted of conspiracy to commit a crime, even though only one (or neither) is convicted of the crime for which they conspired, such as murder. In addition, a crime may be committed when a person plays a role in assisting another person to commit a crime.

A crime may be committed when a person has made an **attempt** to commit— but has not committed—an act defined as a crime. The person must have made a substantial attempt to commit the crime. A very early English case established the crime of attempt. The defendant was accused of putting a lighted candle and some combustible materials in the house he was renting. The house was not burned, but the defendant was convicted. The court said, "The intent may make an act, innocent in itself, criminal; nor is the completion of an act, criminal in itself, necessary to constitute criminality."[12]

Failure to act may also constitute a crime but only when a person has a **legal duty** to act. If a child is drowning and two people watch without making any effort to rescue the child, the lack of action of one may be a crime, whereas that of the other might not meet the requirements of a criminal act of omission. In the first instance, the observer is a parent with a legal duty to aid the drowning child. Conversely, if the other person is not a close relative, has no contractual obligation to the child, and has not placed the child in that position of peril, he or she may not have a legal duty to come to the child's aid. Failure to do so does not constitute a crime, no matter how reprehensible the lack of action may be from a moral point of view.

For an act to be criminal, it must be voluntary. A driver who has a sudden epileptic seizure, loses control of the car, strikes another car, and injures or kills another human being has not necessarily committed a crime. But a driver who has had prior attacks of a similar nature might be found guilty of a crime for recklessly creating a situation of danger to others by driving a car when he or she knows such attacks may occur.

An Unlawful Act

A crime is an act prohibited by *criminal* law. A person cannot be punished for acts that may be considered socially harmful but that are not prohibited by criminal law. As noted earlier, the law must be reasonably clear about the conduct that is prohibited. A statute will be declared void when "men of common intelligence must necessarily guess at its meaning and differ as to its application."[13]

An Intent

For an act to be a crime, the law requires the element of intent, or ***mens rea***, a guilty mind. This is to distinguish those acts that may be harmful to others but for which the actor had no immoral or wrongful purpose. **Negligence** can cause harm to others, who

---

▶ *Mala in se* (see p. 14) Actions that are intrinsically immoral, such as murder, forcible rape, and robbery.

▶ *Mala prohibita* (see p. 14) Actions that are wrong because legislation prohibits them, although there may not be general agreement that they are wrong in themselves, such as the possession of small amounts of marijuana.

▶ Attempt   In criminal law, refers to a crime that may be defined as involving a *substantial* step toward the commission of a crime, combined with the *intent* to commit that crime.

▶ Legal duty   An obligation to another that is imposed by law, such as the duty of a parent to go to the rescue of his or her child.

▶ *Mens rea*   The criminal intent of the accused at the time the criminal act is committed.

▶ Negligence   In law, an act that a reasonable person would not do, or would not fail to do under similar circumstances. Negligence does not require a criminal intent.

Spotlight 1-3   **General Requirements of Culpability**

Model Penal Code, Section 2.02

(1) Minimum Requirements of Culpability. Except as provided in Section 2.05, a person is not guilty of an offense unless he acted purposely, knowingly, recklessly, or negligently, as the law may require, with respect to each material element of the offense.

(2) Kinds of Culpability Defined.

  (a) *Purposely.*

    A person acts purposely with respect to a material element of an offense when:

    (i) if the element involves the nature of his conduct or a result thereof, it is his conscious object to engage in conduct of that nature or to cause such a result; and

    (ii) if the element involves the attendant circumstances, he is aware of the existence of such circumstances or he believes or hopes that they exist.

  (b) *Knowingly.*

    A person acts knowingly with respect to a material element of an offense when:

    (i) if the element involves the nature of his conduct or the attendant circumstances, he is aware that his conduct is of that nature or that such circumstances exist; and

    (ii) if the element involves the result of his conduct, he is aware that it is practically certain that his conduct will cause such a result.

  (c) *Recklessly.*

    A person acts recklessly with respect to a material element of an offense when he consciously disregards a substantial and unjustifiable risk that the material element exists or will result from his conduct. The risk must be of such a nature and degree that, considering the nature and purpose of the actor's conduct and the circumstances known to him, its disregard involves a gross deviation from the standard of conduct that a law-abiding person would observe in the actor's situation.

  (d) *Negligently.*

    A person acts negligently with respect to a material element of an offense when he should be aware of a substantial and unjustifiable risk that the material element exists or will result from his conduct. The risk must be of such a nature and degree that the actor's failure to perceive it, considering the nature and purpose of his conduct and the circumstances known to him, involves a gross deviation from the standard of care that a reasonable person would observe in the actor's situation.

---

may recover damages in a civil suit, but with the exceptions noted later in this section, the law requires a guilty or an immoral mind for acts to be considered criminal. Former U.S. Supreme Court Justice Oliver Wendell Holmes Jr. described the meaning of this distinction when he said, "Even a dog distinguishes between being stumbled over and being kicked."[14]

The intent requirement is complex. Neither court decisions nor scholarly legal writings provide an easily understood meaning. The requirement may vary from crime to crime. In simple terms, an intent to do something means that the actor intends to bring about the consequences of his or her actions or engages in acts that are reasonably certain to bring about the negative effects. The actor does not have to intend the *specific* result that occurs. A person who fires a gun into a crowd, intending to kill a specific person, but who misses that person and kills another could be convicted of murder. In this example, the intent comes from the evidence that the individual purposely and knowingly took the action that resulted in the death of another. Usually, this is the easiest kind of case in which to prove intent, but the required intent need not be that obvious. Criminal intent may be found in cases in which the action is extremely reckless or grossly negligent.

Defining criminal intent in cases of reckless and negligent behavior is not easy. The **Model Penal Code (MPC)**, reproduced in part in Spotlight 1-3, illustrates one way to define those kinds of culpability, as well as the two more common kinds of intent: purposely and knowingly. The MPC was developed by legal scholars of the American Law Institute, and its proposals have been adopted, in whole or in part, in many jurisdictions. For example, the Texas Penal Code closely follows the MPC.[15]

▶ **Model Penal Code (MPC)**   A systematized statement of criminal law by the American Law Institute. This code is often used as the model for state criminal codes.

Intent may not be required in some cases, such as those in which people are held responsible for the criminal acts of others. For example, the owner of a bar might be charged with a crime if one of his employees serves liquor to an underage person, who then drives negligently and kills another. Nor is knowledge that a crime is being committed required in all circumstances. To illustrate, sexual intercourse with a person under the legal age of consent may be defined as the crime of *statutory rape* even though the alleged victim consented to the act. Historically, the law presumed that young women must be protected and thus could not legally consent to sex. In recent years, some of these laws have been revised or eliminated and, in many cases, reworded to include male victims and female perpetrators.

The Concurrence of Act and Intent

For an act to be a crime, the act and the intent must occur together. It is not sufficient to have a criminal intent one day but not commit the act until another day. For example, *A* might intend to kill *B* today but not do so. One week later, after *A* and *B* have resolved their differences, they go hunting. *A* accidentally falls while preparing to shoot a deer. *A*'s gun fires, *B* is killed. *A* should not be charged with murder because, at the time he fired, he did not have the criminal intent required for the crime of murder.

The importance of the concurrence of act and intent, along with the issue of causation (discussed in the next section), has been raised recently in the cases of persons who know they have **AIDS (acquired immune deficiency syndrome)** or are HIV (human immunodeficiency virus) positive and have sexual relations without disclosing to their partners that they have the virus or the disease. The following examples illustrate the legal issues.

Nushawn J. Williams, 22, pleaded guilty to two counts of reckless endangerment after he became the first person to be charged under the recently enacted New York statute that criminalizes knowingly having sexual relations without informing a partner of one's HIV status. Williams also pleaded guilty to other sex-related offenses, including statutory rape. Prosecutors alleged that Williams engaged in unprotected sex with as many as 48 women during one year (four of the women were known to have had children by Williams), but most of the identified women refused to cooperate with the prosecution; thus, charges were not filed in those cases. In an interview, Williams boasted about his sexual activities, claiming that over 300 women were involved. He said, "Yeah, I gave them a death sentence, but it wasn't knowingly." Williams was denied parole in August 2001 and again in July 2003.[16]

In September 2005, a senior medical student, Garry Wayne Carriker, who had graduated from the U.S. Air Force Academy prior to enrolling in medical school, was charged with multiple violations of a Georgia statute prohibiting felony reckless misconduct consisting of having sex without telling his partners that he was HIV positive. The statute in question prohibits acts that might lead to the transmission of infectious diseases, such as hepatitis and HIV. The relevant part of the statute in Carriker's case is as follows:

> (c) A person who is an HIV infected person who, after obtaining knowledge of being infected with HIV:
>
> 1. Knowingly engages in sexual intercourse or performs or submits to any sexual act involving the sex organs of one person and the mouth or anus of another person and the HIV infected person does not disclose to the other person the fact of that infected person's being an HIV infected person prior to that intercourse or sexual act;…is guilty of a felony and, upon conviction thereof, shall be punished by imprisonment for not more than ten years.[17]

HIV- or AIDS-infected persons who are convicted of a crime for having unprotected sex may argue that they did not have an intent to harm the alleged victim. A 1998 Michigan case, however, held that the intent requirement is implicit in the irresponsible conduct. The court made the analogy of driving a car while under the

▶ **AIDS (acquired immune deficiency syndrome)** A deadly disease that attacks the immune system. It is communicated through exchange of body fluids, especially during sexual activity and blood transfusions, but it can also be transmitted in other ways.

influence of a controlled substance. The person may not intend to harm anyone, but the general intent to do so is implicit in that reckless and irresponsible act.[18]

In contrast to the state statutes involved in the preceding examples, some states have chosen to use existing statutes to prosecute the act of having unprotected sex when an individual knows that he or she is HIV positive or has AIDS. In 1993, for example, Texas repealed its statute that criminalized exposing to AIDS/HIV. Legislators noted that the statute had not been used frequently and had some problems; they argued that existing statutes, such as attempted murder, would cover the crime.[19]

In fact, Texas did convict an inmate who, knowing he was HIV positive, spat at a correctional officer and yelled words to the effect that, if he were going down, he would take everyone with him. Despite the defendant's offer of evidence that neither the HIV virus nor AIDS can be transmitted by saliva, under the facts of this case, the jury was permitted to find the inmate guilty of attempted murder. In a similar case, the state of New Jersey upheld the conviction of an HIV positive inmate after he threatened to kill correctional officers by biting and spitting at them.[20]

One final example demonstrates the need to read cases carefully. A Maryland appellate court held that, in the case of Dwight Ralph Smallwood, who was told to use condoms before having sex (because of his HIV status), the state could not assume from his act alone that he had the requisite intent for attempted second-degree murder and assault with attempt to murder when he raped three women without using condoms. The court held that in each case the state must prove specific intent. The court distinguished the New Jersey and Texas cases by the announced intentions of these defendants.[21]

Causation

Causation In criminal law, the requirement that the act be the *cause* of the harmful consequence.

The final element of all crimes is that there must be proof that the result is caused by the act. If *A* shoots and hits *B*, wounding *B* slightly, *A* may be charged with attempted murder (if the elements of that crime can be proved). But *A* should not be charged with murder if *B* dies of causes unrelated to the act of shooting. **Causation** in criminal law is intricate and complex, but legal cause is a crucial element that must be proved before a person is convicted of a crime.

Attendant circumstances Facts surrounding a crime that are considered to be a part of that crime and that must be proved along with the elements of the crime.

In addition to proving an act, an intent, concurrence of the act and the intent, and causation, for some crimes the prosecution must prove the existence of **attendant circumstances**, which are facts surrounding an act. For example, a statute may provide for a higher penalty if the crime is committed against a police officer, in which case the prosecution would have to prove that the victim was a police officer, and in some jurisdictions, might have to prove that the perpetrator knew or should have known that fact.

1-6c   Defenses to Crimes

Defenses Responses by the defendant in a criminal or civil case. They may consist only of a denial of the factual allegations of the prosecution (in a criminal case) or of the plaintiff (in a civil case). If the defense offers new factual allegations in an effort to negate the charges, there is an *affirmative defense*.

In the 1800s, the classical school of criminologists advocated that punishment should fit the crime. All who committed a particular crime should have the same penalty. Others advocated that some exceptions should be made. For example, because of their infancy, children should not have the same criminal responsibility as adults; indeed, children below a certain age should not be charged with crimes. Those who have serious mental problems to the extent that either they do not know what they are doing or they cannot control their actions should not be criminally responsible. Exceptions, or **defenses**, thus crept into the law.

Defenses to criminal culpability have varied over the years, and like all areas of law, this one is in transition, with new attempts at criminal defenses occurring often, although some defenses have been traditional in many societies.[22]

1-7   The Reach of Criminal Law

The acts covered within criminal law vary from time to time and from jurisdiction to jurisdiction. Some of these acts result from reactions to technology. For example, one of the fastest-growing and relatively new crimes in the world today is **identity theft**. Most people would not have an issue with extending criminal law to cover such new crimes as identity theft. Some do, however, contend that expanding the law to cover other acts is unreasonable. The following sections discuss some of those acts.

1-7a   Crimes against Public Morality

Historically, the purpose of criminal law has been the subject of extensive debate. Some people argue that only clearly *criminal* acts should be included and that criminal law should not be used to try to control behavior that many people do not consider wrong. Others take the position that criminal law is the most effective method of social control and therefore should embrace even those acts that some consider to be *mala prohibita* rather than *mala in se*. The issues arise most frequently when criminal law embraces areas of private morality, such as consensual adult sexual behavior and substance abuse, or goes beyond the historical coverage of a crime, such as murder, by including a fetus. We begin with consensual sexual behavior.

Sexual Behavior

In a 1969 publication, two scholars referred to U.S. criminal laws as the most moralistic in history—characterized by sex offense statutes designed "to provide an enormous legislative chastity belt encompassing the whole population and proscribing everything but solitary and joyless masturbation and 'normal coitus' inside wedlock."[23]

In recent years, many states have repealed criminal statutes that proscribe sexual behavior between consenting adults. They have limited criminal statutes to sexual behavior that is the result of force against any person, that is committed consensually but with an underage or a mentally or physically incompetent person, or that is committed in public. Some states retain the common law approach, however, and provide criminal penalties for adult consensual sexual behavior that is considered deviant by some members of the population. In the controversial 1986 *Bowers v. Hartwick* decision, the U.S. Supreme Court upheld the right of states to do so. This case involved consensual sexual behavior between two men in the privacy of their Georgia home, where police had gone for legal reasons. Although this case was not reversed by the U.S. Supreme Court, in 1998 the Georgia Supreme Court held that the state's statute on which the case was based violated the Georgia constitution.[24] As Spotlight 1-4 indicates, in June 2003, the U.S. Supreme Court decided another case, *Lawrence v. Texas*, involving the issue of private and consenting sexual behavior between same-gender persons; in that case, the Supreme Court overruled *Bowers v. Hartwick*.

Child Pornography

The attempts of Congress to prohibit the use of children in pornography serves as another example of the use of criminal law to ban sexual behavior. It is not illegal for adults to view pornography, but it is illegal to produce or possess pornography involving children, as this is seen as sexual exploitation of children. Congress has enacted various statutes aimed at such prohibitions, and some of these have been upheld.[25]

The U.S. Supreme Court has held, however, that the production or possession of *virtual child pornography*, which is created by computer simulations rather than through the use of children, does not violate federal statutes. By a 6-to-3 vote, the Court, emphasizing the First Amendment right to free speech (see Appendix A), ruled that the provisions of the Child Pornography Prevention Act of 1996 (CPPA) that criminalize virtual child pornography are unconstitutional. Although the justices acknowledged the need (and the right) to prohibit children from viewing pornography or being involved in its production, they nevertheless took the position that "speech within the rights of adults to hear may not be silenced completely in an attempt to shield children from it."[26] A big issue in the continued fight against using real children in pornography will

> **Identity theft**   The stealing of an individual's Social Security number or other important information about his or her identity and using that information to commit crimes, such as removing funds from the victim's bank account.

Spotlight 1-4 The U.S. Supreme Court Rules on Same-Gender Sex

Lawrence v. Texas,[1] 539 U.S. 558 (2003)

Justice Kennedy delivered the opinion of the Court:

Liberty protects the person from unwarranted government intrusions into a dwelling or other private places. In our tradition the state is not omnipresent in the home. And there are other spheres of our lives and existence, outside the home, where the state should not be a dominant presence. Freedom extends beyond spatial bounds. Liberty presumes an autonomy of self that includes freedom of thought, belief, expression, and certain intimate conduct....

The question before the Court is the validity of a Texas statute making it a crime for two persons of the same sex to engage in certain intimate sexual conduct.

In Houston, Texas, officers of the Harris County Police Department were dispatched to a private residence in response to a reported weapons disturbance. They entered an apartment where one of the petitioners, John Geddes Lawrence, resided. The right of the police to enter does not seem to have been questioned. The officers observed Lawrence and another man, Tyron Garner, engaging in a sexual act. The two petitioners were arrested, held in custody overnight, and charged and convicted before a Justice of the Peace.

The complainants described their crime as "deviate sexual intercourse, namely anal sex, with a member of the same sex (man)." The applicable state law provides: "A person commits an offense if he engages in deviate sexual intercourse with another individual of the same sex." The statute defines "deviant sexual intercourse" as follows:

(A) any contact between any part of the genitals of one person and the mouth or anus of another person; or
(B) the penetration of the genitals or the anus of another person with an object.

The petitioners exercised their right to a trial *de novo* [a new trial] in Harris County Criminal Court. They challenged the statute as a violation of the Equal Protection Clause of the Fourteenth Amendment and of a like provision of the Texas Constitution. Those contentions were rejected. The petitioners, having entered a plea of *nolo contendere* [meaning the defendant will not contest the charges], were each fined $200 and assessed court costs of $141.25....

[The constitutional challenges were rejected and the convictions were affirmed by the Court of Appeals for the Texas Fourteenth District.]

We granted *certiorari* to consider three questions:

1. Whether petitioners' criminal convictions under the Texas Homosexual Conduct law—which criminalizes sexual intimacy by same-sex couples, but not identical behavior by different-sex couples—violates the Fourteenth Amendment guarantee of equal protection of laws?
2. Whether petitioners' criminal convictions for adult consensual sexual intimacy in the home violate their vital interests in liberty and privacy protected by the Due Process Clause of the Fourteenth Amendment?
3. Whether *Bowers v. Hardwick* should be overruled?

The petitioners were adults at the time of the alleged offense. Their conduct was in private and consensual....

[The U.S. Supreme Court ruled in the affirmative on all issues and, among other statements, made the following]:

The central holding of *Bowers* has been brought into question by this case, and it should be addressed. Its continuance as precedent demeans the lives of homosexual persons....

Bowers was not correct when it was decided, and it is not correct today. It ought not to remain binding precedent. *Bowers v. Hardwick* should be and now is overruled....

The Texas statute furthers no legitimate state interest which can justify its intrusion into the personal and private life of the individual.

Had those who drew and ratified the Due Process Clauses of the Fifth Amendment or the Fourteenth Amendment known the components of liberty in its manifold possibilities, they might have been more specific. They did not presume to have this insight. They knew times can blind us to certain truths and later generations can see that laws once thought necessary and proper in fact serve only to oppress. As the Constitution endures, persons in every generation can invoke its principles in their own search for greater freedom.

1. Lawrence v. Texas, 539 U.S. 558 (2003), citations and footnotes omitted.

be for the prosecution to prove beyond a reasonable doubt that, in any given example of pornography involving children, *actual* children were used.

A 2003 statute enacted by Congress and signed by President George W. Bush was designed to protect children from pornography as well as other forms of sexual abuse, kidnapping, and other crimes. The lengthy statute is entitled the Prosecutorial Remedies and Other Tools to End the Exploitation of Children Today Act of 2003 (the Protect Act).[27] In addition, Congress has enacted statutes designed to prevent children from viewing pornography online. The Communications Decency Act of 1996 was one attempt; that statute was considered too broad by the U.S. Supreme Court.[28] However, a later congressional attempt, the Child Online Protection Act of 2001 (COPA), has been upheld in part.[29]

In March 2006, in an international pornography ring, 13 Americans, including one who admitted downloading 30,000 pornographic images of children, were arrested for violating federal statutes designed to protect children. Several experts, along with a teen victim, Justin Berry, 19, testified before Congress on what was called a $20 billion industry of online sexual exploitation of children. Some of the victims, it was alleged, are as young as 18 months.[30]

There are many other areas involving public morality in which some people take the position that criminal law should not be used to attempt to regulate behavior. Some of those areas are prostitution, sexual behavior between heterosexuals who are not married to each other, and public nudity under some circumstances (such as on beaches designated for that purpose).

Substance Abuse

Substance abuse is another major area in which the use of criminal law to regulate behavior is questioned. Although many people would agree that criminal law is an appropriate mechanism for controlling the sale of certain drugs, there is no general agreement with regard to its use to control the *use* of some drugs, such as marijuana.

Considerable debate has occurred concerning the role of criminal law in attempting to regulate substance abuse. Several reasons are given for including acts related to substance abuse within criminal law. First is the symbolic value of the legislation: by criminalizing the acts, society makes it clear that they are unacceptable. Second, it is assumed that criminalization has a deterrent effect; if the act is a crime, most people will decline to commit it. This reason requires more careful consideration. There is no significant evidence that the threat of criminal punishment is a deterrent to public drunkenness. In fact, in 1986, a California court concluded that jailing public drunks might even be counterproductive.[31]

Some people take the position that alcoholism is a disease, not a condition over which the alcoholic has control. It is not clear which position the U.S. Supreme Court would take on the issue. In 1988, in *Traynor v. Turnage*, a case involving veterans' benefits, the U.S. Supreme Court upheld the statutory categorization of alcoholism as "willful misconduct" when the alcoholism is unrelated to mental illness, but the Court noted that it did not have to decide whether alcoholism is a disease. According to the justices, "It is not our role to resolve this medical issue on which the authorities remain sharply divided."[32]

Since *Traynor v. Turnage*, some medical scientists have reported evidence of a hereditary basis for alcoholism. If sufficient evidence suggests that the tendency toward substance abuse is inherited, we have to face the question of whether the use of alcohol and other drugs should be decriminalized and, if so, in what way. For example, should criminal law retain jurisdiction over the selling of alcohol and other drugs to minors? Should driving under the influence (DUI) of a controlled substance result in *criminal* liability if the driver cannot control his or her drinking? Given the high percentage of highway deaths caused by drunk drivers, one could argue that this criminalization should continue. But does it have a deterrent effect?

It is also maintained that, because the use of alcohol (and other drugs) is related to criminal behavior, substance abuse should come under the jurisdiction of criminal law, but the relationship between substance abuse and crime must be analyzed carefully.

In a recent study published by the Bureau of Justice Statistics (BJS), in which 2002 data were analyzed, 68 percent of men and 69 percent of women in local jails reported substance dependence or abuse. Convicted inmates reported that over 33 percent of the men and 22 percent of the women had been using alcohol at the time of the offense for which they were convicted.[33] Recent evidence also suggests that substance abuse is associated with juvenile delinquent acts.[34] Substance abuse *violations* also account for a large percentage of the increase in crime and, consequently, in jail and prison populations. For example, in the federal system, 55 percent of all inmates in a recent survey were incarcerated because of convictions for drug offenses.[35]

To combat substance abuse among inmates, in 2005 the Office of Justice Programs (OJP) of the U.S. Department of Justice awarded $32.6 million in grants for treatment programs in state and local detention and correctional facilities. The acting assistant attorney for OJP stated:

> The growth of the state and local inmate population and the history of substance abuse among the majority of these inmates indicate the need to break the drug-crime link and increase opportunities for successful transition into communities while ensuring public safety.[36]

Although it is unreasonable to ignore the possible effect of substance abuse present in so many instances when crimes are committed, the concurrence of alcohol or other drug abuse with criminal activity does not necessarily imply a direct cause-and-effect relationship. It is possible that the use of alcohol and other drugs represents a lifestyle adopted by some offenders and has nothing to do with the commission of crimes. In those cases, attempts to enforce laws regulating the abuse of alcohol and other drugs will not have a significant long-term effect on criminal activity. Nevertheless, many scholars who have studied the impact of substance abuse on crime have concluded that the relationship is significant. An example is the work of James A. Inciardi and Anne E. Pottieger, who, although acknowledging that the evidence does not *prove* that substance abuse *causes* crime, concluded the following:

> It is clear to us that drugs are driving crime. That is, although drug use does not necessarily initiate criminal careers among users, it freezes users into patterns of criminality that are more intensive and unremitting than they would have been without drugs.[37]

> **Date rape** Forced sexual acts that occur during a social occasion. The alleged victim may have agreed to some intimacy but not to the activities defined in that jurisdiction as constituting the elements of rape.

Another area in which substance abuse and crime are related is that of **date rape**. It is estimated that each year over 97,000 college and university students are the victims of sexual or other abuse (including date rape) in alcohol-related incidents. Over 100,000 students report that on occasion they were too intoxicated to know whether they engaged in sexual acts.[38]

In some cases, these alleged victimizations occur after the use of so-called club drugs, such as gamma hydroxybutyrate (GHB), which may be dropped into the drinks of unsuspecting dates, who are then victimized by forced sexual acts. GHB causes unconsciousness quickly, and it cannot be smelled or tasted. Victims may have no memory of an alleged sexual attack. Another drug used in date rapes is Ecstasy, which highlighted a famous trial in 2003. In February of that year, Andrew Luster, 39-year-old grandson of the founder of the Max Factor (cosmetics) company, was convicted in absentia (he fled to Mexico during his February trial but was captured in June and returned to the United States to serve his term) of numerous counts of rape and sodomy of unconscious victims, as well as possession of Ecstasy, poisoning, and sexual battery. Luster was sentenced to 124 years in prison.

The seriousness of club drug crimes has led to numerous legislative attempts to curb the drugs' use. A law passed in 2000 increased the penalties for possessing and distributing GHB and moved that drug into the category of drugs that receives the highest regulations under the federal Controlled Substances Act (CSA)—the Schedule I drugs. The CSA divides drugs into five categories, called *schedules*, with the most serious drugs included in Schedule I, about which the statute states the following:

(A) The drug or other substance has a high potential for abuse.

(B) The drug or other substance has no currently accepted medical use in treatment in the United States.

(C) There is a lack of accepted safety for use of the drug or other substance under medical supervision.[39]

Physicians may not prescribe Schedule I drugs unless necessary for government-approved research.

Bills introduced in the U.S. Congress in 2002 and 2003 were designed to crack down on Ecstasy and other club drugs. The Reducing Americans' Vulnerability to Ecstasy (RAVE) Act amended existing federal laws to increase the civil and criminal penalties for persons responsible for putting teenagers at risk of using Ecstasy and other club drugs by preventing the leasing of, renting of, or profiting from any place in which the drugs are used. The bill became law when it was signed by President George W. Bush in April 2003. The RAVE act amends the controlled substance provision of the Comprehensive Drug Abuse and Prevention Act of 1970.[40]

1-7b   The Use of Marijuana for Medicinal Purposes

Another use of criminal law to control substance abuse involves laws prohibiting growing, distributing, and prescribing marijuana for any purpose. The sale and possession of marijuana is a serious offense, with long penalties in many states. In the federal CSA, discussed earlier, marijuana is a Schedule I drug. However, in California and a few other states, *state* law allows the use of marijuana for medicinal reasons with a prescription from a physician.[41] The drug relieves pain and other symptoms in some diseases and is tolerated by some patients who do not respond well to other drugs.

Federal authorities have taken the position that the prescription of marijuana for medicinal reasons violates the federal CSA and have focused on prosecuting those in California who violate this statute. They have had some success, with the U.S. Supreme Court reversing a lower federal court in California and ruling that the necessity defense is not available to a defendant who grows marijuana for medicinal reasons. That means that the defendant charged with violating the federal CSA by growing marijuana cannot defend that this was done because the drug is necessary for medical treatment. The U.S. Supreme Court reasoned that, when Congress included marijuana as a Schedule I drug, meaning it cannot be prescribed by physicians for any reason, and provided no exceptions, that is exactly what Congress meant. However, federal prosecutors wanted to avoid the harsh penalties of the federal statute and thus petitioned the California court to issue an **injunction** prohibiting anyone from providing marijuana for medical reasons. The state court did so, and that permits federal prosecutors to process through the civil rather than the criminal court anyone who grows, sells, or uses marijuana for medicinal purposes.[42]

On the issue of using marijuana for medicinal purposes, a panel of the Ninth Circuit Court of Appeals in California ruled that the government may not revoke the medical licenses of physicians who prescribe marijuana for medicinal reasons. A hearing by the full court was denied, and the U.S. Supreme Court refused to review the case.[43]

Finally, in June 2005, the U.S. Supreme Court decided a case involving the use of marijuana for medical reasons. The two plaintiffs in *Gonzales v. Raich* were using marijuana to ease the pain from their respective diseases; no other medications had given them relief. The Supreme Court held that the CSA is within the proper exercise of federal power "even as applied to the troubling facts of this case." Advocates of the medical use of marijuana must now convince Congress to change the federal statute.[44]

> **Injunction** A prohibitive remedy issued by a court and ordering someone or an agency to do something or stop doing something; based on a request by a party who petitions the court for the relief. There are several kinds of injunctions, including those that are preliminary (effective until a further decision), partial, temporary, or permanent.

1-7c   Fetal Abuse

Another controversial area concerning the use of criminal law is **fetal abuse**. Two areas of focus are discussed here: (1) the abuse of a fetus by a pregnant woman who uses alcohol and other drugs, and (2) the killing of a fetus.

There is sufficient evidence that consumption of alcohol and other drugs by pregnant women may cause harm to their fetuses that warnings are given and criminal sanctions are imposed. The toughest drug laws regarding harm to a fetus are found in South Carolina, which provides that a pregnant woman who uses drugs may be charged with murder if her fetus dies as a result. One woman who used crack cocaine during her pregnancy and gave birth to a stillborn fetus was convicted of murder. Her conviction was upheld in 2003 by the South Carolina Supreme Court, and the U.S. Supreme Court refused to hear the case on appeal.[45] Although the U.S. Supreme Court has not

> **Fetal abuse** The abusing of a fetus, which may or may not lead to its death. In some jurisdictions, any resulting injury may lead to legal culpability. In a few states, killing a fetus may result in murder charges.

ruled on this issue, it has held that a state may not force pregnant women suspected of drug abuse to be drug-tested involuntarily if the primary purpose of the test is to report their actions to the police.[46]

Another expansion of criminal law in the area of fetal abuse is illustrated by the definition of murder in the California criminal statutes. The state previously defined murder as "the unlawful killing of a human being with malice aforethought." The current statute adds "or a fetus" after the words *human being*.[47] (Exclusions are made for legal abortions.) This change in the common law definition of murder, which has been followed in some other states, has led to murder convictions for defendants accused of killing a woman and her fetus. The California position gained national and worldwide focus in the criminal trial of Scott Peterson for the murders of his wife, Laci, who disappeared from their home on Christmas Eve, 2002, and their unborn son, Connor. The double murder charge provided the special circumstances required by California law to try a defendant for capital murder. Peterson was convicted of first-degree murder for his wife's death and second-degree murder for the death of her fetus. He was sentenced to death. As a result of this case, Congress passed a federal statute entitled the Unborn Victims of Violence Act of 2004 (also known as Laci and Connor's Law) to change the federal criminal code and that of the military code to protect unborn children from assault and murder.[48]

1-7d Conclusion on the Reach of Criminal Law

Even if we decide that all of the acts discussed in this section of the chapter should be included within criminal law, we should consider carefully what penalties to assess. What is accomplished by jailing a pregnant woman who uses drugs, other than to prevent her from harming her fetus further? Given that perhaps worthy goal, is it necessary to incarcerate her? What if she has other children to care for? And is that jail term worth the cost to society when new facilities must be constructed to handle the large populations of incarcerated people?

This discussion of criminalizing acts some consider against public morality, legalizing the use of marijuana for medicinal purposes, and fetal abuse raises the issue of whether criminal law is used too extensively and therefore goes beyond the purpose of protecting the public's safety and welfare and interferes with the behavior of private persons. Those who take this position argue that criminal law is being used to encompass acts without victims. They assert that the results are harmful in the long run: police may invade personal rights of privacy in order to enforce the law; minorities and other unpopular groups may be harassed; courts, jails, and prisons may be overcrowded as a result of processing these people through criminal justice systems; underground markets may develop to supply prohibited products, such as alcohol and other drugs; and attempts to enforce unpopular and unsupported criminal statutes may create disrespect for the law. Critical police resources may be diverted from more important functions.

Supporters argue that criminal law is a necessary symbol of morality and that removal of *mala prohibita* acts from criminal law would place society's stamp of approval on the behaviors in question. Resolution of these two positions regarding the use of criminal law to control morality involves religious, moral, and ethical considerations, as well as legal and empirical issues. In the final analysis, the answer may be a personal one. But it is clear that, whatever position is taken, it will have important repercussions on criminal justice systems.

Chapter Wrap-Up

This chapter presents an overview of criminal justice systems and criminal law. Although the systems differ, all may be analyzed first in terms of punishment philosophies: incapacitation, retribution, rehabilitation, deterrence, preservation of social solidarity, and reparation or restitution. In the present-day United States, the philosophies of deterrence and retribution, often combined in the just deserts approach, are dominant. Just a short time ago, U.S. systems were dominated by the philosophy of rehabilitation, and today, some efforts are being made to bring back that emphasis.

The role of discretion in punishment is crucial to criminal justice systems. It exists at all levels, and it cannot be eliminated, but it can be controlled by some measures. If left unchecked, discretion can result in unfairness to defendants.

After an overview of discretion, the chapter looked briefly at the components of criminal justice systems, using a diagram of general U.S. approaches for illustrative purposes. All of the elements of the systems are discussed in more detail throughout the text.

Crucial to all criminal justice systems is the basis for those systems, criminal law. A criminal justice system is based on a society's willingness to grant legal authority to some individuals to impose punishment. Criminal law provides that basis in modern societies, and this chapter began its overview of criminal law by distinguishing between criminal and civil law. Criminal law has existed for centuries, predating and forming the basis for much of our civil law.

Criminal justice systems may be based on either the adversary or the inquisitory model. U.S. systems follow the adversary model, in which all accused persons are presumed innocent and the state must prove their guilt beyond a reasonable doubt. In contrast is the inquisitory system, in which the accused are presumed guilty and must prove their innocence. The adversary system is characterized by due process and equal protection. Other constitutional limitations include the prohibition of statutes that are vague or too broad and the imposition of cruel and unusual punishment.

Criminal law emerges from statutes enacted by the legislative branches of government, administrative rules and regulations, constitutions, and court decisions. All of these are important sources of law.

Criminal law is based on the concept of *crime*, which must be defined legally to fall within criminal justice systems. Crimes are classified as serious (felonies) or less serious (misdemeanors). Crimes may be classified as *mala prohibita*, criminal because they are so designated by society, or *mala in se*, criminal per se. Crimes have elements that must be proved before a person is convicted. Those elements include an illegal act that concurs with a guilty mind, causation, and for some crimes, attendant circumstances. Some acts that fit these elements may not be considered criminal because the accused has an acceptable defense.

Scholars, politicians, and the general public continue to debate what the reach of criminal law should be. This chapter considered whether consensual sexual behavior between adults in private, the use of children in pornography, and substance abuse should be included within the reach of criminal law. It also discussed whether we should legalize the use of marijuana for medicinal purposes. Finally, it analyzed recent developments in criminal law regarding the status of a fetus.

This overview chapter on criminal justice systems and criminal law sets the stage for more detailed analyses of the components of the systems. The next chapter focuses on another foundation important to the understanding of criminal justice systems—the collection and analysis of data on crime, offenders, and crime victims.

Key Terms

administrative law (p. 14)

adversary systems (p. 12)

AIDS (acquired immune deficiency syndrome) (p. 17)

attempt (p. 15)

attendant circumstances (p. 18)

case law (p. 14)

castration (p. 7)

causation (p. 18)

civil law (p. 9)

common law (p. 14)

crime (p. 14)

criminal (p. 5)

criminal justice system (p. 4)

criminal law (p. 9)

cruel and unusual punishment (p. 13)

date rape (p. 22)

defenses (p. 18)

deterrence (p. 6)

discretion (p. 8)

due process (p. 12)

equal protection (p. 12)

felony (p. 14)

fetal abuse (p. 23)

general deterrence (p. 8)

identity theft (p. 19)

incapacitation (p. 6)

individual deterrence (p. 7)

injunction (p. 23)

inquisitory system (p. 12)

jurisdiction (p. 13)

just deserts (p. 8)

legal duty (p. 15)

mala in se (p. 14)

mala prohibita (p. 14)

mens rea (p. 15)

misdemeanor (p. 14)

Model Penal Code (MPC) (p. 16)

negligence (p. 15)

rehabilitation (p. 6)

retribution (p. 6)

sanction (p. 4)

statutory law (p. 13)

Apply It

1. Briefly summarize the recent terrorist and other violent crimes that have occurred on U.S. soil.

2. Explain and distinguish among deterrence, rehabilitation, incapacitation, and retribution. Explain how these punishment and sentencing philosophies relate to the justice model of punishment.

3. Discuss the punishment implications of the cases discussed in Spotlight 1-1.

4. How do you think discretion should be regulated in criminal justice systems? Discuss the process in terms of specific personnel, such as police, prosecutors, judges, and juries. Consider your answer at the end of the course to determine whether your personal views have changed.

5. Contrast civil and criminal law.

6. Distinguish between the adversary and the inquisitory systems of criminal justice.

7. Explain the meaning of due process and equal protection. What other constitutional limitations are placed on criminal law and included in this chapter?

8. Do you think capital punishment is cruel and unusual punishment? How about a life sentence without parole for drug possession? For drug sales? Would your answer to the last two questions depend on the amount of drugs?

9. List and discuss the sources of criminal law.

10. How are crimes classified?

11. Discuss the basic elements of a crime.

12. What are criminal defenses?

13. Should criminal law be used to control any or all of the following: premarital sex, extramarital sex, same-gender sex, driving while intoxicated, use of drugs, use of seat belts?

14. Analyze the U.S. Supreme Court decision concerning the sexual behavior of gay men.

15. What position should criminal law take on the use of marijuana for medicinal purposes?

16. Under what theory should a fetus be considered a person for purposes of homicide statutes?

17. Should pregnant women who use illegal drugs be prosecuted for the *criminal* abuse (or death) of a fetus?

Endnotes

1. See "Clemency Granted to a Mercy Killer," *New York Times* (2 August 1990), p. 9.

2. "What Are Prisons For? No Longer Rehabilitation, but to Punish—and to Lock the Worst Away," *Time* (13 September 1982), p. 38.

3. Cal. Penal Code, Article 1, Section 1170 (2007).

4. U.S. Code, Article 28, Section 994(k) (2007).

5. See Cal. Penal Code, Section 1210.1 (2007); Idaho Code, Section 39-301 (2007).

6. Cal. Penal Code, Section 645 (2007).

7. See, for example, Ernest van den Haag, *Punishing Criminals: Concerning a Very Old and Painful Question* (New York: Basic Books, 1975); and David Fogel, *We Are the Living Proof: The Justice Model for Corrections* (Cincinnati, Ohio: Anderson, 1975).

8. Joint Anti-Fascist Refugee Committee v. McGrath, 341 U.S. 123, 162–163 (1951), Justice Frankfurter, concurring.

9. Thornhill v. Alabama, 310 U.S. 88, 97 (1940).

10. Hazel B. Kerper, *Introduction to the Criminal Justice System* (St. Paul, Minn.: West, 1972), p. 27.

11. Model Penal Code, Section 1.104(1).

12. Rex v. Scofield, Cald. 397, 400 (1784).

13. Connally v. General Construction Company, 269 U.S. 385, 391 (1926).

14. Oliver Wendell Holmes Jr., *The Common Law,* as cited in Morissette v. United States, 342 U.S. 246, 252 (1952).

15. Texas Penal Code, Chapter 6, Sections 6.02–6.03 (2006).

16. "Drifter Gets Four to Twelve Years in H.I.V. Case," *New York Times* (6 April 1999), p. 1B; "Man Guilty of Spreading AIDS Virus Says He Had Hundreds of Sex Partners," *New York Times* (29 July 1999), p. 19; "Niagara Street Fire Damage Is Estimated at $90,000," *Buffalo News* (New York) (1 August 2003), p. 2C.

17. "Med Student Faces Trial in HIV Exposure Cases," *Atlanta Journal-Constitution* (11 September 2005), p. 1. The statute is codified at Official Code of Georgia Annotated, O.C.G.A., Title 16, Chapter 5, Article 4, Section 16-5-60 (2006).

18. People v. Jensen, 586 N.W.2d 748 (Mich.App. 1998).

19. "Texas AIDS Law Off Books in '94: No Convictions Obtained in Statute's Brief History," *Houston Chronicle* (5 September 1993), p. 1C.

20. Weeks v. State, 834 S.W.2d 559, 561 (Tex.Ct.App. 1992), *sum. judgment granted sub nom.,* 867 F.Supp. 544 (S.D.Tex. 1994), *subsequent appeal sub nom.,* 55 F.3d 1059 (5th Cir. 1995). The

New Jersey case is Smith v. State, 621 A.2d 493 (N.J.Sup. 1993), *certification denied,* 634 A.2d 523 (N.J. 1993).

21. Smallwood v. State, 680 A.2d 512 (Md. 1996).

22. For more details on defenses, see Sue Titus Reid, *Criminal Law,* 7th ed. (Los Angeles: Roxbury Publishing, 2007), pp. 93–162.

23. Norval Morris and Gordon Hawkins, *The Honest Politician's Guide to Crime Control* (Chicago: University of Chicago Press, 1969), p. 15.

24. Bowers v. Hardwick, 478 U.S. 186 (1986), *overruled by* Lawrence v. Texas, 539 U.S. 558 (2003). See also Powell v. State, 510 S.E.2d 18 (Ga. 1998).

25. See United States v. X-Citement Video, 513 U.S. 64 (1994). The federal statute is codified at U.S. Code, Title 18, Section 2251 *et seq.* (2007).

26. Ashcroft v. Free Speech Coalition, 535 U.S. 234 (2002).

27. The Prosecutorial Remedies and Other Tools to End the Exploitation of Children Today Act of 2003 (the Protect Act), Public Law 108-21 (2007).

28. The Communications Decency Act of 1996, U.S. Code, Title 47, Section 2236(a)(b) (2007). The case is Reno v. American Civil Liberties Union, 521 U.S. 844 (1997).

29. The Child Online Protection Act, U.S. Code, Title 47, Section 231 (2007). The case is Ashcroft v. American Civil Liberties Union, 542 U.S. 656 (2004).

30. "27 Charged in International Online Child Pornography Ring," *New York Times* (16 March 2006), p. 15; "Child Sex as Internet Fare, through Eyes of a Victim," *New York Times* (5 April 2006), p. 20.

31. Sundance v. Municipal Court, 729 P.2d 80 (Cal. 1986).

32. Traynor v. Turnage, 485 U.S. 535 (1988), *superseded by statute as stated in* Larrabee v. Derwinski, 968 F.2d 1497 (3d Cir. 1992).

33. Jennifer C. Karberg and Doris J. James, Bureau of Justice Statistics, *Substance Dependence, Abuse, and Treatment of Jail Inmates, 2002* (Washington, D.C.: U.S. Department of Justice, July 2005), pp. 1–7.

34. Office of National Drug Control Policy, *Juveniles and Drugs,* p. 5, http://www.whitehousedrugpolicy.gov/drugfact/juveniles/index.html, accessed 15 August 2005.

35. Paige M. Harrison and Allen J. Beck, Bureau of Justice Statistics Bulletin, *Prisoners in 2005* (Washington, D.C.: U.S. Department of Justice, Office of Justice Programs, November 2006), pp. 1, 10.

36. "DOJ Awards $32.6 Million for Treatment of Lockups," *Corrections Professional* 10, no. 16 (13 May 2003): n.p.

37. James A. Inciardi and Anne E. Pottieger, "Drug Use and Street Crime in Miami: An (Almost) Twenty-Year Retrospective," in *The American Drug Scene*, 3d ed., ed. James A. Inciardi and Karen McElrath (Los Angeles: Roxbury Publishing, 2001), pp. 319–342; quotation is on pp. 337–338.

38. National Institute on Alcohol Abuse and Alcoholism (NIAAA), "A Snapshot of Annual High-Risk College Drinking Consequences," http://www.collegedrinkingprevention. gov/statesummaries/snapshot/aspx, accessed 23 May 2006.

39. The Control Substances Act is codified at U.S. Code, Title 21, Section 812 (2007).

40. The Reducing Americans' Vulnerability to Ecstasy (RAVE) Act of 2003 amended the Comprehensive Drug Abuse and Prevention Act of 1970, U.S. Code, Title 21, Sections 801–966 (2007).

41. The California statute is the Compassionate Use Act of 1996, Cal. Health & Safety Code, Section 11362.5 (2007).

42. United States v. Oakland Cannabis Buyers' Cooperative, 532 U.S. 483 (2001), injunction granted sub nom., 2002 U.S. Dist. LEXIS 10660 (N.D.Cal. 10 June 2002).

43. Conant v. Walters, 309 F.3d 629 (9th Cir. 2002), *reh'g. denied, reh'g. en banc, denied sub nom.,* 2003 U.S. App. LEXIS 3932 (9th Cir. 2003), *cert. denied,* 540 U.S. 819 (2003).

44. Gonzales v. Raich, 545 U.S. 1 (2005).

45. State v. McKnight, 576 S.E.2d 168 (S.C. 2003), *cert. denied sub nom.,* 540 U.S. 819 (2003).

46. Ferguson v. Charleston, 532 U.S. 67 (2001).

47. Cal. Penal Code, Section 187(a)(b)(2007).

48. Unborn Victims of Violence Act of 2004, U.S. Code, Title 18, Section 1841 (2007).

Crime, Offenders, and Victims

In October 2000, the Federal Bureau of Investigation (FBI) released crime data for 1999, and for the eighth consecutive year, serious crimes reported to police declined, this time by 7 percent. This was the longest consecutive period of decreases since the FBI had begun keeping records. Murder (including nonnegligent manslaughter) was down 8.5 percent; robberies were down 4 percent; forcible rape fell 4 percent; and aggravated assault declined by 10 percent. Burglaries declined by 10 percent, auto thefts decreased by 7.7 percent, and larceny-thefts dropped by 5.7.[1]

These 1999 figures were encouraging, and even more so was the fact that a year later the FBI announced that there had been virtually no change in serious crimes in 2000, compared with 1999. In 2000, overall serious crimes were down 14 percent from 1996 and 22 percent from 1991.[2] In 2001, crime data showed the first increase in serious crime in a decade, but the volume fell again in the following years. This text will focus on the 2005 data for serious violent and property crimes. That year showed an increase in violent crimes and a decrease in property crimes.[3] Later discussions in this chapter contain more details about the 2005 changes in crime data.

It is important that these (and other) crime data be analyzed carefully in light of changing demographics and other variables, such as the state of the economy; the changing ages of the population; changing local, state, and federal budgets for law enforcement; prison populations; the number of inmates being released; and so on.

It must also be understood that the collection of crime data is not as precise as some would have us believe. Not all crimes are reported to the police, although as Figure 2-1 notes, based on a special report by the **Bureau of Justice Statistics (BJS)**, crime reporting has improved. Not all reported crimes are cleared by arrest; fewer still are cleared by conviction. This means that no data source is complete in its measure of criminal activity. Additional problems exist when comparisons are made among jurisdictions.

Despite the impossibility of detecting all criminal activity or prosecuting and convicting all guilty parties who are detected, crime data serve an important function. Official agencies need the data to determine policies and budgets. Police officials use the data to determine the best use of their limited resources. Crime data may also be used by private citizens who are determined to make their communities safer for all who live there. Social scientists who study

▶ **Bureau of Justice Statistics (BJS)** (see p. 29) A federal agency authorized by Congress to collect and analyze crime data based on surveys of the general population, who are questioned about crime victimizations.

L E A R N I N G
OBJECTIVES

After reading this chapter, you should be able to do the following:

- **List and evaluate the major sources of crime and victimization data.**
- **Recognize the importance of misdemeanors in criminal justice systems.**
- **List and explain the reasons that crime data may not be accurate.**
- **Discuss reasons for the nonreporting of crime by victims.**
- **List and define the eight serious crimes as categorized by the Federal Bureau of Investigation.**
- **Analyze and summarize recent crime data, noting changes in the rates of violent and property crimes.**
- **Explain the meaning of *hate crime*, and analyze the U.S. Supreme Court decision regarding cross burning.**
- **Discuss the demographic characteristics of offenders.**
- **Define *victimology*, and describe and criticize the sources of victimization data.**
- **List the major variables used to analyze victimization data, and explain the meaning of each.**
- **Explain the relationship between victims and offenders according to crime data, and predict your chances of becoming a crime victim, given your current lifestyle.**
- **Consider the effects of the 9/11 terrorist attacks.**
- **Discuss ways in which criminal justice systems have attempted to respond to the needs of victims, and evaluate each.**
- **Evaluate your own fear of crime, and assess whether you alter your lifestyle as a result.**

criminal behavior use crime data, both official and unofficial, in their analyses of why and under what circumstances people commit criminal acts. Crime data may also be used for political reasons in an effort to convince voters of the success or failure of crime prevention efforts. The point is not to dismiss crime data because of problems of inaccuracy but, rather, to consider carefully the various sources of data and to determine which are best for a particular purpose.

This chapter examines and analyzes the most common methods for collecting crime data: official reports of reported crimes, data secured from victims, and data from self-report studies. Following the description of data sources, the discussion compares those sources and analyzes the problems of collecting data by each method. The chapter contains an overview of the amount and types of crime and characteristics of offenders, as determined by official data as well as by data collected from victimization studies. Finally, the chapter looks at crime victims as well as the relationship between victims and offenders, the fear of crime, and how criminal justice systems treat victims.

2-1 Sources of Crime Data

The two major sources of official crime data in the United States are: the *Uniform Crime Reports (UCR)* and the National Crime Victimization Survey (NCVS). Table 2-1 explains the purposes of these two sources and their differences. The *UCR* reports crime data that come to the attention of police through their own observations or through

Reporting to the police of violent crime increased from an annual average of 43%, 1992–99, to 49% in 2000

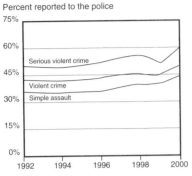

Percent reported to the police

Note: Serious violent crime includes rape, sexual assault, robbery, and aggravated assault and excludes simple assault.

- In 2000, 39% of the 25.4 million violent and property crimes were reported to the police, according to the National Crime Victimization Survey. Violent crimes were reported at a higher percentage than property crimes.

- Violence against females was more likely to be reported than violence against males. Higher percentages of violence against older persons than younger persons were reported to law enforcement.

- Overall, violent crime was more likely to be reported to the police if the victim perceived that the offender was under the influence of drugs/alcohol.

- When violent crime was committed by an armed offender, it was more likely to be reported to the police.

- A higher percentage of violence in which the victim was injured was reported to the police. Ninety percent of violence in which the victim was shot was reported to the police.

- Overall, violent crime committed by strangers was reported to police at a higher percentage than was violent crime committed by nonstrangers.

- Robbery was less likely to have been reported to the police when the victim thought the offender was a gang member (46% for gang members and 59% for nongang members).

- Violent crime was most often reported in an effort to "prevent future violence," "stop the offender," or to "protect others."

- Violent crime was most often not reported to police because it was deemed a "private/personal matter," was considered "not important enough," or was "reported to another official."

Figure 2-1
Reporting Crime to the Police, 1992–2000

Source: Timothy C. Hart and Callie Rennison, Bureau of Justice Statistics, *Reporting Crime to the Police, 1992–2000* (Washington, D.C.: U.S. Department of Justice, March 2003), p. 1.

reports from others. The *UCR* includes two crimes not included by the NCVS—murder and arson. Murder is not included in NCVS data because those data are based on interviews with crime victims. Arson is not included because it is too difficult to measure with the techniques used in the NCVS.

Of the two sources, the *UCR* is used more frequently. Despite their differences, the two sources may complement each other, but a comparison should be based on the realization that the *UCR* and the NCVS are based on different time periods, definitions of the included crimes, and methods of counting crime.

Each source has limitations, as noted in the respective discussions. But neither can estimate the extent to which a few offenders are responsible for large numbers of crimes. These reports disclose only how many crimes were reported (not how many of those crimes were traced to the same offenders) and how many arrests were made (not how many times a particular person was arrested). More specialized studies disclose that a large percentage of those who enter prison to serve time were previously convicted of other crimes. Although these repeat offenders are relatively few, they account for a large amount of crime.

2-1a   *Uniform Crime Reports (UCR)*

The ***Uniform Crime Reports (UCR)*** consists of crime data collected by the FBI. The FBI publishes the official report yearly, usually in the fall. Originally, seven crimes were selected, because of their seriousness and frequency, to constitute the *UCR* crime index.

Uniform Crime Reports (UCR) Official crime data, collected and published by the Federal Bureau of Investigation (FBI) and based on "crimes known to the police"—crimes that are reported to or observed by the police and that the police have reason to believe were committed.

T A B L E 2-1	**Comparison of the _Uniform Crime Reports_ and the National Crime Victimization Survey**	
	Uniform Crime Reports	**National Crime Victimization Survey**
Offenses measured	Homicide Rape Robbery (personal and commercial) Assault (aggravated) Burglary (commercial and household) Larceny (personal and household) Motor vehicle theft Arson	Rape Robbery (personal) Assault (aggravated and simple) Household burglary Larceny (personal and household) Motor vehicle theft
Scope	Crimes reported to the police in most jurisdictions: considerable flexibility in developing small-area data	Crimes both reported and not reported to police: all data are available for a few large geographic areas
Collection method	Police department reports to FBI or to centralized state agencies that then report to FBI	Survey interviews: periodically measures the total number of crimes committed by asking a national sample of 49,000 households encompassing 101,000 persons age 12 and over about their experiences as victims of crime during a specific period
Kinds of information	In addition to offense counts, provides information on crime clearances, persons arrested, persons charged, law enforcement officers killed and assaulted, and characteristics of homicide victims	Provides details about victims (such as age, race, sex, education, income, and whether the victim and offender were related to each other) and about crimes (such as time and place of occurrence, whether or not reported to police, use of weapons, occurrence of injury, and economic consequences)
Sponsor	Department of Justice, Federal Bureau of Investigation	Department of Justice, Bureau of Justice Statistics

Source: Bureau of Justice Statistics, _Report to the Nation on Crime and Justice: The Data_, 2d ed. (Washington, D.C.: U.S. Government Printing Office, 1988), p. 1.

▶ **Index offenses** The FBI's _Uniform Crime Reports_ of the occurrences of the eight crimes considered most serious: murder and nonnegligent manslaughter, forcible rape, robbery, aggravated assault, burglary, larceny-theft, motor vehicle theft, and arson. In June 2004, the FBI discontinued publishing data according to index offenses because of the misrepresentation of crime in an area that can be caused by a very high (or low) volume or rate of only one of these serious crimes in that area.

Known as Part I, or **index offenses**, they included murder and nonnegligent manslaughter, forcible rape, robbery, aggravated assault, burglary, larceny-theft, and motor vehicle theft. Congress added arson to the crime index in 1979 and referred to the crime index as the _modified crime index._

In June 2004, the FBI ceased using the concept of _index offenses_ for reporting data because of its concern that this category was misleading. For example, overall, most serious crimes are property crimes, with larceny-theft constituting almost 60 percent of serious crimes. Thus, if one jurisdiction had a large increase in larceny-theft, that could raise its overall crime index offense data significantly, even though it had an insignificant increase in serious violent crimes.

Each month law enforcement agencies report the number of **crimes known to the police**—that is, the number of Part I offenses verified by police investigation of the complaint. A crime known to the police is counted even if no suspect is arrested and no prosecution occurs. If a criminal activity involves several different crimes, only the most serious one is reported as a Part I, or serious, offense. If a victim is raped, robbed, and murdered, only the murder is counted in the _UCR._ Offenses known to police do not show how many persons were involved in a particular reported crime. The data are used to calculate a **crime rate**. The national crime rate is calculated by dividing the number of Part I reported crimes by the number of people in the country (data obtained from census reports). The result is expressed as a rate of crimes per 100,000 people.

In addition, the _UCR_ reports the number of Part I offenses that are cleared. Offenses are cleared in two ways: (1) when a suspect is arrested, charged, and turned over to the judicial system for prosecution, and (2) by circumstances beyond the control of the police. For example, a suspect's death or a victim's refusal to press charges may signal the end of police involvement in a reported crime. Crimes are considered cleared whether or not the suspect is convicted.

Several persons may be arrested and one crime cleared, or one person may be arrested and many crimes cleared. The *clearance rate* is the number of crimes solved, expressed as a percentage of the total number of crimes reported to the police. The clearance rate is critical in policy decisions because it is one measure used to evaluate police departments. The higher the number of crimes solved by arrest, the better the police force looks in the eyes of the public.

Violent crimes are more likely than property crimes to be cleared by arrest. This is because victims (or families, in the case of murder) are more likely to report violent crimes than property crimes and to act more quickly. Victims of personal violence, as compared with victims of property crimes, are more likely to be able to give police pertinent information that might lead to an arrest. Murder is the crime most likely to be cleared by arrest; burglary is least likely, but motor vehicle theft and larceny-theft also have low clearance rates.

Arrest information in the *UCR* is presented in two forms: (1) the total estimated numbers of arrests by crime for each of the recorded offenses and (2) the number of arrests made during one year for each of the serious offenses per 100,000 population. The *UCR* does not report the number of persons arrested each year because some individuals are arrested more than once during the year. The actual number of arrested persons, therefore, is likely to be smaller than the total number of arrests.

In addition to data on crimes reported and arrest information for Part I offenses, the *UCR* publishes the number of arrests for less serious crimes, known as Part II offenses. Examples of these offenses are other assaults (simple), forgery and counterfeiting, fraud, embezzlement, stolen property, vandalism, prostitution and commercialized vice, other sex offenses, drug abuse violations, driving under the influence (DUI), drunkenness, and disorderly conduct. Although some of the offenses included in Part II are felonies, others are misdemeanors, and they receive little attention in criminal justice texts, but they are important in criminal justice systems.

Recall that Chapter 1 noted that misdemeanors are the less serious criminal offenses, whereas felonies are more serious. Perhaps this is why so little attention is paid to misdemeanors in most textbooks. But in terms of their impact on criminal justice systems and victims, misdemeanors can be extremely important. They occur more frequently than felonies, and attempts to apprehend offenders who commit misdemeanors may lead to accusations that suspects' constitutional rights have been violated.

Chapter 1 also pointed out that some offenses may be misdemeanors the first time they are committed but classified as felonies for subsequent offenses. The Chapter 1 discussion of whether the criminal law should be used to cover consenting sexual behavior between adults in private, child pornography, substance abuse, the use of marijuana for medicinal purposes, or even fetal abuse points to one of the reasons why misdemeanors are important. Attempts to enforce statutes covering the possession of small amounts of marijuana for one's own use or such offenses as some consensual, private sexual acts may lead to the infringement of constitutional rights, such as the right to privacy. Attempts to enforce statutes regulating vagrancy and loitering may lead to violations of a person's right to be governed by statutes that are clear, concise, and not too broad. Arrests in violation of constitutional rights offend our sense of fairness and justice, and force citizens to expend money and energy fighting criminal justice systems.

The lack of focus on misdemeanors is one problem with the *UCR*, but the FBI's reporting system also has other limitations.

Limitations of the *UCR*

The most serious limitation of the *UCR* is that it does not include all crimes that are committed. Some scholars have argued that *UCR* data are significantly lower

> ▶ **Crimes known to the police** (see p. 32)   All serious criminal offenses that have been reported to the police and for which the police have sufficient evidence to believe the crimes were committed.

> ▶ **Crime rate** (see p. 32)   The number of crimes per 100,000 population.

than the actual incidence of crime. The *UCR* does not record all criminal activity for several reasons.

First, not all crimes are reported; in fact, most crimes are not reported to police. There are many reasons for not reporting a crime: Some victims think police will not do anything. Others are embarrassed or believe they will be blamed for the crime. For example, rape victims may think that they will be suspected of encouraging the crime, particularly if the rape was committed by an acquaintance. Rape victims may not want to go through a trial in which they must face the alleged rapist and submit to questions by the defendant's attorney. They may be too embarrassed to relate the details of the crime to the police, prosecution, rape counselors, or even to their own families.

A second factor affecting crime data is the delay in reporting crimes. Delay may be caused by an inability to decide whether to report the crime. There are three reasons for this indecisiveness: Some individuals first want to verify that a crime has occurred. Others take some actions to cope with the crime before calling the police. Still others experience conflict about calling the police, so they try to avoid making a quick decision. Once the decision to call the police has been made, there may be further delays. A phone may not be available. The caller may not know the police number. The caller may have difficulty communicating with the police department dispatcher.[4]

Police decisions also affect the crime data in the *UCR*. Crimes are included in the *UCR* only if the police decide there is sufficient evidence to believe that a crime has been committed. Police have wide discretion in making that decision, and factors such as the seriousness of the crime, the relationship between the complainant and the alleged offender, the desire for informal disposition of the case, and deference shown the police may influence police decisions regarding arrest.

Police individually, or as a department, may want to downplay the amount of crime in their areas. Consequently, they may not record all reported crimes, even when there is sufficient evidence that a crime has been committed.

UCR crime data are also affected by the fact that some crimes are not included within the list of crimes for which data are collected. As noted already, some misdemeanors are not included. Furthermore, some very serious crimes, such as those categorized as **white-collar crime**, are handled informally, or they are handled by administrative agencies rather than by criminal courts and thus are not counted as crimes.

Other kinds of crimes that might be considered serious but that are not recorded as either Part I or Part II offenses are computer crimes, organized crime, identity theft crimes, and corporate crimes. The economic impact of these crimes, along with white-collar crimes, is extensive, resulting in far greater total financial damage to society than the larceny-theft crimes included in the *UCR*.

The National Incident-Based Reporting System (NIBRS)

The FBI recognizes that more data are needed. In 1988, the FBI published details of its new approach: **National Incident-Based Reporting System (NIBRS)**. The NIBRS views crime, along with all its components, as an incident and recognizes that the data constituting those components should be collected and organized for purposes of analysis. The FBI refers to *elements* of crimes, among which are the following:

1. Alcohol and other drug influence
2. Specified location of the crime
3. Type of criminal activity involved
4. Type of weapon used
5. Type of victim
6. Relationship of victim to offender
7. Residency of victim and arrestee
8. Description of property and its value[5]

▶ **White-collar crime** The illegal actions of corporations or individuals, committed while pursuing their legitimate occupations. Examples are consumer fraud, bribery, and embezzlement.

▶ **National Incident-Based Reporting System (NIBRS)** A reporting system used by the FBI in collecting crime data. In this system, a crime is viewed along with all of its components, including the type of victim, type of weapon, location of the crime, alcohol/drug influence, type of criminal activity, relationship of victim to offender, and residence of victims and arrestees, as well as a description of the property and its value. This system includes 22 crimes, rather than the 8 that constitute the FBI's Part I Offenses, or serious crimes.

The NIBRS collects data on additional crime categories beyond the 8 included as Part I offenses and the 21 included as Part II offenses in the *UCR*. Among other differences, the NIBRS reports data on the number of rapes reported with male victims, whereas the *UCR* reports only female victims. According to a July 2005 BJS report, the NIBRS increases our knowledge about crime due to the following:

- Expansion of the number of offense categories included
- Detail on individual crime incidents (offenses, offenders, victims, property, and arrests)
- Linkage between arrests and clearances to specific incidents or offenses
- Inclusion of all offenses in an incident rather than only the most serious offense
- The ability to distinguish between attempted and completed crimes
- Linkages between offense, offender, victim, property, and arrestee variables, which permits examination of interrelationships[6]

2-1b National Crime Victimization Survey (NCVS)

The existence of unreported crime, often called the *dark figure of crime*, which never becomes part of official crime data, led to the establishment of another method of measuring crime. It was thought that, if victims do not report crimes to the police, perhaps they will do so on questionnaires submitted to samples of the general population.

Victimization surveys conducted by the Bureau of Justice Statistics (BJS) are called the **National Crime Victimization Survey (NCVS)**. The NCVS is based on the results of interviews conducted each six months with persons in about 60,000 households. Household members are questioned about whether they have been the victims of forcible rape, robbery, assault, household burglary, personal and household larceny, or motor vehicle theft. In addition, the NCVS conducts research on large samples in 20 of the largest cities in the country, along with 8 impact cities. These surveys include questions on business as well as personal victimizations.

The NCVS is a valuable supplement to the *UCR*. In addition to disclosing some crimes that are not reported to police, these surveys relate the reasons people give for not reporting crimes. However, the data are dependent on victim recall and perception, which may not be accurate. Despite this problem, victimization studies add to our knowledge of criminal activity.

> **National Crime Victimization Survey (NCVS)** Crime data collected by the Bureau of Justice Statistics (BJS) and based on surveys of people to determine who has been victimized by crime.

2-1c Self-Report Data (SRD)

In addition to the *UCR* data and surveys of the population that report how many people have been victimized, self-report studies are used to gather data on the extent and nature of criminal activity. **Self-report data (SRD)** are acquired by two methods: (1) the interview, in which a person is asked questions about illegal activities, and (2) the questionnaire, usually anonymous. Initially, self-report studies were conducted mainly with juveniles, but increasingly, the method is also being used to study adult career criminals.

SRD have been criticized on several grounds. The first problem is that of accuracy. Some respondents, especially juveniles, overreport their involvement in illegal activities, whereas others do not report some or all of their criminal activities. Other criticisms of SRD are that the surveys include too many trivial offenses and sometimes omit serious crimes, such as burglary, robbery, and sexual assault. Furthermore, self-report studies include too few minorities.

Taken together, these criticisms raise serious questions. White respondents tend to report greater involvement in less serious crimes that occur more frequently, and African Americans tend to report illegal acts that are less frequent but more serious. One study found that African American male offenders fail to report known offenses three times more often than white male offenders.[7]

> **Self-report data (SRD)** The process of collecting crime data by asking people about their criminal activity, usually by use of anonymous questionnaires.

Differences by gender have also been reported, but such findings do not invalidate the use of self-reports. However, they do suggest that it may be necessary to compare these results with other measures and to develop more sophisticated methods for data analysis.

2-2 Crime and Offenders: An Overview

All methods of counting and compiling crimes have problems. How crime is defined and how crimes are counted affect the results of all the methods. Crime is recorded and counted according to the policy used to determine whether one or more crimes occurred during the interaction between the offender and his or her victim. Frequently, the issue arises in sex crimes. For example, in one rape case, a defendant was convicted of three counts of forcible genital penetration. The defendant argued that he should have been convicted of only one count because each act lasted only a few seconds and all three occurred during a brief period, 7 to 10 minutes. The court disagreed, stating that the statute's prohibition of "penetration, however slight, of the genital or anal openings of another person by any foreign object, substance, instrument, or device" against the victim's will means that *each penetration* is a separate act. A "violation is *complete* the moment such 'penetration' occurs." The court emphasized that the purpose of the statute is to punish those who commit the "outrage to the person and [violate] feelings of the victim" and that this outrage occurs "each time the victim endures a new, unconsented sexual insertion."[8]

Another issue is that a sex crime that meets the definition of **rape** might be charged in one jurisdiction by another name, such as sexual battery, or might be reduced to a lesser charge, such as lewd behavior. With these caveats, we will look at some crime data.

In the foreword to the 1982 *UCR*, the director of the FBI announced with cautious optimism that the rate of serious crime was down 3 percent from 1981. The cautiousness of his optimism stemmed from the fact that, in the 1970s, crime rates dropped twice, only to turn back upward shortly thereafter. In the 1984 *UCR*, the director announced that crime had declined for the third straight year, with fewer serious offenses reported to law enforcement that year than in any year since 1978. He cautioned that the unprecedented three-year period of decline might be coming to an end because there had been a slight increase in crime during the last quarter of 1984.[9]

The number of crimes reported to the police, along with the crime rate, began climbing in 1984, leading the director of the FBI to say, "There are few social statements more tragic than these."[10] The increase in the number of crime offenses continued through 1991 but began dropping between 1991 and 1992. The numbers continued to decline, and by 1999, had fallen for the eighth consecutive year, but they leveled off in 2000, 2001, and 2002, with only small changes in 2003 and slight decreases in 2004. However, the 2005 data revealed a 2.3 percent increase in the volume of violent crimes and a 1.5 percent decrease in the volume of property crimes. Although experts warn that a year is not a trend, the rise in violent crime is of concern, especially the rise in murder.[11]

Experts do not agree on the explanations for the changes in the volume and rates of crime in recent years. For example, attempts to explain the changes in the crime rates in New York City are illustrated by a *New York Times* article in November 2002 headlined "Reasons for Crime Drop in New York Elude Many." Two of the most reliable crime figures are those of murder and motor vehicle thefts, and murder rates in New York City decreased by 12.7 percent between 2001 and 2002, with motor vehicle thefts decreasing by 5.3 percent. New York City Police Commissioner Raymond W. Kelly cited the city's efforts to increase law enforcement personnel over the previous decade, focusing on serious as well as quality-of-life criminal violations.[12]

Others were not so sure and referred to the 2006 brutal murder and apparent sexual torture of 24-year-old criminology graduate student Imette St. Guillen from Boston.

> **Rape** Historically, unlawful vaginal intercourse with a woman. It is called *forcible rape* if engaged in against the will of the woman by the use of threats or force. It is called *statutory rape* if the sexual intercourse was consensual between a man and a woman who was under the age of consent. More recently, some rape statutes have been rewritten to include male victims and female perpetrators, as well as penetration of any body opening by any instrument, including but not limited to the male sexual organ.

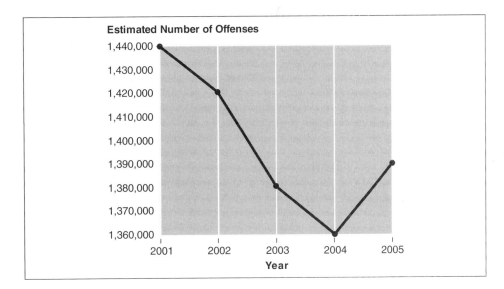

Estimated Number of Offenses

Figure 2-2
Trends in U.S. Violent Crime, 2001–2005
Source: Federal Bureau of Investigation, *Crime in the United States, Uniform Crime Reports 2005,* http://www.fbi.gov/ucr/05cius/offenses/violent_crime/index.html, retrieved 20 November 2006.

Darrell Littlejohn, the bouncer at the bar in which the beautiful John Jay School of Criminal Justice graduate student was last seen, was indicted for this gruesome murder. Yet, despite the publicity given to this murder, New York City is a relatively safe place, according to police strategists. According to the police department's deputy commissioner for strategic initiatives, "If the average New Yorker is concerned about being murdered in a random crime, the odds of that happening are really remote….If you are living apart from a life of crime, your risk is negligible." And in the words of a criminologist who lives and teaches in that city, "People will be shocked at how safe it is to live in New York City."[13]

The FBI's division of serious crimes into two categories—*violent crimes* (murder and nonnegligent manslaughter, forcible rape, robbery, and aggravated assault) and *property crimes* (burglary, larceny-theft, motor vehicle theft, and arson)—is used for further analysis of crime data. We begin with serious violent crimes.

2-2a Violent Crimes

Most of the reported serious crimes in the United States are property crimes, not violent crimes against the person. **Violent crimes** in the *UCR* include murder and nonnegligent manslaughter, forcible rape, robbery, and aggravated assault. The number of violent crimes in the United States, estimated at 1,390,695 in 2005, increased by 2.3 percent between 2004 and 2005. Figure 2-2 graphs the changes in the volume of violent crime in the United States between 2001 and 2005.[14]

The crime of **murder** (which, in the FBI compilation includes nonnegligent **manslaughter**) is defined as the "willful (nonnegligent) killing of one human being by another." In 2005, an estimated 16,692 murders occurred, representing a 3.4 percent increase over 2004. Murder and nonnegligent manslaughter accounted for 1.2 percent of all serious violent crimes in 2005.[15]

The second serious violent crime is *forcible rape*, defined by the *UCR* as "the carnal knowledge of a female forcibly and against her will. Assaults or attempts to commit rape by force or threat of force are included; however, **statutory rape** (without force) and other sex offenses are not included in this category." The FBI reported an estimated 93,934 forcible rapes in 2005, representing a 1.2 percent decrease from 2004, an estimated 3.4 percent increase compared to 2001, and a 2.4 percent decrease when compared to 1996 data.[16]

The third violent crime, **robbery**, is often used to refer to an act that constitutes larceny-theft rather than robbery. Since property is taken in both crimes, what is the

> **Violent crimes** Crimes defined by the FBI's *Uniform Crime Reports* as serious crimes against a person. They include murder and nonnegligent manslaughter, robbery, forcible rape, and aggravated assault.

> **Murder** The unlawful killing of another person with either express or implied malice aforethought.

> **Manslaughter** The unlawful killing of a human being by a person who lacks malice. Manslaughter may be *involuntary* (or *negligent*), the result of recklessness while committing an unlawful act (such as driving while intoxicated), or *voluntary*, an intentional killing committed in the heat of passion.

> **Statutory rape** *See* **Rape.**

> **Robbery** The use of force or fear to take personal property belonging to another against that person's will.

Figure 2-3
Trends in U.S. Property Crime, 2001–2005
Source: Federal Bureau of Investigation, *Crime in the United States, Uniform Crime Reports 2005*, http://www.fbi.gov/ucr/05cius/offenses/property_crime/index.html, retrieved 20 November 2006.

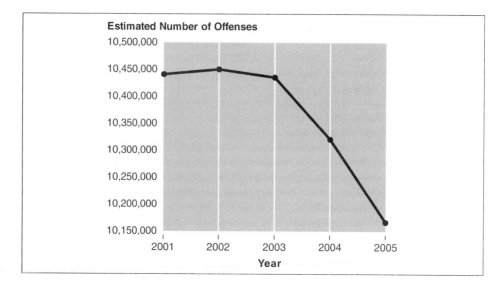

difference? Robbery involves the same elements as larceny-theft (discussed in the next section) but adds two elements that make it a violent crime: (1) taking the property from the person or in the presence of the person *and* (2) using force or threatening to use force. The FBI defines *robbery* as "the taking or attempting to take anything of value from the care, custody, or control of a person or persons by force or threat of force or violence and/or by putting the victim in fear." An estimated 417,122 robberies occurred in 2005, representing a 3.9 percent increase over 2004, but a 22.1 decrease from 1996.[17]

In some cases, the line between larceny-theft and robbery is a fine one, and not all scholars agree on how or where to draw that line. Thus, a crime such as purse snatching, which occurs so quickly that the victim does not have time to offer resistance or to be scared, may be classified as larceny-theft rather than robbery. But the fear that the victim suffers *after* the incident may be greater than the concern a victim has after a burglary or larceny-theft. It is this fear of violence, as well as the possibility of violence, that places robbery in the violent personal crime category.

The fourth violent crime, **aggravated assault**, is defined by the FBI as "an unlawful attack by one person upon another for the purpose of inflicting severe or aggravated bodily injury....Attempts involving the display or threat of a gun, knife, or other weapon are included because serious personal injury would likely result if the assault were completed." Although some aggravated assaults are conducted without a weapon, many involve the use of a deadly weapon. In 2005, an estimated 862,947 aggravated assaults occurred. Aggravated assaults increased 1.8 percent over 2004 but declined 16.8 percent from 1996.[18]

2-2b   Property Crimes

Most of the serious crimes committed in the United States are not violent personal crimes; they are **property crimes**. These crimes involve taking money or property that belongs to others, but they do not involve force against the victims. Four property crimes are included within the FBI's Part I, or serious, crimes: burglary, larceny-theft, motor vehicle theft, and arson. The FBI reported 10,166,159 property crimes in 2005, representing a 1.5 percent decrease from 2004 and a 13.9 percent decline from 1996. These crimes accounted for an estimated property loss of $16.5 billion; two-thirds of the crimes were larceny-theft.[19] Figure 2-3 graphs the estimated trend in the volume of property crime in the United States between 2001 and 2005.

The crime of **burglary** is defined by the FBI as "the unlawful entry of a structure to commit a felony or theft. The use of force to gain entry is not required to classify an offense as burglary." Burglary in the *UCR* is "categorized into three subclassifications:

► **Aggravated assault** Technically, an assault is a threat to commit a battery, but often, the term is used to refer to a battery. Aggravated assault involves a battery inflicted by use of a deadly weapon.

► **Property crimes** Crimes aimed at the property of another person rather than at the person. Serious property crimes include larceny-theft, burglary, motor vehicle theft, and arson.

► **Burglary** The illegal or forcible entering of any enclosed structure in order to commit a crime, usually theft. Some jurisdictions require that the intent be to commit a felony rather than a less serious crime.

forcible entry, unlawful entry where no force is used, and attempted forcible entry For 2005, the FBI reported an estimated 2,154,126 burglary offenses, representing a 0.5 percent increase over 2004. The volume of burglary offenses increased 1.8 percent from 2001 to 2005 but declined 14.1 percent from 1996 to 2005. Burglary accounted for 21.2 percent of all property crimes in 2005.[20]

The most frequently committed property offense is **larceny-theft**, which is defined as the "unlawful taking, carrying, leading, or riding away of property from the possession or constructive possession of another. It includes crimes such as shoplifting, pocket-picking, purse snatching, thefts from motor vehicles, thefts of motor vehicle parts and accessories, bicycle thefts, etc., in which no use of force, violence, or fraud occurs." In the *UCR*, larceny-theft "does not include embezzlement, con games, forgery, and worthless checks. Motor vehicle theft is also excluded from this category inasmuch as it is a separate…[Part 1, or serious] offense." The number of reported larceny-thefts in the United States in 2005 was 6,776,807, representing a decrease of 2.3 percent from 2004 and a 14.3 percent decline from 1996. In 2005, the estimated cost of larceny-theft per victim was $764.[21]

Motor vehicle theft, defined as "the theft or attempted theft of a motor vehicle," does not include thefts of items from within a motor vehicle; those are counted as larceny-theft. In 2005, there were approximately 1.2 million motor vehicle thefts in the United States, representing a 0.2 percent decrease from 2004 and an 11.4 percent decrease from 1996, and accounting for an estimated total property loss of $7.6 billion (an average of $6,173 per stolen vehicle).[22]

The final serious property crime is **arson**, defined by the FBI as "any willful or malicious burning or attempt to burn, with or without intent to defraud, a dwelling house, public building, motor vehicle or aircraft, personal property of another, etc. Only fires determined through investigation to have been willfully or maliciously set are classified as arsons. Fires of suspicious or unknown origins are excluded." Arson did not become a Part I offense until 1979; thus, trend data are not available for this crime as for other Part I offenses. Data are not available for all reporting agencies, and the FBI warns that, as a result, caution must be used in interpreting arson data. During 2005, an estimated 67,504 arson offenses were reported, with an average loss per arson of $14,910. The 2005 data represented a decrease of 2.7 percent from 2004.[23]

This completes the overview of the four violent and four property crimes that constitute Part I offenses in the *UCR*. But beginning with the report on the 1996 data, the FBI has included a section on hate crimes, which is discussed briefly here.

2-2c Hate Crimes

The *UCR* definition of **hate crime** is as follows: "A hate crime, also known as a bias crime, is a criminal offense committed against a person, property, or society which is motivated, in whole or in part, by the offender's bias against a race, religion, disability, sexual orientation, or ethnicity/national origin." Hate crimes may be aimed at property or at persons, but most of them are aimed at persons.

The U.S. Supreme Court has decided cases involving hate crime statutes. A recent one, in which the Court dealt with the characterization of an act as a hate crime or an expression of free speech, is the subject of Spotlight 2-1. In that case, the Court considered whether burning a cross is *prima facie* **evidence** of a hate crime or whether further evidence is required to support the hate crime charge.

2-2d Characteristics of Offenders

The FBI data on criminal offenders comes from arrests. In 2005, U.S. law enforcement officials reported that they had made an estimated 14,094,186 million arrests (excluding traffic infractions), with 603,503 of those constituting arrests for Part I violent crimes and 1,609,327 for Part I property crimes. The largest number of arrests for any offense was for drug abuse violations, accounting for 1.8 million arrests, representing

▶ **Larceny-theft** The unlawful removal and taking away of someone else's property with the intention of keeping it permanently. Historically, small thefts were categorized as *petit larceny* and large thefts as *grand larceny*. The latter was punished by the death penalty, a punishment no longer permitted for larceny-theft in the United States. Some modern theft laws do not distinguish between the two types of larceny-theft.

▶ **Motor vehicle theft** The stealing of an automobile, in contrast to the stealing of an automobile part or larceny-theft *from* an automobile.

▶ **Arson** The willful and malicious burning of the structure of another with or without the intent to defraud. Burning of one's own property with the intent to defraud is included in some definitions. Many modern statutes carry a more severe penalty for the burning of a dwelling than of other real property.

▶ **Hate crime** As defined in the federal criminal code, a crime "that manifests evidence of prejudice based on race, religion, disability, sexual orientation, or ethnicity, including where appropriate the crimes of murder, nonnegligent manslaughter, forcible rape, aggravated assault, simple assault, intimidation, arson, and destruction, damage or vandalism of property."

▶ ***Prima facie* evidence** Evidence that, on its face, is sufficient to constitute a fact unless it is sufficiently refuted.

Spotlight 2-1   Hate Crime versus Free Speech

In 2003, in *Virginia v. Black*, the U.S. Supreme Court considered a Virginia statute that stated "It shall be unlawful for any person or persons, with the intent of intimidating any person or group of persons, to burn, or cause to be burned, a cross on the property of another, a highway, or other public place." The second part of that statute provided that "Any such burning of a cross shall be *prima facie* evidence of an intent to intimidate a person or group of persons." Three separate cases were joined for purposes of the appeal. Barry Black led a Ku Klux Klan rally in which 25 to 30 people gathered on private property, talked about their beliefs, made negative comments about African Americans and Mexicans, and burned a cross. Black was tried before a jury that was instructed that the prosecution must prove that the defendant intended to intimidate, which means to put in fear, but that the intent could be *inferred* by the fact of cross burning.

In a separate incident, Richard Elliott and Jonathan O'Mara, along with another individual, attempted to burn a cross in the yard of an African American, James Jubilee. Jubilee, who lived next door to Elliott, had inquired of Elliott's mother about shots that were fired from behind the Elliott home. Elliott's mother responded that her son shot firearms as a hobby and that he did so in his backyard. In an apparent attempt to "get back" at Jubilee for his complaint about the firearms, Elliott and O'Mara drove a truck onto Jubilee's property, planted a cross, and attempted to burn it. Jubilee saw the partially burned cross the next morning. He said he was "very nervous" because "a cross burned in your yard...tells you that it's just the first round."

In considering these cases, the justices of the U.S. Supreme Court were not in agreement on several of the issues, some of which are procedural and beyond the scope of this text. Relevant here is that a majority of the Court held that it is not unconstitutional to ban cross burning with the intent to intimidate, but for a conviction to be upheld under this statute, prosecutors must prove beyond a reasonable doubt that the cross burning was for the purpose of intimidation rather than as an expression of *symbolic* speech, which is included within the First Amendment right to free speech (see Appendix A). The Court reversed Black's conviction because the jury was instructed that the required intent could be *inferred* from the fact of cross burning. That instruction was not at issue in O'Mara's case because he entered a guilty plea to both charges—attempted cross burning and conspiracy to commit cross burning. In the trial of Elliott on both of those charges, the jury instruction concerning inferred intent was not given. The cases of Elliott and O'Mara were vacated and remanded for further proceedings.

Justice Clarence Thomas wrote a scathing dissent, in which he characterized cross burning as a unique symbol of racial hatred and discrimination.

Source: Virginia v. Black, 538 U.S. 343 (2003).

13.1 percent of the total arrests in 2005. The total arrests in 2005 represented a decrease of 0.2 percent from 2004, although arrests for murder increased by 7.3 percent.[24]

A thorough study of crime includes not only an analysis of the number and type of crimes but also information on the characteristics of those who commit crimes. In this section, after a general overview of sources, data on offenders are discussed by age, race, and gender.

Before the collection of self-report data, most studies of criminals were based on the *UCR* data, which revealed that a higher percentage of the arrestees were young African Americans from the lower socioeconomic class. Many people concluded that persons with these characteristics were more likely to commit crimes, whereas others argued that the data represented discrimination against these groups.

When looking at the data, we should understand that the differences between the crime rates of men and women and of African Americans and whites do not mean that gender or race *causes* the criminal activity or the reaction to that activity. There is some evidence that it is not age, gender, or race that influences official reaction to the alleged offender but, rather, the seriousness of the offense committed and the degree of the offender's involvement in that offense. There is evidence, too, that the differences in crime rates between the SRD and *UCR* data may be explained by the fact that only a small number of African Americans were sampled in the self-report studies. Furthermore, as noted earlier, some studies show that African Americans and whites differ in their tendencies to report certain crimes, but it may also be argued that the differences in crime rates by race are too great to be explained in any way other than discrimination.[25]

Age

Age is a factor most often associated with crimes, most of which are committed by young people. According to the 2005 data:

- In 2005, adults (persons 18 years of age and over) accounted for 84.7 percent of all persons arrested.
- Adults accounted for 84.2 percent of persons arrested for violent crime. Persons under 25 years of age comprised 44.3 percent of all those arrested.
- Adults were arrested most often for drug abuse violations than for any other offense, and juveniles (persons under 18 years of age) were arrested most often for larceny-theft offenses.
- Historically, juveniles have had a high involvement in arson offenses. In 2005, 48.6 percent of persons arrested for arson were juveniles, and of those juveniles, 59.4 percent were under the age of 15.
- Persons under 18 constituted 15.3 percent of the total arrestees in 2005.[26]

Race

Another factor often associated with crime is race, although there is no general agreement on the impact of race on crime. In 2005, most arrestees were white (69.8 percent, compared with 27.8 percent for African Americans), with whites accounting for 61 percent of all arrests for violent crimes and 69.4 percent of all arrests for property crimes. Whites were most often arrested for driving under the influence, African Americans for drug abuse violations. When race and age are considered, white and black juveniles were almost equally represented in arrests for violent crimes, but white juveniles accounted for 67.2 percent of all arrests for property crimes. African American juveniles were most often arrested for simple assaults, white juveniles for larceny-theft.[27]

While analyzing these data, we must realize that, even in cases in which the arrest rates are higher for whites than for African Americans, they may still be disproportionate, as African Americans constitute only approximately 11 percent of the total population. Second, we must consider not only arrest data but also the fact that official and unofficial crime data show differences between African Americans and whites at all levels of criminal justice system activity.

Gender

A third demographic factor associated with crime is gender. Historically, crime rates for men have been significantly higher than those for women, with the exception of those crimes that, by definition, are committed predominantly by women, such as prostitution. Males constituted 76.2 percent of the 2005 arrestees, including 82.1 percent of arrestees for violent crimes and 68.0 percent of all arrests for property crimes. The number of men arrested in 2005 was approximately the same as in 2004; the number of women increased by 0.7 percent. The number of female arrests, although small overall, increased by 9.5 percent in the five-year period 2001–2005, during which time the number of male arrests increased by only 1.7 percent. During that five-year period, the number of women arrested for murder decreased by 9.2 percent, compared to an increase of 10.1 percent for men. However, the number of males arrested for drug violations increased 13.5 percent, compared to an increase of 24.8 percent for women.[28]

2-3   Crime Victims

Historically, the study of victims was not an important focus among social scientists. This has changed in the past two decades, with more attention being given to studying the characteristics and problems of victims, as well as to improving the responses of

Professions 2-1

Careers in Victimology

In recent years, Congress and most states have enacted legislation to provide assistance to crime victims, creating numerous job opportunities in victimology. Provisions for financial assistance require qualified persons to administer the programs. Counseling of crime victims necessitates providing specialized training, especially in the treatment of victims of rape and other sex crimes. Many jurisdictions have established rape crisis centers, whereas others have concentrated on training police and prosecutors to understand the trauma suffered by sex crime victims. Schoolteachers must be informed regarding what to expect, especially from children who have become crime victims.

Background checks for employees in many jobs are important to avoid the negligent hiring of persons who might victimize those with whom they come into contact during work. All individuals who work with victims must be sensitized to the privacy requirements regarding those victims' crime records. Preparing victim impact statements for courts is a new area of crucial paperwork required of probation offi-

cers and others. Requirements that victims be notified of pending court and other important hearings create jobs for persons charged with these responsibilities.

Although we have a long way to go before victims receive sufficient assistance in our criminal justice systems, we have made progress at the national, state, and local levels, and interesting and challenging job opportunities exist for those who wish to work with crime victims.

Check the following websites for information on jobs in criminology and specifically in victimology:

- http://criminaljustice.factexpert.com/596-victimology-job.php
- http://www.princetonreview.com/cte/profiles/dayInLife.asp?careerID=47
- http://jobguide.thegoodguides.com.au/jobdetails.cfm?jobid=425
- http://www.allcriminaljusticeschools.com/faqs/criminology.php

▶ **Victimology** The discipline that studies the nature and causes of victimization, as well as programs for aiding victims and preventing victimization.

▶ **Restitution** Punishment that requires an offender to repay the victim with services or money. This punishment may be imposed instead of or in addition to other punishment or fines and may be a requirement of parole.

criminal justice systems to victims' needs. Professional societies such as the National Organization for Victim Assistance (NOVA) have been instrumental in passing federal and state legislation concerning victims. NOVA has provided national assistance to thousands of victims, and its officials coordinate with local organizations to improve services at that level. Workshops on **victimology** have increased our knowledge and understanding of the problems. Job opportunities have been developed in victimology, as illustrated by Professions 2-1.

Concern with victims' rights and needs has led to national legislation on their behalf. In response to the Victim and Witness Protection Act of 1982,[29] a federal statute, the U.S. attorney general's office issued detailed guidelines concerning the treatment of crime victims and witnesses by prosecutors and investigators in the Department of Justice. These guidelines are designed to protect the privacy of victims and witnesses and to provide medical, social, and counseling services. Notification of court proceedings, **restitution**, and other programs available for the assistance of victims and witnesses are also provided. Some states have gone beyond the federal provisions and have enacted additional legislation to aid victims, and in the 1994 crime bill, Congress included some provisions to enhance victims' rights, with a major focus on domestic violence victims.[30]

Special legislation was also provided to compensate the victims of the 9/11 terrorist attacks. Within 11 days of the attacks, Congress enacted the Air Transportation Safety and System Stabilization Act of 2001 to provide financial compensation for victims who agreed not to sue the airlines or others for negligence. In June 2004, the Victim Compensation Fund was ended, with 97 percent of the 2,973 eligible families taking part in its provisions. A study by the Rand Corporation reported in the fall of 2004 that over $38 billion had been paid to individuals and businesses, with families of victims who died in the 9/11 attacks receiving, on the average, $3.1 million from government and charitable sources. The families of law enforcement officers received an average of $4.2 million each.[31]

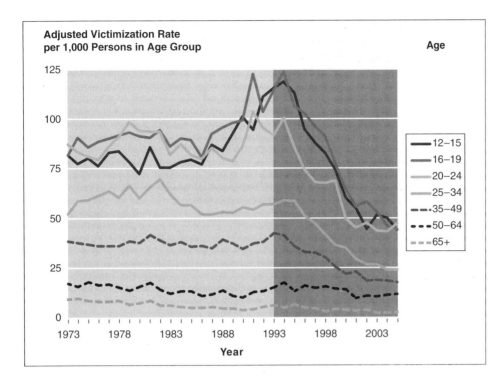

Adjusted Victimization Rate per 1,000 Persons in Age Group

Age

Legend:
- 12–15
- 16–19
- 20–24
- 25–34
- 35–49
- 50–64
- 65+

Year

Figure 2-4
Violent Crime Rates by Age of Victim, 1973–2005
Source: Bureau of Justice Statistics, U.S. Department of Justice, "Victim Characteristics," http://www.ojp.usdoj.gov/bjs/cvict_v.htm, retrieved 20 February 2007.

Victim compensation programs, however, do not solve all of the problems of victims. Many of these programs are not adequately funded and thus do not provide sufficient money to satisfy reasonable claims. Further, a study of prosecutors' offices noted that such programs place heavy burdens on prosecutors, who are primarily responsible for the programs' implementation. Prosecutorial offices must hire additional staff and develop policies and programs that require financial and other resources.[32] Even supervising restitution required by law to be paid by offenders to their victims can be a significant financial burden on prosecutorial offices. Finally, many of the state laws are not written clearly or are not enforced widely.[33]

> **Victim compensation programs** Plans for assisting crime victims in making social, emotional, and economic adjustments.

2-3a Characteristics of Victims

The National Crime Victimization Survey (NCVS) data include information on the demographic characteristics of crime victims. For many years, analyses of victimization data have shown differences in the rates of victimization of specific groups within the population. The most frequent violent crime victims are young people, men (except for rape and sexual assault), African Americans, Hispanics, divorced or separated people, the unemployed, the poor, and residents of central cities.

Age

In general, the younger the person, the more likely he or she is to become a crime victim. The BJS found, as indicated in Figure 2-4, that in 2005, persons between the ages of 12 and 24 were more frequently violent crime victims than persons of all other ages, but "beginning with the 20–24 age category, the rate at which persons were victims declined significantly as the age category increased."[34]

Race

Victimization data show that African Americans suffer higher rates of violent and household crimes than whites, and generally, violent crimes against African Americans are more serious than those committed against whites. Offenders who victimize African

Americans are more likely to use weapons; violent crimes against African Americans involve a gun in twice as many cases as compared with whites. African American victims are more likely than whites to be attacked physically during the crime's commission.[35]

The BJS reported that in 2004,

- "Per every 1,000 persons in that racial group, 26 blacks, 21 whites, and 13 persons of other races sustained a violent crime.
- Black and white persons experienced statistically similar rates of simple assault.
- Black, white, and other races experienced similar rates of rape/sexual assault."[36]

Victimization data also distinguish Hispanic victims. Earlier analyses of data disclosed that Hispanics, whose population is expanding more rapidly than any other racial group in the United States, were more often victimized by violent crimes than were non-Hispanics. They also endured a higher rate of household crimes.[37]

BJS trend data for 1993–2004, however, reveal that crime victimization of Hispanics fell 67 percent. For 2004, BJS reported the following with regard to ethnicity:

- "563,260 Hispanic persons age 12 or older were victims of rape, sexual assault, robbery, aggravated assault and simple assault.
- Violence against Hispanics age 12 or older most often took the form of simple assault (64 percent).
- Hispanic persons age 12 or older experienced 11 percent of all violent crimes and made up 13 percent of the population.
- Hispanics were victims of overall violence at a rate higher than non-Hispanics.
- Hispanics were more likely to be victims of simple assault than non-Hispanics.
- Hispanics and non-Hispanics experienced similar rates of aggravated assault, robbery, and rape/sexual assault."[38]

Gender

Overall, men are more likely than women to be victimized by crime, especially violent crime, although trend data show that the rates are getting closer. Women have higher violent crime victimization rates than men in only the categories of forcible rape and other sexual assaults.

Violent crime rates for both female and male victims decreased between 1973 and 2005, as Figure 2-5 indicates. The BJS victimization data on which that figure is based include the crimes of homicide, forcible rape, robbery, and both simple and aggravated assault.

2-3b   Relationship between Victims and Offenders

Social interaction between offenders and their victims is an important factor in some crimes. Normally, violence in the form of assault or murder is preceded by social interaction, and physical violence is more likely if both the offender and the victim define the situation as one calling for violence. If only one person is prone toward physical violence, the altercation generally will not become a physical one. In this sense, the victim may contribute to his or her own injury or death, but that does not mean the victim *caused* or is responsible for the crime.

The extent of violence committed by those who know each other, especially within the domestic setting, is difficult to estimate. These crimes may not be reported by the victims or by other family members because of fear, embarrassment, or for other reasons, such as a hope that the situation will improve. Many violent crime victims, especially murder victims, know their assailants, but recent data also show a decline in the homicide of intimates, especially male victims. For example, the BJS reported that between 1976 and 2000, the number of men who were murdered by intimates (defined as spouses, ex-spouses, boyfriends, or girlfriends), dropped by 68 percent. The number

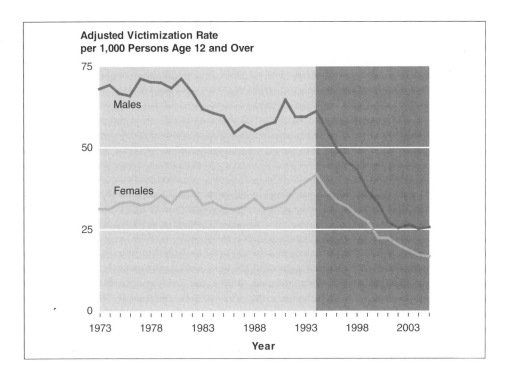

Adjusted Victimization Rate per 1,000 Persons Age 12 and Over

Males

Females

Year

Figure 2-5
Violent Crime Rates by Gender of Victims, 1973–2005
Source: Bureau of Justice Statistics, *U.S. Department of Justice,* "Victim Characteristics," http://www.ojp.usdoj.gov/bjs/cvict_v.htm, retrieved 20 February 2007.

of women who were murdered by intimates declined in 1993 through 1995 (after being stable for two decades) and then stabilized through the year 2000. Intimates remain a significant factor in homicides, however, with the BJS reporting in 2006 that data through the year 2002 showed the following:

- "Spouses and family members made up about 15 percent of all victims.
- About one-third of the victims were acquaintances of the assailant.
- In 14 percent of all murders, the victim and the offender were strangers.
- The victim/offender relationship was undetermined in about one-third of homicides."[39]

The BJS also reports that female, as compared with male, murder victims are much more likely to be victimized by their intimates and that in recent years:

- "About one-third of female murder victims were killed by an intimate.
- About 3–4 percent of male murder victims were killed by an intimate.
- Of all female murder victims, the proportion killed by an intimate was relatively stable until 1995 when the proportion began increasing.
- Of male murder victims, the proportion killed by an intimate has dropped."[40]

One final area of victim abuse involving close associations is that of the abandonment or killing of newborns. In Houston, Texas, for example, an increase in this crime led to the enactment of an ordinance that encourages parents to turn over their newborns to hospitals or fire stations rather than abandon them. The parents are provided legal protection if they take this route. But it is also a growing concern that some mothers in the maternity wards of hospitals are abandoning drug-addicted babies, along with those infected with HIV.[41] Provisions for protecting mothers (or fathers) who abandon their newborn children in ways that will protect those infants are called **Baby Moses laws** and are becoming more common in the United States as well as some other countries.

2-3c Fear of Crime and Citizens' Reactions

Another victimization focus is on the fear of random violence. The fear of violent crime by strangers, who often pick their victims randomly, led U.S. Supreme Court Chief

▶ **Baby Moses laws** Provisions for protecting mothers (or fathers) who abandon their newborn children in ways that will protect those infants. These laws are becoming more common in the United States as well as some other countries. Normally, the laws permit new parents to leave the babies in designated *safe places* and avoid prosecution.

Justice Warren E. Burger to refer in 1981 to the "reign of terror in American cities." One privately funded study of crime concluded that same year that "the fear of crime is slowly paralyzing American society."[42]

The fear of crime may not always be realistic in terms of the probability that crimes will occur, but fear leads to lifestyle changes for many, especially the elderly. A purse snatching may have a far more serious effect on an elderly person than it would have on a younger victim. The elderly are more likely to be injured seriously in any altercation with an assailant. Such direct contact may be much more frightening to an elderly person, and the loss of money may be more serious to a person living on a fixed income. For many elderly, the fear of crime leads to significant lifestyle changes; some even refuse to leave their dwellings.

Women may also adjust their lifestyles to decrease their chances of becoming crime victims. They may be advised by police and others to do so. In various cities, police have reported that a high percentage of forcible rapes are committed against female victims who have been careless—walking alone at night, hitchhiking, sleeping in apartments with unlocked doors or windows, or going out with someone they met at a bar. Other women, because of their fear of crime, may avoid going to places they would like to go in order to reduce the probability that they will be victimized. But they deprive themselves of a lifestyle they prefer. For them, one cost of crime is diminished personal freedom.

One venue in which young women fear personal violence, especially rape, is on college and university campuses. Research shows that women in this venue are more likely to become rape victims than their cohorts who are not in college. In a recent study of college women, researchers found that their fear of rape overshadows their fear of other crimes, especially face-to-face crimes, and that women fear rape even more than murder.[43] Others disagree that women's fear of rape so overshadows their fear of other crimes that it accounts for the greater fear of crime among women than among men. Although clearly "the magnitude of fear [of crime] for women is greater than it is for men," say other researchers, "the patterns of variables that predict fear are similar for both men and women." It is argued that a "generalized fear of personal harm may be the more important predictor, rather than a specific fear of rape." This latter study measured fear of gang violence, and that fear extended to both men and women.[44]

Women and the elderly are not the only ones who make lifestyle changes as a result of a concern with crime. Many people install expensive burglar alarm systems or move to another, hopefully safer, neighborhood. Others refrain from going out at night or from traveling to certain areas. As two scholars have concluded, "Left unchecked, [fear] can destroy the fabric of civilized society, causing us to become suspicious of each other, locking ourselves in our homes and offices, and relinquishing our streets to predators."[45]

Our fear of crime has been enhanced by the events of 9/11, which made it clear that thousands of innocent people can be subject to catastrophic injury, property damage, and even death. The reach of those terrorist acts, along with the bombing of the federal building in Oklahoma City, school shootings, and numerous other highly publicized criminal acts, has resulted in increased security not only at airports and in large cities and at major events but also in schools. The inconvenience and time consumption of some of these security measures (such as long waits at airports) provide constant reminders that we are all subject to random violence.

2-3d   Criminal Justice Systems and Crime Victims

Research in the 1980s and 1990s provided information on how victims react to crime. The findings of this research have led to significant changes in criminal justice systems. It has not been an easy journey for crime victims; nor are all of their problems solved. Victim reaction, however, has been a key factor in these changes.

In 1982, President Ronald Reagan established the President's Task Force on Victims, which was followed in 1984 by the Attorney General's Task Force on Family Violence.

Both commissions interviewed crime victims and others. Most of the victims spoke negatively about their treatment in criminal justice systems.

The criminal justice systems' reaction to some crime victims means that they are victimized twice: once by the criminal and once by the system in a variety of ways. First, the victim may be blamed for the crime. Particularly in the case of sexual assault, the response of the system may be that the victim asked for it by being in a questionable place, such as a bar; by hitchhiking on the highway; by having a questionable reputation; or by wearing provocative clothing. This is referred to as **victim precipitation**.

In addition to being blamed for the crime, victims may perceive that police and others will not be sympathetic to crimes committed by persons known to the alleged victim—that they view those actions as domestic problems, not violence. Some rape victims have complained about the reactions of police and prosecutors, alleging that they have not tried to understand the problems suffered by the victims.

Third, some victims (and others) complain that U.S. criminal justice systems favor defendants over victims. This response should be analyzed in light of later discussions in this text of defendants' rights, but basically, the position is that criminal justice systems have gone too far in protecting defendants to the exclusion of victims. This issue was highlighted in the 2004 legal proceedings involving Kobe Bryant, Los Angeles Lakers star basketball player, who was accused of raping a young employee while he was staying at a resort hotel in Colorado. Bryant, 25, admitted having sex with the complainant, 19, but maintained that he did not rape her. The trial judge ruled that during court proceedings the complainant could not be referred to as a *victim*. The defense had argued that to do so prejudiced the defense, establishing a presumption that a rape occurred.[46] Eventually, the complainant refused to continue to press charges against Bryant, and the criminal charges were dropped. The civil case filed by the complainant was settled out of court, but the terms remained confidential.

Some changes designed to benefit victims have been made within criminal justice systems. Many departments now train police and prosecutors to be sensitive to the needs of adult rape and domestic violence victims, as well as young children who are abused in any way by their families, friends, or strangers. Other departments have special units of officers designated to handle allegations by these or other types of victims.

Police departments have changed their arrest policies in response to victims who have complained that often police do not arrest the offenders, and that if they do, some prosecutors will not file charges. Police response to that complaint has been that most victims will not cooperate, and without their cooperation, most prosecutions of domestic violence cases will not be successful. Victims respond that they are afraid that, if they cooperate, the alleged offenders will retaliate.

In an attempt to remove the responsibility (and thus the increased chances of retaliation by the accused) from the victim, some police departments have instituted a policy of mandatory arrests in domestic battery cases. Mandatory arrests remove from police the discretion to avoid the situation, mediate, or recommend civil action only. If called to the scene of a domestic battering, police must arrest if they have probable cause to believe that battering has occurred.

Legislative and administrative changes in the roles of prosecutors and judges have also been made. Training programs for prosecutors have given them greater understanding of the unique problems suffered by rape, domestic abuse, and child abuse victims. The provision of counseling services for victims; court-ordered counseling for those found guilty of rape, domestic violence, or child abuse; greater restrictions on pretrial release of suspects; and many other changes have occurred.

Earlier in this chapter, we mentioned that some criminal justice systems have responded to victims' needs by establishing victim compensation programs, but some jurisdictions have also enacted legislation to benefit witnesses, and some legislation is designed to benefit both crime victims and witnesses. Congress passed a victim compensation bill that applies to victims and witnesses involved in federal crimes—the Victim and Witness Protection Act of 1982 (VWPA), which has been amended subsequently. The

▶ **Victim precipitation** The concept that a criminal act may have been brought on by the alleged victim's actions.

act contains various provisions designed to prevent harassment of victims and witnesses. It establishes guidelines for fair treatment of crime victims and witnesses in criminal justice systems. It requires victim impact statements at sentencing, contains more stringent bail requirements, and provides that the sentencing judge must order defendants to pay restitution to victims or state reasons for not doing so.[47]

Congress also passed the Victims of Crime Act (VOCA) of 1984, which authorizes that federal funds be distributed by the Office of Justice Programs through its Office for Victims of Crime and Bureau of Justice for state victim compensation and assistance programs. VOCA originally provided that federal funds would stop after 30 September 1988, but Congress reauthorized the program to continue. The money for the fund comes from fines, penalties, and the sale of forfeited goods. The fund is distributed to local agencies and has been used for hiring counselors to work with victims, to compensate victims, and even for technology, such as computers, used to assist victims.[48]

In recent years, additional attempts have been made to compensate victims and to increase their participation in criminal justice systems. Although a proposed amendment to the U.S. Constitution was withdrawn by its sponsors, who stated that they knew they could not get the necessary support for passage, a new federal bill was passed by the U.S. Congress and signed by President George W. Bush in 2004. In part, the Crime Victims' Rights Act provides the following:

1. The right to be reasonably protected from the accused.
2. The right to reasonable, accurate, and timely notice of any public court proceeding, or any parole proceeding, involving the crime or of any release or escape of the accused.
3. The right not to be excluded from any such public court proceeding, unless the court, after receiving clear and convincing evidence, determines that testimony by the victim would be materially altered if the victim heard other testimony at that proceeding.
4. The right to be reasonably heard at any public proceeding in the district court involving release, plea, sentencing, or any parole proceeding.
5. The reasonable right to confer with the attorney for the Government in the case.
6. The right to full and timely restitution as provided in law.
7. The right to proceedings free from unreasonable delay.
8. The right to be treated with fairness and with respect for the victim's dignity and privacy.[49]

Chapter Wrap-Up

This chapter provided an overview of data on crime, offenders, and crime victims, and discussed how those data are secured. The three basic methods for collecting crime data were described and analyzed. The official data of the *Uniform Crime Reports (UCR)* report the amount of crime as recorded by police departments and reported to the FBI.

In recent years, the FBI has recognized the limitations of its method of collecting and recording crime data. Its most significant change, the National Incident-Based Reporting System (NIBRS), is in operation in many states. NIBRS views crime as an incident that involves many elements, including alcohol and drug abuse; the types of victims, weapons, and criminal activity; the victim's and arrestee's residency; the relationship between victims and offenders; and a description of property and property values. The collection of these additional elements of criminal acts significantly enhances our ability to analyze crime.

The second source of crime data is the National Crime Victimization Survey (NCVS). It is valuable because it reveals that

many victims do not report their victimizations to the police. The NCVS provides data on why people do not report victimizations. It does not give any information on arrests, and it is dependent on the accuracy of perception and reporting of crime victims.

The third major source of crime data—self-report data (SRD)—provides information not secured by either of the official methods on characteristics of people who say they have committed crimes. SRD provide valuable data for social scientists who study why crimes are committed, as well as for officials who must make decisions concerning the use of resources aimed at crime control and prevention. SRD allow the study of repeat offenders. The major problem with this approach is that respondents may underreport or overreport crimes.

All the data sources can be used to analyze the nature and extent of crime, but it is important to analyze carefully the time periods and the definitions of crimes being measured before comparing data from the various sources. Data in this chapter come primarily from the *UCR*, with victimization data coming from the NCVS. The data on criminal offenders are analyzed by three major variables: age, race, and gender.

Following the look at data, the chapter explored the recently developed and rapidly expanding study of victimology. It discussed the characteristics of crime victims, along with the problems those victims face in criminal justice systems. The chapter noted that, although they are the most frequently studied, women, the elderly, and children are not the most frequent crime victims. Most violent crimes are committed against African American men, and men are more frequent crime victims than women. Brief mention was made of the smallest victims—newborns who are abandoned by their parents—and the Baby Moses laws designed to encourage parents to give those infants a chance at life and adoption.

The chapter noted some of the specific problems crime victims face within criminal justice systems. It closed with a discussion of efforts to assist crime victims, mentioning such measures as victim compensation, revised court procedures, and victim participation in criminal justice processes.

Like most changes in the system, recognizing the rights of victims creates other needs, such as training programs for professionals within the system and financial backing for those programs as well as for victim compensation plans. Furthermore, victims' rights and defendants' rights may come into conflict. Nevertheless, changes made in the system to help victims may produce positive results, such as increased crime reporting and more arrests and convictions. But what appear to be positive results could create problems for the system and society because of the increased need for jails and prisons. Thus, a study of crime victims provides another example of the need to assess the effect that changes in one aspect of the system have on the rest of the system and on society.

This completes the introductory chapters. We turn now to a look at policing, the criminal justice component through which many people enter criminal justice system processing.

Key Terms

aggravated assault (p. 38)
arson (p. 39)
Baby Moses laws (p. 45)
Bureau of Justice Statistics (BJS) (p. 29)
burglary (p. 38)
crime rate (p. 32)
crimes known to the police (p. 32)
hate crime (p. 39)
index offenses (p. 32)
larceny-theft (p. 39)

manslaughter (p. 37)
motor vehicle theft (p. 39)
murder (p. 37)
National Crime Victimization Survey (NCVS) (p. 35)
National Incident-Based Reporting System (NIBRS) (p. 34)
prima facie evidence (p. 39)
property crimes (p. 38)
rape (p. 36)

restitution (p. 42)
robbery (p. 37)
self-report data (SRD) (p. 35)
statutory rape (p. 37)
Uniform Crime Reports (UCR) (p. 31)
victim compensation programs (p. 43)
victimology (p. 42)
victim precipitation (p. 47)
violent crimes (p. 37)
white-collar crime (p. 34)

Apply It

1. Describe and contrast the major sources of crime data.
2. Why should attention be paid to misdemeanors?
3. What are the limitations of the UCR?
4. Explain and evaluate the FBI's NIBRS system of data reporting.
5. Why are some crimes not reported by victims? If you were a crime victim, would you call the police? Would it depend on the nature of the crime?
6. What are the advantages and disadvantages of self-report studies?
7. What have been the major changes in the amount of crime in the United States in the past decade?
8. What are the major differences between serious violent and property crimes? List and define the four crimes in each of these categories.
9. What is hate crime? Discuss. How does the recent U.S. Supreme Court case on cross burning relate to hate crimes?
10. Discuss the relationship between crime and each of the following: age, race, and gender.
11. What progress has been made recently in the study of victims?
12. Discuss the characteristics of crime victims.
13. Define Baby Moses laws.
14. What lifestyle changes might you consider because of the risk of crime?
15. What, if any, effect did the 9/11 terrorist attacks have on your view of crime?
16. Is the fear of crime realistic?
17. What changes have been made in recent legislation to improve the plight of crime victims?

Endnotes

1. Federal Bureau of Investigation, *Crime in the United States: Uniform Crime Reports 1999* (Washington, D.C.: U.S. Government Printing Office, 2000), pp. 6–50.

2. *Crime in the United States, 2000*, News Release, Federal Bureau of Investigation (22 October 2001), p. 1.

3. Federal Bureau of Investigation, *FBI Releases Its 2005 Crime Statistics*, http://www.fbi.gov/ucr/o5cius/about/crime_summary.html, accessed 20 November 2006.

4. William Spelman and Dale K. Brown, *Calling the Police: Citizen Reporting of Serious Crime* (Washington, D.C.: National Institute of Justice, October 1984), pp. xxiv–xxvii.

5. See Federal Bureau of Investigation, *Uniform Crime Reporting: National Incident-Based Reporting System*, vol. 1, *Data Collection Guidelines* (Washington, D.C.: U.S. Department of Justice, 1 July 1988).

6. Bureau of Justice Statistics, U.S. Department of Justice, *Incident-Based Statistics*, http://www.ojp.usdoj.gov.bjs, accessed 23 May 2006.

7. Michael J. Hindelang, Travis Hirschi, and Joseph G. Weis, "Correlates of Delinquency: The Illusion of Discrepancy between Self-Report and Official Measures," *American Sociological Review* 44 (December 1979): 995–1014.

8. People v. Harrison, 768 P.2d 1078, 1081, 1082 (Cal. 1989).

9. Federal Bureau of Investigation, *Crime in the United States: Uniform Crime Reports 1984* (Washington, D.C.: U.S. Government Printing Office, 1985), p. iii.

10. Federal Bureau of Investigation, *Crime in the United States: Uniform Crime Reports 1985* (Washington, D.C.: U.S. Government Printing Office, 1986), p. iii.

11. Federal Bureau of Investigation, *Crime in the United States: Uniform Crime Reports 2005*, http://www.fbi.gov/05cius/about/crime_summary.html, accessed 20 November 2006.

12. "Reasons for Crime Drop in New York Elude Many," *New York Times* (29 November 2002), p. 28.

13. "New York City Killers, and Those Killed, by Numbers," *New York Times* (28 April 2006), p. 1.

14. Federal Bureau of Investigation, "Violent Crime," *Uniform Crime Reports 2005*, http://www.fbi.gov/ucr/05cius/offenses/violent_crime/index.html, accessed 20 November 2006.

15. Federal Bureau of Investigation, "Murder," *Uniform Crime Reports 2005*, http://www.fbi.gov/ucr/05cius/offenses/violent_crime/murder_homicide.html, accessed 20 November 2006.

16. Federal Bureau of Investigation, "Forcible Rape," *Uniform Crime Reports 2005*, http://www.fbi.gov/ucr/05cius/offenses/violent_crime/forcible_rape.html, accessed 20 November 2006.

17. Federal Bureau of Investigation, "Robbery," *Uniform Crime Reports 2005*, http://www.fbi.gov/ucr/05cius/offenses/violent-crime/robbery.html, accessed 20 November 2006.

18. Federal Bureau of Investigation, "Aggravated Assault," *Uniform Crime Reports 2005*, http://www.fbi.gov/ucr/05cius/offenses/violent_crime/aggravated_assault.html, accessed 20 November 2006.

19. Federal Bureau of Investigation, "Property Crime," *Uniform Crime Reports 2005*, http://www.fbi.gov/ucr/05cius/offenses/property_crime/index.html, accessed 20 November 2006.

20. Federal Bureau of Investigation, "Burglary," *Uniform Crime Reports 2005*, http://www.fbi.gov/ucr/05cius/offenses/property_crime/burglary.html, accessed 20 November 2006.

21. Federal Bureau of Investigation, "Larceny-Theft," *Uniform Crime Reports 2005*, http://www.fbi.gov/ucr/05cius/offenses/property_crime/larceny-theft.html, accessed 20 November 2006.

22. Federal Bureau of Investigation, "Motor Vehicle Theft," *Uniform Crime Reports 2005*, http://www.fbi.gov/ucr/05cius/offenses/property_crime/motor_vehicle_theft.html, accessed 20 November 2006.

23. Federal Bureau of Investigation, "Arson," *Uniform Crime Reports 2005*, http://www.fbi.gov/ucr/05cius/offenses/property_crime/arson.html, accessed 20 November 2006.

24. Federal Bureau of Investigation, "Persons Arrested," *Uniform Crime Reports 2005*, http://www.fbi.gov/ucr/05cius/arrests/index.html, accessed 10 December 2006.

25. See, for example, William Wilbanks, *The Myth of a Racist Criminal Justice System* (Monterey, Calif.: Brooks/Cole, 1987) and Joan Petersilia et al., *Racial Equity in Sentencing* (Santa Monica, Calif.: Rand, February 1988).

26. Federal Bureau of Investigation, "Persons Arrested," *Crime in the United States 2005*, http://www.fbi.gov/ucr/05cius/data/table_38.html, accessed 10 December 2006.

27. Federal Bureau of Investigation, "Persons Arrested," *Crime in the United States 2005*, http://www.fbi.gov/ucr/05cius/data/table_43.html, accessed 10 December 2006.

28. Ibid., Table 35.

29. U.S. Code, Title 18, Section 3663 (2007).

30. See, for example, Title IV, Violence against Women, of the Violent Crime Control and Law Enforcement Act of 1994, Public Law 103-322 (13 September 1994).

31. The Air Transportation Safety and System Stabilization Act of 2001, as amended in 2002, Pub. Law No. 107-72 (2007). See also "New Study Puts Sept. 11 Payout at $38 Billion," *New York Times* (8 November 2004), p. 1.

32. "Victim Rights Impose Burdens on Prosecutors, Study Shows," *Criminal Justice Newsletter* 32, no. 10 (5 June 2002): 3.

33. "States Closing Loopholes in Victim Restitution Laws," *Criminal Justice Newsletter* (16 January 2003), p. 4.

34. Bureau of Justice Statistics, *Victim Characteristics*, http://www.ojp.usdoj.gov/bjs/cvict_v.htm, accessed 24 May 2006.

35. Bureau of Justice Statistics, *Black Victims* (Washington, D.C.: U.S. Department of Justice, April 1990), p. 1.

36. Bureau of Justice Statistics, *Victim Characteristics*.

37. Bureau of Justice Statistics, *Hispanic Victims* (Washington, D.C.: U.S. Department of Justice, January 1990), p. 1; Bureau of Justice Statistics, *Criminal Victimization 1994* (Washington, D.C.: U.S. Department of Justice, May 1997), p. 4.

38. Bureau of Justice Statistics, *Victim Characteristics*.

39. Bureau of Justice Statistics, *U.S. Department of Justice Office of Justice Programs*, "Homicide Trends in the U.S.: Intimate Homicide," http://www.ojp.usdoj.gov/bjs/homicide/intimates.htm, accessed 24 May 2006.

40. Ibid.

41. "A Flurry of Baby Abandonment Leaves Houston Wondering Why," *New York Times* (21 December 1999), p. 12.

42. "The Curse of Violent Crime: A Pervasive Fear of Robbery and Mayhem Threatens the Way America Lives," *Time* (23 March 1981), p. 16.

43. Bonnie S. Fisher and John J. Sloan III, "Unraveling Fear of Victimization among College Women: Is the 'Shadow of Sexual Assault Hypothesis' Supported?" *Justice Quarterly* 20, no. 3 (September 2003): 633–659.

44. Jodi Lane and James W. Meeker, "Women's and Men's Fear of Gang Crime: Sexual and Nonsexual Assault as Perceptually Contemporaneous Offenses," *Justice Quarterly* 20, no. 2 (June 2003): 337–371; quotation is on p. 366.

45. Hubert Williams and Anthony M. Pate, "Returning to First Principles: Reducing the Fear of Crime in Newark," *Crime & Delinquency* 33 (January 1987): 53.

46. "Judge Rules Bryant Accuser May Not Be Called 'Victim,'" *New York Times* (2 May 2004), p. 14.

47. U.S. Code, Title 18, Section 3663 (2007).

48. U.S. Code, Title 42, Section 10601 *et seq.* (2007).

49. Crime Victims' Rights Act, U.S. Code, Title 18, Section 3771(a)(1)-(8) (2007).

Entry into Criminal Justice Systems: Policing

Law enforcement officers occupy the front line in our ever-struggling efforts to combat terrorism and other crimes. Our ability to do what we want, free from the fear of crime, depends on them. But despite the responsibilities and powers granted to these important persons, they cannot deal effectively with crime without the assistance of victims and witnesses, and that cooperation is not always given. However, law enforcement officers are blamed if crime rates increase and if reported crimes are not solved.

Part 2 explores the nature, organization, function, and problems of policing to place this important aspect of criminal justice systems in proper perspective. Chapter 3 covers the history of policing and explains how formal police systems emerged. It differentiates the levels of public police systems in the United States, looks briefly at international policing, and reviews the nature and problems of private policing. The organization and administration of police systems are considered, with a focus on problem- and community-oriented policing.

Chapter 4 describes what police actually do, ranging from performing many services within the community to engaging in the dangerous job of apprehending criminals. Police functions are discussed in the context of legal requirements and empirical social science research. Part 2 closes with Chapter 5, which focuses on the major problems and issues in policing.

The Emergence and Structure of Police Systems

3

Policing is one of the most important functions in criminal justice systems. As stated by a noted expert on policing, "The strength of a democracy and the quality of life enjoyed by its citizens are determined in large measure by the ability of the police to discharge their duties."[1] However, the ability of U.S. police to function effectively and properly has come into serious question in recent years, and this chapter and Chapters 4 and 5 will explore some of the reasons for this, as they examine the past, present, and future of policing in the United States.

This chapter begins with a history of policing to explain the reason for the formal systems of present-day public policing. The history is traced from policing's informal beginnings in other countries to today's formal systems in the United States. The decentralized systems of U.S. policing are examined by their major categories: local, state, and federal policing systems, with the federal discussion focusing on the Federal Bureau of Investigation (FBI) and the newly created Department of Homeland Security (DHS) and Transportation Security Administration (TSA). Relevant federal legislation creating these new agencies and others is discussed. Brief attention is given to international policing, followed by a section on private policing and security.

The chapter then focuses on the organization, administration, and management of police departments. After a brief discussion of early reform efforts, attention is given to policing models, including the professional, problem-oriented, and community-oriented approaches. The chapter closes with a discussion of police strategies in crime reduction.

3-1 The History of Policing

Although formal policing is a relatively modern development, some form of policing has existed for centuries. When societies were small and cohesive, with most members sharing goals and activities, it was usually possible to keep order without a formal **police** structure. The rules and regulations of the society were taught to new members as they were socialized, and most people observed the rules. Others could be coerced

LEARNING
OBJECTIVES

After reading this chapter, you should be able to do the following:

- Discuss the history of U.S. policing, paying special attention to the contributions of the British police.
- Explain the meaning of decentralized policing.
- Distinguish among local, state, and federal policing systems.
- State and evaluate the role and function of the Federal Bureau of Investigation (FBI).
- Comment on recent federal legislation designed to combat terrorism.
- Discuss the nature and purpose of the Department of Homeland Security (DHS).
- Analyze the function and problems of the Transportation Security Administration (TSA).
- Explain the difference between private and public policing, and discuss their comparative growth and importance.
- Note early reform efforts in the organization and administration of policing systems.
- Explain what is meant by a professional model of policing.
- Discuss what is meant by a problem-oriented approach to policing.
- Analyze community-oriented policing.
- Explain and evaluate COMPSTAT.

Police (see p. 54) A government official authorized to enforce the law, provide services, and maintain order, using physical (including deadly) force if necessary.

Frankpledge system In old English law, a system whereby the members of a tithing had corporate responsibility for the behavior of all members over 14 years old. Ten tithings formed a hundred, and hundreds were later combined to form shires, similar to counties, over which a sheriff had jurisdiction.

Tithing In English history, a system of 10 families who had responsibility for the behavior of members over the age of 14. Tithings were also important in protecting the group from outsiders.

Hundred In English law, a combination of 10 tithings as part of the frankpledge system. *See also* **Tithing** and **Frankpledge system**.

Constable An officer of a municipal corporation who has duties similar to those of a sheriff, such as preserving the public peace, executing papers from the court, and maintaining the custody of juries.

Shires *See* **Frankpledge system**.

Sheriff The chief law enforcement officer in a county, usually chosen by popular election.

Watch system A system charged with the duties of overseeing, patrolling, or guarding an area or a person. Watchmen were prominent in the early watch system of policing.

into observing those rules by informal techniques of social control. If that did not work and if rules were violated, crime victims might have handled the situation informally. The victim might also have been permitted to take private revenge against the offender.

In some countries, informal policing was organized beyond the immediate family or individual concerned. England had the **frankpledge system**, in which families were organized into a **tithing** (10 families) and a **hundred** (10 tithings) for purposes of protecting each other, as well as for enforcing laws. The frankpledge was a system of mutual pledge or mutual help, with all adult members responsible for their own conduct and that of others in the system. If the group failed to apprehend a lawbreaker, the English Crown fined all of the group members.

Individual private policing had its limits, however, and as societies grew in size and complexity, public policing was needed. The appointment of constables in England in the 12th century signaled the beginning of public policing in that country. An unpaid **constable** was responsible for taking care of the weapons and the equipment of the hundred, as well as keeping the peace by enforcing laws.

A second kind of police officer emerged when hundreds were combined to form **shires**, which were analogous to counties. The king appointed a shire-reeve to supervise each shire. The shire-reeve was the forerunner of the **sheriff**. Originally, the shire-reeve was responsible only for ensuring that citizens performed their law enforcement functions adequately, but later, the duties were expanded to include apprehending law violators. The shire-reeve, the only paid official, was assisted in his duties by constables.

During the reign of Edward I (1272–1307), the **watch system**, the immediate forerunner to modern police systems, emerged in England. The watch system was developed as a means of protecting property against fire and for guarding the walls and gates of the cities. Watchmen were responsible for maintaining order and monitoring public behavior and manners. The London watchmen carried clubs and swords. They did not wear uniforms and could be distinguished from other citizens only by the lanterns and staffs they carried. Originally, they were to patrol the streets at specified intervals during the night, announcing that all was well. As the city grew, a day shift was added.

In 1326, Edward II supplemented the shire-reeve–supervised mutual pledge system by creating an office of justice of the peace. The justices were appointed by the king, and their initial function was to assist the shire-reeve with policing the counties. Later, the justices assumed judicial functions. As the central government took on greater responsibility for law enforcement in England, the constables lost their independence as officials of the pledge system and were under the authority of the justices, who were assisted by volunteers.

Constables performed functions such as supervising night watchmen, taking charge of prisoners, serving summonses, and executing warrants. The justices performed judicial functions, thus beginning the separation of the functions of the police and the judiciary. This distinction between the police functions of the constable and the judicial functions of the justices, with the constables reporting to the justices, remained the pattern in England for the next 500 years.

The mutual pledge system began to decline, however, as many citizens failed to perform their law enforcement functions within the system. The early police officials were not popular with citizens; nor were they effective. Citizens were dissatisfied with the watch system and its inability to maintain order and prevent crime. English life was characterized by rising levels of crime, a perceived increase in and greater severity of public riots, and an increase in public intoxication resulting from a rise in drinking among the lower classes.

Public drunkenness was a serious problem, resulting in a significant increase in violent street crimes and thefts. The government responded by improving city lighting, increasing the number of watchmen, and increasing the punishment for all crimes. But the watchmen were not able to control the frequent riots that occurred; neither could they protect citizens and their possessions. The public responded by refraining from entering the streets at night without a private guard and by arming themselves. The rich moved to safer areas, leaving behind them the residential segregation characteristic of contemporary society.[2]

The rise of industrialization in England contributed to the need for a formal police force. As more people moved to cities and life became more complex, maintaining law and order became more difficult, and the less formal system of policing was no longer sufficient.

3-1a　Modern Policing: The London Beginning

Magistrate　A judge from the lower courts of the state or federal court system. Usually, magistrates preside over arraignments, preliminary hearings, bail hearings, and minor offenses.

Bow Street Runners　The mid-18th-century London system that gave the police powers of investigation and arrest to constables, who were given some training and paid a portion of the fines in successfully prosecuted cases.

Although scholars debate how and why formal police systems emerged, usually the beginning is traced to England, where Londoners protested the ineffectiveness of the watch system and agitated for a formal police force. Some believed that a police force constantly patrolling the town would reduce and eventually eliminate street crime. Others feared that the concentration of power necessary for a formal police force would lead to abuses, especially if the force were a national one. Eventually, the tension between these two positions was resolved by the establishment of local police systems.

Dissatisfaction with the constable system led the English to experiment with other systems. In the mid-18th century, John Fielding and Henry Fielding, London **magistrates**, instituted a system called the **Bow Street Runners**. The Fieldings selected constables with a year of experience and gave them police powers of investigation and arrest. The constables were given some training and were paid a portion of the fines in the cases they prosecuted successfully.

Increased concern about safety and security in London led citizens to pressure for improved police protection. Between 1770 and 1828, a total of six commissions appointed by the English Parliament investigated policing and made suggestions, but an attempt in 1785 to establish a metropolitan police force was defeated by the opposition of powerful commercial interests. None of the English efforts were successful in establishing a satisfactory police force until 1829.[3]

In 1829, the first modern police force, the Metropolitan Police, was founded in London by Sir Robert Peel. The men employed by the force were called *Peelers* or *Bobbies* after the founder. Working full-time and wearing special uniforms, the officers' primary function was to prevent crime. They were organized by territories, and they reported to a central government. Candidates had to meet high standards to qualify for a job as a police officer in London. The system has been described as follows:

> Peel divided London into divisions, then into "beats." The headquarters for the police commissioners looked out upon a courtyard that had been the site of a residence used by the Kings of Scotland and was, therefore, called "Scotland Yard."...[I]n 1856 Parliament required every borough and county to have a police force similar to London's.[4]

London set the example; the rest of England was slow to follow, but other countries began establishing modern, formal police systems. Some countries developed a centralized police system, but a decentralized system developed in the United States. Most European countries followed the British practice of not arming the police, but the amount of violence led the British to change that tradition in 1994, when some specially trained Bobbies began carrying guns.

Despite its historical reputation for professional and successful policing, Scotland Yard faced a crisis in 1999, when an investigation concluded that it was infected with institutional racism. The force had a poor record of minority recruitment, hiring, retention, and promotion. Only 3 percent of the police officers were minority, but 25 percent of the city's ethnic population were minority. Police were criticized for their overall investigation of the slaying of an 18-year-old black man, Stephen Lawrence, who was stabbed to death at a bus stop in South London by a group of whites in 1993. According to the report, police were insensitive to minorities' rights, including the rights of minorities who worked within the department. The police were ordered to recruit one-fourth of their new officers from ethnic and racial minorities by 2009.[5]

In the spring of 2003, on the 10th anniversary of Lawrence's death, England's prime minister, Tony Blair, in a letter to the Lawrence family, wrote that, although progress had been made,

> There is still a great deal more to do if we are to build a genuinely fair and inclusive society....[There is a] genuine commitment, shared by all our public institutions, to ensure they are really representative and responsive to all the people and communities they serve. One of Britain's great strengths is that it is a country of many races, many cultures and many faiths.... The diversity of our society is respected and celebrated.[6]

Despite the efforts of Blair and Scotland Yard to combat racism, the five men who were accused of murdering Lawrence were not convicted, and in April 2006, Scotland Yard confirmed that the special team that was investigating the case had been disbanded, although the department would investigate any new leads brought to their attention. That same month, another young black, Christopher Alaneme, also 18 at his death in Kent, England, was allegedly abused and tormented by a group of white youths before he bled to death while waiting for a delayed ambulance. The head of Kent's police force, the only black chief constable in Britain, acted quickly and expressed his confidence that the killers would be found and prosecuted: "Racist crime is not something we tolerate in this country and we'll be doing everything possible to find and track and prosecute those people responsible." In this case, however, the police have not been criticized for lack of quick action, as in the case of the investigation of Lawrence's death.[7]

3-1b The Emergence of Policing in the United States

People in the United States saw a variety of policing systems in the early days. Immigrants brought many aspects of the English system to this country. The constable was in charge of towns, and the sheriff had jurisdiction over policing counties. Before the

American Revolution, these positions were filled by governors appointed by the British Crown, but subsequently, most constables and sheriffs obtained their positions by popular elections.

Many of the colonies adopted the English watch system. The New York City system was said to be an example. Bellmen walked throughout the city, ringing bells and providing police services. Later, they were replaced by a permanent watch of citizens and, still later, by paid constables.

One of the most familiar kinds of policing, still in use in some rural areas today, was the **posse**. Under the posse system, a sheriff could call into action any number of citizens over a certain age if they were needed to assist in law enforcement.

> **Posse** The rural police system in which the sheriff may call into action any number of citizens over a certain age if they are needed to assist in law enforcement.

In some early U.S. systems, law enforcement officials were paid by local government. Others were paid by private individuals. "By the early nineteenth century, American law enforcement had become a hodgepodge of small jurisdictions staffed by various officials with different powers, responsibilities, and legal standing. There was no system, although there were ample precedents for public policing."[8]

It did not take long, however, for Americans to realize that these methods of policing did not produce the efficiency and expertise necessary to control the urban riots and increasing rates of crime and violence that accompanied the industrialization, increased complexity, and growth of American cities. A professional police system was needed, and by the late 1880s, most American cities had established municipal police forces, although the county sheriff system continued to provide policing services in rural areas. State police systems were added gradually, followed by the federal system. The state and federal systems, however, were not to supersede the local systems.[9]

One final type of policing that should be mentioned is **vigilantism**, which means *watchman* and refers to the acts of a person who is alert, cautious, suspicious, and ready to take action to maintain and preserve peace. Vigilantism is based on the belief that laws aid persons who are vigilant and who do not sleep on their rights. In colonial days, people (usually only men) formed vigilante committees to stop rebellions and other problems and to catch and punish criminals. These groups operated outside the law but apparently viewed themselves as preserving law.

> **Vigilantism** Literally, "watchman." Action by a person who is alert and on guard, cautious, suspicious, and ready to take action to maintain and preserve peace. Actions of citizens who take the law into their own hands in an effort to catch and punish criminals.

Vigilante committees and groups continue to operate within the United States and often aim their efforts at the suppression of racial and other minority groups, thus constituting a serious threat to the rights of these people. They may, however, also be very helpful, as indicated in Spotlight 3-1, which relates the events of an attempted terrorist act on an airplane.

3-2   Decentralized Policing: U.S. Systems

In the United States, formal police systems are decentralized, operating at local, state, and federal levels.

3-2a   Local Policing

Local policing includes police agencies at the rural, county, and municipal levels. Most studies of police focus on municipal policing. Few criminal justice texts discuss rural policing, and usually only slight attention is given to county police systems, leaving the impression that these levels of policing are not important. This conclusion is erroneous because local and county levels of policing cover significant geographical areas of the country. In fact, the majority of police agencies in the United States are located in small towns, villages, or boroughs.

Rural Policing

Throughout the United States, but particularly in southern and western regions, many towns and villages are too small to support a police department. Some of these areas depend on the county police system for protection. Others have their own systems,

---

Spotlight 3-1   **Vigilantism in the Air**

Passengers say they will take action; pilots have encouraged them to do so if necessary. Another 9/11 will not happen on my flight! That appears to be the reaction of many pilots and passengers after the 9/11 terrorist attacks. The would-be shoe bomber found out the hard way.

Richard Reid, 29, a British citizen, attempted to ignite a bomb on a flight from Paris to Miami. The flight was carrying 197 people in December 2001 when Reid attempted to light a fuse protruding from his shoe. Passengers overpowered Reid, whose shoe carried concealed plastic explosives. Reid entered a guilty plea, stating that he hated the United States and was a follower of Osama bin Laden. On 30 January 2003, when Reid, who had converted to Islam, was to be sentenced, he yelled at the judge, "You will be judged by Allah! Your government has sponsored the torture of Muslims in Iraq and Turkey and Jordan and Syria with their money and weapons." In part, federal judge William Young responded as follows:

> We are not afraid of any of your terrorist co-conspirators, Mr. Reid. We are Americans. We have been through the fire before. You are a terrorist. You are not a soldier in any war. To give you that reference, to call you a soldier gives you far too much stature....
>
> You hate our freedom. Our individual freedom. Our individual freedom to live as we choose, to come and go as we choose, to believe or not believe as we individually choose.
>
> Here, in this society, the very winds carry freedom. They carry it from sea to shining sea. It is because we prize individual freedom so much that you are here in this beautiful courtroom....
>
> See that flag, Mr. Reid? That's the flag of the United States of America. That flag will fly there long after this is all forgotten. That flag stands for freedom. You know it always will.[1]

Reid was sentenced to the maximum term for his crime: life in prison. The issue of vigilantism, however, goes far beyond this case and raises the possibility that, if airline passengers are willing to take physical action against suspected terrorists, what might the results be? For example, in September 2002, passengers aboard a Southwest Airlines flight from Phoenix to Salt Lake City beat and kicked to death a young man who charged the cockpit door.[2] Subsequent to the 9/11 terrorist attacks, cockpit doors were made more secure, and along with other security precautions, they are locked during flights.

1. Quoted in "At Sentencing, Judge Lets Shoe Bomber Know What American Stands For," *St. Louis Post-Dispatch* (17 April 2003), p. 2.
2. The information on the Southwest flight came from "Should Plane Cockpit Doors Be Locked?" *The Straits Times* (Singapore) (31 December 2002), pp. 1, 2.

---

usually consisting of an elected official. This official, who may be called a *constable*, has policing duties similar to those of the county sheriff. Constables might not be trained in law or policing. However, they have the power to enforce laws, to arrest, to maintain order, and to execute processes from the magistrate's courts, which are courts of limited jurisdiction, often called *justice of the peace courts*.

Rural policing is very important but often plagued with financial and personnel problems. One officer cannot police even a small area for 24 hours a day. Frequently, citizens are without police protection; local police officers are overworked; and in many jurisdictions, funds are not available for the support services necessary for adequate policing.

Many rural officers do not have sufficient resources for investigating criminal activity. They are more isolated from other officers. Quick backup services from other officers may be a scarce luxury rather than a daily reality. Working conditions of rural police may be less desirable than those of police officers at other levels. Most salaries are low and not necessarily compensated for by a lower cost of living. Initial training is more limited and may not be geared to the unique problems of rural policing. Most officers must train in urban settings because in many areas there are not enough rural police to justify separate training centers. As a result, those officers may have unrealistic expectations of rural policing. In addition, many rural officers do not have the opportunity for continued education and training.

Budget planning and other activities concerning policing in rural areas might be town projects, with police officers involved in heated discussions from which their urban counterparts might be shielded by police administrators. This high visibility and total immersion in local problems and politics might affect the social life of the officer, who may find it impossible to go anywhere in the area without being viewed as a police officer. For rural officers, long periods of inactivity may lead to boredom and a lowered self-concept. In comparison with urban police, rural police may face greater citizen expectations for a variety of services not connected with law enforcement.

On the positive side, some rural officers enjoy their involvement in community activities with local citizens. The lower crime rates, particularly the lower rates of violence, may increase police security. The lack of complexity in the police system might be seen as a positive rather than a negative factor. Problems associated with a lack of security, when only one officer is assigned to an area, might be eliminated or greatly reduced by cooperation from the next level—county policing. In some areas, rural police are limited to traffic functions and some ministerial duties, with the major law enforcement activities being handled by the county sheriff and county police officers. The county may contract with the rural community to provide these services.

Some rural police view their positions as more expansive than those of urban or state police. For example, in the small New England village in which this author lives, the two police officers always monitor the closing of the school day, with a police car and an officer ever present as the children are leaving to get on the school bus, walk home, or be picked up by their parents or other adults. They respond to motorists stranded in a snowstorm, and they have a presence at most community functions, always available to help. They rush to every call to the volunteer fire department, just in case a resident needs transportation to other housing; they check on the elderly during snowstorms. And many residents feel free to stop by the police offices in the town hall and talk with the officer on hand about a local problem or just to chat.

County Policing

Some county police agencies are rural, but the county system is larger and usually employs a sheriff as the primary law enforcement officer. The county sheriff may have numerous other functions unrelated to law enforcement, such as acting as the county coroner, collecting county taxes, or supervising any number of county government activities. If the department is large enough, the county police department might have a deputy sheriff and law enforcement officers assigned to patrol the county and enforce order.

The sheriff is considered the most important law enforcement officer in the county, but in practice, the functions of the sheriff's office usually are limited to the unincorporated areas of the county, with law enforcement in the incorporated areas handled by the municipal police in the larger cities. Most sheriffs are elected officials. Previously, most sheriffs served for very long periods, but it is becoming difficult, if not impossible, for long sheriff tenures today. In many jurisdictions, political activists have been successful in unseating sheriffs who have served for years.

Larger county police departments may contract their services to smaller county or rural departments. The county department may employ a county **marshal**, a sworn officer whose primary function is to perform civil duties for the courts, such as delivering papers to initiate civil proceedings or serving papers for the arrest of criminal suspects.

Larger county police departments have investigative units that service the district attorneys who bring the prosecutions in the county. These departments are staffed by sworn officers and support personnel. Departments too small for investigative units may contract for such services from the municipal or urban police departments in the area or from the Federal Bureau of Investigation (FBI), discussed later in this chapter.

The movement of drugs into the rural areas of U.S. communities has changed the nature of both county and rural policing. In one feature article on this issue, the sheriff of Jefferson Davis County, Mississippi, noted the increase in violence and related problems in rural areas due to the influx of drug dealers, who have become wealthy through illegal dealing in the legal prescription painkiller Oxycontin, as well as through drug trafficking in crack and powder cocaine, marijuana, and other illegal drugs. According

▶ **Marshal** A sworn law enforcement officer who performs the civil duties of the courts, such as the delivery of papers to begin civil proceedings. In some jurisdictions, marshals serve papers for the arrest of criminal suspects and escort inmates from jail to court or into the community when they are permitted to leave the jail or prison temporarily. Marshals may also transport offenders from one jurisdiction to another, escort fugitives from their places of capture to the jurisdictions in which they will be tried, provide security for designated persons, or fly on planes as an added security measure.

to the sheriff, his office has received calls from teachers warning that students in their classrooms who deal in drugs have threatened to kill each other and from an elderly woman stating that her crack-addicted son's life had been threatened by a drug dealer. A 13-year-old standing outside his home was shot and killed by a drug dealer who was looking for the teen's brother, with whom he had a fight. The sheriff noted the problems in trying to apprehend drug dealers. For example, the officers cannot work undercover to buy drugs because the department does not have the money; successful undercover work would be impossible, anyway, because everyone knows everyone else.[10]

Municipal Policing

Most studies of policing focus on municipal departments; consequently, the discussions in Chapters 4 and 5 apply primarily to municipal policing. In this chapter, we examine the differences between municipal, or urban, policing and policing at the other local levels.

Municipal police departments differ from other local police agencies mainly in their size, organization, complexity, and services. Although they may service smaller geographical areas than rural or county systems, most municipal police systems have more employees and provide more extended services. The complexity of the departments leads to greater problems in staffing, organization, and fulfillment of the public's needs. Many municipal departments have more resources, which may be shared with rural and county systems on a contract basis. On the other hand, citizens' expectations for services from municipal police departments may be greater than expectations at the rural or county level, where the department's mandate may be less defined and more open-ended.

Municipal departments, in contrast to departments at other levels, may encounter more difficult political problems with their governing bodies. The municipal police department competes with other agencies for funding. The costs of policing are highest in urban areas, where population changes may present more problems. Many large cities have experienced significant changes in the numbers of people who live in the city, compared with the number who commute daily to work. The residential tax base goes down as the need for services, order maintenance, and law enforcement increases.

Generally, crime rates are much higher in urban than in rural or county areas. The composition of the urban population may present greater policing problems. Urban areas have a more heterogeneous population, as well as a greater number of unemployed people, transients, and those who have been in trouble with the law.

3-2b State Policing

State police patrol highways and regulate traffic. They have the primary responsibility for enforcing some state laws and providing services, such as a system of criminal identification, police training programs, and a communications system for local law officials. The organization and services provided by state police vary from state to state. No national or central control exists, except for some standards established by the U.S. Department of Justice and the U.S. Department of Transportation.

This lack of centralization stems from the historic distrust of national police systems, as well as from the different law enforcement needs of the individual states. For example, in 1835, the Texas Rangers, a group of uneducated and untrained men, were recruited and given authority to protect the Texas border from the Mexicans. After Texas was admitted to the Union, the Rangers were retained, along with their primary duty of patrolling the southern border of Texas.

The Texas Rangers became the first state-supported police organization in the United States. As police functions expanded, the role of the Texas Rangers was enlarged, as was their training.

The industrialization and expansion of the country led to many problems that could not be handled adequately at the local level, and although Texas had the first state police agency, Pennsylvania's system became the early model for state police in the United States. In the late 1870s, a powerful secret organization, the **Molly Maguires**, responded to anti-Irish riots in Pennsylvania by forming Irish labor unions, which used violence to terrorize the state's coal-producing regions. The Molly Maguires controlled all hiring and firing. Some employers who ignored their mandates were killed. The terrorists threatened the growing Pennsylvania economy, which was heavily dependent on mineral wealth. The state was sparsely settled, and local police authorities could not control the Molly Maguires. "The Pinkerton Detective Agency, a private national organization, was eventually brought in to infiltrate the Molly Maguires, and 20 of its members were convicted of murder and other crimes."[11]

> ▶ **Molly Maguires** A powerful secret police organization in the 1870s in Pennsylvania.

In 1905, Pennsylvania's governor succeeded in convincing that state's legislature to appropriate funds for a constabulary to help prevent future disasters, such as those caused by the Molly Maguires. The movement toward state policing did not happen quickly, however, for many still feared that the next step would be national police and political repression. But the use of automobiles and increased problems with traffic on state roads and highways in the 20th century created an obvious need for state police.

State police are similar to the state patrol. Both have uniformed, sworn officers who carry weapons. They differ primarily in their law enforcement powers. Most state patrol officers engage primarily in traffic control. Although they may be empowered to enforce criminal laws violated in their presence, on the highway, or within sight of or adjacent to the highway, they do not have general powers of law enforcement for all state laws, as state police have. State police, in contrast to state patrol, may have their own investigative units as well as a forensic science laboratory.

State police and state patrol also differ in that many state police systems include specialized forms of policing, such as control over fishing and gaming laws, regulation of gambling and horse racing, and regulation of alcohol sales. The Alcohol Board of Control is a state agency responsible for investigating requests for liquor licenses and has the power to establish rules concerning the conditions under which liquor is sold. This board is in charge of enforcing state laws enacted to regulate the sale of dangerous drugs.

3-2c Federal Policing

Enforcement of criminal laws in the United States historically has been viewed as the function of states, although states may and do delegate some of their powers to local police agencies. The U.S. Constitution does not provide for a central police agency. It gives the federal government specific power to enforce only a limited number of laws. The Constitution also provides that all powers not delegated to the federal government are reserved to the states. The Constitution gives Congress the power to pass laws that are "necessary and proper" for the exercise of congressional powers. Over the years, Congress has passed bills on federal crimes. The U.S. Supreme Court has upheld the power of Congress to do so.

Federal law enforcement includes federal prosecutors and federal police agencies. The federal policing level is complex and encompasses more than 50 enforcement agencies, which are located within various departments, but some of which have been transferred to the newly created Department of Homeland Security (DHS), discussed later in the chapter. Professions 3-1 examines one of the federal police agencies—the U.S. Marshals Service—and also shows how agencies at various levels can and do cooperate to solve crime.

In addition to the U.S. Marshals Service, the Department of Justice (DOJ) encompasses other major investigative agencies, the largest of which is the Federal Bureau of Investigation (FBI).

Professions 3-1

U.S. Marshals Service

The U.S. Marshals Service, located within the Department of Justice, is the oldest federal law enforcement agency, with more than 4,500 employees celebrating the organization's 215th anniversary on 24 September 2004. The service consists of one person from each federal judicial district. The marshals are appointed by the U.S. president, with the advice and consent of the Senate, and are assisted by deputy marshals.

The primary function of U.S. marshals is to transport federal inmates between prison and court and to escort them to homes or jobs when they have temporary leaves. The marshals provide protection for federal jurors, judges, prosecutors, attorneys, and witnesses. They are in charge of seizing and auctioning property that has been taken by officers under federal court orders. As sworn police officers, U.S. marshals may make arrests for federal offenses and perform other police functions, such as controlling riots and executing federal fugitive warrants.

In marking the 215th year of the U.S. marshals, President George W. Bush wrote the following in a letter to the organization's employees:

> U.S. Marshals have contributed to the safety of our Nation by providing security for our courts and witnesses, capturing

fugitives, assisting with prisoner transportation, and responding to emergency situations.[1]

Each year, U.S. marshals capture approximately 34,000 federal fugitives, making more arrests than all other federal agencies combined. U.S. marshals also team with other federal, state, and local law enforcement officers. For example, in April 2006, all participated in Operation FALCON II—Federal and Local Cops Organized Nationally. According to the U.S. marshals, the combined efforts of 25 federal and 120 state law enforcement agencies, 330 county sheriffs, 312 police departments, and 6 foreign agencies resulted in the "largest fugitive sweep to ever primarily focus on violent sex offenders," resulting in arrests of 9,037 fugitives, 462 of whom were wanted for *violent* sex crimes. Another 311 were wanted for other sex crimes, while 783 were sex offenders who had failed to register as required by law.[2]

Additional information about the U.S. Marshals Service and employment opportunities within this agency can be found at http://www.usdoj.gov/marshals.

1. News Release, United States Marshals Service (24 September 2004).
2. U.S. Marshals Operation Falcon II, http://www.usdoj.gov/marshals/falcon2/index.html, (17–23 April 2006), accessed 5 March 2007.

The Federal Bureau of Investigation (FBI)

On 26 July 1908, President Theodore Roosevelt directed the U.S. attorney general to issue an order creating the agency now known as the **Federal Bureau of Investigation (FBI)**. In 1924, J. Edgar Hoover was appointed director of the organization and remained in that position until his death in May 1972. The FBI is the primary agency charged with enforcing all federal laws not assigned to other special agencies. FBI headquarters are located in Washington, D.C. Field officers are located in major cities throughout the United States and in San Juan, Puerto Rico. The director of the FBI is appointed by the president of the United States, by and with the consent of the U.S. Senate.

The investigative work of the FBI is performed by special agents, who are trained at the FBI Academy, located on the U.S. Marine Corps base in Quantico, Virginia. In addition to special agents, the FBI employs individuals who perform such investigative functions as fingerprint examinations, clerical and receptionist duties, computer programming, and laboratory work. Attorneys, accountants, and other professionals are also employed.

The FBI is not a national police force. Primarily, it is an investigative agency. FBI agents may investigate crimes over which the federal government has jurisdiction by statute; they may investigate state and local crimes when requested by those agencies. There is no charge for these services.

The training facilities of the FBI Academy are used by other agencies for training law enforcement officers; some foreign officers are accepted into the program. The academy also provides continuing education and training for officers. Another important function of the FBI, discussed in Chapter 2, is the collection of national crime data.

> **Federal Bureau of Investigation (FBI)**
> A federal agency established in 1908 and delegated the power to investigate all federal laws (unless they are otherwise assigned to another agency). The FBI investigates alleged civil, criminal, and securities violations. Although the agency is a federal one, it can, when invited, assist local and state law enforcement agencies.

Throughout its history, particularly during the long years it was headed by J. Edgar Hoover, the FBI was severely criticized as well as highly praised. During most of its existence, the FBI has had only loose directives from Congress. A strong leader such as Hoover was able to take advantage of that situation and build a powerful, extremely influential organization, which allegedly held extensive control even over the presidents under whom Hoover served.

Among recent FBI directors, Judge Louis J. Freeh was appointed by President Bill Clinton and confirmed in 1993. Freeh's appointment followed the resignation of William Sessions, who was plagued by allegations of ethics violations. Freeh was criticized but remained in office until June 2001.

Prior to the 9/11 terrorist attacks, the FBI had experienced charges of scandals, corruption, favoritism, discrimination against minorities and women, sexual harassment, and other problems. For example, in the spring of 2001, FBI officials admitted that the agency had withheld documents from the attorneys of Timothy McVeigh, who was convicted of capital murder in the 1995 bombing of the federal building in Oklahoma City, Oklahoma. McVeigh's execution was postponed as a result, but after the trial judge refused to grant a second delay, McVeigh did not appeal, and he was executed on 11 June 2001. Also in 2001, a former FBI agent accused of spying for Moscow, Robert P. Hanssen, pleaded guilty to 15 counts of espionage, attempted espionage, and conspiracy. As a result of Hanssen's plea bargain, some charges against him were dropped and he was spared the death sentence, but he will serve life in prison. The Hanssen case, coupled with reports in the spring of 2001 that the FBI could not account for 449 weapons and 184 laptop computers, led some legislators to proclaim that the agency could "no longer manage its basic operations" and that "Lax administrative controls over sensitive materials like these cannot be tolerated." In July 2001, Vermont Senator Patrick J. Leahy commented, "There are some very, very serious management problems at the FBI."[12]

In the summer of 2001, Robert S. Mueller III was confirmed as the new FBI director. In the fall of that year, the Bush administration announced its plan to revamp the FBI, focusing the agency's efforts on counterterrorism, which would require a deemphasis on some of the agency's traditional targets, such as drug enforcement, bank robbery, and some violent crime investigations. In fact, within hours after the 9/11 terrorist attacks, thousands of FBI agents were reassigned to counterterrorism.

Significant changes were made in the FBI, and the June 2003 reports of two investigative groups, constituting the most thorough study of the changes at the FBI, gave encouraging but cautious comments. One report was the work of the General Accounting Office (GAO), which is the investigative agency of Congress. The other was conducted by the National Academy of Public Administration, with the investigation headed by former U.S. attorney general Richard Thornburgh. Both reports stated that the FBI had made significant progress in its reorganization efforts but that important challenges remained. Specifically, the reports considered the efforts of the FBI to update its technology systems, develop programs for sharing intelligence information with other government agencies, and maintain full law enforcement in traditional areas (such as drug trafficking) while focusing on counterterrorism. In particular, the GAO report noted an approximately 15 percent decrease in drug trafficking referrals made by the FBI, compared with the previous year. Approximately 400 FBI agents were transferred from units investigating drugs to units concerned with terrorism. Another concern was the lack of independence of the newly created Terrorism Threat Integration Center. The purpose of this agency is to filter intelligence information concerning terrorism across government agencies, but several lawmakers to whom the reports were presented noted that the Central Intelligence Agency (CIA) runs the Terrorism Threat Integration Center. Some feared that the CIA would not be willing to share some of the terrorism information with other agencies.[13]

The 9/11 Commission Report, the *Final Report of the National Commission on Terrorist Attacks upon the United States* (the commission was established by the U.S.

Congress and President George W. Bush in November 2002), was critical of the FBI. Consider, for example, the following statement from that report:

> Responsibility for domestic intelligence gathering on terrorism was vested solely in the FBI, yet during almost all of the Clinton administration the relationship between the FBI Director and the President was nearly nonexistent. The FBI Director would not communicate directly with the President. His key personnel shared very little information with the National Security Council and the rest of the national security community. As a consequence, one of the critical working relationships in the counterterrorism effort was broken.[14]

The chair of the commission said that reports of the FBI's work both before and after the 9/11 attacks was an "indictment of the FBI. It failed and it failed and it failed and it failed....This is an agency that does not work. It makes you angry. And I don't know how to fix it."[15]

Some changes in the FBI were made in 2005. The bureau, under pressure from the Bush White House, agreed to accept some of the recommendations of a presidential commission. Specifically, the FBI agreed to permit the newly appointed and first director of national intelligence, John D. Negroponte, to assist in the selection of the FBI's intelligence chief, the third-ranking official of the FBI. It was the first time in history that the FBI gave an outsider a significant role in the selection of one of its top officials.

Also by 2005, the FBI had reordered its priorities, with FBI Director Mueller testifying before Congress that the agency's top 10 priorities were as follows: counterterrorism, counterintelligence, cybercrime, criminal intelligence, public corruption, civil rights, violent gangs, criminal enterprises, corporate and securities fraud, and healthcare fraud. In 2006, the director, testifying before the Senate Judiciary Committee, stated, "[T]his year will mark the five-year anniversary of September 11th, and the FBI has changed dramatically since the terrorist attacks of that day. And we will continue to evolve to meet the emerging threats to our country."[16] That the agency has not evolved sufficiently is evidenced by the oversight conclusions of the Office of the Inspector General, which are noted, in part, in Spotlight 3-2.

The FBI, like other federal law enforcement agencies, should be viewed as a supplement to, not a replacement of, state and local agencies. The agency is assisted by other federal agencies. All are aided by recent legislative enactments.

Recent Federal Legislative Enactments

After the 9/11 terrorist attacks, President George W. Bush proposed and Congress enacted several pieces of legislation to create new federal agencies and to empower those agencies and others in the fight against terrorism. The **USA Patriot Act** (Uniting and Strengthening America by Providing Appropriate Tools Required to Intercept and Obstruct Terrorism Act of 2001) was passed by Congress and signed by President Bush in the fall of 2001. The act expanded the powers of the federal government to deal with terrorism. Some of those powers involve the expansion of wiretaps on terrorist suspects' email, telephone conversations, and use of the Internet. Tighter controls were placed on immigration and on money laundering.[17] The USA Patriot Act has been lauded by many but criticized by others, who claim that it violates the constitutional rights of privacy, due process, and free speech and gives the government the power to spy on Americans and others. The act has been challenged in the courts and in Congress, but after a bitter fight, Congress renewed the statute in 2007.

Two federal agencies designed to combat terrorism in the United States are the Department of Homeland Security (DHS) and the Transportation Security Administration (TSA).

The Department of Homeland Security (DHS)

One of the major proposals of the Bush administration after the 9/11 terrorist attacks was the creation of the **Department of Homeland Security (DHS)**. The administration's

USA Patriot Act   The Uniting and Strengthening America by Providing Appropriate Tools Required to Intercept and Obstruct Terrorism Act of 2001, enacted in fall 2001 in response to the 9/11 terrorist attacks. The act expands the powers of the federal government to deal with terrorism. Some of those powers involve using wiretaps on terrorist suspects' email, telephone conversations, and use of the Internet.

Department of Homeland Security (DHS)   The cabinet-level department created after the 9/11 terrorist attacks. Its creation constituted the most extensive federal government reorganization in 50 years. It combines 22 federal agencies and constitutes the third largest federal agency.

Spotlight 3-2 Focus on the Federal Bureau of Investigation

Since the 9/11 terrorist attacks, the Federal Bureau of Investigation (FBI) has been closely scrutinized, with some arguing that the country's major law enforcement agency should have been more vigilant in detecting terrorism. Significant changes have been and continue to be made in the agency, some of which are detailed in this text. This Spotlight highlights a portion of the testimony of the Honorable Glenn A. Fine, inspector general of the U.S. Department of Justice, in his 2 May 2006 testimony before the Senate Judiciary Committee. The Office of Inspector General (OIG) is charged with overseeing the operations of the FBI. Some of the conclusions of the OIG's recent evaluation of the FBI are summarized here.

The FBI has made significant changes and progress since 9/11, but improvement needs to continue in some areas. First, the FBI needs a modern, effective case management and records system. The agency spent millions of dollars developing one system, the Virtual Case File, only to have it collapse. It is being replaced with a system called the Sentinel Project. According to Senator Patrick Leahy, the ranking member of the Senate Judiciary Committee, that system will cost approximately $425 million and will not be fully operational until 2009. Senator Leahy emphasized the importance of the FBI having an effective informational technology (IT) infrastructure, stating that, "The Bureau's effectiveness hangs in the balance, and the American people cannot afford another fiasco."[1]

The OIG found that the FBI had made progress in its ability to develop and manage a major IT project but had the following concerns:

"1. the incomplete staffing of the Sentinel Program Management Office,
2. the FBI's ability to reprogram funds to complete the second phase of the project without jeopardizing its mission-critical operations,

3. Sentinel's ability to share information with external intelligence and law enforcement agencies and provide a common framework for other agencies' case management systems,
4. the lack of an Established Earned Value Management process,
5. the FBI's ability to track and control Sentinel's costs, and
6. the lack of complete documentation required by the FBI's Information Technology Investment Management processes."[2]

In addition to these internal problems, the OIG expressed concern about Sentinel's "ability to connect with external systems in other Department of Justice components, the Department of Homeland Security, and other intelligence community agencies." If the FBI is not able to do that, the other agencies might be forced to spend large sums to alter their communication systems.

The OIG also found that the FBI had problems in the area of civil rights and civil liberties, with violations of one or more of the attorney general guidelines in 87 percent of the confidential informant files that the OIG examined. The OIG found significant difficulties in the ability of the FBI to recruit, train, and retain employees in some areas of expertise within the agency. In addition, the OIG noted that information sharing remains a problem and that the FBI needs to improve its work in this area. In short, the inspector general testified that, although the FBI has made some improvements since 9/11, "more progress is clearly needed."[3]

1. "FBI Oversight," testimony by Patrick Leahy, ranking member, Senate Judiciary, Capitol Hill Hearing Testimony, *Federal Document Clearing House Congressional Testimony* (2 May 2006), n.p.
2. "FBI Oversight," testimony by Glenn A. Fine, inspector general, United States Department of Justice, Capitol Hill Hearing Testimony, *Federal Document Clearing House Congressional Testimony* (2 May 2006), n.p.
3. Ibid.

Transportation Security Administration (TSA)
A federal agency created by the Aviation and Transportation Security Act (ATSA), enacted two months after the 9/11 terrorist attacks. The TSA was developed to take over the security screening functions for all commercial flights in the United States.

wish to make the DHS into a cabinet-level position was approved by Congress. The new agency combines 22 former federal agencies (not including the Central Intelligence Agency [CIA] and the FBI, which remain independent agencies). The new department was initially headed by Tom Ridge, Pennsylvania's former governor. Ridge resigned after the reelection of President George W. Bush. In February 2005, Michael Chertoff was confirmed by the U.S. Senate as the new DHS head.

The creation of the DHS constituted the most extensive federal government reorganization in 50 years. The DHS is the third largest federal agency (after the Defense Department and the Department of Veterans Affairs). Spotlight 3-3 details the major components of the federal legislation that provided for the DHS.

The Transportation Security Administration (TSA)

Another federal agency created since 9/11 is the **Transportation Security Administration (TSA)**, which was created by the Aviation and Transportation Security Act (ATSA), enacted in November 2001. The TSA was developed to take on the security screening

Spotlight 3-3   Federal Law Enforcement and the Homeland Security Act

On November 25, 2002, President George W. Bush signed into law the Homeland Security Act, creating the Department of Homeland Security (DHS), a new Cabinet-level Department that will plan, coordinate, and integrate U.S. Government activities related to homeland security.

The legislation creates a new Office of Inspector General, and transfers all or part of 22 existing agencies to DHS. (For more information, see the DHS website, http://www.dhs.gov.) Most transfers had occurred by March 1, 2003, with full integration during the following months. Several agencies employing officers with arrest and firearm authority are now part of DHS.

The following are transferred as distinct entities reporting directly the DHS secretary:

U.S. Coast Guard
Transferred from the Department of Transportation. In times of war, or on direction of the President, the Coast Guard will still be attached to the Department of Defense, U.S. Navy.

U.S. Secret Service
Transferred from the Department of the Treasury.

In addition to agencies or components that report directly to the Secretary, DHS includes five Directorates: Border and Transportation Security, Emergency Preparedness and Response, Information Analysis and Infrastructure, Science and Technology, and Management.

The Directorates of Border and Transportation Security includes the following:

Federal Law Enforcement Training Center
Transferred from the Department of the Treasury.

Federal Protective Service
Transferred from the General Services Administration.

U.S. Customs Service (except for some revenue functions)
Transferred from the Department of the Treasury.

Immigration and Naturalization Service
The INS is terminated, and its functions are transferred from the Department of Justice.

Transportation Security Administration (TSA)
TSA, which was created in November 2001 and includes the Federal Air Marshals program, is transferred from the Department of Transportation.

The Directorate of Border and Transportation Security will include two major new bureaus with law enforcement duties: The Bureau of Customs and Border Protection (CBP), with about 30,000 employees, will primarily perform border protection and inspection functions. It combines Customs Service and INS inspection services, the Border Patrol, and the Agricultural Quarantine Inspection program. CBP is directed by the Customs commissioner.

The Bureau of Immigration and Customs Enforcement (BICE) will enforce immigration and customs laws within the U.S. Interior. Its 14,000 employees are comprised primarily of Customs Service and INS special agent, INS detention and deportation officers, the INS Immigration Litigation Section, and Federal Protective Service (FPS) employees. Customs air and marine interdiction functions, and intelligence components of INS, Customs, and FPS are also included.

Immigration and citizenship services formerly handled by the INS will reside with the new Bureau of Citizenship and Immigration Services (BCIS). BCIS will report directly to the DHS Deputy Secretary.

The Directorate for Emergency and Preparedness Response includes:

Federal Emergency Management Agency (formerly independent).

Also affected by the Homeland Security Act:

Bureau of Alcohol, Tobacco and Firearms (ATF)
Law enforcement functions transferred from the Department of the Treasury to the Justice Department. Revenue functions remain at Treasury. Legislation incorporates the Safe Explosives Act, creating new ATF enforcement powers related to explosives. The agency name has changed to Bureau of Alcohol, Tobacco, Firearms and Explosives, though ATF initials will still be used.

Source: Bureau of Justice Statistics, *Federal Law Enforcement Officers, 2002* (Washington, D.C.: U.S. Department of Justice, August 2003), p. 5.

---

functions for all commercial flights. This job had been performed by the Federal Aviation Administration (FAA), which was restructured by the statute. The TSA is a part of the DHS and is devoted to securing modes of transportation.

Other Federal Law Enforcement Agencies

Prior to the changes in federal agencies since the 9/11 terrorist attacks, the U.S. Department of Justice (DOJ) contained two other major law enforcement agencies in addition to the FBI: the Drug Enforcement Administration (DEA) and the Immigration and Naturalization Service (INS). The DEA previously was part of the Treasury Department and called the *Bureau of Narcotics*. It was shifted to the DOJ in 1973. The FBI has some drug enforcement powers, too, and engages in some cooperative work with the DEA, although the drug enforcement of the FBI has declined since the bureau has adopted an increased focus on counterterrorism.

The INS was in charge of policing U.S. borders to prevent the entrance of illegal aliens. It drew intense criticism after 9/11, and the agency's functions were moved to the DOJ. As Spotlight 3-3 notes, the enforcement of immigration and customs laws is now the responsibility of the newly created bureau of Immigration and Customs Enforcement (ICE), while the Bureau of Citizenship and Immigration Services (CIS) is in charge of immigration and citizenship. Both of these report to the DHS. This reorganization, however, did not solve major immigration problems, and in the spring of 2006, the U.S. Senate and the U.S. House of Representatives passed separate and significantly different bills concerning the problems of immigration. President Bush stated that he wanted a new immigration bill by the end of 2006; meanwhile, to ease problems at the borders, he sent National Guard troops to the problem areas.

The U.S. Secret Service, formerly in the U.S. Treasury Department, also now reports to the DHS. The Secret Service is responsible for protecting the president and vice president (and their immediate families), as well as former presidents, their spouses and minor children, and during an election campaign, qualified presidential and vice presidential candidates and their spouses. The Secret Service also protects visiting heads of state. In addition, the agency is in charge of investigating forged government checks, other securities, and counterfeiting activities.

Also included within the newly created DHS is the bureau of Alcohol, Tobacco, and Firearms (ATF), which has jurisdiction over laws and licensing requirements regarding the sale of alcohol and other drugs, federal gun control laws, and the collection of taxes connected with these areas. As Spotlight 3-3 notes, this agency was transferred from the U.S. Treasury Department, and its name was changed to the bureau of Alcohol, Tobacco, Firearms and Explosives, although it retains the initials ATF.

Some federal agencies that have law enforcement as well as other functions were not transferred to the DHS. For example, the Internal Revenue Service (IRS), which is in charge of laws regulating federal income tax and its collection, remains within the U.S. Department of the Treasury.

Other federal agencies are concerned with law enforcement, licensing, or both. The Food and Drug Administration oversees the enforcement of the vast number of laws regulating the sale and distribution of pure food and drugs. The Department of Agriculture has an office that investigates fraud in the areas of food stamps, aid to disaster victims, subsidies to farmers and rural home buyers, and other activities over which the department has administrative authority. Additional criminal law enforcement divisions are found in the Securities and Exchange Commission, the Department of Labor, the U.S. Postal Service, and other federal agencies.

3-2d The International Level

The functions that federal agencies may provide for local and state police are illustrated by the participation of the federal government in the International Criminal Police Organization, know as **INTERPOL**, the world's largest international police organization. INTERPOL was established for cooperation among nations involved in common police problems. INTERPOL was founded in 1923 but did not function actively until after its reorganization in 1946. The United States became a member in 1938. The mission of INTERPOL is to "track and apprehend criminal fugitives, thwart criminal schemes, exchange experience and technology, and analyze major trends of international criminal activity." Requests for assistance from INTERPOL can be initiated by any member.[18]

The INTERPOL website states the following:

> Interpol aims to facilitate international police cooperation even where diplomatic relations do not exist between particular countries. Action is taken within the limits of existing laws in different countries and in the spirit of the Universal Declaration of

INTERPOL A world police organization that was established for the purpose of cooperation among nations in common policing problems.

Human Rights. Interpol's constitution prohibits "any intervention or activities of a political, military, religious, or racial character."[19]

3-3   Private Police and Security Forces

In addition to public policing, an important development all over the world is the growth of private policing. Retail businesses employ security guards to protect their premises from shoplifting and to secure the personal safety of employees and shoppers. Security guards are employed to escort female employees from their places of work to their automobiles at night, particularly in high-crime areas. Apartment owners have increased their use of **private security forces**, as have neighborhood associations. Increasingly common are guard gates, at which drivers entering an association's area are required to stop and present adequate identification before being granted permission to enter the premises.

On many college campuses, private security forces are hired for night work in addition to the regular security of the institution. Some serve as escorts for female students who attend night classes. In many large cities, private security forces are hired to patrol housing and business areas. Professional services may be customized to meet the individual needs of customers.[20] The demand for private security and private police has risen as citizens have felt a lack of sufficient security provided by public police.

> **Private security forces** Persons employed by private agencies instead of governmental ones to provide security from criminal activity.

3-3a   Types of Systems

Private security may be *proprietary* or *contractual*. In the case of proprietary, organizations or individuals have their own private investigators and security personnel. For those who cannot afford this approach or who choose not to do so, contracts may be made with professional agencies to provide private security. Regardless of the type of system, a variety of components exist, including security managers, uniformed officers, undercover agents, and electronic specialists or equipment.

The oldest and largest of the firms providing investigative and security services is Pinkerton's, Inc., founded in 1850 by Allan Pinkerton and currently operating 250 offices throughout the United States, Canada, Mexico, Latin America, Europe, and Asia. Pinkerton was the first detective of the Chicago Police Department. Local, state, and federal agencies, as well as private companies and individuals, have employed the services of Pinkerton's. "The term 'private eye' had its source in the unblinking eye that was Pinkerton's trademark for many years." The primary business of Pinkerton's, headquartered in New York City, is to supply private security guards, but the firm also provides private consultants, electronic surveillance devices, and some investigation services.[21]

Private security is also provided by alarm companies. The most frequently used security programs are alarm systems; increasing numbers of systems are being installed in private residences and in businesses. Fire and burglar alarm systems are most common, but alarm companies also install access control systems, fixed security equipment, and perimeter security systems. Most alarm systems are installed by relatively small companies, although some companies have services available nationally. The most sophisticated systems monitor covered premises constantly for increased protection and may be extensive and very expensive.

Private security is provided by armored vehicles with armed guards for transporting precious jewels, money, and other valuables. Courier services provide fast delivery of valuables and papers that must be transported quickly and safely. Private security services may be employed for emptying cash machines, delivering money from businesses to bank drops after hours, and engaging in many other activities for which businesspersons or private citizens feel a need for added security. Other services include security training courses, screening of personnel for businesses, technical countersurveillance to determine whether bugging devices have been installed, security consultation, and drug detection. Some people who want access to their valuables after regular banking hours use private security vaults.

| *Spotlight 3-4* | **Models of Off-Duty Police Employment** |

Officer Contract Model

- Each officer finds own secondary employment.
- Officer independently contracts conditions of work, hours, pay.
- Officer then applies for permission to accept off-duty job.
- Department grants permission provided job meets minimum standards.
- Employer pays office in cash.

Union Brokerage Model

- Union, guild, or association finds paid details.
- Union assigns officers who have volunteered.
- Union sets assignment conditions for paid details.

- Union bargains with the department over status, pay, and condition of paid details.

Department Contract Model

- Police agency contracts with employers.
- Agency assigns officers and pays them from reimbursements by employers.
- Agency assigns off-duty employment coordinator to receive employer requests, issue off-duty work permits, and assign officers to paid details.
- Agency negotiates with union or guild on pay, conditions, and regulations governing employment.

Source: Albert J. Reiss Jr., *Private Employment of Public Police* (Washington, D.C.: U.S. Department of Justice, December 1988), p. 3.

Public police may also be privately employed for additional security. Sociologist Albert J. Reiss Jr. emphasized the increased use of public police for private security. In fact, while on patrol with the police, Reiss remarked that it was impossible to tell which officers were performing as public employees and which off-duty public employees were working in a private capacity. Reiss researched the problems and issues of off-duty police employment, with special emphasis on the particular departments noted in Spotlight 3-4, which also describes the three models for off-duty police employment.

Some police departments place restrictions on off-duty employment. Reiss found that officers generally were forbidden to take any assignments that involved a "conflict of interest between duties as a police officer and duties for the outside employer" and those that constituted "threats to the status or dignity of the police," as well as those that posed an "unacceptable risk of injury that would disable an officer for regular duty." In addition, police departments may limit the jurisdiction in which officers work, the compensation received, and the number of hours worked.[22]

3-3b   Public and Private Policing Compared

Some attempts have been made to study the relationships between public law enforcement and private security systems. A national government study highlighted some of the problems between the two systems, as well as the progress in solving those problems. It was found that the two systems share many goals, such as recovering stolen property, protecting life and property, and deterring and discovering criminal activity. In addition, the study disclosed that public law enforcement officials rated private security personnel as poor in almost every area of their work and that they did not have a high regard for the ability of private security officers to prevent crime.

The study concluded that there was a "climate of suspicion and distrust between private security and law enforcement," although some progress toward cooperative efforts had been made. There was evidence of a willingness to cooperate and to transfer some responsibilities from public law enforcement to private security. Some efforts have been made to integrate the activities and increase the understanding between private security personnel and public law enforcement officers.[23]

Other issues have arisen concerning private police protection. Despite recent legislation in many states, some still do not have licensing requirements for private security. In those jurisdictions, there are few, if any, checks on the quality of security services or on the recruitment or training of security personnel.

Some states have enacted statutes providing for the regulation of private security, but issues remain, such as statutes that are not broad enough to include all types of private security. Increased reliance on private security forces also raises the moral and ethical question of whether society can afford to have a system in which necessary police protection is available only to those who can pay for it.

Perhaps it is ironic that private security has grown because people fear they are not adequately protected by public security, yet so little attention is paid by many to the type of training required of private security guards. Obviously, the federal government was not pleased with private security at airports, as illustrated by the development of the TSA. But serious security breaches have also occurred since the TSA took over U.S. airport security.

3-4 The Organization, Administration, and Management of Police Systems

The organization, administration, and management of any large department presents numerous challenges and problems, but these may be particularly acute in publicly supported police departments. The police department is the largest and most complex agency in many criminal justice systems, with patrol officers exercising immense authority over citizens. The functions performed by these people are varied and complex, although the training for the job is focused primarily on only one of those functions—law enforcement.

Despite the importance of police administration, until recently little attention was given to the issues and problems of organization or administration. Indeed, in contrast to the well-planned development of the English police system, the development of U.S. policing was preceded by little planning because of a basic mistrust of a professional police force. Early systems were characterized by corruption and inefficiency.[24]

3-4a Early Reform Efforts

Widespread corruption, inefficiency, and a realization of the often negative impact of partisan politics on police systems gave rise in the early 1900s to a study of the role of organization and administration in improving the quality of policing and to the increased use of private security guards. These early efforts were assisted by the work of the major reformer August Vollmer, often referred to as the father of modern police management systems or the dean of American chiefs of police. As chief of the Berkeley, California, Police Department, Vollmer instituted a summer program in criminology at the University of California at Berkeley and began an emphasis on the importance of educating police formally.

In 1931, the School of Criminology was founded at Berkeley. In 1933, it granted the first police degree, an AB degree with a minor in criminology. In 1930, the first two-year college police program was begun at the San Jose (California) Junior College, but the first grants to such programs were not offered until 1966. These programs comprised courses in liberal arts, behavioral sciences, public administration, law, and government. Many changes have occurred in criminal justice education, with other programs developing and some, such as Berkeley's, being abolished.

Others who were influential in the development of earlier criminal justice programs were Bruce Smith, who contributed to police professionalism through his writings and as a professional police consultant, and O. W. Wilson. Wilson was influential as a police chief who emphasized advanced training for officers in Wichita, Kansas, in the late 1920s. He was dean of the School of Criminology at Berkeley and authored a widely acclaimed text on police administration. He is perhaps best known for his contributions in the 1960s as Chicago's police superintendent.

Vollmer, Smith, and Wilson influenced the emergence of a professional model for policing, which included not only the use of management skills at the administrative levels of policing but also the application of modern technology in improving police work. The result was a model characterized by "a tight quasi-military organization; rigorous discipline; a streamlined chain of command; higher recruitment standards; a lengthy period of preservice training; the allocation of available personnel according to demonstrated need; and extensive use of vehicles, communications, and computer technology."[25]

3-4b Policing Models

The organization and management of police departments received considerable attention from the President's Commission on Law Enforcement and Administration of Justice (hereafter referred to as the President's Commission). Some of the commission's conclusions, stated in its 1967 report on police, noted the lack of qualified leadership; resistance to change; the lack of trained personnel in research and planning, law, business administration, and computer analysis; the inefficient use of personnel; and departmental organization that did not incorporate "well-established principles of modern business management."[26]

A Professional Model of Policing

The President's Commission graphed one model of departmental organization—the traditional, or professional, model—characterized by a hierarchical structure, with the police chief as the central authority in the organization. Heads of departments, such as internal investigation, community relations, administration bureau, operations bureau, and services bureau, report directly to the chief. Each of these heads has subordinate administrators reporting directly to him or her. Under this model, the police department is organized around specialized functions, such as patrol, traffic, personnel and training, and data processing, all of which are subunits of the major divisions of administration, operations, and services. This model has major units concerned with internal investigations and community relations. Some departments have a unit specializing in crime prevention.

The chain of command in the professional model is clear. Subordinates in each unit report directly to their division heads, who report to the police chief. This model involves many rules and regulations, with little input from subordinates in developing them. It may be a very efficient model for making quick decisions, for prescribing safety measures, and for internally controlling subordinates. The professional model often results in high production output.

The professional model of policing gained momentum with the reports of the 1967 President's Commission and the National Advisory Commission on Criminal Justice Standards and Goals in 1973. According to the 1981 report of the U.S. Commission on Civil Rights, "These two commissions, in particular, gave added impetus to some specific suggestions, such as the more effective use of police personnel and, most emphatically, the requirement that police officers have some college education."[27]

The need for professional police systems became obvious in the 1960s, when television brought into American homes the violent clashes between police and minorities, including the young as well as racial and ethnic groups. The urban riots of the 1960s demonstrated the need to train police in handling orderly protests as well as violence and law enforcement.

During the 1960s, police and other elements of criminal justice systems became the focus of the federal government. In 1965, President Lyndon Johnson appointed the President's Commission on Law Enforcement and Administration of Justice, as noted earlier. This commission issued several reports in 1967. In 1965, Congress established the Office of Law Enforcement Assistance and, in 1968, the **Law Enforcement Assistance Administration (LEAA)**. Until its demise in 1982, the LEAA provided over $7 billion for research, development, and evaluation of various programs in criminal justice, some of which went for hardware in police departments (a source of criticism of the LEAA). Money was provided for police education through the **Law Enforcement**

Law Enforcement Assistance Administration (LEAA) The agency, established by Congress in 1965, that provided funding for the development of police departments, police techniques, police education, and police training. It was abolished in 1982. Money for education was provided through the Law Enforcement Education Program (LEEP).

Law Enforcement Education Program (LEEP) *See* **Law Enforcement Assistance Administration (LEAA)**.

Education Program (LEEP). The result was the development of criminal justice departments throughout the country. Most of them focused on police education or training, discussed in Chapter 4.

The professional model is criticized for being too authoritarian and for establishing policing units that are too specialized. For example, if a police officer assigned to the patrol division encounters a problem with a juvenile, under the professional model, the juvenile should be turned over to the juvenile division, even though the patrol officer in that district may have more knowledge of the individual and his or her background. Controlling traffic and issuing traffic citations are the specialty of the officers in the traffic division; they should be called for handling these problems in the patrol officer's district. The officer may arrest a suspect for violating a crime, but the investigation of that crime will be conducted by a detective in another division. There may be overlap in the record keeping of these various divisions, in addition to the obvious fragmentation of functions.

Problem-Oriented Policing

Dissatisfaction with the professional model has led to an emphasis on an approach to policing that focuses on *problems* rather than *incidents. Problems* consist of incidents that are in some way related—for example, they all occur in the same area of the city— or they are thought to have the same underlying causes. The problem-solving nature of this approach focuses on a less-extensive division of labor, fewer rules and regulations, and fewer levels of authority. The emphasis is on solving problems, and power comes from the ability of employees to succeed in that goal, not from the titles of their positions. Its emphasis is on gaining knowledge and using that knowledge to adapt to new situations. This model provides greater flexibility, which may be necessary for some decisions, while permitting more involvement of subordinates in the police force. It is based on the belief that police effectiveness may be increased if the expertise and creativity of line officers are utilized to develop innovative methods for solving the underlying problems that cause or influence criminal behavior.

Since much of police work requires officers to make on-the-spot decisions, the problem-oriented model may be more effective than the professional model in developing the ability to make decisions effectively. Problem-oriented policing can focus on underlying problems in any or all of the three traditional areas of policing: order maintenance, law enforcement, and community service (all discussed in Chapter 4). It is designed to enhance the effectiveness of policing by identifying underlying problems and attempting to solve those problems.

The problem-solving approach to policing has been emphasized in the writings of Herman Goldstein, who developed his earlier published ideas in a 1990 book. Among other examples, Goldstein discussed a Philadelphia case involving a police sergeant who noted that many noise complaints (505 separate calls in a six-month period) about the same bar had been made to police, who responded to all of these complaints. The officers did not find the noise to be in violation of the city ordinance. After some time, however, officers discovered that the noise about which the neighbors complained was coming from the vibration of the jukebox located at the common wall. The jukebox was moved to another wall, and the noise complaints stopped.[28]

A focus on problem-oriented policing does not mean that police will not respond to calls for service, but the demands created by these calls may lead administrators to rationalize that they do not have the personnel to engage in innovative policing, such as problem-solving approaches. It is necessary to integrate the traditional calls for service with problem-solving policing, and this cannot be done without better management of police time.

Goldstein responded to the time issue by stating,

> A common reaction to problem oriented policing is that the agency has no time available for it....This type of reaction assumes that problem oriented policing is an

add-on. It fails to recognize that the concept raises fundamental questions about how police currently spend their time, both in responding to calls for assistance and in the intervals between calls.[29]

It is argued that the time that police may waste in patrol under the professional policing model can be used more effectively if the police are involved in problem-solving approaches. For example, give police daily assessments of specific problems in their patrol areas and let them work on those problems. As one authority noted, "Many of the citywide crime problems would appear more manageable if officers could deal with them at the neighborhood level."[30]

Problem-oriented policing is based on the concept that officers should become less anonymous and more integrated into the communities they patrol. Returning to foot patrol or using horses or bicycles assists officers in this effort. Police become more visible and more accountable to the public, and they are encouraged to view citizens as partners in crime prevention. Furthermore, more decision making at the patrol level means that those who are best informed of the problems in the community are the ones making important policing decisions.

The problem-solving approach to policing requires that police assume a **proactive** rather than a **reactive** role. That is, police should be more involved, taking the initiative in preventing crime, rather than waiting for others to call in complaints.

The stage for the recent problem-solving approach was set by the emphasis on returning to foot patrol articulated in a 1982 article, "Police and Neighborhood Safety: Broken Windows," written by James Q. Wilson and George L. Kelling. The broken windows concept embodies the belief that minor offenders who disrupt the quality of life should be controlled, thus making neighborhoods safer, resulting in a reduction of fear and of crime. The concept was illustrated by a "Safe and Clean Neighborhoods Program" that began in New Jersey (primarily in Newark) in the mid-1970s and involved putting police back on foot patrol. An evaluation of foot patrol programs by the Police Foundation concluded that the programs did not result in a reduction in crime but that residents *felt* safer within their neighborhoods and *felt* that crime had been reduced. In addition, the officers on foot patrol had "higher morale, greater job satisfaction, and a more favorable attitude toward citizens in their neighborhood" than did their counterparts in patrol cars. Wilson and Kelling concluded that, despite the fact that the overall crime rate did not go down, there were advantages to foot patrol in Newark. The citizens of that city were correct in believing that their neighborhoods were safer because the presence of the police maintained order in the neighborhoods.[31]

Criminologist Gary W. Cordner has analyzed problem-oriented policing and concluded, "In less than two decades, community policing has evolved from a few small foot patrol studies to the preeminent reform agenda of modern policing....[It has become] the dominant strategy of policing."[32] After analyzing the use of problem-oriented policing in San Diego, California, Cordner and Elizabeth Perkins Biebel concluded that, compared to other approaches to policing, "problem-oriented policing offers the most targeted, analytical and in-depth approach."[33]

In his analysis of the problem-solving approach, William V. Pelfrey Jr. called the movement the "first significant role shift for American policing in the past 60 years." The approach, said Pelfrey, is "intended to facilitate the sharing of information, enhance the co-production of neighborhood safety, and ultimately decrease crimes." But, claimed Pelfrey, even in departments that utilize the problem-solving approach, not all officers are involved in it. Rather, most agencies have a "battalion of officers whose primary mission is traditional and reactive" and fewer officers assigned to proactive community policing. That, in effect, creates another level of specialists. In addition, there are some conflicts between the two groups, and they react differently in terms of job satisfaction, time allocation, perceptions of the impact of their work, and their endorsements of various police styles. Pelfrey concluded that the data from his study in Philadelphia suggest that "rather than occasioning significant change, community policing has caused a second layer of concepts to be placed on top of reform era policing."[34]

▶ **Proactive** In policing, preparing for, intervening in, or taking the initiative in finding criminals, rather than depending on the reports of citizens.

▶ **Reactive** In policing, depending on the reports of citizens to find criminal suspects, rather than working independently. It is important because police are not in a position to observe most criminal behavior.

An analysis of one attempt at solving crime through problem solving occurred in St. Louis, beginning in 1994. Residents were concerned about the increasing violence among juveniles, and a woman asked the police to search a house in which she thought guns were located. The police said they could not do that because they did not have sufficient evidence to secure a search warrant. The woman suggested that they just ask for permission to search. That began the *Consent-to-Search* program, with police going to many houses, in response to complaints, and asking for permission to search for guns. They got permission in about 98 percent of the residences. Apparently, the key to their success was that they promised only to confiscate guns and other contraband (such as drugs) but not to prosecute.[35]

The program was highly successful initially and gained national recognition. Program evaluators of the program reported that there were underlying differences between the backers of the program, who believed the program's success depended on keeping the promise not to prosecute, and police, who wanted to get probable cause for search warrants and thus be able to arrest. Further, some police saw the program as a public relations move rather than real police work. The program was suspended in 1996, later revived with significant changes, including the discontinuation of the promise not to prosecute, a reduction of 90 percent in drug seizures, and again, discontinuing the program. The program was again revived, this time with the promise of no prosecution, but police relied on their own intelligence gathering rather than on community tips about which houses should be searched. Consents to search dropped by 50 percent, and gun seizures fell significantly. The investigators concluded that for such programs to be successful, they must have strong support at all levels of the police organization as well as of the community.[36]

Community-Oriented Policing

The influence of problem-oriented policing is seen in the federal development of the Community Oriented Policing Services (COPS), established by the Violent Crime Control and Enforcement Act of 1994.[37] COPS defines *community-oriented policing* as follows:

> [A] policing philosophy that promotes and supports organizational strategies to address the causes and reduce the fear of crime and social disorder through problem-solving tactics and police-community partnerships.[38]

COPS, located within the Department of Justice (DOJ), provides grants to local, tribal, and state law enforcement agencies for hiring and training community policing professionals. An additional mission of COPS is to develop and test innovative policing strategies and to acquire and utilize new techniques for preventing and fighting crime.

The core elements of community policing, as articulated by COPS, are listed in Spotlight 3-5.

Spotlight 3-5   Core Elements of Community Policing

Organizational Elements:
1. Philosophy adopted organization-wide
2. Decentralized decision making and accountability
3. Fixed geographic accountability and generalist responsibilities
4. Utilization of volunteer resources
5. Enhancers

Tactical Elements:
1. Enforcement of laws
2. Proactive, crime-prevention–oriented
3. Problem solving

External Elements:
1. Public involvement in community partnerships
2. Government and other agency partnerships

Source: COPS, http://www.cops.usdoj.gov/default.asp?Item=36, accessed 29 May 2006.

COPS was supported by President Bill Clinton, who announced in his campaign that his administration would put 100,000 more police on the street through a federal hiring program. In early 1994, Clinton announced the "down payment" on his campaign promise, and later that year Congress enacted the new crime bill that contained a provision for the 100,000 promised officers.

Despite Republicans opposition to COPS, by the fall of 1998, money had been appropriated for over two-thirds of the promised 100,000 additional officers, and the Clinton administration was proclaiming that the program was a success. However, the U.S. Department of Justice's inspector general issued a report that sharply criticized the program. The report questioned whether the funds were being used for the intended purpose (putting more officers on the streets and assigning them to community-oriented policing tasks). The auditors reported insufficient controls over how the grants were allocated and spent, concluding that the COPS office "accepts virtually any activity related to law enforcement as community policing." This created confusion concerning the meaning of community-oriented policing. The report raised doubt that the goal of adding 100,000 officers would be met because some agencies were using the grant money to fund current rather than new officers.[39]

President George W. Bush requested that funding for COPS be eliminated from the 2003 budget, but that did not occur. In September 2004, the Senate Appropriations Committee unanimously passed its appropriations act, providing $756 million for the COPS program in 2005. That was roughly $714 million more than President Bush had proposed and $100 million more than the House had proposed. In the final budget, however, Democrats were unable to rescue the COPS program. The 2005 budget slashed funds for the COPS program.[40] Funding remains a problem. In April 2006, even the Republicans criticized the Bush administration for its 2007 budget proposals, and as this text went to press, the president was proposing his 2008 budget, which included a 94 percent cut in the COPS program budget, a drop from $542 million in 2007 to $32 million in 2008.[41]

3-4c   Police Strategies and Crime Reduction

Have the changes in police management and procedures made a difference in crime rates? Perhaps it was inevitable that politicians would claim all of the credit for the crime reductions in their cities during the 1990s. Here we will look at New York City's approach.

Significant attention has been given to the crime reduction in New York City in the 1990s during the administrations of Mayor Rudolph Giuliani and his police commissioner William Bratton, who took office in 1994. The program introduced by Bratton and subsequently adopted in police departments throughout the country is called **COMPSTAT**. COMPSTAT is described by William F. Walsh as "a goal-oriented strategic management process that uses computer technology, operational strategy and managerial accountability to structure the manner in which a police department provides crime-control services." The process has been acclaimed by the Ford Foundation and the John F. Kennedy School of Government at Harvard University and its implementation credited with the decreases in crime in New York City.[42]

According to Walsh, since the return to foot patrol in the 1980s, police departments have been going through a process of "examination, reflection, and experimentation that involves a variety of managerial and operational strategies."[43] At the center of the COMPSTAT approach is the computerization of information about crime. Crime data are processed, mapped, and analyzed, and the results are sent on a regular basis to operational managers, who have the power and the responsibility to discuss the information with their subunits. They are held accountable for appropriate problem-solving responses.[44] Walsh cited specifics with regard to how COMPSTAT was utilized in New York City. He emphasized, however, that the process is not a quick fix to lower crime rates. It requires major changes in organizational

COMPSTAT   A strategic management process acclaimed by numerous organizations today as effective in crime reduction. Utilizes computer technology and other modern management techniques to devise methods of fighting crime.

structure and thinking, and we do not yet know whether its use will have long-term success in reducing crime.[45]

The broken windows concept, discussed earlier in this chapter, is key to New York's approach to the use of COMPSTAT. The emphasis was on cleaning up the streets: arresting minor offenders whose presence may suggest that the police are not in control. Administrators took pride in their claims that New York City became a cleaner and, consequently, safer place to live as the police were responsible for taking back the streets. Not all criminologists agree, however, and some who have studied the crime rates of the 1990s insist that more careful and scientific evaluations are necessary before the conclusions of the politicians and the police can be accepted.[46]

Chapter Wrap-Up

This chapter illustrated the need for formal police systems. It examined the history of informal and formal policing methods in England and the United States. Many factors contributed to the need for formal policing, but in both countries, the increasing complexity that resulted when society became industrialized was crucial. The rising levels of criminal activity, public unrest, and riots that accompanied industrialization demonstrated the inability of informal methods of policing to provide adequate protection.

The formal system of policing that has evolved in the United States—a decentralized system having local, state, and federal levels—results in overlaps and gaps among levels. It also permits states and localities to experiment with methods that might be effective in light of the problems that distinguish their policing needs from those of the federal government. The various levels of policing cooperate in some functions, such as investigation and training. Numerous law enforcement agencies exist at the federal level, and they are available to assist states and local agencies as well. These federal agencies have undergone dramatic changes in recent years, especially since the 9/11 terrorist attacks on U.S. soil.

The changes, such as the development of two new agencies, the Department of Homeland Security and the Transportation Security Administration, have not been without controversy, and neither has the legislation that created and empowered these agencies.

Formal, public policing systems have been the object of criticism for a long time; some citizens have reacted by employing private police or by having security devices installed in their homes or businesses. Conflict between public and private policing developed and continues, although there is some evidence of cooperation between the two. Some states have established minimum requirements for licensing private security firms.

The type of police organization and administration may have a significant effect on policing. The chapter discussed early reform efforts in police organization and administration and then focused on differentiating policing models: the professional model, problem-oriented policing, and community-oriented policing. The chapter closed with a look at police strategies for crime reduction.

This chapter provided a framework in which to examine the nature and functioning of policing, the focus of Chapter 4.

Key Terms

Bow Street Runners (p. 56)
COMPSTAT (p. 76)
constable (p. 55)
Department of Homeland Security (DHS) (p. 65)
Federal Bureau of Investigation (FBI) (p. 63)
frankpledge system (p. 55)
hundred (p. 55)
INTERPOL (p. 68)

Law Enforcement Assistance Administration (LEAA) (p. 72)
Law Enforcement Education Program (LEEP) (p. 72)
magistrates (p. 56)
marshal (p. 60)
Molly Maguires (p. 62)
police (p. 54)
posse (p. 58)
private security forces (p. 69)

proactive (p. 74)
reactive (p. 74)
sheriff (p. 55)
shires (p. 55)
tithing (p. 55)
Transportation Security Administration (TSA) (p. 66)
USA Patriot Act (p. 65)
vigilantism (p. 58)
watch system (p. 55)

Apply It

1. Why do we have a formal system of policing?
2. Explain the meaning of the following to the development of modern policing: Bow Street Runners, Peelers or Bobbies, posses, and Molly Maguires.

3. Define *vigilantism*, and discuss its advantages and disadvantages with regard to air travel today.
4. Compare local, state, and federal police systems. What are the advantages and disadvantages of decentralized policing?

5. What are some of the unique problems of rural law enforcement?

6. What is the role of the county sheriff in most jurisdictions?

7. What is the function of U.S. marshals?

8. Discuss the strengths and weaknesses of the FBI, and comment on the reorganization and reputation of this agency since the 9/11 terrorist attacks. What do you think should be the FBI's role with regard to counterterrorism efforts?

9. What impact have illegal drugs had on rural and county policing in recent years?

10. Discuss two of the recent pieces of federal legislation designed to combat terrorism.

11. Describe the Department of Homeland Security and the Transportation Security Administration.

12. What is the role of private police agencies? Evaluate.

13. How would you describe the administration of early police systems in the United States?

14. Evaluate the traditional, authoritarian model of organizational structure of police departments.

15. Trace the development of the professional model of policing.

16. Describe and analyze the concepts of problem-oriented and community-oriented policing.

17. Explain what is meant by COMPSTAT, and discuss why it is considered, at least by some, to be effective.

Endnotes

1. Herman Goldstein, *Policing in a Free Society* (Cambridge, Mass.: Ballinger, 1977), p. 1.

2. Jonathan Rubinstein, *City Police* (New York: Ballantine Books, 1973), p. 5.

3. David H. Bayley, "Police: History," in *Encyclopedia of Crime and Justice*, vol. 3, ed. Sanford H. Kadish (New York: Free Press, 1983), pp. 1122–1123.

4. Louis B. Schwartz and Stephen R. Goldstein, *Law Enforcement Handbook for Police* (St. Paul, Minn.: West, 1970), p. 34.

5. "Police Race Bias Moves Blasted," *Daily Star* (24 August 2004), p. 6.

6. "10 Years after Their Son Was Killed, Blair's Message to the Lawrences: Still Too Much Racism," *Evening Standard* (London) (22 April 2003), n.p.

7. "Police Chief Vows to Bring Racist Killers to Book," *The Guardian* (London) (final edition) (27 April 2006), p. 6. The information on the Lawrence investigation is from "Lawrence Police Team Disbanded," *Evening Standard* (London) (24 April 2006), p. 19.

8. Bayley, "Police: History," p. 1124.

9. Ibid.

10. "As Drug Use Drops in Big Cities, Small Towns Confront Upsurge," *New York Times* (11 February 2002), p. 1.

11. Robert Borkenstein, "Police: State Police," in *Encyclopedia of Crime and Justice*, vol. 3, ed. Kadish, p. 1133.

12. "Senators Criticize F.B.I. for Its Security Failures," *New York Times* (19 July 2001), p. 16.

13. "F.B.I. Is Retailoring to Meet New Threats but Stretched Thin, Reports Say," *New York Times* (19 June 2003), p. 15.

14. *The 9/11 Commission Report: Final Report of the National Commission on Terrorist Attacks upon the United States, Authorized Edition* (New York: W. W. Norton & Company, 2004), p. 358.

15. "F.B.I. Is Assailed for Its Handling of Terror Risks," *New York Times* (14 April 2004), p. 1.

16. Robert S. Mueller III, Director of the Federal Bureau of Investigation, "FBI Oversight," Testimony before the Senate Judiciary Committee, *Federal News Service* (2 May 2006), n.p.

17. The USA Patriot Act is codified at U.S. Code, Title 18, Section 1229 *et seq.* (2007).

18. Michael Fooner, "INTERPOL," in *Encyclopedia of Crime and Justice*, vol. 3, ed. Kadish, p. 912.

19. "About Interpol," http://www.interpol.int/public/icpo/default.asp. accessed 27 May 2006.

20. See, for example, Off Duty Services, Inc., http://www.offdutyservices.com/, accessed 27 May 2006.

21. James S. Kakalik and Sorrel Wildhorn, *The Private Police: Security and Danger* (New York: Crane Russak, 1977), p. 68.

22. Albert J. Reiss Jr., *Private Employment of Public Police* (Washington, D.C.: U.S. Department of Justice, December 1988), pp. 2–3.

23. William C. Cunningham and Todd H. Taylor, "Ten Years of Growth in Law Enforcement," *Police Chief* 1 (June 1983): 32.

24. The basis for this discussion is the article by Herman Goldstein, "Police Administration," in *Encyclopedia of Crime and Justice*, vol. 3, ed. Kadish, pp. 1125–1131.

25. Ibid., p. 1126.

26. The President's Commission on Law Enforcement and Administration of Justice, *Task Force on the Police, Task Force Report: The Police* (Washington, D.C.: U.S. Government Printing Office, 1967), p. 44.

27. United States Commission on Civil Rights, *Who Is Guarding the Guardians? A Report on Police Practices* (Washington, D.C.: U.S. Government Printing Office, 1981), p. 6.

28. Herman Goldstein, *Problem Oriented Policing* (New York: McGraw-Hill, 1990), p. 81 (n. 6).

29. Ibid., p. 151.

30. David A. Kessler, "Integrating Calls for Service with Community and Problem Oriented Policing: A Case Study," *Crime and Delinquency* 39 (October 1993): 506.

31. James Q. Wilson and George L. Kelling, "Police and Neighborhood Safety: Broken Windows," *Atlantic Monthly* 249 (March 1982): 28–38.

32. Gary W. Cordner, "Community Policing: Elements and Effects," in *Critical Issues in Policing: Contemporary Readings*, 5th ed., ed. Roger G. Dunham and Geoffrey P. Alpert (Long Grove, Ill.: Waveland Press, 2005), pp. 401–418; quotation is on p. 401.

33. Gary Cordner and Elizabeth Perkins Biebel, "Problem-Oriented Policing in Practice," *Criminology and Public Policy* 4, no. 2 (May 2005): 155–180; quotation is on p. 158.

34. William V. Pelfrey Jr., "The Inchoate Nature of Community Policing: Differences between Community Policing and Traditional Police Officers," *Justice Quarterly* 21, no. 3 (September 2004): 579–601; quotations are on pp. 596 and 597.

35. Scott H. Decker and Richard Rosenfeld, *Reducing Gun Violence: The St. Louis Consent to Search Program,* National

Institute of Justice, 2004, http://www.ojpd.usdoj.gov/nij, accessed 29 May 2006.

36. Ibid.

37. Violent Crime Control and Law Enforcement Act of 1994, Public Law 103-322 (13 September 1994).

38. COPS, http://www.cops.usdoj.gov/default.asp?Item=36, accessed 29 May 2006.

39. "Audit Cites Many Problems in Monitoring of COPS Grants," *Criminal Justice Newsletter* 29 (15 December 1998): 3–4; "COPS Grant Progress Overstated, Justice Department Auditor Says," *Criminal Justice Newsletter* 30 (16 March 1999): 4.

40. "Local Government's Priorities Are Tested in FY 2004 Appropriations," *Nation's Cities Weekly* 26, no. 37 (15 September 2003): 1; "Senate Public Safety Appropriations a Mixed Bag for Cities," *Nation's Cities Weekly* 27, no. 39 (27 September 2004): 3; "Congress Cuts Back the Bush...," *Washington Post* (7 December 2004), p. 23; "Cuts to Hit L.A. Hard; COPS, Women's Programs Slashed," *Daily News of Los Angeles* (8 February 2005), p. 1N.

41. "Lawmakers Criticize Budget Cuts for Police," *Washington Post* (6 April 2006), p. 11; "Lieberman Alerts Budget Committee to Major Inadequacies in Proposed Homeland Security Budget," *States News Services* (3 March 2006), n.p.; "Rep. Courtney Slams President's Proposed Cuts to First Responders," *U.S. Federal News* (27 February 2007), n.p.

42. William F. Walsh, "COMPSTAT: An Analysis of a Merging Police Managerial Paradigm," in *Critical Issues in Policing*, ed. Dunham and Alpert, pp. 201–216; quotation is on p. 201.

43. Ibid., p. 202.

44. Ibid., p. 206.

45. Ibid., p. 213.

46. See, for example, Richard Rosenfeld et al., "Did Ceasefire, COMPSTAT, and Exile Reduce Homicide?" *Criminology and Public Policy* 4, no. 3 (August 2005): 419–450; and James J. Willis et al., "COMPSTAT and Bureaucracy: A Case Study of Challenges and Opportunities for Change," *Justice Quarterly* 21, no. 3 (September 2004): 463–496.

Policing in a Modern Society

Police in the United States are expected to prevent crime, apprehend and arrest criminals, enforce traffic ordinances and laws, maintain order in domestic and other kinds of disputes, control or prevent disturbances, and perform numerous miscellaneous services. Police must perform these functions in the context of political, legal, and societal expectations, which may be unrealistic and conflicting.

Some of the functions assigned to police are shared by other persons or agencies, which often results in conflict concerning police roles. But police are given greater discretion and power in performing their tasks than are other agencies. Why? The possibility that disorder, or even violence, will occur convinces us that the police should handle the situation. Therefore, we are willing to grant police the power to act when intervention is necessary.

This chapter focuses on what police do in a modern society, but those functions should be examined in the context of the extensive discretion police have in performing their jobs. The importance of discretion and the possibility of its abuse require that high standards be maintained by those who occupy policing roles. The chapter discussion of discretion is thus preceded by a look at preparing for policing.

The chapter discussion of police functions focuses first on order maintenance and community service before devoting substantial coverage to law enforcement, which begins with an overview of constitutional issues.

The specifics of law enforcement begin with an analysis of traffic stops and other attempts to enforce traffic ordinances. The investigatory stop by police is examined in terms of racial profiling and other issues regarding stop and frisk. The arrest, search, and seizure of suspects is examined by a look at warrants and the meaning of probable cause, along with a summary of the laws regarding home, automobile, and person searches. The final two sections cover the interrogation and investigation of suspects.

4-1 Preparing for Policing

The importance of policing demands that careful attention be given to the recruitment and selection, as well as the education and training, of persons who will become police officers.

L E A R N I N G

OBJECTIVES

After reading this chapter, you should be able to do the following:

- **Describe the importance of police recruitment and selection.**
- **Discuss the role of higher education in policing.**
- **Analyze the importance of police training.**
- **Explain the meaning and importance of discretion in policing.**
- **List and discuss the three major areas of police functions.**
- **Present an overview of the major U.S. constitutional provisions that govern policing.**
- **Discuss recent U.S. Supreme Court decisions regarding traffic stops and searches.**
- **Explain the difference between an investigatory stop and an arrest.**
- **Assess the meaning and importance of racial profiling.**
- **Discuss the meaning of probable cause, and explain the purpose of requiring a warrant for most searches.**
- **Explain what police can and cannot do in searching a home, an automobile, and a person.**
- **Compare the police role of interrogation with that of investigation.**
- **Explain and evaluate the *Miranda* rule and its exceptions.**

4-1a Recruitment and Selection

One difficulty in the recruitment and selection of police is that desirable qualities and characteristics are usually not defined in measurable terms. Perhaps the problem is that, in the past, the focus was on the recruits and their qualities, the assumption being that, if different types of people were attracted to policing, the profession would improve. Some researchers reported that certain types—for example, authoritarian and cynical people—are attracted to policing. Others argued that policing *creates* these personalities.[1]

Successful recruitment of police officers requires more research into the characteristics most highly associated with effective policing. Good policing requires intelligence and the abilities to think independently, to perform different roles and functions, to comprehend and accept other cultures and subcultures, and to understand the importance of freedom and the dangers of abusing authority. Figure 4-1 lists the screening methods used to recruit police in 2003, the latest available data. The figure graphs the percentage of local police officers employed by departments using each method. Note that all departments conducted criminal background checks, 98 percent utilized personal interviews, 73 percent utilized drug testing, and 67 percent conducted psychological evaluations.

It is crucial for police departments to recruit people who have high moral and ethical standards and who have not had previous infractions with the law. Chapter 5 discusses corruption in policing; avoiding that problem requires recruiting persons who will not succumb to the temptations facing law enforcement officers. This is difficult to do, however, as police officials throughout the country have discovered. Officers are recruited from a generation of young people who have grown up in a culture in which it may be considered acceptable to engage in some law violations, such as using illegal drugs. Trying to recruit persons who have never used drugs may be an impossible task, especially in some of the larger cities. Of course, recruiting ethical candidates for jobs is important in most jobs, but as one authority on police ethics notes, it is particularly crucial in policing: Few occupations make as significant moral demands on their

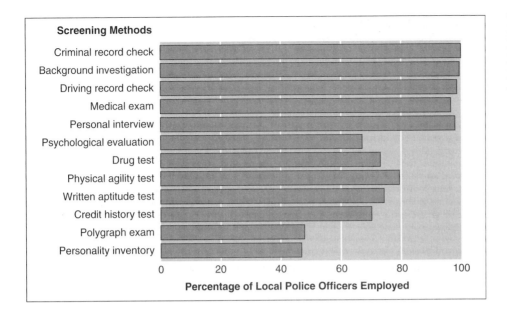

Figure 4-1
Local Police Officers Employed by Departments Using Various Recruit Screening Methods, 2003
Source: Matthew J. Hickman and Brian A. Reaves, Bureau of Justice Statistics, *Local Police Departments, 2003* (Washington, D.C.: U.S. Department of Justice, May 2006), p. 8.

practitioners as policing. Yet no occupation has been as poorly prepared for the moral demands laid on it.[2]

Police recruits need an understanding of the context in which policing occurs, as well as the nature of the job. This information might alleviate the stress caused by recruits' unrealistic expectations.

The success of efforts to recruit persons with high moral and ethical standards into policing and to encourage them to maintain those standards may be analyzed in terms of the subsequent behavior of recruits. In that respect, the New York City Police Department (NYPD) is often the focus of attention. For example, a major investigation into policing in that city occurred upon the arrest of four police officers after a brutal attack on Abner Louima, a Haitian immigrant, at a Brooklyn station house on 9 August 1997. In testimony before the New York City Council, Frank Serpico, a former New York City police officer, stated, "We must create an atmosphere where the crooked cop fears the honest cop, and not the other way around." In the early 1970s, Serpico reported and testified against officers who engaged in corrupt or other forms of illegal behavior. He almost lost his life in his fight against the problems of the NYPD, and his story became a best-selling book and movie, *Serpico*.[3]

Recruiting well-qualified candidates for policing has become a serious problem in some areas. The low salaries and high risk do not attract many applicants. At the same time, in some departments, the need for recruits has increased due to retirements. In the NYPD, for example, after the 9/11 terrorist attacks, the work demands on officers were such that, by the end of fiscal year 2002, many of them had doubled their income through overtime pay, creating an incentive to retire while their salaries reflected those increases. Police with 20 years in the NYPD may retire at one-half the pay of their last 12 months of service.[4] Heavy retirements, which had already risen significantly over the previous year, made recruitment difficult and increased the problems of adjustment on the police force. As one police chief stated, "When there is a sudden intrusion of new rookies, they overwhelm the organization....They are able to impose their values on the organization. They can be resistant to positive mentoring."[5]

In March 2006, New York City Mayor Michael Bloomberg announced that the city would add 800 officers and 400 civilians to the police department, and that represents the first city-financed additions since 1993. It will be difficult, though, with a starting salary of $25,100 for the first six months while they are being trained, followed by $32,700 for the next 12 months, when they are on patrol. In contrast to this starting salary, the Los Angeles Police Department (LAPD) pays $51,000.[6]

4-1b   Education

Most would agree that education is important for police officers, but there is disagreement over the amount and type of education that should be required. The dispute over whether any college education should be mandated is significant. As far back as 1917, a college education for police received significant attention from August Vollmer, when he recruited part-time police officers from students at the University of California. Despite his emphasis on the importance of higher education and his reputation as an outstanding police administrator, Vollmer did not succeed in convincing many police departments to follow his lead. During the Great Depression, when jobs were scarce, police departments recruited college-educated men, but that practice ceased with the end of the Depression.

In 1967, when the average police officer had only slightly more than a high school diploma, the President's Commission on Law Enforcement and Administration of Justice (hereafter referred to as the President's Commission) recommended that the "ultimate aim of all police departments should be that personnel with general enforcement powers have baccalaureate degrees."[7] The federal government provided financial incentives and support for the development of programs for higher education of police officers.

As noted in Chapter 3, one of the provisions of the federal 1994 crime control bill was to put more police on the streets. The money Congress provided for the Community Oriented Policing Services (COPS) program established by the 1994 statute was used in some jurisdictions for enhanced training and education of police. The 1994 statute provided funds for the development in six states (Maryland, North Carolina, Oregon, Nevada, Arkansas, and South Carolina) of programs that were modeled after the military's Reserve Officers Training Corps (ROTC). For college graduates who agreed to serve four years in policing, the program reimbursed up to $30,000 in educational costs. But also as noted in Chapter 3, funding has been an issue.

There has been some improvement in the college education of police recruits, with 9 percent of police departments in 2003 requiring a two-year degree for recruits, as noted in Professions 4-1. Professions 4-1 also contains information about the amount of training required of recruits, as well as the salaries recruits can expect.

One encouraging sign with regard to educating police is the combining of higher education and training, thus reducing the time a recruit must spend in obtaining both. In May 2006, Miami Dade College (Florida) announced that the state's board of education had approved for the college a new bachelor's degree program for law enforcement officers. The degree, entitled *applied science in public safety management*, enables students to earn a bachelor's degree and law enforcement certification in one program, thus reducing by one year the process of receiving each in separate institutions. The program is not limited to police students but is also open to correctional officers, probation officers, crime scene investigators, and security guards.[8]

Those who do not favor college education for police cite several reasons: First, raising educational requirements might discriminate against minority applicants. Second, there is concern that the applicant pool may be too small. Third, some police unions are opposed to higher educational requirements.[9] Finally, many of the criminal justice programs that have provided police education have come under attack. Critics argue that there is too much emphasis on technical skills at the expense of a broad educational background.[10]

Along these lines, the Massachusetts Board of Education announced in the spring of 2003 that it would close some of the units that had been providing criminal justice education for police in that state, which was facing a $3 billion deficit. Under the Massachusetts Quinn bill, cities and towns pay one-half of the cost of higher education expenses for police, while the state pays the other half. Police salaries are increased with each level of higher education obtained (10 percent for an associate degree, 20 percent for a bachelor's degree, and 25 percent for a master's degree; pension costs also increase), and some taxpayers do not believe the expenditure is worth the cost, about

$100 million annually. The state proposed to cut some of the so-called "cop shops" that "specialize in quickie criminal justice diplomas." By 2004, the Quinn bill was still in effect but had been overhauled by the board of education, which instituted new and stricter testing and curriculum standards, "and officers can no longer receive credit for 'life experience' and required police academy training." Additional requirements have been placed on the colleges that offer police education, which are now required to hire more professors with advanced degrees in criminal justice or related fields. Perhaps as a result of the Quinn bill (and overtime pay), police in Boston, Massachusetts, are among the highest-paid law enforcement officers in the country. In 2004, the average Boston patrol officer received total pay of $90,241. That year, the police were demanding pay increases to average 17 percent over the next four years; the mayor was offering 11 percent. An arbitrator settled on 14.5 percent. At that time, base salaries ranged from $49,174 to $77,682. Approximately $9.6 million of the $188.5 million appropriated for police salaries was necessary to pay for the Quinn bill bonuses.[11]

Despite the cost of higher education for police and some of the disadvantages of such education, evidence indicates that higher education is worth the time and expense. A frequently cited study in support of higher education for police is the 1989 publication based on the research by the Police Executive Research Forum (PERF). The authors concluded that, overall, college-educated officers were more responsible and made better decisions than their less-educated counterparts. As such, officers with some college education were not only more effective in performing their jobs but also more efficient in that costs associated with lost personnel time were lower.[12]

Finally, the authors of an analysis of higher education and policing concluded the following:

> We find that higher education has two important roles to play. One is to carry education beyond the classroom in ways that encourage broad reform. The other is to help make improvements in police training and education in ways that, at least will produce higher levels of civility, and might even encourage a more humanistic police professionalism.[13]

4-1c Training

In its 1967 report, the Task Force on Police of the President's Commission emphasized the importance of adequate police training, noting that the problem was particularly acute in small police departments. Many larger departments had expanded police training, but the task force concluded that "current training programs, for the most part, prepare an officer to perform police work mechanically but do not prepare him to understand his community, the police role, or the imperfections of the criminal justice system." Few of the programs reviewed by the commission provided training on the use of police discretion.[14]

The President's Commission recommended that police training include instruction on "subjects that prepare recruits to exercise discretion properly and to understand the community, the role of the police, and what the criminal justice system can and cannot do." The commission recommended "an absolute minimum of 400 hours of classroom work spread over a four- to six-month period so that it can be combined with carefully selected and supervised field training." In-service training at least once a year, along with incentives for officers to continue their education, should be provided.[15] In 1973, the National Advisory Commission on Criminal Justice Standards and Goals put police training into perspective with some harsh comments: "Perhaps no other profession has such lax standards or is allowed to operate without firm controls and without licensing."[16]

In 1981, the U.S. Commission on Civil Rights emphasized the need for formal police training and concluded that most of the examined programs "do not give sufficient priority to on-the-job field training, programs in human relations, and preparation for the social service function of police officers, including intervening in family-related

Professions 4-1

Police Personnel in Local Departments: Education, Training, and Salaries

The following is information published in May 2006 by the Bureau of Justice Statistics concerning the education, training, and salaries of local police in 2003:

Education and Training Requirements

Nearly all (98 percent) local police departments had an education requirement for new officer recruits. Eighteen percent of departments had some type of college requirement, with 9 percent requiring a two-year degree.

In 2003 the percentage of officers employed by a department with some type of college requirement for new officers (33 percent) was about the same as in 2000 (32 percent), but more than three times as high as in 1990 (10 percent).

In the largest jurisdictions new local police recruits were required to complete an average of about 1,500 hours of training compared to about 800 hours in the smallest. On average, about three-quarters of training hours were State mandated, with the remainder an agency requirement....

From 2000 to 2003 there were significant increases in training requirements for local police recruits in jurisdictions with fewer than 250,000 residents. In jurisdictions with 50,000 to 249,999 residents, the average combined field and academy training requirement rose from 1,178 hours to 1,355 hours; with 10,000 to 49,999 residents, from 969 to 1,148; and with fewer than 10,000 residents, from 605 to 855. The average requirement rose slightly in jurisdictions with more than 250,000 residents, from 1,514 to 1,543.

The average annual inservice training requirement for non-probationary officers was 47 hours, including 24 State-mandated hours.

Overall, just 3 percent of departments operated a training academy; however, nearly all of those serving a population of 250,000 or more did so. Nationwide, 45 percent of all officers were employed by a department that operated an academy.

Salaries

The overall average base starting salary for local police chiefs was $48,800 in 2003. Average starting salaries for chiefs ranged from $113,000 in jurisdictions with 1 million or more residents to $32,700 in those with a population under 2,500.

Average minimum starting salaries for first-line supervisors (sergeant or equivalent) ranged from $60,200 in the largest jurisdictions to $27,100 in the smallest, with an overall departmental average of $36,600. When size of department is considered, the average minimum starting salary earned by local police sergeants was about $52,600.

By department the average base starting salary offered to entry-level patrol officers in 2003 was $28,200. Starting salaries ranged from $23,400 in jurisdictions with fewer than 2,500 residents to $39,600 in those with a population of 100,000 to 249,999. When size of department is factored in, it is estimated that new entry-level local police officers started at an average salary of about $35,000 during 2003. This was 12 percent more than in 2000, a 5 percent increase after adjusting for inflation.

By population category inflation-adjusted salaries rose by 4 percent in jurisdictions with 250,000 or more residents, from $36,170 to $37,514. In smaller jurisdictions, the increase was also 4 percent: 50,000 to 249,999 residents, from $36,607 to $38,011; 10,000 to 49,999 residents, from $32,706 to $33,889; fewer than 10,000 residents, from $24,835 to $25,834. [See Figure 1.]

Special Pay

Nationwide, 35 percent of local police departments, employing 62 percent of all officers, offered tuition reimbursement to officers. This included a majority of departments serving 10,000 or more residents.

disturbances." The commission found that in many jurisdictions even firearms training was inadequate and "subject to the ambiguities found in statutes and departmental policies." Because of this ambiguity, the commission concluded that it is imperative that police training expose recruits to situations in which the use of firearms might or might not be appropriate. Alternatives to deadly force should also be demonstrated. Finally, the commission recommended that police receive training in the social services they are expected to perform.[17]

Basic police training includes many areas of expertise, ranging from firing weapons to understanding the ordinances and laws that govern a particular jurisdiction. Much of the training is standard and cannot be detailed here, but it is important to go beyond the traditional, standard training. Let's consider just a few examples. A publication of a five-year study of drug-related deaths of suspects in police custody concluded that approximately one-third of those deaths could have been prevented had police been adequately trained for significant intervention. But prevention requires more than "just an officer standing outside [the cell] and seeing if someone is sleeping; it requires a

An estimated 32 percent of departments offered education incentive pay to qualifying officers, including a majority of those serving a population of 10,000 or more. About half (53%) of all local police officers worked for a department that offered this type of pay.

Twenty-one percent of local police departments, employing 30 percent of all local police officers, offered merit pay to qualifying sworn personnel.

Twenty-one percent of departments, employing 52 percent of all officers, offered shift differential pay to full-time officers. This included a majority of the departments serving a population of 100,000 or more.

Thirteen percent of departments offered special skills pay, including more than half of the departments serving 1 million or more residents and more than a third of those serving a population of 50,000 to 999,999.

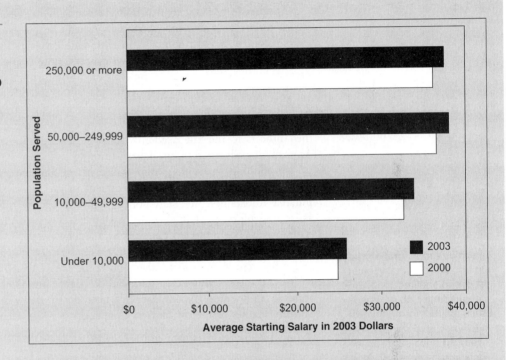

Figure 1
Average Base Starting Salary for Entry-Level Officers in Local Police Departments, 2000 and 2003

Source: Matthew J. Hickman and Brian A. Reaves, Bureau of Justice Statistics, *Local Police Departments, 2003* (Washington, D.C.: U.S. Department of Justice, May 2006), pp. 9, 11.

more active process of rousing and checking." The study found that jailers and medical examiners need more training in recognizing drug problems. Police and correctional officers must be constantly vigilant to prevent cell deaths.[18]

Gang violence is a serious problem in many neighborhoods and even in some schools, and in this area, we see another example of cooperation between federal and local agencies. In May 2006, the U.S. Department of Justice announced that it was adding another $300,000 to Projects Safe Neighborhoods, a project originally aimed at reducing the availability of guns and then moving into preventing gang activity. The new money will be granted primarily to local police departments to enable officials to pay officers overtime for investigating gang activity. The remaining 30 percent will be utilized to train school police officers and security personnel to become familiar with gang signs, clothing, graffiti, tattoos, and symbols.[19]

Another area in which police need special training is patrolling in and around schools. With the increase in violence on school grounds and inside school buildings, security has become increasingly important. In Troy, Michigan, a special force of police officers on bicycles patrols school grounds as well as parks and special events within the city. These officers must be specially trained. They receive 40 hours of classroom and practical training, which includes instruction on how to repair and maintain a bicycle. They must be in excellent physical condition, for, as one of these special officers said, "You've got to be able to pedal quick and under control."[20]

Despite the special training needed for policing in and around schools, a 2001 poll of school resource officers revealed that they were not required to have any special training beyond that required of all police officers. The executive director of the National Association of School Resource Officers stated as follows: "Because policing a school is so tremendously different than policing the street, the need for training is very [important]....Administrators need to commit to making sure officers are specially trained."[21]

Another important area of police training is in the skills needed to dissect crime scenes for relevant evidence, especially when the evidence is buried. For example, a course entitled "Skeletal Remains in Homicide Investigations," initiated by one sheriff's department in 1994 to train its own officers, now trains other local law enforcement agents as well as FBI agents in the craft of sifting through graves to find evidence.[22]

It is, of course, expensive to train law enforcement officers, and most departments do not have the resources to train their officers in all areas of expertise. Some departments take advantage of the courses at other local departments, whereas others send their officers to the FBI Academy or to the Drug Enforcement Administration (DEA) Academy for advanced or specialized training.

In addition to helping train police in other departments, police may help other professions train to assist law enforcement in preventing crimes, such as terrorism. In Indiana, for example, the state police began a program in June 2003 to train truckers to assist law enforcement in spotting national security and highway safety threats on the state's roads. The project is financed by a federal grant.[23]

Increased training for law enforcement officers, along with additional equipment and other resources, is expensive, and some local departments do not have the funds to finance these ventures. In addition to grants provided by the federal government, some local law enforcement agencies take advantage of the offerings of local colleges and universities. The East Haven, Connecticut, Police Department, for example, saved about $80,000 in 2003 by taking advantage of the reduced rates provided by the state's community college system. Police and administrators were provided training and permitted to purchase computers and other equipment at the college's bulk rate price. At the successful completion of the training, the officers received college credit and certificates.[24]

The importance of adequate police training was emphasized by a 1989 U.S. Supreme Court decision, *City of Canton, Ohio v. Harris*, in which the Court held that inadequate police training may result in civil liability for the municipality under which the police department operates. The Supreme Court placed limitations, stating that liability may exist "only where the failure to train amounts to deliberate indifference to the rights of persons with whom the police come into contact."[25] The case is discussed in Spotlight 4-1.

4-2 Police Discretion

Chapter 1 includes a discussion of discretion and notes that wide discretion exists in criminal justice systems. That discretion is extreme and critical in policing. Police have wide discretion in determining whether to begin the formal processing of criminal justice systems. When they see a person who appears to be violating the law, police may refuse to acknowledge that action. Or they may investigate the situation and decide that they do not have sufficient reason to think a crime has been committed. They might also decide that a crime has been committed but not by the suspect, or that the suspect may have committed the crime but for some reason should not be arrested.

Spotlight 4-1 | The Importance of Adequate Police Training: The U.S. Supreme Court Speaks

[In 1989, the U.S. Supreme Court emphasized the importance of police training. Portions of the case *City of Canton, Ohio v. Harris* follow.]

In this case, we are asked to determine if a municipality can ever be liable...for constitutional violations resulting from its failure to train municipal employees. We hold that, under certain circumstances, such liability is permitted....

In April 1978, respondent Geraldine Harris was arrested by officers of the Canton Police Department. Harris was brought to the police station in a patrol wagon.

When she arrived at the station, Harris was found sitting on the floor of the wagon. She was asked if she needed medical attention, and responded with an incoherent remark. After she was brought inside the station for processing, Mrs. Harris slumped to the floor on two occasions. Eventually, the police officers left Mrs. Harris lying on the floor to prevent her from falling again. No medical attention was ever summoned for Mrs. Harris. After about an hour, Mrs. Harris was released from custody and taken by an ambulance (provided by her family) to a nearby hospital. There, Mrs. Harris was diagnosed as suffering from several emotional ailments; she was hospitalized for one week and received subsequent outpatient treatment for an additional year.

Some time later, Mrs. Harris commenced this action, alleging many state law and constitutional claims against the city of Canton and its officials. Among these claims was one seeking to hold the city liable...for its violation of Mrs. Harris' right, under the Due Process Clause of the Fourteenth Amendment, to receive necessary medical attention while in police custody....

We hold today that the inadequacy of police training may serve as the basis for liability only where the failure to train amounts to deliberate indifference to the rights of persons with whom the police come into contact....Only where a municipality's failure to train its employees in a relevant respect evidences a "deliberate indifference" to the rights of its inhabitants can such a shortcoming be properly thought of as a city "policy or custom" that is actionable....

Moreover, for liability to attach in this circumstance, the identified deficiency in a city's training program must be closely related to the ultimate injury. Thus, in the case at hand, respondent must still prove that the deficiency in training actually caused the police officers' indifference to her medical needs. Would the injury have been avoided had the employee been trained under a program that was not deficient in the identified respect? Predicting how a hypothetically well-trained officer would have acted under the circumstances may not be an easy task for the fact finder, particularly since matters of judgment may be involved, and since officers who are well-trained are not free from error and perhaps might react very much like the untrained officer in similar circumstances. But judge and jury, doing their respective jobs, will be adequate to the task.

Source: City of Canton, Ohio v. Harris, 489 U.S. 378 (1989), footnotes and citations omitted.

How the officer exercises discretion may be influenced by several factors. Consider this hypothetical scenario: A police officer, while out on patrol at midnight on a Friday night, observed a car weaving down the highway, going five miles over the speed limit. The officer turned on the police car siren and lights and directed the driver to stop. After checking the operator's driver's license, the officer inquired where the person was going and why she was speeding. The driver replied that she did not realize she was speeding but that she was in a hurry to get home because a contact lens was causing pain. Something apparently had flown into her eye and blurred her vision temporarily. She considered it unsafe for a woman alone to stop by the side of a highway late at night, and she was attempting to get to her home only a mile away.

When asked where she had been, the driver replied that she was an *A* student in a criminal justice program and had been at a friend's house, studying, since the library closed at 11 P.M. When asked whether she had been drinking, the driver replied that she had consumed only one beer. The driver answered all questions politely and nondefensively.

What would you do if you were the police officer? Would you ticket the driver for speeding? Would you believe her response about the contact lens? Would you believe what she told you about drinking only one beer? Would it make any difference in your decision if you had stopped her at 3 A.M. rather than at midnight? You could, of course, give the driver a verbal warning and let her go. You could give her a speeding ticket. If you had sufficient reason to think that she had been drinking to the point that she was legally impaired, you could ask her to get out of the car and perform some simple tests.

Or you might arrest her and take her to the police station to begin official processing through the criminal justice system.

Now, think about the results of your decision. If the driver is telling the truth and you decide to arrest her, what have you accomplished by your action? Is it not possible that the negative effect of the arrest and subsequent experiences she has in the criminal justice system will outweigh any benefit that society will get from this arrest? On the other hand, if she has been drinking too much, is it not possible that an arrest will cause her to think before she gets into a car again after drinking? Or will it have no effect on her behavior? What about the behavior of her friends and other persons, who will certainly hear about your actions?

Perhaps by now you have decided what action you would take. Let's add more facts to the scenario. Suppose that, when you begin to talk to the driver, she curses you and tells you to mind your own business. Would this affect your decision to write a speeding ticket or give her roadside tests for intoxication?

Police must make decisions such as these daily. Selective enforcement of laws is necessary because our system cannot process all cases of law violations, even if we choose to do so. Police discretion is important because police are the primary persons responsible for the initial entry of someone into the criminal justice system. The necessity to exercise discretion without adequate guidelines puts tremendous pressure on police.

In recent years, attention has been given to the need to prepare police for the appropriate use of discretion. The need for guidelines is recognized, although there is no agreement on what those guidelines should be or which agency should formulate them. Legislatures enact statutes for general guidance and delegate to police departments, as administrative agencies, the power to develop more specific rules. Courts have the responsibility for interpreting the guidelines, statutes, and policies in terms of state and federal constitutions.

Numerous studies have been done of police discretion and the factors involved in police decision making. This vast research was analyzed and summarized in a recent article by Laure Weber Brooks, who found four categories of variables: organization variables, neighborhood variables, situational variables, and officer characteristics. *Organization variables* include such variables as the way in which the department is organized, the rotation shifts, the size of the department, the extent and type of specialty units within the department, and the extent of professionalism within the department. *Neighborhood variables* include the racial and socioeconomic composition of the population and the crime rate. *Situational variables* include the race, gender, and socioeconomic characteristics of the suspects and of the alleged victims, along with the demeanor and attitudes of each. The characteristics of the encounter, such as the seriousness of the offense, may also be a factor. *Officer characteristics* include the officer's race, gender, attitudes, the extent and type of experience, and education. Brooks concluded that all four of these variables may be influential in police decision making and that further research is needed.[26]

The key, however, is that although police may use many reasons for making decisions, they may *not* use *extralegal* rather than legal factors to decide whether to stop, arrest, or take other actions. More will be said about that in subsequent discussions in this and other chapters.

4-3   Police Functions

Although in the popular image police may spend most of their time apprehending and arresting criminals, these functions constitute a very small, though significant, part of the daily lives of police officers. Police also perform a variety of functions not directly related to law enforcement. These functions have been categorized as *order maintenance* and *community service*, which we will discuss prior to our analysis of law enforcement.

There appears to be agreement that law enforcement, order maintenance, and community service are the three basic areas of police functions, but there is no agreement on whether they *should* be. Nor is there agreement on how police time and resources should be allocated among the three areas. It is clear, however, that the areas are not discrete; there is considerable overlap. Attention to an order maintenance problem or provision of a particular service may prevent a situation from escalating into criminal behavior. Engaging in order maintenance functions and services may alert the police to criminal law violations. Finally, police are expected to prevent crime, and that may occur while they are performing any of their three main functions.

Before we analyze police functions in more detail, it is important to emphasize that all police functions involve an enormous amount of paperwork, which consumes considerable police time, a fact rarely mentioned in discussions on policing. Perhaps this oversight is typical of other professions, and those who enter have no prior concept of the incredible detail expected of them in filing reports. With police, however, expectations are particularly important because, if the paperwork is not done properly, cases may be dropped or evidence may be excluded. The defendant may be acquitted, or civil actions may be brought against the police. Reports must be filed immediately to preserve accuracy, and police rarely have access to sufficient staff assistance in writing and filing their reports. Thus, paperwork is a tedious and time-consuming, but very important, police function.

4-3a   Order Maintenance

Police are charged with maintaining order, particularly in areas in which crime might erupt. James Q. Wilson, a noted authority on the subject, defined *order* as the absence of disorder, by which he meant behavior that tends to disrupt the peace and tranquility of the public or that involves serious face-to-face conflict between two or more persons. Wilson believed that the key to order maintenance is the management of conflict situations to bring about consensual resolution. In his view, order maintenance is the primary police function, and it is important because police encounter more problems in this area than in community service or law enforcement (with the exception of traffic violations). Wilson considered order maintenance more important than law enforcement for several reasons.[27]

First, many police departments receive more calls for help in order maintenance than in law enforcement. Some of these complaints result in arrests, but most do not. Police may be called to quiet down noisy neighbors or to intervene in disputes between friends and associates who cannot solve their differences and who appear to be on the brink of fighting. Public drunks wandering around the city alarm some people, who call the police to handle the situation. Some of these activities violate local ordinances, but many of the situations involve activities that are not criminal, although they may be obnoxious to those who call the police.

Order maintenance is an important police function for a second reason. Maintaining order may subject the police and others to physical danger. A large protest group may turn into a riot. Some domestic disputes lead to violence between the participants or against the police, and many domestic problems occur late at night, when other resources and personnel are not available to the complainant.

A third reason listed by Wilson as underscoring the importance of order maintenance is that, in this area, police exercise

> substantial discretion over matters of the greatest importance (public and private morality, honor and dishonor, life and death) in a situation that is, by definition, one of conflict and in an environment that is apprehensive and perhaps hostile.[28]

George L. Kelling analyzed order maintenance in the context of earlier policing reforms. He found that, as professionalism in policing was emphasized, the evaluation of individual police and of police departments focused on tangibles, such as arrests and quick response times of police to citizen calls. Police departments did not recognize or reward police behavior that did not lead to arrests. Police concentrated on crime prevention, arrests, and apprehension of criminals, thus emphasizing law enforcement over order maintenance or provision of services. This approach, said Kelling, decreased police corruption and improved the internal management of policing, but it resulted in less emphasis on order maintenance.[29]

Kelling argued that the focus on law enforcement had not lowered crime rates significantly but that a decreased involvement of police in order maintenance had resulted in negative effects. His position was that increased police attention to order maintenance improves relationships between the police and the community, which results in greater cooperation of citizens with the police. Citizen fear of crime is reduced, community support of the police is improved, police feel less isolated from the community, and crime detection and prevention increase.[30] Kelling, along with Wilson, advocated a significant enlargement in the time allocated to order maintenance in policing. Neither believed this approach would endanger law enforcement.[31]

The Kelling and Wilson position was challenged by Carl B. Klockars, who argued that American police maintain "an extraordinarily strong crime-fighting mandate," seen by them and others as the primary mission of policing. To reduce that emphasis by increasing resources for order maintenance is undesirable, according to Klockars. It would not reduce crime significantly because the police do not have control over many of the factors that produce crime. The financial cost would be much greater and would be at the sacrifice of a reduction in the number of calls for service to which police could respond quickly.

Klockars suggested that one solution might be to use foot patrols in high-density areas, particularly business areas. The increased costs might be financed partially by voluntary, tax-deductible contributions by businesspeople, who stand to gain the most from the increased presence of police in the area. The problem with that suggestion, warned Klockars, is that one study of a foot patrol experiment in Newark disclosed that commercial residents perceived "a deterioration in their neighborhoods: more activity on the street, more crime-related problems, reduced safety, more victimization, poorer police service, and greater use of protective devices." Klockars was not arguing against order maintenance but only against an extended and more systematic and costly approach, which would require significant changes in the administrative structure of police departments.[32]

Two types of situations illustrate the importance of police involvement in order maintenance. The first concerns police monitoring and intervention, when necessary, of college and university sporting or campus events. Many of these events are "traditional," and if police know in advance what is expected to happen, they can be in a position to prevent riots and injuries. Police must understand what can be expected—for example, only a few students become disorderly; thus, to avoid escalating the situation, police should learn to distinguish between those students who are only observers and those who are preparing to become involved in violence. To avoid so-called "party riots," police might require students to obtain permits when they plan to host a large gathering. This enables police to know when such a gathering is planned and to set conditions, such as limits on how many may attend, minimum standards regarding the event, and limits regarding alcohol consumption. "These restrictions can lessen the likelihood of a disturbance, as well as hold the hosts responsible for any negative outcomes."[33]

A second area in which police might maintain order is in assisting offenders with their reentry into society. A study by the Urban Institute's Justice Policy Center referred to police as the "eyes and ears on the street." According to this report, "the primary mission of law enforcement is to maintain peace and order." When offenders leave incarceration and return to the community, residents are, realistically, fearful that additional crimes may be committed. Making contact with these offenders is part of policing, so it is natural that police should be involved in the offenders' reentry into society. The report concluded:

> The benefits of police reentry partnership can be tremendous, the most important of which are crime reduction and approved prospects for released prisoners leading productive and law-abiding lives.[34]

4-3b   Community Service

In addition to law enforcement and order maintenance, police perform a variety of other services for the community. Wilson maintained that these services are expected of police as a result of historical accident and community convenience, that there is no good reason for police to perform these services, and that the services should "be priced and sold on the market."[35]

Removal of unnecessary community service does not mean that the police should not continue to be involved in community services either directly or indirectly related to crime prevention or order maintenance. For example, many police departments provide the equipment and officers to visit community groups and individual homes to assist residents in marking their possessions so that stolen items may be identified more quickly and easily. Officers give talks on crime prevention, emphasizing to residents what they can do to diminish the possibility that they will become crime victims. Educating women on rape prevention is a frequent topic of these sessions. Visiting with schoolchildren to educate them in crime prevention is another type of police community service.

One way to solve police time commitment problems is to train and assign special officers for community service. Community service officers generally have less training, less education, and lower salaries than other officers. The community service program, however, provides career opportunities for qualified young people who cannot or do not wish to fulfill all of the assignments required of police officers.

4-4   Law Enforcement

The third major area of police functions is law enforcement. Police are empowered to detect and prevent crime, even if to do so means using force, although there are limitations on the force that may be used. The ability of police to handle crime is limited, however, and they are dependent on citizens for assistance, although they do not always get that assistance.

The law enforcement function of policing cannot be understood adequately except in the context of the legal requirements that police officers performing this function must observe. Thus, before discussing particular law enforcement activities, we will look at the legal context of law enforcement.

4-4a   Constitutional Provisions: An Overview

Any discussion of law enforcement must consider it in the context of the federal and state constitutions under which it operates. The legal right to use coercive force to intervene in the daily lives of people is a tremendous police power, and it cannot be unrestricted.

In Chapter 1, we discussed the constitutional concepts of due process and equal protection. This chapter considers the application of these constitutional rights to the police functions of stopping and questioning a suspect; arresting and conducting searches of the person, home, or automobile of a suspect; and the practices of custodial interrogation and initial investigation. The discussion begins with a brief look at traffic control, an area of law enforcement in which many police officers engage and one that may lead to the detection of serious crimes.

4-4b   Traffic Control and the Enforcement of Traffic Laws

Traffic control is an important aspect of law enforcement. Police enforce state and local ordinances governing the operation of motor vehicles. This function includes enforcing requirements that vehicles be licensed and inspected, as well as ticketing motorists who commit moving violations. Normally, violations of this type involve a simple procedure in which the police officer signs a statement, noting the violation, and gives a copy to the driver, explaining that the ticket, if unchallenged, may be handled by mail or in person at the police station. Court appearances are not required unless the motorist decides to challenge the ticket, and most do not do so. The officer may decide not to issue a ticket; a verbal or written warning may be given instead.

The enforcement of statutes and ordinances designed to regulate the flow of traffic and to create safe conditions for drivers and pedestrians is also an important police function. Driving with excessive speed on any street or highway, speeding in school zones or failing to stop for school buses, and driving under the influence of alcohol or other drugs are dangerous activities. Further, the apprehension of people who violate traffic ordinances may lead to disorder and violence. Thus, it is important that trained police officers be in charge of such apprehensions, which may lead police to evidence of criminal activity, such as stolen automobiles, violations of substance abuse laws, escaped felons, wanted persons, burglaries, and other crimes.

Some aspects of police discretion concerning moving violations have, however, been questioned. One example is the stopping of drivers who are not wearing seat belts in jurisdictions in which a statute requires drivers and passengers to wear them. A controversial case involving this issue occurred in Texas, which permitted police to stop and arrest drivers who were not buckled up (a misdemeanor in that state), in contrast to some jurisdictions that permit a stop and arrest for failure to wear a seat belt *only* if the driver has committed a moving violation.

In *Atwater v. City of Lago Vista*, the police stopped Gail Atwater, who was driving her two children, ages four and six, home from soccer practice in a town near Austin, Texas, in 1997. The children were not wearing seat belts, which was required by law. The officer had stopped Atwater on a prior occasion, thinking her son was not wearing a seat belt, but he was. Atwater alleged that when she was stopped this second time, and arrested, the officer yelled at her, frightening her children. A friend took the children home, but Atwater was handcuffed and taken to the police station, where she was booked, photographed, and kept for about one hour before she was released on $310 bond. Eventually, the case was settled by a $50 fine, the maximum permitted. Atwater sued the arresting officer, the police chief, and the city. The defendants won a summary judgment (dismissal on the grounds that insufficient facts are presented to sustain the allegation) at the trial court level, and that was upheld by the Fifth U.S. Circuit Court of Appeals. The U.S. Supreme Court affirmed, holding that the officer's actions were reasonable.[36]

The U.S. Supreme Court acknowledged that "Atwater's claim to live free of pointless indignity and confinement clearly outweighs anything the city can raise against it specific to her case." The Court agreed that Atwater suffered "gratuitous humiliations imposed by a police office who was [at best] exercising extremely poor judgment." But the U.S. Supreme Court recognized the problems involved with a scenario in which "every discretionary judgment in the field be converted into an occasion for constitutional review." And if changes are to be made concerning the authority of the police to arrest for minor offenses, those changes should be made by legislators and police officials, not by the courts. The Supreme Court noted that even Atwater's attorney did not cite examples of any other "comparably foolish" arrests. The Court concluded that "the country is not confronting anything like an epidemic of unnecessary minor-offense arrests." Accordingly, the U.S. Supreme Court concluded:

> [W]e confirm today what our prior cases have intimated.... The standard of probable cause applies to all areas, without the need to balance the interests and circumstances involved in particular situations. If an officer has probable cause to believe that an individual has committed even a very minor criminal offense in his presence, he may, without violating the Fourth Amendment, arrest the offender.[37]

4-4c   The Investigatory Stop

Pretextual stop A stop allegedly for a minor traffic offense but actually conducted as a pretense to look for a more serious offense, such as the possession of illegal drugs.

Problems arise when police make a **pretextual stop** (a stop allegedly for a minor traffic offense but actually conducted as a pretense to look for a more serious offense, such as the possession of illegal drugs). The key case on this issue, *Whren v. United States*, was decided in 1996. In *Whren*, the initial stop was made by District of Columbia Metropolitan Police plainclothes vice-squad officers, who were traveling in an unmarked car in an area known for high levels of illegal drug trafficking. The officers observed two young African American males in a dark Nissan Pathfinder truck waiting for an unusually long time at a stop sign, with the driver looking into the lap of his passenger. When the officers made a U-turn to follow the vehicle, the driver turned without signaling and took off at what the officers considered an unreasonable speed. The officers overtook the truck when it was stopped behind traffic at a signal. One officer got out, approached the truck, and told the driver to put the vehicle in park. The officer observed the passenger holding two large plastic bags of what appeared to be crack cocaine. The driver and the passenger were arrested, and quantities of various illegal drugs were seized. Both men were charged with four counts of violating federal drug laws. On appeal, the petitioners challenged the legality of the stop and the resulting seizure of the drugs. They argued that the stop had not been justified by probable cause to believe, or even reasonable suspicion,

> that the petitioners were engaged in illegal drug-dealing activity; and that [the officer's] asserted ground for approaching the vehicle—to give the driver a warning concerning traffic violations—was pretextual.[38]

The defense further argued that, if police are permitted to search in such situations, they might harass persons (such as, in this case, minorities) for whom they otherwise could not make a stop for lack of reasonable suspicion that a violation had occurred. The U.S. Supreme Court held that an officer who is suspicious of the behavior of the occupants of a motor vehicle but does not have grounds for stopping them may do so when a traffic violation occurs. That stop may then be used to pursue the other suspicions of illegal acts.[39]

In another 1996 case, the U.S. Supreme Court examined the issue of whether police must tell drivers detained for alleged traffic violations that they are free to leave before they ask them for permission to search their vehicles. In *Ohio v. Robinette*, decided by a vote of eight-to-one, the justices held that "sweet-talking" drivers into consenting to a vehicle search is permitted and that police are not required to tell the drivers that they are free to leave and thus are not required to consent to the search. After all, drivers should know enough to resist pressure from police. This might be questioned when it is understood that the officer does have the power to write a ticket for the alleged traffic violation.[40]

In 1997, in *Maryland v. Wilson*, the U.S. Supreme Court held that during a routine traffic stop, police may order occupants of the car (as well as the driver) out of the car without any reason to suspect them of wrongdoing. In *Wilson*, a police officer signaled a stop to a driver whose car was traveling at a speed of 64 in a 55-mile-per-hour area. The driver initially refused to stop, and during the 1.5-mile pursuit, the officer noticed three passengers in the car, each turning from time to time to look at the officer. After the car stopped, the driver exited and walked back to the officer's car. The driver was trembling and appeared very nervous, but he produced a valid state driver's license. The officer instructed the driver to return to the car and retrieve the rental papers. When the driver complied, followed by the officer, the officer noted that one of the passengers was sweating and appeared to be nervous. The officer asked that passenger to exit the vehicle, and when he did, a quantity of crack cocaine fell to the ground. The passenger was arrested, charged with possession of cocaine with intent to distribute, tried, and convicted. The U.S. Supreme Court held that the evidence was properly admitted at trial. As part of its reasoning, the Supreme Court stated:

> [D]anger to an officer from a traffic stop is likely to be greater when there are passengers in addition to the driver in the stopped car. While there is not the same basis for ordering the passengers out of the car as there is for ordering the driver out, the additional intrusion on the passenger is minimal. We therefore hold that an officer making a traffic stop may order passengers to get out of the car pending completion of the stop.[41]

A law professor has stated that, as a result of these three cases, motorists are left "to fend for themselves when confronted with the authority and power of the police."[42] Others argue that, in all of these cases, the officer in question observed facts that supported a reasonable belief that additional law infractions were being committed.

Another issue arises when, in stopping motorists, police take actions that are not based on individualized suspicion. In November 2000, the U.S. Supreme Court held that, when this allegedly occurs, the officer's *purpose* in making the stop should be considered in deciding whether the police action was legitimate. The case of *City of Indianapolis v. Edmond* was brought by motorists in Indianapolis, Indiana, who asked the federal court to prohibit police from stopping them for the purpose of detecting illegal drugs. In *Edmond*, while police were checking driver's licenses and car registrations, other officers circled the cars with their canines to search for illegal drugs. Although the U.S. Supreme Court refused to uphold this practice, in which police admitted that the primary purpose was to detect motorists with illegal drugs, the issue of whether it would be permissible to make suspicionless stops if drug offenses were a secondary purpose was not answered.[43]

The U.S. Supreme Court distinguished *Edmond* from an earlier case, in which the Court had held that police may make suspicionless stops of motorists to check for drivers under the influence of alcohol. In Michigan Department of *State Police v. Sitz*, the Supreme Court emphasized that the stops were brief and for the purpose of enabling officers to detect and remove drunk drivers from the highways, a purpose that, according to the Supreme Court, was clearly aimed at protecting public safety. In contrast, according to Justice Sandra Day O'Connor, who wrote the majority opinion, the stops in *Edmond* were "ultimately indistinguishable from the general interest in crime control."[44]

In September 2003, the U.S. Supreme Court again entertained the issue of when the police may stop motorists about whom they have no reason to suspicion illegal acts. *Illinois v. Lidster* involved a fatal hit-and-run accident in Chicago, Illinois. One week after the accident, police stopped all motorists at the same intersection at the same late hour and handed them a flier describing the accident and requesting information concerning any witnesses to it. One driver nearly hit the officer with his car and was given a sobriety test, arrested for drunk driving, tried, and convicted. In a 4-to-3 vote, the Illinois Supreme Court held that the roadblock was an unconstitutional stop, not a valid investigatory tool, and overturned the conviction. The U.S. Supreme Court justices' questions during the oral arguments on this case raised many issues. Justice Antonin Scalia asked one counselor if it would be reasonable for the police to stop every car to ask, "Sir, or Madam, have you seen any crime committed in the last six months?" The attorney responded that, normally, that would be bad, but it might be reasonable in a city with "rampant lawlessness," many unsolved crimes, and a population of persons afraid of law enforcement. In *Lidster*, the police roadblock did not uncover any additional witnesses, but a local television station's coverage of the roadblock did produce a witness who was able to identify a suspect. This might suggest that television coverage would suffice and that such police roadblocks are ineffective as well as intrusive. The U.S. Supreme Court upheld the roadblock, however, ruling that it is constitutional for the police to establish "information-seeking checkpoints" in their efforts to combat crime.[45]

Whatever the case, the apprehension of traffic violators and their passengers, as well as of persons suspected of having committed crimes in other environments, begins with the investigatory stop, which may or may not lead to an arrest. One issue in this initial stop is racial profiling.

Racial profiling The reaction by law enforcement officers to potential suspects based solely on their race or ethnicity.

Racial Profiling

In the area of traffic and other stops, police have been accused of engaging in pretextual stops based on **racial profiling**, in which persons are stopped for traffic violations by police who have stereotyped them as more serious law violators because of their race or ethnicity. Such traffic stops of African Americans have been referred to by some critics as *driving while black*. Police in New Jersey were accused of racial profiling after they shot three unarmed men during a traffic stop in April 1998. The white officers had stopped a van carrying African American and Latino men and subsequently claimed that they had stopped the van because their supervisors had taught them that minorities were more likely to be involved in drug offenses. The officers claimed that they shot the men in self-defense. A study in New Jersey found that state troopers were engaging in racial profiling in many of their stops and that, in comparison with troopers' treatment of whites, African Americans and other minorities were treated in a discriminatory manner after they were stopped. In December 1999, state officials and the U.S. Department of Justice entered into a consent agreement on the issue. Included in that agreement was the provision of an independent monitor to report on whether troopers were following the terms of the consent agreement. Race as a reason for stopping a driver is permitted only if it is relevant to a description of a crime suspect for whom the police are looking.[46]

In 2002, the troopers involved in the shooting of the three unarmed men in the 1998 shooting were permitted to plead guilty to misdemeanor charges of obstructing the investigation and lying about the facts shortly after the incident. They avoided prison time and were fined $280 each. The officers had already lost their jobs. The judge noted that one of the officers had been involved in a previous shooting and had returned to work too quickly and without adequate counseling. The judge also noted that the men were following the policies they had been taught. To the officers, the judge said, "You are victims not only of your own actions but of the system which employed you." Both officers signed statements that they would never again seek employment as law enforcement officers.[47]

In 2005, New Jersey began requiring all police officers in the state, along with some civilians, to take a half-day training course designed to eliminate racial profiling.[48]

In 2001, the U.S. Department of Justice (DOJ) released a study (conducted by the Bureau of Justice Statistics [BJS] and mandated by a 1994 law requiring the publication of data on the police use of force) of approximately 80,000 U.S. residents, age 16 and over. The study reported that African American motorists are more likely than white motorists to be stopped by police, to be stopped more than once in the same year, to be given a ticket, to be handcuffed, to be subjected to a search of the person and of the vehicle, to be subjected to force, and to be arrested. The BJS emphasized that the data could reflect actual violations rather than profiling and thus did not *prove* racial profiling.[49] More information published by the BJS on drivers and police is reported in Spotlight 4-2.

The lack of such studies to prove racial profiling does not, however, mean that profiling is not an important issue. A study published in 2001 by the Police Executive Research Forum (PERF) revealed that the way police see their actions differs from the public's perception of them. The public believes that racial profiling exists and that it damages the ability of police to work effectively in areas characterized predominantly by minority populations. The PERF report contained numerous recommendations for improving policing and its effect on minorities, and concluded that racial and ethnic differences should never be the sole justification for police action because they do not support probable cause or even reasonable suspicion.[50]

A recent analysis of policing by criminologist Geoffrey P. Alpert and his colleagues found evidence to support the belief that police are more likely to view minority suspects, as compared to nonminority suspects, suspiciously. However, they also concluded that minority status does not influence police in their decision to stop and question suspects.[51]

Other criminologists have concluded from their research that "young black and Hispanic males are at increased risk for citations, searches, arrests, and uses of force after other extralegal and legal characteristics are controlled." But minority drivers are no more likely than white drivers to be carrying illegal items, such as drugs.[52] Similar findings were released in 2005 in Texas, where an analysis of millions of traffic stops in

Spotlight 4-2 Characteristics of Drivers Stopped by Police

General Characteristics of Drivers Stopped by Police in 1999...

- Among drivers age 16 to 24, blacks (17.1 percent) did not differ significantly from either whites (20.1 percent) or Hispanics (15.5 percent) in the probability of being stopped. White drivers age 16 to 24 were somewhat more likely than their Hispanic counterparts to be pulled over.
- The average number of stops was greater for young black males (2.7 percent) than young white males (1.7 percent) and marginally greater than for young Hispanic males (1.8 percent).

Drivers' Opinions of the Legitimacy of the Stops

- Both blacks (74.0 percent) and Hispanics (81.6 percent) were less likely than whites (86.0 percent) to feel they were stopped by police for a legitimate reason.
- Of drivers stopped more than once, whites (84.4 percent) were more likely than both blacks (70.2 percent) and Hispanics (70 percent) to feel the stop was legitimate.
- Among male drivers age 16 to 24, blacks (75.7 percent) were not significantly less likely than whites (83.2 percent) or Hispanics (76.0 percent) to feel the stops were legitimate.

Reason for Traffic Stop

- Few drivers were not informed of the reason for being stopped by police. No significant differences were found between white (1.5 percent), black (2.0 percent), or Hispanic (1.2 percent) drivers in the likelihood of being informed by the officer of the reason for the traffic stop.

- Males stopped for speeding were more likely to be ticketed (70.3 percent) than females (66.5 percent).
- Drivers age 16 to 24 who were stopped for speeding were ticketed (73.6 percent) more often than drivers over 24 (66.8 percent).
- Among drivers stopped for speeding, blacks (75.7 percent) and Hispanics (79.4 percent) were more likely than whites (66.6 percent) to be ticketed.

Searches Conducted by Police during Traffic Stops

- In 1999, 6.6 percent of traffic stops involved a search of the driver, the vehicle, or both.
- Police were more likely to conduct a search of the vehicle and/or driver in traffic stops involving black male drivers (15.9 percent) or Hispanic male drivers (14.2 percent), compared to white male drivers (7.9 percent).
- Of the nearly 1.3 million searches of vehicles and/or drivers conducted following traffic stops in 1999, 37 percent were accompanied by an arrest of the driver.

Police Use of Force in Traffic Stops and in Other Situations

- Approximately 422,000 persons age 16 or older said the police used or threatened to use force against them at least once during 1999.
- Traffic stops accounted for 139,000 police use-of-force incidents, 33 percent of the 422,000 incident total.
- Of the 139,000 force contacts that occurred during a traffic stop, the majority involved a male driver (98.2 percent of those contacts). Males accounted for 81.4

2002 and 2003 found that minorities were far more likely than whites to be stopped and searched, but were not more likely to be carrying illegal items, such as drugs. In response to these findings, the executive director of the Texas Police Chiefs said, "Do we believe racial profiling exists? Yes. Do we condone that? Absolutely not." As a result of the problems in Texas, the state enacted legislation requiring that every law enforcement agency that engages in traffic stops on a regular basis must keep data concerning race.[53]

In April 2000, the Ninth Circuit Court of Appeals held that it is not permissible to use ethnicity as a factor in deciding whether to stop an individual suspected of a crime. The court noted the large number and rapid growth rate of Hispanics in California and concluded that, despite a 25-year-old U.S. Supreme Court decision ruling that racial appearance was an appropriate factor for deciding whether a person should be stopped by police, this practice is not currently acceptable. "Hispanic appearance is, in general, of such little probative value that it may not be considered as a relevant factor where particularized or individualized suspicion is required." The case of *United States v. Montero-Camargo* involved three Mexicans who were stopped by the U.S. Border Patrol in 1996, about 115 miles east of San Diego. The agents, responding to a tip, gave five factors they considered in their decision to stop the suspects, one of which was their Hispanic appearance. The U.S. Supreme Court refused to review the case, thus permitting the decision to stand.[54]

percent of the remaining 282,000 force contacts that occurred at times other than a traffic stop.

- Persons under 25 were involved in just over half of all force contacts with police in 1999.
- Most (76.1 percent) of the 422,000 people involved in a police use-of-force incident said the force was excessive.

Characteristics of Drivers Stopped by Police...

Driver Race/Ethnicity

Whites were 76.7 percent of licensed drivers and 77 percent of drivers stopped by police in 1999. Blacks were 9.8 percent of licensed drivers, but 11.6 percent of stopped drivers, while Hispanics accounted for 9.9 percent of licensed drivers and 8.4% of stopped drivers. An additional 3.6 percent of licensed drivers were persons of other races, who were also 3 percent of drivers stopped by police.

Driver Gender, Age, and Race/Ethnicity

Young white males (those age 16 to 24) were 5.2 percent of licensed drivers and 12.3 percent of the 19.3 million drivers pulled over by police....Young black males accounted for 0.8 percent of licensed drivers and 1.6 percent of traffic stops, while young Hispanic males were 1.1 percent of licensed drivers and 2 percent of stopped drivers. Young males of other races formed 0.4 percent of persons with a license and 0.6 percent of drivers involved in a traffic stop.

Likelihood of Drivers Being Stopped...

Driver Race/Ethnicity

Black drivers were somewhat more likely than white drivers to be stopped at least once (12.3 percent of blacks versus 10.4 percent of whites). Blacks were significantly more likely than both Hispanics (8.8 percent) and drivers of other races (8.7 percent) to be stopped at least once. There was also some indication that black drivers (3.0 percent) were more likely than both white drivers (2.1 percent) and Hispanic drivers (2 percent) to be stopped more than once.

Driver Gender, Age, and Race/Ethnicity

Among persons age 16 to 24:

- Blacks (17.1 percent) did not differ significantly from either whites (20.1 percent) or Hispanics (15.5 percent) in the probability of being stopped.
- Whites (20.1 percent) were somewhat more likely than Hispanics (15.5 percent) to be pulled over.
- No significant differences by race were found in the probability of being stopped more than once.

Among persons over age 24:

- Blacks (11.2 percent) were significantly more likely than whites (8.9 percent) to be pulled over and somewhat more likely than Hispanics (7.8 percent).
- Blacks (2.2 percent) were significantly more likely than Hispanics (1.3 percent) and somewhat more likely than whites (1.5 percent) to be stopped more than once by police.

Source: Erica Leah Schmitt et al., Bureau of Justice Statistics, *Characteristics of Drivers Stopped by Police, 1999* (Washington, D.C.: U.S. Department of Justice, March 2002), pp. 1, 2, 3.

Research by criminologists suggests that police can do something about perceptions of racial profiling. Police can offer legitimate reasons for stops. "Several studies have shown that citizens, and blacks especially, are much more likely to cooperate with officers when they are given a reason for the stop, and that people put a premium on officers being polite, listening to citizens, and explaining their actions." It is also possible that if officers are required to explain to motorists why they were stopped, police officers might be less likely to engage in racial profiling.[55]

Another study of racial profiling by police concluded with the observation that requiring police to attend sensitivity training will not "have much impact on a practice that reflects the values of the community to which the police are accountable."[56]

There have been some efforts to eliminate racial profiling. In February 2003, the California Highway Patrol settled a three-year lawsuit by agreeing to discontinue using traffic stops as a pretext to search for drugs. The lawsuit was brought by a Latino lawyer, Curtis Rodriguez, who was stopped and searched by the highway patrol in 1998. According to the American Civil Liberties Union, California was the first state to announce that it would discontinue asking motorists for permission to search their cars when they are stopped for traffic violations. The agreement also specified that the highway patrol would compile and analyze extensive data collected about each highway stop.[57]

Spotlight 4-3	## The *Lawson* Case and the Abuse of Police Discretion to Stop and Question

Thirty-six-year-old Edward Lawson—tall, black, muscular, and long-haired—walked almost everywhere he went. Lawson was stopped by police approximately 15 times between March 1975 and January 1977. Police in California were relying on a California statute that prohibited a person from loitering or wandering

> upon the streets or from place to place without apparent reason or business and who refuses to identify himself and to account for his presence when requested by any peace officer to do so, if the surrounding circumstances are such as to indicate to a reasonable man that the public safety demands such identification.[1]

Each time he was stopped, Lawson refused to identify himself. He was arrested five of the times he was stopped, convicted once, and spent several weeks in jail. The *Lawson* case illustrates the tension between the police claim that in order to combat crime they must be able to stop and question people who look suspicious and the right of

citizens to be free of unreasonable intrusions into their privacy.

Lawson appealed his convictions to the U.S. Supreme Court, which reversed them on the grounds that the statute under which Lawson was convicted was vague. The problem with the California statute was not the initial police stop. According to the Court, "Although the initial detention is justified, the State fails to establish standards by which the officers may determine whether the suspect has complied with the subsequent identification requirement." The U.S. Supreme Court held that giving a police officer such discretion "confers on police a virtually unrestrained power to arrest and charge persons with a violation" and therefore "furnishes a convenient tool for 'harsh and discriminatory enforcement by local prosecuting officials against particular groups deemed to merit their displeasure.'"[2]

1. Cal. Penal Code, Section 647(e) (1977).
2. Kolender et al. v. Lawson, 461 U.S. 352, 360, 361 (1983).

Racial profiling may also occur in nontraffic situations. Spotlight 4-3 discusses *Kolender et al. v. Lawson*, which illustrates police abuse of the discretion to stop and question a suspect. For several reasons, this case is very important, despite the fact that it was decided in 1983. First, it is still good law. Second, it was decided by the U.S. Supreme Court. Third, it stands against the recent decisions, discussed earlier, in which the Supreme Court has refused to restrict police in stopping and searching, especially in the area of traffic control. Finally, it is argued by some that the stop in *Lawson* represented a case of racial bias, which is not permitted.

The *Lawson* case makes it clear that police may not use a vague statute for purposes of stopping, questioning, and otherwise harassing individuals. But the case also makes it clear that police may stop and question individuals. How can police tell when they can go beyond initial questioning and make an arrest, or as the next section discusses, frisk?

Finally, some researchers have concluded that drug arrests of minorities suggest racial disparity. In a 2006 journal article on drug arrests in Seattle, three sociologists concluded that the higher arrest rate of blacks in that city is not explained by race-neutral factors such as crime rates but, rather, by police perceptions and the organizational response to those perceptions.[58]

Stop and Frisk

The police may be notified or they may observe a situation that gives them a reasonable basis for stopping a pedestrian or a driver. At this initial stop, police have wide discretion, provided they do not use extralegal reasons, such as race, for making that stop. They can decide not to make the stop. They can stop but not arrest the suspect. They can release the suspect with a verbal or written warning. The police must make important judgment calls at the stage of stopping and questioning suspects, for it would be an inefficient use of police time and, in most cases, a violation of suspects' constitutional rights for police to arrest persons when there is no probable cause to believe they are violating the law.

Some discretion must be allowed the police officer who, based on experience, perceives that a crime might have been committed and that the suspect may be armed, thus constituting a threat to the life or health of the officer or others. It is permissible for the police to conduct pat-down searches, or **frisk** the suspect in some cases, as illustrated by the following example.

In *Terry v. Ohio*, Detective Martin McFadden of the Cleveland, Ohio, Police Department noticed two men standing on a street corner in front of several stores. The men made many trips up and down the street, peering into store windows. They talked to a third man, whom they followed up the street after his departure. McFadden, who had 39 years of experience as a police officer, suspected that the men were casing the stores for a robbery. He approached the men, identified himself as a police officer, and asked their names. The men mumbled responses, at which point the detective spun one of the men, Terry, around and patted his breast pocket. Officer McFadden removed the pistol that he felt and then frisked the second man, on whom he also found a pistol. The third man was frisked but did not have a weapon.[59]

In *Terry*, the U.S. Supreme Court emphasized that even brief detention of a person without probable cause for an arrest is a seizure of that person. These stops constitute a serious intrusion that can lead to strong resentment. But police officers are injured and killed in the line of duty. They cannot be expected to take unreasonable risks; thus, they may conduct a search that is limited in time and scope.

In *Terry*, the U.S. Supreme Court looked at the totality of the circumstances, holding that if, during the pat-down search, the police feel an object that might be a weapon, they may continue the search until they are satisfied that it is not a weapon. The Supreme Court did not, however, answer the question of whether they could seize a **contraband** item that is not a weapon. In 1993, the Supreme Court decided that issue. In *Minnesota v. Dickerson* the Court held that, if during a *Terry* search and before an officer has concluded that the suspect is not armed, the officer feels an item "whose contour or mass makes its identity immediately apparent," that item may be seized without a warrant. The discovery of the contraband would not constitute any greater invasion of privacy than had occurred during the permissible weapons search and thus is acceptable. The Supreme Court referred to this as the *plain feel* doctrine. But officers may not go beyond the permissible scope of the weapons search to examine the item suspected of being contraband but not a weapon.[60]

The totality of the circumstances rule articulated by the U.S. Supreme Court in the *Terry* case was emphasized again in 2002 when the Court, in *United States v. Arvizu*, upheld a border patrol agent's search. Agent Clinton Stoddard was working at a checkpoint about 30 miles north of a border town when he was notified that a magnetic sensor had been triggered on a back road near his location. Stoddard concluded that a motorist might be trying to avoid the main road checkpoint because he or she was smuggling illegal drugs or immigrants. Stoddard drove to the road in question and pulled over to get a good look at an oncoming minivan as it passed him. Based on his observations and his knowledge, he concluded that the driver might be smuggling. Stoddard's suspicions were based on a number of factors:

- The car was a minivan, a type of car often used by smugglers.
- The car was on a back road often used by smugglers.
- The time was during shift changes, when detection might be interrupted.
- The driver slowed down sharply as he approached Stoddard's car, did not look at Stoddard, and appeared stiff and rigid.
- Three children in the minivan waved mechanically, as if they might have been told to do so.
- The knees of the children were unusually high, as if they might have their feet resting on objects.
- There were no picnic grounds in the area, so it was unlikely the family was on an outing for recreational purposes.[61]

Stoddard signaled the van to pull over and asked for permission to search the car. He was granted permission; he found 130 pounds of marijuana. At his trial, Arvizu

▶ **Frisk** An action by a law enforcement officer or a correctional officer consisting of patting down or running one's hands quickly over a person's body to determine whether the suspect or inmate has a weapon or other contraband. This is in contrast to a body search, which is a more careful and thorough examination of the person.

▶ **Contraband** Any item (such as weapons, alcohol, or other drugs), possession of which is illegal or violates prison rules.

asked the court to exclude the marijuana. The court refused, but the Ninth Circuit Court of Appeals reversed, stating, among other comments, that if every strange act of a child "could contribute to a finding of reasonable suspicion, the vast majority of American parents might be stopped regularly." The U.S. Supreme Court reversed, holding that the totality of the circumstances and the agent's experience should be considered in making a determination whether the officer had reason to pull over a car and request permission to search it. According to a unanimous Supreme Court, "This process allows officers to draw on their own experience and specialized training to make inferences from and deductions about the cumulative information available to them that 'might well elude an untrained person.'"[62]

Law enforcement officers might also have reason to stop a motorist if the driver takes flight. In 2000, in a unanimous opinion in *Illinois v. Wardlow*, the U.S. Supreme Court held that under some circumstances, the flight of a person who sees a law enforcement officer provides reasonable grounds for the officer to stop and search. But the justices disagreed on how the facts of a Chicago case should be analyzed in light of that principle. In *Wardlow*, the defendant fled when he saw several police cars in an area of the city known for heavy trafficking in illegal narcotics. One officer chased Wardlow down an alley and found that he was carrying a loaded gun. In a controversial 5-to-4 decision, Chief Justice William H. Rehnquist, writing for the majority, concluded that in an area of that type, an unprovoked flight constituted grounds for a stop and search. According to Rehnquist, "The determination of reasonable suspicion must be based on commonsense judgments and inferences about human behavior." Rehnquist also stated, "Headlong flight—wherever it occurs—is the consummate act of evasion; it is not necessarily indicative of wrongdoing, but it is certainly suggestive of such." Justice John Paul Stevens stated in his dissenting opinion that the facts did not justify the search:

> Among some citizens, particularly minorities and those resident in high crime areas, there is also the possibility that the fleeing person is entirely innocent, but, with or without justification, believes that contact with the police can itself be dangerous, apart from any criminal activity associated with the officer's sudden presence.[63]

4-4d   Arrest, Search, and Seizure

The process of stopping and questioning suspects may lead to an **arrest**, which is a crucial step in criminal justice proceedings because most cases are initiated by arrest. **Search and seizure** may accompany arrest, but a clear understanding of these processes requires a brief introduction to the Fourth Amendment of the U.S. Constitution. That amendment prohibits only *unreasonable* searches and seizures (see Appendix A). This provision of the U.S. Constitution is pertinent to our discussion because, under some circumstances, stopping and arresting a person may constitute a seizure of the person and therefore must follow proper procedures or be ruled unreasonable by the courts.

Warrants and Probable Cause

With some exceptions, arrests and searches may not be made until the police secure a **warrant**. A 1948 decision emphasized the purpose of the **search warrant**, but the principle also applies to arrests. According to the U.S. Supreme Court,

> The point of the Fourth Amendment, which often is not grasped by zealous officers, is not that it denies law enforcement the support of the usual inferences which reasonable men draw from evidence. Its protection consists in requiring that those inferences be drawn by a neutral and detached magistrate instead of being judged by the officer engaged in the often competitive enterprise of ferreting out crime.... When the right of privacy must reasonably yield to the right of search is, as a rule, to be decided by a judicial officer, not by a policeman or government enforcement agent.[64]

The Fourth Amendment requires that a warrant shall not be issued except upon a finding of **probable cause**. Probable cause is required as well in those exceptions in

---

▶ Arrest The act of taking an individual into custody in order to make a criminal charge against that person.

▶ Search and seizure The examination of a person or a person's property and the taking of items that may be evidence of criminal activity. It generally requires a search warrant. Unreasonable searches and seizures are prohibited.

▶ Warrant A court-issued *writ* authorizing an officer to arrest a suspect or to search a person, personal property, or a place.

▶ Search warrant *See* **Warrant**.

▶ Probable cause In search warrant cases, a set of facts and circumstances that leads to the reasonable belief that the items sought are located in a particular place. In arrest cases, the facts and circumstances lead to the reasonable belief that the suspect has committed a crime.

which arrest, search, and seizure are permitted without a warrant. To constitute probable cause, the facts of the situation must be such that, upon hearing those facts, a reasonable person would conclude that in all probability a crime had been committed.

How is probable cause established? Facts sufficient to lead a reasonable person to conclude that a crime has been committed by a particular person or that a particular kind of contraband may be found at a specified location may be secured in various ways. One of the most controversial ways occurs when the facts come from an **informant**, who may have a history of criminal activity, or from an anonymous source. The U.S. Supreme Court considered the latter in *Illinois v. Gates*. In *Gates*, the police received an anonymous letter alleging that two specified people, a husband and wife, were engaging in illegal drug sales and that on 3 May 1978 the wife was going to drive their car back to Florida. The letter stated that the husband would fly to Florida to drive the car to Illinois with the trunk loaded with drugs and that the couple had about $100,000 worth of drugs in the basement of their Illinois home.

> **Informant** A person who gives information to law enforcement officials about a crime or planned criminal activity.

After receiving this information, a police detective secured the couple's address. The officer found that the husband had a reservation to fly to Florida on 5 May 1978. The flight was put under surveillance, which disclosed that the suspect took the flight. It was confirmed that he spent the night in a motel room registered to his wife and that the next morning he left in a car with a woman. The license plate of the car was registered to the husband suspect. The couple was driving north on an interstate highway used frequently for traffic to Illinois.

The police detective in possession of these facts signed a statement under oath concerning the facts and submitted that statement to a judge, who issued a search warrant for the couple's house and automobile. The police were waiting for them when they returned to their Illinois home. Upon searching the house and car, the police found drugs, which the state attempted to use against the couple at trial. The couple's motion to have the evidence suppressed at trial was successful, and the Illinois Supreme Court upheld the lower court on this issue.

The U.S. Supreme Court disagreed and looked at the totality of the circumstances, holding that, in this case, independent police verification of the allegations from the anonymous source provided sufficient information on which a magistrate could have probable cause to issue the warrants. The Supreme Court emphasized that probable cause is a fluid concept based on probabilities, not certainties. All of the circumstances under which information is secured must be considered and weighed in determining whether probable cause exists for issuing a warrant.[65]

The U.S. Supreme Court has established rules that must be followed when police secure information from known informants. There must be underlying circumstances that would lead a reasonable person to conclude that the informant is reliable and credible in what he or she is saying, and there must be underlying circumstances that provide a basis for the conclusions drawn by the informant. If the informant is a police officer, credibility might not be questioned, although it is necessary to show why that person has reason to have such information. When the informant is a known or suspected criminal, as is frequently the case, establishing credibility is more difficult.

Although the U.S. Supreme Court upheld the use of an informant in the *Gates* case, the Court ruled against such use in a 2002 case, *Florida v. J.L.* This case involved an anonymous call to the Miami-Dade, Florida, police, who were told that a young African American male, wearing a plaid shirt and carrying a gun, was standing at a particular bus stop. Police went to the stop and found three African American males, one of whom was wearing a plaid shirt. That young man made no suspicious or threatening movements; no gun was obvious. The police had no reason, except for the anonymous tip, to suspect any of the three young men of illegal activity. The police frisked all three suspects and found a gun in the pocket of J.L., who was wearing the plaid shirt. J.L. was only 15, a juvenile, so his name was kept confidential. J.L. was charged with possessing a firearm while under the age of 18 and carrying a concealed weapon. The trial court granted the defendant's motion to exclude the gun, an intermediate appellate court reversed, the Florida Supreme Court upheld the trial court, and Florida appealed. Florida sought review in the U.S. Supreme Court because other courts had held that such evidence is admissible. The U.S. Supreme Court agreed to hear the case to settle the dispute.

The U.S. Supreme Court referred to its holding in *Terry v. Ohio*, discussed earlier, noting the differences between the two cases. In *J.L.*, the officers did not observe any behavior that was suspicious. They had no reason, other than the anonymous tip, to believe that any of the young men were armed and dangerous. According to the Supreme Court, the anonymous tip alone was not sufficient to warrant the search and thus the evidence secured by means of that illegal search was properly excluded from trial. Police may not search for weapons without reasonable suspicion, as established in *Terry*.[66]

Some searches and seizures are permissible without a warrant, without probable cause, and without consent. One exception to the warrant requirement is a search that occurs when an officer makes a lawful arrest. The U.S. Supreme Court has emphasized, however, that the right to search the person without a search warrant or the suspect's consent, even when the arrest is proper, is a limited privilege.

After an arrest, some warrantless searches, such as searches of possessions or of the person when the suspect is booked into jail (inventory searches), are proper. Routine searches at the border are also permitted. Inspections and searches of regulated industries are permitted, too, as are searches at certain fixed checkpoints, such as checks for drivers under the influence of controlled substances. As Spotlight 4-4 notes, warrantless searches are also permissible under exigent circumstances.

Warrantless searches may also be conducted legally when a person consents to the search. This consent may be given prior to arrest, at the time of arrest, or later at the police station. It may involve searching possessions, automobiles, homes, or persons. The critical factor is whether the consent is made knowingly and voluntarily. In some circumstances, consent to a search may be given by a third party, but these circumstances are limited.

In 1996 in *Ornelas v. United States*, the U.S. Supreme Court held that, when judges are confronted with a warrantless search, they are to consider the facts that led to the stop or search and then determine whether those facts "viewed from the standpoint of a reasonable police officer" constitute probable cause. The decisions of trial judges on this matter are to be reviewed by appellate judges only for clear error, and during that review, due weight must be given to the consideration of the facts by local law enforcement officers and trial judges. Appellate review of such cases should be undertaken *de novo* (from the beginning). Again, the U.S. Supreme Court emphasized its "strong preferences for searches conducted pursuant to a warrant."[67]

Spotlight 4-4   Exigent Circumstances and Warrantless Searches

Police are permitted to conduct warrantless searches in limited cases, including those with exigent circumstances. In a 1994 California case, the court refused to suppress evidence seized in a warrantless search of a home by police, who were responding to an anonymous call concerning domestic violence. Police were greeted at the door by a woman who said she was alone and safe. But police saw a man in the house, and the woman appeared to have been hit recently. The woman told police she had just fallen down the stairs.

Police entered the home and seized the illegal drugs that were in plain view. The California court held that the officers entered the home under exigent circumstances. They knew that the woman had lied about being alone, and they had reason to suspect she had been hit recently, perhaps by the man they saw in the home. For her protection, they had a right to enter. While they were in the home legally, police were justified in seizing illegal drugs that were in plain view.[1]

1. People (California) v. Higgins, 26 Cal.App.4th 247 (4th Dist. 1994), *review denied*, 1994 Cal. LEXIS 5620 (Cal. Oct. 13, 1994).

Under some circumstances, arrests may be made without a warrant. Historically, under English common law, police were permitted to make lawful arrests without a warrant if they had probable cause to believe that a *felony* had been committed and that it had been committed by the person to be arrested. Today, either by court decisions or by statutes, this rule exists in most jurisdictions. But historically, under the common law, in cases of less serious offenses, *misdemeanors*, police were permitted to arrest without a warrant only if the act constituted a breach of peace that occurred within the presence of the officer.

Today, most jurisdictions permit police to make a warrantless arrest for any misdemeanor committed in their presence. If the offense is not committed in the officer's presence, however, most jurisdictions require a warrant for an arrest of a suspected misdemeanant, even if the officer has overwhelming evidence that the suspect committed the offense. "Committed in the presence of the officer" does not mean that the officer must have seen the crime committed; usually, it is interpreted to mean that the officer has probable cause to believe that the misdemeanor was committed in his or her presence.

An arrest without a warrant is a serious matter, however, and the U.S. Supreme Court has placed restrictions on this procedure. Persons arrested without a warrant are entitled to a prompt judicial determination of whether probable cause existed. The Court has interpreted *prompt* to mean 48 hours under most circumstances. If a weekend is involved and the judicial determination of probable cause will not be held within 48 hours, the state has the burden of showing that the delay beyond that period was reasonable.[68]

The U.S. Supreme Court has held that investigation of a homicide is not one of the recognized exceptions to the requirement of a warrant before a search. In *Flippo v. West Virginia*, decided in 1999, the police were called by a minister, James M. Flippo, to a cabin he was occupying with his wife. Flippo told officers that he and his wife had been attacked; the wife was dead when police arrived. Flippo was taken to the hospital for treatment of injuries that he claimed occurred during the attack. The area outside the cabin was searched for signs of forced entry and footprints. Police reentered the cabin when a police photographer arrived. They processed the crime scene and conducted a search. Inside a briefcase, they found a photograph of a man, later identified as a member of Flippo's congregation, who appeared to be taking off his pants. Prosecutors used that photograph at the trial, arguing that Flippo was having a sexual relationship with another man and that, when his wife found out and objected, he had a motive to kill her. Flippo argued that the evidence should have been excluded.

The U.S. Supreme Court agreed with Flippo, ruling that a homicide scene is not an exception to the warrant requirement before a search is executed. The Supreme Court did not, however, rule on whether the admission of the tainted evidence constituted **harmless error** or **reversible error**. Nor did the Court rule on the issue of whether Flippo consented to a search by virtue of calling 911 and asking the police to come to the cabin. Consent, said the Supreme Court, is a fact to be determined by the lower court as it is a factual (in contrast to a legal) question.[69]

One general issue regarding search and seizure that should be noted before we go into specific areas for searches is that of the anticipatory search. In 2006, the U.S. Supreme Court upheld the constitutionality of an **anticipatory search warrant**, referring to a warrant that is issued for a search at a particular place at a particular time in the future. The case of *United States v. Grubbs* involved a defendant, Jeffrey Grubbs, who purchased from a website a videotape containing child pornography. The website was operated by an undercover postal inspector. On the basis of these facts and an affidavit that the videotape would be delivered to Grubbs' home at a controlled time and that the warrant would not be executed until the package had been delivered and taken into the home, federal agents secured a search warrant. That warrant contained two attachments describing what the authorities expected to find, along with the location of the home. The attachments, but not the affidavit, were included in the body of the

Harmless error Minor or trivial errors not deemed sufficient to harm the rights of the parties who assert the errors. Cases are not reversed on the basis of harmless errors.

Reversible error An error in a legal proceeding, such as a trial, that is considered sufficient to require the reversal of a conviction or a sentence.

Anticipatory search warrant A warrant that is issued for a search at a particular place at a particular time *in the future*. It is based on evidence of a *triggering* event that gives probable cause to believe that the evidence, contraband, or fugitive will be at that place at that time.

warrant. The package was delivered to Grubbs' home, where his wife signed for it and took it into the house. A few minutes later, when Grubbs left the home, he was detained by federal agents, who then entered the home and began the search. Grubbs was given the search warrant, which contained the attachments but not the affidavit. Grubbs admitted that he had the tape. At trial, he filed a motion to suppress the videotape because the search warrant did not contain the affidavit stating the triggering events and was thus defective. His motion was denied. Grubbs then entered a guilty plea but reserved his right to appeal.[70]

The U.S. Supreme Court first confronted the issue of whether anticipatory search warrants were constitutional. Grubbs argued that they are not constitutional because they violate the requirement that warrants must be issued only upon probable cause. So, if the police execute the warrant before the stated triggering event has occurred, they do not have reason to believe the items in question are at the searched place; thus, they have no probable cause. The Court rejected this position and stated in part:[71]

United States v. Grubbs

Because the probable cause requirement looks to whether evidence will be found when the search is conducted, all warrants are, in a sense, "anticipatory." In the typical case where the police seek permission to search a house for an item they believe is already located there, the magistrate's determination that there is probable cause for the search amounts to a prediction that the item will still be there when the warrant is executed....

Anticipatory warrants are, therefore, no different in principle from ordinary warrants. They require the magistrate to determine (1) that it is now probable that (2) contraband, evidence of a crime, or a fugitive will be on the described premises (3) when the warrant is executed.

The second issue the U.S. Supreme Court faced in *Grubbs* was whether the anticipatory warrant was defective because it did not contain the affidavit with the triggering information. The Court held that it was not defective because the Fourth Amendment (see Appendix A) "does not require that the triggering condition for an anticipatory search warrant be set forth in the warrant itself."[72]

Home Searches

The U.S. Supreme Court has said that the "physical entry of the home is the chief evil against which the wording of the Fourth Amendment is directed."[73] The Supreme Court recognizes a difference between searches and seizures within a home or an office and the search of a person's property in other places.

An example of an unreasonable entry into and search inside of a home occurred in *Mapp v. Ohio*. Police had received information that a person wanted for questioning in a bombing was hiding out in a two-family dwelling. Mapp and her daughter by a previous marriage lived on the top floor of the home. When police arrived at the home and knocked on the door, Mapp called her attorney and then denied entrance to the officers without a warrant. The police advised their headquarters of that response and put the house under surveillance. About three hours later, with more officers on the scene, police attempted entry again. When Mapp did not come to the door quickly, the officers forced their way into the house. Mapp's attorney arrived, but the police would not let him enter the house or see Mapp.[74]

Mapp demanded to see a search warrant. The officers produced a paper they claimed to be a search warrant. Mapp grabbed that paper (which was not a warrant) and tucked it into her bosom. The officers retrieved the paper and handcuffed Mapp for being belligerent. Mapp complained that the officers were hurting her. The officers took the complaining and handcuffed suspect to her bedroom, where they conducted a search. They searched other rooms as well and found obscene materials in a basement trunk.

The seized evidence was used against Mapp at trial, and she was convicted of "knowingly having had in her possession and under her control certain lewd and lascivious books, pictures, and photographs." The U.S. Supreme Court ruled that the evidence seized in Mapp's home could not be used against her in a state trial. The Court referred to the seizure as a "flagrant abuse" of the "constitutional…right to privacy free from unreasonable state intrusion."[75]

Even if police have a right to search a home, there is an issue of the permissible *scope* of that search. Several factors must be considered. In *Chimel v. California*, police officers searched a house thoroughly after they entered with an arrest warrant but without a search warrant. The U.S. Supreme Court reversed the defendant's conviction and limited the areas that may be searched for weapons, if necessary, to protect the life of the officer and others. The suspect may also be searched to the extent necessary to prevent the destruction of evidence. The officer may search the area "within the immediate control" of the arrestee, such as a gun lying on a table near the suspect.[76]

In 1971, the U.S. Supreme Court held that police may seize evidence without a warrant while they are within the home to execute a lawful arrest, provided that the evidence is in plain view.[77] In 1987, the Court held that probable cause is required to invoke the **plain view doctrine**.[78]

In 1990, the U.S. Supreme Court held that an officer who is executing an arrest warrant within a private dwelling may search rooms other than the one in which the arrest is made. The Court called this a *protective sweep* search, but there are limitations. Although the search does not require probable cause or even reasonable suspicion, it is permitted only for the purpose of locating another person who might pose danger. Thus, the officers may "look in closets and other spaces immediately adjoining the place of arrest from which an attack could be immediately launched." To go further, the officers must have "*articulable* facts which, taken together with the rational inferences from those facts, would warrant a reasonably prudent officer in believing that the area to be swept harbors an individual posing a danger to those on the arrest scene." The Supreme Court emphasized that this warrantless search is permissible only for the protection of those present and cannot extend to a full search of the premises, "but [it] may extend only to a cursory inspection of those spaces where a person may be found." The protective sweep must be brief; it may last "no longer than is necessary to dispel the reasonable suspicion of danger and in any event no longer than it takes to complete the arrest and depart the premises."[79]

The U.S. Supreme Court has elaborated on the scope of the lawful search of a home's **curtilage**. The Court has held that a barn 60 yards from a house and outside the area surrounding the house enclosed by a fence is not part of the curtilage. The Court stated that

> curtilage questions should be resolved with particular reference to four factors: the proximity of the area claimed to be curtilage to the home, whether the area is included within an enclosure surrounding the home, the nature of the uses to which the area is put, and the steps taken by the resident to protect the area from observation by people passing by.[80]

The U.S. Supreme Court has ruled that the Fourth Amendment does not prohibit warrantless searches and seizures of garbage that is left outside a home's curtilage. The Court reasoned that, since the garbage is readily accessible to the public, its owner has no reasonable expectation of privacy.[81] The Court left unanswered the issue of whether the Fourth Amendment prohibits warrantless searches of garbage left *within* the curtilage, but in 1991, a lower federal appellate court ruled that such a search would not be unlawful, provided the garbage was left under circumstances in which it was readily accessible to the public. That test was interpreted to include garbage left on a driveway

▶ **Plain view doctrine**   The legal doctrine that permits a law enforcement officer who is legally searching a place for particular items to seize those that are in plain view but not listed on a search warrant.

▶ **Curtilage**   The enclosed ground and buildings immediately around a dwelling.

50 feet south of the house and 20 feet from the unattached garage, 25 to 30 feet west of the street, and 18 feet west of the public sidewalk. The garbage in question was halfway up the driveway, a bit closer to the sidewalk than to the garage, and technically within the curtilage. The Seventh Circuit Court of Appeals ruled that, despite that location, the garbage was abandoned and exposed to the public; consequently, its owner had no reasonable expectation of privacy with regard to its contents. The U.S. Supreme Court refused to review the case, thus allowing the Seventh Circuit's ruling to stand.[82]

The U.S. Supreme Court has also held that police may prevent a person outside his or her home from entering that home while police secure a search warrant. In 2001, in *Illinois v. McArthur*, the Court approved the decision of police to prevent Charles McArthur from reentering his home after police received a tip from McArthur's wife, Tera McArthur, that "Chuck has dope in there." Tera McArthur had summoned the police to keep the peace while she removed her personal belongings from the trailer in which she had lived with her husband. After she finished, Tera told police about the drugs. By that time, Charles McArthur was on the porch. Police asked him for permission to search the trailer; he refused. Police then told McArthur that he could not reenter the trailer unless he was accompanied by a police officer. Approximately two hours later, the police, with a search warrant, entered the trailer, found less than 2.5 grams of marijuana, and arrested McArthur. McArthur moved to have the drugs excluded as evidence, arguing that they were seized during an improper search. The trial court granted the motion; the U.S. Supreme Court ruled 8-to-1 that the seizure was proper. The Court held that the restriction on McArthur's freedom to return unaccompanied to the inside of the trailer was reasonable because

- The police had probable cause to believe that illegal drugs were inside the trailer.
- The police had good reason to fear that McArthur might destroy the drugs if he returned to the inside unaccompanied.
- The police made reasonable efforts to reconcile the need to protect McArthur's right to privacy while maintaining good law enforcement.
- The police limited the restraint to a reasonable time period, approximately two hours.[83]

State constitutions, statutes, and courts may provide *greater* protection than the federal Constitution requires. For example, the New Jersey Supreme Court has held that police need a search warrant to open and examine garbage bags left at curbside for collection.[84]

Another type of search regarding the home and its curtilage is the *aerial* search. The U.S. Supreme Court has held that aerial searches may be conducted without a warrant.[85] But in a 5-to-4 decision in 2001, the Court held that it is unconstitutional to use a thermal imaging device (from a public street) to detect heat radiating from the external surface of a private home to determine whether marijuana is being grown within the home.[86]

Another issue concerning searches of the home is the long-standing principle of "knock and announce," meaning that police who arrive at a dwelling to search with or without a warrant must knock and announce their presence prior to entering. In 1995, the U.S. Supreme Court elevated that principle to a constitutional dimension.[87] The rule may be relaxed under exigent circumstances, such as if there is reason to believe the evidence sought will be destroyed or the suspects are armed and dangerous. The Court left it to lower courts to devise rules under which the knock-and-announce rule could be waived. However, in 1997, in *Richards v. Wisconsin*, the Supreme Court struck down a blanket exception to the rule. *Richards* involved a felony drug investigation. The lower court had held that police are never required to knock and announce before entering if they have a search warrant for a felony drug investigation, the assumption being that they already have reasonable cause to believe that exigent circumstances exist in such cases. The Supreme Court upheld the no-knock in this case because the justices considered the officers' decision not to knock and announce reasonable under the circumstances of that case, but the Court rejected the blanket rule permitting no-knock in all cases involving alleged felony drug violations. The Court held that a case-by-case analysis was required.[88]

In 1998, the U.S. Supreme Court answered the question of whether damage to property during a no-knock entry of a home should be considered in determining whether the entry was reasonable. In *United States v. Ramirez*, in order to prevent a suspect from having access to weapons thought to be stored in a garage, police broke a window in the attached garage before they announced their presence to the suspect in the house. When the suspect was told that the forced garage entry was caused by police, not burglars, he surrendered. The Supreme Court held that, under these circumstances, it was reasonable for police to break the garage window without first announcing their presence.[89]

In 1999, in *Minnesota v. Carter*, the U.S. Supreme Court held that individuals who are paying a short-term visit to a home for commercial purposes do not have the reasonable expectation of privacy that is protected by the Fourth Amendment. In *Carter*, the officer peered through a gap in a blind at a window in an apartment and saw three people bagging cocaine. The suspects were arrested and convicted of state drug offenses. The trial court ruled that the officer's observations did not constitute a search under the Fourth Amendment and that the respondents did not have a reasonable expectation of privacy; thus, the search was reasonable. The U.S. Supreme Court agreed, noting that the expectation of privacy that one has in a commercial setting is less than that in one's home or even during an overnight stay as a social guest in a friend's home.[90]

Another case concerning home searches is one in which the U.S. Supreme Court considered the time that police must wait for forcible entry after announcing their presence and intent. In *United States v. Banks*, police arrived at an apartment to execute a search warrant for drugs. They knocked and yelled, "Police search warrant." When the resident, LaShawn L. Banks, did not answer the door within 15 to 20 seconds (he was in the shower), the police entered forcibly and found crack cocaine, three guns, and $6,000 in cash. During the oral arguments before the Supreme Court, attorneys and the justices discussed the issue of whether one should be permitted to complete a shower. The justices were not at all interested in that issue and upheld the search, although they did not answer the question of how long police should wait after knocking before entering forcibly.[91]

One final issue we will consider concerning home searches was decided by the U.S. Supreme Court in March 2006. *Georgia v. Randolph* involved a domestic dispute situation. Scott Randolph and his wife, Janet, who lived in Americus, Georgia, separated, and she went to her parents' home in Canada, taking their son with her. She returned home over a month later, and the record was not clear whether she was there for purposes of attempting a reconciliation or to remove possessions. She called police to tell them that her husband had taken their son. When police arrived, she told them that her husband was a cocaine user and that the habit had caused financial problems. The husband returned shortly thereafter, said that he had removed the son because he feared that his wife would take the son out of the country again, and that he was not a drug abuser but that his wife had problems with alcohol and other drugs. One officer went with the wife to retrieve the son. When they returned, she again told the officer that her husband had drug problems and that there was evidence of drugs in the house. The officer asked for permission to search. The husband refused. The wife consented and directed the officers to her husband's room. The police found evidence of drugs (a straw). One officer left to get an evidence bag from his car and call his supervisor, who then told him to get a search warrant before continuing the search. When he returned to the house the wife revoked her consent. Both of the Randolphs were taken to the police station, and the police returned to the house with a search warrant, found more evidence, and arrested the husband for drug offenses. He was indicted for cocaine possession. His motion to suppress the evidence was denied on the grounds that the wife had common access to the property and thus had the legal ability to consent. Randolph was convicted and appealed.

The U.S. Supreme Court articulated the issue as follows: "whether one occupant may give law enforcement effective consent to search shared premises as against a co-tenant who is present and states a refusal to permit the search." The Court ruled by a 5-to-3 margin (Justice Samuel Alito did not vote because he was not on the bench during oral arguments) to suppress the evidence, stating as follows:

> This case invites a straightforward application of the rule that a physically present inhabitant's express refusal of consent to a police search is dispositive as to him, regardless of the consent of a fellow occupant.[92]

Automobile Searches

Some of the rules concerning warrantless automobile searches were discussed earlier in connection with traffic violation stops, but the U.S. Supreme Court has decided a number of cases that go beyond that scenario.

In *Carroll v. United States*, the U.S. Supreme Court held that, when police stop an automobile and have probable cause to believe it contains contraband, it is not unreasonable to search that vehicle. However, the Court did not deal with the scope of that permissible search. In *Chambers v. Maroney*, the Supreme Court held that a search warrant is not necessary "where there is probable cause to search an automobile stopped on the highway; the car is moveable; the occupants are alerted; and the car's contents may never be found again if a warrant must be obtained." Each case must be judged on its facts, for the U.S. Supreme Court has made it clear that not all warrantless car searches are lawful.[93]

In 1991, the U.S. Supreme Court clarified some of the procedural problems in *Carroll*, *Maroney*, and other cases, holding that "the police may search an automobile and the containers within it where they have probable cause to believe contraband or evidence is contained."[94]

In 1981, in *Robbins v. California*, the U.S. Supreme Court held that, when police stopped a car for proceeding erratically, smelled marijuana smoke as the door was opened, searched the car, and found two packages wrapped in opaque plastic, they went beyond the scope of a legitimate search without a warrant when they opened the packages.[95] One year later, in *United States v. Ross*, the Supreme Court reconsidered its position by examining the extent to which police officers, who have stopped an automobile legitimately and who have probable cause to believe that contraband is concealed somewhere within it, may conduct a probing search of compartments and containers within the vehicle if its contents are not in plain view. "We hold that they may conduct a search of the vehicle that is as thorough as a magistrate could authorize in a warrant 'particularly describing the place to be searched.'" The U.S. Supreme Court emphasized that such searches must be based on probable cause.[96]

In 1985, the U.S. Supreme Court held that a warrantless search of packages held for three days after seizure by customs officials was not unreasonable. Customs officials had been observing what appeared to be a drug-smuggling operation. They saw several packages removed from two small airplanes, which had landed in a remote section of the airport. The packages were loaded onto two pickup trucks. The customs officers approached the trucks, smelled marijuana, and saw packages that were wrapped in plastic bags and sealed with tape. Some of the individuals were arrested, and the packages were seized and placed in a Drug Enforcement Agency (DEA) warehouse. Three days later, without a search warrant, officers opened the packages and found marijuana. In ruling that the search was proper even without a warrant, the U.S. Supreme Court held that the warrantless search of a vehicle need not occur contemporaneously with the lawful seizure of the items. The Court emphasized, however, that officers may not hold vehicles and their contents indefinitely before they complete a search.[97]

As noted earlier, in some cases, police may conduct warrantless vehicle searches. This may be done to protect the police from danger, to protect the owner's property while the police have custody of the vehicle, and to protect police against claims that items were stolen from the vehicle while it was in police custody.[98] Furthermore, the U.S. Supreme Court held that, when a driver who was stopped for an illegal turn consented to a search of his car, police could legally examine the contents of a closed container within that car.[99]

The search of vehicles may also include buses. In 1991, the U.S. Supreme Court held that when police board long-distance buses and, without reasonable suspicion that anyone on those buses is smuggling drugs, ask passengers for permission to search their luggage for narcotics, they are not violating those passengers' constitutional rights per se.[100] In 2002, the U.S. Supreme Court ruled that, when police board a bus to check for drugs or for other purposes, they are not required to tell passengers that they have a right to refuse to cooperate. Reasonable people understand that they are free to leave the bus or to answer questions; thus, when the police board the bus, that action does not constitute a seizure, ruled the Court. Among the three dissenters, Justice David Souter wrote that the "officers took control of the entire passenger compartment" and that "no reasonable passenger could have believed" that he or she was free to refuse to cooperate.[101]

In an earlier decision in 2000, however, the U.S. Supreme Court ruled by a 7-to-2 margin that police do not have the right to feel the personal bags that passengers take onto buses. In *Bond v. United States*, the Supreme Court emphasized that when passengers board buses "for whatever reason," they may take personal items in bags that are placed in the overhead racks. In *Bond*, the petitioner was a passenger on a Greyhound bus that left California headed for Little Rock, Arkansas. As required by law, the bus stopped at a permanent border patrol checkpoint in Sierra Blanca, Texas, where a border agent boarded the bus to check passengers' immigration status. As the agent walked the aisle, he squeezed the soft luggage in the overhead bins. He felt a "brick-like" object in the soft bag in the rack over Bond's head. Bond acknowledged that was his bag and consented to a search. The agent found a "brick" of methamphetamine. Bond was arrested, charged, and convicted of illegal drug possession.[102]

In 1999, the U.S. Supreme Court held that an officer who has probable cause to conduct a warrantless search of an automobile may search all containers that might hold the object of the search. This includes containers that belong to a passenger. In *Wyoming v. Houghton*, a police officer who stopped an automobile noted that the driver had a hypodermic syringe in his shirt pocket. The driver, David Young, was stopped for speeding and driving with a defective brake light. Young admitted that he used the syringe to take drugs. Two passengers were also in the front seat. The officer searched the car, including a purse on the back seat. The respondent in this case, Sandra K. Houghton, claimed the purse, which contained her driver's license with her correct identification. When questioned before this search, Houghton had told the officer that she was Sandra James and that she had no identification. When asked why she had lied, Houghton told the officer she did that "in case things went bad." Upon further search, the officer found a brown pouch, which Houghton denied was hers. She admitted ownership of the black wallet-type container. Officers found illegal drugs and drug paraphernalia and a syringe in each, but the amount of drugs in the syringe within the black container (60 cc of methamphetamine) was not sufficient to support the felony conviction in this case. Fresh needle marks were noticed on Houghton's arms. She was arrested and charged with felony possession of methamphetamine in a liquid amount greater than three-tenths of a gram. Her motion to have the contraband excluded was denied; she was convicted. A divided Wyoming Supreme Court reversed the conviction, stating that the officer should have known that the purse did not belong to the driver, and there was no probable cause to search the possessions of the passengers. Thus, the evidence against Houghton should have been excluded, as the search violated the Fourth and Fourteenth Amendments. By a 6-to-3 vote, the U.S. Supreme Court reversed, holding that the police had probable cause to search the car and thus were permitted to search the appellee's belongings that might have contained the items for which the police were searching.[103]

In *Maryland v. Pringle*, decided in 2003, the U.S. Supreme Court considered the following fact pattern. The appellant was a passenger in the front seat of a car; another passenger was in the back seat. The police had probable cause to stop the driver of the car because he was speeding. The driver and the passengers consented to a search, during which the police found cocaine in the back seat armrest and a significant amount of cash in the glove compartment. None of the occupants claimed possession of the drugs or the cash. All three occupants of the car were arrested and charged with possession of illegal drugs. Joseph Pringle argued successfully to a Maryland appellate court that the police did not have probable cause to arrest him, and thus the illegal drugs and questionable cash should not have been admitted as evidence against him, although he acknowledged that those items were his property. The U.S. Supreme Court disagreed and held that the arrest was proper. According to the Supreme Court, a reasonable officer could have thought any or all of the car's occupants were responsible for the contraband; thus, the officers had probable cause to arrest all three occupants.[104]

Finally, we consider the issue of whether police violate a suspect's constitutional rights when they use a drug-detecting dog to sniff a vehicle after they signal the driver to pull over in a routine traffic stop. In *Illinois v. Caballes*, police stopped Roy Caballes because he was driving 71 miles per hour in a 65-mile-per-hour zone on Interstate 80. Upon request, Caballes provided police with his driver's license, vehicle registration, and proof of insurance. Caballes was asked to join the police officer in his squad car; when he did, a warning ticket for speeding was issued. Caballes refused to grant the officer's request to search his car. The officer asked Caballes if he had ever been arrested, and he replied in the negative. But the police dispatcher informed the officer that Caballes had been arrested twice on suspicion of distributing marijuana. While the officer was writing the ticket, another officer arrived with a dog trained to sniff for drugs; the dog smelled drugs; Caballes's car was searched, marijuana was found, and Caballes was arrested for drug trafficking. The U.S. Supreme Court agreed to review the case to determine whether the Fourth Amendment (see Appendix A) prohibition against unreasonable searches and seizures requires police to have a reasonable suspicion before they use drug-sniffing dogs during a legitimate traffic stop. The Supreme Court held that a well-trained narcotics-detection dog, used, as in the *Caballes case*, to sniff only the outside of the vehicle during a legitimate traffic stop, is permitted by the Fourth Amendment.[105]

Body Searches

The search of body cavities is the most controversial search and seizure issue. Some body cavity searches are permitted, but there are limitations on the type, time, place, and method of search. The classic case involving body searches was decided in 1949, when three deputy sheriffs of Los Angeles County, relying on some information that a man named Rochin was selling narcotics, went to Rochin's home and entered the home through an open door. The officers forced open the door of the second-floor bedroom, where they found Rochin, partially clothed, sitting on the bed where his wife was lying. The officers saw two capsules beside the bed and asked, "Whose stuff is this?" Rochin grabbed the capsules and swallowed them. The officers, applying force, tried to remove the capsules and, when they were unsuccessful, handcuffed Rochin and took him to the hospital. They ordered his stomach pumped, and the drugs were used as evidence in the subsequent trial, at which Rochin was convicted. In *Rochin v. California*, the U.S. Supreme Court stated why this search and seizure was illegal.

Rochin v. California

[T]he proceedings by which this conviction was obtained do more than offend some fastidious squeamishness or private sentimentalism about combating crime too energetically. This is conduct that shocks the conscience, illegally breaking into the privacy of the petitioner, the struggle to open his mouth and remove what was there, the forcible extraction of his stomach's contents—this course of proceeding by agents of government to obtain evidence is bound to offend even hardened sensibilities. They are methods too close to the rack and the screw to permit of constitutional differentiation.[106]

The U.S. Supreme Court no longer uses the Rochin test of shocking the conscience, but rather, utilizes an objective test based on the Fourth Amendment. Clearly, some body cavity searches are permitted. For example, safety and security within jails and prisons are sufficient reasons for strip-searching inmates, although the Ninth Circuit Court of Appeals has held that a blanket policy of strip-searching all felony arrestees is unconstitutional.[107]

The Ninth Circuit held that it was illegal to conduct a strip and visual search of the vagina and anus of each of three women who were arrested for shoplifting rings. No rings were found, and no charges were filed. The court noted that, even if the women had secreted rings in their body cavities, they were in no danger to themselves. Furthermore, officials could have monitored their behavior until a search warrant was secured. Thus, no exigent circumstances existed for conducting a warrantless body cavity search.[108]

Earlier, we noted that border searches are permissible. Body cavity searches may also be conducted at the borders into the country whenever customs officials have reason to believe a person is smuggling contraband by carrying the contraband, usually illegal drugs, therein. This crime is referred to as *alimentary canal smuggling*. Probable cause is not required for the search of body cavities in these cases; customs officials need only have a reasonable suspicion that a traveler is committing the crime of alimentary canal smuggling to conduct the search.

The U.S. Supreme Court has decided a case on this issue. *United States v. Montoya de Hernandez* involved a woman who arrived in Los Angeles from Bogota, Colombia. Customs officials became suspicious when, while examining her passport, they noted that she had made numerous recent trips to Miami and Los Angeles. She was carrying $5,000 in cash and told officers that she planned to purchase goods for her husband's store, but she had made no hotel reservations or any appointments with merchandise vendors. Customs officials suspected that she was smuggling drugs within her body. A pat-down search by a female officer disclosed that the suspect's abdomen was firm and that she was wearing plastic underpants lined with a paper towel.[109]

Officials asked the suspect to consent to an X-ray, which at first she agreed to do, but subsequently, she withdrew her consent. At that point, she was given three choices. She could return to Colombia on the next available flight, submit to an X-ray, or remain in detention until she produced a bowel movement, which would be monitored. She chose to return to Colombia, but no flight was available, so she was detained for 16 hours. During that time, she refused to use the toilet facilities provided for her (a wastebasket placed in a restroom). She refused to eat or drink. Officials obtained a court order for an X-ray and a body search of her rectum. They found a cocaine-filled balloon. During the next four days of detention, the suspect excreted numerous balloons filled with cocaine, totaling more than half a kilogram of the drug.

In upholding the body search as legal, the U.S. Supreme Court stated that the right to privacy is diminished at the border. The suspect's rights are important, but the government has an interest in preventing drug smuggling. The test used by the Court for border searches is whether, after considering all of the facts involved, customs officials reasonably suspect that the traveler is smuggling contraband in his or her alimentary canal.

In contrast is a case involving proposed surgery to remove a bullet from a suspect who refused to consent to the surgery. The U.S. Supreme Court held that this search and seizure would be unreasonable. The prosecution claimed that the bullet would link the suspect to the crime. Initial investigation had shown that the surgery would involve only a minor incision, which could be conducted with a local anesthetic; on the basis of that evidence, the lower court granted the request to conduct the surgery. Further evidence indicated that the bullet was embedded deeply and that removal would require a general anesthetic.

The U.S. Supreme Court noted that the interest of individuals in their right to privacy, as well as health and life, must be considered against the government's interest in combating crime. A surgical procedure to remove evidence may be unreasonable and therefore illegal if it "endangers the life or health of the suspect…and [intrudes] upon the individual's dignitary interest in personal privacy and bodily integrity." In this case, the Supreme Court said there was considerable medical uncertainty regarding the safety of the procedure.[110]

One example of illegal body searches does not involve an appeal because the case was settled out of court. In New York City, 50,000 or more people were eligible to share in a settlement of $50 million for damages sustained when they were strip-searched after arrests for such minor offenses as disorderly conduct, loitering, and subway violations. The searches were conducted by jail guards in Manhattan and Queens over a 10-month period in 1996 and 1997. The individual awards ranged from $250 to $22,500. The higher awards were available to plaintiffs who could prove significant emotional damages.[111]

The settlement ended those claims, but in October 2003, a judge ruled that the allegations brought by 20 persons of illegal strip searches by New York police in Brooklyn were sufficient to state a cause of action for trial. Those persons and others with similar claims could sue the police department for searching them (after arrests on minor charges), even when there was no reason to suspect that they were concealing illegal drugs or other contraband. One Haitian man, Paul G. Brumaire, who was arrested on a misdemeanor charge evolving from a dispute with a tenant, said he was forced to undress and bend over in front of laughing officers. One officer was holding a metal wand, normally used as a metal detector. Brumaire said he began to think of Abner Louima, the Haitian who was sodomized by New York City police, resulting in the criminal trials of several officers.[112]

An interesting body search and seizure case was decided by the Texas Court of Criminal Appeal in April 2003. On 20 December 1997, a Houston police officer received a call from a "concerned citizen" that a man named McGee and two other men were selling crack cocaine at a particular intersection and that McGee was hiding the drugs between his buttocks. The officer went to the intersection, found three men who matched the description, smelled marijuana, and saw blue smoke surrounding the men. Based on his experience, the officer decided the smoke came from marijuana. He asked for identification and confirmed the names with those given by the caller. The officer checked for weapons and found none. McGee admitted that someone smoked marijuana but that he did not do so. The police found a cigar containing marijuana on the ground. The men were handcuffed and transported to a nearby fire station. The Texas court noted the following additional facts. The U.S. Supreme Court declined to hear the case.[113]

McGee v. Texas

At the fire station, Officer Rowan took McGee to a secluded area of the station and compelled McGee to drop his pants, bend over, and spread his buttocks. Officer Rowan proceeded to perform a visual search of McGee's anal region. The officer testified that he saw several rocks of crack cocaine wrapped in red plastic in plain view lodged between McGee's buttocks. He further testified that the crack cocaine was not inside McGee's anus, but that when the cocaine was exposed, McGee attempted to push it into his anus. Officer Rowan testified that he was able to retrieve the drugs before McGee pushed them into his anus without digitally probing the anus. McGee was then charged with possession of cocaine.

Before trial, McGee presented his motion to suppress evidence, which the trial court denied after a hearing. McGee then pled guilty to the charge of possession of cocaine weighing less than one gram and was sentenced to 90 days' confinement.... [McGee appealed, arguing that the evidence should have been excluded because it was the result of an illegal search and seizure and that the arrest was illegal. The court of appeals agreed. The state sought review by the Texas Court of Criminal Appeals, which reversed the lower appellate court. Among other comments, the court stated the following.]

The [U.S.] Supreme Court has upheld the use of visual body cavity searches based on suspicion short of probable cause.... [In this case] the arresting officer had probable cause to believe that McGee was engaged in illegal activity. Probable cause is the highest level of justification employed by the courts. While we do not create a per se rule that probable cause always justifies a body cavity search, in this instance we find from the totality of the circumstances that Officer Rowan had sufficient justification to believe that a search was necessary....

The Court of Appeals was incorrect in holding that the cocaine should have been suppressed. We reverse the judgment of the Court of Appeals and reinstate the judgment of the trial court.

4-4e   Interrogation

Another important law enforcement function of policing is interrogation. Police must be able to question suspects, but that need to question must be balanced with the Fifth Amendment provision that no person "shall be compelled in any criminal case to be a witness against himself" (see Appendix A). For much of our history, it was assumed that most decisions regarding police interrogation and the admission of evidence obtained by those interrogations were governed by state, not federal, law. Jurisdictions recognized various police practices, and coercion of confessions was not uncommon. In 1964, the U.S. Supreme Court declared that "today the admissibility of a confession in a state criminal prosecution is tested by the same standard applied in federal prosecutions since 1897," which meant that the Fifth Amendment's prohibition against self-incrimination was applicable to the states.[114]

In 1964, in *Escobedo v. Illinois*, the U.S. Supreme Court spoke of "the right of the accused to be advised by his lawyer of his privilege against self-incrimination." Although *Escobedo* concerned the Sixth Amendment right to counsel (see Appendix A), it was considered important in the movement toward interpreting the Fifth Amendment as constituting a right not to testify against oneself.[115]

In 1966, the U.S. Supreme Court decided *Miranda v. Arizona* by a 5-to-4 decision, which set off a flurry of reaction from liberals and conservatives but established the constitutional rights of the accused concerning interrogation. The Supreme Court engaged in a lengthy examination of police manuals, which stated, among other things, how to use psychological coercion to elicit a suspect's confession. The Court examined the facts of the *Miranda* case. Ernesto Miranda was arrested, taken into custody, and identified by a complaining witness. He was held and interrogated for two hours by police, who admitted that they did not tell him he had a right to have an attorney present. The police obtained from Miranda a written confession, which stated that his confession was voluntary, that he had made it with full knowledge that it could be used against him, and that he fully understood his legal rights. That confession was admitted into evidence at the trial, and Miranda was convicted.

Miranda warning The rule, stemming from *Miranda v. Arizona*, that stipulates that anyone in custody for an offense that might result in a jail or prison term must be warned of certain rights before being questioned by law enforcement officials. These rights include the right to remain silent, to be told that anything said can and will be held against the suspect, the right to counsel (which will be appointed if the suspect cannot afford to retain private counsel), and the right to cease talking at any time. If the warning is not given or is given and violated, any information obtained from the suspect may be inadmissible as evidence at trial. The rights may be waived if done so willingly and knowingly by one who has the legal capacity to waive them.

The Arizona Supreme Court upheld the conviction, emphasizing that Miranda did not ask for an attorney. The U.S. Supreme Court reversed the conviction in a lengthy decision discussing the dangers of establishing psychological environments in which the accused, even if innocent, would confess. To protect suspects from impermissible psychological interrogation, the Court handed down the ***Miranda*** **warning**, which consists of the following:

- The right to remain silent
- The right to notice that anything said by the suspect may and will be used against him or her at trial
- The right to the presence of an attorney, who will be
- Appointed (that is, paid for by the government) if the suspect is indigent[116]

The suspect may waive the right to an attorney, but that waiver must be made voluntarily, knowingly, and intelligently. If the suspect indicates a willingness to talk but subsequently wishes to remain silent, police should not continue their interrogation.

The U.S. Supreme Court has decided numerous cases interpreting *Miranda*. For example, in *Davis v. United States*, the Court voted 5-to-4 to uphold the conviction of a defendant for murdering a fellow serviceman on naval grounds. After he received the *Miranda* warnings, Davis signed a waiver of his right to counsel and began talking. Later, he stated, "Maybe I should see a lawyer." At that point, officers stopped questioning Davis about the crime and began inquiring whether he wanted counsel. Davis said he did not wish to speak with an attorney, and interrogation resumed. Davis's statements were used against him, and he was convicted. On appeal, the Supreme Court upheld the admission of this evidence. In the opinion written for the majority, Justice Sandra Day O'Connor stated that the Court was not willing to go beyond previous cases and hold that police may not question a suspect who *might* want an attorney. The suspect must *request* an attorney.[117] This case is not to be confused with the Court's previous holdings that once a suspect has invoked the right to counsel, the police must cease interrogation.[118]

By far the most important of the recent decisions concerning *Miranda* was *Dickerson v. United States*, decided by the U.S. Supreme Court in 2000. In this case, decided by a 7-to-2 vote, the Court reaffirmed *Miranda*, with Chief Justice William H. Rehnquist writing the opinion and calling *Miranda* a part of American culture. *Dickerson* involved a 1968 congressional statute, which provided that, in determining whether a confession is voluntary, courts should weigh several factors, only one of which is whether the *Miranda* warning was given. The issue before the Supreme Court in the *Dickerson* case was whether the federal statute was an unconstitutional attempt by Congress to overrule *Miranda*. It had been assumed that *Miranda* established an irrebuttable presumption that a confession is not voluntary if it is made prior to the giving of the *Miranda* warning. The argument was that the U.S. Constitution does not require this presumption; thus, Congress has the power to reverse the rule by statute, which it did in this 1968 law.[119]

Section (b) of the federal statute provides as follows:

(b) The trial judge in determining the issue of voluntariness shall take into consideration all the circumstances surrounding the giving of the confession, including (1) the time elapsing between arrest and arraignment of the defendant making the confession, if it was made after arrest and before arraignment, (2) whether such defendant knew the nature of the offense with which he was charged or of which he was suspected at the time of making the confession, (3) whether or not such defendant was advised or knew that he was not required to make any statement and that any such statement could be used against him, (4) whether or not such defendant had been advised prior to questioning of his right to the assistance of counsel; and (5) whether or not such defendant was without the assistance of counsel when questioned and when giving such confession.[120]

The presence or absence of any of the previously mentioned factors to be taken into consideration by the judge need not be conclusive on the issue of the voluntariness of the confession. Federal prosecutors had made little or no effort to enforce this statute until the *Dickerson* case.

In *Dickerson*, the U.S. Supreme Court ruled that the *Miranda* rule is constitutional; it rests on the principles of due process as guaranteed by the Fourteenth Amendment and the Fifth Amendment's privilege against self-incrimination. Thus, Congress did not have the power to reverse the requirement by statute. Reversal would have required a constitutional amendment. *Dickerson* did not answer all of the *Miranda* questions, however, but during its 2003–2004 term, the U.S. Supreme Court decided three cases involving the issue of whether police may question suspects first and then issue the *Miranda* warning after those suspects have confessed. The case of *Missouri v. Seibert* involved a mother who was accused of conspiring for her 17-year-old retarded son to die in a fire in their mobile home in order to cover up evidence that a younger son had died by neglect. Five days after the fire, when Patrice Seibert was sleeping in the waiting room at the hospital, police interrogators awakened her and questioned her about the fire, using repeatedly the phrase, "Donald was also to die in his sleep." The interrogators said they were instructed to question the suspect and get a confession before giving her the *Miranda* warnings. Seibert confessed, was tried, and convicted. The Missouri Supreme Court reversed the conviction on the grounds that Seibert's constitutional rights were violated when she was not first given the *Miranda* warning; thus, her confession could not be used at her trial. The legal issue was whether her confession could be used because it was voluntary. The U.S. Supreme Court affirmed the Missouri Supreme Court's ruling, holding that questioning a suspect first tended to thwart the purpose of the *Miranda* warning and thus the confession violated Seibert's constitutional rights.[121]

In the second case, *United States v. Fellers*, John Fellers was convicted of drug charges. The police had gone to Fellers's home, told him they were there to discuss his involvement in drug distribution, and asked to talk with him. Fellers invited the police into his home, after which they told him that a grand jury had indicted him on drug charges and that they had a warrant for his arrest. The police named four of the persons with whom the indictment stated Fellers had conspired. Fellers told the officers that he knew the four and had used drugs with them. Fellers was arrested and taken to the county jail, where he was given his *Miranda* warning for the first time. Fellers then repeated his earlier statement. He petitioned the judge to exclude these statements from his trial. The statements made at his home were excluded. Those made at the jail were admitted, and he was convicted. On appeal, Fellers argued that the jailhouse statements should have been excluded as the "forbidden fruits" (evidence obtained as the result of an illegal search or an illegal interrogation) of the statements made in his home in violation of his constitutional rights. The U.S. Circuit Court of Appeals for the Eighth Circuit held that Fellers's jailhouse statements were properly admitted at his trial because they had been made voluntarily and thus were not tainted by the failure of the arresting officers to give the *Miranda* warnings *before* the statements were made. The U.S. Supreme Court found that the police had deliberately elicited the statements from Fellers at his home, in violation of his Sixth Amendment right to counsel. The Court sent the case back to the Eighth Circuit for a determination of whether the testimony secured as the result of the police violation of Fellers's constitutional right at his home tainted the testimony elicited from Fellers at the jailhouse, thus requiring that the jailhouse confession also be excluded. The Eighth Circuit held that there was no evidence that the police used the illegally secured testimony of Fellers at his home to elicit his jailhouse confession. The policies that support excluding from trial any evidence that is illegally obtained were, according to the court, fulfilled by the exclusion of the testimony Fellers made at his home. The exclusion of his jailhouse testimony would not promote the fairness of the trial process because it was not unfair to Fellers; thus, it was properly used against him. The Eighth Circuit upheld the convictions but sent the case back to the trial court for resentencing, noting that the court had erred in its determination of Fellers's sentence.[122]

The third case on the *Miranda* warning, *United States v. Patane*, involved the use of physical evidence secured before the police gave the *Miranda* warning. Colorado Springs, Colorado, police went to the home of Samuel Patane to arrest him, a felon accused of violating a domestic restraining order. After Patane was arrested and handcuffed, one officer began reading him the *Miranda* warning, but Patane stopped the officer. When the police later asked him about a gun, Patane told them where it could be found. That weapon, secured from Patane before he had heard his full *Miranda* rights, was admitted at his trial. Patane was convicted of being in possession of a firearm, which is illegal for felons. On appeal, the Tenth Circuit Court of Appeals held that the gun should not have been admitted as evidence because it was obtained during a search that violated the suspect's *Miranda* rights. The U.S. Supreme Court reversed and remanded the case, stating that the fruits of an unwarned but voluntary statement from a suspect may be admitted against that person at trial.[123]

These three cases, along with another one, *Yarborough v. Alvarado*[124] (which involved the *Miranda* warnings as they apply to juveniles and is discussed in Chapter 12), decided by the U.S. Supreme Court during its 2003–2004 term, gave the Supreme Court an opportunity to further refine the implications of the *Miranda* decision.

The issues of police interrogation continue. In a 2003 article, Yale Kamisar, noted law professor and author of numerous scholarly publications on police interrogation (and other topics), wrote a special piece for the *National Law Journal* in which he spoke about the importance of tape-recording police interrogations. Referring to the *Miranda* decision statement that the secrecy surrounding police interrogation "results in a gap in our knowledge as to what in fact goes on in the interrogation rooms," Kamisar noted, "37 years later, we know little more about actual police interrogation practices than we did at the time of *Miranda*. The 'swearing contest' between police and suspect as to what was said [a contest usually won by the police] has not let up." Kamisar noted that police often tape confessions but not interrogations prior to those confessions. He referred to a narrowly defeated bill in Illinois that would have required police to videotape or audiotape all police interrogations. That bill died after the law enforcement community successfully lobbied against it, complaining that it would increase the defendants' rights and hinder public security. Said Kamisar, "Why making a complete record of what happened during interrogations would expand the rights of the accused was not made clear. Illinois has, however,...passed a new bill to take effect in two years that will require videotaping of interrogations in murder cases." Kamisar concluded his article with this statement:

> It is not because a peace officer is more dishonest than the rest of us that we should demand an objective recording of the critical custodial events. Rather, it is because we are entitled to assume that the police are no less human—and equally inclined to reconstruct and interpret past events in a favorable light—that we should not permit them to be the judges of their own cause.[125]

Finally, it is important to understand that *Miranda* applies only to a *custodial* interrogation. Police are free to ask questions in noncustodial circumstances without giving the required warning. But frequently, however, the issue is what constitutes a custodial situation. In a 2003 Texas case, the U.S. Supreme Court refused to uphold a decision in which police went to the home of Robert Kaupp, 17, who was awakened at 3 A.M. and told, "[W]e need to go and talk." Kaupp was convicted of a 1999 murder and sentenced to 55 years in prison. The U.S. Supreme Court rejected the lower court's decision that Kaupp was not under arrest, as he was free to refuse to cooperate with the officers. Thus, his answers to police questions were admissible in court. The Supreme Court stated that a "group of police officers rousing an adolescent out of bed in the middle of the night with the words 'we need to go and talk' presents no option but 'to go.'...It cannot seriously be suggested that when the detectives began to question Kaupp, a reasonable person in his situation would have thought he was sitting in the interview room as a matter of choice, free to change his mind and go home to bed." The U.S. Supreme Court vacated the lower appellate court's decision, sent the case back for reconsideration, and instructed the court that Kaupp's confession should be excluded "unless…the state can point to testimony undisclosed on the record before us, and weighty enough to carry the state's burden despite the clear force of the evidence shown here."[126]

4-4f   Investigation

Crime scene investigation has become a popular topic in the United States, capturing the attention of millions on television shows such as *CSI: Crime Scene Investigation*, *CSI: Miami*, and *CSI: New York*.[127] A popular board game based on the TV series enables players to serve as interns assigned to solve a horrible Las Vegas crime. Further, with the assistance of a $2 million federal grant, the University of New Haven has established the nation's first national crime scene investigation training center, located in the university's Henry C. Lee Institute of Forensic Science. Dr. Lee is an internationally known forensics expert, who stated that this center "is going to provide a real CSI training center for the country." According to a legal account, "At the school crime lab, workers, lawyers and other law enforcement officials will take intensive, hands-on, week-long classes about the basics of processing crime scenes and protecting evidence. The school will also offer specialized classes on other investigative tools, from ballistics tests to the science of blood stains."[128]

Searching and seizing, along with interrogation, illustrate the investigative function of policing. The success or failure of the prosecution of a suspect for a particular crime often depends on the investigative abilities of the police before, during, or after the suspect's arrest. Evidence may be destroyed quickly or never found. Without physical evidence, it may be impossible to link the alleged criminal activity to the suspect.

In large police departments, criminal investigations may be the responsibility of specialists, and police officers may not be closely involved in the process. In many cases, however, the police officer who makes the arrest is a critical element in the investigative process. In some police departments, the patrol officer's investigative function is limited. Most of this work, at least in serious cases, is conducted by specialized officers in the criminal investigation unit of the department. These investigators conduct various kinds of activities, ranging from the maintenance of field activity records to total crime scene management, including such other activities as collecting body fluids, photographing crime scenes, following up on investigations, sketching crime scenes, obtaining search/arrest warrants, conducting interviews/interrogations, and attending autopsies.

Police use many investigative techniques. Fingerprinting is one of the most effective methods. This technique has been available in the United States since it was first used around 1900 by London's Scotland Yard. The use of computers to assist with fingerprint identification has increased investigative techniques in this area.

Another technique is the use of deoxyribonucleic acid, or DNA, "which carries the genetic information that determines individual characteristics such as eye color and body size." Some argue that DNA is close to 100 percent accurate, compared with traditional blood and semen tests, which are only 90 to 95 percent accurate. Advocates call this process *DNA genetic fingerprinting*.[129]

DNA results have been used to free inmates who were convicted and have served years in prison. The results have been used to win acquittals for defendants as well as to convict others. But the use of DNA remains controversial; courts do not agree on whether testimony regarding DNA should be admitted, although the trend is toward admitting the evidence. Some courts have admitted certain methods of DNA testing while excluding others or have instructed trial courts to examine the testing methods more carefully. Lawyers may also challenge the methods of collecting and analyzing DNA evidence.

Chapter Wrap-Up

This chapter is the second of two on policing, and it began with a discussion of preparing for policing, which looked at the issues surrounding the recruitment, selection, education, and training of police.

Police exercise wide discretion in criminal justice systems, and the chapter devoted a section to the explanation and analysis of why discretion is necessary and how it might be abused. Discretion cannot be abolished; thus, controlling it is a necessity.

The primary focus of the chapter, however, was on the functions that police must perform in an increasingly complex society. Those functions are numerous, but they are categorized as law enforcement, order maintenance, and community service. The latter two were discussed briefly before greater attention was given to law enforcement.

The controversy over the importance of order maintenance was noted within the context of the contributions of several experts on policing. Order maintenance may be a crucial function of policing, as the absence of order may lead to law violations, even serious criminal acts, such as the violent crimes of aggravated assault and murder. Likewise, the community service function of policing may prevent or reduce actions that might lead to law violations. Furthermore, many of the activities police are called upon to perform occur after hours, when other organizations have closed for the day.

The discussion of law enforcement began with a brief overview of the constitutional limitations on policing, for it is clear that police could make more arrests and conduct more thorough investigations if they did not have to observe defendants' due process rights. U.S. criminal justice systems place great emphasis on the right of individuals to be free from unreasonable governmental intrusion. This does not mean that police cannot arrest, search and seize, interrogate, and investigate, but only that these functions must be performed within the limits of state and federal statutes, constitutions, and court decisions. Those limits are being challenged in many cases.

The Fourth Amendment's prohibition against unreasonable search and seizure and the Fifth Amendment's provision that a person may not be forced to incriminate himself or herself are the key constitutional bases of what police may and may not do in law enforcement. The investigatory stop, brief detention, arrest, and searching and seizing are important police activities regulated by constitutional requirements, court interpretations of those requirements, and departmental policies.

A look at a few key cases on the law of stop, arrest, search, and seizure should make it obvious that it is impossible to state what *the law* is in these areas. The facts of a particular case must be analyzed carefully in light of previous court decisions, statutes, and constitutional provisions. Reasonable minds may differ as to the conclusion in any given case. It is important to analyze case law carefully, looking at the rule of a case as well as the reasons for that rule.

In some situations, police are permitted to stop, arrest, search, and seize without a warrant, although the U.S. Supreme Court prefers warrants. Again, it is impossible for police to know in every case whether they face exceptions to the warrant requirement. Frequently, law enforcement is ambiguous, leaving considerable discretion to the individual officer, who may be second-guessed by the courts. Despite the need to analyze individual cases in terms of their unique facts, some general principles of constitutional law govern the law enforcement function of policing. Those were discussed in the chapter, with attention paid to some of the major U.S. Supreme Court cases governing each aspect of law enforcement, from the initial stop to the searching and seizing of homes, automobiles, and persons.

Interrogation is another important law enforcement function. The U.S. Supreme Court has decided many cases in this area. The *Miranda* warning must be given in cases in which a person might be deprived of his or her liberty, but it is not always clear when interrogation has begun and the warning must be given. Failure to comply with *Miranda* requirements may result in the exclusion of evidence from the trial, an issue discussed in Chapter 5.

Investigation was the final police function discussed in this chapter. Traditionally, police have spent considerable time investigating crimes at the scene of their occurrence without significant effectiveness. Recently, investigative techniques have been improved by the use of forensic science, especially DNA. Some continue to question the reliability of DNA testing or challenge the methods of collecting and analyzing DNA evidence.

Policing has changed in many ways in recent years. This chapter touched on only a few areas in which changes have been attempted. Chapter 5 focuses on the primary problems and issues of policing.

Key Terms

anticipatory search warrant (p. 105)
arrest (p. 102)
contraband (p. 101)
curtilage (p. 107)
frisk (p. 101)
harmless error (p. 105)

informant (p. 103)
Miranda *warning (p. 116)*
plain view doctrine (p. 107)
pretextual stop (p. 94)
probable cause (p. 102)
racial profiling (p. 96)

reversible error (p. 105)
search and seizure (p. 102)
search warrant (p. 102)
warrant (p. 102)

Apply It

1. If you were in charge of recruiting persons into policing, what characteristics would you emphasize? What emphasis would you place on higher education and why? What type of training would you require and why? How would you assess the ethical and moral standards of recruits? What standards would you require for policing, and what efforts

would you suggest for maintaining those standards within police forces?

2. What effect do you think the 9/11 terrorist attacks have had on policing? What types of training would prepare police for such terrorist acts?

3. Discuss the importance of discretion in policing.

4. What is meant by *order maintenance* in policing?

5. What should be the role of police with regard to service functions within the communities they serve?

6. Explain briefly the constitutional provisions that govern policing.

7. What functions do police have in traffic control and the enforcement of traffic laws and ordinances? Discuss the recent U.S. Supreme Court cases in this area.

8. Under what circumstances may police stop, question, and arrest a suspect? When may police frisk?

9. Explain racial profiling and its implications.

10. Why are warrants usually required for arrest and search?

11. Under what circumstances may police search without a warrant? Arrest without a warrant?

12. What is the meaning of *probable cause*, and how may it be established?

13. When may police search a home? How much of the home may be searched? Explain the plain view doctrine, and define *curtilage*.

14. After knocking and announcing, how long must police wait before entering a home forcibly to execute a search warrant?

15. Do you believe police should be permitted to use drug-sniffing dogs at the scene of a normal traffic stop?

16. Explain the *plain feel* doctrine.

17. Under what circumstances may an automobile be searched?

18. Under what circumstances may body searches be conducted?

19. What is the *Miranda* warning? Why is it important? What did the U.S. Supreme Court hold in *Dickerson v. United States*? What right-to-counsel issues has the U.S. Supreme Court decided recently?

20. What is DNA testing, and why is it controversial?

Endnotes

1. See Arthur Niederhoffer, *Behind the Shield: The Police in Urban Society* (Garden City, N.Y.: Anchor Books, 1969), pp. 109–160.

2. John Kleinig, *The Ethics of Policing* (New York: University of Cambridge, 1996), front cover, as cited in a review of the text by Richard N. Holden, *Criminal Justice Review* 22 (September 1997): 113.

3. "Ex-Cop Serpico Testifies on NYPD," *Miami Herald* (24 September 1997), p. 8.

4. "New York Police Overtime Soars: Extra Pay May Speed Retirement," *New York Times* (2 November 2002), p. 1.

5. "Los Angeles Police Officials Admit Widespread Lapses," *New York Times* (19 February 2000), p. 12, quoting Edward A. Flynn, police chief of Arlington County, Virginia.

6. "Counting Heads Along the Thin Blue Line," *New York Times* (26 March 2006), Section 4, p. 4.

7. The President's Commission on Law Enforcement and Administration of Justice, *The Challenge of Crime in a Free Society* (Washington, D.C.: U.S. Government Printing Office, 1967), p. 109.

8. "College Adding New Degree Program," *Miami Herald* (22 March 2006), n.p.

9. See Patrick Murphy, foreword to David L. Carter et al., *The State of Police Education: Policy Direction for the 21st Century* (Washington, D.C.: Police Executive Research Forum, 1989), pp. iii–iv.

10. For an analysis of higher education and policing, see Agnes L. Baro and David Burlingame, "Law Enforcement and Higher Education: Is There an Impasse?" *Journal of Criminal Justice Education* 10 (Spring 1999): 57–74.

11. "A Costly Gift to Police," *Boston Globe* (29 April 2003), p. 20; "Proposed Police Standards Raise Opposition in House," *Providence Journal* (16 March 2004), p. 1C; "Boston Police among Highest Paid in Nation," *Boston Globe* (29 March 2004), p. 1; "Raises from the Mayor Outpace Private Sector," *Boston Globe* (2 August 2007), p. 1. The Quinn bill is codified at ALM GL Chapter 41, Section 108L (2007).

12. Carter et al., *The State of Police Education*, p. 15.

13. Baro and Burlingame, "Law Enforcement and Higher Education"; quotation is on p. 70.

14. The President's Commission on Law Enforcement and Administration of Justice, *Task Force Report: The Police* (Washington, D.C.: U.S. Government Printing Office, 1967), p. 138.

15. The President's Commission on Law Enforcement and Administration of Justice, *The Challenge of Crime in a Free Society*, pp. 112–113.

16. National Advisory Commission on Criminal Justice Standards and Goals, *A National Strategy to Reduce Crime* (Washington, D.C.: U.S. Government Printing Office, 1973), p. 83.

17. The U.S. Commission on Civil Rights, *Who Is Guarding the Guardians? A Report on Police Practices* (Washington, D.C.: U.S. Government Printing Office, October 1981), p. 155.

18. "Training Could Prevent Many Police Cell Fatalities," *Birmingham Post* (11 June 2003), p. 6.

19. "Feds Taking New Aim at Gangs," *Hartford Courant* (Connecticut) (4 May 2006), n.p.

20. "Bike Cops Get Road-Ready: Training Helps Officers Learn Skills and Stamina to Patrol on Two Wheels," *Detroit News* (25 June 2003), p. 1K.

21. "Ensure School-Based Officers Are Trained to Work on Campus," *School Violence Alert* 7, no. 12 (27 November 2001): n.p.

22. "Cops Get Grisly Lesson in Unearthing Clues: County Police Training Program Draws Officers from Across Nation," *Asbury Park Press* (29 May 2003), p. 1B.

23. "Homeland Security," *Indianapolis Star* (13 June 2003), p. 3B.

24. "Community College/Police Training Partnership," *Public Management* 85, no. 2 (1 March 2003): 22.

25. City of Canton, Ohio v. Harris, 489 U.S. 378 (1989).

26. Laure Weber Brooks, "Police Discretionary Behavior: A Study of Style," in Roger G. Dunham and Geoffrey P. Alpert, *Critical Issues in Policing: Contemporary Readings*, 5th ed. (Long Grove, Ill: Waveland Press, Inc., 2005), pp. 89–105.

27. James Q. Wilson, *Varieties of Police Behavior: The Management of Law and Order in Eight Communities* (Cambridge, Mass.: Harvard University Press, 1968), pp. 16, 17, 21.

28. Ibid., p. 21.

29. George L. Kelling, "Order Maintenance, the Quality of Urban Life, and Police: A Line of Argument," in *Police Leadership in America: Crisis and Opportunity*, ed. William A. Geller (Chicago: American Bar Foundation, 1985), p. 297.

30. Ibid., p. 308.

31. See James Q. Wilson and George L. Kelling, "Police and Neighborhood Safety: Broken Windows," *Atlantic Monthly* 249 (March 1982): 29–38.

32. Carl B. Klockars, "Order Maintenance, the Quality of Urban Life, and Police: A Different Line of Argument," in *Police Leadership*, ed. Geller, p. 316, quoting *The Newark Foot Patrol Experiment* (Washington, D.C.: Police Foundation, 1981), p. 88.

33. *Student Party Riots*, available from the COPS Office Response Center, cited and quoted in "Police Urged to Review Policies to Prevent Student Party Riots," *Criminal Justice Newsletter* (17 April 2006), p. 5.

34. *Police Reentry and Community Policing: Strategies for Balancing Public Safety*, Urban Institute Justice Policy Center, as cited in "Natural Role Seen for Police in Prisoners Reentry Programs," *Criminal Justice Newsletter* (17 April 2006), p. 6.

35. Wilson, *Varieties of Police Behavior*, p. 5.

36. Atwater v. City of Lago Vista, 533 U.S. 924 (2001).

37. Atwater v. City of Lago Vista, 533 U.S. 924 (2001).

38. Whren v. United States, 517 U.S. 806 (1996).

39. Whren v. United States, 517 U.S. 806 (1996).

40. Ohio v. Robinette, 519 U.S. 33 (1996).

41. Maryland v. Wilson, 519 U.S. 408 (1997).

42. Tracey Maclin, "Open Door Policy: Court Rulings on Traffic Stops Undercut Fourth Amendment Protections," *American Bar Association Journal* 83 (July 1997): 46.

43. Indianapolis, Indiana v. Edmond, 531 U.S. 32 (2000).

44. Indianapolis, Indiana v. Edmond, 531 U.S. 32 (2000), referring to Michigan Dept. of State Police v. Sitz, 496 U.S. 444 (1990). See also United States v. Martinez-Fuerte, 428 U.S. 543 (1976), permitting suspicionless stops of motorists for the purpose of intercepting illegal immigrants.

45. Illinois v. Lidster, 747 N.E.2d 419 (Ill. 2d Dist. 2001), aff'd., 779 N.E.2d 855 (Ill. 2002), rev'd., 540 U.S. 419 (2004). The comments from the justices are reported in "When Can Drivers Be Halted? Justices Take Up Issue Anew," *New York Times* (6 September 2003), p. 25.

46. "New Jersey Enters into Consent Decree on Racial Issues in Highway Stops," *Criminal Law Reporter* 66 (5 January 2000), p. 251.

47. "New Jersey Troopers Avoid Jail in Case That Highlighted Profiling," *New York Times* (15 January 2002), p. 1.

48. "Fighting Profiling: Training for All Cops," *New Jersey Lawyer* 14, no. 27 (4 July 2005): 39.

49. Bureau of Justice Statistics, *Contacts between Police and the Public: Findings from the 1999 National Survey* (Washington, D.C.: U.S. Department of Justice, 2001), reported in "Survey Shows Harsher Treatment of Minorities in Traffic Stops," *Criminal Justice Newsletter* 31, no. 8 (14 March 2001): p. 4.

50. *Racially Biased Policing: A Principled Response*, available on the Internet at http://www.policeforum.org, or in print from the Police Executive Research Forum, 1120 Connecticut Avenue NW, Suite 930, Washington, D.C., 20036.

51. Geoffrey P. Alpert et al, "Police Suspicion and Discretionary Decision Making during Citizen Stops," *Criminology* 43, no. 2 (May 2005): 407–434.

52. Robin Shepard Engel and Jennifer M. Calnon, "Examining the Influence of Drivers' Characteristics during Traffic Stops with Police: Results from a National Sample," *Justice Quarterly* 21, no. 1 (March 2004): 49–90; quotation is on p. 49.

53. "Study in Texas Sees Race Bias in Searches," *New York Times* (25 February 2005), p. 14. See also *Racial Profiling: Texas Traffic Stops and Searches—A First Look at the Nation's Most Comprehensive Racial Profiling Dataset: Texas Traffic Stops and Searches*, cited in "Large Study of Traffic Stops Finds Race Disparities in Texas," *Criminal Justice Newsletter* (17 February 2004), p. 3.

54. United States v. Montero-Camargo, 208 F.3d 1122 (9th Cir. 2000), cert. denied, 531 U.S. 889 (2000).

55. Ronald Weitzer and Steven A. Tuch, "Perceptions of Racial Profiling: Race, Class, and Personal Experience," *Criminology* 40 (May 2002): 435–456; quotation is on p. 452. See also Lorie Fridell et al., *Racially Biased Policing: A Principled Response* (Washington, D.C.: Police Executive Research Forum, 2001).

56. Albert J. Meehan and Michael C. Ponder, "Race and Place: The Ecology of Racial Profiling African American Motorists," *Justice Quarterly* 19, no. 3 (September 2002): 399–430; quotation is on pp. 426–427.

57. "California Ending Searches during Minor Traffic Stops," *New York Times* (28 February 2003), p. 16.

58. Katherine Beckett et al., "Race, Drugs, and Policing: Understanding Disparities in Drug Delivery Arrests," *Criminology* 44, no. 1 (February 2006): 105–138.

59. Terry v. Ohio, 392 U.S. 1 (1968).

60. Minnesota v. Dickerson, 508 U.S. 366 (1993).

61. United States v. Arvizu, 534 U.S. 266 (2002).

62. United States v. Arvizu, 534 U.S. 266 (2002).

63. Illinois v. Wardlow, 528 U.S. 119 (2000).

64. Johnson v. United States, 333 U.S. 10, 13–14 (1948).

65. Illinois v. Gates, 462 U.S. 213 (1983); United States v. Miller, 925 F.2d 695 (4th Cir. 1991), cert. denied, 502 U.S. 833 (1991).

66. Florida v. J.L., 529 U.S. 266 (2000).

67. Ornelas v. United States, 517 U.S. 690 (1996).

68. County of Riverside v. McLaughlin, 500 U.S. 44 (1991).

69. Flippo v. West Virginia, 528 U.S. 11 (1999).

70. United States v. Grubbs, 126 S.Ct. 1494 (2006).

71. United States v. Grubbs, 126 S.Ct. 1494 (2006), citations and footnotes omitted.

72. United States v. Grubbs, 126 S.Ct. 1494 (2006).

73. United States v. U.S. District Court, 407 U.S. 297 (1972).

74. Mapp v. Ohio, 367 U.S. 643 (1961).

75. Mapp v. Ohio, 367 U.S. 643 (1961).

76. Chimel v. California, 395 U.S. 752 (1969).

77. Coolidge v. New Hampshire, 403 U.S. 443 (1971).

78. Arizona v. Hicks, 480 U.S. 321 (1987).

79. Maryland v. Buie, 494 U.S. 325 (1990).

80. United States v. Dunn, 480 U.S. 294 (1987).

81. California v. Greenwood, 486 U.S. 35 (1988).
82. United States v. Hedrick, 922 F.2d 396 (7th Cir. 1991), *cert. denied*, 502 U.S. 847 (1991).
83. Illinois v. McArthur, 531 U.S. 326 (2001).
84. State v. Hempele, 576 A.2d 793 (N.J. 1990).
85. See California v. Ciraolo, 476 U.S. 207 (1986); and Florida v. Riley, 488 U.S. 445 (1989).
86. Kyllo v. United States, 533 U.S. 27 (2001).
87. Wilson v. Arkansas, 514 U.S. 927 (1995).
88. Richards v. Wisconsin, 520 U.S. 385 (1997).
89. United States v. Ramirez, 523 U.S. 65 (1998).
90. Minnesota v. Carter, 525 U.S. 83 (1999).
91. United States v. Banks, 282 F.3d 699 (9th Cir. 2002), *rev'd., remanded*, 540 U.S. 31 (2003), and *rev'd., remanded*, 355 F.3d 1188 (9th Cir. 2004).
92. Georgia v. Randolph, 125 S.Ct. 1515 (2006), citations and footnotes omitted.
93. Carroll v. United States, 267 U.S. 132 (1925); Chambers v. Maroney, 399 U.S. 42 (1970). See also Florida v. Myers, 466 U.S. 380 (1984) (*per curiam*), upholding the warrantless search by police of a car that was impounded and had been subjected to a previous legitimate inventory search.
94. California v. Acevedo, 500 U.S. 565 (1991).
95. Robbins v. California, 453 U.S. 420 (1981).
96. United States v. Ross, 456 U.S. 798 (1982).
97. United States v. Johns, 469 U.S. 478 (1985).
98. See Colorado v. Bertine, 479 U.S. 367 (1987); Florida v. Wells, 495 U.S. 1 (1990).
99. Florida v. Jimeno, 500 U.S. 248 (1991).
100. Florida v. Bostick, 501 U.S. 421 (1991).
101. United States v. Drayton, 536 U.S. 194 (2002).
102. Bond v. United States, 529 U.S. 334 (2000).
103. Wyoming v. Houghton, 526 U.S. 295 (1999).
104. Maryland v. Pringle, 540 U.S. 366 (2003).
105. Illinois v. Caballes, 545 U.S. 405 (2005).
106. Rochin v. California, 342 U.S. 165 (1952), *overruled as stated in* Lester v. Chicago, 830 F.2d 706 (7th Cir. 1987).
107. Fuller v. M.G. Jewelry, 950 F.2d 1437 (9th Cir. 1991).
108. Fuller v. M.G. Jewelry, 950 F.2d 1437 (9th Cir. 1991).
109. United States v. Montoya de Hernandez, 473 U.S. 531 (1985).
110. Winston v. Lee, 470 U.S. 753 (1985).
111. "New York to Pay $50 Million over Illegal Strip-Searches," *New York Times* (10 January 2001), p. 1; "New York Judge OKs $50 Million Illegal Strip Search Settlement," *Jet* (2 July 2001), p. 38.
112. "Suit Accuses Brooklyn Police of Improper Strip-Searches in Minor Cases," *New York Times* (final edition) (30 October 2003), p. 1.
113. McGee v. Texas, 105 S.W.3d 609 (Tex.Crim.App. 2003), *cert. denied*, 540 U.S. 1004 (2003).
114. Malloy v. Hogan, 378 U.S. 1 (1964).
115. Escobedo v. Illinois, 378 U.S. 478 (1964).
116. Miranda v. Arizona, 384 U.S. 436, 478–479 (1966).
117. Davis v. United States, 512 U.S. 452 (1994).
118. See Edwards v. Arizona, 451 U.S. 477 (1981); Minnick v. Arizona, 498 U.S. 146 (1990).
119. Dickerson v. United States, 530 U.S. 2326 (2000).
120. U.S. Code, Chapter 18, Section 3501 (2007).
121. Missouri v. Seibert, 2002 Mo. App. LEXIS 401 (Mo. Ct. App. 2002), *aff'd.*, 540 U.S. 519 (2004).
122. United States v. Fellers, 285 F.3d 721 (8th Cir. 2002), *rev'd., remanded*, 540 U.S. 519 (2004), *and aff'd. in part and remanded in part*, 397 F.3d 1090 (8th Cir. 2005).
123. United States v. Patane, 304 F.3d 1013 (10th Cir. 2002), *rev'd., remanded*, 542 U.S. 630 (2004).
124. Yarborough v. Alvarado, 541 U.S. 562 (2004).
125. Yale Kamisar, "Interrogating Suspects," *National Law Journal* 25, no. 84 (9 June 2003): 43.
126. Kaupp v. Texas, 538 U.S. 626 (2003).
127. "Improved Numbers Shelter CBS from the Fallout," *New York Times* (25 November 2004), p. 1C.
128. "Prosecution and Defense," *Connecticut Law Tribune*, 28, no. 44 (4 November 2002): 12.
129. Debra Cassens Moss, "DNA—the New Fingerprints," *American Bar Association Journal* 74 (1 May 1988): 66.

Problems and Issues in Policing

5

Policing is a job that arouses great controversy. Police may use deadly force, and in some circumstances, they would be negligent if they did not do so. Police are expected to stop and question persons who appear to have violated laws, but they may be criticized for doing so. Police are expected to obey all laws, but not all police meet that expectation. Police are expected to be well trained and have enough education to use reasonable judgment and discretion, but they may be stressed and bored if they are too highly educated or trained. They are expected to be alert on the job, but the dull aspects of many patrol assignments may make it difficult to remain alert at all times. In short, policing is stressful.

In considering the problems in policing, we must realize that no problem is pervasive. This chapter discusses issues that arise in policing, but does not suggest that all police, or even most police, encounter the problems and do not resolve them successfully. Policing, like all jobs, involves some persons who are corrupt, incompetent, or in some other way unprofessional; however, many police officers work very hard to serve the public, and they do an excellent job. And many police officers find their work challenging and rewarding.

Policing presents officers and administrators with some serious dilemmas. Conflicts arise over allocation of officers' time; investigations may compromise officers' integrity or lead the public to question officers' investigative techniques. Processing domestic violence calls, confronting the drug scene, and dealing with the reality that some suspects or victims may have communicable diseases are situations that, among others, create serious problems for police.

Role conflicts, the threat of danger, methods of evaluating job performance, job satisfaction, and other issues create stressful situations that lead to professional and personal problems. The dangers of terrorism, especially since the 9/11 terrorist attacks, concern all of us, but police must face the possibility of rescue and investigation, including people whose lives depend on their success. Some police react in the same way many people react to stress: they confront the issues and deal with them successfully. They may become involved in a police subculture in which they feel comfortable and accepted while off duty. Others may become involved in corruption or overzealous law enforcement, or they may succumb to the use of illegal drugs or even drug trafficking. A few turn to brutality against crime suspects. The line between appropriate and excessive use of deadly force is not

L E A R N I N G
OBJECTIVES

After reading this chapter, you should be able to do the following:

- **Explain the meaning of dilemmas in policing.**
- **Summarize the external political pressures of policing.**
- **Explain time allocation pressures in policing.**
- **Define *proactive* and *reactive* policing, and discuss each in the context of domestic violence.**
- **Assess the impact of various stressors on policing.**
- **State what we can do to decrease domestic violence among police.**
- **Explain and analyze the impact of police subcultures.**
- **Discuss the nature and extent of police misconduct.**
- **Explain the proper use of deadly force in the context of fleeing felons and vehicle pursuits.**
- **Discuss the nature and implications of police brutality.**
- **Discuss violence against police.**
- **Explain how police activities may be controlled by police departments.**
- **Explain and evaluate the exclusionary rule.**
- **Suggest ways in which federal regulations might improve policing.**
- **Discuss the control of policing by community relations and through civil actions.**
- **Explain the legal actions that citizens may take if they are mistreated by negligently trained police officers.**
- **Discuss the impact that affirmative action programs have had on policing and what might be expected in the future.**

easy to draw, but court decisions give some guidelines. When the line is crossed, civil liability attaches, and civil lawsuits against police are increasing. The control of policing is not easy but is attempted through police department regulations, federal regulations, courts, and community relationships.

The final section of the chapter focuses on affirmative action policies. The efforts of police departments to recruit minority and female applicants have increased the representation of these groups. Court cases have chipped away at affirmative action policies, but the U.S. Supreme Court has upheld some affirmative action policies.

5-1 Dilemmas in Policing

In any work environment, it is necessary to make adjustments to conflicting demands and pressures, but conflicts may be greater in policing than in most jobs or professions. We expect the police to solve and prevent crimes. We want them to respond cheerfully, quickly, and efficiently to a host of public needs. At the same time, police are expected to be polite, even when being attacked verbally or physically, and to be effective in securing evidence of crimes without violating suspects' constitutional rights. They must use violence when necessary, not when unnecessary, and the line between those two is not clearly established. Police should report ethical and legal violations of their colleagues, but frequently, internal pressures are against such reports. All of the dilemmas police face are enhanced by external political pressures.

5-1a External Political Pressures

Police are accountable to local, state, and federal agencies. Legal restrictions may be placed on police at any of these levels. Furthermore, police departments must compete with other public agencies for funding, and to be competitive, they must show that, although they are using their existing resources efficiently and prudently, local, state, and federal problems have grown beyond their ability to cope without additional resources.

The wide discretion police have in law enforcement may create political problems. Police are supposed to enforce laws that are violated; however, if they arrest a prominent, influential citizen, they may find that strict enforcement is not expected or even tolerated. Failure to enforce laws whenever prominent, influential citizens are involved creates political pressures from those against whom those laws are enforced. Political pressure to control the poor and minorities leads to allegations that policing is for the purpose of protecting the majority's status quo, with little regard for the rights of all people. A police administrator might find it impossible to be responsive to the needs of all of his or her constituents because of political influences that could cause the administrator to lose the job. Political pressures from local, state, and federal levels permeate policing and cannot be ignored. The fact that these external pressures may conflict with internal pressures makes the situation even more difficult and stressful for police.

The internal values of a police department may be at odds with those of the external constituency. To make the situation even more complicated, both the external and internal values and pressures may not be suitable for the current challenges of policing. One issue that creates conflict within and outside of the police department is how police should allocate their time.

5-1b Allocation of Police Time

There is little agreement on how police should allocate their time among law enforcement, order maintenance, and community service, the three major functions of policing discussed in Chapter 4. Studies of why people call police departments illustrate this time pressure. James Q. Wilson sampled calls to the Syracuse (New York) Police Department in 1966 and found that only 10.3 percent of those calls related to law enforcement, compared with 30.1 percent for order maintenance. Requests for services dealing with accidents, illnesses, and lost or found persons or property constituted 37.5 percent (the largest category of calls), whereas 22.1 percent of the calls were for information.[1]

In another study, published in 1971, Albert J. Reiss Jr. analyzed calls to the Chicago Police Department. His findings were similar to those of Wilson in one respect: 30 percent of the calls were for noncriminal matters. But Reiss found that 58 percent of the calls were related to law enforcement matters.[2] In 1980, Richard J. Lundman published the results of his study of police activities in five jurisdictions. Lundman found law enforcement to be the most frequent category of functions in which police engaged, consuming slightly less than one-third of all police time.[3]

The inconsistent findings of these studies may be attributed to the different methodology used for assessing police time allocation. Wilson and Reiss analyzed calls made to police departments; Lundman observed officers on patrol. Perhaps a more important variable in explaining the difference lies in the failure to specify carefully which activities would be included in each category.

Carefully defined, narrow categories may produce a more accurate picture of police time allocation. Eric J. Scott categorized more than 26,000 calls to police departments. According to Scott's 1981 publication, 21 percent of the calls were for information, 17 percent concerned nonviolent crimes, 12 percent were for assistance, 22 percent were for public nuisances, 9 percent were for traffic problems, 8 percent were citizens offering information, and 7 percent were concerned with interpersonal conflict. Other categories were violent crimes (representing only 2 percent of the calls), medical assistance, dependent persons, and calls regarding internal operations. Each of the categories was subdivided into more specific categories. For example, the category *assistance* included animal problems, property checks, escorts and transports, utility problems, property discoveries, assistance to motorists, fires, alarms, crank calls, unspecified requests, and other.[4]

According to Scott, the failure of other investigators to define each category carefully was a serious problem because "the addition or subtraction of a particular call from some categories can cause a large change in the percentage of calls attributable to that category."[5] Scott was concerned with the problem of coding calls as crime or noncrime. Many police activities involve a little of each and cannot be coded accurately into two discrete categories. As a result, the various studies are not comparable, as it is not possible to determine how specific types of calls in the various studies were coded.

These studies of the allocation of police time have important implications for police recruitment, as well as for understanding the role conflicts of those already in policing. If people are attracted to policing because they think most of an officer's time is spent in exciting chases of dangerous criminals and have no concept of the often dull periods of waiting for action, they might be unhappy as police officers. If they have no concept of the service functions of policing and are not trained to perform those functions, life on the beat might come as an unpleasant surprise.

An additional problem is that police officers may encounter supervisors who do not give equal credit to successful performance of the three police functions. Catching dangerous criminals might result in a faster promotion than performing order maintenance or community service functions successfully. Police officers may experience a similar response from their colleagues and from the community.

5-1c   Proactive versus Reactive Policing: Domestic Violence

Regardless of how police activities are categorized, police clearly do not spend most of their time engaging in the stereotype held by many: catching dangerous criminals. In fact, many police officers spend very little time in actual crime detection. Most police work is *reactive*, not *proactive*; that is, police are dependent on the assistance of victims, witnesses, and other citizens to report crimes.

There have been some changes in recent years. In Chapter 3, we examined problem-oriented and community-oriented policing, whereby police identify and try to eliminate problems that may be creating a criminal situation. Police have become proactive in other areas, too, such as identifying and arresting domestic violence offenders.

In recent years, more attention has been paid to **domestic violence**, which involves spouses abusing each other, parents abusing children, and children abusing each other or their parents. Some studies include courtship violence, also referred to as *intimate partner violence (IPV)*, which includes violence toward a former spouse, girlfriend, or boyfriend. As noted in Figure 5-1, according to the Bureau of Justice Statistics (BJS), the percentage of households in which a member experienced IPV was down in 2004 as compared to 1994. The data in Figure 5-1 are based on interviews with IPV victims. According to respondents, less than half of 1 percent of all households reported IPV in 2004. Figure 5-1 shows that between 2002 and 2004, there was no significant change in the percentage of households experiencing IPV.

According to the BJS, during 2004, women were more likely than men to be victimized by an intimate. Approximately 7 in 10 women who reported being raped stated that they were assaulted by an intimate or a friend or an acquaintance or a relative.[6] In an analysis of data on family violence, the BJS reported that, although the rates between 1993 and 2002 fell by 60 percent, family violence continued to account for a significant portion of violent crimes in the United States, as high as 33 percent of all violent crimes in 18 states and the District of Columbia. Further, two-thirds of all murders of persons

Domestic violence   The causing of serious physical harm or the threatening of such harm to a member of one's family or household, including spouses, ex-spouses, parents, children, persons otherwise related by blood, persons living in the household, or persons who lived there formerly. May include relationships of persons who do not live together but who have had or currently have intimate relationships, such as courtship.

Intimate partner violence (IPV)   Violence toward a current or former spouse, girlfriend, or boyfriend.

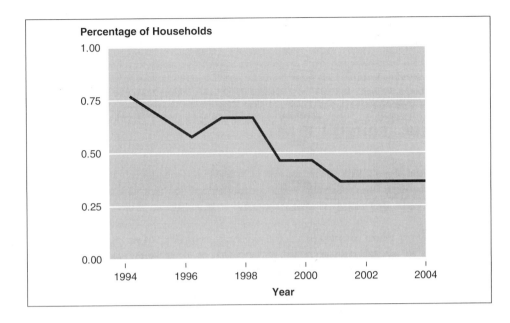

Percentage of Households

Figure 5-1
Intimate Partner Violence,
1994–2004
Source: Patsy Klaus, *Crime and the Nation's Households, 2004,* Bureau of Justice Statistics Bulletin (Washington, D.C.: U.S. Department of Justice, April 2006), p. 2.

under the age of 13 are committed by family members. And 15 percent of the nearly 500,000 inmates incarcerated for violent crimes committed crimes against a family member.[7] Spotlight 5-1 contains additional information regarding family violence.

Data reported by the National Center for Injury Prevention and Control, based on analyses of other studies, indicate that each year, almost 5.3 million incidents of IPV occur among women 18 and over, and 3.2 million incidents of IPV victimize men. Most of these victimizations are relatively minor assault, such as pushing and shoving, but some are serious, resulting in approximately two million injuries and 1,300 deaths each year. Additionally, each year more than one million women and 371,000 men are stalked by intimates. During their lifetimes, approximately 29 percent of women and 22 percent of men experience some form of physical, sexual, or psychological IPV. Finally, between 4 percent and 8 percent of pregnant women are victims of IPV.[8]

IPV is not limited to heterosexual couples. The first lesbian couple to enter into Vermont's civil union provision on 1 July 2000 stated in December 2005 that they were ending their relationship, and one partner applied for and obtained a restraining order against the other, claiming that she knocked a hole in the wall while they were arguing and threatened to harm a friend.[9]

In earlier times, violence among intimates, and especially within the family, was considered a domestic problem, not a crime, and if police intervened at all, they did so mainly as mediators, not as law enforcement officers. Arrests were rarely made. In recent years, legislation has changed this. For example, the federal Violence against Women Act of 1984 provides some protection for victims of domestic violence, sexual assault, and stalking. In 1996, the Department of Justice published its final rules covering federal grants authorized by this legislation. Included are provisions for programs that train police for handling domestic violence cases, for developing policies providing sanctions for officers who refuse to arrest in such cases, for developing guidelines for when to arrest in domestic violence cases, and so on.[10] After the passage of that act, many states enacted statutes giving police discretion to arrest in misdemeanor cases they had not witnessed. Many police departments began training officers in how to handle domestic violence, and some jurisdictions instituted a policy of mandatory arrests in domestic violence cases. But the evidence on the results of police arrests in domestic violence cases is contradictory.

Under a mandatory arrest policy, the police officer must arrest the alleged perpetrator of domestic violence if there is sufficient evidence that violence has occurred. This

Spotlight 5-1 Highlights of Family Violence Data

Family Violence Reported to Police

Approximately 60 percent of family violence victimizations were reported to police between 1998 and 2002. The reporting rate among female victims was not significantly greater than the reporting rate among male victims.

The most common reason victims of family violence cited for not reporting the crime to police was that the incident was a "private/personal matter" (34 percent). Another 12 percent of non-reporting family violence victims did not report the crime in order to "protect the offender."

Among the 2.1 million incidents of family violence reported to police between 1998 and 2002, 36 percent resulted in an arrest.

Family Violence Recorded by Police

Family violence accounted for 33 percent of all violent crimes recorded by police in 18 states and the District of Columbia in 2000. Of these more than 207,000 family violence crimes, about half (53 percent, or 110,000) were crimes between spouses.

Among crimes recorded by police, 2 percent of family violence involved a firearm, compared to 6 percent of nonfamily violence. A weapon was used in 16 percent of family and 21 percent of nonfamily violence.

About 6 percent of all violent crime recorded by police in 2000 involved more than one offender victimizing a lone victim. The exception was stranger crime, in which 14 percent of incidents involved multiple offenders victimizing a lone victim.

About 49 percent of family violence crimes recorded by police resulted in an arrest. Males comprised 77 percent of suspected family violence offenders arrested in 2000.

State Prosecution of Family Assault

Of the approximately 1,500 defendants charged with felony assault during May 2000 in the state courts of 11 large counties, about a third were charged with family violence.

Among felony assault defendants charged with family violence in state courts, 84 percent had at least one prior arrest for either a felony or a misdemeanor (not necessarily for family violence), and 73 percent had been previously convicted of some type of felony or misdemeanor (not necessarily family violence).

Nearly half of felony assault defendants charged with family violence were released pending case disposition.

Among the 1,500 felony assault cases, the probability of the case leading to conviction (felony or misdemeanor) was

greater for family assault defendants (71 percent) than nonfamily assault defendants (61 percent).

State courts sentenced 83 percent of persons convicted of assault (both family and nonfamily) to either prison or jail. Among felony assault defendants convicted in state courts:

- Sixty-eight percent of incarceration sentences for family assault were to jail.
- Sixty-two percent of incarceration sentences for nonfamily assault were to prison.
- Forty-five percent of persons sent to prison for family assault received a sentence of more than two years, compared to 77 percent of nonfamily assault offenders sent to prison.

Federal Prosecution of Domestic Violence

Persons suspected of domestic violence made up 4 percent of the total 18,653 federal suspects referred to U.S. attorneys for alleged violent crimes from 2000 to 2002.

Of the 757 suspects referred to U.S. attorneys for domestic violence offenses between 2000 and 2002, most were firearm-related domestic violence offenses, rather than interstate domestic violence offenses:

- The Bureau of Alcohol, Tobacco, Firearms and Explosives accounted for 80 percent of all referrals for firearm-related domestic violence.
- The FBI accounted for 72 percent of all interstate domestic violence referrals.

Federal courts convicted 90 percent of defendants adjudicated for an interstate domestic violence offense. Among defendants convicted in federal courts:

- Seventy-nine percent of convictions were the product of a guilty plea, and the remaining 21 percent were the product of conviction following a trial.
- Most were male (96 percent), under age 40 (67 percent), white (72 percent), and non-Hispanic (95 percent).
- Four in five defendants had a prior adult conviction.

Of 47 federal defendants sentenced for an interstate domestic violence offense between 2000 and 2002, 91 percent received a prison term with a median length of 60 months.

Source: Matthew R. Durose et al., Office of Justice Programs, Bureau of Justice Statistics, *Family Violence Statistics* (Washington, D.C.: U.S. Department of Justice, June 2005), p. 2.

approach has resulted in more arrests in domestic violence cases in which police act on their own, without waiting for victims to insist on pressing charges.

Some of the earlier evaluations of higher arrest rates in domestic violence cases show that this approach—as compared to a nonarrest policy—is more successful in preventing further domestic violence. In assessing the results of the Minneapolis Domestic Violence Experiment, Lawrence W. Sherman and Richard A. Berk concluded that

> arrest was the most effective of three standard methods police use to reduce domestic violence. The other police methods—attempting to counsel both parties or sending assailants away—were found to be considerably less effective in deterring future violence in the cases examined.[11]

The Minneapolis findings were not replicated in a similar study in Omaha, Nebraska, however, leading its authors to suggest that their findings

> will undoubtedly cast some doubt on the deterrent power of a mandatory or even a presumptory arrest policy for cases of misdemeanor domestic assault. At this point, researchers and policymakers are in the awkward position of having conflicting results from two experiments and no clear, unambiguous direction from the research on this issue.[12]

Other studies report that the first time an offender is apprehended by police after a domestic violence call is the most potent one and that arrest is most effective at that time. Arrest also is more effective if followed by court-mandated treatment. Subsequent monitorings of these offenders reveal that the more educated the offender, the more likely it is that he or she will not repeat domestic violence offenses.[13]

Lawrence W. Sherman examined what is known or not known about domestic violence, particularly the effect of arrest, and concluded that,

> after more than a decade of evaluating arrest for misdemeanor domestic violence, we still have much to learn. The jigsaw puzzle of diverse results in different cities has not been put together, and too many pieces are still missing.[14]

Another study regarding policing spousal violence reported that, although police were not likely to arrest in such cases (arrests were not made in 76 percent of the cases), arrests were no more likely in other types of violence cases.[15] And an analysis of police responses to domestic violence in the past few decades concluded that authorities had yet to develop a set of tools or responses that "work well across a variety of situations in reducing the likelihood of future violence" within domestic environments.[16]

In another analysis, criminologists Richard B. Felson and Jeff Ackerman examined arrests for domestic and other assaults. These researchers emphasized the importance of looking at the types of violence and the degree of seriousness and suggested that "moral outrage" about domestic violence could lead some researchers to overlook these important variables. The fact that police refused to arrest in a situation involving minor domestic violence does not mean that police are treating that situation differently than a minor assault against a nonspouse or an intimate. In short, domestic violence should not be examined in isolation but, rather, in the general context of violence. Felson and Ackerman concluded that police decisions regarding arrests are affected by the relationship between the suspect and the victim. In particular:

> The police are less likely to arrest strangers than nonstrangers for assault because they are often unable to identify them. On the other hand, when the police are able to identify the suspect, they show lenience when the suspect knows the victim. Their leniency is not due to a tolerance for intimate violence or violence against women; they are more likely to make an arrest in incidents involving intimate violence than in incidents involving other nonstrangers. Rather, leniency in nonstranger incidents is due to the reluctance of victims to sign complaints, the absence of witnesses, and the unwillingness of the police to arrest suspects for minor acts of violence against people they know.[17]

Felson and Ackerman, along with Catherine A. Gallagher, published the results of a later study in 2005, in which they analyzed National Crime Victimization Survey data to determine whether domestic violence is more likely to be repeated under two circumstances: reporting it to the police and arrest of the suspect. The investigators concluded that there is a strong deterrent effect when such incidents are reported to the police but that the deterrent effect of arrest is very small. Further, there is no strong evidence of retaliation by the suspect against the alleged victim who calls police. The investigators concluded that the best deterrent effect with regard to domestic violence incidents is for the victim and third parties to report those incidents to the police.[18]

These and other studies suggest that we need to continue evaluating the best ways to handle domestic violence, a situation that remains one of conflict for police. Even where mandatory arrest policies are in effect, police encounter alleged victims who refuse to cooperate. Many spouses do not want their partners arrested; if police insist and make the arrest, the complaining partner may become hostile, belligerent, and even violent. Thus, what appears to be a positive change in policing may result in greater role conflict for police officers, including violence against them. Mandatory arrests may also increase the number of cases beyond a reasonable level for some prosecution offices. Researchers who studied the situation in Milwaukee, Wisconsin, after the adoption of a mandatory arrest policy in domestic violence cases in 1987 concluded the following:

> Good intentions do not always result in good public policy. Arresting more batterers does not necessarily result in more prosecutions. Our results show that prosecuting more domestic violence cases can increase court delay, increase pretrial recidivism, and lower conviction rates. The domestic violence literature is becoming filled with examples of how well-intended policies regarding domestic violence can backfire....Good intentions of policy makers need to be balanced with a realistic view of how the criminal justice system functions and what the actual effects of new policies are likely to be.[19]

Some recent research evidence, however, indicates that most laws do have the effect of reducing domestic violence, although fewer of those laws "appear to influence police involvement and none relate to more arrests. This suggests that laws may deter would-be offenders from harming family and partners."[20]

Other variables that should be considered in analyzing domestic violence and policing are those involving reasons that victims do or do not report the violence. Richard B. Felson and three of his colleagues analyzed the reasons for reporting or not reporting domestic violence. They found several reasons domestic violence victims are less likely than other victims to report violence: privacy concerns, fear of reprisal, and the desire to protect their assailants. But they also found that domestic violence victims are *more* likely to report violence than are other victims because they see the violence as more serious, as it occurs in the home. The researchers concluded, "As a result of these and other offsetting factors, victims of domestic violence are just as likely as other victims of assault to call the police."[21]

One final area of domestic violence and policing that is gaining more attention is police violence against their own intimate partners. That issue is discussed in the next section and in Spotlight 5-2, in an analysis of police suicides.

5-1d Stress

In recent years, increasing attention has been given to stress and its effects on people in various occupations and professions. A variety of harmful physical results occur when individuals do not handle stress successfully. Although all people may be affected in some way by on-the-job stress, studies have found evidence of particularly high stress rates in some jobs; policing has been called the most stressful.

Attention to the stressors of policing is evident in such books as *CopShock: Surviving Posttraumatic Stress Disorder (PTSD)*, written by Allen R. Kates, member, American Academy of Experts in Traumatic Stress. The book recounts the experiences of officers who have felt stress, talks about how to deal with the results of stress, and provides resources on the topic.[22]

Another book, *Managing Police Stress*, was written by a former police officer, Wayne D. Ford, who shot and killed a suspect in self-defense. Subsequently, Ford had a heart

Spotlight 5-2   Police Suicides

Suicide is always a shock to the family and friends of the person who chooses to end his or her life, but the suicide of a police officer is perhaps less expected and thus even more shocking. When that officer has been accused of domestic abuse and kills his or her spouse before committing suicide, the reaction is rage as well as shock, especially as details are released that show the possibility that at least some people should have known of the difficult situations and perhaps intervened.

On 26 April 2003, David Brame, police chief in Tacoma, Washington, fatally shot his wife, Crystal, and then killed himself. Two young children (ages eight and five) witnessed the killings. Records show that in 1981 two psychologists concluded that Brame should not be hired as a rookie officer. A woman claimed that in 1988 Brame had raped her. In 2001, a city human resource official reported that Brame's past might embarrass the city. There were reasons to take Brame's gun from him the day before he killed his wife and himself. After she filed for divorce in early 2003, Crystal spoke to her family and others about years of alleged domestic violence by her spouse. Some evidence indicates that police officials knew about the allegations, and investigations are ongoing. Crystal's family filed a $75-million lawsuit against the police department and the city. The suit was settled for $12 million in 2005.[1]

In the adjacent state of Oregon, at midnight on 26 April 2003, 32-year-old police detective Benjamin Crosby went to the Sherwood Police Department holding cell while off duty and shot himself. He had left a note outside, warning that his body was inside. In an apparent effort to answer questions, he had left several letters about his action, stating, "This is a suicide, not a homicide." He had left a letter for his

seven-year-old son. Detective Crosby had been depressed; his wife declined comment.[2]

The 1995 bombing of the federal building in Oklahoma City, resulting in the deaths of 168 persons, also claimed at least one police officer who was on duty during the tragedy. In 1996, Sergeant Terrance Yeakey, 30, took his own life. He left no note, but friends suggested that, although he had saved four people in the Oklahoma City disaster, he may have felt guilty about not saving more. Sergeant Yeakey was one of the first officers to arrive on the scene, but after he rescued four persons, he fell two stories in the building, injuring his back.[3]

Police suicides are not limited to the United States. In a 2003 Hong Kong, China, report, two police suicides were noted, with the comment that police commit suicide for the same reasons as many other people: depression, marital stress, and work problems. One of the examples cited was an officer who had killed himself after losing his pension savings through gambling. Another was suffering from psychosis. One of the writers stated, "Every profession has working problems; it depends on how you face them." He noted, however, the importance of training people to understand and accept those problems.[4] In June 2003, a Singapore news source reported the increase in police suicides in India and noted that "at least five stressed-out policemen a day seek premature retirement."[5]

1. Summarized from multiple media sources.
2. "Sherwood Officer Remembered for His Caring," *The Oregonian* (29 April 2003), p. 1B.
3. "Policeman in Bombing Rescue in Oklahoma City Is a Suicide," *New York Times* (11 May 1996), p. 9.
4. "Tragic Police Suffer Like the Rest of Us," *Hong Kong Imail* (26 June 2003).
5. "Cops on the Edge," *The Straits Times* (Singapore).

attack while on duty, thus enduring another stressing event that can affect any professional. Ford's book is based on the material of his two days of seminars on police stress.[23]

Some police departments have developed stress reduction programs. An example is one sponsored by the National Institute of Justice: "Program for the Reduction of Stress for New York City Police Officers and Their Families," authored by W. W. Genet. This program expanded on a previous one that was developed after 21 officers in that city committed suicide in 1994 and 1995. The purpose was to establish a volunteer peer support program. The program involves, among other techniques, the following:

- The use of volunteer peer support officers
- The creation of a database of mental health clinicians trained on issues experienced by police personnel and their families
- The establishment of a 24-hour help line
- Interagency and public-private collaborations.[24]

Stress in policing is not confined to patrol officers. Undercover officers may experience the same stresses as patrol officers, along with some other stressors, such as the need for secrecy, unique to undercover work. Police administrators may also experience stress.

This discussion may imply that stress in policing is no different from stress in other occupations and professions. But there is one major difference; police are trained to injure or kill, and if the situation requires, they are expected to do so. Indeed, they may be sanctioned for not using their weapons. It is this requirement, say some officers, that is unique in creating stress in policing.

Long before the tragic and shocking terrorist events of 9/11, the U.S. Commission on Civil Rights emphasized the need to provide stress management programs and services for police. The commission noted that most police departments lacked such programs, despite the emphasis on stress as "an important underlying factor in police misconduct incidents."[25]

Police and Suicide

One reaction to stress is to take one's own life. Suicides among police have received more attention in recent years, especially because some of the suicides have involved violence against others. For example, in 2002, Edward Lutes, a 17-year veteran of the Seaside Heights (New Jersey) Police Department, killed five people and injured his boss before killing himself. Lutes was angry at his neighbors, one of whom was tried but acquitted of sexually molesting Lutes's daughter. The neighbor and his wife took care of the daughter each morning after Lutes left for work and before the daughter went to school. Lutes killed both neighbors and then crossed the street and killed another couple and their son. He then drove 20 miles to the police chief's home and shot and wounded him before shooting himself. Lutes was found dead in his car. These shootings occurred shortly after a retired Newark (New Jersey) police officer, John W. Mabie, 72, was arrested and indicted for killing his granddaughter and three neighbors not far from the neighborhood in which Lutes and his murder victims lived.[26] In October 2003, Mabie entered guilty pleas to the murder counts. Spotlight 5-2 discusses other examples of police suicides.

There are numerous formal efforts to prevent police suicides. One example is NPSF—the National P.O.L.I.C.E. Suicide Foundation. The services of NPSF extend beyond police to such law enforcement officers as those with the Internal Revenue Service (IRS), paramedics, firefighters, and other emergency workers. The stated mission of NPSF is "to provide suicide awareness and prevention training programs and support services that will meet the psychological and spiritual needs of emergency workers and their families."[27]

The Impact of AIDS

A second major source of stress for police is the fear of contracting the human immunodeficiency virus (HIV), which causes acquired immune deficiency syndrome (AIDS). AIDS is a deadly disease that affects the immune system, leaving the body unable to fight infections. It can be acquired through exchanges of body fluids, including sexual activity with an infected person, through use of an unsterile needle, and by means of a transfusion of tainted blood. The virus can also be transmitted by a pregnant woman to her fetus.

One other issue of concern is police officers who have AIDS. Although there is no evidence that AIDS is transmitted by casual contact, many people are concerned about contacts with persons infected with AIDS. Colleagues may react negatively to an officer who has AIDS.

In August 2000, a news article focused on New York City police officers with AIDS who had come to the attention of a retired officer, who counseled them and shared his own experiences with the disease. Stephen P. Yurcik described his counselees, who did not even know each others' names, as follows:

> To their fellow officers, they are indistinguishable from the rest of the 40,000 men and women who police New York City, but in their own minds, AIDS has set them a world apart. For many, it weighs them down not only with the fear of death, but also with a secret they are desperate to keep from their fellow officers.[28]

In 2003, the village of Westmont, Illinois, settled a suit with a plaintiff who claimed he was refused a job with the police department because he is HIV positive. The applicant, who received $125,000 in the settlement, was a police academy graduate who had worked in another police department. The Westmont department required medical examinations of its applicants, but in the settlement, the department agreed that it would no longer test its applicants for HIV. The department also agreed that medical exams would be limited to issues relevant to policing. The plaintiff in this case, who refused to reveal his name, called the settlement "an encouragement for people who have been discriminated against, that they do have rights and they can stand up for them." A federal district court had refused to dismiss the case. The settlement ended the litigation.[29]

And in 2006, a federal lawsuit was filed in Welch, a small community in West Virginia, against the police department, alleging that the police failed to provide CPR to a gay man for fear that the man was HIV positive and would infect officers.[30]

The Impact of Terrorism

Perhaps the greatest stressors police face as a group are those related to terrorism. This is not to suggest that police have any greater concern or fear for themselves personally but that the demands placed on law enforcement by the 9/11 terrorist attacks have created significant problems. Not only the FBI but also many local departments reassigned officers from their usual jobs to counterterrorist task forces. Some officers were required to leave their jobs and serve in the war in Iraq. Others were killed in the 9/11 terrorist attacks; many retired. Police departments were required to answer and investigate many calls concerning substances that might be deadly anthrax or that might be related to suspected terrorists. Local departments located in cities with airports faced the need to provide those facilities with added security.

A little over a month after the 9/11 terrorist attacks, officials expressed concern that the diversion of FBI agents to counterterrorism task forces and a deemphasis on drug-related offenses and bank robberies placed increasing pressure on local departments to provide law enforcement in these areas. And most departments were already facing budget problems as a result of terrorism and other problems. Even the canine patrol was overworked in many cities, with the added calls for bomb checks. In Los Angeles, for example, officers received 44 bomb threat calls on one day; none were substantiated.

Crime prevention may suffer, but local departments must do their part in assisting federal officials to prevent terrorism. As Figure 5-2 shows, most are attempting to do so, with approximately 90 percent of local police departments serving populations of 250,000 or more reporting in the latest data (for 2003) that they have a written plan in place for handling a terrorist attack.

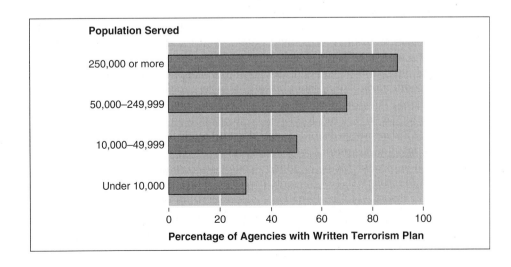

Figure 5-2
Local Police Departments with Anti-Terrorist Plans
Source: Matthew J. Hickman and Brian A. Reaves, Bureau of Justice Statistics, *Local Police Departments, 2003* (Washington, D.C.: U.S. Department of Justice, May 2006), front cover.

State police have also been taking a more active role in counterterrorism since 9/11. A survey of the 50 states, reported in 2005, indicated that 70 percent of state police agencies reported that they had increased their allocations for resources for homeland security responsibilities. According to the report, state police agencies are more important than ever in assisting the interaction of local and federal law enforcement agencies. State patrol officers are critical in patrolling the state highways and would play a critical role if mass evacuations were required in disaster areas.[31]

Finally, a big issue for local police departments in their fight against terrorism is funding, much of which comes from the federal Department of Homeland Security (DHS). In June 2006, for example, New York City's antiterrorism funding from DHS was cut sharply. DHS began using a risk-based allotment formula, resulting in increased allotments for cities such as Charlotte, North Carolina; Omaha, Nebraska; and Louisville, Kentucky; but with reductions for others, including both cities hit by the 9/11 attacks. Federal funding for New York City and Washington, D.C. was cut by 40 percent, to $124.5 million for the former (the highest allocation for any city) and $46.5 million for the latter.[32]

5-2 The Police Subculture

Subculture A group of significant size whose behavior differs significantly from the behavior of the dominant groups of society.

One way of handling dilemmas, role conflicts, and stress is to withdraw into a more comfortable situation. If sufficient numbers of a group do so, a subgroup, or **subculture**, forms. The subculture has values and expectations that distinguish it from the dominant culture and that solidify its members.

Police can become isolated from people who might be their friends if it were not because of the officers' authority and responsibility to regulate the daily lives of citizens. Traffic violations and laws regulating the use of alcohol and other drugs are examples. It would be difficult to form a close relationship with someone who was expected to enforce traffic or other laws that you might violate from time to time. Thus, many police confine their personal lives to their own families and other police and their families.

Earlier studies suggested that police were a homogeneous group who formed subcultures and manifested a distinct personality type. They were said to be authoritarian, cynical, punitive, rigid, physically aggressive, assertive, and impulsive risk takers.[33] Police were viewed as people who looked for negatives and who stereotyped situations, making quick judgments whenever they thought crime was involved. Such attitudes may lead to violence.

It was assumed that the best way to alleviate police cynicism was to increase their professionalism, but some studies reported that, although "commitment to a professional ideology reduces cynicism among police," the relationship between these two variables was more complex than earlier researchers had thought.[34] Thus, it is necessary to look more carefully at the dimensions of each of the variables: cynicism and professionalism.

There is some evidence of a relationship between professionalism and cynicism among police chiefs, although there are some differences when comparing chiefs with other police officers. Also, there are differences based on the duration of service. For example, cynicism "is highest for police chiefs during their early years and gradually declines with experience." Cynicism varies according to the size of the chief's police agency, with those in larger agencies showing less cynicism.[35]

Some evidence indicates that police officers, like police chiefs, become less cynical as their length of service increases.[36] Taken as a whole, research on police cynicism underscores the importance of looking carefully at all variables that might account for cynicism and analyzing those variables in their full complexity. It is not sufficient to find cynicism and professionalism (or any other trait) among police officers or chiefs and draw the conclusion that the relationship is a simple one. On the other hand, professionalism is important in policing, as it is in other occupations and professions.

Policing is also characterized by the *blue code of silence*, which means that police will not testify against each other or even report any improper behavior. In a 2001 lawsuit, a female officer was awarded $3 million in her claim against the Cook County (Chicago) Forest Preserve Department of Law Enforcement. Officer Cynthia Spina, one of approximately 100 officers in the department, only 9 of whom were women, complained about sexual harassment for four years. She alleged that she had been touched inappropriately, that sexual materials had been mailed to her home, and that she had often been subjected to sexual comments and stories. She had reported the behavior, but no action was taken as a result of her report. According to Spina's lawyer, the key witness in her client's successful case was Penny Harrington, the former police chief of Portland, Oregon, and the head of the National Center for Women in Policing. Harrington "explained police culture and practices, what the 'code of silence' is, and what breaking it means for a police officer, and why Spina is essentially unemployable as a police officer due to her courage in confronting this harassment and retaliation." Harrington explained how officers shun and isolate those among them who complain to officials about the behavior of other officers. A clinical forensic psychiatrist testified that Spina suffered from "an adjustment disorder brought on by the stress of the harassment and the department's failure to respond." A federal judge, stating that $3 million for years of sexual harassment was "monstrously excessive," gave the plaintiff the option of accepting $300,000 or going to trial again on the issue of damages only. The case was settled in March 2003, with $375,000 for Spina and $1.15 million for attorneys' fees.[37]

Victor E. Kappeler, Richard D. Sluder, and Geoffrey P. Alpert defined three elements that characterize police culture: bravery, autonomy, and secrecy. According to these investigators, "The police subculture stresses these sentiments and teaches new officers the value of adopting these attitudes—and the consequence of not conforming." They also advocate that the police subculture is dominated by two cultural themes: the need for solidarity and the isolation of police from the rest of society.[38]

5-3 Police Misconduct

Police officers have many opportunities for engaging in improper behavior, and they have the power to coerce individuals to comply. One area of misconduct that has received some attention lately is sexual misconduct, but in recent years, most reported police misconduct has involved *corruption*, defined as follows:

> A public official is corrupt if he accepts money or money's worth for doing something that he is under a duty to do anyway, that he is under a duty not to do, or to exercise a legitimate discretion for improper reasons.[39]

The possibility for corruption varies, with the greater opportunities available in larger cities, but corruption can be found in all types of police departments.

James Q. Wilson analyzed police corruption according to the type of organization in a police department. He defined three types of law enforcement styles and found those styles to be related to the degree of police corruption.[40] According to Wilson, most police corruption is found in departments characterized by the *watchman style*, in which police are expected to maintain order, not regulate conduct. Low salaries and the expectation that police will have other jobs increase the probabilities that police will be involved in corruption.

Corruption is found to a lesser degree in departments characterized by the *legalistic style*, with its emphasis on providing formal police training, recruiting from the middle class, offering greater promotional opportunities, and viewing law as a means to an end, rather than an end in itself. Formal sanctions are used more frequently than informal ones, with police giving less attention to community service and order maintenance than to law enforcement.

Corruption is not a serious problem in the third type of style, the *service style*. In this management style, law enforcement and order maintenance are combined, with an emphasis on good relationships between the police and the community. Police command is decentralized, with police on patrol working out of specialized units. Higher education and promotional opportunities are emphasized, and police are expected to lead exemplary private lives.

Lawrence W. Sherman analyzed police corruption according to types. The first, the *rotten apples*, refers to a department characterized by a few police officers who accept bribes and engage in other forms of corruption. Generally, those people are uniformed patrol officers, but they are loners who will accept bribes for overlooking traffic violations, licensing ordinances, or crimes. Some officers work in groups, termed *rotten pockets*, accepting bribes for nonenforcement of the law. Many members of the vice squad are found in this type.[41]

The second type of corruption, according to Sherman, is *pervasive organized corruption*, describing the highly organized hierarchical organization of the political processes of the community, which goes beyond the police force. Some police departments are characterized by widespread but unorganized corruption, labeled as *pervasive unorganized corruption*.[42]

5-3a   The Knapp Commission and Its Aftermath

In 1970, in response to allegations of corruption in New York City, Mayor John V. Lindsay issued an executive order establishing the Knapp Commission. The 1972 commission's report disclosed widespread police corruption. Rookies were initiated into the system quickly, many became corrupt, and some grew cynical. The commission found that police were involved with organized crime (the most lucrative form of corruption); payoffs from citizens, especially for traffic citations; and the acceptance of money for overlooking violations of licensing ordinances.[43]

New York City Police Department officials contend that only a very small percentage of police officers are involved in corruption. They say that undercover tests of integrity, whereby some officers are assigned to make secret reports on the behavior of other officers, have eliminated most corruption. Others contend that corruption has not been eliminated in the New York City Police Department or any other; they hold that corruption is inevitable. According to one authority,

> corruption is endemic to policing. The very nature of the police function is bound to subject officers to tempting offers….Solutions, so far, seem inadequate and certainly are not likely to produce permanent results.[44]

There is evidence that, even after the Knapp Commission report, corruption continued in the New York City Police Department, but the nature of it changed. According to one federal prosecutor, between 1972, when the Knapp Commission ended its work, and 1993, when the Mollen Commission (discussed in the following section) began its work, the "pervasive low-level corruption…was greatly lessened, if not eliminated," but "the serious corruption got worse."[45]

5-3b   The Mollen Commission

In the fall of 1993, the Mollen Commission, headed by former judge Milton Mollen, began a study of police corruption in New York City. In referring to the commission's interim report, published in December of that year, a *New York Times* editorial stated these findings:

> [P]ockets of police corruption and brutality exist because the ingrained culture of the Police Department tolerates wrongdoing, even protects the wrongdoer. The panel recommends shaking up the department's anti-corruption bureaucracy, and appointing an outside panel to conduct investigations.[46]

The final report of the commission was issued in July 1994. This report concluded that corruption was less common in New York City than it was during the Knapp

Commission study, but that its nature had changed. In 1994, more officers sought opportunities to move beyond bribery to violating other laws. Some officers stole routinely from drug dealers after stopping them for traffic violations, and some used violence to carry out their thefts. The commission found that corruption flourished in some parts of New York City because of opportunities but also because the police culture placed a greater emphasis on loyalty than on integrity. The majority of New York City's officers were not involved in corruption, but they feared reporting those who were.[47]

The Mollen Commission coined a new word to characterize the pervasive falsifications they found by police: *testilying*. That word was used in the spring of 2003, when the Houston (Texas) Police Department was under fire for corruption for falsifying information in its crime lab, although in reference to this scandal, a state representative, Harold Dutton, said, "We have a name for that in Texas, and that is perjury." Noted appellate attorney and Harvard Law School professor Alan M. Dershowitz has stated that testilying occurs because too many people focus on guilt or innocence, rather than on the process itself. Dershowitz told the U.S. House of Representatives Judiciary Committee that,

> clearly, the most heinous brand of lying is the giving of false testimony that results in the imprisonment or even execution of an innocent person. Less egregious, but still quite serious, is false testimony that results in the conviction of a person who committed the criminal conduct but whose rights were violated in a manner that would preclude conviction if the police were to testify truthfully.[48]

The Mollen Commission's 1994 conclusion that the NYPD could not police itself and needed an independent commission to do so was followed in 1995 with the origination of the Mayor's Commission to Combat Police Corruption. The commission consists of six commissioners, all lawyers, who serve without pay; four staff lawyers; and a $500,000 budget. Since June 2005, the commission has been headed by Michael F. Armstrong, who served as chief counsel to the Knapp Commission. This latest police commission conducts audits on the NYPD and analyzes its anticorruption strategies.[49]

By far the most shocking incident of corruption in the NYPD is recent. In April 2006, a jury convicted two highly decorated former NYPD detectives of eight murders and other charges associated with their links to organized crime. Louis Eppolito, 57, and Steven Caracappa, 64, could have been sentenced to life in prison without parole for their respective roles in what one prosecutor called "the bloodiest, most violent betrayal of the badge this city has ever seen." Bail was revoked immediately after the verdict, and the two defendants were jailed. At the trial, the prosecution offered evidence that the two defendants themselves carried out two of the eight murders and delivered the victims of the other six to their Mafia colleagues. Eppolito and Caracappa were charged with carrying out the murders between 1986 and 1990. During those years, they were employed by the NYPD and, charged the prosecution, also on the payroll of Mafia families. Both defendants were sentenced to the maximum: life in prison without the possibility of parole.[50]

Subsequently, despite overwhelming evidence that Caracappa and Eppolito were guilty of conspiring to take part in at least eight murders for the Mafia, the trial judge reversed these convictions for a technical reason—the **statute of limitations** (five years) had expired for conspiracy. He left open the possibility that the two men could be tried on a drug indictment (for both) and a money laundering indictment for Eppolito. The judge denied bail for both men. One article referred to the former police detectives as having an unusual legal status that one might call "guilty but acquitted."[51]

Corruption in police departments is not confined to the NYPD, however, and many in that department take great pride in their jobs, referring to themselves as "New York's Finest," as the title of Professions 5-1 notes. Professions 5-1 contains information on the NYPD, which might interest some students; those who prefer to check out another police department with the possibility of applying can check the website for that city.

▶ **Statute of limitations** The time limit in which to bring a charge for a crime. The statute of limitations may differ from jurisdiction to jurisdiction, but most have no limitations on filing murder charges.

Professions 5-1

Become a Police Officer; Join New York's Finest

Benefits

Salary*

Start receiving full pay and benefits from your first day of recruit training ($25,100 per annum). Upon the completion of the Police Academy (six months), your annual salary increases to $32,700. Salaries will continue to increase every year, and upon completion of 5½ years of service, base salary will increase to $59,588. [See Figure 1.] In addition to these base salaries, there is overtime earning, holiday pay, night differential, and uniform allowance.

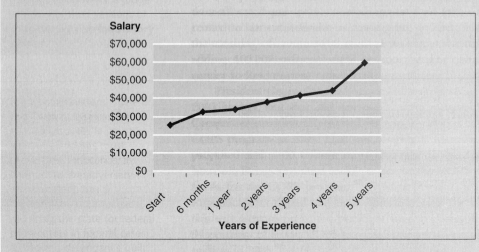

Salary

Figure 1
Salary Increases Over the First 5½ Years

Annual Base Salaries for Officers Hired during January 2006 or After
Police Academy (first six months): $25,100 (annualized)
Upon completion of six months: $32,700

Upon completion of 1½ years: $34,000
Upon completion of 2½ years: $38,000
Upon completion of 3½ years: $41,500
Upon completion of 4½ years: $44,100
Upon completion of 5½ years: $59,588

Allegations of corruption have also arisen in other police departments, but the frequency and magnitude, along with the media attention, are greater in large departments. Spotlight 5-3 discusses a recent corruption scandal in the Los Angeles Police Department.

5-3c   Drugs and Policing

The nation's declared war on drugs presents criminal justice systems and police with one of their most frustrating problems. The escalation of drug trafficking has resulted in violence, distorted and ruined lives, enormous expense, and a crushing blow to all elements of criminal justice systems. Jails and prisons are overcrowded, due in large part to drug offenders, many of whom are creating a new underworld within prisons, with the result that some prison correctional officers have been corrupted. Civil cases are backed up for years to enable courts to process the drug cases.

Police face the difficulty of confronting the massive drug problem without sufficient resources, whereas drug offenders have resources to tempt officers who earn relatively low salaries in highly stressful jobs. Police patrol officers are at high risk of corruption by drug dealers because of the arrest power, but drugs also lead to corruption at other levels of law enforcement. Police have been known to extort money or property from

Additional Benefits

- 20 paid vacation days your first year
- 27 paid vacation days after 5 years of service
- Unlimited sick leave with full pay
- A choice of paid medical programs
- Prescription, dental, and eye glass coverage
- Annuity fund
- Deferred Compensation Plan
- Optional retirement at one-half salary after 20 years of service
- Annual $12,000 Variable Supplement Fund (upon retirement)
- Annual banking of $12,000 Variable Supplement Fund after 20 years of service (if not retiring)
- Excellent promotional opportunities
- Educational opportunities
- Additional benefits are available to military personnel

Career Opportunities

The NYPD administers promotional exams for each rank above police officer every two to three years.
It's a great place to advance....

- 1 in 6 uniformed members of the NYPD are Detectives. A Detective's (3rd grade) average earning is $88,000.** (Promotion to Detective is not based on a promotional exam; it's based on merit.)
- 1 in 7 uniformed members of the NYPD are Sergeants. A Sergeant's average earning is $91,000.**
- 1 in 20 uniformed members of the NYPD are Lieutenants. A Lieutenant's average earning is $105,000.**

Retirement Benefits

After 20 years of service, a retired Police Officer will receive:

- Estimated earnings of $46,000 per year, comprised of 50 percent of salary, longevity, night shift differential, overtime, and an annual $12,000 payment from a Variable Supplement Fund
  - A retired Police Officer could receive approximately $1.75 million when retired, assuming a life expectancy of 80 years. This figure is based on the age of appointment of 22 and the age of retirement of 42.
  - The dollar amount of $1.75 million is estimated on 2003 salaries and is not adjusted for inflation or for future raises.
  - This dollar amount will be higher for uniformed members who retire above the rank of Police Officer.
- Full health benefits
- Annuity Fund and Deferred Compensation Plan
  - The amount of the funds depends on the market value of the portfolio that the officer has chosen while active.

*These salaries do not include overtime earnings, night-shift differential, holiday pay and uniform allowance. There is also longevity pay every 5 years up to 20 years of service.
**These salaries include base salary, average overtime and night shift differential, holiday pay, and uniform allowance. The above ranks do enjoy the same additional benefits described above.

Source: "Join New York's Finest: The Nation's Premier Crime Fighters," http://www.nypd2.org/html/recruit/salary.html, accessed 6 June 2006.

drug dealers in exchange for not arresting them, to steal the drugs they seize from suspects, to accept bribes for tampering with evidence or committing perjury, to sell information about forthcoming drug raids, and so on.

A specific example of great proportion occurred in Tulia, Texas, population 5,000, where 38 defendants were convicted of drug offenses and sentenced to a total of 750 years in prison. These defendants were convicted primarily on the basis of the undercover work and testimonies of Tom Coleman, who lied about the evidence. Coleman was convicted of perjury and sentenced to 10 years probation but could not be charged with the more serious offense of aggravated perjury because the statute of limitations had run out. The defendants were incarcerated, but after the case was exposed nationally on *60 Minutes*, the Texas governor pardoned all of the inmates.[52]

5-4 Violence and the Police

Historically, police have been viewed as agents who are necessary for establishing law and order, often by applying justice on the spot. Although violence between police and citizens had been reported earlier, the violence and unrest that occurred in the 1960s led to demands for larger and better-trained police forces. During that decade, predominantly white police and minority citizens clashed in hot, crowded cities. Many student protesters also found themselves in conflict with the police, and the police experienced

Spotlight 5-3   The Los Angeles Police Department under Scrutiny

In September 1999, an officer of the Los Angeles Police Department (LAPD) was apprehended for stealing cocaine from an evidence room. This incident led to criminal allegations against the officer, Rafael Perez, and an investigation that resulted in the firing of numerous officers in the Rampart Division of the LAPD. The report on what was to be known as the Rampart corruption scandal was issued in March 2000 and included a list of 108 recommendations for changes. The department was criticized for a lack of training and supervision of officers, a lack of attention to citizen complaints, a "startling lack" of internal auditing, a "near universal ignorance" of the department's policies concerning the use of informants, and the framing and shooting of innocent persons.

The 350-page report concluded that mediocrity flourished within the LAPD, with internal policies often ignored by officers and others. The report began with an investigation of the anti-gang unit but was expanded to include other units. Police Chief Bernard C. Parks, in issuing the report, stated that many of the problems resulted from "people failing to do their jobs with a high level of consistency and integrity....Unfortunately, we found this to be true at all levels of the organization, including top managers, first-line supervisors, and line personnel." Parks concluded, "Clearly, pride in one's work and a commitment to do things correctly the first time seem to have waned."[1]

In February 2000, Perez was sentenced to five years in prison for stealing cocaine. Part of his plea bargain was that he would not be charged with other crimes to which he admitted, such as framing innocent persons by planting evidence on them and lying about these cases in court hearings, but that plea bargain did not prohibit federal prosecutors from charging Perez with any federal crimes he may have committed, which they did. In April 2001, Perez was released after serving only part of his five-year state sentence after the judge ruled that he had met the terms of his plea agreement and that he had been treated unfairly by being incarcerated in jail rather than in prison. Prison time, in contrast to jail time, may result in obtaining more days off a sentence due to good behavior. However, in a federal case, Perez was sentenced to two years in a federal prison for violating the civil rights of Javier Francisco Ovando, a former gang member who is paralyzed from the waist down after being shot by Perez and officer Nino Durden, who then planted a gun on Ovando and claimed that he was threatening them. Ovando was an innocent man who served nearly 3 years (of a 23-year sentence) but was freed as a result of the investigation into police corruption in the LAPD.

In November 2000, the city of Los Angeles settled with Ovando for $15 million, the largest settlement for police abuse in that city to that date. In April 2001, Durden, Perez's former partner, pleaded guilty to federal civil rights charges and for possessing an illicit weapon that he used to frame Ovando. Durden was sentenced to five years in prison.

In November 2000, Los Angeles officials agreed to enter into a consent decree to avoid an investigation by the U.S.

---

disillusionment with a system that they did not believe protected their interests. They, too, became more active. Police unions were established; these were viewed by some as a representation of police hostility.

In short, the 1960s brought open violence between police and citizens, and the 1970s brought more cases of police violence and corruption. Meanwhile, crime rates began to rise, and citizens demanded greater police protection. Demands for a more professionalized police force were heard, along with allegations of police misconduct through the unreasonable use of force.

Police are entitled to use force. The issue lies with how much and under what circumstances. The perception of some is that police use excessive force and that they do it frequently. Kenneth Adams conducted a thorough review of the literature and summarized what we know about police use of force into three categories:

1. What we know with substantial confidence
2. What we know with modest confidence
3. What we do not know

In the first category, Adams stated that we know with substantial confidence that police do not use force often; that the force they use most frequently involves shoving, grabbing, or pushing, rather than more serious force; and that force by police usually occurs when they are effecting an arrest and the suspect is resisting. With modest confidence, we know that the use of force by police tends not to be related to gender, age,

Department of Justice (DOJ). The decree mandated reforms in the LAPD. In late 2001, an independent monitor, appointed in June of that year, concluded that those reforms were on schedule.[2] In early 2003, the district attorney announced that his office was completing its investigation of the Rampart scandal and would not be prosecuting any additional officers, stating that Durden had implicated only himself and Perez. The *Los Angeles Times* concluded otherwise after obtaining copies of secret debriefings of Durden. In an article published on 1 March 2003, the *Times* stated as follows:

> As a result of the [Rampart] investigation, more than 100 convictions were overturned and taxpayers have paid more than $40 million to settle lawsuits. Eight officers were charged with on-duty crimes. Four officers, including Durden, pleaded guilty or no contest to crimes. Three other officers were convicted of corruption-related offenses by a jury, but the judge in the cases overturned the jury's verdict. [The district attorney] is appealing the judge's decision. One officer was acquitted of wrongdoing.[3]

In December 2004, prosecutors dropped charges against those three officers.

The Rampart scandal in the LAPD led to the resignation of Bernard Parks and the appointment of a new police chief in October 2002. William J. Bratton had formerly served as the police commissioner in New York City, and prior to that, in Boston. Although Bratton is not a minority (the two previous chiefs were African American; neither was appointed to a second five-year term), it was predicted that he would be accepted by the minority community, but some residents were skeptical. As one alleged, "The problem here is nobody trusts the police....It is no secret that the LAPD. is racist, that they profile black people,

and they plant evidence. How does one man change a community's mind? No one has that answer."[4]

By April 2005, after the completion of yet another investigation, the city had settled almost all of the 200 civil suits filed in the wake of the Rampart scandal and paid almost $70 million to plaintiffs, with the largest settlement going to Ovando, mentioned earlier. The city attorney stated, "This marks the end of an unfortunate and dark chapter in our city's history." Chief Bratton said he hoped the closing of the Rampart scandal would lead to a cleaner and more diverse and respected LAPD.[5]

In February 2006, a Los Angeles jury awarded $5 million to each of these LAPD officers accused in the Rampart corruption scandal. The federal jury concluded that Sergeant Edward Ortiz, Officer Paul Harper, and former Sergeant Brian Liddy were victims of fake arrest and malicious prosecution. All three were acquitted of corruption-related charges in April 2000.[6]

Source: Summarized by the author from media sources unless otherwise noted by endnote.

1. "Los Angeles Police's Report Cites Vast Command Lapses," *New York Times* (2 March 2000), p. 14; "LAPD Issues Self-Critical Report, but Others Seek Outside Control," *Criminal Justice Newsletter* 30 (20 March 2000): 2.
2. "LAPD Reforms Are on Track, Independent Monitor Says," *Criminal Justice Newsletter* 31, no. 21 (24 November 2001): 3.
3. "Transcripts on Rampart Belie D.A," *Los Angeles Times* (1 March 2003), p. 1, Part 2.
4. "Naming of New Police Chief Raises Minorities' Hopes," *New York Times* (4 October 2002), p. 21.
5. "Los Angeles Paying Victims $70 Million for Police Graft," *New York Times* (1 April 2005), p. 19.
6. "Three Cops Get $15 Million in Rampart Scandal," *VPI Release* (10 February 2006).

and ethnicity; that the use of force typically occurs when the suspects are mentally ill or are under the influence of alcohol or other drugs; and that the use of force is committed by a small percentage of police but they represent a disproportionate number of incidents.[53]

In some of the previous conclusions, Adams indicated that more research is needed. Clearly, research is needed in the final category: what we do *not* know about police use of force. We do not know the incidence of the use of force. We do not know the influence of the following on police use of force: training, discipline, the use of technology, police department policies, or department organization. And finally, we do not know very much about the situations and the transactions that evoke police use of force, other than police tend to respond to interpersonal disturbances and violent crime. Situations such as a fleeing person are also likely to evoke their response.[54]

Police use of force does not always involve excessive force; nor is the force always deadly, but it is the use of deadly force that, understandably, evokes the most intense response, particularly when that force is perceived as unreasonable.

5-4a   Police Use of Deadly Force

Police use of **deadly force** has been defined as "such force as under normal circumstances poses a high risk of death or serious injury to its human target, regardless of whether or not death, serious injury, or any harm actually result."[55] Police officers may

> **Deadly force** Force likely to cause serious bodily injury or death.

use deadly force under some circumstances. If they use deadly force improperly, the officers (and the police department and the city) may be liable to the injured person (or, in the event of death, to the family of the deceased) in a civil suit.

Excessive use of force may occur while police are apprehending suspects either on foot or in vehicles, or it may occur when suspects are already apprehended. We will consider first the use of force in attempts to apprehend suspects.

Fleeing Felon Rule

> **Fleeing felon rule** The common law rule that permitted police to shoot at any fleeing felon. The rule has been modified to require circumstances involving (1) the threat of serious injury to or death of an officer or others, (2) the prevention of an escape if the suspect threatens the officer with a gun, or (3) the officer having probable cause to believe that the suspect has committed or has threatened to commit serious bodily harm.

In the past, shooting any fleeing felon was permitted. Because all felonies were punishable by death, it was assumed that any felon would resist arrest by all possible means. The **fleeing felon rule** developed during a time when apprehending criminals was more difficult than it is today. Police did not have weapons that could be used for shooting at a long distance; nor did they have communication techniques that enabled them to quickly notify other jurisdictions that a suspect had escaped arrest. Therefore, if fleeing felons were not apprehended immediately, they could escape and begin a new life in another community without fear of detection by the police.

As more powerful and efficient weapons were developed, it became easier for police to apprehend escaping felons, and many did so by the use of deadly force, even though the fleeing felons were not dangerous. Such actions were not necessary to protect the officer and others; nor were they necessary to apprehend felons. Despite these developments, however, most jurisdictions adopted the common law rule that permitted police officers to use deadly force in apprehending fleeing felons. This practice was condemned by many commentators and scholars, but it was considered legal until 1985, when the U.S. Supreme Court ruled that Tennessee's fleeing felon statute was unconstitutional under the facts of the case.

Tennessee v. Garner involved an unarmed youth who was killed by a police officer as he fled from an unoccupied house. The officer could see that the fleeing felon was a young male and apparently unarmed. But the officer argued that he knew that, if the youth got over the fence, he could escape, so he fired at him. The Tennessee statute allowed an officer to shoot a suspect if it appeared to be necessary to prevent the escape of a felon.[56]

In *Garner*, the U.S. Supreme Court emphasized that, to be lawful, police use of deadly force must be reasonable. Deadly force is reasonable under the following circumstances:

- To prevent an escape when the suspect has threatened the officer with a weapon
- When there is a threat of death or serious physical injury to the officer or others
- If there is probable cause to believe that the person has committed a crime involving the infliction or threatened infliction of serious physical harm and, where practical, the police officer has given some warning

A statute that permits an officer to shoot a fleeing felon may be constitutional in some instances; however, when used against a young, slight, and unarmed youth who was suspected of burglary, deadly force was unreasonable and therefore unlawful.

Vehicle Pursuits

A second area in which police may be involved in deadly force is in vehicle pursuits. High-speed chases may end in injury or death to the suspect (see the discussion in Spotlight 5-4 of the Benton Harbor, Michigan, high-speed chase), the police pursuer, or innocent bystanders. Earlier studies report some data suggesting that such pursuits are not worth the results in property damage, human injuries, and deaths. Likewise, some courts have held police departments liable for the consequences of such pursuits. Consequently, police departments restrict the types of cases in which vehicle pursuits are permitted or forbid them entirely.

The Los Angeles Police Department (LAPD) provides an example of recent policy changes, which took effect in May 2003. Los Angeles had more police pursuits than any other city, and almost 60 percent of those were the result of traffic violations or other minor infractions. In 2002, Los Angeles had 721 police vehicle pursuits, with 200 of those resulting in crashes that injured 63 people. In 2001, the department had 781 pursuits, which caused 6 deaths and 139 injuries. Under the new policy, police may engage in vehicle pursuits only in serious cases and with a helicopter tracking them. According to one LAPD commander, "We're balancing protecting the public by apprehending criminals while at the same time trying not to endanger the public....The pursuit is probably one of the most dangerous activities involved in law enforcement."[57]

In a national study of 1,200 police departments, Geoffrey P. Alpert found that 90 percent had written policies governing police vehicle pursuits. Although some of those policies were old, dating back to the 1970s, one-half had been revised or drafted within the previous two years. Most of the changes involved making the policies more restrictive. Alpert reported "strikingly effective" results after changes were made in policies. For example, in Miami, Florida, a change in policy in 1992, providing that only violent felonies warrant pursuits, was followed by an 82 percent drop in pursuits. In contrast, Omaha, Nebraska's policy was changed to a more permissive one in 1993 and was followed by an increase in pursuits of over 600 percent the following year.[58]

Over one-half of all traffic accidents that occur during police high-speed chases occur within the first two minutes of the chase, according to a study by the Pursuit Management Task Force, a panel composed of local, state, regional, and federal law enforcement agencies. The most common and most effective technique for stopping the vehicle being pursued is the "spike strip," which is placed in the road. The strip deflates the tires of the pursued vehicle. Other techniques are being developed.[59]

Police Brutality

In a classic and frequently cited article on police brutality published in 1968, sociologist Albert J. Reiss Jr. began his discussion with a 1903 quotation by a former New York City police commissioner:

> For three years, there has been through the courts and the streets a dreary procession of citizens with broken heads and bruised bodies against few of whom was violence needed to affect an arrest. Many of them had done nothing to deserve an arrest. In a majority of such cases, no complaint was made. If the victim complains, his charge is generally dismissed. The police are practically above the law.[60]

During the summer of 1966, Reiss conducted a study of police-citizen interactions in Boston, Chicago, and Washington, D.C. In discussing the results of that study, Reiss pointed out the difficulty of defining police brutality, but he emphasized the importance to the citizen of the status degradation aspect of police behavior, "the judgment that [inmates] have not been treated with the full rights and dignity among citizens in a democratic society."[61]

Police brutality may cause serious injury or even death, and police use of deadly force is at the root of most of the controversy surrounding questionable police behavior. Some of the most publicized allegations of police brutality in recent years are discussed in Spotlight 5-4. Some of the widespread media attention is justified, and in some cases, police are found guilty of crimes for their use of force against citizens. But it is important to put these incidents into perspective and remember that, as discussed previously, most people who have encounters with police report that those interactions do not include violence.

A second type of violence involving police occurs when citizens engage in violence *against* the police.

5-4b Violence against the Police

Law enforcement officers are at a higher risk of workplace violence than are other types of employees. In 2002, a total of 56 law enforcement officers were killed feloniously

Spotlight 5-4   Police Brutality: The 1990s and Beyond

Allegations of police brutality in recent years have focused on several highly publicized cases. Spotlight 5-3 discussed corruption in the Los Angeles Police Department (LAPD), along with some incidents of violence. Here we look at the Rodney King case in that city, as well as examples of police brutality in other cities.

Los Angeles: 1991

The brutality of white police officers against an African American suspect might have gone unnoticed, but an eyewitness taped the actions of 3 March 1991. National television brought the details of a police beating into our homes, as we saw Rodney King, a 25-year-old African American suspect, fired on by a white police officer carrying a 50,000-volt Taser stun gun. Three other officers kicked and beat the suspect on his head with their night sticks, causing injuries to his neck, legs, and kidneys. King suffered multiple skull fractures, a broken ankle, a crushed cheekbone, internal injuries, severe bruises, and some brain damage.

All four officers in the King incident were charged with assault with a deadly weapon and excessive force by an officer under color of law (acting in their capacity as federal, state, or local employees). Two were charged with filing a false police report, and one was charged with being an accessory after the fact. In the spring of 1992, the officers were tried by a jury in Simi Valley, California, a predominantly white community to which the trial had been moved when defense attorneys successfully argued that their clients could not get a fair trial in Los Angeles. All of the officers were acquitted of the assault and secondary charges, but the jury could not reach a verdict on the excessive force charge against one officer. The judge declared a mistrial on that charge. The prosecutor announced plans to retry the officer, and the judge ruled that the trial would be held in Los Angeles.

The reaction in Los Angeles was violent. The resulting rioting and looting led to 60 deaths, although later reports indicated that approximately 15 of those were not related to the rioting. Still, it was the "most deadly U.S. disturbance in the 20th century."[1]

All four police officers were tried on federal charges of violating Rodney King's civil rights. Two officers, Timothy Wind and Ted Briseno, were acquitted. Officer Laurence Powell and Sergeant Stacey Koon were found guilty and sentenced to prison for two-and-one-half years. A federal appeals court upheld the convictions but ordered the trial court to reconsider the sentences, ruling that they were too short. The case was appealed to the U.S. Supreme Court, which upheld some but not all of the reasons for the trial court judge's sentence. The case was sent back for reconsideration by the trial judge in light of the Supreme Court's analysis of federal sentencing guidelines. On reconsideration, the original sentence was not changed.[2]

New York City Trials: 1999, 2000

Before the end of his trial in May 1999, New York City police officer Justin A. Volpe entered a guilty plea to beating and sodomizing Abner Louima, a Haitian immigrant. The acts occurred in the police station house in 1997. Volpe also admitted that he threatened to kill Louima if he told anyone about the incident. Volpe admitted his guilt only after several other officers testified against him and it appeared that he would be convicted. A conviction could have resulted in a life sentence; Volpe was sentenced to 30 years in prison.

The New York City trial continued for the other officers who were tried with Volpe. After an 18-hour deliberation, the jury acquitted Thomas Bruder and Thomas Wiese of beating Louima in a patrol car but convicted Charles Schwarz of holding Louima while Volpe sodomized him. In March 2000, Schwarz, Bruder, and Wiese were found guilty of conspiracy to obstruct justice in their attempts to cover up the brutalizing of Louima.[3] An appellate court reversed those charges in March 2002. That summer, Schwarz was retried and found guilty of perjury, but the jury could not reach an agreement on the other charges against him, including two civil rights charges. The prosecutors announced that they would try Schwarz again, but the prosecution and the defense reached a plea agreement shortly before the scheduled trial. Schwarz entered a guilty plea to perjury and was sentenced to up to five years in prison. In April 2006, his plea for early release was denied. He will be eligible for release in 2007. Louima settled his civil suit against the police for $8.7 million.

In 1999, an Albany, New York, jury acquitted four white New York City police officers who fired 41 times in the shooting death of Amadou Diallo, an unarmed West African immigrant. An anonymous juror reportedly stated that the prosecution did not prove its case beyond a reasonable doubt.[4]

---

while in the line of duty. In 2003, the number was 52, but an additional 80 officers were accidentally killed in the line of duty in 2003, up from 76 in 2002. In 2004, 57 officers were feloniously killed while in the line of duty, and 82 more were killed in accidents in the line of duty. In 2005, 55 officers were feloniously killed; and of those, 36 were employed in city police departments. Fifty-four of the victims were men; eight were black.[62]

Not all police deaths in the line of duty are felonious deaths; many are the results of accidents or natural causes. Furthermore, not all police who are confronted with

Detroit, Michigan: 2003

Years of complaints of misconduct by police in Detroit, Michigan, led the city's mayor to request the U.S. Department of Justice (DOJ) to investigate, beginning in 2000. Several police shootings were the focus of the inquiry, but the allegations also included mistreatment of inmates. In 2002, the DOJ made 175 recommendations for changes; more were presented to the city in March 2003. In 2003, the DOJ and the city agreed to a federal monitor to oversee the department. It was estimated that the changes required for the Detroit Police Department to meet the federal mandate could exceed $100 million, with a cost of $50 million alone for remodeling the holding cells at the jail. Providing adequate screening for medical problems of inmates, along with proper care for those who are sick, is another major expense. Improved training of officers is expensive and may require overtime pay. No longer will inmates receive bologna on two slices of bread for lunch. Rather, their food must come from a menu approved by a dietician. Police must conduct a campaign to inform citizens on how to make complaints and must buy new video cameras for holding cells and squad cars. The costs could be even more expensive, given the time constraints ordered for some changes. The city encountered these costs just as it laid off employees in the face of budget and funding cuts. Some civil rights activists claimed that the consent decrees were not strong enough and that the DOJ was entering into them because it wished to settle cases, rather than file lawsuits against police departments. DOJ officials pointed out that they could still sue if the federal monitors determined that police departments were not in compliance.[5]

In October 2004, Sheryl Robinson Wood, the federal monitor reported that few changes had been made and that the Detroit Police Department had failed to improve. Specifically, Wood stated that the department had complied with only 2 of the 98 consent requirements, although she did acknowledge that the greatest improvement had come in the previous three months. It was estimated that it would cost the city at least $98 million to bring the police department into compliance with the federal consent agreements.[6]

As of January 2006, with one-half of the monitoring period over, Wood reported that Detroit was not even close to fulfilling the federal mandate. The city had missed numerous improvement deadlines. Wood's required quarterly report noted that the city had complied with only 8 of the 80 requirements for improvement. The city has paid over $4 million in monitoring costs and estimates that the total cost of required improvements would be approximately $100 million.[7]

Benton Harbor, Michigan: 16 June 2003

The death of Terrance Shurn, a 28-year-old African American, after he lost control of his motorcycle and crashed into a wall during a high-speed chase by white police officers on 16 June 2003, led to two nights of rioting in Benton Harbor, Michigan. Rumors that police had bumped the motorcycle spread quickly, but police investigations denied that. Benton Harbor, with its predominantly African American population, had a history of poverty, high unemployment, and racial tensions. Shortly after the riots, an 18-year-old teen, Coleman Tavon Edwards, shot a police officer. Edwards was convicted of assault with intent to murder and sentenced to 18 to 45 years in prison, as well as two years on a weapons charge. A committee appointed to investigate the riots made its report in October 2003, urging improved relationships between the police and the community and "eradicating substandard housing in the city, where poverty and joblessness are rife."[8]

In 2005 Edwards' convictions were upheld by the Michigan Court of Appeals, and the state supreme court denied review.[9]

1. "One-Fourth of L.A. Riot Deaths Found Unrelated to Violence," *St. Petersburg Times* (2 June 1992), p. 4.
2. "Court Recommends Longer Sentences in Beating of King," *New York Times* (20 September 1994), p. 1. The case is United States v. Koon, 34 F.3d 1416 (9th Cir. 1994), *aff'd. in part, rev'd. in part, remanded,* 518 U.S. 81 (1996).
3. "Three Are Guilty of Cover-Up Plot in Louima Attack," *New York Times* (7 March 2000), p. 1.
4. "Pressed on Not-Guilty Verdicts, Diallo Juror Points to Prosecution," *New York Times* (27 February 2000), p. 1.
5. "Detroit Reform Tab May Top $100 Million," *Detroit News* (29 June 2003), p. 1; "Detroit Agrees on Monitor for the Police," *New York Times* (12 June 2003).
6. "Detroit Police Fail to Improve: Federal Monitor Says Department Has Made Little Progress in First Year of Sweeping Overhaul," *Detroit News* (19 October 2004), p. 1B.
7. "Detroit Police Reform Failing," *Detroit News* (19 January 2006), p. 1B.
8. "Cops Out in Force in Benton Harbor As Governor Vows Help," *Chicago Sun-Times* (20 June 2003), p. 3; "National Briefing Midwest: Michigan: Recommendations by Panel on Rioting," *New York Times* (22 October 2003), p. 18; "Teen Draws 20-Year Sentence: State Trooper Shot Week after June Riots," *South Bend Tribune* (21 October 2003), p. 1.
9. People v. Edwards, 2005 Mich.App. LEXIS 1902 (Mich.Ct.App. 2005), *appeal denied,* 706 N.W.2d 18 (Mich. 2005).

violence by others are killed, although some of them are seriously injured. Police also encounter hostility that may result in verbal abuse. It is debatable which comes first and which causes which, but there are indications that both verbal and physical violence against police officers are accompanied by violence by police officers.[63]

Violence against the police has serious repercussions. Officers who survive may have physical injuries or psychological problems that preclude further work as police officers. Families and friends of those who are killed are also victims of such violence. In additional to financial problems, they may develop feelings of hostility and fear, experience difficulty making decisions, may feel alone in social situations, suffer from emotional problems, develop sleep disorders, and have guilt feelings about their interactions with the deceased prior to his or her death.

5-5   The Control of Policing

Although only a minority of police officers may be guilty of misconduct, any misconduct is serious and should be subject to discipline. Policies and programs should be developed to avoid as much misconduct as possible. Police misconduct may be controlled from within or outside the department.

5-5a   Regulation by Police Departments

Regulation of police conduct is not easy, given the number of persons involved, the extent of the potentially compromising situations, and the limitations on funding for recruitment and training, but the efficient operation of any department requires the internal disciplining of employees. In the case of police departments, it is important that the public's image of internal operations also be positive. The U.S. Commission on Civil Rights emphasized that it is essential that police departments have an effective system of internal discipline that will "include clear definition of proper conduct, a reliable mechanism for detecting misconduct, and appropriate sanctions, consistently imposed, when misconduct has been proven." Policies must be clearly articulated.[64]

Police departments should enforce their written policies actively and fairly. If officers believe that they will not be reprimanded for violating departmental policies, those policies may be ineffective in curbing police abuse of discretion. The Commission on Civil Rights recommended that "every police department should have a clearly defined system for the receipt, processing, and investigation of civilian complaints." Once a violation of policy is found, "discipline imposed should be fair, swift, and consistent with departmental practices and procedures."[65] Police departments should take measures to identify violence-prone officers in an attempt to avert problems.

A study funded by the federal office of Community Oriented Policing Services (COPS) and conducted by the Police Executive Research Forum (PERF) reported that approximately one-fourth of the larger law enforcement agencies have an *early warning system*, which is designed to detect officers who might abuse their power. According to PERF, there is evidence that these systems, which are expected to be in force in many more departments within the near future, are successful in reducing problem behaviors. The early warning systems analyze citizen complaints, officer firings, high-speed chases, reports of the use of force, and other criteria to identify officers who are potential problems. Generally, the first reaction will be for the officer's immediate supervisor to talk with him or her and document what the officer is told and his or her response. This information should be reviewed by a higher-ranking commander. Some departments involve the higher-ranking person directly; some require the identified officers to attend special training classes. Officers who are identified early as potential problems may never become problems. Another advantage of early intervention is to alert supervisors to their roles in identifying and preventing problem behavior. The researchers emphasized that, for early intervention programs to be successful, they must involve accountability of supervisors and higher-up commanders. Examples of potential identifiers are frequent traffic stops of women or minorities.[66]

Another way in which local police departments can help control policing is to establish clearly written policies to assist officers in their decision making. The BJS found that of local police departments reporting on 2003 data, 95 percent had a written policy concerning the use of deadly force, 90 percent had a written policy on the use of nonlethal force, and 84 percent had written policies concerning the handling of juveniles, but only 59 percent had policies concerning the handling of the mentally ill, and only 62 percent had policies concerning racial profiling.[67]

5-5b Federal Regulations

Another method for regulating local and state police is for federal agencies to be involved. We noted in Spotlights 5-3 and 5-4 that federal monitors have been assigned to some police departments. These monitors are appointed after federal investigations, often with federal courts ordering the monitoring system. Various federal statutes have enacted measures designed to improve local and state policing. Some of these statutes provide funds for increasing the number of police or for assisting police departments with training or acquiring the necessary equipment to improve their programs. And the FBI Academy at Quantico, Virginia, is used for training officers from non-FBI agencies.

5-5c Regulation by Courts

If police departments do not control themselves sufficiently, the courts can be used. Courts have two major ways of controlling policing: excluding evidence and providing a forum for civil lawsuits against police officers and their departments.

The Exclusionary Rule and Its Exceptions

If police seize evidence illegally or secure confessions improperly, the evidence may be excluded from trial. This procedure is the result of the U.S. Supreme Court's **exclusionary rule**. In 1914, the Supreme Court held that the Fourth Amendment (which prohibits unreasonable searches and seizures; see Appendix A) would have no meaning unless courts prohibited the use of illegally seized evidence. Consequently, when the police conducted an illegal search, the evidence they seized could not be used in *federal* cases. In 1961, the Court held that the exclusionary rule also applies to the states.[68]

> **Exclusionary rule** Evidence secured as the result of illegal actions by law enforcement officers should be excluded from a legal proceeding, such as a trial.

The exclusionary rule is controversial, mainly because it applies after the fact. When illegally seized evidence is excluded from a trial, we know who the suspect is and may believe that guilt is obvious. Thus, for instance, when a judge rules that a gun allegedly used in a murder cannot be admitted at the suspect's trial because the evidence was obtained illegally by the police, and the suspect goes free because there is not enough legal evidence for a conviction, there may be strong public reaction of disbelief and outrage.

The exclusionary rule serves a symbolic purpose. According to one scholar, it is "a symbol of our system of criminal procedure. It is lauded as a crowning achievement of a free society."[69] If police violate individual rights to obtain evidence to convict alleged criminals, the government, in a sense, is supporting crime. When this occurs, the government becomes a lawbreaker, and in the words of a noted jurist, "it breeds contempt for law; it invites…anarchy."[70]

The second reason for the exclusionary rule is a practical one: it is assumed that the rule prevents police from engaging in illegal searches and seizures. According to the U.S. Supreme Court, the exclusionary rule "compels respect for the constitutional guarantee in the only effectively available way—by removing the incentive to disregard it."[71] It is difficult to know whether that statement is true because most illegal searches conducted to harass or punish take place in secret and may not be reported. Research on the issue is inconclusive. There is evidence, however, that the rule has led some police departments to increase the quantity and quality of police training, thus educating officers in what they may and may not do regarding search and seizure.[72]

In recent years, the exclusionary rule has come under severe attack, with many people calling for its abolition or modification. Most of their arguments are the reverse of the arguments in favor of the rule. First is the argument of the symbolism of abolition, based on the view that, when people see guilty persons going free as a result of a technicality, they lose respect for law and order, and criminal justice systems are weakened. The public's perception of letting guilty people go free is crucial.

Second, the abolitionists contend that the exclusionary rule should be eliminated because it results in the release of guilty people. The rule "is attacked as one of the chief technical loopholes through which walk the guilty on their way out of the courthouse to continue their depredations."[73] It makes no difference how many: one is too many, argue the abolitionists.

Third, the possibility of having evidence excluded from trial because it was not properly seized leads defendants to file numerous motions to suppress evidence, which consumes a lot of time and contributes to court congestion. In criminal cases, objections to search and seizure are the issues raised most frequently.

The U.S. Supreme Court has recognized some exceptions to the exclusionary rule. Under the **good faith exception**, illegally obtained evidence is not excluded from trial if it can be shown that police secured the evidence in good faith; that is, they had a reasonable belief that they were acting in accordance with the law. In *Massachusetts v. Sheppard*, the Supreme Court held that when police conduct a search in good faith, even if the technical search warrant is defective, the seized evidence should not be excluded from the trial.[74] In 1995, the Supreme Court ruled that an arrest based on incorrect information due to a clerical error could stand because, when analyzed objectively, there was no evidence that the arresting officer was not acting reasonably.[75]

The U.S. Supreme Court has interpreted the U.S. Constitution to permit the use of evidence seized by officers who had a warrant to search one apartment but searched the wrong apartment and found illegal drugs. In *Maryland v. Garrison*, the Supreme Court reasoned that, because the search was in good faith, and because excluding its use in such cases would not deter police, who thought they were searching an apartment included in the warrant, nothing positive would be gained by applying the exclusionary rule in this fact pattern.[76]

The U.S. Supreme Court has held that a defendant's federal constitutional rights are not violated when police officers lose or destroy evidence that might have been used to establish the defendant's innocence, provided the officers' actions were made in good faith. The case of *Arizona v. Youngblood* involved Larry Youngblood, who had been convicted of the kidnapping, molestation, and sexual assault of a 10-year-old boy. The police failed to refrigerate the victim's semen-stained clothing or to make tests capable of showing whether the semen had come from Youngblood. The results of such tests might have shown that Youngblood was not the offender. William H. Rehnquist, writing for the majority, argued that the omission could "at worst be described as negligent."[77]

Since the U.S. Supreme Court adopted the good faith exception to the exclusionary rule, some state courts have held that it does not apply under their state constitutions, and thus all illegally seized evidence must be excluded at trial, regardless of the motivation of the officer who seized the evidence. Because this involves enlarging, not reducing, a U.S. Supreme Court interpretation of the federal Constitution, as it decreases the amount of evidence that can be used against a defendant, such lower court rulings are permissible.

The U.S. Supreme Court has also recognized a second major exception to the exclusionary rule: the **inevitable discovery rule**. According to this rule, illegally seized evidence will be admitted at trial if it can be shown that, eventually, the evidence would have been discovered by legal methods. Writing for the Court in *Nix v. Williams*, Chief Justice Warren E. Burger said, "Exclusion of physical evidence that would inevitably have been discovered adds nothing to either the integrity or fairness of a criminal trial."[78]

In a 1990 case, the U.S. Supreme Court further demonstrated its relaxing of the exclusionary rule. In 1980, the Court had held that the Fourth Amendment prohibits police from entering a suspect's home without a warrant and without the suspect's consent to effect a felony arrest. The Court stated that its reason for this rule was to protect the physical integrity of the home. In 1990, the Court ruled that even a violation of this earlier case does not invalidate a statement made by the accused *after* the warrantless entry of the home if the accused makes a statement to police *outside* the home. It is not necessary to exclude the statement, despite the illegal entry into the home. The prohibition against the warrantless entry of the home is to protect the home's physical integrity, "not to grant criminal suspects protection for statements made outside their premises, where the police have probable cause to make an arrest."[79]

> **Good faith exception** The provision that illegally obtained evidence will not be excluded from a subsequent trial if it can be shown that police officers secured the evidence in good faith, meaning that they had a reasonable belief that they were acting in accordance with the law.

> **Inevitable discovery rule** Evidence secured illegally by police will not be excluded from the suspect's trial, provided it can be shown that the evidence would have been discovered anyway under legal means.

In 1991, a sharply divided U.S. Supreme Court permitted the use of coerced confessions in some circumstances. In 1967, the Supreme Court had articulated the *harmful error rule*, which holds that, if a confession is coerced, it must be excluded at trial. But in *Arizona v. Fulminante*, the Court held that the Constitution does not require the automatic exclusion of the coerced confession. Rather, a coerced confession is to be considered like any other trial error; it is to be analyzed under the circumstances, and the trial court is to make a decision regarding whether it is a harmful error beyond a reasonable doubt. If so, it must be excluded; if not, it is a *harmless error*, and the evidence may be used against the suspect.[80]

In addition to the exclusionary rule, courts assist in the regulation of police actions through civil cases, as noted in the next section.

Civil Actions

The use of civil lawsuits to bring actions against police (or other authorities) who violate citizens' civil rights is thought to be an effective deterrent for such illegal actions. Even if these lawsuits do not deter other violations, civil actions permit abuse victims (or their survivors) to recover monetary damages for their physical injuries (or death) and for emotional, psychological, and economic damages.

Civil actions are brought under the Civil Rights Act of 1964 and are commonly called *1983 actions*, after the section of the U.S. Code in which the provision for such actions is codified.[81] Section 1983 actions may be brought by persons who are injured as a result of police negligence, as in high-speed chases that result in injuries (or death) to bystanders. Suits may also be brought for police mistreatment. Civil actions against police represent a growing body of civil law and increasing expenses for the municipalities that are legally responsible for those actions.

Civil suits against police may be brought not only for intentional or malicious conduct. *Negligence* is also a basis for liability, especially negligence in hiring and training. In 1989, for example, the U.S. Supreme Court held that inadequate police training may result in civil liability for the municipality under which the police department operates. Spotlight 4-1 discussed the case of *City of Canton, Ohio v. Harris*.[82] As that spotlight notes, the case involved civil liability for the misconduct of police. Some examples are pertinent here. In 2003, the Mississippi Supreme Court held that police who engage in high-speed chases through densely populated areas can be held responsible in civil actions for any injuries or deaths they cause. In *Jackson v. Brister*, police were summoned to a bank in which a customer was attempting to cash a forged check. When the customer saw the police, she fled the bank in her car, followed by the police. The high-speed chase ended when the customer's car hit another car, killing the driver. The driver's estate sued for civil damages, and the court ruled that the usual immunity provided to police for civil damages does not apply when officers act recklessly in disregard for human life. The police department policy permits such pursuits only when the officer knows the suspect has committed a felony and it is reasonable to assume that the suspect is more dangerous to the community than is the risk of a high-speed chase. In this case, the officers could have gotten the license plate number, tracked down the suspect, and arrested her. The high-speed chase was not necessary.[83]

5-5d Community Relations

Another method of controlling police activities is through community involvement and improved police-community relationships. It is vital that relationships between police and the community be improved. Police are not able to apprehend most criminals without the support of citizens. The U.S. Commission on Civil Rights emphasized that the men and women who are authorized to make arrests depend to a great extent on the cooperation of the public. "Perhaps the most valuable asset these officers can possess is credibility with the communities they serve."[84]

The importance of these contacts is emphasized by studies showing that citizens who have positive images of the police are more likely to report crimes than are those with negative images. Those most likely to have negative images of the police are members of the lower socioeconomic class, African Americans, and other nonwhites—persons who feel a general alienation from the political process and those who perceive an increase in crime in their neighborhoods.

As noted in Chapter 4, community-oriented policing is in vogue today. Earlier studies disclosed that some positive results, such as crime reduction, follow community-oriented policing.[85] Crime prevention programs are also important. Police educate the community about various approaches to crime prevention. Community organization activities in which police and the community work together to identify community problems are helpful. Herman Goldstein, who has written extensively about numerous criminal justice issues, concluded that full development of the overall concept of community policing, including a "concern with the substance of policing as well as its form," could "provide the integrated strategy for improving the quality of policing."[86]

We have already noted that violence by the police may evoke violence against the police. Earlier commissions underscored police violence as a catalyst for urban rioting in the 1960s.[87] But they also noted the impact of race in explaining violence by and against the police. For example, the U.S. Commission on Civil Rights emphasized the importance of hiring more racial minorities and upgrading their positions on police forces when it cited the study of the National Minority Advisory Council on Criminal Justice, which stressed the far-reaching effects of police brutality.[88] Efforts to increase diversity in policing deserve analysis.

5-6   Affirmative Action Recruitment and Hiring

Diversity in police departments is increasingly being recognized as one way to improve the services police offer to the community, as well as to improve the community's perception of police.

The need to recruit women and racial minorities was emphasized by the U.S. Commission on Civil Rights, which concluded,

> Serious underutilization of minorities and women in local law enforcement agencies continues to hamper the ability of police departments to function effectively in and earn the respect of predominantly minority neighborhoods, thereby increasing the probability of tension and violence.
>
> While there has been some entry of minorities and women into police service in recent years, police departments remain largely white and male, particularly in the upper-level command positions. Utilization figures for women hardly approach tokenism, although studies have indicated that as a rule women perform at least as well as men on the force.

In light of that finding, the commission recommended that "[p]olice department officials should develop and implement affirmative action plans so that ultimately the force reflects the composition of the community it serves."[89]

The U.S. Commission on Civil Rights found that efforts by police departments to recruit women and racial minorities may be hindered by the community's perceptions that the department is not committed to such recruitment. Such perceptions are created in different ways. For example, newspaper reports of the way police handle cases involving women and racial minorities, complaints of former members of the police force, and the treatment received by women and minorities who applied but were turned down as recruits by the police department may affect perceptions. Perceptions of race and gender discrimination are created by the lack of advancement opportunities for women and racial minorities within police departments, as well as by the high rates of attrition during training. The commission concluded that, in addition to an emphasis on recruitment, "minorities and women, through the implementation of equal opportunity programs, should hold positions that lead to upward mobility in the ranks, allowing them to compete for command positions."[90]

Recruitment of women and minority officers has had some help from the courts, with both groups having filed successful affirmative action cases under federal statutes. Women have successfully argued that they were discriminated against in hiring, on-the-job assignments, and promotions. After a decade of decisions on affirmative action policies concerning minorities and women, in 1987 the U.S. Supreme Court held that it is permissible for employers to give preferential treatment in jobs on the basis of gender and race.[91] More recently, the U.S. Supreme Court has decided two cases involving university admissions that may be applicable to hiring as well.

In 2003, the U.S. Supreme Court looked at two admissions policies from the University of Michigan. One involved a law school admissions policy; the second involved undergraduate admissions. The law school admissions policy was upheld; the undergraduate policy was rejected.

In the undergraduate case, *Gratz v. Bollinger*, the University of Michigan used a 150-point scale for admissions. An applicant needed 100 points for guaranteed admission. Applicants from underrepresented minority groups were given 20 points for that fact alone. The U.S. Supreme Court ruled that using race as an admissions factor in that way—that is, using a mechanical formula—is unconstitutional.[92] The law school, however, used race as only one factor among others, such as grade point average, score on the law school admission test, teacher recommendations, alumni connections, and personal essays. In *Grutter v. Bollinger*, the U.S. Supreme Court upheld this practice.[93] Although one could argue that both systems are race-conscious and that the real differences are only symbolic, some legal scholars believe that the important difference is public perception.

Justice Sandra Day O'Connor, who wrote the majority opinion upholding the Michigan Law School's policy (and who also voted in the majority rejecting the undergraduate admission policy), stated the importance of affirmative action in this comment: "In order to cultivate a set of leaders with legitimacy in the eyes of the citizenry, it is necessary that the path to leadership be visibly open to talented and qualified individuals of every race and ethnicity." According to Justice O'Connor (who also stated that she hoped affirmative action will not be necessary in 25 years), the law school policy represents a "highly individualized, holistic review of each applicant's file" and does not use race in a "mechanical way." Further, the policy utilizing race must be narrowly tailored so that race is used as a *plus* factor.

The importance of diversity in many areas of life was emphasized by the members of over 300 organizations who signed 60 briefs submitted to the U.S. Supreme Court in support of the University of Michigan affirmative action policies prior to the hearing of those cases. The briefs provided compelling reasons to uphold affirmative action. For example, one submitted by the military (including General Norman Schwarzkopf, who commanded the allied forces during the Persian Gulf War) insisted that the United States cannot be properly defended without diversity in the troops. Businesses (such as Coca-Cola, General Electric, and Microsoft) included in their statements that diversity in education admissions is crucial to their recruiting of a diverse workforce, which they believe is necessary for their significant contributions to the international marketplace. According to the comments of the senior vice president and general counsel at Merck, a pharmaceutical company, "Diversity creates stronger companies….The work we do directly impacts patients of all types around the globe. Understanding people is essential to our success."[94]

In his dissent in the law school admission case, U.S. Supreme Court Justice Clarence Thomas, the only African American on the Court, stated the following:

> I believe blacks can achieve in every avenue of American life without the meddling of
> university administrators. Because I wish to see all students succeed whatever their
> color, I share, in some respect, the sympathies of those who sponsor the type of

Figure 5-3

Female and Minority Local Police Officers, 1987 and 2003

Source: Matthew J. Hickman and Brian A. Reaves, Bureau of Justice Statistics, *Local Police Departments 2003* (Washington, D.C.: U.S. Department of Justice, May 2006), p. iii.

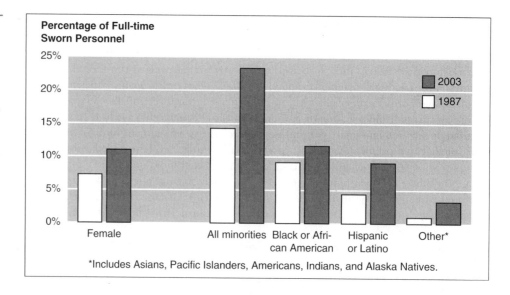

discrimination advanced by the University of Michigan Law School. The Constitution does not, however, tolerate institutional devotion to the status quo in admissions policies when such devotion ripens into racial discrimination.[95]

These recent decisions by the U.S. Supreme Court will have an impact on police hiring. Clearly, some form of affirmative action is still considered constitutional; clearly, a mechanical system is not acceptable. And there is a practical issue: if minorities believe that their representation in a given police force will be too small, they may not apply. But both women and minorities have been involved in policing for a long time, although they represent a small percentage of law enforcement officers, and most hold subordinate roles. Still, their numbers have been increasing, as noted in Figure 5-3, and these latest decisions may increase their representation. In 2003 (the latest BJS published data), racial and ethnic minorities constituted 23.6 percent of sworn officers in local police departments, while women comprised 11.9 percent. Figure 5-3 graphs the differences in each category, comparing 1987 and 2003.

Chapter Wrap-Up

This chapter focused on some problems and issues connected with policing in a complex society. Political pressures from within the department, along with pressures from the community and other outside forces, create problems. Problems may be related to the role conflicts of policing. Most officers receive more training in law enforcement than in order maintenance and performance of community services. Many of them view policing primarily as law enforcement; superiors may evaluate them by their work in that area. However, studies reveal that officers spend less time in law enforcement than in other police functions. Nor are the lines always clear regarding law enforcement. For example, today most departments view domestic violence as a law enforcement issue, not a social problem, but not all police administrators, officers, or the public agree. But domestic violence among police has also become an issue.

Police encounter numerous stressors on their jobs. Some are due to the nature of the job and varying citizen expectations, and many citizens have no hesitation in complaining if all police functions are not performed quickly, efficiently, and adequately. The real problem may lie in our unrealistic expectations of police. In theory, we want them to enforce all laws; however, in reality, we will not tolerate full enforcement—police will not and cannot do that, anyway. We expect the police to prevent crime, but that is not always possible either. We think that they should be authoritarian in enforcement situations yet maintain a supportive and friendly approach in others. We authorize them to handle all kinds of emergencies, yet we do not provide them with the resources or authority for these functions. No matter what police do, they encounter conflicts.

Most important, we cannot separate policing and its context from the rest of our society. As one authority on policing concluded, the actions of the police "mirror the social relations of American society. Until those relations change, we will continue to have a police problem."[96]

Stress may become a major issue for police, some of whom commit suicide as a result. The spread of AIDS has created stress for officers who are infected, as well as for those who do not know how to react to AIDS-infected colleagues. The concern with and planning for the prevention of terrorist attacks has placed stress on law enforcement officers and administrators. The development of a police subculture is one way police cope with these and other stressors.

Police misconduct is another problem and has been widely studied. Reports vary as to the pervasiveness and nature of misconduct, but it is clear that at least some police are involved in drug transactions and other illegal acts. Departmental efforts to eradicate this illegal behavior are not always successful.

Police use of deadly force has become a critical issue in some departments. Police are permitted to use some force, but the *abuse* of that responsibility is a focus of concern. Court decisions have required changes in the use of deadly force, for example, and some police departments have responded with a greater emphasis on proper training in the use of deadly force. In addition, some have established more detailed departmental policies on the use of vehicular pursuits. Despite these changes, some police use excessive force, leading to allegations of police brutality.

Violence and brutality by police came into national focus in the widely publicized beating of Rodney King, an African American, by white police officers. Violence against police and police violence against citizens lead to serious repercussions, as illustrated by the deadly and destructive Los Angeles riots after the state acquittals of the officers tried in the King case. Recent allegations of police violence have refocused attention on this serious problem of policing. Violence against police is also an important concern in today's world.

Efforts to control improper policing have come from department regulations, court decisions, civil actions against police, and the improvement of community-police relations. The most controversial of these efforts has been the U.S. Supreme Court's exclusionary rule, whereby evidence obtained by police in violation of a suspect's constitutional rights may be excluded from that individual's trial. The Court has created some exceptions to the exclusionary rule, such as good faith and inevitable discovery. Civil actions against police may serve as a deterrent to improper police behavior, and an increasing number of these suits are being filed under the federal code.

Further problems and issues in policing surround affirmative action programs aimed at employing more women and racial minorities. These groups argue that the police cannot understand their problems and gain the support of their members unless the groups are represented adequately among police officers and administrators. Others argue that recruitment efforts have lowered standards or that court decisions upholding affirmative action programs for increasing the number of women and racial minorities on a police force are unfair and create internal problems for police. The U.S. Supreme Court's upholding of some affirmative action policies in 2003 may give a green light to universities and businesses—including law enforcement agencies—to attempt to achieve greater diversity in admissions and hiring.

Despite problems in policing, many officers are satisfied with their profession. Problems exist in any profession, and perhaps it is good that we are never free of the opportunities for improvement that problems present. Policing is not for everyone; however, for those who enjoy a challenging, exciting job in which there is opportunity for service as well as hard work, policing is a viable choice.

Joseph Wambaugh, a former police officer and an author of best-selling novels, in assessing his life in both professions, said he did not miss the tedium and bureaucracy of policing, but he did miss the loyalty and camaraderie of his former police colleagues. "I find a lot of disloyalty in show business. In police work, it's totally different....For the period of time that you're working together [in policing], you are absolutely loyal to each other." Wambaugh concluded, "Being a cop was a good life."[97]

Key Terms

deadly force (p. 143)
domestic violence (p. 128)
exclusionary rule (p. 149)

fleeing felon rule (p. 144)
good faith exception (p. 150)
inevitable discovery rule (p. 150)

intimate partner violence (IPV) (p. 128)
statute of limitations (p. 139)
subculture (p. 136)

Apply It

1. What external political situations might affect policing?
2. How should police spend most of their time? Why?
3. What is meant by *proactive* and *reactive* policing, and what changes are being made in the former?
4. What is the relationship between domestic violence and policing?
5. What are the major stressors in policing?
6. What is meant by a *subculture*? How does that concept apply to policing?
7. Discuss the extent and result of police corruption, with particular reference to the influence of drugs.
8. What is the *fleeing felon rule*? Contrast its historical meaning with the U.S. Supreme Court's ruling currently in effect.
9. Analyze the reasons for and concern with police vehicle pursuits.
10. Discuss police brutality in the context of a recent example.
11. What is the relationship between violence against the police and violence by the police?
12. Distinguish between police department regulations and civil lawsuits as methods of controlling policing.
13. How have changes in federal regulations affected law enforcement?
14. State the purpose of the *exclusionary rule*, and analyze whether that purpose is being met. What exceptions has the U.S. Supreme Court permitted?
15. Discuss civil liability that may result from inadequate training of police.

16. What has been the result of efforts to recruit women and racial minorities into policing? Do you think this is important? If so, why? If not, why not? What effect will recent U.S. Supreme Court decisions regarding college and university admissions policies have on affirmative action recruiting?

Endnotes

1. James Q. Wilson, *Varieties of Police Behavior: The Management of Law and Order in Eight Communities* (Cambridge, Mass.: Harvard University Press, 1968), p. 19.

2. Albert J. Reiss Jr., *The Police and the Public* (New Haven, Conn.: Yale University Press, 1971), pp. 63, 64, 71.

3. Richard J. Lundman, "Police Patrol Work: A Comparative Perspective," in *Police Behavior: A Sociological Perspective*, ed. Richard J. Lundman (New York: Oxford University Press, 1980), p. 55.

4. Eric J. Scott, *Calls for Service: Citizen Demand and Initial Police Performance*, National Institute of Justice (Washington, D.C.: U.S. Department of Justice, July 1981), pp. 24–30.

5. Ibid., p. 27.

6. Bureau of Justice Statistics, U.S. Department of Justice, "Crime Characteristics," http://www.ojp.usdoj.gov/bjs/cvict_htm, accessed 2 June 2006.

7. Matthew R. Durose et al., Office of Justice Programs, Bureau of Justice Statistics, *Family Violence Statistics* (Washington, D.C.: U.S. Department of Justice, June 2005), pp. 1–8.

8. "Intimate Partner Violence: Fact Sheet," National Center for Injury Prevention and Control, http://www.cdc.gov/ncipc/factsheets/ipvfacts.htm, accessed 2 June 2006.

9. "1st Gay Couple Ending Relationship," *Chicago Tribune* (16 December 2005), News, Zone 3, Across the Nation, p. 42.

10. Violence against Women Act of 1994, U.S. Code, Title 42, Chapter 136, Section 1381 (2007). The final rule is published in the *Federal Register*, Volume 61, Section 40727-34 (6 August 1996).

11. Lawrence W. Sherman and Richard A. Berk, *The Minneapolis Domestic Violence Experiment* (Washington, D.C.: Police Foundation, 1984), p. 1.

12. Franklyn W. Dunford et al., "The Role of Arrest in Domestic Assault: The Omaha Police Experiment," *Criminology* 28 (May 1990): 204.

13. Maryann Syers and Jeffrey L. Edleson, "The Combined Effects of Coordinated Criminal Justice Intervention in Woman Abuse," *Journal of Interpersonal Violence* 7 (December 1992): 490–502.

14. Lawrence W. Sherman, "The Influence of Criminology on Criminal Law: Evaluating Arrests for Misdemeanor Domestic Violence," *Journal of Criminal Law and Criminology* 83 (Spring 1992): 1–45; quotation is on pp. 44–45.

15. David A. Klinger, "Policing Spousal Assault," *Journal of Research in Crime and Delinquency* 32 (August 1995): 308–324.

16. Robert C. Davis and Barbara Smith, "Domestic Violence Reforms: Empty Promises or Fulfilled Expectations?" *Crime & Delinquency* 41 (October 1995): 541–552; quotation is on p. 541.

17. Richard B. Felson and Jeff Ackerman, "Arrest for Domestic and Other Assaults," *Criminology* 39, no. 3 (August 2001): 655–676; quotation is on p. 672.

18. Richard B. Felson et al., "Police Intervention and the Repeat of Domestic Assault," *Criminology* 43, no. 3 (August 2005): 563–588.

19. Robert C. Davis et al., "Increasing the Proportion of Domestic Violence Arrests That Are Prosecuted: A Natural Experiment in Milwaukee," *Criminology and Public Policy* 2, no. 2 (March 2003): 263–282; quotation is on p. 280.

20. Laura Dugan, "Domestic Violence Legislation: Exploring Its Impact on the Likelihood of Domestic Violence, Police Involvement, and Arrest," *Criminology and Public Policy* 2, no. 2 (March 2003): 263–283; quotation is on p. 283.

21. Richard B. Felson et al., "Reasons for Reporting and Not Reporting Domestic Violence to the Police," *Criminology* 40, no. 3 (August 2002): 617–648; quotation is on p. 617.

22. Allen R. Kates, *CopShock: Surviving Posttraumatic Stress Disorder (PTSD)* (Tucson, Ariz.: Holbrook Street Press, 1999).

23. Wayne D. Ford, *Managing Police Stress* (Walnut Creek, Calif.: The Management Advantage, 1998).

24. W. W. Genet, National Institute of Justice, *Program for the Reduction of Stress for New York City Police Officers and Their Families, Final Report*, http://www.ncjrs.gov/rr/vol2_2/16.html, accessed 3 June 2006.

25. The U.S. Commission on Civil Rights, *Who Is Guarding the Guardians? A Report on Police Practices* (Washington, D.C.: U.S. Government Printing Office, October 1981), p. 156.

26. "Ex-Cop Indicted in Killing of Kin, 3 Neighbors," *The Record* (Bergen County, N.J.) (4 September 2002), p. 3.

27. "What Is the National P.O.L.I.C.E. Suicide Foundation?" http://www.psf.org/about.htm, accessed 2 June 2006.

28. "A Silent Fraternity: Officers with H.I.V.," *New York Times* (2 August 2000), p. 23.

29. "Westmont Settles Job Bias Suit; Police Applicant Is HIV-Positive," *Chicago Tribune* (30 May 2003), p. 4 Metro. The case is Roe v. Village of Westmont, 2003 U.S. Dist. LEXIS 245 (N.D. Ill. 2003).

30. "Police Chief Accused of Denying Gay Man CPR," *Fox News*, http://www.foxnews.com/story/0,2933,186683,00.html, accessed 3 June 2006.

31. "State Police Key in Terrorism Prevention," *State News* 48, no. 6 (1 June 2005): 1.

32. "In N.Y., Anti-Terrorism Cuts Called 'Knife in the Back,'" *Los Angeles Times* (2 June 2006), p. 18.

33. See Arthur Niederhoffer, *Behind the Shield: The Police in Urban Society* (Garden City, N.Y.: Doubleday, 1969).

34. Eric D. Poole and Robert M. Regoli, "An Examination of the Effects of Professionalism on Cynicism among Police," *Social Science Journal* 16 (October 1979): 64.

35. John P. Crank et al., "Cynicism among Police Chiefs," *Justice Quarterly* 3 (September 1986): 343–352.

36. Dennis Jay Wiechman, "Police Cynicism toward the Judicial Process," *Journal of Police Science and Administration* 7 (September 1979): 340–345.

37. "Police Officer Subjected to 'Code of Silence' for Complaining about Harassment Wins Substantial Verdict," *Criminal Law Reporter* 45 (April 2002): 113; "Judge Slashes $3 Million Jury Award," *Chicago Daily Law Bulletin* (3 June 2002). The case is Spina v. Forest Pres. Dist., 204 F.Supp 2d. 764 (N.D.Ill. 2002).

38. Victor E. Kappeler, Richard D. Sluder, and Geoffrey P. Alpert, "Breeding Deviant Conformity: The Ideology and Culture of Police," in *Forces of Deviance: The Dark Side of Policing*, 2d ed. (Prospect Heights, Ill.: Waveland, 1998), pp. 83–108, reprinted in *Critical Issues in Policing: Contemporary Readings*, 5th ed., by Roger G. Dunham and Geoffrey P. Alpert (Long Grove, Ill.: Waveland, 2005), pp. 231–257; quotation is on p. 254.

39. Lawrence W. Sherman, ed., *Police Corruption: A Sociological Perspective* (Garden City, N.Y.: Doubleday, 1974), p. 6.

40. Wilson, *Varieties of Police Behavior*, Chapters 5–7, pp. 140–226.

41. Sherman, ed., *Police Corruption*, pp. 7–8.

42. Ibid., pp. 1–39.

43. *The Knapp Commission Report on Police Corruption* (New York: Braziller, 1972).

44. Herman Goldstein, *Policing a Free Society* (Cambridge, Mass.: Ballinger, 1977), p. 218.

45. "Badges of Dishonor: In the Annals of Police Corruption, Experts Say They've Never Heard of a Case Like This," *Newsday* (New York) (14 March 2005), p. 7.

46. "Pursuing Corrupt Cops," *New York Times* (30 December 1993), p. 12.

47. "Police Corruption in New York Found Rarer but More Virulent," *Criminal Justice Newsletter* 25 (15 July 1994): 1–2.

48. "A Choice Word for Crime Lab Mess," *Houston Chronicle* (26 April 2003), p. 31.

49. "Metro Briefing: New York: Manhattan: New Anticorruption Chief," *New York Times* (3 June 2005), p. 4.

50. "Police Officers Were Hitmen for the Mafia," *Daily Telegraph* (Australia) (8 April 2006), p. 22.

51. "Judge in Mob Case Denies 2 Ex-Detectives Bail," *New York Times* (26 July 2006), p. 18.

52. "Perry Shouldn't Delay in Pardoning Tulia 35," *Austin America-Statesman* (31 July 2003), Editorial, p. 14; *60 Minutes* (4 July 2004).

53. Kenneth Adams, "What We Know about Police Use of Force," in *Use of Force by Police: Overview of Local and National Data*, National Institute of Justice Research Report (Washington, D.C.: U.S. Department of Justice, 1999), reprinted in Dunham and Alpert, *Critical Issues in Policing*, pp. 453–460.

54. Ibid., pp. 462–465.

55. Catherine H. Milton et al., *Police Use of Deadly Force* (Washington, D.C.: Police Foundation, 1977), p. 41.

56. Tennessee v. Garner, 471 U.S. 1 (1985).

57. "New Pursuit Rules Held a Week: Police Intend to Work Out Kinks before Changing Policy," *Daily News of Los Angeles* (3 May 2003), p. 3N.

58. Geoffrey P. Alpert, National Criminal Justice Reference Service, *Police Pursuit: Policies and Training* (Washington,

D.C.: U.S. Department of Justice, 1997), as cited in "Police Tightening Policies on High-Speed Chases, Study Finds," *Criminal Justice Newsletter* 28 (1 July 1997): 6.

59. "Most Police Chase Accidents Occur in First Two Minutes, Study Finds," *Criminal Justice Newsletter* 29 (3 August 1999): 7.

60. Albert J. Reiss Jr., "Police Brutality," *Transaction Magazine* 5 (1968), reprinted in *Police Behavior: A Sociological Perspective*, ed. Richard J. Lundman (New York: Oxford University Press, 1980), pp. 274–275.

61. Ibid., p. 276.

62. Federal Bureau of Investigation, *Crime in the United States 2002* (Washington, D.C.: U.S. Department of Justice, 2003), p. 323; *Crime in the United States 2003*, p. 365; *Crime in the United States, 2004*, p. 370; "Law Enforcement Officers Feloniously Killed," http://www.fbi.gov/ucr/killed/2005/feloniouslykilled.htm, accessed 17 March 2007.

63. Milton et al., *Police Use of Deadly Force*, p. 3.

64. U.S. Commission on Civil Rights, *Who Is Guarding the Guardians?* p. 35.

65. Ibid., pp. 157, 159. See also pp. 58–79.

66. *Early Warning Systems: Responding to the Problem Police Officer* (Rockville, Md.: U.S. Department of Justice, 2001), as cited in "Police Creating Warning Systems for Potential Problem Officers," *Criminal Justice Newsletter* 31, no. 17 (19 September 2001): 4.

67. Matthew J. Hickman and Brian A. Reeves, *Local Police Departments, 2003*, Bureau of Justice Statistics (Washington, D.C.: U.S. Department of Justice, May 2006), p. iv.

68. Weeks v. United States, 232 U.S. 383 (1914); Mapp v. Ohio, 367 U.S. 643 (1961).

69. Lawrence Crocker, "Can the Exclusionary Rule Be Saved?" *Journal of Criminal Law & Criminology* 84 (Summer 1993): 310–351; quotation is on pp. 310–311.

70. Olmstead v. United States, 277 U.S. 438, 485 (1928), Justice Brandeis, dissenting.

71. Elkins v. United States, 364 U.S. 206, 217 (1960).

72. See Stephen H. Sachs, "The Exclusionary Rule: A Prosecutor's Defense," *Criminal Justice Ethics* 1 (Summer/Fall 1982): n.p.

73. Crocker, "Can the Exclusionary Rule Be Saved?" p. 311.

74. Massachusetts v. Sheppard, 468 U.S. 981 (1984). See also United States v. Leon, 468 U.S. 897 (1984) (decided the same day).

75. Arizona v. Evans, 514 U.S. 1 (1995).

76. Maryland v. Garrison, 480 U.S. 79 (1987).

77. Arizona v. Youngblood, 488 U.S. 51 (1988).

78. Nix v. Williams, 467 U.S. 431 (1984).

79. New York v. Harris, 495 U.S. 14 (1990), referring to the previous case, Payton v. New York, 445 U.S. 573 (1980).

80. Arizona v. Fulminante, 499 U.S. 279 (1991).

81. U.S. Code, Chapter 42, Section 1983 (2007).

82. City of Canton, Ohio v. Harris, 489 U.S. 378 (1989).

83. Jackson v. Brister, 838 So.2d 274 (Miss. 2003).

84. U.S. Commission on Civil Rights, *Who Is Guarding the Guardians?* p. 2.

85. See Jerome H. Skolnick and David H. Bayley, *The New Blue Line: Police Innovation in Six American Cities* (New York: Free Press, 1986); Albert J. Reiss Jr., *Policing in a City's Central District: The Oakland Story* (Washington, D.C.: National Institute of Justice, 1985).

86. Herman Goldstein, "Toward Community-Oriented Policing: Potential, Basic Requirements, and Threshold Questions," *Crime & Delinquency* 33 (January 1987): 28.

87. U.S. Commission on Civil Rights, *Who Is Guarding the Guardians?* p. vi.

88. National Minority Advisory Council on Criminal Justice, *The Inequality of Justice: A Report on Crime and the Administration of Justice in the Minority Community* (October 1980), pp. 15–16, as quoted in U.S. Commission on Civil Rights, *Who Is Guarding the Guardians?* p. 2.

89. U.S. Commission on Civil Rights, *Who Is Guarding the Guardians?* p. 2.

90. Ibid., p. 154.

91. See Johnson v. Transportation Agency, 480 U.S. 616 (1987).

92. Gratz v. Bollinger, 539 U.S. 244 (2003).

93. Grutter v. Bollinger, 539 U.S. 306 (2003).

94. "300 Groups File Briefs to Support the University of Michigan in an Affirmative Action Case," *New York Times* (18 February 2003), p. 14.

95. Grutter v. Bollinger, 539 U.S. 306 (2003).

96. Michael K. Brown, *Working the Street: Police Discretion and the Dilemmas of Reform* (New York: Russell Sage, 1981).

97. Quoted in Claudia Dreifus, "A Conversation with Joseph Wambaugh," *Police Magazine* (May 1980), pp. 37–38.

3

Processing a Criminal Case: Criminal Court Systems

The processing of a criminal case involves a complex series of stages that center on the criminal courts. The chapters in Part 3 examine the pretrial, trial, and appellate procedures of criminal court systems. Chapter 6 explores the structure of courts, how they are administered, what role judges play in the court system, and what might be done about the current crisis in courts created by the increase in cases.

Attorneys play important roles in the trial of criminal cases. Prosecutors and defense attorneys are seen popularly as fighting their battles in the drama of criminal courtrooms. Their roles are far more complex, however, than the media portray. Chapter 7 looks at the differences between the prosecution and the defense, and analyzes their roles in criminal justice systems. Particular attention is given to prosecutorial discretion. Chapter 7 also covers pretrial procedures, including the frequently used and highly controversial process of plea bargaining.

Chapter 8 focuses on the trial of a criminal case, examining each step of the trial and explaining the roles of defense, prosecution, and judges. But perhaps the most controversial process in criminal justice systems is the sentencing of persons who are found guilty. Chapter 8 examines recent trends in sentencing, along with the sentencing process and an analysis of issues raised by sentencing. The chapter closes with a discussion of appeals.

Criminal Court Systems

The importance of courts in American criminal law cannot be overemphasized. Courts supervise most aspects of criminal justice systems. The actions that occur within courts affect all other aspects of criminal justice systems. The judicial branch of the government is separate from the legislative and executive branches, and the separation of powers is important. However, a survey commissioned by the American Bar Association (ABA) and published in 2005 revealed that most of the survey respondents had limited knowledge of this important separation of powers. Although 82 percent of the respondents replied that the separation of powers is "very important" or "important," 48 percent did not know what is meant by *separation of powers*. Perhaps more shocking is that 40 percent of the respondents could not name the three branches of government to which the doctrine applies, and 44 percent could not name the basic function of the judicial branch.[1]

Today, courts are under more severe attack than ever before. In 2005 the president of the ABA expressed his concern regarding the "alarming increase in rhetorical and physical attacks on the judiciary" and concluded that we need to teach our citizens the reasons our country established an independent judiciary. Michael Greco concluded his brief remarks with these words:

> Those who would tear down our courts, for short-term political or other gain threaten the very fabric of our republic. It is our responsibility to ensure that judges are able to decide cases fairly and without fear of retribution, and that the judiciary receives the resources and respect it must have to do its job. If we do not protect our courts, our courts cannot protect us.[2]

This chapter begins with an introduction to some legal concepts that must be understood for an adequate explanation of courts. It examines court structures, pointing out the distinctions between federal and state court systems. Both systems have trial and appellate courts; those types are discussed and distinguished. The highest court in the United States, the U.S. Supreme Court, is examined in more detail. The next major section of the chapter examines the judge's role. The final section focuses on court congestion and discusses solutions to this major problem.

L E A R N I N G
OBJECTIVES

After reading this chapter, you should be able to do the following:

- **Discuss the judicial branch of government, define basic legal terminology regarding courts, and distinguish between trial and appellate courts.**
- **Diagram the levels of state and federal court systems, and explain what happens at each level.**
- **Discuss the history and purpose of the U.S. Supreme Court, and explain and evaluate its functions and operations.**
- **Describe the role of judges in criminal trials.**
- **Explain and evaluate the sentencing role of trial judges.**
- **Contrast the role of an appellate judge with that of a trial judge.**
- **List and explain two methods for selecting judges.**
- **Explain briefly the training, retention, and control of judges.**
- **Describe court congestion and suggest remedies.**

6-1   The Judicial Branch of Government

The framers of the U.S. Constitution established three branches of government at the national level—legislative, executive, and judicial—and provided for the establishment of one supreme court. They envisioned a separation of the powers of these three branches, although there is some overlap. Federal **judges** and the U.S. Supreme Court justices are appointed by the president, representing the executive branch, and confirmed by the Senate, representing the legislative branch. Because courts have limited enforcement powers, they rely on the executive branch for enforcement of their decisions. The court system must depend on the legislative branch of government for financial appropriations.

In U.S. criminal justice systems, a separate judicial branch is viewed as necessary for assuring that the constitutional and statutory rights of citizens are not controlled by political pressures. In practice, however, political pressures may enter into the selection of judges, as well as into the organization and administration of courts and the judicial decision-making process. As mentioned previously, the judiciary has come under attack recently, and there is danger of damaging the delicate balance of powers among the three branches of government. In 2005, ABA's president Greco appointed a commission to develop ways to improve the understanding that U.S. citizens have of civics in general and the separation of powers in particular. That commission, named the ABA Commission on Civic Education and the Separation of Powers, is composed of representatives from all three branches of government. The committee's honorary co-chairs are retired U.S. Supreme Court justice, Sandra Day O'Connor, and former U.S. senator, Bill Bradley.

> **Judge** An elected or appointed officer of the court who presides over a court of law. The final and neutral arbiter of law who is responsible for all activities within that court system.

6-1a   Definitions of Legal Terms

For a complete understanding of criminal court systems, it is necessary to understand some legal terms and concepts. *Jurisdiction* refers to a court's power to hear and decide a case. This power is given by the constitution or statute that created that court. A court's jurisdiction may be limited to a certain age group (e.g., juvenile courts, with jurisdiction over juvenile delinquency, child custody, and adoption proceedings) or to a particular type of law (e.g., criminal, civil, bankruptcy). Some courts have jurisdiction only over minor offenses, or *misdemeanors*. Others hear only the more serious kinds of offenses, called *felonies*. Some courts hear only civil cases, others only criminal cases. This text is concerned primarily with courts that have jurisdiction over criminal law, although at appellate levels, most courts hear both criminal and civil cases.

It is important to distinguish original from appellate jurisdiction. *Original jurisdiction* refers to the jurisdiction of the court that may hear a case first—that is, the court that may try the facts. *Appellate jurisdiction* refers to the jurisdiction of the court that may hear the case on appeal. When more than one court may hear a case, those courts have *concurrent jurisdiction*. When only one court may hear a case, that court has *exclusive jurisdiction*.

The subject of jurisdiction arose in a highly publicized case in January 2000, after Michael Skakel, a nephew of the late Senator Robert F. Kennedy, was arrested and charged with the murder of Martha Moxley, age 14, almost 25 years earlier. Skakel, a neighbor and friend of Moxley's, was 15 at the time of her murder, which would have given the juvenile court jurisdiction over him at the time of the murder. That jurisdiction would have ended when Skakel reached 21. The defense argued that no court had jurisdiction over Skakel in the year 2000. The prosecutor argued that the adult criminal court had jurisdiction because Skakel was 39 at the time of his arrest. The trial judge ruled that the adult criminal court had jurisdiction to try the case.

In June 2002, Skakel was convicted of Moxley's murder; he was sentenced to 20 years to life in prison. Although his appeals on issues of law have been declined, in April 2007, he was granted a hearing on his motion for a new trial.[3] The Connecticut Superior Court was considering that motion, based on arguments of new evidence, when this text went to press.

Another limitation on courts is that they hear only actual cases and controversies. Courts do not decide hypothetical issues, and normally they do not give advisory opinions. Only when a dispute involves a legal right between two or more parties will a court hear the case. If the controversy ends before the completion of the trial or the appeal, usually the court will not decide the case, as the issue is **moot**, meaning that it is no longer a real case because no legal issue between the parties remains to be resolved. Thus, if a defendant has appealed the exclusion of evidence at trial but the case is decided on a plea bargain, there is no reason for the appellate court to hear the appeal on the evidence issue: that issue is moot once the defendant and the prosecution have agreed to a plea that has been accepted by the trial court judge.

Because law needs stability, courts follow the rule of *stare decisis* ("to abide by, or adhere to, decided cases"), whereby previous decisions become precedents for current and future decisions. But law is flexible, and courts may overrule (specifically or by implication) their previous decisions, although this is not done often.

It is important to distinguish between the rule of the court and the **dicta** of the judges or justices. Dicta refers to judicial comments on issues that are not part of the court's ruling. These comments, even if they represent the opinion of a majority of the court, must be recognized as dicta and not confused with the holding or rule of law of the court. For this reason, it is necessary to read cases carefully.

Most appellate court judges and justices issue written opinions that are recorded in official reports. Decisions of the U.S. Supreme Court are recorded officially in the *United States Reports*, but this official printing may take a year or longer. When recent U.S. Supreme Court cases are cited in this text, endnotes reference those cases as printed in the *Supreme Court Reporter* (S.Ct.), the *U.S. Law Week* (USLW), or a legal computer service, such as Lexis-Nexis, which also provides access to important information, such as the prior decisions in those cases, as well as any subsequent court action. Today, U.S. Supreme Court cases are also available on the Internet.

Decisions of the U.S. Supreme Court are binding on all lower federal courts. They are also binding on state courts when applicable—that is, where *federal* statutory or constitutional rights are involved.

Moot   The term used to describe a controversy that has ended or evolved to the stage at which a court decision is no longer relevant or necessary.

Stare decisis   Literally, "let the decision stand." The doctrine that courts will abide by or adhere to the rulings of previous court decisions when deciding cases having substantially the same facts.

Dicta   The written portions of a judge's opinion that are not part of the actual ruling of the court and are not legally binding precedents for future court decisions.

6-1b   Trial and Appellate Courts

Trial and appellate courts exist at the state and federal levels. Both are involved in making and interpreting laws, but generally, trial courts try the facts of the case, and appellate courts are concerned only with law. There are exceptions.

Trial courts are the major fact finders in a case. The trial jury (or judge if the case is not tried before a jury) decides the basic questions of fact. In a criminal trial, for example, the trial jury decides whether the accused committed the crime for which he or she is being tried, whether a defense (such as insanity) was proved, and so on. In making these findings, the jury considers evidence presented by both the defense and the prosecution. Because the trial judge and jury hear and see the witnesses, they are in a better position than the appellate court to decide whether those witnesses are credible. Thus, it is argued, the appellate court should be confined to issues of law and not be permitted to reverse a trial court's decision regarding ultimate fact issues, such as guilt or innocence.

After the judge or jury has made a decision at the trial level, the defendant, if found guilty, may **appeal** that decision. At the appellate level, the **appellant**, the defendant at trial, alleges errors in the trial court proceeding (e.g., admission of an illegal confession or exclusion of minorities from the jury) and asks for a new trial. The **appellee**, the prosecution at trial, argues that either errors did not exist or that the errors did not prejudice the appellant and therefore a new trial should not be granted.

Appeal cases are heard by judges or justices, rather than juries. The appellate court looks at the trial court record, considers written briefs submitted by attorneys who use them to establish and support their legal arguments, and may hear oral arguments from counsel for the defense and the prosecution regarding alleged errors of law during the trial. The appellate court makes a ruling on those issues. The court may hold that no errors were committed during the trial, in which case the appellate court *affirms* the lower court's decision. It may hold that there were errors but that the errors did not prejudice the defendant, and thus the conviction stands. The court may hold that there were errors and that one or more of those errors prejudiced the defendant, which means that the defendant could not have received a fair trial. In that case, the appellate court may reverse the case and send it back for another trial with instructions concerning the errors. This process is referred to as *reversed and remanded*. The court may also reverse the case *with prejudice*, meaning that no further trials may be permitted on those charges.

In essence, appellate courts are assessing the work of trial courts. This system allows appellate courts to exercise some administrative control over trial courts, thus achieving more uniformity among courts than would exist otherwise. Trial court judges and juries exercise considerable power in criminal justice systems, however, as most cases are not appealed. In cases that are appealed and retried, the lower court frequently reaches the same decision on retrial.

In addition to the power to hear and decide cases appealed on facts of law in criminal trials, appellate courts have the power of **judicial review** over acts of the legislative and executive branches of government if those acts infringe on freedoms and liberties guaranteed by the state statutes and state constitutions (in state cases) and by the U.S. Constitution or federal laws (in federal cases). This power of judicial review represents the great authority of courts. The U.S. Supreme Court also has the power to declare acts of the president or of Congress unconstitutional.

The highest court of each state determines the constitutionality of that state's statutes in relation to its constitution. The U.S. Supreme Court is the final decision maker in the process of judicial review of federal statutes and U.S. constitutional issues.

6-2   The Dual Court System

The United States has a dual court system consisting of state and federal courts, as diagrammed in Figure 6-1. State crimes are prosecuted in state courts, and federal crimes are tried in federal courts. State crimes are defined by state statutes, federal crimes by Congress.

▶ **Appeal**   The stage in a judicial proceeding in which a higher court is asked to review a decision of a lower court.

▶ **Appellant**   The losing party in a lower court, who seeks a review of the decision by a higher appellate court.

▶ **Appellee**   The winning party in a lower court, who argues on appeal against reversing the lower court's decision.

▶ **Judicial review**   The authority of an appellate court to check the decisions of lower courts as well as those within the executive and legislative branches of government within its jurisdiction to determine whether any of those acts are in violation of statutes or constitutions. Also, the power of an appellate court to review the actions of a trial court or a lower appellate court.

Figure 6-1

The U.S. Dual Court System

Note: Arrows indicate general avenues of appeal; there may be some exceptions. State court systems are explained in more detail in Spotlight 6-1.

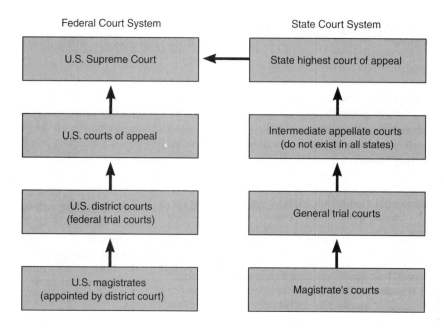

Some acts violate both federal and state statutes, in which case the defendant may be tried in a state or a federal court or both. For example, the four Los Angeles police officers who were acquitted of charges in a California *state* court (review again Spotlight 5-4) were tried in a *federal* court for the violation of Rodney King's federal civil rights; two were convicted.

Lower federal and state courts constitute separate systems. Cases may not be appealed from a state court to a federal court, except to the U.S. Supreme Court, and then only when a federal statutory or constitutional right is at issue. Federal and state courts may hear only cases over which they have jurisdiction. Many of the cases brought in federal courts by state inmates are appropriate to those courts because the inmates are alleging that federal rights have been violated.

A closer look at the structure and organization of state and federal court systems facilitates understanding of the subsequent material in this chapter, as well as the analysis of pretrial and trial processes in subsequent chapters. This discussion begins with the state court systems, since most criminal cases are tried in state and local courts.

6-2a   State Courts

Considerable variation exists in the organization of state court systems. Diversity exists within states, too, leading to problems that have prompted some states to move toward a unified court system. Despite the variety in systems, it is possible to make some general observations that provide an overview of state court systems. This discussion focuses on courts that process criminal cases (although they may also process civil cases). The main aspects of the structure, function, and jurisdiction of state courts are summarized in Spotlight 6-1.

Courts of Limited Jurisdiction

In discussions about courts, frequent references are made to lower courts. These are the courts of limited jurisdiction, so-called because, legally, they are entitled to hear only specific types of cases. Usually, jurisdiction is limited to minor civil cases and criminal misdemeanors. Jurisdiction over criminal cases may be limited to certain kinds of misdemeanors, such as those that carry a jail or short prison term or some other, less serious, sanction.

Jurisdiction may be limited to certain activities of the courts. The judge or magistrate who presides over courts of limited jurisdiction may conduct some pretrial

Spotlight 6-1	Structure and Jurisdiction of State Court System

Court	Structure	Jurisdiction
Highest state appellate court (usually called the supreme court)	Consists of five, seven, or nine justices, who may be appointed or elected; cases decided by this court may not be appealed to the U.S. Supreme Court unless they involve a federal question, and then there is no right of appeal except in limited cases.	If there is no intermediate appellate court, defendants convicted in a general trial court have a right of appeal to this court; if there is an intermediate appellate court, this court has discretion to limit appeals with few exceptions, such as in capital cases.
Intermediate appellate court (also called court of appeals; exists in approximately half of the states)	May have one court that hears appeals from all general trial courts or may have more than one court, each with appellate jurisdiction over a particular area of the state; usually has a panel of three judges.	Defendants convicted in general trial court have right of appeal to this level.
General trial courts (also called superior courts, circuit courts, district courts, court of common pleas)	Usually, state is divided into judicial districts, with one general trial court in each district, often one per county; courts may be divided by function, such as civil, criminal, probate, domestic.	Jurisdiction to try cases usually begins where jurisdiction of lower court ends, so this court tries more serious cases; may have appellate jurisdiction over cases decided in lower courts.
Courts of limited jurisdiction (also called magistrate's courts, police courts, justice of peace courts, municipal courts)	Differ from state to state; some states divide the state into districts, with each district having the same type of lower court; in other states, courts are located in political subdivisions, such as cities or townships, in which case the structure may differ from court to court; may not be a court of record, in which case the system will permit trial *de novo* in general trial court; particularly in rural areas, magistrates may not be lawyers and may work only part-time.	May be limited to specific proceedings, such as initial appearance, preliminary hearing, issuing of search and arrest warrants, setting of bail, appointing of counsel for indigent defendants; jurisdiction of cases is limited to certain types, usually the lesser criminal and civil cases; some jurisdictions may hear all misdemeanors; others are limited to misdemeanors with minor penalties.

procedures, such as issuing warrants for searches or arrests, deciding bail, appointing counsel for indigent defendants, or presiding over the initial appearance or preliminary hearing.

Lower courts, which are called by various names, as noted in Spotlight 6-1, should not be considered unimportant due to their limited jurisdiction. Certainly, their ability to grant or deny bail or some other method of pretrial release is a tremendous power. Despite the importance of lower courts, many are underfinanced and staffed by part-time judges with limited staff and resources.

General Trial Courts

General trial courts are called by various names, as noted in Spotlight 6-1. Usually, these courts have a wider geographical base than lower courts. In large areas, the general trial court may be divided by functions: traffic cases, domestic cases, civil cases (excluding domestic and traffic cases), probate, estates and wills, and criminal cases. Smaller jurisdictions may have fewer divisions. A civil and a criminal division is one frequently used model.

In most systems, the jurisdiction of general trial courts begins where the jurisdiction of the lower courts ends and includes the more serious cases. If the lower court is not a court of record, meaning that the court does not make provision for a transcript of the proceedings, a case appealed from the lower court to the general trial court may

Professions 6-1

Careers in Criminal Court Systems

A wide variety of positions exist in criminal court systems. Not all require a law degree, but those of lawyers and judges generally do.

Lawyers perform various functions in court systems. *Prosecutors* represent the government and prosecute cases; *defense attorneys* represent those who are accused of violating criminal law. Lawyers must receive a law degree (usually a three-year program) and pass the state bar. Although some states are reciprocal and permit attorneys from other states to be admitted to practice through a petitions process, many require that the bar be taken in that state. Some permit attorneys from other states to become members of the bar by taking only part of the exam, provided they have passed the bar of another state and have engaged in some years of practice.

Most *judges* are lawyers. Some of them have practiced law; others have not. Judges may or may not have received special training for their roles, although it is becoming more common to provide judicial training.

Paralegals may perform some legal functions in criminal court systems, but they are not recognized as lawyers and generally must be supervised by attorneys. They have some legal training, but it is not as extensive as that required for a law degree. *Legal assistants* and *law clerks* may assist attorneys, but they, too, must be supervised. Although the position of law clerk (generally held by law students) usually does not pay well, that is not the case with legal assistant and paralegal positions, which, in some jurisdictions, are relatively high-paying.

The *court clerk*, normally a position that does not require formal legal training, is the court officer charged by statute or court rules with the responsibility of maintaining all court records. The court clerk files the pleadings and motions and records any decisions made by the court. These are very important functions because judgments are not enforceable if they have not been filed properly. The court clerk is assisted by a staff, which in large jurisdictions may include a deputy for each of the court's divisions (such as traffic, probate, civil,

and criminal). Various personnel may be employed to handle the paperwork of the court.

The *bailiff*, perhaps best known for pronouncing, "Hear ye, hear ye, this court of the Honorable Judge Smith is in session; all rise" before the judge's entry into the courtroom, has a variety of functions. The bailiff is charged with keeping order in the courtroom and may eject or otherwise discipline people who do not observe proper courtroom behavior. The bailiff may transport defendants to and from the court, pass papers and exhibits to and from attorneys and the judge, run errands for the judge, and guard the jury during its deliberations. In some courts, a deputy sheriff performs the bailiff's functions. In federal courts, a deputy marshal may serve as bailiff. And in state courts, the bailiff's position may carry a different title, such as *court service officer*.

In courts of record, a verbatim account of all proceedings is kept by a *court reporter*. The proceedings are not transcribed unless one or both of the parties request it, in which case there is a fee. If a criminal defendant is indigent, the state pays for the transcript when it is required for an appeal. Court reporters also record proceedings outside of court when attorneys are securing evidence for trial by questioning witnesses. Court reporters must have extensive training, and generally, the pay is very good. Many court reporters have their own businesses; others are employed by the courts.

The *minute clerk* is an employee of the court who records an outline of what happens during the proceedings but does not maintain a verbatim account. The minute clerk might record the charges against the defendant, summarize the process of selecting the jury, perhaps note the time spent in that process, list the names of the jurors and alternates, summarize the presented evidence, and record the court's decision.

Larger court systems employ other professionals. *Counselors* or *social workers* may be available, along with *psychologists, statisticians, probation officers,* and *clerical personnel.*

De novo Literally, anew or fresh. A trial *de novo* is a case that is tried again, as if no decision had been previously rendered. In some jurisdictions, the first appeal from a lower court may be a trial *de novo*. The term may be used to refer to other proceedings, such as hearings.

be tried **de novo**, which means a new trial. In that instance, the evidence will be presented again. Over time, however, evidence may be destroyed, and witnesses may die or forget. So the probability of being convicted when a case is tried *de novo* at this level may be lower than the probability of conviction in the lower court.

Both of the court levels discussed thus far are at the trial level. Before considering state appellate courts, it is important to note the personnel and their functions in trial courts. These may vary among jurisdictions, but most are fairly common and are noted in Professions 6-1. Some of these positions are also characteristic of appellate courts.

Intermediate Appellate Courts

All states provide for at least one appeal from an adverse decision in a criminal trial, but only about half of the states have an intermediate appellate court, usually called a *court of appeals.* In states that have an intermediate appellate court, only one court may hear all appeals, or courts in various districts may hear appeals from their respective geographical areas. Defendants who have been convicted in general trial courts have a right to appeal to this court where it exists. If it does not exist, they have a right to appeal to the highest court; however, if the state has an intermediate appellate court, the defendant may not have a right to appeal to more than one appellate court, except in capital (death penalty) cases. Thus, the defendant who loses an appeal at the intermediate appellate level may have no other appeal unless he or she has other legal issues that might be raised—for example, in a federal court.

Highest State Appellate Courts

If the state does not have an intermediate appellate court, cases may be appealed from the general trial courts to the highest court, which in most states is called the *state supreme court*. Justices of this court are either elected or appointed, and the court may have five, seven, or nine justices. In states having intermediate appellate courts, except in a few types of cases, the highest appellate court has the power to limit the cases it hears and decides. This court has the final decision on cases that involve legal issues pertaining to the constitution or statutes of the state in which the case is brought. If the case involves any federal issues, the defendant may appeal to the U.S. Supreme Court, although that Court hears only a limited number of the cases for which review is requested.

Two states have two final appellate courts. Texas and Oklahoma have a final court of appeals for criminal cases and a second one for civil cases. Cases may not be appealed from one of these courts to the other.

6-2b   Federal Courts

In the federal court system, U.S. magistrates, judicial officers appointed by the district court (as noted in Figure 6-1), may have full jurisdiction over minor offenses, along with jurisdiction over some of the pretrial steps of more serious offenses. The basic trial courts in the federal system are the U.S. district courts. These courts hear cases in which individuals have been accused of violating federal criminal laws. They try civil cases that meet specified criteria. Each state has at least one federal district court, and some states have several. In the federal district courts, cases are prosecuted by U.S. attorneys and presided over by federal trial judges. These are appointed positions.

Cases appealed from federal district courts go to the appropriate intermediate federal appellate courts. These courts, referred to as *circuit courts*, are called the United States Court of Appeals for the First (Second, and so on) Judicial District. Decisions of the federal appellate courts are not binding on state courts unless they involve federally created procedural rights that have been held to apply to the states or federally protected constitutional rights, such as the right to counsel. The decision of one federal court of appeals is not binding on another federal appellate court. If federal circuit courts decide similar cases differently, the resulting conflict may be resolved only by the U.S. Supreme Court, the final appellate court in the federal system. The importance of that Court warrants a closer look, but first, it is appropriate to note some issues in the federal court system.

Each year, the chief justice of the U.S. Supreme Court gives a state of the federal court system. In his January 2006 report, recently appointed Chief Justice John G. Roberts Jr. continued in the path of his mentor, the late Chief Justice William H. Rehnquist, asking for higher salaries for the federal judiciary. In his January 2007 report, Roberts again pressed for higher judicial salaries.

The 2006 yearly salaries of federal judges and justices were as follows:

District judges—$165,200
Appellate judges—$175,100
Associate justices of the U.S. Supreme Court—$203,000
Chief justice of the U.S. Supreme Court—$212,100[4]

According to Roberts, the issue of judicial pay has been ignored for too long "and has now reached the level of a constitutional crisis that threatens to undermine the strength and independence of the federal judiciary." The chief justice explained that, when adjusted for inflation, federal judicial salaries show a 23.9 percent decline since 1969. He noted that some young law graduates have beginning salaries that exceed those of the federal judges before whom they practice. The chief justice emphasized that federal judges and justices do not have a constituency in Congress to lobby for them and that a bill to raise judicial salaries by 16.5 percent died in Congress in 2006 without coming to a vote. Chief Justice Roberts continued:

> If judicial appointment ceases to be the capstone of a distinguished career and instead becomes a stepping stone to a lucrative position in private practice, the Framers' goal of a truly independent judiciary will be placed in serious jeopardy.[5]

A law professor who analyzed federal judicial salaries and tenure spoke in favor of increased salaries because federal judges deserve them ("compensation ought to bear some relationship to a job's value") but emphasized that, despite relatively low salaries, many lawyers still apply for federal judgeships. Federal judges are appointed for life, they retire at full pay, they do not have the pressures of private lawyers to bill enough hours to meet the firm's demands, they do not face civil liability for their actions, and they enjoy great prestige. The professor continued with these comments:

> Meanwhile, practicing lawyers report extraordinary levels of job dissatisfaction, sometimes bordering on outright despair. Those high salaries come at an equally high cost, exacting their toll in time and stress. It is hardly surprising, therefore, that lawyers are abandoning private practice at a far greater rate than federal judges are leaving the bench.[6]

In March 2003, President George W. Bush signed legislation that gives all federal judges a cost-of-living raise each year. Prior to the enactment of this legislation, federal judges did not receive this raise automatically; Congress was required to determine their raises. Almost all other federal employees, however, already received cost-of-living raises.[7]

6-3 The U.S. Supreme Court

The U.S. Supreme Court is the only specific court established by the federal Constitution, which designates a few cases in which the Supreme Court has original jurisdiction. The Court has appellate jurisdiction under such exceptions and regulations as determined by Congress. In the debates of the Constitutional Convention, it was recognized that the Supreme Court would have the power to review state court decisions whenever those decisions affect *federal* rights.

The basic function of the U.S. Supreme Court is to interpret federal laws and the federal Constitution. In fulfilling this judicial review function, the Court is often accused of making law or of reshaping the Constitution. Technically, the Court does not make but, rather, *interprets* law. A former member of the Court said that the justices "breathe life, feeble or strong, into the inert pages of the Constitution and of statute books." One constitutional lawyer pointed out that "it matters who does the breathing."[8]

Nine justices sit on the U.S. Supreme Court. The Court began its 2006–2007 term with eight men, one of whom is African American, and one woman. Upon the death of Chief Justice William H. Rehnquist in 2005, Judge John G. Roberts Jr. was nominated and confirmed as the chief justice, who presides over the Court. Justice Sandra Day O'Connor retired in 2005 and was replaced by Justice Samuel Alito. The other U.S. Supreme Court justices are: Ruth Bader Ginsburg, Stephen Breyer, John Paul Stevens, Antonin Scalia, Anthony M. Kennedy, David Hackett Souter, and Clarence Thomas. Professions 6-2 contains pertinent information concerning what one might expect to see and hear during a Supreme Court session.

A case gets before the U.S. Supreme Court if the Court grants a **writ of *certiorari*** on an appealed case. A *writ* is an order from a court authorizing or ordering that an action be done. *Certiorari* literally means "to be informed of." When the Supreme Court grants a writ of *certiorari*, in effect it is agreeing to hear a case appealed from a

▶ **Writ of *certiorari*** *Certiorari* literally means "to be informed of." A *writ* is an order from a court giving authority for an act to be done or ordering that it be done. A writ of *certiorari* is used by courts that have discretion to determine which cases they will hear. Today, this writ is most commonly associated with the U.S. Supreme Court.

Professions 6-2

The U.S. Supreme Court

General Procedures

Welcome to the Supreme Court of the United States.

This is your Supreme Court and we hope you find your visit here enjoyable, interesting and informative. However, we do ask you to recognize our restrictions and requirements for visitors. In order to maintain the atmosphere one might expect in the nation's highest court, we would appreciate your cooperation.

Please refrain from smoking and restrict food and beverages to the cafeteria, snack bar, and vending machine alcove.

Be as quiet as possible. There are Court employees working in their offices near the public areas of the building who would appreciate not being disturbed.

Oral Argument

You are about to attend an oral argument. A case selected for argument usually involves interpretations of the U.S. Constitution or federal law. At least four Justices have selected the case as being of such importance that the Supreme Court must resolve the legal issues.

An attorney for each side of a case will have an opportunity to make a presentation to the Court and answer questions posed by the Justices. Prior to the argument each side has submitted a legal brief—a written legal argument outlining each party's points of law. The Justices have read these briefs prior to argument and are thoroughly familiar with the case, its facts, and the legal positions that each party is advocating.

Beginning the first Monday in October, the Court is scheduled to hear up to four one-hour arguments a day, three days a week, in two-week intervals (with longer breaks in December and February), concluding the oral argument portion of the term in late April. Typically, two arguments are held in the mornings beginning at 10 A.M. and two in the afternoons beginning at 1 P.M. on Monday, Tuesday, and Wednesday. In the recesses between argument sessions, the Justices are busy writing opinions, deciding which cases to hear in the future, and reading the briefs for the next argument session. They grant review in approximately 100–120 of the more than 7,000 petitions filed with the Court each term. No one knows exactly when a decision will be handed down by the Court in an argued case, nor is there a set time period in which the Justices must reach a decision. However, all cases argued during a term of Court are decided before the summer recess begins, usually by the end of June.

During an argument week, the Justices meet in a private conference, closed even to staff, to discuss the cases and to take a preliminary vote on each case. If the Chief Justice is in the majority on a case decision, he decides to write it himself or he may assign that duty to any other Justice in the majority. If the Chief Justice is in the minority, the Justice in the majority who has the most seniority assumes the assignment duty.

Draft opinions are privately circulated among the Justices until a final draft is agreed upon. When a final decision has been reached, the Justice who wrote the opinion announces the decision in a Court session and may deliver a summary of the Court's reasoning. Meanwhile, the Public Information Office releases the full text of the opinion to the public and news media.

Participants in the Courtroom

Justices. The Justices enter the Courtroom through three entrances behind the Bench. The Chief Justice and two senior Associate Justices enter through the center, and three Associate Justices enter through each side. They also sit on the Bench in order of seniority with the Chief Justice in the middle, and the others alternating from left to right, ending with the most junior Associate Justice on the far right, as you face the Bench.

Clerk. The Clerk of the Supreme Court or his representative sits to the left of the Bench. His responsibilities in the Courtroom include providing the Justices with materials about the case if the Justices desire additional documents and notifying the appropriate Court personnel when an opinion can be released to the public. He also swears in new members of the Supreme Court Bar.

Marshal. The Marshal or his representative sits to the right side of the Bench. His roles are to call the Court to order, maintain decorum in the Courtroom, tape the audio portions of argument, and time the oral presentations so that attorneys do not exceed their one-half hour limitations.

Marshal's Aides. Marshal's aides are seated behind the Justices. They often carry messages to the Justices or convey messages from a Justice to a member of his or her staff.

Attorneys. The attorneys scheduled to argue cases are seated at the tables facing the Bench. The arguing attorney will stand behind the lectern immediately in front of the Chief Justice. On the lectern there are two lights. When the white light goes on, the attorney has five minutes remaining to argue. The red light indicates that the attorney has used all the allotted time.

Attorneys who are admitted as members of the Supreme Court Bar may be seated in the chairs just beyond the bronze railing. Any member of the Supreme Court Bar may attend any argument, space permitting.

Others

Law Clerks. Each Justice has the option of employing up to four law clerks as assistants. These clerks are law school graduates who have previously clerked for a federal judge on a lower court. The clerks often listen to oral arguments. They are seated in the chairs flanking the Courtroom on the right.

Special Guests. Guests of Justices are seated in the benches to the right of the bench and are seated in order of the seniority of the Justice who invited them. The row of black chairs in front of the guest section is reserved for retired Justices and officers of the Court, such as the Reporter of Decisions or the Librarian, who attend oral argument from time to time.

News Media. Members of the Supreme Court press corps sit to the left of the Bench in the benches and chairs facing the guest section. The press enter the Courtroom from the hallway on the left.

Source: Free Pamphlet available at the U.S. Supreme Court, Washington, D.C.

lower court and is ordering that court to produce the necessary documents for that appeal. If the Court denies *certiorari*, it is refusing to review the case, which means that the decision of the lower court stands. Four of the justices must vote in favor of a writ of *certiorari* for it to be granted. If an even number of justices is sitting and there is a tie vote, the decision being appealed is not granted *certiorari*, and the lower court's decision stands. In an average term, the Court hears only about 3 percent of the cases filed. In recent years, the U.S. Supreme Court has decreased the number of cases it decides. The Court has decided as many as 150 cases a year, but in recent years, the number has been around 80 per year.

One of the reasons for limiting the number of cases is the time required for oral arguments, as well as for the deliberations and opinion writing of the justices. The second reason the U.S. Supreme Court hears only a percentage of the cases filed was emphasized by a former chief justice of the Court:

> To remain effective, the Supreme Court must continue to decide only those cases which present questions whose resolution will have immediate importance far beyond the particular facts and parties involved.[9]

The U.S. Supreme Court may hear cases when lower court decisions on the issues in question have differed. The Court's decision becomes the final resolution of the issue, unless or until it is overruled by a subsequent U.S. Supreme Court decision, by a constitutional amendment, or by congressional legislation.

Cases that are accepted for review by the U.S. Supreme Court must be filed within a specified time before oral arguments. The attorneys who argue before the Court are under considerable pressure. They must be well prepared and are subject to being interrupted at any time by a justice's question. Attorneys are expected to argue their cases without reading from the prepared briefs. Each is limited to 30 minutes (sometimes an hour) for oral arguments.

Most U.S. Supreme Court decisions are announced in written opinions, which represent majority opinions in many cases. A **concurring opinion** may be written by a justice who voted with the Court but disagreed with one or more of its reasons, who agreed with the decision but for reasons other than those in the Court's opinion, or who agreed with the Court's reasons but wishes to emphasize or clarify one or more points. Thus, in some cases, the opinion of the Court represents the views of a plurality of the justices. Opinions concurring in part, dissenting in part, and dissenting entirely may also be written.

Judicial opinions, especially those of U.S. Supreme Court justices, are a very important part of U.S. legal systems. These opinions are read carefully by lawyers, who use the reasoning and conclusions of law in future cases. The justices circulate among themselves drafts of their opinions, which remain secret until the Court announces its decision in the case. Rarely is a written opinion the sole product of the justice whose name appears as the author.

Decisions of the U.S. Supreme Court are handed down on opinion days, usually three Mondays of each month of the term, although at times the Court also issues opinions on other days. The announced decisions are public, and the media pick up those portions of the decisions thought to be of greatest interest. Decisions of the U.S. Supreme Court are also available on the Internet.

> ▶ **Concurring opinion**
> A judge's written opinion agreeing with the result in a case but presenting other reasons for the decision or emphasizing some of the reasons stated by the majority opinion.

6-4 Judges in Criminal Court Systems

Historically, judges have been held in high esteem by the U.S. public. In recent years, however, the position of judge has come under severe criticism. In their decisions on pretrial releases, judges have been accused of releasing dangerous persons who prey on the public, commit more crimes, and terrorize citizens. In their sentencing decisions, judges have been accused of coddling criminals. Judges are easy scapegoats, and some critics are taking the opportunity to accuse them of causing most of the critical problems in the handling of criminals. Although some of the criticism is justified, much of it is not.

Judges begin their participation in criminal justice systems long before the trial. They determine whether there is probable cause to issue a search or an arrest warrant. After arrest, a suspect must be taken before a neutral magistrate or judge, who will determine whether there is probable cause to hold the alleged offender. Judges determine whether the accused is released on bail or some other pretrial procedure, or is detained in jail, awaiting trial.

Judges hear and rule on motions made by attorneys before trial. They approve plea bargains made between the prosecution and the defense. Judges play a critical role in the criminal trial. They hear and rule on motions made before, during, and after the trial, and in most cases, they determine the sentences of convicted offenders. Judges (or justices) at the appellate level determine whether cases should be reversed or affirmed.

6-4a   Trial Judges

At a trial, judges are referees. Theoretically, they are neither for nor against a particular position or issue but, rather, are committed to the fair implementation of the rules of evidence and law. They are charged with the responsibility of ensuring that attorneys follow the rules.

In the role of referee, the judge has immense power. If the defense makes a motion to have evidence suppressed on the grounds that it was allegedly obtained illegally, the judge's decision whether or not to grant that motion might be the deciding factor in the outcome of the case. Without the evidence, the prosecution might not be able to prove its case. Likewise, the judge's decision to admit evidence offered by the defendant, such as the testimony of a psychiatrist regarding the defendant's mental state, may be the deciding factor in the ability of the defense to convince the jury of its position.

Although trial judges' decisions may be appealed, most are not. Many decisions that are appealed are not reversed, and even if the defense wins on appeal, considerable time is lost—time that might have been spent by the accused in jail. Furthermore, the U.S. Supreme Court has emphasized that it is important to *prevent* problems at trial whenever possible, and that responsibility lies with the trial judge.

Another important responsibility of the trial judge is to rule on whether **expert witness** testimony may be admitted. Many issues in criminal cases are beyond the common knowledge of jurors, so it is necessary to submit expert testimony. In addition to deciding whether the area of expertise is acceptable, the judge must determine whether the offered expert is qualified to testify about that evidence. Generally, judges make these decisions after hearing oral arguments from the defense and the prosecution, and some judges require written motions by attorneys prior to those arguments.

Another responsibility of the trial judge is to decide whether there is sufficient evidence to send a case to the jury for a decision on the evidence presented or whether the case should be dismissed for lack of evidence. Even if the judge sends the case to the jury and the jury finds the defendant guilty, the trial judge may reverse that decision if he or she believes the evidence is not sufficient to determine guilt beyond a reasonable doubt. This power is given to judges so they can serve as a check on jurors who might be influenced by passion or prejudice despite the evidence in the case.

The role of the trial judge in deciding whether to accept a jury verdict is illustrated by the trial and conviction of au pair Louise Woodward, discussed in Spotlight 6-2.

After hearing the evidence in a case, a judge may direct the jury to return a verdict of **acquittal**. This may occur before the judge hears all the evidence, as well as after a jury verdict of guilty. Once the verdict of acquittal has been entered, the defendant may not be retried on the same issue; to do so would violate the defendant's constitutional right not to be tried twice for the same offense.

Another role of the judge is to instruct the jury regarding the law in the case it must decide. In addition, the judge must monitor all activities of the trial, ensuring that

> **Expert witness**   A person with extensive training or education in a particular field, such as medicine, who testifies at depositions or at trials concerning a critical issue of that case, such as what caused the death of the deceased.

> **Acquittal**   Legal verification of the innocence of a person in a criminal trial.

Spotlight 6-2   Judicial Power in Question: The Au Pair Case

In a case that gained international media attention in 1997, Louise Woodward, age 19, was convicted of second-degree murder in the death of Matthew Eappen, 8 months old. Woodward was a British au pair whom Matthew's parents had hired to take care of the baby and his older brother. Woodward was charged with murder after she called 911 to report that Matthew was not responsive. The prosecution argued that Woodward had shaken the baby and knocked his head against a wall or the tub. The defense claimed that Matthew died of a skull injury he had incurred several weeks prior to his death.

The defense asked the judge to instruct the jury on murder charges only, taking the gamble that, if the jury had to choose between murder and acquittal for Woodward, it would choose acquittal. The defense was wrong. After deliberating for 27 hours, the jury found Woodward guilty of second-degree murder; she faced life in prison.

At a subsequent hearing, the trial judge, Hiller B. Zobel, listened to arguments from both the defense and the prosecution, took a few days to contemplate, and then announced his decision: Louise Woodward's conviction for second-degree murder was not supported by the evidence. "Having considered the matter carefully, I am firmly convinced that the interests of justice…mandate my reducing the verdict to manslaughter. I do this in accordance with my discretion and my duty."[1]

The judge ruled that, had the jury been instructed on manslaughter, it might have chosen that option, which he believed was one rational conclusion based on the evidence. He did not believe the evidence supported a murder conviction. At a subsequent hearing, the judge sentenced Woodward to the time she had already served and set her free.

The Woodward case illustrates the judge's power to change a jury's decision if he or she believes such is required by the evidence. Some argue that this power is a plus in the system; others suggest that it is unreasonable and unfair. After the Woodward decision, the Massachusetts Society for the Prevention of Cruelty to Children published a letter signed by 49 child abuse specialists, stating that the prosecution's expert evidence at trial was overwhelmingly supportive of the theory that Woodward had shaken the baby and thus had caused his death. The case appeared to turn on the controversial scientific evidence, and perhaps one result of the case was a closer look at the presentation of such evidence in criminal trials.[2]

After serving only 279 days in prison, Woodward returned to her home in England, and in 2002, she received a law degree from London's South Bank University. Subsequently, she won a coveted place on the Legal Practice course at the Manchester Metropolitan University, becoming "the first convicted killer to be allowed on such a top course." Some of the students were furious when they discovered her identity. One said, "Louise is a convicted killer who uses a different name. Nobody told us she was on the course. We all found out by accident and were speechless." The student continued, "She may have paid her debt in America for what she did, but many of us still find it goes against the grain to have her sitting alongside us, on probably the best law course you can get."[3]

In the fall of 2004, Woodward gave interviews to several media stations in the United States. She proclaimed her innocence, stating that she was haunted by Matthew's death. She said that she did not know what had happened to him; she only knew what had not happened—she had not shaken him violently. In March 2005, Woodward quit her job as a lawyer to become a dance instructor.[4]

Matthew Eappen's family moved from the home in which Matthew died. The parents and brother were joined by two more children.

An attempt has been made to enact legislation to require that nannies be trained and certified, including training in first aid.[5]

In March of 2007, Woodward announced that she was planning marriage and a family and that she had evidence that might result in reopening her criminal case and exonerating her. The prosecution's star expert on the shaken baby syndrome said he no longer believed that the baby's death could have been caused in that manner. But Woodward could not escape infamy, even 10 years after her trial. She was featured as number one in the list of the 10 most notorious offenders in Massachusetts.[6]

1. "Excerpts from the Judge's Decision Reducing Conviction of Au Pair," *New York Times* (11 November 1997), p. 16.
2. "Pediatric Experts Express Doubt on Au Pair's Defense," *New York Times* (12 November 1997), p. 14.
3. "Killer Nanny Is Training to Be Legal Eagle," *Daily Star* (1 February 2003), p. 27.
4. "Baby Killer Woodward Leaves Law for Dance," *UPI Press Release* (29 March 2005).
5. "Matthew's Law to Make Nannies Safe," *The Mirror* (14 November 2002), p. 30.
6. "I Want A Baby of My Own," *Daily Mail* (London) (8 March 2007), p. 46; "Woodward No. 1 for Infamy," *Liverpool Daily Echo* (14 April 2007), p. 4. (29 March 2005).

the defendant's constitutional and statutory rights are protected, that all rules and regulations are followed, and that all participants and spectators (including the media) behave appropriately.

The role of the trial judge at sentencing is one of the most important of all judicial functions. Despite the importance of sentencing, until recently little attention was paid to preparing judges for this role. Nor was there any emphasis on the importance of thorough presentence reports by probation or other officers of the court to assist judges in making the decision. Likewise, little attention was given to appellate review of judicial sentencing.

Concern with the extensive power of judges over sentencing, along with other sentencing issues, has led to sentence reform, which is discussed in Chapter 8. Clearly, the purpose of most of the reform efforts has been to reduce judicial sentencing power, thought to cause sentence disparity. Some of the alleged disparity results from a consideration of legally acceptable factors, such as the defendant's prior record and the nature of the current charge(s). However, some of the differences may be the result of unacceptable factors, such as the gender, age, race, or ethnicity of a defendant, as well as of the personalities, backgrounds, and prejudices of the sentencing judges. Therefore, before concluding that judicial sentencing differences are unfair, unreasonable, or unconstitutional, all the variables involved in the decision-making process must be considered.

The sentencing decision is a difficult one; it may be impossible to achieve justice at this stage. As one judge concluded, "I am sure that I speak for my many colleagues when I state that the imposition of a criminal sentence is the most delicate, difficult, distasteful task for the trial judge."[10]

In all of these and other activities at trial, not only the decision but also the demeanor and attitude of the judge are important. The judge's behavior may influence the attitudes and decisions of jurors, witnesses, and victims at the trial, as well as the general public's image of criminal justice systems. In addition, the judge influences the flow of cases through the criminal courts. Poor management of a caseload contributes to court congestion and risks impairing the rights of defendants to a speedy trial.

6-4b Appellate Judges

As noted earlier, the decisions of trial judges may be reversed on appeal. In most cases, however, appellate courts defer to trial courts on issues in which trial judges have an advantage because of their direct observation of the events that occurred at trial. Only a fraction of cases are reversed on appeal, but those cases are important not only to the individual defendants but to the justice system as well.

Frequently, appellate judges and justices are faced with interpreting the laws and constitutions of their jurisdictions in ways that will have an effect on more than the parties before the court. In that respect, their decisions have a much broader impact than the decisions of trial courts. Usually, their decisions, in contrast to those of trial courts, are accompanied by written opinions, thus placing an even greater responsibility on judges to articulate why they decided a specific issue in a particular way.

6-4c Judicial Selection, Training, and Retention

The first issue in deciding how to select, train, and retain judges is to decide what qualities are desired. Historically, judges have been white, male, and Protestant, with conservative backgrounds. Only recently have more women and minorities joined the judiciary, and scholars continue to debate whether race and gender impact judicial decision making.

Judges should be impartial and fair. They should be able to approach a case with an objective and open mind concerning the facts. If for any reason a judge cannot be objective in a case, he or she should withdraw from that case, a process known as **recusal**. Objectivity enables the judge to be fair, to insist that attorneys play by the rules of the game, and to see that due process is not violated. They should be well educated in substantive law, procedural rules, and evidence. Judges should be able to

▶ **Recusal** The removal of oneself from a proceeding, such as done by a judge who has a conflict of interest in a case.

think and write clearly. Their opinions are of great importance to attorneys and other judges, who use them to analyze how future cases might be argued and decided. Judges should have high moral and ethical standards, enabling them to withstand political and economic pressures that might influence decisions. They should be in good physical, mental, and emotional health. They should be good managers because they have considerable power over the court system. They should be able to assume power sensibly, without abuse, and to exercise leadership in social reform where necessary and desirable.

The late Irving R. Kaufman, a federal judge on the Second Circuit, addressed the issue of the qualities and characteristics that should be considered in the selection of federal judges, but his suggestions are also applicable to state and local judges. According to Kaufman,

> a judge's comportment must at all times square with the ideals of justice and impartiality that the public projects on us in our symbolic role. A judge must be reflective, perhaps even a bit grave, but must always demonstrate an openness consistent with our tradition of giving each side its say before a decision is rendered. [A judge should be able to] separate the dignity of the office from a sense of self-importance.[11]

Finding persons with the desired judicial qualifications is not always easy. Several methods have been used for selecting judges in the United States. During the colonial period, judges were appointed by the king, but after the Revolution, this practice ceased. In a majority of the colonies, judges were appointed by the legislators. In some colonies, the appointment was made by the governor, with or without the required approval of his council.

As the colonies became states, they gradually began to select judges by popular election, but that method came under criticism, with frequent allegations that undue political influence led to the selection of incompetent and corrupt judges. Today, most states use the election process for some of their judges. Another method of selecting judges, the merit plan, is traced to Albert M. Kales, one of the founders of the American Judicature Society. The plan was first adopted by Missouri in 1940. It is referred to as the *Missouri plan* or, less commonly, the *Kales plan* or *commission plan*.

Merit selection plans vary extensively from state to state, but most plans include a nonpartisan commission, which solicits, investigates, and screens candidates when judicial openings occur. The commission sends a select number of names (usually three to five) to the executive branch, where an appointment is made. The new judge may serve a probationary period (usually a year) and may be required to run unopposed on a general election retention ballot. Voters are polled with a yes or no vote to decide whether this judge should be retained in office. A judge who receives a majority of votes (which is usually the case) will be retained. A merit selection plan does not assure that politics will not enter into the selection process, but arguably, the prescreening by a nonpartisan commission places only qualified candidates in a position for election. Criticisms remain, however, and politics plays an important role.

In an effort to avoid public pressures on judicial decision making, federal judges, along with U.S. Supreme Court justices, are appointed and hold their jobs for life. Technically, they are appointed by the president of the United States and confirmed by the Senate, but usually, the attorney general or the deputy attorney general recommends individuals, and the president accepts those recommendations. Members of the U.S. House of Representatives and the U.S. Senate are also influential in nominating the candidates for judicial positions. The constitutional provision for the appointment of federal judges and justices has been interpreted to mean that they hold their appointments for life. They may be removed only for bad behavior, but that process is very difficult and is not often undertaken, even when there are good reasons to do so.

Most U.S. jurisdictions do not have required formal training for judges, although training is mandatory in many other countries. Despite the lack of requirements for judicial training, we are making progress in providing training programs for newly appointed or elected judges. Most states provide some training, and many are offering continuing education courses for judges already on the bench.

Recruiting the right kind of attorneys and giving them proper training in the judiciary is important, but retention of our best judges is becoming a serious problem. In the past, a judicial appointment, especially to the federal bench, was the ultimate aim of many lawyers. But the increasing number of resignations of federal judges has led some to refer to the revolving door of the federal judiciary, with some of the best candidates refusing nominations or accepting them, staying a few years, and then leaving. For those who do stay, morale may be affected as they realize the substantial pay cut they take by leaving private practice to accept an appointment to the bench. According to the Judicial Conference, "It is no wonder that underpaid judges are leaving when law clerks who join major law firms as first-year associates can earn more in their first year than any federal judge earns."[12]

Judicial salaries vary significantly from state to state. Although, generally, salaries are higher in the federal system, the level of compensation of federal judges was described by the late Judge Irving R. Kaufman in an open letter to President Ronald Reagan: "And as you know, we receive for our services little more than those fresh-faced lads a few years out of Harvard at the larger New York firms."[13] Salaries of federal judges have increased since Judge Kaufman made that statement, and as noted earlier, federal judges now get cost-of-living raises, but the salaries have not kept pace with the increases in other professions.[14]

Judicial salaries will never compete with those in private practice, and some highly qualified attorneys will not be attracted to judicial positions as a result, but it is reasonable to expect that the prestige of being a federal judge, along with a job for life, is appealing. One professional group with which federal judges can be compared is that of senior law professors and law school deans. In 1969, the salaries of federal district court judges were about 30 percent higher than those of senior law professors and 20 percent higher than those of law deans. That is no longer the case, with law deans earning over $300,000 and senior law professors earning an average of around $210,000.[15] As noted earlier in the chapter, in 2006, federal district court judges were earning a salary of $165,200.

Another problem judges face is that of stress. Judges handle issues that are very important and highly controversial but that must be decided. As Judge Kaufman said, "Much tension accompanies the job of deciding the questions that all the rest of the social matrix has found too hard to answer."[16]

In addition to the stresses faced by any professional person, judges face several stressors not common to other professions. There is a lonely transition from the practice of law to a position about which they may know very little except as outside observers. Usually at the peak of their legal careers when they become judges, they must give up many of their positions and even their friendships. Additional stresses on judges come from the judicial code of conduct that places limitations on their financial and social lives. For example, contacts that might compromise a judge's decisions must be avoided, close associations with attorneys who might appear before them must be restricted, and they are limited in terms of when and with whom they may discuss cases. Spotlight 6-3 contains the code of conduct for federal U.S. judges.

One final area of stress for judges and justices is violence. Violence has invaded courtrooms in some parts of the country, as illustrated in March 2005, when a man entered the Atlanta courtroom of Superior Court Judge Rowland W. Barnes and shot and killed him and his court reporter, Julie Ann Brandau. The alleged gunman, Brian Nichols, 33, was a defendant in a criminal trial presided over by Judge Barnes. It was alleged that Nichols overpowered his guard, Cynthia Hall, who was critically injured, took her weapon, and went to the judge's chambers, where he overpowered another

Spotlight 6-3　Code of Conduct for U.S. Judges

The seven canons, listed below, of the Code of Conduct for U.S. judges apply to circuit judges, district judges, bankruptcy judges, magistrate judges, and judges in the Court of International Trade and the Court of Federal Claims. The code includes an explanation for each of the canons; refer to the source listed at the end of this Spotlight to find those explanations.

Canon 1

A judge should uphold the integrity and independence of the judiciary.

Canon 2

A judge should avoid impropriety and the appearance of impropriety in all activities.

Canon 3

A judge should perform the duties of the office impartially and diligently.

Canon 4

A judge may engage in extra-judicial activities to improve the law, the legal system, and the administration of justice.

Canon 5

A judge should regulate extra-judicial activities to minimize the risk of conflict with judicial duties.

Canon 6

A judge should regularly file reports of compensation received for law-related and extra-judicial activities.

Canon 7

A judge should refrain from political activity.

Source: Administrative Office of the United States Courts, http://www.uscourts.gov/guide/vol2/ch1.html, accessed 12 June 2006, emphasis and capitalizations deleted.

deputy, handcuffing him and stealing his gun. After killing Barnes and Brandau, Nichols allegedly went to the parking garage, overpowered and pistol-whipped a reporter, and stole his car. Outside the courthouse, a third murder victim, Sergeant Hoyt Teasley, was shot in the abdomen and killed. Other acts of violence were attributed to Nichols after he left the courthouse area and before he was captured.

These acts of violence at the Fulton County courthouse and in the city of Atlanta occurred less than two weeks after violence against a Chicago judge's family. Upon arriving home one day, Judge Joan Humphrey Lefkow of the United States District Court, who had previously been the target of death threats for which a suspect, Matthew Hale, was convicted, found her husband, Michael F. Lefkow, 64, and her mother, Donna Humphrey, 89, both dead of gunshot wounds. A suspect was arrested and charged with the murders.

Many courthouses do provide security checks on all persons who wish to enter, and in high-profile cases, it is now customary to have extra courthouse security, such as metal detectors and additional security personnel, but it would be prohibitively expensive to provide around-the-clock protection to all judges.

6-4d　Judicial Control

At the opposite extreme of the problem of how to retain good judges is the delicate issue of how to get rid of bad ones. Like all other professions, the judiciary is characterized by some who engage in questionable behavior in their professional and personal lives. Their shortcomings may affect their abilities to function effectively as judges. Although the sexual behavior of most adults may be considered their private business as long as it is consensual and does not involve minors, the public consider it their business when judges engage in illicit sexual behavior. Sexual harassment by anyone is unacceptable, but sexual harassment by a judge is even more shocking. Excessive drinking may be tolerated in some circles, but excessive drinking by a judge, particularly one charged with driving while intoxicated, is unacceptable.

How do we control improper judicial behavior? It is not easy to unseat judges, even after they have been convicted of a crime. Usually, they are asked to resign, but if they do not do so, it may take months or even years to go through disciplinary channels to unseat them. Elected judges may be unseated by a recall vote. When judges are appointed, however, the process is more difficult. At the federal level, where judges serve for life and may be removed only by impeachment and conviction by Congress, legislation provides some avenues for disciplining judges. The Judicial Councils Reform and Judicial Conduct and Disability Act of 1980 provides several sanctions: certify disability, request the judge to retire, strip the judge of his or her caseload "on a temporary basis," and censure or reprimand privately or publicly.[17]

Another method for controlling judicial misconduct and compensating those who are victimized by judges is to permit federal civil rights charges to be brought against judges. In 1997, the U.S. Supreme Court considered a case appealed from a lower federal court, which had held that the federal civil rights statute involved in a Tennessee case did not provide notice that it covered simple or sexual assault crimes. The Supreme Court held that the statute need not specify the *specific* conduct covered and sent the case back for the lower court to reconsider the issue in light of the Supreme Court's holding that the rule is "whether the statute, either standing alone or as construed [interpreted], made it reasonably clear at the relevant time that the defendant's conduct was criminal."[18]

This case, *United States v. Lanier*, involved allegations that Judge David Lanier sexually assaulted five women in his judicial chambers. Judge Lanier had presided over the divorce and custody hearings of one of the complainants. It was alleged that when the woman interviewed for a secretarial position at the courthouse in which he worked, Judge Lanier suggested to her that he might have to reexamine her daughter's custody case. The woman charged that as she left the interview, the judge "grabbed her, sexually assaulted her, and finally committed oral rape."[19]

Judge Lanier was convicted in 1992 and served 2 years of his 22-year sentence before a federal appeals court released him on his own recognizance after its decision that the statute did not apply to the facts of his case. After the U.S. Supreme Court heard the case, ruled that the statute in question applied, and sent the case back to the lower court, that court ordered Judge Lanier to appear on 22 August 1997 for a hearing. He did not appear; the court issued a warrant for his arrest and subsequently dismissed his appeal. The judge was located and arrested two months later in Mississippi, where he was living under an assumed name. In December 1997, he entered a plea of guilty to eluding arrest to avoid prison. The judge is back in prison, now serving a 25-year sentence.

6-5   Crisis in the Courts

Numerous problems exist in our criminal courts, some of which are mentioned in the discussions in this chapter. But by far the most serious problem is the pressure placed on courts, on defendants, and on society by the increased number of cases tried and appealed. This increase has led to a crisis in our courts, and the crisis continues, despite additional judges in both the state and the federal court systems.

The greatest number of criminal offenses in federal criminal courts fall into the categories concerned with drugs, leading to recommendations that most drug cases be tried in state courts. In addition to drug cases, the federal court caseload has grown because of the increased number of crimes that have been made *federal* offenses by statute. Over a decade ago, Chief Justice William H. Rehnquist warned against this trend of "one new federal statute after another," but his warnings have not been heeded.[20]

Shifting federal cases to state courts might ease the problem in federal courts, but state courts also face case backlogs. In 2000, Chief Justice Rehnquist emphasized that the crises in state courts were greater than those in federal courts, with many systems facing serious funding cuts. Rehnquist concluded, "It seems likely for the foreseeable future that a regime of fiscal austerity will predominate at the national and state levels."[21]

The problems in funding courts have led many states to shift the requirement of funding local courts to the state, with at least 33 states, including Minnesota, Missouri, California, New York, Colorado, and Pennsylvania, already having moved in that direction.[22]

Problems in funding courts have led to cuts in personnel, including judges, court-appointed attorneys, and prosecutors. This is occurring at a time when court loads are increasing; thus, courts are more crowded. Among other problems, court congestion

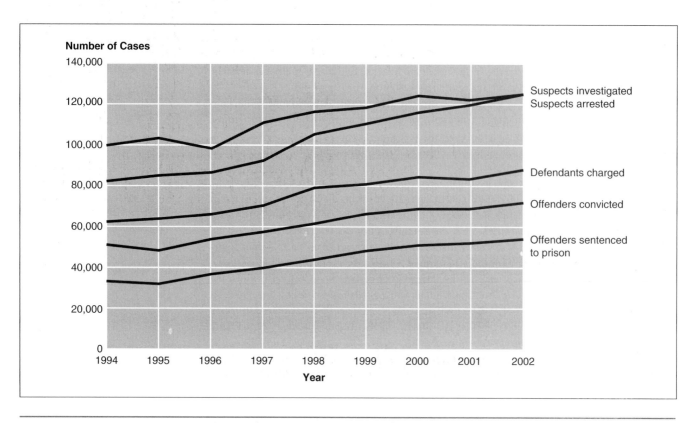

Figure 6-2
Federal Criminal Case Processing, 1994–2002

Source: Bureau of Justice Statistics, *Federal Criminal Case Processing, 2002: With Trends 1982–2002,* http://www.ojp.usdoj.gov/bjs/pub/pdf/fccp02.pdf, accessed 12 June 2006.

results in delayed trials. It is argued that justice delayed is justice denied. That concept is based on the belief that, when a trial is delayed for a significant time, there is a greater chance for error. Witnesses may die or forget. Crowded court dockets have created pressures that encourage plea bargaining and mass handling of some cases. Delayed trials may deny defendants their constitutional right to a speedy trial.

For the accused who are not released before trial, court congestion may mean a long jail term in already-overcrowded facilities. Because their court-appointed attorneys are so busy with other cases, defendants may not see them during that period. The accused are left with many questions, no answers, and a long wait, often under crowded conditions in local jails. Those who are incarcerated before trial face more obstacles in preparation for trial.

Obvious injustices are created by overcrowded courts that must decide cases presented by overworked prosecutors and defense attorneys. The image of inefficiency and injustice that the crowded court dockets and delayed trials project colors public perceptions of criminal justice systems.

In 2005, filings in federal bankruptcy and in federal appeals courts reached record highs. In 2006, however, for the first time in 11 years, case filings in federal appeals courts dropped. Criminal appeals were down 5 percent over 2005, while civil appeals dropped 3 percent. The only type of appeals that increased in 2006 involved sex crimes, which rose 19 percent. In 2006, federal bankruptcy filings dropped 37.6 percent, falling to their lowest level in 10 years. In contrast, the filings in federal district courts increased in 2006, but only by 1 percent.[23]

Federal criminal case processings remain high, however, after a steady increase between 1994 and 2002, as noted in Figure 6-2.

In addition to the delays caused by overcrowded court dockets, there are other reasons for court delays. One is the use of a **continuance**, or postponement. The purpose of granting continuances is to guarantee a fair hearing. The defense or the prosecution may need more time to prepare; additional evidence might have come to light and need evaluating; additional witnesses may need to be located.

Another reason for congestion in criminal courts is that courts must handle some cases that perhaps should be processed in some other way. Criminal law is used in an effort to control behaviors such as some types of alcohol and other drug abuse, consenting sexual behavior between adults in private, prostitution, and gambling. This is not to suggest that we should be unconcerned with these activities but only to question the reasonableness of using criminal law to regulate them. Removal of some or all of these actions from the criminal court system would reduce the number of cases in those courts.

Yet another reason for court congestion may be the filing of frivolous lawsuits. This occurs in civil cases, but some inmates have filed numerous and frivolous lawsuits as well. For example, one inmate filed five product liability lawsuits in one year in New York. He alleged that (1) a scoop of yogurt contained glass, which cut his mouth and paralyzed his lip; (2) his head was burned by Revlon's Flex protein conditioner; (3) a can of shaving cream exploded in his face; (4) a television set caught fire and burned his clothes; and (5) a Nuprin tablet caused severe kidney damage and left him comatose. The judge dismissed the cases, stating that the court "cannot tolerate this type of cynical abuse of the judicial process." The judge also ordered the removal of the inmate plaintiff's word processor, computer, printer, and any other instruments used in filing the frivolous claims. The inmate was barred from filing any new products liability cases without the judge's permission, and he was ordered to pay a $5,000 fine to the court clerk.[24]

Many suggestions have been made for solving court congestion. The first is to reduce the number of offenses covered by criminal law. Building new court facilities and expanding the number of judges, prosecutors, defense attorneys, and support staff are other possible solutions. Better management of court proceedings and court dockets may also be helpful. Court personnel need to update their equipment and make use of improved technology. Some courts are using computers to speed up the paperwork. Other courts have been reorganized for greater efficiency.

Other suggestions are to use lay judges, volunteers who would handle misdemeanor cases, such as disorderly conduct, petit larceny, prostitution, and criminal mischief, as a method of relieving pressures in the regular court system. Volunteers may be used as prosecutors in some cases, while special courts, such as drug courts, mental health courts, and domestic violence courts, some of which are discussed in Chapter 11, are becoming more common.

Another suggestion is the use of alternatives to courts, based on the assumption that, in many cases, courts could and should be avoided. Although most of the alternatives, such as arbitration and mediation, apply primarily to civil cases, some are also used in criminal cases. The expanded use of plea bargaining, whereby defense and prosecution reach an agreement out of court, is an example.

The costs of these proposals must be evaluated. We are not talking only about the cost of enlarging the judiciary. Expanding courts and increasing the number of judges involves the direct cost of the expansions along with support staff and an increase in the number of prosecutors, defense attorneys, courtrooms, other facilities, and police and correctional personnel and facilities.

> ▶ **Continuance** The adjournment of a trial or another legal proceeding until a later date.

Chapter Wrap-Up

An understanding of the nature and structure of criminal court systems is necessary for a study of the activities taking place within those systems. Terminology is also important. If a court does not have jurisdiction, it cannot hear and decide a case. Cases must be brought before the proper court, and this is determined by the seriousness of the offense, the type of offense, or both.

Some courts hear criminal cases; others hear civil; some hear both. Some hear petty offenses or misdemeanors, whereas others have jurisdiction over felony cases.

Trial courts must base their decisions on facts, which may or may not establish whether the defendant committed the alleged criminal act or acts. Usually, appellate courts are concerned only with questions of law. They ask, "During the trial, did the trial court commit any serious errors in law, such as the admission of evidence that should have been excluded, and if so, was that error prejudicial to the defendant's right to a fair trial?" If so, the case is reversed and sent back for retrial, for resentencing, or both. The appellate court might find less serious errors in law and not reverse the case.

Criminal cases may be appealed, but not necessarily to the highest court. Cases in the state system may not be appealed to the lower federal appellate courts. If a federal constitutional right is involved in a state case, the U.S. Supreme Court may hear that case. Cases decided in state courts must be followed in the states in which they are decided but are not binding on other states' courts.

Decisions at one level or jurisdiction may be used by other courts as reasons for their decisions if the judges choose to do so. Decisions of the U.S. Supreme Court are binding on all lower federal courts and on state courts when a federal right is involved. However, because the Supreme Court hears only a few of the cases it is asked to hear, many issues remain unsettled because federal courts in different jurisdictions decide similar cases differently.

The primary figure in court efficiency and administration is the judge. Despite the importance of judges in U.S. court systems, some who become judges are not trained in judicial decision making or trial and appellate procedures. Some have had limited experience as trial lawyers, yet they are given vast powers in criminal justice systems. Most perform admirably; some need to be disciplined or removed, but the system is not very well equipped for those processes.

Today, courts are criticized for being in a state of crisis as a result of the large backlog of cases, criminal and civil, at both the trial and appellate levels. Some steps must be taken to reduce this backlog. Lawyers and judges have a great responsibility to solve this problem, but the role of the public is important, too.

Significant changes cannot be made in court systems without public support, especially financial support. Changes are needed in all areas of criminal justice systems. Significant changes in the courts also affect the other criminal justice areas. If we create more courts, so that we can try, convict, and sentence more people to prison, yet do not build adequate facilities to accommodate that increase, we push the problems from one area of the system to another. Courts must be analyzed and altered in the total social context in which they operate.

Key Terms

acquittal (p. 171)
appeal (p. 163)
appellant (p. 163)
appellee (p. 163)
concurring opinion (p. 170)

continuance (p. 179)
de novo (p. 166)
dicta (p. 162)
expert witness (p. 171)
judge (p. 161)

judicial review (p. 163)
moot (p. 162)
recusal (p. 173)
stare decisis (p. 162)
writ of certiorari (p. 168)

Apply It

1. Distinguish the judicial branch from other branches of government.
2. What is meant by *jurisdiction?* How does it apply to the dual court system?
3. What is the difference between trial and appellate courts?
4. What is the relationship between state and federal courts?
5. What are the levels of courts in each of the two main court systems, state and federal?
6. What is the purpose of the U.S. Supreme Court, and how does a case get before the Court? What happens to a case that is appealed to but not accepted by the Court? What changes would you suggest in the operation of the Supreme Court in order to handle the increasing workload it faces?

7. What are the main roles of judges in trial courts? In appellate courts?
8. How are judges and justices selected? What are the advantages and disadvantages of each method?
9. Should an effort be made to recruit more female and minority judges? Why or why not? What methods do you suggest if you think more should be recruited?
10. What actions do you think should be sufficient to disqualify a person for a state judgeship? A federal judgeship? Appointment to the U.S. Supreme Court?
11. To what extent, if any, should public opinion be permitted to influence judicial appointments? Judicial retention?
12. How would you suggest that the current caseload crisis in trial and appellate courts be resolved?

Endnotes

1. "Lawyers Have a Lot to Teach," *American Bar Association Journal* 91 (October 2005): 6.
2. Ibid.

3. State v. Skakel, 888 A.2d 985 (Conn.Sup.Ct. 2006), *cert. denied*, 127 S.Ct. 578 (2006).

4. "'Unfair' Pay Hurts Judicial System: Roberts," *Chicago Daily Law Bulletin* (2 January 2007), p. 10001.

5. Ibid.

6. Steven Luber, "Judging Pay," *The American Lawyer* (March 2003), n.p.

7. "President Signs Legislation Authorizing Judicial COLA," *Federal Human Resources Week* 9, no. 43 (3 March 2003): n.p.

8. "Court at the Crossroads," *Time* (8 October 1984), p. 28, referring to a remark by Floyd Abrams in response to the earlier remark by former U.S. Supreme Court Justice Felix Frankfurter.

9. Chief Justice Fred M. Vinson, quoted in Ronald L. Carlson, *Criminal Justice Procedure*, 2d ed. (Cincinnati, Ohio: Anderson, 1978), p. 243.

10. United States v. Wiley, 184 F.Supp. 679 (D.Ill. 1960).

11. Irving R. Kaufman, "An Open Letter to President Reagan on Judge Picking," *American Bar Association Journal* 67 (April 1981): 443.

12. Judicial Conference, "Fact Sheet: The Need for a Federal Judicial Pay Increase," http://www.uscourts.gov/newsroom/judicialpayincrease.htm, accessed 12 June 2006.

13. Kaufman, "An Open Letter," p. 444.

14. Judicial Conference, "Fact Sheet."

15. Ibid.

16. Quoted in "By and Large We Succeed," *Time* (5 May 1980), p. 70.

17. Judicial Councils Reform and Judicial Conduct and Disability Act of 1980, Public Law No. 96-458, incorporated into Complaints of Judicial Misconduct or Disability, USCS Ct. App. Fed. Cir. R 51 (1994).

18. United States v. Lanier, 520 U.S. 259 (1997).

19. United States v. Lanier, 520 U.S. 259 (1997).

20. "Troubling Review: Rehnquist Sees Rough Times Ahead of Federal and State Courts," *American Bar Association Journal* (January 1994), p. 94.

21. Ibid.

22. "Push on to Shift Larger Share of Court Funding to State," *Chicago Daily Law Bulletin* (6 December 2005), p. 1.

23. "Caseload Edges Lower: Feds Report," *Chicago Daily Law Bulletin* (13 March 2007), p. 10001.

24. "Judge Ensures Frivolous Suits Will Stop," *St. Petersburg Times* (30 March 1994), p. 9.

Prosecution, Defense, and Pretrial Procedures

7

The adversary philosophy that characterizes U.S. criminal justice systems applies not only to the trial and appeal of a criminal case but also to many activities that occur prior to a trial. This chapter examines those critical pretrial procedures, but first it is necessary to examine the role that lawyers play. Underlying the adversary philosophy is the belief that the best way to obtain the facts of a criminal case is for each side to have an advocate, or attorney, to present evidence and cross-examine the witnesses on the opposing side.

Attorneys are important figures at various stages in criminal justice systems. This chapter examines the important functions of each side and then focuses on the pretrial procedures in which they engage, along with the judge and other participants in criminal cases. The chapter begins with a general overview of lawyers and the legal profession.

7-1 Lawyers and the Legal Profession

Lawyers have created controversy historically throughout the world. One of William Shakespeare's characters in *Henry VI* exclaimed, "The first thing we do, let's kill all the lawyers," and English poet John Keats said, "I think we may class the lawyer in the natural history of monsters." According to a popular news magazine, lawyers have been "charged with the practice of witchcraft, demagoguery, corrupting justice, hypocrisy, charging outrageous fees, pleading unjust causes, and misusing language."[1]

During the 17th century, the American colonies operated under a legal system without lawyers. Lawyers were so distrusted and scorned that most people handled their own cases. The Puritans preferred to keep law and religion as one. Their law was the Bible, and many of their criminal laws were taken verbatim from that source. In Massachusetts, it was illegal for a lawyer to take a fee for his work. For 70 years after Pennsylvania was settled, the colony had no lawyers.[2]

As legal matters became more complicated, people began to recognize the need for experts trained in law, and the legal profession developed into one of power and wealth. In the 50 years before the American Revolution, the profession flourished. Of the 55 men who served in the Continental Congress, 31 were lawyers, as were 25 of the original signers of the Declaration of Independence.

Between 1830 and 1870, as a result of the rejection of anything English and out of fear of a legal aristocracy, the American bar fell into disfavor again. During this

L E A R N I N G
OBJECTIVES

After reading this chapter, you should be able to do the following:

- **Discuss briefly the historical background of the legal profession.**
- **Explain the organization and structure of prosecutorial systems.**
- **Recognize the importance and problems of prosecutorial discretion regarding whether to prosecute.**
- **Evaluate ways to control prosecutorial discretion and especially prosecutorial misconduct.**
- **Explain the role of the defense attorney.**
- **Explain and analyze the right to be represented by defense counsel.**
- **Discuss the reasons for private defense counsel in contrast to public defense counsel.**
- **Distinguish among public defender programs, assigned counsel programs, and contract systems for providing defense counsel.**
- **Explain the meaning of effective assistance of counsel and the right to refuse counsel.**
- **List and explain the major steps in the criminal justice pretrial process.**
- **Explain the importance of bail to defendants.**
- **List and explain the ways in which a defendant may be released pending trial.**
- **Explain the process of entering a plea in a criminal case.**
- **Discuss the arguments for and against plea bargaining.**

frontier era, with its dislike for specialists, practicing law was considered a natural right. Michigan and Indiana permitted any male voter of good moral character to practice law. After 1870, there was a move toward professionalism, which resulted in the improvement of legal education, along with higher law school admission standards, the licensing of lawyers, and the beginning of a strong bar association.[3]

The public view of lawyers improved in the United States, and in the 1900s, public opinion polls revealed that, generally, lawyers were accorded high prestige.[4] In 1975, however, a Louis Harris public opinion poll found that "the public had more confidence in garbage collectors than in lawyers, or doctors or teachers."[5]

The image of the legal profession in the United States was tarnished by the criminal activities of high-level politicians during the administration of President Richard M. Nixon. Prosecution of some of those politicians in the Watergate scandal led to prison terms. (The Watergate scandal was so-called because of the illegal entrance into the offices of the Democratic National Headquarters in Washington, D.C.'s Watergate, a building containing condominiums as well as offices and businesses.) Many of the people involved in Watergate were attorneys. In addition to violating the law and the ethics of the legal profession, they violated the ethical principles of many Americans. According to one writer, the result was that "the pedestal on which lawyers traditionally have been placed is crumbling faster than at any other time in history."[6]

During the years since the Watergate scandal, the image of the legal profession has remained tarnished. The highly publicized and internationally televised trial of O. J. Simpson, acquitted of murder in the deaths of his ex-wife and her friend, also exacerbated that tarnished image.

Attacks on lawyers have also come from within the legal profession. The 1977 criticisms by U.S. Supreme Court Chief Justice Warren Burger were widely publicized.

Professions 7-1

An Open Letter to American Lawyers

[Reprinted here is part of an open letter written to members of the American Bar Association (ABA) via email on 10 September 2002 by the ABA president, Alfred P. Carlton Jr.]

The seasons have now cycled since that moment when we saw a blue September sky turn the darkest of gray. One year ago, forces from outside our imagination attacked innocent and earnest people for no other reason than they were workaday participants in the wondrous journey that is America....[Carlton discussed many of the values that are important to Americans and to the world before he continued.]

Such an allegiance to these ideals is not just rhetorical. It is written into, and facilitated by, our laws. It is our law, above all else, that binds us all to a common moral code. Our law protects us from tyranny, rewards our creativity, punishes our corruptness. Our law facilitates that which is the greatest moral concept our species has ever had the temerity to develop—the concept of justice. As lawyers, you and I see justice every day.

Fair hearing, due process, presumption of innocence, are the foundations on which everything else rests. It is you and I, the American lawyer, whose calling it is to ensure that justice is done.

Most of us become lawyers because of a desire to be involved in the operation of the social construct. As officers of the court, we seek to ensure that our vast universe of human endeavor moves with the grace of justice. We are sworn to pursue this calling with our common oath to "uphold, defend and protect the Constitution and the laws of the United States of America."

I hope all lawyers have felt, as I have, a renewed passion for our chosen profession in these new times. No matter how far removed your daily work seems from the founding principles of this nation we know that it is not. Justice exists every day, each a fair hearing, each served by due process. The law is, and always will be, our collective shelter from the storm.

Burger warned that society was moving toward excessive litigation, and he predicted that if we did not stop that trend and devise "substitutes for the courtroom process...we may well be on our way to a society overrun by hordes of lawyers hungry as locusts competing with each other, and brigades of judges in numbers never before contemplated." Justice Burger recognized the great contribution lawyers had made in the United States but warned that "unrestrained, they can aggravate the problem."[7]

A lack of understanding of the adversary system may influence the public's image of lawyers, especially of those who practice in criminal justice. The public's image of justice may be confused with the attorney's obligation to protect the adversary system. On one occasion, a federal judge drove Supreme Court Justice Oliver Wendell Holmes in a horse-drawn carriage to a session of the U.S. Supreme Court. The judge said, "Well, sir, good-bye. Do justice." Justice Holmes turned and scowled, "That is not my job. My job is to play the game according to the rules."[8]

Law and lawyers play a critical role in the administration of justice in any society. The 9/11 terrorist acts caused some U.S. lawyers to renew their commitment to their chosen profession, as illustrated by the excerpts (reprinted in Professions 7-1) from a letter sent by the president of the American Bar Association (ABA) to all of the association's members.

The terrorist attacks in 2001 were preceded and followed by a decline in the economy due to a weakening of the high technology market and other reasons. The decline in the U.S. economy affected some law firms as well as other businesses. For example, a May 2003 publication reported that one large law firm had cut more than 30 lawyers from its Chicago headquarters, cut its number of summer associates in half, and withdrawn 8 of 15 job offers to 2003 graduates. In addition, the income per partner was predicted to be down about 14 percent that year. A spokesperson stated that the law partners were trying to focus "on right-sizing the firm in response to what's going on in the economy generally." The firm, one of the 10 or 12 most profitable in the nation, was expected to remain in that category even with the cutbacks. The firm had about 320 lawyers and, in addition to its U.S. offices, had 10 offices overseas. Despite these predictions, however, the firm had collapsed by the end of 2003, as did another large

Chicago law firm, Peterson and Ross, which was 110 years old and employed 50 lawyers. An even larger law firm to collapse in 2003 was in San Francisco: Brobeck, Phleger & Harrison, with approximately 500 attorneys. According to a December 2003 legal journal, "The collapse [of two Chicago law firms]...showed that even the most venerable firms were not immune to the pressures of a changing market and a struggling economy." The publication went on to note the following:

> In early 2003, Altheimer & Gray was snapping up new attorneys for its new San Francisco office; by June, the firm announced its demise. Even in the last months of the firm's existence, it employed about 300 attorneys worldwide, about 130 of whom worked in Chicago.[9]

The economic slump found more lawyers looking for employment, with the unemployment rate in the legal profession at 1.2 percent in 2003 (representing 11,000 unemployed out of 940,000 lawyers). Although that figure was much less than the overall unemployment rate of white-collar professionals (about 9 percent, according to the U.S. Department of Labor), it was the highest unemployment rate for lawyers since 1997 and represented a sharp rise from the 1999 rate of 0.6 percent. Not all lawyers are suffering economically, however. The most vulnerable areas are those that were among the most profitable in the 1990s—for example, high-tech areas. The most profitable in 2003 were bankruptcy, patent prosecution, and litigation.[10]

Improvements in the economy in 2004 were reflected in law firm profits. The status of the Am Law 100, referring to the 100 largest law firms in America, is published by *American Lawyer Magazine* in September each year, reflecting the previous year's profits. The 2005 report stated that the combined gross income of the 100 firms increased by 8 percent over the previous year, for a total of $46 billion, with only a 2 percent increase in involved partners. The average partner in those firms received $960,000, a 9 percent increase over the previous year. The editor-in-chief of the magazine stated:

> The nation's largest law firms continued to demonstrate their amazing ability to convert revenue into compensation for partners. On average, 42 cents of every dollar that firms took in last year went to the firms' partners, a level of efficiency that most of their clients would envy....For the second consecutive year, revenue per lawyer, the key metric of law firm economic health, grew faster than head count. That hasn't happened in a decade and resulted from an unending flow of big-ticket litigation, the return of deals and finance, and slower growth in head count.[11]

One other issue that should be noted is that of disciplining lawyers. Spotlight 7-1 looks at this issue in light of recent cases.

Our discussion of the roles lawyers play in the prosecution and defense of criminal cases begins with the prosecution.

7-2   Prosecution

▶ **Prosecution**   The process that occurs when the state (or federal government) begins the formal process in a criminal case. The action is taken by a prosecuting attorney.

▶ **Defendant**   The person charged with a crime and against whom a criminal proceeding has begun or is pending.

The **prosecution** of a criminal case is the process by which formal charges are brought against a person accused of committing a crime. Formal prosecutions are a modern phenomenon. In the American colonies, although an attorney general or a prosecutor had the authority to initiate prosecutions, many criminal prosecutions were left to the alleged victims. There was considerable abuse of the system, with some victims initiating criminal prosecutions to pressure a **defendant** to make financial settlements with them. Because the penalties for many criminal offenses were severe, it was not uncommon for the accused to settle financially—thus, in effect, buying freedom from criminal prosecution.

Such abuses led to the exercise of the power of public prosecution by the colonial attorney general. Soon, it became evident that one attorney general and one colonial court could not handle all the prosecutions in a colony. Gradually, a system developed by which prosecutors in each county brought local prosecutions in the emerging county

Spotlight 7-1   Lawyers in Legal Trouble

What should the legal system do when lawyers violate the rules, or even the law? Judges have the power to discipline lawyers, with punishments ranging from fines to contempt of court citations, which could result in a jail sentence. When lawyers violate the civil or criminal laws, they may be prosecuted. This Spotlight examines a few recent examples.

During the death penalty case of Zacarias Moussaoui, the only person tried for the 9/11 terrorist acts, Transportation Security Administration (TSA) attorney Carla J. Martin was accused of providing information in order to coach government witnesses. The judge held an evidentiary hearing and declared that there was no question that Martin had communicated improperly with government witnesses, which was a violation of the judge's sequestration order. According to the judge, the evidence confirmed the accusation that Martin sent the first day's trial testimony to the potential witnesses and suggested how they might testify. The judge also found that Martin had not told the truth in response to some questions asked of her. Martin could be charged with contempt or witness tampering. She was placed on administrative leave and was under investigation by the U.S. Attorney's Office and a Pennsylvania lawyer disciplinary board; the judge refused to permit those witnesses to testify.[1]

The second case involves indictments of a law firm and of two partners of that firm. Milberg Weiss Bershad & Schulman, a plaintiff securities firm, along with partners David J. Bershad and Steven G. Schulman, are facing a 20-count indictment, handed down in May 2006, for conspiracy to obstruct justice, perjury, fraud, and bribery. Prosecutors allege that the purpose of the conspiracy "was to conceal the fact that some $11.3 million in illegal kickbacks had been secretly paid by Milberg Weiss to lead plaintiffs in class action cases filed by the firm." Among lawyers, it is considered unethical to give referral fees to nonlawyers. In addition, statutes prohibit such actions. Prosecutors allege that the illegal acts took place over two and one-half decades. All defendants entered not guilty pleas in July 2006, and the trial was scheduled to begin on 8 January 2008. In addition to the above indictments, two other lawyers were charged: Seymour M. Lazar, an entertainment lawyer and

investor, and his attorney, Paul T. Selzer. Others were named as co-conspirators.[2]

The final case involves a criminal conviction. Attorney Lynne Stewart was convicted of aiding her clients, who were involved in terrorist acts. Stewart represented Sheik Omar Abdel-Rahman, known as the "blind cleric," who was convicted of plotting to bomb several New York City landmarks, including the World Trade Center, along with others accused of terrorist acts. Stewart was charged with aiding and abetting a terrorist organization by helping her clients communicate with them. Stewart, who is in her 60s, faced 30 years in prison. Her sentencing was postponed several times because she was recovering from treatment for breast cancer. She was free on bail pending sentencing. Asked if she would take the Rahman case again, she stated the following:

> Well, I'd like to think I would. First, because everyone is entitled to a lawyer—and I saw that as a lifelong New Yorker who watched the towers go up and saw them destroyed, not believing what I was seeing. And second, because what has happened to me proves that the laws I was found guilty of violating can now make it virtually impossible to defend unpopular, hated clients.
>
> Many people detest me for the sort of law I practice and the clients I represent....What should matter most is the chilling effect my prosecution and conviction could have, if allowed to stand, on everyone's freedom—even people who can't stand me, who think freedom is an abstract thing.[3]

In 2006, Steward was sentenced to 28 months in prison. Many were outraged at the judge's leniency, but he stated that he took into consideration Stewart's age, health, and the fact that she frequently represented indigent defendants. In April 2007, Stewart was disbarred in New York.

1. "In Trouble over Sequester Break," *ABA Journal Report* (24 March 2006), http://www.abanet.org/journal/ereport/m.24terror.html, accessed 25 March 2006), pp. 1–3.
2. Martha Neil, "Milberg Weiss Indicted: Charges in Alleged Fee-Sharing Scheme Hit Firm, Two Partners," *ABA Journal Report* (19 May 2006), pp. 1–3, http://www.abanet.org/journal/ereport/my19milad.html, accessed 19 May 2006; "More Milberg Charges Possible," *Los Angeles Times* (1 February 2007), p. 1C.
3. Roger Franklin, "Defending the Indefensible," *New Zealand Herald* (2 April 2005), n.p.

courts. These county prosecutors were viewed as local and autonomous, not as arms of the colonial government.[12]

The system of public prosecution differed from colony to colony. Some counties distinguished between violations of state statutes and violations of local ordinances and had a separate prosecution system for each. Today, all states have local and state prosecution systems. Local jurisdictions may have local ordinances applicable only to those jurisdictions, and local prosecutors are responsible for prosecuting violations of those ordinances. Serious offenses are designated by state statutes, although generally, they are prosecuted in local courts by local prosecutors. The federal criminal justice system also has prosecutors, referred to as *U.S. attorneys*.

7-2a The Organization and Structure of Prosecution Systems

Most local and state prosecutors are elected officials, although the elected prosecutor may appoint other attorneys to serve as deputy (or assistant) prosecutors within the office. Election means that prosecutors may be subject to the pressures of local and state politics, but it is argued that the election of this important official makes the prosecutor more accountable to the people. Prosecution systems may be categorized as local, state, or federal.

Local prosecution systems exist at the rural, suburban, and urban levels. The advantages of rural prosecution are numerous. Generally, small towns and rural areas have lower crime rates, and case processing may be more informal. Caseloads are lighter, so rural district attorneys may have more time to prepare cases. Most prosecutors are acquainted with the other lawyers, judges, and court personnel on a professional as well as a social level. Cases are usually handled individually, and most personnel, from the judge to the probation officer, may give each case considerable attention.

In rural areas, most cases are settled by guilty pleas. Since rural judges and juries tend to give harsher sentences, defense attorneys are less likely to advise their clients to go to trial, and more defendants are willing to plead guilty without a trial. Rural prosecutors handle a different type of population and different types of cases than do urban prosecutors. Violent crimes, such as armed robbery or murder, are rare.

One disadvantage of rural prosecution is that salaries are low; many prosecutors maintain a private law practice in order to survive financially. Another disadvantage is that many rural prosecutors must function without a full-time staff, adequate office equipment, or resources to investigate crimes. Criminal justice systems may be affected, too: when the sole prosecutor has an unexpected illness or emergency, the court cannot process cases. Also, in small villages, the police chief may prosecute misdemeanors.

The second type of local prosecution system is *suburban prosecution*. Suburban prosecutors usually have more funds and resources than those in rural offices. Land development, population increases, and growth in the tax base in suburban areas provide greater resources for their criminal justice systems.[13]

The third type of local prosecution system is *urban prosecution,* which is more complex than rural and suburban prosecution because the volume of crime is higher in most large urban areas and the types of crimes include the more serious violent personal crimes, such as armed robbery and murder. Caseloads are also heavier. Some urban prosecutors are so busy that they may not see the files of cases involving less serious offenses until a few minutes before they arrive in court to prosecute the cases.

Generally, the salaries of urban prosecutors are not competitive with those of attorneys in private practice, and for that reason, it is difficult to attract the most qualified attorneys to prosecution. Many who do become prosecutors may not stay long because of low salaries or job burnout or because they view the job only as a training ground. On the positive side, most salaries for urban prosecutors are higher than those in suburban and rural areas. Offices are better equipped and better staffed, and some attorneys find the variety in the types of crime prosecuted in large cities to be a challenge not found in other areas of legal work, particularly in rural and suburban areas.

Urban prosecution offices may include programs not available in smaller offices. In recent years, many urban prosecution offices have added programs for crime victims and witnesses. Special prosecutors may be trained to work with adult rape victims, as well as with children who are victims of sexual and other forms of abuse.

A second major type of prosecution occurs at the *state* level. These systems differ from state to state, but most are headed by a state attorney general, usually an elected official, who is the chief prosecutor for the state. The state attorney general has jurisdiction throughout the state for prosecuting violations of state statutes, although some of that responsibility may be delegated to local levels. The attorney general may issue opinions on the constitutionality of state statutes. He or she may appoint assistant attorney generals.

Many young attorneys view the office of the state attorney general as a good place to gain experience in a legal career. It is excellent preparation for other types of law practice and provides young lawyers with valuable contacts in the legal profession.

The final type of prosecution system occurs at the *federal* level and was provided for by the Judiciary Act of 1789. Federal prosecutors, or U.S. attorneys, are appointed by the president (who often accepts the recommendations of the members of the U.S. Senate and the U.S. House of Representatives from the area in which the U.S. attorney will work) and are approved by the Senate. These officials and their assistant U.S. attorneys, along with other lawyers in the U.S. Department of Justice (DOJ), have jurisdiction for prosecuting alleged violations of federal statutes. Additional information on federal prosecutors is featured in Professions 7-2.

The DOJ is headed by the attorney general, an attorney who is appointed by the president and confirmed by the Senate. During the first term of President George W. Bush, John Ashcroft served as the U.S. attorney general. Ashcroft resigned in early 2005, and Alberto R. Gonzales was appointed and confirmed. By March 2007, however,

Professions 7-2

Federal Prosecutors

At the federal level, cases are prosecuted by attorneys who are called *United States attorneys* or U.S. attorneys. The chief prosecutor is the U.S. attorney general. The positions are political appointments and require a law degree. Special prosecutors may be appointed by the attorney general. An example was the appointment of Kenneth Starr to head the investigation of allegations of impropriety by President Bill Clinton, his wife, Hillary Rodham Clinton, and their associates in the failed Whitewater venture. Although Starr was criticized for taking his investigations further and delving into allegations of sexual improprieties by the president, he was given permission by Attorney General Janet Reno to extend his investigation into those allegations.

Some of the functions of U.S. attorneys, along with their method of appointment, are described in this excerpt:

> The United States Attorneys serve as the chief Federal law enforcement officers within their respective districts. They are appointed by the President, confirmed by the Senate, and report to the Attorney General through the Deputy Attorney General. Each United States Attorney is responsible for establishing law enforcement priorities within his or her district. Each United States Attorney is also the chief litigator representing the United States in civil judicial proceedings in the district. The United States Attorneys, too, carry out the important role of liaison with Federal, state and local law enforcement officers and members of the community on programs such as the Attorney General's Anti-Violent Crime Initiative, juvenile violent crime and drug demand reduction, and the Weed and Seed Program....
>
> Assistant United States Attorneys constituted 54 percent of all Department of Justice attorneys and about 60 percent of those Department attorneys with prosecution or litigation responsibilities. Most new Assistant United States Attorneys

have prior litigation experience with a prosecuting attorney's office, a law firm, or another government agency. In addition to their prior legal experience, Assistant United States Attorneys nationwide have an average of eight years' experience in United States Attorneys' offices.

> While the civil caseload is larger numerically, about 75 percent of the United States Attorneys' personnel were devoted to criminal prosecutions and 25 percent to civil litigation. Ninety percent of all attorney work hours spent in the United States District Court were devoted to criminal prosecutions and ten percent to civil litigation....
>
> The United States Attorneys continued to make the best use of resources during Fiscal Year 1996 by promoting coordination and cooperation among Federal, state and local law enforcement through continued use of their Law Enforcement Coordinating Committees (LECC). The LECCs bring together Federal agencies such as the Federal Bureau of Investigation, Drug Enforcement Administration and Bureau of Alcohol, Tobacco and Firearms, along with state and local prosecutors' offices, state police agencies, and local sheriffs' and police departments, thereby enhancing the effectiveness of the criminal justice system....
>
> The United States Attorneys, their Assistants, Victim-Witness Coordinators and other members of their staffs worked with community, business, and social service representatives to provide assistance to the victims and witnesses of crime, to identify and address the particular violent crime problems within their local communities, to develop and implement prosecution and redevelopment strategies for selected neighborhood sites under the Weed and Seed program, and to encourage and initiate local activities to deter both drug use and violent crime among America's children.[1]

1. *United States Attorneys Annual Statistical Report* (Washington, D.C., U.S. Department of Justice, 1997), pp. 1–3.

Gonzales was under fire from Congress, some of whose members claimed that the DOJ firing of eight U.S. attorneys was politically motivated. U.S. attorneys are responsible to the attorney general, to whom they report through the deputy attorney general, but generally, they are free to develop their own priorities within the guidelines provided by the DOJ. This freedom may result in greater job satisfaction for the attorneys who occupy these positions and provide the needed flexibility for federal prosecutions to be concentrated on the types of crime characteristic of specific areas. But it may also result in different types of law enforcement throughout the federal system, which in turn may lead to charges of unjust practices.

7-2b   Community Prosecution: A New Approach

> **Community-oriented prosecution**   Similar to community-oriented policing, utilizes a more integrated, solution-based approach to crime, going beyond traditional criminal justice systems to look at such issues as quality of life.

According to the American Prosecutors Research Institute (APRI), many prosecutorial offices are moving from a traditional to a **community-oriented prosecution** system. In discussing their research on this issue, APRI referred to the *broken windows* concept discussed in Chapter 3 as the basis for community-oriented policing systems. Like community-oriented policing, community prosecution focuses on problem solving. APRI defines the concept as "a more integrated solutions-based approach to eradicate crime." Community prosecution utilizes tools beyond the criminal justice system, such as mediation and civil sanctions to solve problems that prosecutors working with community residents identify. Quality-of-life issues, such as prostitution, disorderly conduct, drug solicitation, vandalism, and graffiti, dominate this approach. The systems vary, but APRI has identified the following most common elements of community prosecution:

- A focus on problem solving, public safety, and quality-of-life issues
- Inclusion of the community's input into the criminal justice systems, including the courtroom (e.g., admission of community impact statements to be considered at sentencing)
- Partnerships with the prosecutor, law enforcement, public and private agencies, and the community
- Varied prevention, intervention, and enforcement methods (e.g., use of tools other than criminal prosecution to address problems)
- A clearly defined focus area, which has traditionally been defined as a targeted geographic area
- An integrated approach involving both reactive (e.g., prosecuting crimes identified by the police) and proactive strategies (e.g., anticipatory actions aimed at addressing problems at their root cause).[14]

7-2c   The Prosecutor's Role

> **Prosecuting attorney**   A government official responsible for representing the state (or federal government) against an offender in criminal proceedings.

According to the American Bar Association's criminal justice standards, the duty of the **prosecuting attorney** is to "seek justice, not merely to convict."[15] In a criminal case, the prosecutor is responsible for assessing the allegations and the evidence and deciding whether to bring charges against persons accused of committing crimes. If charges are brought, the prosecutor must turn over certain evidence to the defense, decide whether to plea bargain a case, recommend to the judge that the charges be dropped if additional evidence suggests that is the just approach, or if the case goes to trial, develop and present the evidence against the accused. Prosecutors also participate in the sentencing phase of a criminal case. Most of these functions are discussed in this chapter; the importance of this section is to assess the role of discretion in prosecutorial decisions whether to charge or proceed with a case.

Prosecutorial Discretion: An Overview

The prosecutor in most jurisdictions has extensive discretion in deciding whether to bring formal charges against the accused. Statutes vary among the states, but generally, they provide that the prosecutor or assistant prosecutors of a particular jurisdiction shall appear at all trials and shall prosecute all actions for crimes committed in their jurisdictions. These statutes have been interpreted to mean that prosecutions must be brought by prosecutors or their assistants and not that prosecutors must file charges in *all* crimes brought to their attention. Consequently, prosecutors have the discretion to refuse to prosecute; this discretion is virtually unchecked, as noted by a New Jersey appellate court:

> A decision to prosecute or not to prosecute is to be accorded judicial deference in the absence of a showing of arbitrariness, gross abuse of discretion or bad faith....It is fundamental that the mental processes of public officials by means of which governmental action is determined are generally beyond the scope of judicial review.[16]

The decision to prosecute may also be highly criticized. A Florida case is illustrative. In November 2001, Terry King was beaten to death with a baseball bat while he slept in a recliner in the living room of his home. King's sons, Alex, 12, and Derek, 13, confessed to the slaying and to burning the house to destroy the evidence. Subsequently, they recanted their statements and alleged that a family friend, Ricky Chavis, committed the murder to cover up a sexual relationship with Alex. Prosecutors first tried Chavis on the basis of the boys' allegations and then the teenage brothers, on the basis of their prior confessions, thus representing two different and contradictory theories: either Chavis committed the murder or the boys did. Either the boys were lying when they said Chavis committed the murder, or they were lying when they confessed. Chavis was acquitted, but that fact was withheld until the brothers were tried and convicted of second-degree murder. The boys filed a motion for a new trial, and the judge reversed their convictions, reasoning that the trial of the boys and of Chavis under the contradictory theories denied the boys due process. The trial judge ordered mediation, rarely ever done in murder cases, to avoid another trial. The King teens entered pleas to third-degree murder. Derek received a sentence of 8 years, Alex of 7.

Although Chavis was acquitted of sexually molesting Alex King, he was convicted of falsely imprisoning him (Chavis hid the King boys in his trailer for two days after their father's murder). Chavis was sentenced to 5 years in prison on that charge. Subsequently, he was found guilty of trying to cover up the King murder, witness tampering, and being an accessory after the murder. He was sentenced to 30 years on the accessory charge and 5 years for witness tampering. The sentences are being served consecutively, and Chavis must spend at least 29 years in prison before he is eligible for parole.[17]

The King boys are serving time in separate Florida juvenile detention centers, having been moved there 29 days after being sent to the Florida reception center for adult offenders. The prosecutors were furious with that decision, with one stating, "The lady of justice has been beaten, gang-raped, and left for dead....This serves as a warning to all juveniles that if they commit murder, they could possibly serve 29 days in state prison....That should strike fear in all their hearts."[18]

The King case raised legal questions concerning the transfer of the juveniles to an adult criminal court (discussed in Chapter 12), but for purposes of this discussion, it has resulted in criticism of the prosecutorial decision to try the teens and Chavis under two different and contradictory theories. Consider the possibility that all had been convicted under the contradictory theories. According to one media analysis,

> Instead of figuring out which [theory] was true, prosecutors decided to give each of the contradictory theories a shot. It was an outrageous move....The prosecutors had an obligation to decide on a single theory of the case before going to trial. It was an abdication of their role, and perhaps an ethical violation, for them to ask jurors to find defendants guilty beyond a reasonable doubt when the prosecutors themselves were so uncertain about who committed the crime....In the future, prosecutors should decide who they think is guilty and then ask a jury to convict, and not the other way around.[19]

A case that led many to conclude that the prosecutor had not used his discretion wisely was that of the rape charges brought against three Duke University lacrosse players by prosecutor Michael Nifong in the spring of 2006. As the evidence began to unfold and be made public, legal authorities suggested that Nifong was too personally involved in prosecuting the case and recommended that a special prosecutor be appointed or that all charges be dropped. In the fall of 2006, Nifong dropped the rape charges but left standing kidnapping and lesser sexual offense charges. Under intense pressure, Nifong recused himself in early 2007 and was facing ethics and other professional violations that could lead to disbarment. In April 2007, officials dropped all charges against the three defendants and criticized Nifong for prosecuting them.

In conclusion regarding prosecutorial discretion, it should be noted that prosecutors have even more discretion than police. The impact of police arrest power may be minimized by prosecutors who refuse to file formal charges against arrestees. Although the prosecutor has no direct control over the police, this power to decline prosecution may affect the way police operate. If the prosecutor repeatedly refuses to prosecute certain types of offenses, the police may stop making arrests when suspects appear to have committed those offenses. Vigorous prosecution of some crimes might encourage police to be more diligent in arresting suspects for those crimes.

The Prosecutorial Decision

What influences prosecutors in their decisions whether or not to prosecute? It is, of course, possible that extralegal factors, such as race or gender, influence prosecutorial decisions. If so, the accused may have legal recourse, but it is difficult to win these cases. In 1996, the U.S. Supreme Court decided an important case on prosecutorial discretion. In *United States v. Armstrong* the Court held that a defendant who alleges racial bias regarding a prosecutorial decision must show that similarly situated persons of other races were not prosecuted. At issue in this case was the fact that African Americans are more frequently prosecuted for crack cocaine possession, while whites are more frequently prosecuted for powder cocaine possession. In the federal system, the penalty for possession of the less expensive crack cocaine is 100 times that of the penalty for possession of powder cocaine. In *Armstrong*, African American defendants argued that this penalty differentiation, in effect, constitutes racial disparity. The U.S. Supreme Court held that the defendants in *Armstrong* had not met the requirements for proving race discrimination—that is, they did not prove that actual racial bias had occurred.[20] In an earlier case involving alleged prosecutorial discrimination, the Supreme Court said, "The conscious exercise of some selectivity in enforcement is not in itself a federal constitutional violation."[21] Efforts have been made to change the 100 to 1 ratio between the penalties of crack and powder cocaine, but thus far, these efforts have not succeeded.

Practical reasons may lead to a refusal to prosecute, especially in cases that involve a lot of time, resources, and expense. Other reasons are:

- There may not be enough physical evidence to support a conviction.
- Other evidence may be tainted because of the manner in which it was collected or other violations of defendants' rights.
- Witnesses may be unsure of the alleged facts, unwilling to testify, or not convincing enough to cause prosecutors to conclude that their testimony will be meaningful and effective.
- Prosecutors may secure a guilty plea to another charge in exchange for declining prosecution on other charges.
- Prosecutors may agree not to charge (or to drop charges) if the accused enters a treatment program.
- It may not be in the interests of justice to prosecute a particular case.

These and other reasons for declining to prosecute may also apply to a prosecutor's decision to request a dismissal after a case has been filed.

Prosecutorial discretion cannot be eliminated, but it can be subjected to some controls. One method is to establish guidelines, such as those in the federal system.

Federal Limitations on Prosecutorial Discretion

U.S. Attorney General John Ashcroft imposed limits on prosecutorial discretion at the federal level in the fall of 2003, when he established guidelines that, in general, prosecutors should bring the most serious charges possible in a given case. The former U.S. attorney general, Janet Reno, had given federal prosecutors wide discretion in making decisions concerning charges. Ashcroft emphasized that it is the duty of federal prosecutors to "be fair, uniform, and tough," and continued with these words: "It is the policy of the Department of Justice that federal prosecutors must charge and pursue the most serious, readily provable offense or offenses that are supported by the facts of the case except in limited, narrow circumstances." According to Ashcroft, the *most serious offense* means the one that will, upon conviction, result in the most severe sentence under the federal sentencing guidelines. A charge that is not *readily provable* is one in which the prosecutor has a "good faith doubt, for legal or evidentiary reasons, as to the government's ability readily to prove a charge at trial." In other words, prosecutors should not file weak charges in order to gain an advantage in plea bargaining, which is discussed later in the chapter.[22]

A noted scholar in the sentencing area assessed the Ashcroft memo, suggesting that the exceptions "largely swallowed the rule." In particular, he noted that prosecutors could still bargain when:

- [T]heir cases were weak,
- [T]hey could get useful information from a defendant,
- [I]mmigration and drug cases clogged the courts,
- [W]hen [sentence] enhancements would remove any incentive for a defendant to plead guilty,
- [O]r when the prosecutors could get written approval from their superiors.[23]

In essence, prosecutors have more leverage under the federal sentencing guidelines because those guidelines contain more severe sentences, but as we will discuss subsequently, the U.S. Supreme Court has changed the impact of those federal guidelines. Still, the prosecutor has considerable discretion in bringing charges, even in the federal system.

Deciding the Specific Charge

Once the prosecutor decides to prosecute, he or she must decide the appropriate charge(s) to bring. Many criminal statutes overlap. Some offenses such as first- or second-degree murder, are defined by degrees of seriousness. There may be evidence that the suspect has committed more than one crime. The prosecutor must decide which charges to make in each case, and there is no requirement that the suspect be charged with all possible crimes. In jurisdictions in which separate charges may not be prosecuted in the same trial, or for other reasons, prosecutors may decide to bring charges only on the more serious charges.

Once the prosecutor has decided on specific charges, formal charges must be made. The law specifies where and how those charges are to be filed with the court. The prosecutor prepares an **information**, a document that names a specific person and the specific charge(s) against that individual. The information is only one method by which formal charges are made, however. Another method is an **indictment** by a **grand jury**. In some cases, the law *requires* a formal grand jury indictment, but even then, the prosecutor may have considerable influence over the grand jury's decision. Although the grand jury is viewed as a safeguard against unfounded criminal charges, and thus serves as a check on the prosecutor, most grand juries follow prosecutors' recommendations, especially in urban jurisdictions faced with a large number of alleged criminal

> **Information** A formal written document used to charge a person with a specific offense. Prosecutors issue informations, in contrast to *indictments*, which are issued by grand juries.

> **Indictment** The written accusation of a grand jury, formally stating that probable cause exists to believe that the suspect committed a specified felony.

> **Grand jury** A group of citizens, convened by legal authority, who evaluate evidence to ascertain whether a crime has been committed and whether there is sufficient evidence against the accused to justify prosecution. If so, the grand jury may return an indictment. In some jurisdictions, grand juries are empowered to conduct investigations into alleged criminal activities.

violations, many of which may be serious crimes. In smaller jurisdictions, especially in rural areas, grand juries may have more time to consider cases and thus be less influenced by prosecutors.

When charging decisions are made, most prosecutors have scant evidence about the defendant or the alleged crime. Charging decisions may be based on intuition, personal beliefs about the usefulness of punishment, the relation of the crime to the possible penalty, and even personal bias or prejudice. Most prosecutors must make charging decisions without adequate guidelines or established goals. Where goals and guidelines exist, they differ from one jurisdiction to another. However, some general goals of prosecution are commonly accepted.

Charging Goals

One goal of charging decisions is crime reduction. Prosecutors attempt to control crime by prosecuting and, therefore, incapacitating offenders and presumably deterring potential criminals. Charging practices may be affected by decisions to concentrate on cases involving repeat offenders and the use of habitual criminal statutes with enhanced penalties. Thus, defendants who are convicted of multiple specified crimes may be given longer prison terms than they could receive for each crime individually or for all of them cumulatively. In addition, crime control efforts may focus on high-rate, dangerous offenders.

Another goal of charging decisions is the efficient use of resources in the prosecutor's office. Funds and staff limit the number of cases that can be processed. The cost of prosecuting some cases may be too great, and charging decisions must emphasize early case disposition in offices that cannot afford many trials.

Still another goal may be the rehabilitation of the defendant. The prosecutor may set the level of charge for a defendant with the goal of diverting that person into an alternative treatment program, such as job training or alcohol or other drug rehabilitation, rather than incarceration in prison.

Prosecutorial Discretion and Judicial Review

One way to control prosecutorial discretion is by the exercise of judicial review. Defendants who think they have been treated unfairly might appeal their convictions on the basis of prosecutorial misconduct. This is possible but difficult, as noted in the discussion earlier in this chapter concerning the *Armstrong* case.

The landmark case using the equality principle to overturn a prosecutor's decision is over a century old. In 1886, the U.S. Supreme Court held that, if the prosecutor uses a law that is fair and impartial as written and applies it with "an evil eye and an unequal hand," so that the prosecutor creates discrimination, the defendant has been denied equal protection of the laws, and the decision may be overturned.[24]

In short, appealing a prosecutor's decision is difficult and rarely successful—unless the prosecutor has engaged in misconduct or a criminal act.

Prosecutorial Misconduct

Prosecutors may engage in various types of misconduct, most of which, because of their wide discretion and the lack of judicial review, will go unchallenged. There are, however, some acts for which courts and bar associations hold prosecutors responsible.

Overcharging is one type of prosecutorial misconduct for which judicial review may be a remedy. Prosecutors abuse their discretion when they file charges that are not reasonable in light of the evidence available at the time the charges are filed. Overcharging may be done on purpose to coerce the defendant to plead guilty to a lesser charge.

Allegations of overcharging are difficult to prove. Prosecutors may legally charge a suspect with any crime for which there is sufficient evidence to connect that person. If the prosecutor decides not to file the most serious charge(s) that could be filed, and if the defendant refuses to plead guilty to the lesser charge(s), the prosecutor may file the more serious charge(s). This is not an abuse of discretion.

Spotlight 7-2 Prosecutorial Misconduct

All attorneys who serve the courts should be held to a high standard of conduct. This includes how they act and what they say, both in and out of court. Defense and prosecution attorneys may be placed under a complete or restricted gag order by the judge. If they violate the order and discuss the case, for example, with the media, they may be sanctioned. Attorneys may also be sanctioned for making improper comments during court proceedings. When their statements or actions are challenged by the opposing side, courts analyze the questioned statements in the context in which they were made and consider whether the effect of the words was to deny the defendant a fair trial.

Consider the case of *Darden v. Wainwright*. Among other questionable comments, the prosecutor stated that the defendant "shouldn't be out of his cell unless he has a leash on him and a prison guard at the other end of that leash. I wish [Mr. Turman] had had a shotgun in his hand when he walked in the back door and blown [sic] his [Darden's] face off. I wish I could see him sitting here with no face, blown away by a shotgun."[1]

The crime involved in *Darden* was a particularly heinous one. Darden was attempting an armed robbery of Mrs. Turman in a furniture store in 1973. When Mrs. Turman's husband unexpectedly came in the back door, Darden shot him. As Mr. Turman was dying, Darden attempted to force Mrs. Turman into a sexual act. A young neighbor entered the store and tried to help Mr. Turman but was shot three times by Darden, who fled after the assault. In his rush to escape, Darden had an automobile accident. A witness to that accident testified that Darden was zipping his pants and buckling his belt. Officers traced the car and, with this evidence, charged Darden with the crimes against the Turmans.

During the trial, in addition to the comment quoted earlier in this Spotlight, the prosecutor said repeatedly that he wished Darden had used the gun to kill himself. The U.S. Supreme Court held that, although the prosecutor's comments were improper, they were not sufficient to deny Darden a fair trial. Four justices dissented. In 1988, Darden was executed in Florida's electric chair.

1. Darden v. Wainwright, 477 U.S. 168 (1986).

Prosecutorial misconduct can involve withholding evidence that would be favorable to the defense. A landmark 1963 Supreme Court case held that prosecutors who suppress evidence favorable to defendants are violating the due process rights of those defendants.[25]

Prosecutorial misconduct can occur in or out of court by the manner in which the prosecutor talks or acts. Spotlight 7-2 summarizes one case. There is a fine line, however, between prosecutorial misconduct and questionable judgment. To illustrate, prosecutors may reprosecute defendants after a mistrial, although it is reasonable to question numerous reprosecutions of the same defendant. For example, in 1998 after the fifth trial of Curtis Kyles for the 1984 murder of Delores "Dee" Dye in a New Orleans supermarket parking lot after a botched robbery attempt ended in a hung jury, the prosecutor decided not to retry the man who had endured five trials over a 14-year period. One of Kyles's defense attorneys concluded that the prosecution in these cases was more concerned about its own reputation than about justice. Fourth and fifth prosecutions are rare, but a few have occurred.[26]

In June 2003, the Center for Public Integrity, a research firm located in Washington, D.C., and concerned with ethics and accountability in governments, published a report on prosecutorial misconduct. The study included 11,452 cases in which appellate courts had reviewed allegations of prosecutorial misconduct since 1970. In 2,012 of those cases, the appellate judges reversed; allegations of misconduct were not addressed by the appellate judges in 731 cases. In 8,709 of the cases, the judges found that prosecutors had behaved inappropriately but concluded that the behavior in question did not warrant reversals of the convictions. Some of the types of misconduct were as follows:

- Failing to disclose evidence that would aid the defense
- Mishandling physical evidence or using false or misleading evidence
- Making inflammatory remarks in front of the jury
- Characterizing the evidence to the jury in an unfair and misleading way

- Behaving improperly at the grand jury hearing
- Harassing or showing hostility toward the defendant or defense counsel
- Discriminating on the basis of gender, race, ethnicity, or for other reasons, in jury selection
- Making attempts to introduce evidence that is not admissible
- Charging suspects when the prosecutors have no credible evidence against them[27]

The following example of prosecutorial misconduct is an actual case cited by the Center for Public Integrity study. A 17-year-old woman alleged that she had been sexually assaulted by a 19-year-old man, who said the sexual act was consensual. The alleged victim was examined at a hospital, and the evidence supported the defendant's account rather than hers. When the alleged victim appeared before the grand jury to testify, the prosecutor asked her if she had been examined by a gynecologist at the hospital. The woman answered yes. The prosecutor did not present any evidence concerning the findings of that physician, thus misleading the grand jury, which indicted the defendant, who was convicted. An appellate court overturned the conviction and chastised the prosecutor with this statement:

> The results of the exam were not given to the grand jurors [even though the prosecution conceded that the evidence would have been helpful to the defense]...It is essential that the jurors be informed of the relevant facts. [The medical report] directly contradicts the victim's claim of anal and vaginal penetration and does not support her claim of a one-and-a-half-hour struggle. The grand jurors...were skillfully misled....The state treated this grand jury as a rubber stamp, its playtoy....Given the nature of the medical report, the failure to present it can be termed an intentional subversion of the process.[28]

Some prosecutors go beyond misconduct and commit crimes—some committing the same type of crimes they so vigorously prosecute. An example is the case of Richard J. Roach, who was elected district attorney for five counties in the Texas Panhandle. Roach was so enthusiastic about prosecuting drug offenders that he would bound into his office in the morning, declaring, "Let's go." Although Roach had previously spent time in a drug treatment center, he had resumed his illegal habit. In February 2005, FBI agents entered a courtroom and arrested Roach for suspicion of violating drug and weapons offenses. Roach plea bargained quickly, pleading guilty to possessing a firearm while using illegal drugs, and resigned his position. The remaining charges against him were dropped.[29]

Finally, although there is not necessarily any misconduct involved, prosecutors may be blamed for their failures to gain convictions. After the acquittal of the New York City police officers in the shooting death of unarmed suspect Amadou Diallo, prosecutors were blamed for not being sufficiently aggressive in their prosecution, for lacking passion, and for not presenting the evidence in a way that appealed to the jurors. Some critics blamed the prosecutors for the acquittals.[30]

7-3 Defense

One of the most effective ways to control prosecutorial misconduct is to provide adequate defense counsel for those accused of crimes. This section focuses on the role of the attorney as defense counsel in U.S. criminal justice systems, giving particular attention to the right to counsel.

7-3a The Defense Attorney's Role

Defense attorney The counsel for the defendant in a criminal proceeding, whose main function is to protect the legal rights of the accused.

The **defense attorney** is charged with the responsibility of protecting defendants' constitutional rights at all stages of the legal proceedings, which begin long before trial. The first encounter that a defense attorney usually has with a client is at the jail. Normally, after arrest and booking, a suspect is permitted one phone call. That call is usually to a lawyer or to a friend, requesting that the friend call a lawyer. If the suspect cannot afford an attorney, the judge appoints counsel at the first court appearance. Usually, defendants who can afford to retain counsel are visited by their attorneys before that court appearance.

The defense attorney's first responsibility is to interview the client and obtain as many facts as possible. The attorney must gain the confidence of the client, so that the defendant is willing to disclose all facts. The attorney should explain that this information is confidential between the attorney and the defendant. The defense attorney may begin an investigation by interviewing witnesses or friends, going to the scene of the alleged crime, and securing physical evidence. The attorney will talk to the prosecutor to see what information the police and prosecution have secured against the defendant.

The initial interview with the defendant is a very important one. Defendants may be confused about the law. They may have little or no understanding of their constitutional rights. They may not understand the importance of certain facts to the defense. The attorney must be able to elicit the needed information while maintaining a sense of perspective and understanding.

As soon as the defense attorney has enough information, he or she should advise the defendant concerning the strategy that could be used in the case. It might be reasonable for the defendant to plead guilty rather than go to trial. Negotiating pleas before trial is a frequent and very important procedure. The defense attorney should explain to the defendant the pros and cons of pleading guilty, but the attorney must be careful about encouraging a guilty plea when there is evidence that the defendant is not guilty. Even in those cases, a particular defendant, because of his or her prior record or the nature of the alleged offense, might be advised to plead guilty to a lesser offense rather than risk conviction on a more serious charge. All of these issues involve trial strategy, which includes knowing what to expect from the prosecutor as well as trying to predict what the judge and jury will do, should the case go to trial.

In some cases, defense attorneys talk to their clients' families and inform them of what to expect during the initial stages of the criminal justice process. Families and friends might also be valuable sources of information for the attorney in preparing a defense, as well as in sentencing recommendations if the defendant is found guilty. Getting the facts from defendants and their families and friends is a difficult task in many cases. It is emotionally draining as well, and many defense attorneys are not trained for this process. Defense attorneys devise strategies to elicit information from clients. Some use sworn police statements to shock the defendant into being honest. Others appear nonjudgmental and use hypothetical questions to allow clients to save face. Some attorneys admit that they browbeat their clients by being tyrannical. Others try to be friendly, but they may resent the time required to discover the facts.

The defense attorney must keep track of the scheduled procedures for the remainder of the time the case is in the criminal justice system. Defense attorneys are criticized for missing deadlines, being unprepared for hearings, and attempting to delay the proceedings by asking for a continuance. Sometimes, continuances are justified because there has not been sufficient time to prepare for the hearing. At other times, the requested delays are unreasonable and should be denied by the trial judge.

Some private defense attorneys have attempted to delay proceedings because they have not been paid by their clients. It is difficult to collect fees after a case has ended, particularly when the defendant is not pleased with the result. Some attorneys handle this problem by requiring that defendants pay in advance. They require a retainer fee, and when that amount of money has been exhausted by the attorney's time and expenses, another fee is required before the attorney continues with the case.

Even while obtaining facts and other forms of evidence from defendants and others, most defense attorneys begin preparing the case for trial, should that occur. Trial strategy is important, and an unprepared attorney does a disservice to the defendant. If the case results in a trial and the defendant is convicted, the defense attorney must be prepared to present evidence at sentencing. He or she must also prepare for an appeal if the case warrants one, although some defendants, for their appeals, retain lawyers who specialize in that process.

7-3b   Defense and the Right to Counsel

The defense of a criminal case is extremely important in an adversary system. If the prosecutor tries to prove the case against the defendant by introducing evidence that has been seized or a confession that has been elicited in violation of the defendant's rights, the defense attorney may ask the court to exclude that evidence. If the prosecutor files charges for which there is insubstantial evidence, the defense attorney may petition the court to dismiss those charges.

The primary job of a defense attorney is to protect the legal rights of the defendant and thereby preserve the adversary system. It is not the function of the defense attorney to judge the guilt or innocence of the defendant; that is a factual question to be decided by the jury (or the judge if the case is not tried to a jury). The defense attorney gathers and presents evidence and witnesses that support the defense and examines the evidence and witnesses introduced by the prosecutor.

This basic defense function is critical. The adversary system requires that, for a person to be convicted of a criminal offense, all of the elements of that offense be proved by the prosecutor and the question of guilt decided by a jury or judge. The evidence must be strong enough to determine the defendant's guilt beyond a reasonable doubt, a much tougher burden than that required in a civil case. The prosecution may fail in this burden, as illustrated by the high-profile case of Terry L. Nichols, who, along with Timothy McVeigh (who was convicted of murder and executed), was charged with the *federal* crimes associated with the bombing of the federal building in Oklahoma City in April 1995. Nichols was found guilty of manslaughter (along with the conspiracy charges), but not of murder, and he was sentenced to life in prison. Some of the jurors, who spoke after they had deadlocked on the penalty issue, said the government did not prove beyond a reasonable doubt that Nichols was guilty of murder or that he should be given the death penalty. Oklahoma subsequently tried Nichols for murder under its *state* statute. He was convicted and sentenced to life in prison.

The most important aspect of the defense of a criminal case is that the accused has a **right to counsel**. The drafters of the U.S. Constitution recognized that in a criminal trial the state's powers are immense, compared with those of the defendant. The Sixth Amendment to the U.S. Constitution states that "in all criminal prosecutions, the accused shall enjoy the right…to have the Assistance of Counsel for his defense" (see Appendix A). Many scholars consider the right to counsel to be the most important of all the defendant's constitutional rights. The use of counsel by those who can retain private attorneys has been accepted, but the right to have counsel appointed at the expense of the state (or federal government in a federal trial) has been the subject of considerable litigation.

It is important to an understanding of the right to counsel to note that the Bill of Rights, the first 10 amendments of the U.S. Constitution, was included to restrain the federal government's power. Today, most of those rights have been applied to the states through the due process clause of the Fourteenth Amendment, which specifies that states may not deny life, liberty, or property without due process of law (see Appendix A). It took the U.S. Supreme Court over a century, however, to rule that most of the rights contained in the Bill of Rights also apply to the states. The evolution of the right to appointed counsel is an example.

Appointed Counsel

The right to appointed counsel, which means counsel provided at government expense, has not always been recognized in the United States. In 1932 in *Powell v. Alabama*, the U.S. Supreme Court gave limited recognition to the right.[31] In *Powell*, a state case, nine African American youths were charged with the rape of two white Alabama women.

Right to counsel   The right to be represented by an attorney at crucial stages in the criminal justice system. Indigent defendants have the right to counsel provided by the state.

Eight of the defendants were convicted and sentenced to death. Several issues were raised on appeal; two of them pertained to the lack of counsel.

In *Powell*, the U.S. Supreme Court focused on the issue of whether appointed counsel should have been provided for defendants because they could not have afforded to retain counsel even if they had been given the opportunity to do so. In discussing the right to counsel, the Supreme Court emphasized that the right to be heard would have little meaning unless accompanied by a right to counsel. The Court held that there was a right to appointed counsel but limited that right to the facts of the case, one of which was that the crimes involved carried the death penalty. At the time *Powell* was decided, almost half the states already provided appointed counsel in capital cases. In federal trials, appointed counsel was provided by a congressional statute.

In a 1938 *federal* case, the U.S. Supreme Court held that there is a right to appointed as well as to retained counsel and that this right is not limited to capital cases.[32] In 1942, the Supreme Court refused to apply the right to appointed counsel to state cases. In *Betts v. Brady*, the Supreme Court established a fundamental fairness test, holding that an indigent defendant in a state trial would be entitled to appointed counsel in a noncapital case only where it could be shown that circumstances necessitated appointed counsel for the defendant to receive a fair trial.[33] *Betts v. Brady* was a controversial case, but it remained the law until 1963, when it was overruled, as the following discussion explains.

On 8 January 1962, the U.S. Supreme Court received a large envelope from Florida inmate number 003826. Clarence Earl Gideon, a pauper who had been in and out of prison most of his life, had printed his request in pencil. He was not a violent man, but he had committed several nonviolent crimes. In this case, he was charged with breaking and entering a poolroom with the intent to commit a misdemeanor, a felony under Florida law. Gideon requested that the state appoint an attorney for him. The judge responded that he was sorry but that the laws of Florida did not provide for appointed counsel except in capital cases. Gideon responded, "The United States Supreme Court says I am entitled to be represented by counsel." Gideon conducted his own defense. He was convicted and sentenced to five years in the state prison.

Gideon appealed to the U.S. Supreme Court, which agreed to hear the case and appointed a prestigious Washington, D.C., law firm to defend Gideon. The result was one of the few occasions in which the Supreme Court has overruled an earlier decision by name. In *Gideon v. Wainwright*, the Court reversed its ruling in *Betts v. Brady* and applied the right to appointed counsel to state cases. According to the Court,

> In our adversary system of criminal justice, any person haled into court, who is too poor to hire a lawyer, cannot be assured a fair trial unless counsel is provided for him. This seems to us to be an obvious truth.... [The Court quoted *Powell*:] 'He lacks both the skill and knowledge adequately to prepare his defense, even though he may have a perfect one. He requires the guiding hand of counsel at every step in the proceedings against him. Without it, though he be not guilty, he faces the danger of conviction because he does not know how to establish his innocence.'[34]

Gideon was convicted of a felony; consequently, his case extended the right to appointed counsel only to felony cases. In 1972, the U.S. Supreme Court held that the right to appointed counsel also extends to misdemeanors for which a conviction might result in the "actual deprivation of a person's liberty." In *Argersinger v. Hamlin*, the Supreme Court held that, without a "knowing and intelligent waiver, no person may be imprisoned for any offense, whether classified as petty, misdemeanor, or felony unless he was represented by counsel at his trial."[35]

The U.S. Supreme Court clarified *Argersinger* in *Scott v. Illinois*, decided in 1979. Aubrey Scott was fined but not given a prison sentence, although the statute under which he was convicted for shoplifting provided for either punishment. In ruling that Scott was not entitled to appointed counsel, the Supreme Court emphasized the difference between actual imprisonment and any other form of punishment.[36]

Gideon, Argersinger, and *Scott* concern the right to appointed counsel at trial. In 1967, the U.S. Supreme Court held that the Sixth Amendment right to counsel applies during "critical stages" in criminal proceedings.[37] The right applies when the court begins adversarial judicial proceedings, and it is not necessary for the defendant to ask for an attorney. At the stage when the right to counsel begins, if an attorney is not provided, any further judicial proceedings are improper and will result in the reversal of a conviction.

In 2002, the U.S. Supreme Court extended the right to appointed counsel in a case in which the defendant was not actually incarcerated but, rather, received a suspended sentence. In *Alabama v. Shelton,* the defendant, LaReed Shelton, was convicted of a third-degree assault, a misdemeanor, for his role in a fight occurring after a traffic accident. Shelton was told repeatedly that in representing himself he might commit errors that would harm his case, but he was never told that he had a right to an appointed attorney. After his conviction, the court sentenced Shelton to 30 days in the county prison, but the sentence was suspended, and Shelton was placed on unsupervised probation for two years. He was ordered to pay restitution in the amount of $516.69, along with a $500 fine. Shelton appealed to the Alabama Supreme Court, which agreed with him; the U.S. Supreme Court affirmed (by a 5-to-4 vote), with Justice Ruth Bader Ginsburg writing the following:

> Deprived of counsel when tried, convicted, and sentenced, and unable to challenge the original judgment at a subsequent probation revocation hearing, a defendant in Shelton's circumstances faces incarceration on a conviction that has never been subjected to the crucible of meaningful adversarial testing. The Sixth Amendment does not countenance this result.[38]

The general right to counsel does not apply to all pretrial stages, although it has been applied to most. The right to appointed counsel applies to some but not to all appeals. States may extend constitutional rights beyond those mandated by U.S. Supreme Court interpretations of the federal Constitution, and some have done so.

The right to counsel involves a right to refuse counsel. Defendants may choose to give up their right to counsel and represent themselves. The **waiver** of the right to counsel must be made voluntarily and knowingly. Judges know that the trial process is complicated, and they guard against the possibility that defendants will create an unfair disadvantage by appearing *pro se* (representing themselves). Judges question defendants carefully about their knowledge of criminal law and procedure and their understanding of the advantages of having counsel present. But if the defendant insists, he or she must be given the right to proceed to trial without counsel, although most judges require standby counsel to be present with the defendant to explain the basic rules, formalities, and etiquette in the courtroom. However, some defendants refuse all such advice and proceed on their own, although they must observe court rules.

Private Defense Counsel

Many defendants prefer to retain (hire) their own defense counsel, and they must do so if they are not eligible for an attorney provided at public expense. It is a common belief that the defense attorney with the best reputation for winning cases is one who works privately and charges very high fees, but this is not always the case. In many jurisdictions, the defense attorneys who try cases regularly and are familiar with the local prosecutors and judges have a better chance of gaining an acquittal in a difficult case.

Finding a competent, affordable defense attorney may be difficult. Few standards exist for measuring the competency of attorneys in criminal defense work. Some are selected by references from former clients. Others are selected from advertising on radio or television. In some cities, the local bar association makes referrals on request. Defendants should choose an attorney who is a competent trial lawyer and negotiator, but the personality and style of the attorney might be important as well. It is wise to avoid attorneys who guarantee results or who have a reputation for plea bargaining all

▶ **Waiver** The giving up of one's rights, such as the right to counsel or to a jury trial. Waivers must be made knowingly and intelligently; that is, the defendant must understand what is being relinquished. Some rights may not be waived.

▶ **Pro se** Literally, "on behalf of self." Acting as one's own attorney.

or most cases rather than going to trial. On the other hand, an attorney who insists on a trial might not provide the best representation for some clients.

The right to counsel includes the right to an attorney of one's choice. In June 2006, the U.S. Supreme Court held that the conviction of a defendant who was refused the right to retain his preferred attorney should be reversed. In *United States v. Gonzalez-Lopez*, the defendant, Cuauhtemoc Gonzalez-Lopez, charged with marijuana possession in the eastern federal district court in St. Louis, initially retained a local attorney but subsequently retained Joseph H. Low IV, an experienced California defense attorney who had recently secured a favorable plea bargain in the same court. When lawyers, such as Low, are not already admitted to practice before the court in which their client is scheduled to be tried, they must request the judge to admit them provisionally to try the case. Usually, this request is granted, but there were issues of procedural impropriety on the part of Low, and the judge revoked the temporary provision. Low was also unsuccessful on appeal. Gonzalez-Lopez was represented by other counsel. Low was denied permission to assist and was, in fact, ordered not to sit at counsel table and to have no contact with the defendant during the proceedings. The defendant was convicted and sentenced to 24 years in prison. The U.S. Supreme Court justices agreed that the trial judge should have granted the motion for Low to represent Gonzalez-Lopez, but they disagreed on what remedy should be provided as a result of this error. The justices split 5-to-4, with the majority holding that, even though the trial was fair, the right to defense counsel includes the right of defendants to retain the attorney of their choice. The U.S. Supreme Court ruled that the right to counsel is so important that when defendants are, in effect, denied the opportunity to retain the attorney of their choice, their conviction must be reversed, and they are entitled to a new trial, represented by the counsel they choose to retain and that they believe to be the best.[39]

Whether defendants have private or appointed counsel, they are entitled to the *effective* assistance of counsel, although the nature and meaning of that is not clear.

The Right to Effective Assistance of Counsel

The right to effective assistance of counsel is not mandated by the U.S. Constitution, but it has been held to be implied by that document. After all, the right to counsel would have little or no meaning without effective counsel. The U.S. Supreme Court used the concept of "effective and substantial aid" in *Powell v. Alabama*, discussed earlier. In several subsequent cases, the U.S. Supreme Court has also considered the meaning of the effective assistance of counsel.

The definition and application of the term *effective assistance of counsel* has, for the most part, been left to the lower courts. In 1945, the District of Columbia Court of Appeals articulated the standard that representation would not be considered ineffective unless counsel's actions reduced the trial to a "farce or mockery of justice." Other lower courts adopted this standard; some courts developed higher standards, such as "reasonably effective assistance."[40] In 1984, the U.S. Supreme Court adopted the "reasonably effective assistance" standard then used by all the lower federal courts and stated that no further definition was needed than the establishing of a two-pronged test, explained in *Strickland v. Washington* as follows:

> First, the defendant must show that counsel's performance was deficient. This requires showing that counsel made errors so serious that counsel was not functioning as the "counsel" guaranteed the defendant by the Sixth Amendment. Second, the defendant must show that the deficient performance prejudiced the defense. This requires showing that counsel's errors were so serious as to deprive the defendant of a fair trial, a trial whose result is reliable.[41]

Although a court may conclude that counsel was ineffective based on a single error, *Strickland* requires the court to consider the *totality of circumstances* of the case, and there is a strong presumption that counsel provided effective assistance. The problem

Spotlight 7-3	Ineffective Assistance of Counsel: A U.S. Supreme Court Update

Since it decided *Strickland v. Washington* in 1984 and established the requirement of reasonably effective assistance of counsel, as discussed in the text, the U.S. Supreme Court has given more insight into what it means to have effective assistance of counsel. In 2001, the Court stated, "Authority does not suggest that a minimal amount of additional time in prison cannot constitute prejudice." To the contrary, ruled the justices, "our jurisprudence suggests that any significant jail time has Sixth Amendment [which establishes the right to counsel; see Appendix A] significance." The case, *Glover v. United States*, involved a defendant who argued on appeal to the U.S. Supreme Court that he had ineffective counsel for the following reason. The federal sentencing guidelines provide for a grouping of certain crimes, and that grouping results in a shorter sentence. Paul Glover's crimes were not grouped together, placing him in a sentencing range between 78 and 97 months in prison. Had his crimes been grouped, his sentence would have been in the range of 63 to 78. The result was that his sentence was 6 to 21 months longer than it would have been otherwise. He appealed to the lower federal courts and lost the appeal, with both courts refusing to reach the issue of ineffective assistance of counsel on the grounds that an increase of 6 to 21 months was not sufficiently significant to constitute prejudice to Glover. The U.S. Supreme Court disagreed; the case was reversed and remanded to the lower federal court, which sent it back to the district (trial) court, which scheduled a new sentencing hearing.[1]

In June 2003, the U.S. Supreme Court decided, by a 7-to-2 vote in *Wiggins v. Smith*, that the failure of Kevin Wiggins's trial lawyer to conduct a "reasonable investigation" into his client's social background denied Wiggins his Sixth Amendment right to the effective assistance of counsel.[2]

Writing for the majority in *Wiggins*, Justice Sandra Day O'Connor pointed out that the *Strickland* case requires an appellant to show that the attorney's behavior prejudiced the client's defense. According to *Strickland*, a "defendant must show that there is a reasonable probability that, but for counsel's unprofessional errors, the result of the proceeding would have been different. A reasonable probability is a probability sufficient to undermine confidence in the outcome."

Justice O'Connor continued with these words:

> In assessing prejudice, we reweigh the evidence in aggravation against the totality of available mitigating evidence. In this case, our review is not circumscribed by a state conclusion with respect to prejudice, as neither of the state courts below reached this prong of the Strickland analysis.
>
> The mitigating evidence counsel failed to discover and present in this case is powerful. As Selvog [a licensed social worker] reported based on his conversations with Wiggins and members of his family, Wiggins experienced severe privation and abuse in the first six years of his life while in the custody of his alcoholic, absentee mother. He suffered physical torment, sexual molestation, and repeated rape during his subsequent years in foster care. The time Wiggins spent homeless, along with his diminished mental capacities, further augment his mitigation case. Petitioner thus has the kind of troubled history we have declared relevant to assessing a defendant's moral culpability. [As stated in *Penry v. Texas*] "evidence about the defendant's background and character is relevant because of the belief, long held by

comes in deciding which facts are sufficient to constitute ineffectiveness. Let's consider some examples.

The first case was emphasized by Massachusetts Senator Edward M. Kennedy in his comments in March 2003, recognizing the 40th anniversary of the *Gideon* decision. In August 2002, Wallace M. Fugate III was executed in Georgia. Fugate, who had no prior record when he was charged with the capital murder of his former wife, was represented by lawyers who, according to Senator Kennedy, admitted that they were not familiar with "the most basic criminal and death penalty precedents. They did not ask for plea negotiations or request funds for an investigator. They filed only three motions, none exceeding two pages in length." They did not present any mitigating circumstances, and the sentencing hearing lasted only 27 minutes.[42]

Senator Kennedy cited a second case, also in 2002, in which the U.S. Supreme Court refused to hold that an appellant had received ineffective assistance of counsel. According to Kennedy, in *Bell v. Cone* (see Spotlight 7-3), the Supreme Court upheld "the performance of a lawyer who failed to interview witnesses, present mitigating evidence or even plead for his client's life at the sentencing hearing." The senator continued:

> The [U.S. Supreme] Court's constitutional jurisprudence on this fundamental issue has now deteriorated to the point that it is unclear whether a defendant is "prejudiced"

this society, that defendants who commit criminal acts that are attributable to a disadvantaged background…may be less culpable than defendants who have no such excuse."[3]

In contrast, in 2002, the U.S. Supreme Court upheld the death sentence of a Tennessee death row inmate, Gary Cone, who argued that he received a death sentence rather than life in prison because his attorney did not give him effective assistance of counsel. Cone was convicted of brutally murdering an elderly couple in their home. The previous day, Cone had robbed a jewelry store and shot a bystander and a law enforcement officer who attempted to apprehend him. Cone alleged that, because his attorney did not present mitigating evidence during the sentencing hearing, did not put Cone on the stand to testify, and did not present a final argument in the case, his representation constituted ineffective assistance of counsel. It was also noted that Cone's attorney was treated for mental illness and subsequently committed suicide.

The U.S. Supreme Court held that Cone's allegations against his attorney were too minor to constitute ineffective assistance of counsel; indeed, the defense counsel may have had strategic reasons for the choices he had made in representing Cone. The Court emphasized the *Strickland* test, which requires the appellant to prove that "there is a reasonable probability that, but for counsel's unprofessional errors, the result of the proceeding would have been different" and that counsel's representation "fell below an objective standard of representation." Cone's case failed to meet those tests.[4]

Finally, on 20 June 2005, in *Rompilla v. Beard*, the U.S. Supreme Court reversed the death penalty sentence of Ronald Rompilla. The Pennsylvania case, decided by a 5-to-4 vote, involved public defenders who did not search the records (located in the same courthouse) of their client's rape conviction 14 years earlier, despite the fact that the prosecution had informed the defense that they planned to use that case as evidence of the defendant's prior act of violence, an aggravating factor supporting the death penalty. According to Justice David Souter, who wrote the majority opinion, "no reasonable lawyer would forgo examination of the file" under the circumstances. The file indicates that Rompilla is of limited mental capacity, was an abused child, and most probably suffered from fetal alcohol syndrome and schizophrenia. Subsequent investigations by Rompilla's appellate lawyers uncovered evidence that the father locked Rompilla and his brother in a small dog pen that was "filthy and excrement filled," that the brothers went to school in rags, and that Rompilla dropped out in the ninth grade. According to Justice Souter, a competent lawyer would have uncovered this information and presented it to the jury; such information might have produced a result different from the death penalty.[5]

A noted law professor, citing the cases discussed in this Spotlight, declared, "The basic themes of fundamental fairness in the administration of the death penalty have penetrated the Supreme Court as well as the general public."[6]

1. Glover v. United States, 531 U.S. 198 (2001), *on remand, remanded* 2001 U.S. App. LEXIS 4258 (7th Cir. 2001), *on remand, summ. judgment granted*, 149 F.Supp. 2d 371 (N.D. Ill. 2001).
2. Wiggins v. Smith, 539 U.S. 510 (2003).
3. Wiggins v. Smith, 539 U.S. 510 (2003), footnotes omitted.
4. Bell v. Cone, 535 U.S. 685 (2002).
5. Rompilla v. Beard, 545 U.S. 374 (2005).
6. "Justices Overturn a Death Sentence, Citing an Inadequate Defense Counsel," *New York Times*, Late Edition-Final (21 June 2005), p. 16.

when a defense lawyer sleeps through substantial portions of his capital trial. In 2000, a panel of the 5th U.S. Circuit Court of Appeals ruled in *Burdine v. Johnson* that he is not. Fortunately, that ruling was overturned by the full 5th Circuit. But five of the judges dissented.[43]

The *Burdine* case involved the appeal of Calvin Jerold Burdine. After spending 16 years on death row for a 1984 murder, Burdine filed a writ of **habeas corpus**, claiming that he should be released from prison because he was prejudiced at his trial when his attorney fell asleep. The Fifth Circuit Court of Appeals agreed with Burdine and ordered a new trial. The U.S. Supreme Court refused to hear the case of the Texas sleeping counsel, thus allowing the Fifth Circuit decision to stand. A federal district court ordered Burdine released from death row after the prosecution failed to meet the deadline for procedures concerning a new trial, but a federal appellate court reversed.[44] Burdine remained in prison, awaiting a new trial, which was scheduled for March 2003. However, in June 2003, the prosecution offered and the defense accepted a plea bargain that will keep Burdine off death row, but he will spend most, if not all, of the rest of his life in prison. Under the terms of the agreement, Burdine pleaded guilty to aggravated assault with a deadly weapon, felony possession of a weapon, and capital murder. He was given a life sentence for each charge, with the sentences running consecutively.[45]

▶ **Habeas corpus** Technically, a written court order requiring that the accused be taken to court to determine the legality of custody and confinement. Also refers to writs that inmates file regarding the alleged illegality of their confinement or the conditions of that confinement.

In 2002, the U.S. Supreme Court upheld the conviction and death sentence of a man whose appeal was based on his argument that his assistance of counsel was ineffective because his court-appointed lawyer had previously represented the victim in another case. A bitterly divided Supreme Court held 5-to-4 in *Mickens v. Taylor* that the appellant did not show that he was prejudiced in the case.[46] Recall that showing prejudice is one of the *Strickland* requirements.

In a 1988 case, the Nevada Supreme Court held that a defense attorney's efforts to further his own career rather than pursue the best interests of his client constituted ineffective assistance of counsel. The defendant was charged with first-degree murder for killing her sleeping husband, who had previously abused her. Counsel advised her to plead not guilty on the grounds of self-defense, allegedly believing that an acquittal on that basis would enhance his own career. Technically, self-defense does not apply in such cases; however, the defense has been permitted in some battered person syndrome cases, in which the defendant (usually a woman) had been abused previously (and frequently) by her intimate partner but was not threatened at the time she committed the otherwise criminal act. Considerable publicity is given to cases in which that defense is used successfully. Counsel's advice to his client concerning the case implied his own professional motives, leading the appellate court to reverse the defendant's conviction for first-degree murder.[47] Spotlight 7-3 contains more information about ineffective assistance of counsel, as it discusses recent cases on the issue.

It is important to understand that if a defendant does not agree with the actions of the defense counsel or with the trial's result (e.g., conviction), it does not constitute ineffective assistance of counsel requiring a new trial. In the case of the two former New York City police detectives, Louis J. Eppolito and Stephen Caracappa, discussed in Chapter 5, who were convicted of racketeering, including eight mob murders, the defendants charged their respective attorneys with inadequate representation, which, they claimed, resulted in their convictions. Among other issues, Eppolito alleged that his attorney refused to let him testify. The lawyers were cleared (interestingly, the prosecutors who fought against the defense lawyers during the trial supported them in these allegations of inadequate defense). But, as also noted earlier, the defendants were acquitted due to technical reasons, although they were being held without bail on lesser charges.

Defense Systems for Indigents

Court-appointed counsel for indigent defendants represents a critical part of U.S. criminal justice systems. Approximately 80 percent of jail inmates and 75 percent of prison inmates are represented by appointed rather than by retained counsel. In recent years, funding of indigent defense programs has been threatened, while demand for these defense services has increased. Underfunding of public defender systems at all levels may have a greater impact on minorities than on white defendants, leading to allegations of racism.

Defense counselors' caseloads are too high, salaries are too low to attract many of the brightest law graduates, and capital case appeals have increased and are complicated, with an insufficient number of well-trained attorneys to handle them. There are many examples of indigent defense programs that are improperly staffed, overcrowded, and lack adequate resources. Some jurisdictions are trying to improve their systems. For example, in June 2005, Montana legislators, facing a lawsuit from the American Civil Liberties Union, passed a statute revamping the state's public defender law. Under the previous system, some accused waited in jail longer than the maximum sentence that could be imposed for the crimes for which they were charged. A study had branded Montana's public defender system as "ineffective, inefficient, unethical, [and] conflict-ridden."[48]

In 2003, during the 40th anniversary year of the *Gideon* case, the American Bar Association (ABA) held hearings on the status of the right to counsel in the United States. Witnesses from across the country testified concerning the issues, leading the

---

Spotlight 7-4 — Gideon's Broken Promise: America's Continuing Quest for Equal Justice

The nine findings of the American Bar Association's hearings on the status of defense systems in the United States are as follows:

- Forty years after *Gideon v. Wainwright*, indigent defense in the United States remains in a state of crisis, resulting in a system that lacks fundamental fairness and places poor persons at constant risk of wrongful conviction.
- Funding for indigent defense services is shamefully inadequate.
- Lawyers who provide representation in indigent defense systems sometimes violate their professional duties by failing to furnish competent representation.
- Lawyers are not provided in numerous proceedings in which a right to counsel exists in accordance with the Constitution and/or state laws. Too often, prosecutors seek to obtain waivers of counsel and guilty pleas from unrepresented accused persons, while judges accept and sometimes even encourage waivers of counsel that are not knowing, voluntary, intelligent, and on the record.

- Judges and elected officials often exercise undue influence over indigent defense attorneys, threatening the professional independence of the defense function.
- Indigent defense systems frequently lack basic oversight and accountability, impairing the provision of uniform, quality services.
- Efforts to reform indigent defense systems have been most successful when they involve multi-faceted approaches and representatives from a broad spectrum of interests.
- The organized bar too often has failed to provide the requisite leadership in the indigent defense area.
- Model approaches to providing quality indigent defense services exist in this country, but these models often are not adequately funded and cannot be replicated elsewhere absent sufficient financial support.

Source: Gideon's Broken Promise: America's Continuing Quest for Equal Justice, a report on the American Bar Association's hearings on the right to counsel in criminal proceedings (December 2004), p. v, available at http://www.abanet.org/legalservices/sclaid/defender/brokenpromise, accessed 11 July 2006.

ABA to entitle its report, *Gideon's Broken Promise: America's Continuing Quest for Equal Justice*. The nine main findings of that report are reproduced in Spotlight 7-4.

Three models are used for organizing the provision of defense counsel for indigent defendants in states and localities:

- Public defender programs
- Assigned counsel programs
- Contract systems

Most public defender systems are public law firms whose mission is to provide counsel in criminal cases for defendants who cannot afford to retain private counsel. Most public defender systems are located in metropolitan areas. They are supported publicly and administered by an attorney, usually called the **public defender**.

Like prosecutors, public defenders have the advantage of specializing in criminal cases. This increases their expertise and efficiency, but it may contribute to professional burnout. Like prosecutors, many public defenders work with tremendous caseloads, leaving them insufficient time to devote to any particular case. In addition, inadequate budgets result in a lack of support staff and equipment.

Better recruitment and more intensive training of attorneys would improve public defender programs. Training programs should include an emphasis on efficiency and ethical standards, as well as negotiation and trial skills. If the office does not have a formal training program, efforts might be made to assign new personnel to a more experienced attorney for a period of observation or to contract with private agencies or other public defender offices for training programs.

The burden of improving public defender services rests in two places. Both the legal profession and society must assume the responsibility for protecting constitutional guarantees. Criminal defendants will never be popular, but the public must provide the money and resources necessary to make the system work as a protective device to ensure that no one is denied the constitutional right to be defended by counsel.

▶ **Public defender** An attorney retained and paid by the government to represent indigent defendants in criminal proceedings.

Assigned counsel   An attorney appointed by and paid for by the court to represent a defendant who does not have funds to retain a private attorney.

The second method of providing counsel for indigents is an **assigned counsel** program. Under this model, attorneys are assigned to defend particular indigent defendants. Normally, assignments are made by the judge scheduled to preside over the trial, but some jurisdictions have moved to a more formal and organized system in an attempt to coordinate assignments throughout a jurisdiction. Most assignments are made from lists of attorneys who have volunteered to participate in the program, although in some jurisdictions, all attorneys are expected to participate in the assigned counsel program. A minority of jurisdictions have some procedures for assessing the qualifications of attorneys who participate in assigned counsel cases, but the majority have no qualifications beyond a license to practice law. Most areas that have assigned counsel systems do not have formal provisions for removing names from the list of participating attorneys.

Assigned counsel are paid on a fee schedule determined by state statute or by local bar regulations. These fees are usually too low, however, to attract a sufficient number of lawyers. And in recent years, overall funding has been a problem. Most states have faced budget shortfalls, with many cutting their budgets, including staff as well as programs.

In general, the money received by assigned counsel is less than the average fees paid to private defense attorneys and in most jurisdictions is considerably less. In some systems, maximum fees are established, making it impossible for assigned counsel to be paid an adequate fee for all hours worked in a complicated case.

Contract system   System for providing defense attorneys in which a governmental agency contracts with a local bar association, a private law firm, or a private attorney to provide legal services for indigent defendants.

The third model is the **contract system**, which is not used widely. Most of the counties that utilize this method are small (fewer than 50,000 people). In the contract system, a bar association, a private law firm, or an individual attorney contracts with a jurisdiction to provide legal assistance for indigent defendants.

Despite problems in funding legal aid, there have been some encouraging signs at the state level. In 2005, legal aid groups in Illinois, which ranked at the "bottom of the 10 most populous states" in its funding of legal aid, secured an increase in funding of between $500,000 and $2 million. In previous years, budget problems in that state had led to cuts in the number of attorneys working in legal aid and the closing of some legal aid offices, especially in the state's rural areas.[49]

There has also been some improvement in legal aid at the federal level. In late 2004, Congress passed and President George W. Bush signed the Justice for All Act of 2004, which contains a provision known as the Innocence Protection Act. This act includes grants to states to improve the quality of legal representation in capital cases.[50] The big issue, however, is funding for indigent defense programs, and the Bush administration has proposed to cut funding. In February 2006, the administration proposed to cut funding for Legal Services Corporation (LSC—a nonprofit corporation that provides legal aid in both civil and criminal cases for indigent persons) from $329.8 million in 2006 to $310.86 for fiscal year 2007, which began 1 October 2006. LSC proposed a budget of $411.8 million. Congress appropriated $326.5 million. For fiscal year 2008, LSC requested a $430.6 million budget, which was almost $120 million above President Bush's proposed budget for that agency.[51]

According to one senator who urged his colleagues to increase legal aid funding,

> We stand on this floor every day, and we recite the Pledge of Allegiance to the flag.... In the process of doing that, we pledge to support "liberty and justice for all." You simply cannot have justice in this country if you do not have adequate access to its court system.[52]

The prosecution and the defense begin playing their respective roles and interacting with each other during a series of important pretrial procedures, the focus of the rest of this chapter.

7-4   Pretrial Procedures

This section explores the important processes and procedures that occur prior to the trial of a criminal case. It is important to understand, however, that the stages in the criminal justice process of any trial are not discrete. They do not always happen one after the other; some stages overlap. Nor are the functions of the police, prosecutors, defense attorneys, and judges limited to particular stages. Citizens—as victims, witnesses, or members of a jury—function at different levels as well.

7-4a   Steps in the Criminal Justice Process

Figure 1-1 in Chapter 1 diagrams the steps in the criminal justice process. References to that figure are made in this chapter to help you visualize the processes. The specific stages occurring before trial are enumerated in Spotlight 7-5 for easy reference.

The stages in the criminal justice process are very important for two reasons. First, most people who are arrested are not tried in a criminal court. After the initial investigation, there may not be sufficient evidence for an arrest. There may be sufficient evidence, but the police may not be able to locate the suspect, or for some other reason, the police may not arrest. Those who are arrested may not be prosecuted, for any number of the reasons discussed previously. Second, after the prosecutor files charges, those charges may be dropped by the prosecutor, which may require judicial approval, or dismissed by the judge. This action may occur during any of the court sessions before or after the trial begins.

The procedures listed in Spotlight 7-5 begin with the report of an alleged crime, which may be followed by a formal arrest and **booking**. In the second step, the alleged crime must be investigated. Early investigation of a reported crime is very important; later, evidence may be lost or destroyed, or witnesses may disappear. Thus, police prefer to question potential witnesses at or near the scene of a crime as soon as possible. Police use various methods in investigating an alleged crime. Defense attorneys may use the same methods or even retain private investigators to search for evidence that would assist in the defense of the case. They check for physical evidence by analyzing the victim's clothing and looking for hair, blood, or other evidence that might associate the accused with the reported crime. They look for a weapon or weapons that might have been used in the crime. They question all parties who might know something about the alleged crime or the suspect, looking for information such as motive as well as any evidence linking a specific individual with the crime.

Securing physical evidence that a crime has occurred may involve searching the suspect's automobile, home, or office. It may involve securing physical evidence from the accused. For example, police may obtain body fluids or hair samples from the suspect. Police cannot compel suspects to testify against themselves; that would be a violation of the Fifth Amendment (see Appendix A) However, the U.S. Supreme Court has held that some forms of evidence may be secured from suspects without violating their due process rights. Thus, samples of hair, fiber, blood, and saliva may be seized and tested for deoxyribonucleic acid, or DNA, a genetic code by which individuals may be identified and connected to a crime.

The results of tests on evidence may lead the prosecution to decide not to file charges or to drop charges already filed. In earlier stages, the police may decide not to

▶ **Booking**   The official recording of the name, photograph, and fingerprints of a suspect, along with the offense charged and the name of the officer who made the arrest.

Spotlight 7-5	**Steps in the Criminal Justice Process before Trial**

1. Report of a crime
2. Investigation prior to arrest
3. Arrest
4. Booking
5. Postarrest investigation
6. Prosecutor's decision to charge suspect with a crime
7. Initial appearance
8. Preliminary hearing
9. Grand jury review
10. Arraignment
11. Pretrial motions
12. Pretrial conferences

arrest after conducting a preliminary investigation. For example, a person suspected of driving under the influence may be given a field test for alcohol and perform so well that the officer decides not to pursue the matter.

Police may be required to file detailed reports, even if they decide not to pursue the investigation, and this is true especially if the reported crime is a felony. Usually, the reports are filed on a printed form that contains questions about the offense, location, description of any vehicle, weapons, injuries, and location of the injured parties or damaged property.

These initial investigations at the time of a crime or shortly after a crime has been reported may be followed by more intensive investigations by the police or prosecution. Investigations may continue throughout the case and for a very long time before a case is settled—even before an arrest. In the case of the Unabomber, the investigation went on for 17 years before Theodore "Ted" Kaczynski was arrested. Kaczynski, age 53 at the time of his arrest in 1996, was suspected of carrying out 16 mail bombings, which killed 3 people and wounded 23 others over a 17-year period. Kaczynski is a former math professor who received his Ph.D. from the University of Michigan at Ann Arbor and taught at the University of California at Berkeley. He was convicted and is serving a life term in prison.

Examinations may be required of violent crime victims to secure physical evidence of the alleged crime. Psychological examinations of victims may be given to obtain evidence that might be useful to the prosecution. A psychological or psychiatric examination of a defendant may be ordered at some point before trial in order to determine whether the defendant is mentally competent to stand trial. In the Unabomber case, the trial was postponed after the judge ordered that the suspect be examined to determine whether he was competent to stand trial. Kaczynski had previously been declared competent, but his actions shortly before and during the week the trial was to begin led the judge to order the competency examinations.

During investigations, both sides look for testimonial as well as for physical evidence. Both sides may use the services of an expert witness to testify regarding a crucial element of the case. An expert witness is an individual who has specialized knowledge in a recognized area, such as medicine. Both the prosecution and the defense also look for eye witnesses to the crime. One frequently used method of obtaining eye-witness identification of a suspect is to conduct lineups. A **lineup** involves several people. The witness (who may also be the alleged victim) is asked to look at all of the people in the lineup and decide whether he or she can identify the person(s) who allegedly committed the crime. Lineups are permissible, provided they are conducted properly. In the Duke lacrosse rape case, mentioned earlier, the defense protested the manner of the lineup, which featured only Duke lacrosse players.

It is improper in most instances to ask a witness to identify the suspect in a **showup**, which involves only that suspect. This kind of identification procedure has been condemned by courts but allowed under limited circumstances. Pictures may be shown to witnesses for identification of suspects, although restrictions are placed on this procedure. It must be shown that the witnesses had a good opportunity to see the suspect. The pictures must be viewed soon after the alleged crime, while the memory of the witnesses is clear. Multiple witnesses may not view the pictures in the company of each other. The police may not make suggestive comments regarding the pictures and the suspect. Usually, it is not permissible to offer the witness only one photograph, that of the accused.

If the investigation convinces the prosecutor that sufficient evidence is available to lead a reasonable person to think that a particular suspect committed a crime, and if the prosecutor decides to file formal charges against the suspect, in most cases, that suspect must be taken before a magistrate for an **initial appearance**. The initial appearance is for the purpose of having the court determine whether there is probable cause to charge the suspect with the crime.

A suspect who has been retained in custody must be taken before the magistrate without unreasonable delay. The time involved in processing the suspect at the police

Lineup A procedure in which a group of people are placed together in a line to allow the complainant or an eyewitness to identify the alleged offender.

Showup An identification procedure during a police investigation. It involves showing the alleged victim only one person rather than several, as in a *lineup*. It is permitted only in extraordinary circumstances.

Initial appearance The first appearance of the accused before a magistrate. If the accused is detained in jail immediately after arrest, he or she must be taken quickly to a magistrate for the initial appearance. At that point, the magistrate decides whether there is probable cause to detain the suspect and, if so, tells the suspect of the charges and of his or her constitutional rights, including the right to an attorney.

station usually means that the initial appearance cannot take place until the following day. If the suspect is booked on a weekend, the initial appearance cannot take place until the following Monday, unless special provisions have been made. In some metropolitan areas, because of the high volume of weekend arrests, magistrates' courts hold special sessions on weekends to permit initial appearances earlier than usual and thus decrease the amount of time suspects must spend in jail before their initial appearances.

Most initial appearances are brief. Magistrates verify the names and addresses of the defendants and inform them of the formal charges and of their constitutional rights. Although the procedures differ among jurisdictions, at this stage in many areas, the process of appointing counsel is started. Most defendants who have retained counsel have their attorneys with them at their initial appearances.

If the defendant is charged with a minor offense, such as a misdemeanor, he or she may enter a plea at the initial appearance. Many defendants enter guilty pleas at this stage. Defendants who do not plead guilty are informed of the next stage in the proceeding. Defendants charged with felonies may not enter a plea at the initial appearance. In some felony cases, the defendant is not required to appear in court at this stage, although defense counsel will do so. For defendants who have been detained in custody to this point, magistrates make determinations whether to release them pending trial. If the police have released defendants after booking, then at the initial appearance, magistrates review the terms of those releases and decide whether they were properly made under the circumstances.

In some jurisdictions, the initial appearance is followed by a **preliminary hearing**, at least in cases involving felonies. Normally, the preliminary hearing occurs between one and two weeks after the initial appearance. During the interval between these two stages, some or all charges may be dropped as prosecutors discover that there is insufficient evidence to proceed. If the charges are not dropped, a preliminary hearing is held to determine whether there is probable cause to continue with those charges. A preliminary hearing is not required in all jurisdictions. If it is not required, prosecutors may take the case directly to a grand jury where that is required. If a grand jury is not required, prosecutors may proceed on their own.

At the preliminary hearing, the prosecution and the defense must present sufficient evidence to enable the magistrate to decide the issue of probable cause. Normally, the preliminary hearing is open because of the First Amendment right (see Appendix A) of the press to cover and of the public to know about such hearings. The hearing may be closed if a defendant shows that he or she cannot get a fair hearing without closure. Defendants may waive the preliminary hearing, and many choose to do so, but the waiver must be a knowing and intelligent one.

In the United States, an official criminal charge begins in one of two ways. First, the prosecutor may initiate the proceedings by returning an information. That may be done in cases not requiring action by the grand jury or when the grand jury review is waived. Second, the case may begin with a grand jury indictment, which some states require in felony cases, although the states differ in the crimes for which an indictment is required. Some states limit the requirement to serious felonies. In federal courts, grand jury indictments are required for the prosecution of capital or otherwise infamous crimes, with the exceptions noted in the Fifth Amendment (see Appendix A).

The grand jury is composed of private citizens, usually 23 persons, although some states have reduced the number. Originally, a majority vote was required for a decision, but today, some states, particularly those with grand juries smaller than 23, require more than a majority vote. The grand jury review differs from the initial appearance and the preliminary hearing in that in this review only the prosecution presents evidence. The defendant does not have a right to present evidence or to be present. The grand jury is not bound by all the evidence rules that are required at a trial. The deliberations are secret.

The basic function of the grand jury is to hear the prosecutor's evidence and to decide whether there is probable cause to return an indictment. An indictment returned

> **Preliminary hearing** An appearance before a lower court judge to determine whether there is sufficient evidence to submit the case to the grand jury or to the trial court. Preliminary hearings may include the bail decision.

True bill The prosecutor's indictment returned with the approval of the grand jury. After hearing the prosecutor's evidence, the grand jury determines that the indictment is accurate—that is, it is a *true bill*.

Presentment A document issued by a grand jury that states that probable cause exists to believe that the suspect committed the crime. Presentments are issued without the participation of the prosecutor. *See also* **Indictment**.

Arraignment A hearing before a judge, during which the defendant is identified, hears the formal reading of the charges, is read his or her legal rights, and enters a plea to the charges.

Nolo contendere Literally, "I will not contest it." In a criminal case, this plea has the legal effect of a guilty plea, but the plea cannot be used against the defendant in a civil action based on the same act. The plea might be used in a case involving a felony charge of driving while intoxicated. A guilty plea could be used as evidence of liability in a civil action of wrongful death filed by the family of the victim who died in the accident, whereas a *nolo* plea requires that the plaintiff in the civil action *prove* liability.

Motion A document submitted to the court, asking for an order or a ruling.

Discovery A legal motion requesting the disclosure of information held by the opposing counsel and intended for use in the forthcoming trial.

by a grand jury is called a **true bill**. The *indictment* is the official document stating the name of the accused, the charge, and the essential facts supporting that charge. In returning that indictment, the grand jury is not bound by the magistrate's decision at the preliminary hearing. Generally, a grand jury indictment is not required in misdemeanor or petty offense cases. Those are begun officially when the prosecutor returns an information.

Once it is in session, the grand jury may initiate investigations. This may be done, for example, when there are allegations of widespread corruption in public agencies. The grand jury may also be used to investigate organized crime. When the grand jury begins an official prosecution in this manner—that is, by action on its own knowledge without the indictment presented by the prosecutor—it returns a **presentment**, which is an official document, an accusation asking for the prosecutor to prepare an indictment.

In theory, the grand jury serves as a check on prosecutorial discretion. The U.S. Supreme Court recognized this important function when it said that the grand jury serves the significant function of standing between the accuser and the accused, whether the latter is an individual, a minority group, or another entity, to determine whether a charge is founded on reason or was dictated by an intimidating power or by malice and personal ill will.[53]

In many cases, however, the grand jury is an arm of the prosecution. In fact, in most cases presented by prosecutors to grand juries, the indictment is returned as a true bill. Of course, some procedures must be observed by the grand jury, and the body of case law is extensive and at times conflicting. Like the selection of trial juries (discussed in Chapter 8), the selection of the grand jury may not involve systematic exclusion because of race or other suspect categories, such as gender.

After the indictment or information is officially filed with the court, an **arraignment** is scheduled. At that hearing, judges or magistrates read the indictments or informations to the defendants, inform them of their constitutional rights, and ask for pleas to the charges. If a defendant pleads not guilty, a date is set for trial. If a defendant pleads guilty, a date is set for formal sentencing, unless that takes place at the arraignment, as is often the case with less serious offenses.

In some jurisdictions a defendant is permitted to plead **nolo contendere**, which literally means "I do not contest it." That plea in a criminal case has the legal effect of a guilty plea. The difference is that the plea may not be used against that defendant in a civil case. Thus, if the defendant pleads *nolo* to felony charges of driving while intoxicated and leaving the scene of an accident, that plea may not be used in a civil case filed by a victim who suffered injuries and property damage in the accident.

Throughout the pretrial proceedings, both sides may file motions. A **motion** is a document submitted to the court, asking for a rule or an order. Some motions are inappropriate before trial; a motion for a new trial is an example. Other motions may be made before the trial begins. The defense may make a motion to suppress evidence on the allegation that the evidence was secured in violation of the defendant's rights. Defendants may make motions to dismiss the case because of insufficient evidence. There could be other reasons: the defense might attack the technical sufficiency of the charging document, question the composition of the grand jury, or claim prosecutorial misconduct.

It is common for the defense to file a motion requiring the prosecutor to produce evidence, a process called **discovery**. Discovery procedures are defined by court rules and procedural statutes, but the nature of discovery rules varies from permitting extensive discovery to allowing rather limited discovery. Discovery is a two-way street. The prosecution and the defense are entitled to certain information that the other side plans to use at trial. Lists of witnesses, prior statements obtained from those witnesses, and the nature of physical evidence are the kinds of information that the prosecution and defense might obtain. Prosecutors and defense attorneys may be sanctioned for violating discovery rules.

Under some circumstances, both the prosecution and the defense may obtain oral statements from witnesses outside of court and before trial. These statements are called **depositions**. They are taken under oath, are recorded verbatim (usually by a court reporter), and may be used in court. They are permitted when there is a court order or rules of procedure that allow depositions. Attorneys for both sides are present. Witnesses or other parties may also be given **interrogatories**, a series of questions that are to be answered truthfully, with the respondents signing notarized statements of oath that the answers are correct.

Discovery is very important in criminal as well as in civil cases. The deposition is one of the best tools for gathering information (although it is not permitted, or may be limited, in criminal cases). Although we are accustomed to movies and television shows in which surprise witnesses appear unexpectedly in court and change the nature of the case, or known witnesses blurt out an incriminating fact to the surprise of everyone, this normally does not occur in actual cases.

Another motion the defense might file is for a change of **venue**, which is the place of trial. If the case has received considerable media attention, the defense may succeed with the argument that the defendant could not get a fair trial in that jurisdiction, and therefore, a change of venue should be granted. Changing the venue of a trial is usually controversial, and extended hearings may be held in court over this issue.

Although many defense motions might be filed before trial, these motions do not usually result in dismissals. The prosecutor might file motions, too, including a motion to drop the case or change the charges. In some jurisdictions, once formal charges have been filed, prosecutors may not drop or change those charges without the court's permission. Frequently, the prosecutor files a motion to drop or lower charges as a result of plea bargaining, discussed later in this chapter.

In addition to motions that the prosecution and defense might wish to make individually, or other issues they want to discuss with the judge, there are times when both sides want to meet with the judge to ask for more time to secure evidence, to prepare pretrial motions, to negotiate a plea, or to handle any other pretrial matters. In some instances, these arrangements are made between the attorneys and do not require the judge's presence or approval. In other cases, the judge might keep a tight hold on the management of the case and not permit any changes (such as an extension of the discovery period) without judicial approval.

Pretrial conferences can also be referred to as *status conferences*. They may be informal, with the prosecution and the defense discussing the status of the case, enumerating the issues on which they agree, so that no court time is wasted on arguing issues that are not in dispute. The judge may ask each attorney to estimate the time he or she expects to take to present the case. The answer is important for time management in courts, and the defense and prosecution might be limited by their predictions during these conferences; thus, the estimates should be made only after close scrutiny of the evidence each attorney thinks should be presented.

Both the prosecution and the defense use the pretrial period to prepare for trial. Preparation includes further investigating and testing physical evidence, repeatedly attempting to locate witnesses who have not yet been found, interviewing witnesses, obtaining depositions of expert and other witnesses, and reviewing those depositions and all other information pertinent to the trial. Attorneys spend time with their own witnesses, ensuring that they know what information the witnesses will give at trial and preparing them for the questions that might be asked by opposing counsel.

Attorneys keep records of the expenses of trial preparation, which include costs of their own time (even if they are public defenders paid by the case and not by the hour or prosecutors on salary, most keep an hourly record of their activities), as well as out-of-pocket costs for investigations, depositions, interrogatories, and expenses for expert witnesses and other matters. Most attorneys who require retainers in advance for criminal cases in all probability still keep an annotated record of the time they spend on the case.

▶ **Deposition** Oral testimony taken from the opposing party or a witness for the opposing party. Depositions are taken out of court but under oath. They are recorded verbatim, usually by a court reporter. Attorneys for both sides are present. Depositions may be used when the deposed is not able to appear in court. They may also be used to impeach the testimony of a witness in court.

▶ **Interrogatories** A set of questions given to a party thought to have pertinent information that may be used at a trial or other legal proceeding. The party completing the interrogatories must sign an oath that the statements are correct.

▶ **Venue** The location of a trial. A *change of venue* is the removal of a trial from the location where it normally would be held to another location, either to avoid public pressure or to obtain an impartial jury.

> **Subpoena** A command, issued by a court, ordering a person to appear in court (or at another designated place) at a specified time and place for the purpose of giving testimony on a specified issue. Persons may be ordered to bring documents pertinent to the case. That order is called a subpoena *duces tecum*.

Lists of witnesses who will be called for trial must be prepared, and the proper papers for notifying those witnesses must be filed. If the witnesses do not want to appear, the attorney may request a court order to subpoena them. A **subpoena** is an order to appear in court at a particular time and place and to give testimony on a specified subject or issue. As a precautionary measure, subpoenas might be issued to all potential witnesses to make it more difficult for them to change their minds and refuse to appear in court or at a deposition to testify. Witnesses may also be ordered to produce documents or papers that are important to the trial.

Pretrial conferences are very important to attorneys as they assess and prepare their cases. For example, the prosecutor may decide that the defense position is strong enough that a guilty verdict is unlikely. The attorneys may offer and accept (or reject) plea bargains for a plea to the charge(s) or to lesser charges. Many issues may be discussed during these pretrial conferences.

7-4b   Release or Detention: Bail or Jail?

Once a person has been charged with a crime and arrested, the decision whether to release or detain that individual pending trial is an important one. According to the U.S. Supreme Court, for the defendant, it is a time "when consultation, thoroughgoing investigation and preparation…[are] vitally important."[54] During this period, the defendant retains an attorney or is assigned counsel. The defense counsel and the prosecutor negotiate and consider plea bargaining. Witnesses are interviewed, and other attempts are made by both sides to secure evidence for the trial. Uncovering additional evidence may change the nature of the case and may even result in dropping or reducing charges before trial.

The Bail Decision

For society, the issue of whether the defendant is released or detained before trial is critical. Public outcries, accusing courts of coddling criminals, are common when persons charged with serious crimes are released. When those releasees commit additional crimes, the responses are even more critical.

> **Bail** Money or property posted to guarantee that the defendant will appear for a legal proceeding, such as a trial, sentencing, or imprisonment. If the defendant does not appear, the court may require that the money or property be forfeited.

The procedures by which the **bail** decision is made vary among jurisdictions, but a hearing is required, and the defendant is entitled to the benefit of counsel at that hearing. In the federal system, the hearing must take place within 24 hours of arrest. In some jurisdictions, there are statutes specifying what types of offenses are bailable. In others, there are specifications concerning what the magistrate may consider in making the decision. In many cases, however, the magistrate has wide discretion in the bail decision, and there is virtually no check on this discretion.

The magistrate also has wide latitude in setting the amount of bail. In the federal system, the factors most closely related to the level of bail, in order of importance, are the seriousness of the current charge, the district in which the bail hearing occurs, and the offender's criminal record.[55]

A defendant who is detained may petition the court to reduce the amount of bail or to grant bail if it has been previously denied. Some judges grant these motions, particularly when the defense has had more time to gather evidence that favors the defendant's pretrial release.

The Eighth Amendment to the U.S. Constitution prohibits requiring excessive bail (see Appendix A). This provision has been interpreted to mean that, when bail is set, its amount may not be excessive, but there has been no clear definition of what that means. In 1951 in *Stack v. Boyle*, the U.S. Supreme Court considered this issue and stated that bail set at a "figure higher than an amount reasonably calculated to fulfill this purpose [assuring the presence of the defendant at trial] is 'excessive' under the Eighth Amendment."[56] But many factors can be involved in calculating whether a particular defendant might flee if released. For example, in the case of Mary Winkler, who was accused of shooting and killing her husband in Tennessee in 2006, bail was set at

$750,000, which, her attorneys argued, was the same as no bail for a defendant who could not afford that amount. Winkler spent five months in jail before making bail. In May 2007, she was convicted of voluntary manslaughter and thus avoided a life sentence. Her sentence was pending as this text went to press.

Until recently, the only legitimate purpose of bail was to secure the presence of the accused at trial. In 1970, with the passage of the District of Columbia Court Reform and Criminal Procedure Act, **preventive detention** was recognized as a legitimate purpose of bail. The statute was upheld in 1981.[57] It permits judges to deny bail to defendants charged with dangerous crimes if the government has clear evidence that the safety of others would be endangered if the accused were released. In addition, bail can be denied in cases involving persons who had been convicted of violent crimes while on probation or parole. Other jurisdictions followed the District of Columbia in passing statutes or changing their constitutions to permit the denial of bail for preventive detention. And in 1984 in *Schall v. Martin*, the U.S. Supreme Court upheld the preventive detention of juveniles.[58]

The most controversial changes in bail, however, occurred in the Bail Reform Act of 1984, a federal statute that permits judges to deny bail if they have sufficient reason to think a defendant poses a dangerous threat to the community. The defendant is entitled to a prompt hearing on that issue, but if the hearing is not prompt, the government is not required to release a defendant who otherwise meets the criteria for detention. If there is sufficient evidence to charge the defendant with drug or certain other serious offenses, there is a presumption of dangerousness. This means that bail may be denied unless the defendant can prove to the court that he or she is not dangerous. This burden is a difficult one to sustain.[59]

In 1987, the U.S. Supreme Court decided a case challenging the Bail Reform Act's provision for the preventive detention of dangerous persons. *United States v. Salerno* involved the detention of defendants charged with numerous acts associated with organized crime. At the **pretrial detention** hearing, the government presented evidence that both defendants were in high positions of power in organized crime families. The government contended that the only way to protect the community was to detain these persons pending trial.[60]

Most recently, the preventive detention of suspects was questioned in relation to the detainees suspected of ties to terrorist acts. In November 2003, the U.S. Supreme Court agreed to hear a case involving the issue of whether foreigners suspected of terrorism may be held indefinitely at the U.S. naval base at Guantanamo Bay, Cuba. After the 9/11 terrorist attacks, the Bush administration took the position that, in the country's efforts to combat terrorist acts, it was permissible under the USA Patriot Act (see Chapter 3) to detain indefinitely those labeled by the administration as *enemy combatants*. Over 650 persons were held indefinitely at Guantanamo Bay under rather secret circumstances. The Bush administration argued that military tribunals, rather than U.S. courts, must hear the claims of these foreign nationals, who were captured by U.S. troops fighting in Afghanistan to disarm al-Qaeda, the terrorist group held responsible for the 9/11 terrorist attacks. The detainees argued that their cases should be heard by U.S. courts because the United States controls the military base on which they were held, even though the base is located in Cuba.

In 2004, in *Rasul v. Bush*, the U.S. Supreme Court ruled that all persons in U.S. custody, even foreign nationals, have a right to know why they are being detained, a right to consult with an attorney, and a right to a hearing before a neutral judge. According to the Supreme Court, this also applies to the foreigners captured during the war on terror and held at the U.S. military base in Guantanamo Bay, Cuba.[61] Thus, the detainees may have hearings to challenge their respective detentions, and many are in the process of doing so. The following are the brief facts about two of the so-called enemy combatants, a designation that has no specified termination point.

Yaser Esam Hamdi, who was born in Louisiana but moved to Saudi Arabia as a child, was a suspected terrorist whose Taliban unit surrendered in Afghanistan in

▶ **Preventive detention** *See* **Pretrial detention**.

▶ **Pretrial detention** The detention of a defendant in jail between arrest and trial, either because the judge has refused bail or the defendant cannot meet the requirements of bail. Generally, the purpose is to assure the presence of the accused at trial. Also, *preventive detention* involves defendants who are detained because they are thought to present a danger to themselves, to others, or to both if released pending trial.

November 2001. Hamdi was held, often in isolation, for over two years without charges being filed against him. In June 2004, in *Hamdi v. Rumsfeld*, eight justices of the U.S. Supreme Court ruled that Hamdi was entitled to an attorney and his day in court, stating that "a state of war is not a blank check for the president." The Supreme Court justices did not, however, agree on what should be done with Hamdi, who was being held at a military brig in South Carolina. The Court remanded the case to the lower court for resolution.[62] Subsequently, Hamdi was released to return to Saudi Arabia without U.S. officials ever charging him with a crime. As part of the agreement for his release, Hamdi was required to give up his U.S. citizenship and not sue the U.S. government for his detention.

Jose Padilla, an American citizen who was born in New York and grew up in Chicago, was suspected of plans to detonate a so-called dirty bomb to attack the United States. These bombs are conventional explosives designed to spread radioactive material. Padilla was seized at Chicago's O'Hare Airport and was detained for almost two years without being charged with a crime. During that time, he was not permitted to see a judge, an attorney, or even his own family. After the decision in *Hamdi*, it was logical that Padilla would win his case, since he was arrested on American soil. In February 2005, U.S. District Judge Henry F. Floyd, in Spartanburg, South Carolina, ruled that within 45 days, Padilla must be either charged with a crime, released from detention, or the judge's order appealed. He was released, but in September 2005, the Fourth Circuit Court of Appeals reversed the decision, holding that it was necessary for national security reasons to hold Padilla. Subsequently, a divided U.S. Supreme Court refused to review the case.[63]

In January 2006, the Bush administration's request to remove Padilla from military custody in South Carolina to civilian custody in Florida was granted, and Padilla was removed to a Miami, Florida, jail and held without bail pending his trial.[64] Florida had indicted Padilla, who once lived in that state, for charges unrelated to his enemy combatant status. He was accused of being part of a terror cell in North America and of conspiring with two other persons to murder, kidnap, and maim persons overseas. In June 2006, a federal judge called the case "light on facts" and ordered government attorneys to produce evidence of alleged facts. In late February 2007, Padilla was declared competent to stand trial, which began in April 2007.[65]

In June 2006, the U.S. Supreme Court dealt President Bush a severe blow by holding in a 5-to-3 vote that the president had overstepped his authority when he created special military tribunals to try the detainees at Guantanamo Bay. The Court agreed with the president that the detainee, Salim Ahmed Hamdan, who admitted to being Osama bin Laden's driver, was dangerous and that the United States had the authority to detain him at Guantanamo Bay as an enemy combatant. However, regarding Hamden's trial, the Court stated that the executive branch is "bound to comply with the rule of law that prevails in this jurisdiction." In short, said the justices, the president did not have the authority without congressional authorization to establish the tribunals. The American Bar Association president called the decision "a significant victory for the rule of law and our cherished constitutional protections," while President Bush proclaimed that he would work with Congress to remedy the situation.[66]

The Bail System

The bail system developed for practical reasons. It began in England, probably before A.D. 1000. Before urbanization and the development of modern courts, judges traveled from one jurisdiction to another to hold court sessions. They could not get to any one place often; consequently, it was necessary to devise a way of detaining the accused before the judges arrived. The bail system developed because the detention facilities were recognized as horrible places of confinement and were expensive.

An opportunity to make money in the bail system resulted in the development of the bail **bond** system. In return for a fee, the bail bondsperson posts bond for the defendant. If the defendant does not appear at trial, the bond money must theoretically

▶ **Bond** A written document indicating that the defendant or his or her sureties assure the presence of that defendant at a criminal proceeding and that, if the defendant is not present, the court may require that the security posted for the bond be forfeited.

Spotlight 7-6   Methods of Pretrial Release

Both financial bonds and alternative release options are used today.

Financial Bond

Fully secured bail The defendant posts the full amount of bail with the court.

Privately secured bail A bondsperson signs a promissory note to the court for the bail amount and charges the defendant a fee for the service (usually 10 percent of the bail amount). If the defendant fails to appear, the bondsperson must pay the court the full amount. Frequently, the bondsperson requires the defendant to post collateral in addition to the fee.

Deposit bail The courts allow the defendant to deposit a percentage (usually 10 percent) of the full bail with the court. The full amount of the bail is required if the defendant fails to appear. The percentage bail is returned after disposition of the case, but the court often retains 1 percent for administrative costs.

Unsecured bail The defendant pays no money to the court but is liable for the full amount of bail should he or she fail to appear.

Alternative Release Options

Release on recognizance (ROR) The court releases the defendant on the promise that he or she will appear in court as required.

Conditional release The court releases the defendant subject to his or her following specific conditions set by the court, such as attendance at drug treatment therapy or staying away from the complaining witness.

Third-party custody The defendant is released into the custody of an individual or agency that promises to assure his or her appearance in court. No monetary transactions are involved in this type of release.

Citation release Arrestees are released pending their first court appearance on a written order issued by law enforcement personnel.

Source: Bureau of Justice Statistics, *Report to the Nation on Crime and Justice: The Data,* 2d ed. (Washington, D.C.: U.S. Department of Justice, 1988), p. 76.

be forfeited to the court. In reality, the forfeiture provision is rarely enforced; however, since some bondspersons post bond without having the money available, some jurisdictions require them to prove that they can pay the forfeiture, should that be necessary. Abuses of the bail bond system led to alternative methods for pretrial release, as defined in Spotlight 7-6.

7-4c   The Guilty Plea

The guilty plea is very important in U.S. criminal justice systems because approximately 90 percent of defendants plead guilty. Although many guilty pleas are entered after plea bargaining begins, defendants may choose to plead guilty without any negotiation between the prosecution and the defense. Various reasons account for this decision. Some defendants are guilty and see no reason to go to trial, thinking that they have no chance of an acquittal or a conviction on a lesser offense. They may not want to engage in any kind of plea bargaining because, as in a trial, that might take more time than they are willing to devote to the process. Some defendants want a quick decision. This may be true particularly if they have been denied bail and must wait in jail until a plea bargain is reached or the trial occurs. Still other defendants may not want to experience the public exposure of the evidence the prosecution will present at trial.

In cases involving minor offenses, most defendants are placed on probation. That means they do not have to serve time in jail or prison. They might prefer to plead guilty and get on with their lives. Pleading guilty may save the family money in the case of defendants who do not qualify for publicly supported counsel. Getting back to work enables defendants to continue supporting their families and to reduce the stress placed on everyone by an indecisive situation.

Defendants who plead guilty may be familiar with the court process and the reputation of the prosecutor in that jurisdiction. If the prosecutor has a reputation for recommending stricter sentences for defendants who insist on trials, compared with those who plead guilty, the defendant may be willing to enter a guilty plea. If juries in that jurisdiction have a reputation for being tough on defendants, that information might lead the defendant to plead guilty.

The defense attorney may encourage the defendant to plead guilty. In many cases, this is the best advice that an attorney can give a defendant and should not be viewed as a dereliction of the defense attorney's duty to the client. If defendants have little chance of an acquittal, they are entitled to know that. In addition, most attorneys will explain what may be expected financially and otherwise if the case goes to trial. In other cases, it may be bad advice to counsel defendants to enter a guilty plea. In all cases, however, the final decision about whether or not to plead guilty should be made by the defendant.

In deciding whether to plead guilty, the defendant may consider carefully the implications of studies showing that defendants who plead guilty are less likely to be sentenced to prison than defendants who go to trial and are convicted. Many who plead guilty receive shorter sentences than those who go to trial. The difference, however, may be related to the nature of the offense or to other factors that are not in themselves related to whether guilt is determined by a guilty plea or by a trial.

Jurisdictions vary in the processes by which defendants plead guilty, but generally, the plea is entered in open court and recorded on a form signed by defendants and defense counsel. By signing this form, defendants swear that they are of sound mind, that they are not under the influence of alcohol or other drugs, that they understand fully that they are waiving the rights associated with a trial, and that nothing has been promised in return for their signatures on this form. The form contains the sentence recommended by the prosecutor. The judge is not required to follow that recommendation but usually does.

After the form is completed, the defendant, the defense attorney, and the prosecutor appear before the magistrate or judge for formal entering of the plea. At that time, the judge questions the defendant. Before the plea is accepted, the judge must be convinced that the plea is a knowing and intelligent one and was made voluntarily. The U.S. Supreme Court has made it clear that, because a defendant who pleads guilty gives up several constitutional rights, including the right to a trial by an impartial jury, a guilty plea requires "an intentional relinquishment or abandonment of a known right or privilege" and must be declared void if it is not a knowing and intelligent plea.[67]

If the judge decides that the plea is a knowing and intelligent one, he or she may accept that plea, in which case, a formal record is made with the court. Generally, the form specifies how long the defendant has for an appeal on a sentence imposed by the court. Defendants who change their minds and wish to withdraw their guilty pleas may petition the court to do so. If that request is made prior to sentencing, the judge may grant it; usually, motions to withdraw a guilty plea after sentencing are not granted. There is no absolute right to withdraw a guilty plea at any time.

7-4d   Plea Bargaining

> **Plea bargaining**   The process of negotiation between the defense and the prosecution before or during the trial of a defendant. The process may involve reducing or dropping some charges or a recommendation for leniency in exchange for a plea of guilty on another charge(s). Plea bargaining may also result in no changes in the charges or sentence recommendation.

One of the most controversial practices in U.S. criminal justice systems is **plea bargaining**, the process in which the prosecution and the defense attempt to negotiate a plea. The negotiation may involve reducing charges, dropping charges, or recommending a sentence. Plea bargaining became a part of U.S. criminal justice systems after the Civil War but was not practiced widely until the 1990s. Little attention was paid to the process until crime commissions began their studies in the 1920s.

It was not until the 1970s that the U.S. Supreme Court recognized plea bargaining as appropriate and even essential to criminal justice systems. In 1971, the Court approved plea bargaining as a means of managing overloaded criminal dockets, referring to the process as "an essential component" of the criminal process, which "properly administered … is to be encouraged."[68] The plea bargaining process may not involve threatened physical harm or mental coercion that might result in an involuntary plea by the defendant.

On 19 January 2001, the day before he was leaving office, President Bill Clinton and the special prosecutor's office entered into a plea arrangement by which Clinton agreed to some admissions regarding his behavior with a White House intern, and the special prosecutor agreed not to charge him with any crimes. Clinton also agreed to surrender his law license for five years. Many felt this arrangement was best for the country. It avoided the possibility of a long, expensive, and emotional trial. It permitted the new president, George W. Bush, to begin his administration without the cloud of Clinton's problems, and it allowed Clinton to move forward with his life.

Defendants may reject plea bargains to their detriment. Perhaps the best-known recent example is that of Lionel Tate, who at age 14 was sentenced to life without parole after he was convicted in a Florida adult criminal court for murder (during aggravated child abuse) in the 1999 death of Tiffany Eunick, when Tate was 12 and she was 6. Prior to the trial, the prosecutor offered Tate a plea bargain consisting of 3 years in a juvenile correctional facility, followed by a year of house arrest and probation for 10 years. Tate rejected the plea bargain offer and went to trial. The jury did not believe Tate's testimony that he accidentally killed Eunick while he was imitating pro wrestlers, and Tate was convicted. Under Florida law, a conviction for first-degree murder carries an automatic sentence of life without parole. Florida Governor Jeb Bush considered but rejected Tate's first request for clemency, stating, "We must never forget that the life of a six-year-old girl has been lost." The governor also stated at that time, "I am not sure it is right to consign such a young child to a life without any hope, even when that child is guilty of a truly horrendous crime."[69]

In December 2003, a three-judge panel of Florida's Fourth District Court of Appeals reversed Tate's conviction and life sentence and ordered a new trial. Of the issues on appeal, the appellate court ruled that one required reversal, holding that the defense request to have Tate's mental competency evaluated posttrial should have been granted. The appellate court did state that the "evidence was clear that the victim was brutally slain" and that it would have taken "tremendous force to inflict" the injuries Eunick sustained.[70] It was not stated why the defense had not requested a competency hearing earlier in the process. Tate was to remain incarcerated for at least 15 days, during which time the state could request a hearing of the appeal. If the state did not do so, Tate's defense lawyers planned to file a motion that their client be released pending the results of his new trial.[71]

Rather than retry Tate, the prosecution offered him the same plea deal they had offered before his trial: 3 years in a juvenile institution followed by a year of house arrest and 10 years on probation. Tate accepted the plea bargain and was released in January 2004 to the custody of his mother, as he had already served the required time. Under the terms of the plea deal, Tate was also required to undergo psychiatric counseling and to perform 1,000 hours of community service. Tate was released from prison four days prior to his seventeenth birthday.[72]

In September 2004, Tate was accused of violating the terms of his probation by staying out late at night. For a month, he was placed in another home, but the family found the visitations by probation officers to be stressful and requested that Tate be moved. A judge permitted Tate to return to his mother's home.[73] In June 2005, Tate was again apprehended, accused of robbing a pizza deliveryman at gunpoint; he was jailed without bail. In 2006, Tate entered a guilty plea but was later, at his request, permitted to withdraw his plea to robbery but was refused withdrawal on the weapons charge, since not possessing a weapon was part of his original probationary terms. Tate was sentenced to 30 years in prison for the weapons violation.[74]

There is no legal right to a plea bargain. According to the U.S. Supreme Court, the states and Congress may abolish plea bargaining; however, where it does exist, it is not improper to offer leniency "and other substantial benefits" to defendants in exchange for a guilty plea.[75] In 1984, the U.S. Supreme Court upheld a prosecutor's withdrawal of an offer that had been accepted by a defendant. After he had accepted the prosecutor's offer, the defendant was told that the offer was a mistake and was being withdrawn. He appealed; the federal appellate court agreed with the defendant that the withdrawal was not permissible. However, the Supreme Court disagreed, reversed the lower federal court, and stated that an agreement to a plea bargain is an "executory agreement that does not involve the constitutional rights of the accused until it is embodied in the formal pleas." In upholding the prosecutor's withdrawal of the plea, the Court said, "The Due Process Clause is not a code of ethics for prosecutors" but, rather, is concerned "with the manner in which persons are deprived of their liberty."[76]

The reasons for allowing plea bargaining, as well as some of the prosecutorial activities permissible in the process, were articulated by the U.S. Supreme Court in *Bordenkircher v. Hayes*, decided in 1978. This case involved a defendant who was indicted by a grand jury on the charge of uttering a forged instrument (passing a hot check), an offense carrying a prison term of 2 to 10 years. After the defendant's arraignment on the charge, the prosecutor offered to recommend a five-year sentence if the defendant pleaded guilty to the indictment. If the defendant did not plead guilty, the prosecutor said that he would return to the grand jury and ask for an indictment under the Kentucky Habitual Criminal Act (since repealed). Conviction under that act would have resulted in a life term in prison because the defendant had two prior felony convictions.

Defendant Hayes did not plead guilty. The prosecutor secured the indictment under the Habitual Criminal Act. The jury found Hayes guilty of uttering a forged instrument and in a separate proceeding found that he had two prior felony convictions. As required by statute, upon conviction under that act, Hayes was sentenced to life in prison. The U.S. Supreme Court noted the need for plea bargaining; acknowledged that it is not a right; and held that, although one may not be punished for exercising constitutional rights, the give-and-take of plea bargaining leaves the defendant free to accept or reject an offer. "To hold that the prosecutor's desire to induce a guilty plea is an 'unjustifiable standard,' which, like race or religion, may play no part in his charging decision, would contradict the very premises that underlie the concept of plea bargaining itself."[77] Four justices dissented in *Bordenkircher*, arguing that the facts of the case constituted prosecutorial vindictiveness, which the U.S. Supreme Court had held was impermissible.

In 1995, the U.S. Supreme Court decided a plea bargaining case that might reduce the use of this practice. Although the Court was interpreting a federal statute, the principle of the case may be used in other situations. *United States v. Mezzanatto* involved a statute specifying that incriminating statements made by defendants in the course of a plea bargain may not be used against them at trial. The defendant in this case agreed to the prosecutor's demand during plea bargaining that, if the informal process was not effective and the case went to trial, he would not invoke that provision. Thus, the issue was whether the defendant should be permitted to waive the statutory provision. The U.S. Supreme Court held that the exclusionary provision of the federal rule could be and was waived by the defendant. Lower federal courts had split in their decisions on the issue.[78] It is possible that some defendants will be less candid in plea bargaining sessions as a result of this decision.

Plea bargaining may occur during any stage of the criminal process, but most defense attorneys begin negotiations as soon as possible. The longer a defendant has been in the system, the less likely prosecutors are to plea bargain because of the time and effort already spent on the case. Prosecutors may want to initiate plea bargaining early to dispose of a heavy caseload. On the other hand, they might stall on the process, thinking that defendants will be more cooperative the longer they have to wait, especially if they are being detained in jail.

Plea bargaining may be initiated by either the prosecution or the defense. Prosecutors may refuse to discuss any kind of bargain and insist on a trial. Likewise, defendants may refuse to bargain and insist on a trial, but defendants who enter a guilty plea cannot withdraw it merely because they chose the wrong strategy.

Normally, plea bargaining begins early in the pretrial procedures and is completed before the date set for trial. A high-profile murder case illustrates the use of plea bargaining very early in the criminal justice process. In November 2003, the prosecution in King County (Seattle), Washington, offered a plea deal to Gary L. Ridgway, who was accused in the murders of 48 young women in the Green River area of Seattle. Many of the victims were prostitutes or runaways who had been sexually assaulted and strangled. This case, which baffled police for 20 years, is unusual in that plea bargains normally are not offered in cases involving multiple murders, but the prosecution's position was that the plea deal was the only way to bring closure to all of the cases. Ridgway, showing no emotion, entered a guilty plea to all 48 cases, making him the deadliest serial killer in U.S. history. A statement made previously by Ridgway was read in court: "I killed the 48 women....In most cases, when I murdered these women, I did not know their names. Most of the time, I killed them the first time I met them, and I did not have a good memory for their faces. I killed so many women, I have a hard time keeping them straight." When asked in court whether that statement was true, the defendant said, "Yes, it is." The statement continued as follows:

> I placed most of the bodies in groups which I called clusters. I did this because I wanted to keep track of all the women I killed. I liked to drive by the clusters around the county and think about the women I placed there.[79]

Ridgway had been charged with only seven of the Green River killings and was scheduled to go on trial in 2004; the prosecution was asking for the death penalty. By entering guilty pleas, Ridgway spared his own life. He was sentenced to one prison life term for each murder.

In April 2005, another controversial plea bargain was announced. Eric Rudolph pleaded guilty to multiple terrorist acts in the 1990s. Rudolph's bombings at Atlanta's Olympic games in 1996, at an Atlanta office building (an abortion clinic inside that building was thought to be the target), at an Atlanta bar frequented by gays and lesbians in 1997, and at an abortion clinic in Birmingham, Alabama, in 1998 resulted in the deaths of two persons, including a police officer, and injuries to over 100 others. Rudolph was a fugitive and listed on the FBI's 10 Most Wanted, but he eluded law enforcement officials until his capture in 2003 near Murphy, North Carolina, while he was scavenging for food. Rudolph was to be tried first in Alabama, where prosecutors were seeking the death penalty. After jury selection began, the prosecution announced that they had struck a plea bargain with Rudolph. He would plead guilty to all of the bombings in return for a life sentence. In an 11-page statement released by his attorneys, Rudolph made no apologies, but lashed out at what he called a morally corrupt government that permits abortions and makes accommodations for gays and lesbians. Some victims were angry that Rudolph did not get the death penalty; others were relieved that there would not be a trial and that they had some explanation for his terrorist acts.

It is possible for the parties to negotiate a final plea after the trial has begun. In the case of Ted Kaczynski (the Unabomber discussed earlier in this chapter), a few weeks before the scheduled date of the trial, the defense offered to plead guilty in exchange for a sentence of life without parole. The U.S. Department of Justice, however, recommended that the plea be rejected, and it was. This decision was questioned by some who pointed out the irony that, after the defendant's alleged attempt at suicide, "having insisted on the death penalty, the government is now engaged in the bizarre exercise of trying to prevent Mr. Kaczynski from killing himself so that it can continue to spend enormous amounts of money and court time trying to execute him." The *New York Times* editorialist concluded that pressing a capital trial in this case "will only prolong this costly legal farce." The amount of evidence suggesting that the defendant was mentally ill probably would have been sufficient to trigger a successful appeal if he had been convicted.[80] A plea was accepted in this case, and the defendant was sentenced to life without parole. Kaczynski, who was representing himself at the time of the plea, subsequently claimed that the plea was involuntary. He appealed his conviction, but it was upheld by the federal appellate court, and the U.S. Supreme Court refused to hear the case, thus permitting the conviction to stand.[81]

Once a plea bargain is reached, the defense and prosecution submit formal papers to the judge, who must accept or reject the agreement. The judge is not required to abide by any promise made by the prosecution. Thus, after plea negotiations, it is possible for the defendant to enter a guilty plea with the understanding that a particular sentence will be imposed and subsequently be faced with a different, even harsher sentence.

Generally, judges may not participate in plea negotiations in federal cases, although some state and local jurisdictions permit this practice. When judges participate in plea bargaining, they may suggest directly or indirectly the sentence that might be imposed in the case, encourage defense attorneys and prosecutors to reach a settlement, nudge defendants to accept the plea negotiation decision, or intervene actively in the negotiations.

Some jurisdictions permit victims to be a part of the plea negotiations if they choose to do so. Some victims do not want to participate; others may be too vindictive or too lenient. At a minimum, however, victims should be kept informed of the proceedings at all stages in the pretrial procedures. Whether they should participate actively in plea negotiations is controversial. Some argue that it would give defendants a chance to begin the rehabilitation process by being confronted by the victim, and it would give victims an opportunity to see the defendant as a whole person. Others take the position that the participation of victims would be disruptive to the system and would have a negative impact on victims.

One final issue regarding plea bargaining is important. Recall that earlier in this chapter we discussed the directive issued by U.S. Attorney General John Ashcroft concerning prosecutorial discretion. Ashcroft called for charging suspects with the most serious crimes in most cases. At the same time, the attorney general all but called for the elimination of plea bargaining. This directive was certain to increase the number of federal trials at a time when federal court dockets were already overcrowded. One sentencing expert stated, "If even just a small fraction of the 96 percent of all defendants who currently plead guilty end up going to trial, the courts will be overrun in no time." The federal directive came at a time when, primarily because of budget cuts, many states were looking for ways to reduce the number of trials and the amount of time offenders serve in prison. The result could be significantly longer prison terms for federal offenders than for state offenders convicted of the same or similar crimes.[82] But, as noted earlier in this chapter, there are several exceptions to the directive, thus weakening it considerably, and John Ashcroft is no longer the U.S. attorney general.

Chapter Wrap-Up

This chapter discussed the attorneys who prosecute and defend in criminal cases, and then provided an overview of the pretrial procedures in which they engage. This chapter began with a historical overview of the legal profession before turning to the prosecution of a criminal case. In its analysis of the prosecution, the chapter looked briefly at the historical emergence of public prosecution, contrasting that approach with the method of private prosecution that was its predecessor in the United States and that still exists in some other countries.

U.S. public prosecution systems are varied. Although most prosecutors are elected officials, their functions and the structures of their offices differ, depending on the size of the jurisdiction and the complexities of local needs. State systems of prosecution, like those at the federal level, may be quite large. They differ from local systems in some respects. State and federal prosecutors may issue opinions on the constitutionality of their respective state and federal statutes. In addition, they are charged with the prosecution of state and federal crimes, and like local prosecutors, they

must make important decisions on which cases to prosecute and which charges to bring in each case.

This authority to determine whom to prosecute and which charges to bring when there are several options gives prosecutors tremendous power. Generally, a decision not to prosecute ends the case. Once the initial decision to prosecute has been made, prosecutors may drop charges. Charges may be dropped for a lack of evidence or for political or personal reasons. This power is virtually unchecked. Even when the prosecutorial decision to drop charges occurs after the defendant has made a court appearance and the judge must approve the prosecutor's decision, the prosecutor has immense power in the final determination. Frequently, judges defer to prosecutors, who may insist that they are overworked, that their resources are limited, and that there is not enough evidence to continue the prosecution.

Such extensive power may lead to abuse. Prosecutors may abuse their discretion in many ways. They may charge defendants with crimes for which they have little or no evidence in order to coerce the defendants to plead guilty to crimes for which they have sufficient evidence. This avoids trials and reduces prosecutors' caseloads while providing them with "victories."

The next focus of the chapter was on the defense of a criminal case. The discussion began with an overview of the defense attorney's role, followed by a discussion of the right to counsel. The evolution and current status of the right to appointed counsel for indigent defendants was explored, culminating with the critical *Gideon* decision in 1963, in which the U.S. Supreme Court held that the right to appointed counsel for indigents is not limited to capital cases but applies to other felonies as well. In 1972, the right to appointed counsel for indigents was extended. In *Argersinger v. Hamlin*, the Supreme Court held that no one may be sentenced to incarceration, even for a short time or for a petty offense, without having had benefit of counsel at trial.

The right to appointed counsel does not exist at all pretrial and posttrial stages, although it does exist at critical stages. The right to counsel also involves a right to refuse counsel. Defendants may serve as their own attorneys, provided their waivers of counsel have been made knowingly and intelligently. They may retain private counsel if they prefer and can afford to do so.

The right to counsel implies a right to effective counsel, which the U.S. Supreme Court defined in *Strickland v. Washington* as involving a two-pronged test. The defendant must show that counsel was deficient and that the deficiency resulted in prejudice to the defendant, who as a result did not get a fair trial. This standard is very difficult to prove, but the courts must consider the totality of the circumstances in making their decisions concerning whether a defendant had effective assistance of counsel. The chapter updated the issue of effective assistance of counsel by looking at cases decided since *Strickland*.

The discussion of defense closed with an explanation of the three major models by which appointed counsel are provided: public defender programs, the assigned counsel programs, and contract systems, noting how they differ from each other and from the use of privately retained defense counsel.

The interaction of the defense attorney and the prosecutor is important during criminal proceedings. The pretrial procedures that are the focus of their interaction were the subject of the chapter's final section. These procedures include some of the most critical issues and most difficult procedures in criminal justice systems. All of the pretrial court hearings are crucial, for at any stage, failure to find probable cause must result in the defendant's release. If any rights of the accused are violated during arrest, interrogation, investigation, or search and seizure, the evidence secured as a result of those violations may be excluded from the trial. Without the illegally seized evidence, many cases must be dismissed for lack of probable cause. The initial appearance, the preliminary hearing, the grand jury review, and the arraignment are concerned with the issue of determining whether there is sufficient evidence to continue the case.

The roles of the prosecution and the defense in these stages are critical. Prosecutorial discretion to drop the charges after the police have arrested a suspect may negate police crime control efforts. However, that discretionary power may serve as a check on overzealous police officers. Even after formal charges are filed with the court, either through a prosecutorial information or a grand jury indictment, the prosecutor has considerable influence in getting those charges dismissed. This dismissal may be done for good reasons, such as lack of evidence, or for bad reasons, such as

discrimination or political pressure. Prosecutors have great power at the stage of grand jury review because grand juries usually return a true bill on indictments submitted by the prosecution.

The role of defense attorneys is to protect defendants' rights at all pretrial stages and to plan the defense strategy should the case go to trial. The role of judges is important as well. They preside over all formal court hearings and have the power to grant or deny motions, to grant or deny bail in most cases, and to accept or reject guilty pleas. To a great extent, judges control the timing of all the stages, as they set dates for the court hearings and for the trial. If a guilty plea has been accepted, judges usually have the power to impose sentencing at that time.

Two critical procedures discussed in this chapter raise controversial issues in our criminal justice systems: the decision whether to release or to detain defendants pending trial and the practice of plea bargaining. The decision whether to release a defendant on bail or to allow another alternative requires the judge to predict whether that person would appear for trial if released prior to trial. With recent legislation in some jurisdictions permitting pretrial detention for preventive purposes, some judges have the power to detain if they think the defendant is a danger to society. These are not easy decisions in a world in which predicting human behavior is inaccurate, yet the decision to detain imposes great burdens on defendants, who are inconvenienced and may lose their jobs, endure the indignities and embarrassments of a jail term, and in some cases, suffer physical attacks by other inmates. For those who are acquitted of the crimes for which they are charged, pretrial detention is an incredible injustice. For society, pretrial release may mean more crime; however, pretrial detention creates the need for more facilities, thus increasing the cost of criminal justice systems.

Plea bargaining is another procedure that raises many issues. The practice is necessary as long as we have high crime rates and insufficient facilities and personnel to try all cases. The practice allows the flexibility necessary if the system is to respond with any degree of concern for the circumstances of individual cases. But that flexibility may lead to abuse of discretion, resulting in bitter defendants, some of whom have reasonable justification for believing that the system has treated them unfairly. Plea bargaining may entice defendants to plead guilty to crimes they did not commit rather than risk their constitutional right to trial. Such a choice might, and usually does, result in conviction.

Like previous chapters, Chapter 7 discussed issues relating to the 9/11 terrorist attacks. Such issues include prosecutorial discretion and plea bargaining, as well as the detention of foreign nationals for unlimited periods of time at the U.S. naval base in Guantanamo Bay, Cuba, without formal charges or access to attorneys. In 2004, the U.S. Supreme Court held that this policy violates the constitutional rights of those detainees. In June 2006, the U.S. Supreme Court held that President Bush exceeded his constitutional authority by ordering that the enemy combatants be tried by military tribunals.

Many of the subjects discussed in this chapter are important to Chapter 8 as well. Attorneys and judges are the major professionals in the trial, as well as during pretrial procedures. Plea bargaining may continue. Many of the motions made at pretrial may be made during the trial. The issue of whether a detained defendant should be released from jail may be reconsidered; likewise, the decision to release a defendant pending trial may be revoked when changes in the circumstances warrant that decision. Both prosecution and defense may continue the investigation to secure more evidence to present at trial, particularly during a long trial. The stages in criminal justice systems are not separable. Some procedures and issues, however, are peculiar to the criminal trial, the focus of Chapter 8, which also discusses the stages of sentence and appeal.

Key Terms

arraignment (p. 210)
assigned counsel (p. 206)
bail (p. 212)
bond (p. 214)
booking (p. 207)
community-oriented prosecution (p. 190)
contract system (p. 206)
defendant (p. 186)
defense attorney (p. 196)
depositions (p. 211)
discovery (p. 210)
grand jury (p. 193)

habeas corpus (p. 203)
indictment (p. 193)
information (p. 193)
initial appearance (p. 208)
interrogatories (p. 211)
lineup (p. 208)
motion (p. 210)
nolo contendere (p. 210)
plea bargaining (p. 216)
preliminary hearing (p. 209)
presentment (p. 210)
pretrial detention (p. 213)

preventive detention (p. 213)
pro se (p. 200)
prosecuting attorney (p. 190)
prosecution (p. 186)
public defender (p. 205)
right to counsel (p. 198)
showup (p. 208)
subpoena (p. 212)
true bill (p. 210)
venue (p. 211)
waiver (p. 200)

Apply It

1. Contrast the public's current views of U.S. lawyers with historical views.
2. Why did a system of public prosecution develop, and what is the difference between public and private prosecution? Which system do you think is better?
3. Compare local, state, and federal prosecution systems.
4. What is the main function of a prosecutor? Why is the prosecutor allowed so much discretion in fulfilling that role? What are the problems with allowing such discretion?
5. How can prosecutorial discretion be kept within reasonable limits? Evaluate one example of prosecutorial misconduct discussed in the chapter.
6. What is meant by the *right to counsel*? Describe briefly what that right means today, compared with its historical meaning in the United States.
7. What is the importance of the *Gideon* case?
8. What is the scope of the right to appointed counsel? Should it be expanded? Should it apply to the detention of those suspected of terrorist acts? If not, why not? If so, under what circumstances?
9. Do you think a defendant should have the right to refuse counsel? Explain your answer.
10. What does the U.S. Supreme Court mean by *effective assistance of counsel*? If you had the opportunity to define that term for the Court, what would you include?
11. Enumerate and explain the three major systems by which appointed counsel are provided.
12. How would you suggest improving the availability and quality of legal defense counsel?
13. Would you prefer to be a defense attorney or a prosecuting attorney? Why?
14. Define each of the major steps in the criminal justice process before trial.
15. What restrictions are placed on the securing of physical evidence from a suspect?
16. Describe the main purposes of the *initial appearance, preliminary hearing,* and *arraignment.*
17. What is a *grand jury indictment*? How does that process differ from a prosecutor's information?
18. Distinguish between *depositions* and *interrogatories*.
19. What should be considered in deciding whether to release a defendant prior to trial?
20. What is the *bail bond system*, and why is it controversial today?
21. Which of the alternatives to a bail bond system do you think is most feasible? Why?
22. What should be the goals and purposes of detention prior to trial? Should foreign nationals be treated differently from others? Should it make a difference where they are detained? How did the U.S. Supreme Court rule on this issue?
23. Describe the process of pleading guilty before trial. Does it make any difference whether the plea is a negotiated one?
24. Do you think plea bargaining should be abolished? Why? If it is, what might result?
25. Evaluate some of the recent high-profile cases involving plea bargaining.
26. What do you think about the directive by John Ashcroft that essentially eliminated plea bargaining in the federal system?

Endnotes

1. Quoted in "Those #*X!!! Lawyers," *Time* (10 April 1978), p. 66.
2. Alexis de Tocqueville, "The Temper of the Legal Profession in the United States," in *Before the Law: An Introduction to the Legal Process,* ed. John J. Bonsignore et al. (Boston: Houghton Mifflin, 1974), p. 151.
3. James Willard Hurst, *Growth of American Law* (Boston: Little, Brown, 1950), p. 6.

4. See Peter H. Rossi, "Occupational Prestige in the United States, 1925–1963," *American Journal of Sociology* 70 (November 1964): 286–302.

5. Bailey Morris, "Lawyers' Images of Yesteryear Are Crumbling Fast," *Washington Star* (13 September 1976), p. 1A.

6. Ibid.

7. "Burger Warns about a Society Overrun by Lawyers," *New York Times* (28 May 1977), p. 1.

8. Whitney North Seymour Jr., *Why Justice Fails* (New York: Morrow, 1973), p. 7.

9. "Tough Market? Just Ask Altheimer & Gray How Tough," *Chicago Daily Law Bulletin* (8 May 2003), p. 1; "Law Firms Collapse, Others Merge in Whirlwind 2003," *Chicago Lawyer* (December 2003), p. 12.

10. "The Attorney, Unemployed," *Broward Daily Business Review* 44, no. 101 (2 May 2003): 8.

11. "New Data on Large Firm Finances," *Law Office Management and Administration Report* (September 2005), p. 3.

12. See Abraham S. Goldstein, "Prosecution: History of the Public Prosecutor," in *Encyclopedia of Crime and Justice,* vol. 3, ed. Sanford H. Kadish (New York: Macmillan, 1983), pp. 1286–1289.

13. Joan E. Jacoby, *The American Prosecutor: A Search for Identity* (Lexington, Mass.: D.C. Heath, 1980), pp. 55–61, 64–65, 71–74, 275, 277, 278.

14. M. Elaine Nugent, *The Changing Nature of Prosecution: Community Prosecution vs. Traditional Prosecution Approaches,* p. 7, http://www.ndaa-apri.org, accessed 13 June 2006.

15. *ABA Standards for Criminal Justice: The Prosecution Function,* Standard 3-1.2, approved by the ABA House of Delegates, February 1992.

16. State v. Mitchell, 395 A.2d 1257 (Sup.Ct.App.Div. N.J. 1978).

17. "Man Guilty of Concealing Boys' Killing of Father," *New York Times* (6 March 2003), p. 20.

18. "Kings Sent to Juvenile Facilities," *Pensacola News Journal* (17 December 2002), p. 1.

19. "Prosecutorial Outrage in Florida," *New York Times* (21 October 2002), p. 22.

20. United States v. Armstrong, 517 U.S. 456 (1996).

21. Oyler v. Boles, 368 U.S. 448, 456 (1962).

22. "Ashcroft Imposes New Limits on Prosecutors' Charging Discretion," *Criminal Justice Newsletter* (1 October 2003), p. 7.

23. Albert W. Alschuler, "Disparity: The Normative and Empirical Failure of the Federal Guidelines," *Stanford Law Review* 58, no. 1 (1 October 2005): 85.

24. Yick Wo v. Hopkins, 118 U.S. 356 (1886). In the *Yick Wo* case, a public board that was authorized to issue laundry licenses denied licenses to Chinese applicants and granted licenses to most white applicants.

25. Brady v. Maryland, 373 U.S. 83 (1963).

26. "Tried and Tried Again: Defense Lawyers Say the D.A. Went Too Far Prosecuting a Louisiana Man Five Times for Murder," *American Bar Association Journal* 84 (April 1998): 38.

27. Steve Weinberg, "Breaking the Rules: Who Suffers When a Prosecutor Is Cited for Misconduct," Center for Public Integrity, http://www.publicintegrity.org, accessed 11 July 2006.

28. State v. Gaughran, 615 A.2d 1293 (N.J. Superior, 1992).

29. "A Zealous Prosecutor of Drug Criminals Becomes One Himself," *New York Times* (15 February 2005), p. 14; "I Inject, Your Honor," *Texas Monthly* (April 2005), n.p.; "Drug Plague upon the Panhandle; Former District Attorney Just Another Casualty in Region Where Methamphetamine Pervades," *Austin (Texas) American-Statesman* (6 March 2005), p. 1.

30. See, for example, "Prosecution in Diallo Case Now Finds Itself Accused," *New York Times* (28 February 2000), p. 19.

31. Powell v. Alabama, 287 U.S. 45 (1932). See also Wayne R. LaFave and Jerold H. Israel, *Criminal Procedure* (St. Paul, Minn.: West, 1985), pp. 473–475. This source was used for the historical background discussion of the right to counsel.

32. Johnson v. Zerbst, 304 U.S. 458 (1938).

33. Betts v. Brady, 316 U.S. 455 (1942), *overruled,* Gideon v. Wainwright, 372 U.S. 335 (1963).

34. Gideon v. Wainwright, 372 U.S. 335 (1963).

35. Argersinger v. Hamlin, 407 U.S. 25, 37 (1972).

36. Scott v. Illinois, 440 U.S. 367 (1979).

37. United States v. Wade, 388 U.S. 218 (1967).

38. Alabama v. Shelton, 535 U.S. 654 (2002).

39. United States v. Gonzalez-Lopez, 2006 U.S. LEXIS 5165 (U.S. 2006).

40. Diggs v. Welch, 148 F.2d 667 (D.C.Cir. 1945); *cert. denied,* 325 U.S. 889 (1945).

41. Strickland v. Washington, 466 U.S. 668 (1984).

42. Edward M. Kennedy, "Sen. Kennedy: Georgia Case Mocks *Gideon* Promise," *Fulton County Daily Report* 3, no. 25 (25 March 2003): n.p. The case is Wallace M. Fugate III v. Head, 261 F.3d 1206 (11th Cir. 2001), *cert. denied,* 535 U.S. 1104 (2002).

43. Kennedy, ibid.

44. Burdine v. Johnson, 66 F.Supp. 2d 854 (S.D. Tex. 1999), *stay denied, mot. granted, in part, denied, in part,* 87 F.Supp. 2d 711 (S.D. Tex. 2000), *vacated, remanded,* 231 F.3d 950 (5th Cir. 2000), *and on reh'g., aff'd.,* 262 F.3d 326 (5th Cir. 2001), *cert. denied,* 535 U.S. 1120 (2002).

45. "Burdine Pleads Guilty, Gets Three Consecutive Life Sentences," *Texas Lawyer* 19, no. 16 (23 June 2003): 8.

46. Mickens v. Taylor, 535 U.S. 162 (2002).

47. Lawson v. State, 766 P.2d 261 (Nev. 1988).

48. "Montana Aims to Fix Public Defender System," *Chicago Tribune,* final edition (21 June 2005), p. 11.

49. "2005 Year in Review," *Chicago Lawyer* (December 2005), p. 13.

50. Justice for All Act of 2004, Public Law 108-405 (2007).

51. "Legal Aid Funding Edged Up," *Chicago Daily Law Bulletin* (14 July 2006), p. 10001; "Legal Aid Agency Angles for Bigger Money Pot," *Chicago Daily Law Bulletin* (9 February 2007), p. 1.

52. "ABA Calls for Boost in Federal Legal Aid Funds," *Chicago Daily Law Bulletin* (10 July 2006), n.p.

53. Wood v. Georgia, 370 U.S. 375, 390 (1962).

54. Powell v. Alabama, 287 U.S. 45, 57 (1932).

55. See U.S. Code, Title 18, Section 3142(c)(1) (2007).

56. Stack v. Boyle, 342 U.S. 1 (1951).

57. United States v. Edwards, 430 A.2d 1321 (D.C.Ct.App. 1981), *cert. denied,* 455 U.S. 1022 (1982).

58. Schall v. Martin, 467 U.S. 253 (1984).

59. The Bail Reform Act can be found in U.S. Code, Chapter 18, Sections 3141 et.seq. (2007).

60. United States v. Salerno, 481 U.S. 739 (1987).

61. Rasul v. Bush, 542 U.S. 466 (2004), footnotes omitted.

62. Hamdi v. Rumsfeld, 316 F.3d 450 (4th Cir. 2003), *vacated, remanded,* 542 U.S. 507 (2004), *on remand, remanded,* 378 F.3d 426 (4th Cir. 2004).

63. Padilla v. Hanft, 389 F.Supp.2d 678 (D.S.C. 2005), *rev'd.,* 423 F.3d 386 (4th Cir. 2005), *and cert. denied,* 126 S.Ct. 1649 (2006).

64. "Justices Let U.S. Transfer Padilla to Civilian Custody," *New York Times* (5 January 2005), p. 21.

65. "Judge Orders Details on Padilla," *Sun-Sentinel* (Fort Lauderdale, Fla.) (21 June 2006), p. 5B; "U.S. Judge Finds Padilla Competent to Face Trial," *New York Times* (1 March 2007), n.p.

66. "High Court Blocks Tribunals: Gitmo Commissions Violate Military Rules, Geneva Conventions," *ABA Journal Report* (30 June 2006), pp. 1–2. The case is *In re* Hamden, 126 S.Ct. 2981 (2006).

67. Johnson v. Zerbst, 304 U.S. 458 (1938).

68. Santobello v. New York, 404 U.S. 257, 260-61 (1971).

69. "Grant Clemency to Lionel Tate," *Sun-Sentinel* (Fort Lauderdale, Fla.) (2 July 2003), p. 24.

70. Tate v. State, 864 So.2d 44 (Fla.Dist.Ct.App. 4th Dist. 2003), *reh'g. denied,* 2004 Fla.App. LEXIS 2309 (Fla.Dist.Ct.App. 4th Dist. 12 February 2004).

71. "New Trial for Boy with Life Term in Killing of Playmate in Florida," *New York Times* (11 December 2003), p. 1.

72. "Florida Youth Who Got Life Term for a Killing Is Freed at 16," *New York Times* (27 January 2004), p. 12.

73. "National Briefing South: Florida: Teenager Can Serve Probation at Home," *New York Times* (30 November 2004), p. 16.

74. "Two Reprieves Lost: Tate Gets 30 Years," *Los Angeles Times* (20 May 2006), p. 8.

75. Corbitt v. New Jersey, 439 U.S. 212 (1978).

76. Mabry v. Johnson, 467 U.S. 504 (1984).

77. Bordenkircher v. Hayes, 434 U.S. 357, 360–365 (1978).

78. United States v. Mezzanatto, 513 U.S. 196 (1995).

79. "In Deal for Life, Man Admits Killing 48 Women," *New York Times* (6 November 2003), p. 1.

80. "The Unabomber Travesty," *New York Times* (10 January 1998), p. 24.

81. United States v. Kaczynski, 239 F.3d 1108 (9th Cir. 2001), *cert. denied,* 535 U.S. 933 (2002).

82. "New Plea Bargain Limits Could Swamp Courts, Experts Say," *New York Times* (24 September 2003), p. 1.

Trial, Sentencing, and Appeal

8

Chapter 7 noted that most cases are not tried, and in 2003, yet one more study, this one from the University of Wisconsin, confirmed this fact in the federal system, pointing out that since 1962, the number of both civil and criminal trials has decreased. The study reported that between 1962 and 2000 the number of federal criminal cases going to trial fell from 5,096 to 3,574. In percentages, this means that in 1962 approximately 15 percent of federal criminal cases went to trial, compared with 5 percent in 2000. The percentage of federal civil cases going to trial in 2000 was 1.8, compared to 11.5 percent in 1962. One federal judge described these changes as follows: "What's documented here…is nothing less than the passing of the common law adversarial system that is uniquely American."[1]

The reason we have fewer trials, despite the larger number of cases, is that more cases are resolved out of court. In the civil arena, more cases are settled through negotiations that might include mediation or arbitration; in the criminal area, more are resolved through plea bargains. In both the civil and the criminal venues, these changes may be occurring because of the increased complexity and the high cost of trials. Another reason might be the changes in sentencing practices, which are discussed in this chapter.

For the cases that do proceed to trial, especially in the criminal area, it is important to know the rules and constitutional principles that govern the processes involved. This chapter begins with a discussion of defendants' constitutional rights at trial and explains the major processes that occur during criminal trials.

Sentencing, which may occur even in cases that are not tried, is a critical part of criminal justice systems and is discussed at some length in this chapter. The concept and process of sentencing is explained; types of sentences are discussed, with particular emphasis on the death penalty; and significant attention is given to current sentencing issues. These issues include sentence disparity and the recent punitive approaches of three strikes and you're out and truth in sentencing, which have dominated sentencing in recent years. But the chapter also pays attention to the recent diminishing of sentences through a treatment approach.

Finally, the chapter discusses appeals and writs, the procedures through which convictions and sentences are challenged.

LEARNING
OBJECTIVES

After reading this chapter, you should be able to do the following:

- **State an overview of defendants' constitutional rights.**
- **Explain the defendant's right to a speedy, public trial by an impartial jury.**
- **Discuss the variables of gender, race, age, and disability in jury selection.**
- **List and explain the stages in the trial and appeal of a criminal case in the United States.**
- **Explain how evidence is presented in a criminal trial, and discuss the various types of evidence and objections to evidence.**
- **Distinguish the prosecution's case from the case of the defense.**
- **Discuss the role of the jury in deciding a criminal case.**
- **Explain and analyze the concept and process of sentencing and sentencing strategies.**
- **Discuss the sentencing hearing and decision.**
- **List and define the major types of sentences.**
- **Describe the use of sentencing guidelines by states and the federal government.**
- **Explain the difference between indeterminate and determinate sentencing, and evaluate each.**
- **Explore the meaning, causes, and consequences of sentence disparity.**
- **Discuss the meaning and impact of three strikes and truth in sentencing legislation.**
- **Consider the impact of a treatment approach to sentencing.**
- **Describe appeals and writs.**

8-1   Constitutional Issues at Trial

This analysis of constitutional issues at trial is not meant to be exclusive. It must be understood in the context of the discussions in earlier chapters, but it focuses on the constitutional issues and rights that pertain primarily to a trial in a U.S. adult criminal court.

8-1a   Speedy Trial

> **Trial**   In criminal law, court proceedings during which a judge, a jury, or both listen to the evidence as presented by the defense and the prosecution, and determine whether the defendant is guilty beyond a reasonable doubt or should be acquitted. *See also* **Mistrial**.

The right to a speedy **trial** is embodied in the Sixth Amendment (see Appendix A) to the U.S. Constitution. The U.S. Supreme Court has held that this right "is as fundamental as any of the rights secured by the Sixth Amendment."[2]

In 1974, Congress passed the Speedy Trial Act, which, with its subsequent amendments, provides that, for suspects in federal cases, an indictment or an information charging the suspect must be filed within 30 days of the arrest or of the time when the suspect is served with a summons on the charge. That period may be extended for 30 days in a felony charge if the grand jury was not in session during that time. It is possible for the defendant to be tried so quickly that there would not be adequate time for preparing a defense. The Speedy Trial Act provides that, without the consent of the defendant, "the trial shall not commence less than thirty days from the date on which the defendant first appears through counsel or expressly waives counsel and elects to proceed pro se [on his or her own]."[3]

Some delays are permissible under the Speedy Trial Act. Several are listed in the act, including the obvious ones, such as those delays caused by examinations to determine whether the defendant is competent to stand trial, delays caused by the defendant's mental incompetence to stand trial, and delays caused by deferred prosecution when that is agreed upon by the prosecutor, the defendant, and the court. The act permits delays caused by continuances requested by the defense or the prosecution when they are granted to serve the ends of justice.

The federal Speedy Trial Act applies only to prosecutions in federal courts, but most states have statutes covering the implementation of state and federal rights to a speedy trial. For example, a New York statute, entitled Rights of persons accused of crime, provides as follows:

> In all criminal prosecutions, the accused has a right to a speedy and public trial, by an impartial jury, and is entitled to be informed of the nature and cause of the accusation; to be confronted with the witnesses against him; and to have compulsory process for obtaining witnesses in his favor.[4]

The Texas rules of criminal procedure provide specifically that an adult trial court shall entertain a motion to set aside an indictment, an information, or a complaint if the state is not prepared to go to trial within a specified time after these methods of beginning criminal cases have begun. The time permitted is 180 days for a felony case, 90 days for a misdemeanor punishable by more than 180 days in prison, and 60 days for a misdemeanor punishable by less than 180 days in prison or by a fine only.[5]

In addition, most states have procedural or statutory rules denoting how many days may elapse between arrest and trial. Texas, for example, provides as follows:

> Insofar as is practicable, the trial of a criminal action shall be given preference over trials of civil cases, and the trial of a criminal action against a defendant who is detained in jail pending trial of the action shall be given preference over trials of other criminal actions.[6]

A speedy trial can differ from state to state in time. For example, in 2006, after three Duke University lacrosse players were arrested on rape charges, it was announced that their trial would not occur until the following year. As noted in Chapter 7, the rape charges were dropped but less serious charges retained, although in the spring of 2007, all charges were dropped, and the prosecutor was facing ethics charges.

8-1b Public Trial

The Sixth Amendment also guarantees the right to a *public* trial. This right does not mean that the defendant may be tried by the media. If it can be shown that the defendant cannot get a fair trial because of publicity in the jurisdiction in which the case is to be tried, the trial should be moved to another jurisdiction.

Media publicity in criminal cases raises a delicate problem: the conflict between the First Amendment (see Appendix A) free speech right of the press and the public's right to know and the defendant's right to a trial by an impartial jury not biased by media information.

The U.S. Supreme Court has had several occasions to consider the conflict between the defendant's right to a fair trial and the First Amendment rights of the press. In a 1966 case, the Court overturned the conviction of Dr. Sam Sheppard, who had served 10 years in prison after his conviction for murdering his wife. On retrial, Sheppard was acquitted. In overturning Sheppard's conviction the Supreme Court said,

> Murder and mystery, society, sex and suspense were combined in this case in such a manner as to intrigue and captivate the public fancy to a degree perhaps unparalleled in recent annals. Throughout the preindictment investigation, the subsequent legal skirmishes and the nine-week trial, circulation-conscious editors catered to the insatiable interest of the American public in the bizarre.... In this atmosphere of a "Roman holiday" for the news media, Sam Sheppard stood trial for his life.[7]

In subsequent cases, the U.S. Supreme Court has continued to wrestle with the rights of defendants versus those of the press and the public. The Court has held that, under some circumstances, the former must give way to the latter. For example, in *Globe Newspaper Co. v. Superior Court*, the Court invalidated a Massachusetts statute that had been interpreted to mean exclusion of the press from *all* trials when sexual offense victims under the age of 18 were testifying. The Court ruled that each case must be examined in terms of its own facts, such as "the minor victim's age, psychological maturity and understanding, the nature of the crime, the desires of the victim, and the interests of parents and relatives."[8]

In some highly publicized cases, it has been argued that the defendant cannot get a fair public trial in *any* jurisdiction. Timothy McVeigh, who was tried on capital charges and convicted for the murders resulting from the bombing of the federal building in Oklahoma City, Oklahoma, on 19 April 1995, argued unsuccessfully that he could not get a fair trial. In addition to immense publicity about the bombing and its victims, the media carried articles stating that McVeigh had confessed to his attorneys. After two of these articles were published, McVeigh's attorneys asked the court to dismiss the charges against their client—or in the alternative, to grant a long continuance. The district court denied the motions, and the federal appellate court affirmed. The venue of the trial was moved from Oklahoma to Denver, Colorado, an action, claimed the appellate court, that significantly lessened the chance of prejudice in jury selection. Members of the jury pool were subjected to numerous questions in an attempt to secure jurors who could analyze the evidence objectively, and the appellate court was not convinced that McVeigh did not have fair jurors.[9] McVeigh was scheduled to be executed in May 2001, but after it was discovered that the Federal Bureau of Investigation had failed to disclose over 3,000 pages of documents to the defense, that execution was postponed. McVeigh was executed in June 2001.

In 2006, the Florida jury selection for the trial of John Couey, accused of raping and burying alive Jessica Lunsford, a neighbor, was moved from the county in which Jessica was killed to another county. The judge had hoped to pick a jury in the second county and then try the case in the original county. During jury selection, however, the judge ended the process, declaring that an unbiased jury could not be selected there either. Prospective jurors had developed opinions about the case, some indicating that they had dreamed about the horrors of Jessie's death, others stating that they had heard that Couey confessed—thus, he must be guilty. This case and others that attract worldwide media attention raise the issue of whether the accused can, within a reasonable period of time after the crime, get a fair trial. In 2007, Couey was tried, convicted, and sentenced to death.

8-1c Trial by Jury

The Sixth Amendment also guarantees the defendant in a criminal case the right to a trial by **jury**. Technically, the jury that sits in a trial is called the **petit jury**. The word *petit* means minor, small, or inconsequential, but in this context, it is used to distinguish the trial jury from the larger grand jury, not to carry the connotation of inconsequential.

The importance of the right to a jury trial, along with a brief history of its evolution, was emphasized by the U.S. Supreme Court in 1968 in *Duncan v. Louisiana*. This case involved a defendant who was charged with simple battery, a misdemeanor punishable by a maximum of two years' imprisonment and a $300 fine. A Louisiana trial court denied Duncan's request for a jury trial. At that time, the Louisiana constitution granted jury trials only in cases in which convicted defendants could be sentenced to imprisonment at hard labor or to capital punishment. Duncan was convicted, sentenced to 60 days in the parish prison, and fined $150. The Louisiana Supreme Court denied his request for an appeal. Duncan appealed to the U.S. Supreme Court, alleging that he had been denied his constitutional right to a jury trial. That Court agreed, as illustrated by the following brief excerpt.[10]

▶ **Jury** In a criminal case, a group of people who have been sworn in to listen to the evidence during a trial and to decide whether the defendant is guilty or not guilty. In some jurisdictions, a jury may recommend or even determine the sentence.

▶ **Petit jury** *Petit* literally means "small, minor, or inconsiderate." A trial jury, in contrast to a grand jury. *See also* **Jury**.

Duncan v. Louisiana

A right to jury trial is granted to criminal defendants in order to prevent oppression by the Government.... Providing an accused with the right to be tried by a jury of his peers gave him an inestimable safeguard against the corrupt or overzealous prosecutor and against the compliant, biased, or eccentric judge.... [T]he jury trial provisions in the Federal and State Constitutions reflect a fundamental decision about the exercise of official power—a reluctance to entrust plenary powers over the life and liberty of the citizen to one judge or to a group of judges.... The deep commitment of the Nation to the right of jury trial in serious criminal cases as a defense against arbitrary law enforcement qualifies for protection under the Due Process Clause of the Fourteenth Amendment, and must therefore be respected by the States.

Although it held that Duncan was entitled to a jury trial, the U.S. Supreme Court did say in passing "that there is a category of petty crimes or offenses which is not subject to the Sixth Amendment jury trial provision." Further, the right to a jury trial may be waived, provided it is done knowingly, intelligently, voluntarily, and in writing, and it is accepted by the trial court judge.

The U.S. Constitution does not specify how many jurors must be present for the defendant's right to a jury trial to be legal. Although 12 is the usual number of petit jurors, the U.S. Supreme Court has upheld the use of smaller juries in some cases. But there must be at least six jurors, and a jury that small must be unanimous. A unanimous vote is required in all federal jury trials.

The Sixth Amendment provides for the right to trial by an *impartial* jury, which means a number of things, including the right to a jury not prejudiced unduly by media publicity. As previously noted, in some cases the location of the trial must be moved to eliminate the impact of extensive publicity in the area in which the crime occurred. However, that might not be possible because of extensive national publicity. In those instances, the trial judge may order the jury sequestered for the trial, but a very long sequestration might work against the defense (or the prosecution, if the sequestration is perceived as prolonging the trial unnecessarily) and certainly is disruptive to the lives of the jurors, their families and friends, and their employers.

Some states have mandatory requirements for sequestration in serious cases. In 2001, the New York legislature unanimously enacted a statute deleting its 100-year requirement that all juries that deliberate for more than a day be sequestered (since 1995, exceptions had been made for some low-level criminal cases). The bill was signed by the governor within hours and became effective immediately. New York had the strictest sequestration requirements in the country. Under the present law, juries may be sequestered only upon orders of the trial judge.[11]

The Sixth Amendment further provides for a trial by a jury of the defendant's peers, which the U.S. Supreme Court has interpreted to involve implications for the exclusion of people from the jury on the basis of specific characteristics, such as gender, race and ethnicity, and religion. Despite the acceptance of the process of excusing some potential jurors, our statutes and court decisions establish guidelines on exclusions that may be made in the composition of juries.

Juries must be representative of the community, but that does not mean that juries must mirror the community and reflect the various distinctive groups in the population. Defendants are not entitled to a jury of any particular composition, but the jury wheels, pools of names, panels, or venires [lists of persons summoned to serve in the jury pool for a particular case] from which juries are drawn must not systematically exclude distinctive groups in the community and thereby fail to be reasonably representative thereof.[12]

Spotlight 8-1 Race and Jury Selection: The *Batson* Rule

[In *Batson v. Kentucky*, the U.S. Supreme Court held that it is unconstitutional to exclude African Americans from juries when there is evidence that the exclusion is based on race. The Court stated:]

Petitioner, a black man, was indicted in Kentucky on charges of second-degree burglary and receipt of stolen goods. The prosecutor used his peremptory challenges to strike all four black persons on the venire, and a jury composed only of white persons was selected....

Exclusion of black citizens from service as jurors constitutes a primary example of the evil the Fourteenth Amendment was designed to cure....

The Equal Protection Clause guarantees the defendant that the State will not exclude members of his race from the jury venire on account of race, or on the false assumption that members of his race as a group are not qualified to serve as jurors....Racial discrimination in selection of jurors harms not only the accused whose life or liberty they are summoned to try. Competence to serve as a juror ultimately depends on an assessment of individual qualifications and ability impartially to consider evidence presented at a trial. A person's race simply "is unrelated to his fitness as a juror."...

The harm from discriminatory jury selection extends beyond that inflicted on the defendant and the excluded juror to touch the entire community. Selection procedures that purposefully exclude black persons from juries undermine public confidence in the fairness of our system of justice....

Although a prosecutor ordinarily is entitled to exercise permitted peremptory challenges "for any reason at all, as long as that reason is related to his view concerning the outcome" of the case to be tried, the Equal Protection Clause forbids the prosecutor to challenge potential jurors solely on account of their race or on the assumption that black jurors as a group will be unable impartially to consider the State's case against a black defendant.

[The Court discussed procedures for contesting the peremptory challenges and concluded that the conviction in this case should be reversed.]

Source: Batson v. Kentucky, 476 U.S. 79 (1986), citations and footnotes omitted.

> **Peremptory challenge**
> A challenge that may be used by the prosecution or the defense to excuse a potential juror from the jury panel. No reason is required. Each attorney gets a specified number of peremptory challenges. Peremptory challenges are distinguished from *challenges for cause*, which are unlimited and based on a reason for disqualification, such as a conflict of interest with the case.

It is not clear what is meant by *the community*, but exclusions based on race and gender are not permitted. It is the *systematic* exclusion of particular groups of persons from the jury pool or jury selection that constitutes a constitutional issue, illustrated primarily by the U.S. Supreme Court's rulings regarding the exclusion of African Americans from juries. In 1880, the Supreme Court held that a statute permitting only white men to serve on juries was unconstitutional. In 1965, the Court held that it was permissible to exclude individual African Americans by using a **peremptory challenge** (a challenge that does not require the attorney to state a reason), but the Court left open the issue of systematic exclusion of African Americans.[13]

Other decisions were made in the intervening years, but the key decision did not come until 1986 in *Batson v. Kentucky*, in which the defendant proved that he was a member of a cognizable racial group whose members were excluded from the jury under circumstances that raised an inference that they were excluded because of race. Portions of *Batson* are included in Spotlight 8-1.

In *Batson*, the U.S. Supreme Court articulated a three-pronged test to use when analyzing an allegation that the peremptory challenge was used to eliminate a potential juror because of race:

- A defendant must show a *prima facie* (on its face) case that a peremptory challenge was based on race.
- If the defendant makes that showing, the prosecution must give a race-neutral explanation for why the juror in question was challenged.
- The trial court judge must consider the evidence submitted for the preceding two reasons and determine whether the defendant has shown purposeful discrimination based on race.[14]

Since *Batson*, lower courts and the U.S. Supreme Court have dealt with variations in fact patterns in which the case might apply, including holding that a criminal defendant does not have to be of the same race as the excluded juror to object to race-based exclusions because excluded jurors have a constitutional right not to be excluded from juries based on their race; holding that *Batson* applies equally to the removal of white as well as African American potential jurors and to the defense, as well as to the prosecution; holding that a defendant may challenge a prosecutor's race-based exclusion of a potential juror, regardless of whether the defendant and the excluded juror are of the same race; and holding that *Batson* applies to civil as well as to criminal cases.

In 2003, the U.S. Supreme Court again considered the issue of jury selection and racial bias. The case came from Texas and involved a death-row inmate, Thomas Miller-El, an African American, who was within one week of his scheduled execution when the U.S. Supreme Court agreed to review his case. Miller-El argued that his conviction was a violation of his constitutional rights because the prosecution eliminated 10 of 11 African Americans from the jury pool. The prosecution claimed that it did so because those potential jurors had indicated that they would hesitate to impose the death penalty. Miller-El presented compelling evidence of a larger pattern of racial discrimination in jury selection in that county. His motion to strike the jury (prior to his conviction) had been rejected, and he was convicted by a jury consisting of only one African American. He was sentenced to death. Miller-El's appeal was rejected by the lower appellate courts, and he asked the U.S. Supreme Court to hear his case. The Court heard the case and decided *Miller-El v. Dretke* by an 8-to-1 vote, holding that Miller-El should have been granted a hearing by the federal circuit court of appeals. The Supreme Court chastised the lower federal court (the Fifth Circuit Court of Appeals), urging that court to rethink its "dismissive and strained interpretation of the proof in the case and to give more serious consideration to the significant evidence pointing to unconstitutional discrimination against black jurors during the jury selection process." Instead of following the orders of the U.S. Supreme Court, the Fifth Circuit gave no relief and quoted extensively from the one dissenting vote in the U.S. Supreme Court's decision, that of Justice Clarence Thomas. One journalist referred to this as "something akin to plagiarism," whereas a former federal judge proclaimed that the lower federal court "just went out of its way to defy the Supreme Court." In a subsequent appeal to the U.S. Supreme Court, Miller-El was again successful. In June 2005, the Court, by a 6-to-3 vote, in an opinion written by Justice David Souter, detailed the various tactics and "trickery" that the prosecution had used to exclude African Americans from Miller-El's jury. The tactics included asking different questions of whites and of African Americans (in an apparent attempt to encourage African Americans to disqualify themselves by stating opposition to the death penalty), as well as shuffling the jury pool when too many African Americans appeared in the front of the panel. Justice Souter stated that the prosecution's explanation of its use of its peremptory challenges to exclude African Americans because they were opposed to the death penalty "reeks of afterthought." Justice Clarence Thomas, in a dissenting opinion longer than that of the majority, concluded that the prosecution's position was "eminently reasonable."[15] Miller-El will be retried, and prosecutors will again ask for the death penalty.

In 2005, the U.S. Supreme Court also held that, to state a *prima facie* case under *Batson*, a criminal defendant is *not* required to prove that "peremptory challenges...were more likely than not based on race." That standard is too strict.[16]

Gender is another important category in jury selection. Women have a right to serve on juries, and defendants have a right to have women serve as jurors. Thus, in 1994, the U.S. Supreme Court's decision in *Batson* was extended to include gender. *J.E.B. v. Alabama ex. rel. T.B* was a civil rather than a criminal case, but it is likely that the holding will apply to criminal cases as well. In this case, Alabama sued J.E.B. to establish paternity and award child support to T.B. (the real names are omitted to protect the child), who alleged that J.E.B. was the father of her minor child. During jury selection, the state used most of its peremptory challenges to remove men from the jury pool, whereas the defense used most of its peremptory challenges to remove women from the pool. An all-female jury was empaneled. The U.S. Supreme Court held that the prosecution's use of peremptory challenges to exclude men from the jury was unconstitutional because the prosecution did not show "an exceedingly persuasive justification" for doing so. One of the dissenting opinions noted that for every man the prosecution excluded, the defense excluded a woman; thus, men were not singled out for discriminatory treatment.[17]

Two other categories that might be the basis for exclusion or failure to include are age and disability. The U.S. Supreme Court has not held that defendants have a right to a jury of peers of their own age. In 1985, a lower federal court reversed one of its earlier decisions and held that a young defendant did not have a right to a new trial because young adults from ages 18 to 34 had been underrepresented on the jury. The court held that a "mere statistical disparity in the chosen age group" is not sufficient to establish a violation of the Sixth Amendment right to a jury of one's peers. The defendant must show that the underrepresented group is identified and limited by factors or characteristics that can be defined easily; that the group may be distinguished by a common thread of similarity in attitude, ideas, or experience; and that the group has a community of interest. The U.S. Supreme Court refused to hear the case, thus permitting the lower court's decision to stand.[18]

Disability is another issue that must be considered in jury selection. With the emphasis on the rights of persons with disabilities, exemplified by the passage of and the numerous cases being brought under the Americans with Disabilities Act (ADA), consideration must be given to extending the right to serve on juries to those whose physical or mental challenges might have precluded such service in the past.

Finally, those who serve on juries must conduct themselves properly both inside and outside the courtroom.

8-1d Other Constitutional Issues at Trial

Some constitutional rights of defendants discussed in earlier chapters in connection with the police or with pretrial procedures are also applicable during a criminal trial. Some of those rights take on their fullest meaning during the trial. For example, defendants must be notified of the charges against them. That notice must occur during the early pretrial stages, but formal charges must be read to the defendant at the trial. A confession obtained or evidence secured in violation of a defendant's rights should not be introduced during the trial because of the exclusionary rule, discussed previously.

Defendants have the right to compel witnesses to testify on their behalf and the right to confront and to cross-examine witnesses who testify against them. These rights and others have been interpreted to mean that defendants have a right to be present at their trials. That right, however, is subject to the defendant's good behavior, as illustrated by the classic case of *Illinois v. Allen*, which involved a defendant who appealed his conviction for armed robbery on the grounds that he had been improperly excluded from his trial.

At the beginning of the trial, Allen insisted on being his own lawyer, rejecting the services of his court-appointed counsel. Defendants have the right to refuse counsel, but generally, attorneys will be appointed and available for defendants who choose to exercise that right. In the *Allen* case, when the defendant began questioning prospective jurors, the judge interrupted him and asked him to confine his questions to the matters relating to their qualifications. Allen responded in an abusive and disrespectful manner. The judge asked appointed counsel to proceed with the examination of prospective jurors. Allen continued to talk, "proclaiming that the appointed attorney was not going to act as his lawyer. He terminated his remarks by saying, 'When I go out for lunchtime, you're [the judge] going to be a corpse here.'"

Allen took a file from his court-appointed attorney, tore it, and threw it on the floor. The judge warned Allen that he would remove him from the trial if he continued in this manner, but the warning had no effect on Allen's conduct. Allen was removed from the courtroom, and the examination of the potential jurors continued in his absence. Later, Allen was returned to the court but was removed again after another outburst. During the presentation of the state's case, Allen was occasionally taken to the courtroom for identification, but he used vile and abusive language in responding to a question from the judge. After assuring the court he would behave, Allen was permitted to be in the courtroom while his attorney presented the case for the defense.

Justice Hugo Black delivered the opinion for the U.S. Supreme Court, which upheld the right of the trial judge to exclude Allen from his own trial. Justice Black pointed out that the trial judge had three constitutionally permissible options in this case. He could have cited Allen for **contempt of court**, excluded him from the trial, or bound and gagged him and left him in the courtroom. Each option was discussed, with the Court noting the possible prejudicial effect that binding and gagging the defendant might have had on the jury:

> Not only is it possible that the sight of shackles and gags might have a significant effect on the jury's feelings about the defendant, but the use of this technique is itself something of an affront to the very dignity and decorum of judicial proceedings that the judge is seeking to uphold.[19]

The U.S. Supreme Court noted that another problem with gagging is that this procedure prevents the defendant from meaningful contact with his attorney. For that reason, the Court refused to hold that the state must use this method in lieu of excluding the defendant from the trial. Further, the Court emphasized the importance of maintaining decorum in the courtroom and concluded that

> if our courts are to remain what the Founders intended, the citadels of justice, their proceedings cannot and must not be infected with the sort of scurrilous, abusive language and conduct paraded before the Illinois trial judge in this case.[20]

8-2 The Trial Process

In this section, the stages of a criminal trial are discussed in the order in which they generally occur. Spotlight 8-2 lists those stages, and the discussion follows the order in that list. These stages are not always distinct, however, and some of the procedures may occur at various stages. For example, motions might be made throughout the trial. An obvious motion is one to dismiss or to declare a **mistrial**, which is made by defense counsel after the prosecutor or a prosecution witness has said something improper. A defense motion for change of venue (change of place of trial) might be made before and during the trial as increased media attention to the trial leads the defense to argue that it is impossible for the defendant to have a fair trial in that area.

8-2a Opening of the Court Session

When it is time for the trial court session to begin, the bailiff arrives and calls the court to order with such words as "Hear ye, hear ye, the court of the Honorable Judge Decider is in session—all rise." At that point, everyone in the courtroom should rise. The judge, usually dressed in a robe, enters the courtroom and sits, after which everyone else may sit. The judge announces the case, "The State of California versus Susan Jones, Case No. 45629-16." The judge asks whether the prosecution is ready; if so, the judge asks whether the defense is ready. If both sides are ready, the case begins with jury selection, assuming that the court has no additional business regarding the case, such as pretrial motions, that needs to be heard prior to the beginning of the trial.

After the jury has been selected and sworn in, the judge reads the indictment or information and informs the court that the defendant has entered a plea of not guilty (or not guilty by reason of insanity, if that is permitted), and the trial begins with opening statements. Variances may occur in these procedures; for example, the jury may be selected and sent home (or sequestered), while attorneys argue various motions before the judge.

8-2b Jury Selection

Jurisdictions differ in their procedures for selecting persons to form the pool from which jurors will be selected. Those selected are notified by means of a **summons**, a

Contempt of court An act (usually committed in violation of a court order or rule) considered as embarrassing, humiliating, or as undermining the power of the court. May be civil or criminal.

Mistrial A trial that cannot stand, that is invalid. Judges may call a mistrial for such reasons as an error on the part of the prosecution or the defense, the illness or death of any of the parties participating in the legal proceedings, jury tampering, or the jury's inability to reach a verdict.

Summons A formal document issued by the court to notify a person that his or her presence is required in court for a particular reason at a specified time and date.

Spotlight 8-2   **Stages in the Trial and Appeal of a U.S. Criminal Case**

1. Opening of the court session
2. Jury selection
3. Opening statement by the prosecutor
4. Opening statement by the defense attorney
5. Presentation of evidence by the prosecutor
6. Cross-examination by the defense
7. Redirect examination by the prosecutor
8. Cross-examination by the defense
9. Presentation of the defense's case by the defense attorney
10. Cross-examination by the prosecutor

11. Redirect by the defense
12. Cross-examination by the prosecutor
13. Rebuttal proof by the prosecutor
14. Closing statement by the prosecutor
15. Closing statement by the defense
16. Rebuttal statement by the prosecutor
17. Submittal of the case to the jury
18. The verdict
19. Postverdict motions
20. Sentencing
21. Appeals and writs

formal document the court issues to notify a person that his or her presence is required in court for a particular reason at a specified time and date. The potential juror, after arriving at the designated place, may sit all day and not be picked for a jury. If that happens, he or she may be instructed to return for jury selection the following day. This procedure may go on for days, but many judges try to avoid this inconvenience to potential jurors.

Usually, the members of the jury pool are seated in the courtroom before the judge enters for jury selection. After the formal opening of the court session, the judge instructs the jury pool about procedures. The minute clerk begins by selecting names from a jury wheel, drawing names out of a fishbowl, or using some other similar procedure. As each name is drawn, the minute clerk reads and spells the name. The first selected person sits in the first seat in the jury box and so on until the jury box is filled or contains the number the judge wishes to process at one time.

Questioning of the potential jurors follows, a process called ***voir dire***, which means "to tell the truth." The defense attorney and the prosecuting attorney *voir dire* the jury pool; that is, they question each potential juror and decide whether or not they will approve the selection of that person. Judges may also question potential jurors. In the federal system, judges may refuse to permit attorneys to question prospective jurors. Normally in the federal system, jury selection takes only a few hours; in some states, the process may take weeks or even months.

After they are questioned, potential jurors may be excused from jury duty in two ways. First, if they are excused for *cause*, they are presumed to be biased in the case. Bias may be presumed on the basis of the potential jurors' answers to the questionnaire or to questions in court, association with or knowledge of the defendant or some other person involved in the trial, personal financial interest in the case, or a background that might prejudice them. For example, a person whose spouse has been murdered might be presumed to be prejudiced against a defendant on trial for murder. Attorneys are entitled to an unlimited number of challenges for cause. The judge may also exclude potential jurors for cause.

The second way a potential juror may be excused is by *peremptory challenge*, which means that the attorneys may excuse without cause. No reason need be given; that is the purpose of the challenge. But the peremptory challenge may not be used for extralegal reasons, such as to exclude minorities from the jury, as noted earlier in this chapter. States vary in the number of peremptory challenges permitted.

Some attorneys retain consultants to assist them in the questioning and selection of jurors. Through empirical studies, social scientists have provided information on characteristics that are related to opinions and therefore may influence the decision of a juror. In a particular case, a retained jury consultant may conduct a survey to determine factors that might influence a juror in that town on that case.

▶ **Voir dire**   To speak the truth. The process of questioning prospective jurors to determine their qualifications and desirability for serving on a jury.

8-2c Opening Statements

After the jury is selected, attorneys may make opening statements. The prosecutor makes the first opening statement. This is the prosecution's chance to outline what he or she intends to prove during the trial. The opening statement is very important; it should be planned carefully and delivered convincingly.

The opening statement should be brief but long enough to present an adequate statement of the facts the prosecution expects to prove. It should be interesting but not overly dramatic. The prosecutor must be certain not to overstep his or her boundaries and raise the ire of the judge, the defense, and the jury. Inflammatory and prejudicial statements are not permitted.

The defense is entitled to follow the prosecution with an opening statement, and many defense attorneys do so. The same principles apply to the defense as to the prosecution. The opening statement should raise the jury's interest to listen further but should not be too long or too dramatic. A defense attorney has the option of waiving the opening statement until the prosecution has presented its evidence. Some do so in order to hear that evidence before revealing the defense. Prosecutors, knowing that this might occur, may make comments in their opening statements that would lead the jury to expect the defense to make a statement or to be suspicious if the defense does not do so.

Like the prosecution, the defense attorney should not include information that is misleading in the opening statement. For example, a defense attorney in the Scott Peterson case said in his opening statement that the defense would show that Peterson could not be guilty. That was more than the attorney could deliver, and he was criticized by legal analysts for that assertion. Although that may not have been a major influence on the jury, Peterson was convicted of first-degree murder in the death of his pregnant wife, Laci, and second-degree murder in the death of their unborn son. The jury recommended the death sentence, and the judge imposed that sentence.

8-2d Presentation of the Evidence

Before looking at the types of evidence that the prosecution and the defense may present, it is necessary to understand some general rules of evidence and to look at the categories of evidence that apply to both the prosecution and the defense. The rules of evidence in criminal cases are contained in statutory and case law. They are complex, and they differ from one jurisdiction to another; however, a few general rules are important to a basic understanding of the criminal trial.

Any evidence presented must be *relevant, competent,* and *material* to the case. The meaning of those words has been litigated often, and over time, changes have been made concerning admissible evidence. For example, in rape cases, historically the defense was permitted to ask the complainant about her prior sexual experiences, to imply that the alleged rape was a voluntary sexual act, not one of force. If she had had sexual relationships with other men, particularly if it could be inferred that she had been promiscuous, a rape conviction was unlikely. Today, many jurisdictions have changed that rule. Some permit such questions only if the evidence is relevant to motive or conduct during the alleged crime or if the evidence shows that the alleged victim had sex with someone other than the accused. Other jurisdictions do not permit any questions about the victim's sexual experiences other than with the defendant and may limit that evidence to the case on trial. This change in what is defined as material evidence may not only affect the outcome of the case but also may make it much more likely that victims will report rapes and agree to testify at trial.

Attempts by the prosecution or the defense to introduce evidence or to ask questions thought by the opposing side to be incompetent, irrelevant, or immaterial may be countered by an objection by opposing counsel. If the objection is sustained, the evidence is not admitted. If the objection involves a question posed to the witness, the judge tells the witness not to answer the question. If the question has been answered already, the judge instructs the jury to disregard the answer, unless the information is so prejudicial that the judge declares a mistrial, which means the case cannot continue with that jury. A new jury must be selected or the charges dropped.

An important evidence rule is that of *discovery*, which refers to the process during which one side obtains the information that will be presented in court by the other side, Although in a criminal case, the defense is not required to discover all of its evidence, the prosecution is required to present evidence that might exonerate the defense. The purpose of discovery is to prevent surprises in the trial and to enable each side to prepare adequately for its cross-examination of the evidence introduced by the other side. If discovery procedures are violated, the judge may impose fines or a more severe sanction, such as excluding the evidence in question or even citing the attorney for contempt.

Several types of evidence may be presented. **Demonstrative evidence** is real to the senses, in contrast to evidence presented by the testimony of other people. Examples of demonstrative evidence are the weapon used in a crime, blood samples, hair samples, and clothing. The integrity of demonstrative evidence may be, and often is, challenged.

> ▶ **Demonstrative evidence**   Real evidence. The kind of evidence that is apparent to the senses, in contrast to evidence presented by the testimony of other people.

Some evidence may be competent, relevant, and material to the case but be excluded because it has been secured in violation of the defendant's rights or because it is considered too prejudicial or inflammatory. Deciding which evidence to admit and which to exclude is the judge's responsibility. He or she may be overruled on appeal, but many of the decisions made at the trial (or pretrial) stages stand, and often, they are crucial to the outcome of the case.

A second type of evidence that may be introduced at trial is that of witnesses, which is referred to as *testimonial evidence*. Witnesses may be called by the prosecution or by the defense, and they are sworn in before they are permitted to testify. If they do not tell the truth, they may be prosecuted for perjury. There are several types of witnesses.

The testimony of a *victim-witness* is a preferred type of testimonial evidence. In many cases, prosecutors drop charges if victims will not agree to testify against the accused. For example, after the woman who alleged that she was raped by basketball star Kobe Bryant indicated to the prosecution that she did not want to testify, the rape charges were dropped. The prosecution apparently thought that, without her testimony, it would have been difficult, if not impossible, to get a conviction.

Eyewitnesses who are not the victims of the alleged crime are also prime candidates for being called to testify in criminal cases, although some psychologists question the use of eyewitnesses, finding evidence that some jurors place too much weight on their testimonies.

The defense or the prosecution may also call *expert witnesses* Expert witnesses testify regarding subjects on which they have expertise beyond that of the average person. To illustrate, ballistics experts may be called to testify about the specifics of when and where a gun was fired and what kind of gun was used. Medical experts might testify to the cause of death in a murder case. Psychiatrists might testify concerning the mental or emotional state of the defendant at the time of the crime. Before expert evidence may be admitted, the judge must rule that the science about which the expert will testify is advanced sufficiently to qualify. The judge must also rule on whether a particular person is qualified to testify on the subject in question. The attorney who introduces the expert offers evidence to qualify that person. Typically, experts are asked where they received their education and training, how much experience they have, and whether they have testified previously in the type of case before the court. Opposing counsel may challenge the expert's credentials, but in most cases, they are accepted, although after the expert finishes testifying, opposing counsel will try to discredit the content of the testimony during cross-examination. Both the prosecution and the defense might present experts from the same field. If the experts disagree, it is the jury's responsibility to determine credibility. A particular expert may be allowed to testify to some but not all issues about which the attorney wishes to question him or her.

Generally, witnesses must testify to facts, not opinion, although in some instances, opinions are allowed. But witnesses are not permitted to testify to the ultimate question of fact in a criminal case: the guilt or innocence of the defendant. One way for counsel to get around the requirement of factual, not opinion, testimony is to ask hypothetical questions concerning facts similar to those in the case on trial. The expert witness may answer these hypothetical questions.

In most instances, experts and other witnesses are permitted to testify only to what they know, not to what they have heard from others, which constitutes **hearsay evidence**. Hearsay evidence is not admissible because there is no opportunity to cross-examine the source of the information. However, there are a number of exceptions to the hearsay evidence rule, such as a *dying declaration*. Since it might be presumed that one who is dying has no reason to lie, courts may permit the individual to testify (either in a deposition or at trial) to information that otherwise would be considered hearsay.

One further distinction important to the presentation of evidence is the difference between *direct* and *circumstantial* evidence. For example, a witness who testifies that he or she saw the defendant using the alleged weapon is providing **direct evidence**. Much evidence, however, is not direct; rather, it is *inferred* from a fact or series of facts and is called **circumstantial evidence**. To illustrate, in the Oklahoma City federal bombing trial, the prosecution was not able to present a witness who could testify that he or she saw Terry L. Nichols at the federal building in Oklahoma City when it was bombed. The evidence linking Nichols to that crime was inferred from other testimony, and that testimony did not involve inferences that he was there but, rather, that he had some involvement in the planning of the crime. The lack of direct evidence may account for the jury's decision to convict Nichols of manslaughter rather than murder. Subsequently, Nichols was tried in a state court in Oklahoma and convicted of multiple murders, but he was spared the death penalty.

After the prosecution presents its witnesses, in a process called **direct examination**, the defense attorney may question those witnesses through **cross-examination**. The defense may reserve the right to cross-examine a witness later in the trial. After the defense cross-examines a prosecution witness, the prosecutor may follow with additional questions, in a process called *redirect examination*. If that occurs, the defense may cross-examine the witness again. The same process occurs in reverse after the defense has presented its witnesses.

8-2e The Prosecution's Case

The prosecution is the first to present evidence in a criminal case. Its case may include the presentation of demonstrative evidence, as well as the testimony of the alleged victim, other witnesses, and experts. Usually, police officers involved in the arrest or the investigation of the case are called to testify. The prosecutor's presentation of evidence may consume days, weeks, even months in some trials and may involve very complicated evidence.

After the defense has rested its case, the prosecutor has the option of presenting additional proof to rebut the case presented by the defense. Not all prosecutors choose to exercise this option to present what is called *rebuttal* evidence. When the option is exercised, the prosecution may call or recall police officers or others to testify regarding facts that have been in dispute among witnesses at the trial.

8-2f The Defense Attorney's Case

After the prosecution has presented its case and all cross-examinations and redirect examinations have occurred, the prosecution rests and the defense presents its case. At this point, some special issues arise.

First, the defendant has a right not to testify (see Appendix A, Fifth Amendment). The reason is that even innocent persons might appear guilty if they take the stand. If the defendant does not testify, neither the prosecution nor the judge may make unfavorable comments about that fact.

> **Hearsay evidence** Secondhand evidence of which the witness does not have personal knowledge but merely repeats what the witness says he or she heard another person say. Hearsay evidence must be excluded from a trial unless it meets one of the exceptions to the hearsay rule.

> **Direct evidence** Evidence offered by an eyewitness who testifies to what he or she saw, heard, tasted, smelled, or touched.

> **Circumstantial evidence** Evidence that may be inferred from a fact or a series of facts. *See also* **Direct evidence**.

> **Direct examination** The examination of a witness, which is conducted by the attorney who called the witness to testify.

> **Cross-examination** The questioning of a court witness by adversary counsel after one attorney concludes the direct examination.

Some defendants choose to testify. In that case, they are sworn in, and they may be prosecuted for perjury if they testify falsely. They may be cross-examined by the prosecutor. Rules vary, but generally, the rules applied to other witnesses also apply to the defendant. In most jurisdictions, this means that the cross-examination may encompass only those subjects covered on direct or redirect examination. Where that is the case, the defense attorney has the ability to limit the subject matter about which the prosecution may ask questions to the subjects the defense attorney includes in direct examination. Some jurisdictions, however, permit the prosecution to go beyond those subjects once the defendant takes the stand.

The defense may call *character witnesses*, who testify about the defendant's character; if that occurs, the prosecution may call witnesses to testify to the defendant's bad character. The prosecution may not begin this line of evidence. Character witnesses, like all other witnesses, may be subjected to stringent cross-examination. This is difficult for many people, and therefore, it is important that attorneys who plan to call character or other kinds of witnesses spend time with those witnesses, preparing them for trial.

Another important element of the defendant's case is the presentation of defenses. Commission of a criminal act, even with the required criminal intent, is not sufficient for a guilty verdict if the defense proves a legally acceptable reason that the law should not be applied to this defendant. Many defenses might be raised. Infancy, intoxication, duress, involuntary action, entrapment, public duty, legal impossibility, self-defense or defense of others, action under authority of law (e.g., a justifiable killing by a police officer), and insanity are some examples. Jurisdictions differ regarding which of these defenses are acceptable and under what conditions. Differences exist in the type of proof required for the defense to be successful.[21]

8-2g Closing Statements

After all of the evidence has been presented in a case, attorneys may offer closing statements. The closing statement is given first by the prosecution, then by the defense; this may be followed with a rebuttal by the prosecutor. In the closing statement, as in the entire trial, the prosecutor must be careful not to go too far. If he or she does so, the judge must determine whether the statements are so prejudicial or erroneous that they might have undue influence on the jury's determination of guilt. If so, they are considered **prejudicial errors**, and the judge orders a mistrial. If not, they are considered *harmless errors*. Prejudicial errors and harmless errors may be committed by the defense or the prosecution and may refer to actions or comments made at various stages in the criminal process.

▶ **Prejudicial errors** Errors made during legal proceedings that affect the rights of parties substantially and thus may result in the reversal of a case.

The defense offers a closing statement after that of the prosecutor, unless the defense chooses to waive this step. The defense should also be careful not to go beyond the evidence or be too emotional, but as a practical matter, defense attorneys' closing statements are rarely the subject of appeal. This is because the prosecution may not appeal an acquittal; if the defendant is convicted and the defense appeals, that appeal will be concerned only with alleged errors made by the prosecution or rulings made by the judge.

8-2h Submittal of the Case to the Jury

After all of the preceding steps have been completed, most cases are submitted to a jury. The judge may not direct the jury to return a guilty verdict. However, in many jurisdictions, trial judges, on their own or by granting a motion from the defense, may order a **directed verdict**, a direction to the jury to return a verdict of not guilty.

▶ **Directed verdict** Upon a finding of insufficient evidence to convict a defendant, the judge may direct the jury to return a verdict of not guilty. The judge may not direct a verdict of guilty.

Why would a trial judge have that power? If the evidence is so weak that it is unreasonable to conclude beyond a reasonable doubt that the defendant is guilty, it would be a travesty of justice to send the case to the jury, let the jury return a guilty verdict, and then make the defendant wait for an appeal to get justice.

Before the case is given to the jury for deliberation, the judge has the responsibility of charging the jury, which means instructing jurors on matters of law relating to the case they must decide. In many jurisdictions, patterned jury instructions are given for the most commonly raised issues. The judge accepts suggested instructions from the prosecution and the defense and usually schedules a conference with them on the proposed instructions. The judge determines the final instructions (which may be subject to appeal) and presents them orally to the jury. The charge of the judge is very important, for it can be influential, perhaps determinative, in the jury's decision.

The jury charge should be as clear and as simple as possible without distorting the meaning of the law. The law as applied to many cases is complicated and difficult to understand, especially for people who are not legally trained, yet it is the jury's responsibility to apply that law to the case it has heard. It is the duty of the trial judge to explain the law in terms that the jury can understand. If the judge's charge is too complicated or is an inaccurate interpretation of the law in the case, the defense may appeal. In some instances, the case is reversed and requires a new trial.

The judge's charge must explain to the jury the law that applies to the case, and it must clarify what the jury may do. For example, if the defendant has been charged with first-degree murder but the law permits the jury to return a guilty verdict for second-degree murder, that must be explained, along with the elements that must be proved for conviction of each of those charges. The judge should explain the meaning of evidence and distinguish among the types of evidence. If conflict exists in the testimonial evidence, the jurors need to understand that they are the final determiner regarding the credibility of the testimony. This is true particularly when expert opinions conflict. Jurors may expect conflict between the testimony of a victim and that of a defendant but be very confused when two physicians give contradictory statements. Experts do differ; the jury is to decide whom to believe. On the other hand, jurors may ignore the testimony of any or all experts.

The judge may instruct the jury to disregard certain evidence that has been admitted but that for some reason should not be considered. In the federal as well as in some state systems, the judge is permitted to summarize and comment on the evidence when the charge is given to the jury. This is an immense responsibility, for the judge's obligation to be a neutral party continues throughout the trial unless the right to a jury trial is waived and the judge determines the ultimate fact of guilt or innocence.

The judge might cover many areas of law in the instructions. The details of each charge depend on the nature of the case being tried. Two issues deserve further attention in this section: (1) the presumption of innocence and (2) the burden and standard of proof.

In U.S. criminal justice systems, the defendant is presumed innocent. The **presumption of innocence** is an important principle. It means that the prosecution has the responsibility of proving every element required for conviction and that the defendant does not have to prove innocence. The defendant can do nothing and still be acquitted if the government does not prove its case.

> **Presumption of innocence** A cornerstone of the adversary system. It provides that a defendant is innocent unless and until the prosecution proves guilt beyond a reasonable doubt.

Most judges instruct the jury regarding the presumption of innocence, although the U.S. Supreme Court has held that it is not constitutionally required that an instruction be given. According to the Supreme Court, all circumstances must be examined to determine whether the defendant had a fair trial without an instruction on the presumption. If so, the case will not be reversed for failure to give the instruction.

The presumption of innocence is essential in protecting those who are falsely accused. Innocent people are convicted in some cases, and these convictions may be devastating to their personal and professional lives. The criminal justice system is impaired when the rights of innocent persons are violated, particularly when a violation leads to a conviction (or in some cases, execution).

The standard of proof in a criminal case is **beyond a reasonable doubt**. That burden is a heavy one; it means that, when jurors look at all the evidence, they are convinced, satisfied to a moral certainty, that guilt has been established by the facts. Some judges refuse to define *beyond a reasonable doubt* on the assumption that not much more can be said. We all understand those words, and any attempt to define them further might be confusing or misleading.

> **Beyond a reasonable doubt** The standard for evidence required for a conviction in an adult criminal court or a juvenile court. A lack of uncertainty. The facts presented to the judge or jury are sufficient to lead a reasonable person to conclude without question that the defendant committed the act for which he or she is charged.

After the charge is read to the jury, the bailiff takes the jurors to the jury room to deliberate. These deliberations must be conducted in secret. It is the bailiff's responsibility to ensure that no one talks to the jurors; nor are the jurors permitted to seek advice. If they need further instruction, they may send the bailiff to ask the judge, who may or may not give that instruction, depending on the nature of the request. Any communication between the jury and the judge is conducted within the presence of counsel for both the prosecution and the defense.

If the jurors are sequestered, the bailiff (or another court person, such as a deputy sheriff) escorts them not only in and out of the courtroom but also to all meals and to the hotel rooms where they are staying. Access to television and newspapers is not permitted unless special arrangements are made to avoid any possibility that jurors are exposed to media accounts of the trial. For example, jurors might be offered newspapers only after the articles about the trial have been removed.

Normally, when the jurors deliberate, they have access to the demonstrative evidence that has been introduced during the trial. If they have been permitted to take notes during the trial, they may have their notes for the deliberation. Generally, the trial judge has the discretion to decide whether jurors may take notes.

In some trials, jurors deliberate for hours and do not reach verdicts. They report to the judge, who may tell them to go back and try again. The number of times a judge may send them back and how long they must deliberate is a matter of jurisdictional rules and judicial discretion, but the judge may not require jurors to deliberate for an unreasonable period of time. The definition of *reasonable* depends on the complexity of the trial. If the jury cannot reach a verdict, it is deadlocked, also called a *hung jury*, and the judge should declare a mistrial.

Mistrials may also be declared under other circumstances, such as the serious illness or death of the judge or one of the attorneys or jurors. Mistrials may be declared during the trial as a result of a prejudicial error made by one of the parties involved in the trial. Other reasons include prejudicial media publicity that comes to the attention of the jury and efforts of someone to bribe some or all of the jurors.

If the jury is not deadlocked and returns a verdict, the verdict may be not guilty. In that case, the judge may order a verdict of acquittal, and the case is ended. The judge may not reverse a not guilty verdict. The judge may, but rarely does, reverse a guilty verdict. This may happen if the judge believes the evidence was not sufficient to support the guilty verdict. In addition, as noted in Chapter 6, the judge may find the defendant guilty of a lesser charge than the one on which the jury based its verdict. In the case discussed in that chapter, involving defendant Louise Woodward, the jury was instructed only on murder charges and found the defendant guilty of second-degree murder, but the judge reduced that conviction to manslaughter.

After the verdict and before sentencing, the attorneys may file postverdict motions. If the jury returns a guilty verdict, the defense may file a motion for a judgment of acquittal. That motion may also be made before the case goes to the jury and probably is more appropriately done at that time. The motion is based on the argument that the evidence is not sufficient to support a guilty verdict. The court may be more likely to grant that motion before the jury has returned a verdict, particularly in a close case.

The more common motion made by the defense after a guilty verdict is a motion for a new trial. This motion may be made on several specific grounds or on general grounds; that is, a new trial is in the interest of justice. Court rules or statutes may enumerate the specific grounds on which this motion may be based.

8-3 Sentencing

After a guilty verdict, the court imposes a sentence, which may or may not involve a jury recommendation to the judge. In some jurisdictions, the jury determines the sentence. In others, the jury is permitted to make a sentencing recommendation, but the judge does not have to follow it, although there are exceptions in capital cases.

Frequently, the sentencing process takes place at a later hearing to allow time for presentence reports. The court may hold an extensive sentencing hearing, or the judge may impose a sentence without a hearing, depending on the rules of the jurisdiction and, in some cases, the preferences of the judge. Sentencing is an important stage, and in recent years, it has come under intense scrutiny by the public and the media, as well as by the courts.

8-3a   The Concept and Process of Sentencing

A **sentence** is a term of punishment imposed by a court on a convicted offender. Sentencing is one of the most controversial topics in criminal justice systems. It can be one of the simplest or one of the most complex processes. Sentencing involves numerous people, ranging from the legislators who formulate sentencing laws to the probation officers who compile the presentence reports judges use in making sentence decisions.

> **Sentence**   The punishment that the court imposes on a convicted offender.

An understanding of sentencing is complicated because sentencing differs significantly from state to state, from court to court within a state, from county to county, and even from time to time within any of these jurisdictions. Sentencing policies in the federal system differ from those in the states. Finally, attitudes about what is and is not appropriate in sentencing also differ.

Sentencing Strategies

Four main strategies are used for sentencing: indeterminate, presumptive, mandatory, and determinate sentences. Most states use a combination of these. An **indeterminate sentence** involves legislative specifications of sentence ranges that permit judges to exercise discretion in determining actual sentences. In its purest form, the indeterminate sentence would be from one day to life, but usually, it involves legislative specification of a maximum and minimum term for each offense. For example, if the legislative sentence for armed robbery is not more than 25 or less than 10 years, judges have discretion to set the sentence at any point in between.

> **Indeterminate sentence** A sentence to confinement without a definite term. Parole boards or professionals determine when the offender should be released.

Another sentencing strategy is the **presumptive sentence**. In presumptive sentencing, the normal sentence is specified for each offense, but judges are permitted to deviate from that norm. Some jurisdictions require that any deviation from a presumptive sentence be accompanied by written reasons for the deviation. Furthermore, the law may specify which conditions and circumstances may be considered for deviating from the presumptive sentence.

> **Presumptive sentence** The normal sentence is specified by statute for each offense. Judges are permitted to deviate from that sentence but usually may do so only under specified circumstances or must give reasons for the deviation.

A **mandatory sentence** is one that must be imposed upon conviction. Mandatory sentences are specified by legislatures (or by Congress) and usually involve a prison term. The mandatory approach leaves the judge no discretion is sentencing. For example, if the provision is for a specific prison term, the judge may not suspend the sentence or impose a different term as an alternative to prison.

> **Mandatory sentence** A sentence having a length imposed by the legislature, with no discretion given to the trial judge. If the defendant is convicted, the specified sentence must be imposed.

In recent years, a popular approach in many jurisdictions, including the federal, has been the statutory requirement of imposing mandatory minimum sentences. Generally, these sentences are very long. Some examples are discussed later in this chapter, but at this point, it is important to note that U.S. Supreme Court Associate Justice Anthony M. Kennedy, in speaking before the annual meeting of the American Bar Association (ABA) in August 2003, called for that organization to review the nation's use of long mandatory sentences. Justice Kennedy noted that the United States

- Has the highest rates of incarceration in the world
- Spends approximately $40 billion a year incarcerating inmates
- Has an African American inmate population that constitutes approximately 40 percent of all of the inmates in the country[22]

In response to Justice Kennedy's challenge to revisit the federal sentencing guidelines, which, according to Kennedy, should be revised downward, the ABA appointed the Justice Kennedy Commission, which was chaired by Stephen A. Saltzburg, a law professor at George Washington University Law School. Justice Kennedy said that in many cases mandatory minimum sentences "are unwise and unjust." He compared the cost of incarceration to the cost of education, with these poignant words:

> When it costs so much more to incarcerate a prisoner than to educate a child, we should take special care to ensure that we are not incarcerating too many persons for too long.... It requires one with more expertise in the area than I possess to offer a complete analysis, but it does seem justified to say this: Our resources are misspent, our punishments too severe, our sentences too long.[23]

In August 2004, the ABA adopted some of the recommendations of the Kennedy Commission, "including repealing mandatory sentencing laws, and employing 'guided discretion' sentencing systems 'to avoid unwarranted and inequitable disparities in sentencing among like offenses and offenders, but permit courts to consider unique characteristics of offenses and offenders that may warrant an increase or decrease in a sentence.'" The ABA also adopted resolutions that would require law enforcement agencies to implement policies to eradicate ethnic and racial profiling, establish standards permitting inmates to request reductions of their sentences when exceptional circumstances occur, implement policies to ensure safe correctional facilities, and design programs to assist inmates with the problems of returning to society after incarceration.[24]

Another type of sentencing strategy is the **determinate sentence**, which requires a specific sentence for a particular crime, although the trial judge may have the option of suspending that sentence or imposing probation (or some other sanction, such as work service) rather than a jail or prison term. However, once the judicial sentence is imposed, the parole board does not have the discretion to reduce the sentence by offering early parole. The determinate sentencing scheme may involve a provision for mandatory parole after a specified portion of the determinate sentence has been served. It may include a provision for sentence reduction based on **good time credits** the inmate earned.

Determinate sentences may include a provision for raising or lowering the sentence if there are **mitigating circumstances** or **aggravating circumstances**. For example, the determinate sentence for rape might be 15 years; however, if a weapon is used to threaten the victim, there may be a provision for increasing the penalty. Likewise, if there are circumstances that reduce the moral culpability of the offender, the sentence might be reduced. An example is extreme passion in a homicide, as when the accused finds his or her spouse in bed with another and, in a fit of anger, kills that person.

In any of the sentencing strategies, the power to determine sentence length may be altered by other factors. Power may be given to the governor to commute a sentence of life to a specified term of years or to commute a death sentence to a life sentence. The governor may also have the power to **pardon** an offender. In the case of a federal crime, the pardoning power resides with the president of the United States.

Two cases illustrate state pardons. In 2000, Elaine Bartlett was granted a pardon in New York after serving 16 years of a 20-years-to-life sentence under the state's strict drug possession laws, which among other provisions require that a defendant spend at least 15 years in prison.

In August 2003, Texas Governor Rick Perry pardoned 31 African Americans and 4 whites who were convicted after they were arrested in a drug sting in 1999 in Tulia, a small (population 5,000), predominantly African American Texas town, after the key witness against them, Tom Coleman, a white undercover narcotics agent, was indicted on three charges of perjury. The late Ed Bradley of CBS's *60 Minutes* described the case as "one of the worst miscarriages of justice in recent memory" and noted that the defendants were sentenced to a total of 750 years. Coleman was convicted of aggravated perjury and sentenced to 10 years probation.[25] Coleman's appeal was rejected. Under Texas law, each of the pardoned inmates may receive $25,000 per year of false imprisonment.

▶ **Determinate sentence**
A sentence for a specific crime and determined by the legislature. The parole board, correctional officials, or a judge cannot make changes in the sentence length. In some jurisdictions, the trial judge may have the power to suspend the sentence or to impose probation rather than the legislatively specified prison term.

▶ **Good time credit**   Credit resulting in a reduction of prison time. Awarded for satisfactory behavior in prison.

▶ **Mitigating circumstances**
Circumstances that do not justify or excuse a crime but that, because of justice and fairness, make the crime less reprehensible. They may be used to reduce a crime to a lesser offense, such as to reduce murder to manslaughter. Mitigating circumstances must be considered before the death penalty can be imposed. *See also* **Aggravating circumstances**.

▶ **Aggravating circumstances**
Circumstances that are above and beyond those required for the crime but that make the crime more serious. May be used in reference to many crimes, but the concept is critical particularly in capital punishment cases, where it is required.

The Sentencing Hearing

For less serious offenses, particularly when the case is not tried before a jury, the judge may pronounce sentence immediately upon finding the defendant guilty or upon accepting a guilty plea. Sentencing may be immediate when the judge has no option but to assess the statutory penalty. Sentencing may be set for a future date but may not involve any special investigations, with the judge taking recommendations from the defense and the prosecution. However, the trend is toward having a separate sentencing hearing. After the trial verdict, the judge sets a formal date for sentencing, leaving sufficient time to consider appropriate presentence investigations. It is common in capital cases to have a separate hearing on the issue of whether the defendant will be sentenced to death, life, or a term of years, depending on the legislative options in that jurisdiction.

The **presentence investigation (PSI)** may include information based on interviews with the defendant, family, friends, employers, or others who might have information pertinent to a sentencing decision. Medical, psychiatric, or other reports from experts may be included. Information on prior offenses, work records, school records, associates, pastime activities, attitudes, willingness to cooperate, and problems with alcohol or other drugs might be included as well.

If the PSI is conducted thoroughly, it is a time-consuming job. In some jurisdictions, the reports are prepared by the Department of Corrections (DOC). Most of these departments have diagnostic facilities and may be better equipped to conduct the investigations than probation officers, who conduct the PSI in many jurisdictions.

The Sentencing Decision

Judges decide most sentences (unless the legislature has removed all judicial discretion), but in some cases (usually in serious offenses, such as first-degree murder), juries have sentencing power. The judge is not required to follow the jury's recommendation in all jurisdictions, although U.S. Supreme Court decisions place some restrictions on judges. Many of those decisions relate to sentencing in capital cases; they are complex and extensive and beyond the scope of this text. This discussion is limited to the general procedures that are followed during the sentencing process, with the mention of a case the U.S. Supreme Court decided during its 2003–2004 term.

In 2004, the U.S. Supreme Court decided the case of *Blakely v. Washington*, which raised the issue of whether the Supreme Court's decision in *Ring v. Arizona* applies to noncapital cases. In *Ring*, the Supreme Court held that the aggravating circumstances used to make a defendant eligible for a capital sentence must be decided by a jury, not by a judge. Likewise, mitigating circumstances must be decided by a jury.[26]

In *Blakely*, the U.S. Supreme Court faced the question of whether *Ring* applies to noncapital sentences for which state legislation requires the consideration of aggravating and mitigating circumstances. *Blakely* also raised issues concerning sentencing guidelines. The case came from Washington State, which provided by statute that, for a variety of reasons, a trial judge may increase a sentence up to the statutory maximum. Ralph Howard Blakely was sentenced to 90 months in prison after his conviction for kidnapping his wife. Kidnapping in Washington is a felony and could result in a sentence of up to 120 months. According to the sentencing guidelines of that state, given the circumstances of Blakely's crime, he should have received a 53-month sentence, but the judge increased that to 90 months after finding evidence of domestic violence and deliberate cruelty. The judge made those findings after a special sentencing hearing, during which the standard of proof was *a preponderance of the evidence*, rather than the *beyond a reasonable doubt* standard of proof of the trial phase. Blakely appealed, arguing that the latter standard should apply and that a jury should make the decision. The Washington appellate court rejected those arguments. The U.S. Supreme Court reversed, stating that it was adhering to the 2000 controversial precedent case of *United States v. Apprendi*, in which the Supreme Court had ruled that any fact (other than a prior

▶ **Pardon** (see p. 242) An act by a state governor or the U.S. president (in federal cases) that exempts a convicted offender from punishment or, in the case of those already serving terms, further punishment and removes the legal consequences of the conviction. Pardons may also be granted after a person is released from prison. They may be absolute or conditional; individual or granted to a group, or class, of offenders; and full or partial, in which case the pardon remits only part of the punishment or removes some of the legal disabilities resulting from the conviction.

▶ **Presentence investigation (PSI)** An investigation of the background and characteristics of the defendant. It may include information that would not be admissible at the trial. It is presented to the judge to be used in determining sentence.

conviction) that could be used to enhance a sentence must be submitted to the jury and found to be true beyond a reasonable doubt.[27]

In 2004, the U.S. Supreme Court decided two cases that involved issues left unresolved by *Blakely:* (1) whether the defendant's Sixth Amendment rights are violated if a trial judge alone conducts fact finding at the sentencing hearing and (2) whether the federal sentencing guidelines were still viable.

The first case involved a defendant, Freddie J. Booker, who was convicted of possessing and distributing crack cocaine. The amount of cocaine found on Booker when he was arrested (92.5 grams), combined with his 23 prior convictions, would, under the federal sentencing guidelines, result in a sentence of slightly less than 22 years. Because at the time of his arrest, however, Booker told police that in the previous few months he had sold 20 ounces of cocaine, at the sentencing hearing, the trial judge added that amount to the 92.5 grams. The judge also added an obstruction of justice conviction based on his own determination that Booker had committed perjury at the trial. The result of these add-ons was a 30-year sentence, which was reversed by the court of appeals.

The second case involved Duncan Fanfan, who was convicted of conspiracy to distribute at least 500 grams of powder cocaine. At the sentencing hearing, the prosecution offered evidence that Fanfan also dealt in crack cocaine, which carries a longer sentence. Initially, the federal sentencing judge sentenced Fanfan to 16 years in prison; however, based on *Blakely,* decided four days previously, the judge gave the defendant only a 6½-year sentence. That sentence was based on the amount of drugs involved in the jury decision. In agreeing to review the case, the U.S. Supreme Court bypassed the First Circuit Court of Appeals in Boston and accepted the case directly from the trial decision.

In January 2005, the U.S. Supreme Court handed down its decisions in both *United States v. Booker* and *United States v. Fanfan,* with a 5-to-4 vote. Justice John Paul Stevens, writing for the majority in one opinion, emphasized that the right to a trial by jury guaranteed by the Sixth Amendment (see Appendix A) is violated when a sentence is based on facts determined by the judge but not the jury. The second opinion, written by Justice Stephen G. Breyer, reduced the federal sentencing guidelines to an advisory role. According to Breyer, "The district courts, while not bound to apply the guidelines, must consult those guidelines and take them into account when sentencing." But Breyer noted that Congress could act to change the federal sentencing guidelines, when he said, "The ball now lies in Congress' court. The national legislature is equipped to devise and install, long-term, the sentencing system compatible with the Constitution, that Congress judges best for the federal system of justice." It can be presumed that this ruling, at least for now, leaves federal sentencing decisions up to trial judges, which could and probably will result in widely varying sentences, a situation the federal guidelines were designed to avoid. Meanwhile, we can expect many defendants who were sentenced under the federal guidelines to appeal those sentences. Even Justice Breyer said, "Ours is not the last word." Congress did not act, however, and cases were accumulating on appeal, as lower federal courts issued conflicting rulings. Thus, in November 2006, the U.S. Supreme Court accepted two cases on the issue of the role of federal sentencing guidelines after *Booker.* Decisions in *Rita v. United States* and *Claiborne v. United States* were expected by the end of June 2007.[28]

One final sentencing decision is important to this discussion. In *Shepard v. United States,* decided in March 2005, the U.S. Supreme Court reexamined the role of judges in sentencing. Recall that in *Apprendi,* discussed earlier, the Court ruled that any fact that is used to enhance a sentence, other than a prior conviction, must be determined by a jury. The *Shepard* case involved a defendant who had previously entered guilty pleas to four burglaries, but his plea agreement did not contain the necessary details of those crimes. The federal statute under which Shepard entered a guilty plea to being a felon in possession of a firearm, the Armed Career Criminal Act (ACCA), permits enhanced penalties for offenders who are convicted of specified prior violent felonies. This provision includes burglaries but only if they are committed within a building or an enclosed space, such as a house. The burglary of a car or a boat does not meet the requirement for an enhanced penalty. Since Shepard's plea agreement did not note the required details of his burglary, and the district court ruled that the prosecutor did not present other evidence showing that Shepard's prior burglaries counted, the judge imposed a three-year sentence. The appellate court ruled that the trial judge should have looked at police reports to obtain the needed information, and in effect, ordered the lower court to impose the 15-year mandatory, minimum sentence.

The U.S. Supreme Court reversed the decision of the appellate court, ruling by a 5-to-4 vote that *Apprendi* and other recent cases limit trial judges to official court documents when they consider the nature of prior offenses for purposes of enhancing a sentence; thus, it was inappropriate to go beyond Shepard's plea agreement to determine whether his prior burglaries met the requirements for an enhanced sentence under the ACCA.[29]

In jurisdictions in which the jury has sentencing power, the judge instructs the jury concerning the law and its application to sentencing. Many factors might be considered in the sentencing decision. Those factors may be designated by statute. Some states have formalized and restricted the factors that may be considered. Many require that evidence of aggravating or mitigating circumstances be presented. Some jurisdictions use sentencing formulas, which indicate the weight to be given to specific factors, such as the nature of the crime.

If the defendant has been convicted of more than one offense, the judge usually has the authority to determine whether the sentences are to be imposed concurrently or consecutively. With a **concurrent sentence**, the defendant satisfies the terms of all sentences at the same time. For example, if the defendant is sentenced to 20 years for each of three counts of armed robbery, the total number of years served will be 20 if the sentences are concurrent. With a **consecutive sentence**, the defendant will have to serve 60 years (unless the term is reduced by parole or good time credit or is commuted or pardoned). Most multiple sentences are imposed concurrently.

After the sentence is determined, the judge reads the sentence to the defendant, and the sentence is recorded in court records. If the sentence involves incarceration, the defendant generally is taken into custody immediately (or returned to custody if he or she had not been released before trial). The judge may allow the defendant some time to prepare for incarceration, but that rarely occurs and generally applies only in the cases of government officials or other people who might, in the eyes of the judge, need time to get their affairs in order and who would not be a danger to society or flee the jurisdiction.

One final issue concerning the sentencing decision should be noted. In some jurisdictions, crime victims are permitted to express their concerns and opinions on issues such as sentencing. The role of victims in sentencing was limited by the U.S. Supreme Court in a 1987 decision, *Booth v. Maryland*, in which the Court held that the defendant's constitutional rights are violated when Victim Impact Statements (VIS) contain information such as the severe emotional impact of the crime on the family, the personal characteristics of the victim, and the family members' opinions and characterizations of the crime and the offender. When the issue arose in the sentencing phase of a capital case, the Court emphasized its concern that, in such serious cases, decisions should be based on reason, not on emotion. Thus, the jury should not hear this type of information, which "can serve no other purpose than to inflame the jury and divert it from deciding the case on the relevant evidence concerning the crime and the defendant."[30]

In 1991, the U.S. Supreme Court reversed itself on the ruling in *Booth* and another case. In *Payne v. Tennessee*, the Court ruled that a VIS may be used at capital sentencing hearings. "A state may legitimately conclude that evidence about the victim and about the impact of the murder on the victim's family is relevant to the jury's decision as to whether or not the death penalty should be imposed."[31]

In 1995, the Washington Supreme Court upheld that state's provision for admitting victim impact evidence during the sentencing phase of a capital trial. The U.S. Supreme Court refused to hear an appeal, thus permitting the lower court decision to stand.[32]

> **Concurrent sentence**
> A sentence for more than one offense served at the same time. For example, if an offender receives a three-year prison term for robbery and a five-year prison term for assault, these sentences to be served concurrently, the total prison sentence is five years.

> **Consecutive sentence**
> A term of imprisonment for more than one offense that must be served one following the other. If an offender receives a three-year term for robbery and a five-year term for assault, the defendant has an eight-year term.

8-3b   Types of Sentences

In some jurisdictions, judges have numerous sentencing options. In addition to incarcerating defendants for short jail terms or for longer prison terms, judges may place offenders on probation or impose fines. Judges may use a combination of these possibilities along with others, such as work assignments. Sentencing options differ from jurisdiction to jurisdiction and vary by crime, but it is possible to examine the *types* of sentences. They are listed and defined in Spotlight 8-3 and are discussed briefly in this section.

A **fine** is a punishment in which the offender is ordered to pay a sum of money to the state in lieu of or in addition to other forms of punishment. Fines are used in combination with probation and other alternatives to confinement. Historically, fines were used primarily in cases involving traffic violations or other nonviolent offenses. Recently, with the increasing interest in victim compensation, including compensation for violent and property crimes, some jurisdictions have begun to assess fines against offenders convicted of violent crimes. Fines are used in conjunction with incarceration as well, with the latter being extended beyond the original sentence if the fine is not paid.

Another type of sentence that is growing in use is **restitution**, which requires offenders to reimburse victims financially or with services. The primary rationale for restitution is victim compensation; retribution is another. It is also argued that the state should assist crime victims, and restitution provides one source of revenue at the expense of the offender. And there is some evidence, especially among juveniles, that there is a greater chance of reducing the number of repeat offenders if defendants participate in some form of restitution, either financial or work service.

Restitution may be combined with work assignments. The work assignments may be designed to benefit only the victim or a larger group, as in the case of **community work service** assignments. Some administrative questions are left open by the statutes providing for restitution or community work service. Some are ambiguous about the kind of work that may be assigned. Others require work programs or restitution of a nature that aids the victim but also fosters rehabilitation of the offender. Usually, community work service

Fine   The payment of a sum of money to a court by the convicted defendant in addition to or instead of other punishment(s).

Restitution   Punishment that requires an offender to repay the victim with services or money. This punishment may be imposed instead of or in addition to other punishment or fines and may be a requirement of parole.

Community work service   Punishment assigning the offender to community service or work projects. Sometimes, it is combined with restitution or probation.

Spotlight 8-3   **Types of Sentences**

- **Death penalty** In most States, for the most serious crimes such as murder, the courts may sentence an offender to death by lethal injection, electrocution, exposure to lethal gas, hanging, or other method specified by State law.
- **Incarceration** The confinement of a convicted criminal in a Federal or State prison or a local jail to serve a court-imposed sentence. Confinement is usually in a jail, administered locally, or a prison, operated by the State or Federal Government. In many States, offenders sentenced to one year or less are held in a jail; those sentenced to longer terms are committed to a State prison.
- **Probation** The sentencing of an offender to community supervision by a probation agency, often as a result of suspending a sentence to confinement. Such supervision normally entails specific rules of conduct while in the community. If the rules are violated, a sentence to confinement may be imposed. Probation is the most widely used correctional disposition in the United States.
- **Split sentences, shock probation, and intermittent confinement** A penalty that explicitly requires the con-

victed person to serve a brief period of confinement in a local, State, or Federal facility (the "shock") followed by a period of probation. This penalty attempts to combine the use of community supervision with a short incarceration experience. Some sentences are periodic rather than continuous; for example, an offender may be required to spend a certain number of weekends in jail.
- **Restitution and victim compensation** The offender is required to provide financial repayment or, in some jurisdictions, services in lieu of monetary restitution, for the losses incurred by the victim.
- **Community service** The offender is required to perform a specified amount of public service work, such as collecting trash in parks or other public facilities.
  Fines An economic penalty that requires the offender to pay a specified sum of money within limits set by law. Fines are often imposed in addition to probation or as alternatives in incarceration.

Source: Bureau of Justice Statistics, *Report to the Nation on Crime and Justice: The Data*, 2d ed. (Washington, D.C.: U.S Department of Justice, 1988), p. 96.

orders impose strict rules on the offender and, in many cases, are combined with probation, which is the most frequently used sanction for criminal activity.

Probation is used nearly three times as often as incarceration. It is a sentence in which the defendant is released into the community for a specified period, theoretically under supervision. It has been argued that probation is not a sentence, but it is in the sense that it may be imposed only by the judiciary, which may set terms and conditions for the sentence. These are discussed in more detail, along with other aspects of probation, in Chapter 11. It is important to understand at this point, however, that probation may be imposed in lieu of or in combination with a fine, restitution, or community service. It may be imposed in conjunction with a brief period of incarceration or with electronic monitoring, also discussed in Chapter 11.

Another type of sentencing, **corporal punishment**, is not a legal sentence in the United States at this time. The last statute to be repealed was the Delaware whipping statute in 1973. In the past three decades, however, some scholars have argued for a return to corporal punishment, considering it a less expensive and more humane punishment than incarceration.

Another type of sentence that was used extensively in the past is **capital punishment**. Over the years, capital punishment has been in and out of favor, with abolition movements beginning in the 1700s, gaining momentum in the late 1800s, and leading to actual abolition of the death penalty in many states during the 20th century, only to have it reinstated in most. We have already looked at some of the constitutional issues surrounding capital punishment. Spotlight 8-4 presents other issues, along with a brief history of recent developments in U.S. capital punishment.

One final and critical point about capital punishment is the number of death row inmates who have been exonerated because new evidence pointed to the fact that they did not commit the crimes for which they were given the death sentence. According to the Death Penalty Information Center, over 123 death row inmates have been exonerated since 1973, with 6 exonerations in 2004 and 12 in 2003. The number per state is graphed in Figure 8-1.

The final major type of punishment is confinement, or **incarceration**. Offenders may be incarcerated in a jail (generally used for those awaiting trial or sentenced to short terms, usually less than a year) or in a prison (used for offenders who have been convicted of serious crimes and sentenced to death or to long terms of confinement) or

> ▶ **Corporal punishment**
> Physical punishment, such as beatings or whippings.

> ▶ **Capital punishment**
> Punishment by death for those convicted of capital crimes.

> ▶ **Incarceration**
> Imprisonment in a jail, a prison, or another type of penal institution.

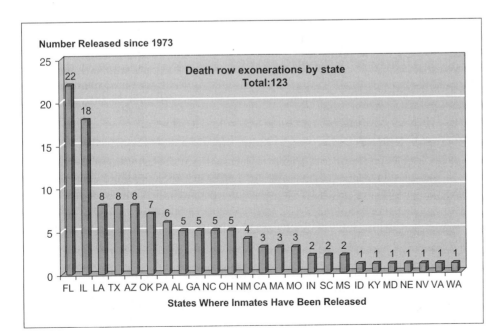

Figure 8-1
Innocence and the Death Penalty
Source: Staff Report, House Judiciary Subcommittee on Civil and Constitutional Rights, October 1993, with updates from the Death Penalty Information Center, http://www.deathpenaltyinfo.org/FactSheet.pdf, accessed 24 March 2007.

Spotlight 8-4   **Capital Punishment in the United States: A Brief History**

In 1972 in *Furman v. Georgia*, the U.S. Supreme Court held that, although capital punishment is not per se unconstitutional, it is unconstitutional when in its application it involves discrimination caused by arbitrary and capricious administration of the sentence. *Furman* invalidated most capital punishment statutes in existence at the time, but the Supreme Court left the door open for new legislation providing for capital punishment if it is applied without violating defendants' constitutional rights.[1]

By 1976, 36 states had responded with new capital punishment statutes, although some of those have been challenged in the courts. In 1977, the constitutional issues were satisfied in the case of the Utah statute, and Gary Gilmore became the first person executed since 1967. In May 1979, after a long and complicated legal battle, John Spenkelink, convicted of murdering a man with a hatchet, was the first involuntary inmate to die of capital punishment in the United States since 1967 (Gilmore refused to appeal his sentence and asked that it be carried out). Spenkelink was executed in Old Sparky, Florida's electric chair.

The movement toward capital punishment was highlighted in 1995, when New York revived the death penalty after 18 years, making New York the 38th state with capital punishment. Governor George E. Pataki signed the bill with two pens owned by slain police officers. Former New York Governor Mario Cuomo had vetoed death penalty legislation 12 times. In June 2004, the state's highest court ruled that the legislation was unconstitutional as constructed, and by November 2004, legislators were predicting that, with the changing political climate, there was little chance the statute would be revised.[2]

In 1999, the U.S. Supreme Court agreed to decide whether electrocution as the only method of capital punishment in Florida constituted cruel and unusual punishment. In January 2000, however, the Florida legislature enacted a new statute, which provides that inmates under a death sentence may choose between electrocution and lethal injection. The Supreme Court dismissed the Florida appeal because the issue, which came from a death row inmate who would be able to choose lethal injection, was moot.[3]

At the end of its 2005–2006 term, the U.S. Supreme Court analyzed the constitutionality of the use of lethal injection for execution. In *Hill v. McDonough*, a unanimous Court held that a Florida inmate may challenge the choice of drugs and the manner in which the state proposed to administer them in his execution. However, just one month earlier, the Court had refused to review *Abdur' Rahman v. Bredesen*, which also involved a challenge to lethal injection.[4]

During its 2005–2006 term, in *Kansas v. Marsh*, the U.S. Supreme Court upheld the Kansas law mandating the death penalty if a jury finds that the aggravating and mitigating circumstances in a given case are equivalent. The Court also held, in *House v. Bell*, that even after a defendant has exhausted all regular appeals in a death penalty case, if new evidence is available, the defendant can ask for a new review of the case.[5]

A recent issue that has received considerable attention in the media as well as in the courts is the possibility that innocent people may be convicted of capital murder and executed. After evidence (primarily DNA) showed that a death row inmate in Illinois was innocent, in 2000 Governor George H. Ryan announced that he would impose a moratorium on

---

may be confined in a community treatment center. These facilities, along with the issues surrounding confinement and incarceration, are discussed in Chapters 10 and 11.

8-3c   Current Sentencing Issues

There are many issues in sentencing. This section considers four: (1) sentence disparity, (2) three strikes and you're out legislation (3) truth in sentencing legislation, and (4) treatment practices.

Sentence Disparity

▶ **Sentence disparity** Inequalities and differences in sentencing as, for example, when people found guilty of the same crime receive sentences varying in length and type, without reasonable justification for those differences.

Although there is great concern about alleged **sentence disparity**, its meaning is not clear. Some use the term to refer to any differences that they think are unfair or inappropriate. Thus, the differences between legislatively determined sentences in two jurisdictions might be viewed as disparate. Others limit the definition of the term to the differences in sentences imposed by judges in similar cases. Some include any differences; others look to the circumstances surrounding the crime before determining whether sentences are disparate.

Sentence disparity may stem from legislative, judicial, or administrative decisions. Sentence length may vary from jurisdiction to jurisdiction because legislatures establish different terms for the same crime. Legislatures may differ with regard to whether a defendant with multiple sentences serves them concurrently or consecutively. Legislative the death penalty in Illinois until the completion of an inquiry on why so many innocent people had been given the death sentence. This action gave significant impetus to the current movement toward a moratorium on executions, although some states (e.g., Texas and Florida) continued with them. Before Ryan left office in January 2003, he pardoned four death row inmates and commuted to life the rest of the death row sentences. His successor continued the execution moratorium. In the fall of 2003, the Illinois legislature overrode the governor's veto on a new capital punishment bill designed to decrease the chances of sending an innocent person to death row. The governor indicated that he would keep the moratorium on capital punishment in place until it could be determined whether the new statute accomplishes its purpose.[6] In 2004, the Illinois Supreme Court upheld the commutations made by Governor Ryan.[7]

In June 2001, the U.S. Supreme Court reversed the death sentence of Johnny Paul Penry, a Texas death row inmate, who came within three hours of execution on 16 November 2000. The case was decided on narrow procedural grounds involving jury instructions and did not reach the issue of whether the mentally ill may be executed.[8] But in 2002, the U.S. Supreme Court held that it is unconstitutional to execute a mentally retarded (but not necessarily mentally ill) person. *Atkins v. Virginia* involved a man who was sentenced to death for a murder he committed when he was 18. Daryl R. Atkins has an IQ of 59. The U.S. Supreme Court left it to the states to determine when a person is mentally retarded and did not provide much guidance for making that determination. In

March 2003, Texas executed James Colburn, who had been diagnosed as paranoid schizophrenic since he was 14. Colburn had made approximately 15 suicide attempts, claiming that voices in his head told him to take his own life. But there was also evidence that Colburn knew what was happening to him, understood the process, and even apologized to the victim's family before he was executed.[9]

According to the Death Penalty Information Center, as of 9 May 2007, 1,075 persons had been executed since 1976, with 60 of those executions occurring in 2005, 53 in 2006, and 18 in 2007. Of the 3,350 inmates on death row as of 9 May 2007, 1,397 are black, 359 are Hispanic, 1,517 are white, and 77 are other.[10]

1. Furman v. Georgia, 408 U.S. 238 (1972).
2. "Lawmakers See Little Chance to Fix Flaws in New York's Death Penalty Statute This Year," *New York Times* (18 November 2004), p. 25. The case is People v. Lavalle, 783 N.Y.S.2d 485 (2004).
3. "New York Revives Death Penalty after Eighteen Years," *New York Times* (8 March 1995), p. 1. See New York Penal Code, Section 60.06 (2007).
4. Hill v. McDonough, 126 S.Ct. 2096 (2006); Abdur' Rahman v. Bredesen, 181 S.W.3d 292, *cert. denied*, 126 S.Ct. 2288 (2006).
5. Kansas v. Marsh, 126 S.Ct. 2516 (2006); House v. Bell, 126 S.Ct. 2064 (2006).
6. "At Last, Death Penalty Reform," *Chicago Tribune* (20 November 2003), p. 30.
7. People ex rel. Madigan v. Snyder, 804 N.E.2d 546 (Ill. 2004).
8. Penry v. Johnson, 532 U.S. 782 (2001).
9. Atkins v. Virginia, 536 U.S. 304 (2002); "A Mentally Ill Killer Is Executed in Texas," *New York Times* (27 March 2003), p. 12.
10. "Facts about the Death Penalty," *Death Penalty Information Center*, http://www.deathpenaltyinfo.org, retrieved 12 May 2007.

sentences may be disparate if within a system there are sentences that are considered unfair. Sentence disparity may also result from decisions made by others. For example, prosecutors may influence a sentence. In the plea bargaining process, the prosecutor may offer a deal that involves a lesser penalty for one offense if the offender pleads guilty to another or to several other offenses.

Sentencing disparity may also occur because juries have considerable discretion, even when they are not empowered to determine sentences. If they think that the judge will be too harsh or if they perceive that the legislative sentence is unfair, jurors may refuse to convict. In that case, juries have the ultimate power to decide sentences.

Administrative discretion may also result in sentence disparity. Although parole has been abolished in some states, where it does exist, parole authorities have great latitude in deciding actual time served. Even when the legislature specifies by statute the percentage of a term that must be served before an offender is eligible for parole, the parole board has the power to determine when, if ever, that person will be released before the end of the actual sentence (parole is discussed in Chapter 11).

Most of the allegations of sentence disparity have involved the variables of race, ethnicity, and gender. Earlier studies examining these variables in sentencing did not agree on whether discrimination existed and, if it did, to what extent and why. Modern scholars do not agree either, and the debate continues. A few studies are illustrative.

Issues of Race and Gender Some criminologists argue that criminal justice systems are racist in sentencing. Michael J. Lynch and W. Byron Groves, in their explanation of radical criminology (an approach to the study of crime and criminals that suggests a connection between economic reality and social phenomena, such as racism), referred to numerous studies that support this position.

> These studies show that minorities, particularly blacks, are discriminated against in the sentencing process. Blacks receive longer sentences than whites for the same crime, and blacks who victimize whites receive longer sentences than blacks who victimize blacks. Recent research…on rape indicates that this bias remains in force today.[33]

In a 1994 publication, law professor Michael Tonry reported his analysis of jail and prison data and concluded that racial disparities in sentencing had "steadily gotten worse since 1980." Tonry attributed this to politically motivated decisions by Republican administrations to increase penalties for drug violations, when they knew that such increases would impact minorities negatively but would not result in a significant reduction of the crime rate. Tonry gave several reasons for his conclusions. He charged that drug arrests are easier to make in inner-city minority areas than in areas dominated by the middle and upper classes. Increased penalties have been aimed primarily at the illegal use of crack cocaine, used by minorities more frequently than powder cocaine, "a pharmacologically indistinguishable drug used primarily by middle-class Whites."[34]

In *United States v. Armstrong*, discussed earlier, the differences between African Americans and whites in drug sentences were raised by African American defendants, who claimed that they were denied equal protection because of the higher sentences (approximately 100-to-1) for the illegal distribution or possession of crack, as compared with powder cocaine. In *Armstrong*, the U.S. Supreme Court held that the African American defendants had not shown racial discrimination. According to the Court, the fact that 88.3 percent of all federal prosecutions for crack cocaine violations were against African Americans did not in itself prove racial discrimination.[35] The U.S. Sentencing Commission has recommended changing the 100-to-1 ratio, but thus far, Congress has not done so.

It has also been alleged that sentence disparity is related to the offender's gender. Some researchers say that women are treated differentially at every stage in U.S. criminal justice systems and that this treatment is sexist; that is, women are discriminated against *because* of their gender.

Others say that the system is more lenient toward women than toward men at every level and that, in particular, women receive lighter sentences than men for the same offenses. That, too, must be analyzed in terms of the legal factors courts may consider in sentencing, such as prior convictions and the seriousness of the current offense. It is argued that, when these factors are analyzed, there is little or no evidence of gender bias in sentencing.[36]

In one study, Darrell J. Steffensmeier reviewed the empirical evidence concerning the differential sentencing of women and concluded that, although preferential treatment exists, it is of small magnitude. He argued that the "changing sex role definitions and the contemporary women's movement have had little impact on sentencing outcomes of either male or female defendants" and that the differentials by gender have been diminished.[37]

In a much later study, Steffensmeier and his colleagues analyzed gender and imprisonment decisions during a two-year period in Pennsylvania. They found support for earlier research, concluding that, in general, women received more lenient sentences than men. However, unlike some of their predecessors, these scholars concluded that the differences were due to "the type or seriousness of the crime committed and the defendant's prior record, not the defendant's gender (or, for that matter, age, race, or other background/contextual variables)."[38]

After a review of the literature on the general issue of disparity in race and gender in the criminal justice system, two scholars, Ronald L. Akers and Christine S. Sellers, concluded as follows:

> Research evidence does not show that racism and sexism blatantly infest the criminal justice system. At the same time, it does not show that the system is free of bias. The

preponderance of research findings, however, support the conclusion....that the criminal justice system makes decisions based more on legally relevant variables than on extra-legal variables.[39]

Efforts to Control Sentencing   Most allegations of sentence disparity are aimed at judges, and many of the recent changes in sentencing laws have been aimed at controlling or removing judicial discretion in sentencing. Various solutions to sentence disparity have been proposed, but most of the reform efforts have centered on two approaches: either controlling judicial discretion or removing it from the sentencing process. This is done primarily through the imposition of sentencing guidelines, or requirements. Sentencing guidelines are seen as a way to control discretion without abolishing it, while correcting the extreme disparity that can result from individualized sentencing.

Basically, guidelines work as follows. A judge has an offender to sentence. Without guidelines, the judge may consider the offender's background, the nature of the offense, and other variables. When guidelines are available, presumably the relevance of these and other variables has been researched. Thus, the judge has a benchmark of an appropriate penalty in such circumstances. However, the judge may decide that it is reasonable in a given case to deviate from the guidelines; in that situation, reasons should be given.

Sentencing guidelines may be based on an empirical analysis of what *has* been done in the jurisdiction, not a philosophy of what *ought* to be done. Sentencing guidelines may be based on what it is thought *should* be done. This may occur in a variety of ways. The guidelines may be recommended by a committee and accepted and thus mandated by the legislature, or they may be adopted by judges to apply to their jurisdictions.

Sentencing guidelines have, however, been challenged in many cases, at both the federal and state levels. In 2003, U.S. Department of Justice (DOJ) officials announced that they would begin monitoring federal judges who sentenced below federal guidelines. This move was understood by some to mean that the DOJ would be making a list of judges who exercise more discretion than the DOJ thinks wise. Specifically, federal prosecutors were directed to notify the DOJ when federal judges sentence below the guidelines; decisions would then be made concerning whether those sentences should be appealed. Attorney General John Ashcroft issued a policy statement in a memo to federal prosecutors on 28 July 2003, which included these words:

> The public in general and crime victims in particular rightly expect that the penalties established by law for specific crimes will be sought and imposed by those who serve in the criminal justice system.[40]

The federal judiciary reacted sternly to this memo and to a law enacted 30 April 2003 as a part of the PROTECT (Prosecutorial Remedies and Other Tools to end the Exploitation of Children Today) Act of 2003. Among other provisions, the PROTECT Act limits the cases in which a federal judge may issue a lighter sentence than the federal sentencing guidelines, gives Congress (without the permission of the sentencing judge) access to certain documents from the case, and requires the reporting of lighter sentences. The act also requires that, when a federal court of appeals reviews a sentencing decision of a federal district court, it must do so *de novo*, which means anew, as if the hearing had not been held before. Some federal judges protested the new law and called for its repeal, with some retiring rather than enforce the law. In September 2003, the Judicial Conference of the United States, which is headed by the U.S. Supreme Court (at that time, Justice William H. Rehnquist) and includes the 27 federal judges who make policy for the federal judiciary, called for a repeal of the law.[41]

In January 2004, Chief Justice Rehnquist focused his annual state of the judiciary on the PROTECT Act. The chief justice stated that the law "could appear to be an unwarranted and ill-considered effort to intimidate individual judges in the performance of their judicial duties." The chief justice continued by declaring, "It seems that the traditional interchange between the Congress and the judiciary broke down" when the law was passed without any formal input from the judiciary. The chair of the House Judiciary Committee, Representative F. James Sensenbrenner Jr., said there was no breakdown in communication. Congress knew the judiciary would oppose the bill, but it was necessary because federal judges were using "downward departures" (that is, lighter sentences) in applying the federal sentencing guidelines.[42] But, as noted earlier in this chapter, significant changes have been made in the impact of the federal sentencing guidelines as a result of the *Booker* and *Fanfan* cases decided by the U.S. Supreme Court in 2005.

The proposal to reduce or remove judicial sentencing discretion was manifested primarily in the adoption of determinate sentencing, which began in the 1970s. One of the most rigid of the new determinate sentencing statutes was that of California, the state that pioneered the indeterminate sentence and that used it most extensively.[43] The California statute removes the rehabilitation philosophy and substitutes punishment as the reason for incarceration. It specifies that sentences are not to be disparate and that defendants charged with similar offenses should receive similar sentences. The judge may decide on the basis of aggravating or mitigating circumstances to raise or lower the presumed sentence, but written reasons must be given for deviating from it. However, in January 2007, the U.S. Supreme Court held that this sentencing provision is unconstitutional because it violates a defendant's right to a jury trial under the Sixth Amendment (see Appendix A).

Cunningham v. California involved a defendant who was convicted of continuous sexual abuse of a child. Under the terms of the California sentencing statute, the defendant could be sentenced to (1) a lower-term sentence of six years, (2) a middle-term sentence of 12 years, or (3) an upper-term sentence of 16 years. The statute required the trial judge to sentence the defendant in this case to the middle term unless he could find one or more aggravating circumstances. The judge found six aggravating circumstances and one mitigating factor (no prior record), concluded that the aggravating factors outweighed the mitigating factor, and sentenced the defendant to 16 years in prison. The U.S. Supreme Court held that the determination of aggravating and mitigating factors should have been decided by the jury, not the judge, and remanded the case. According to Justice Ruth Bader Ginsburg, who wrote the opinion for a majority of six justices, "Factfinding to elevate a sentence from 12 to 16 years, our decisions make plain, falls within the province of the jury."[44]

Other provisions of the California sentencing statute presumably will survive. For example, the statute abolishes the parole board, with its discretion to determine release, but it provides that all releasees be placed under parole *supervision* for one year upon release.

California has also become less punitive in some respects. The state permits sentences to be reduced by good time credits earned during incarceration, and as we will see in Chapter 11, it has moved away from harsh punishment toward a treatment philosophy for some nonviolent drug offenders. However, the harsh and determinate punishment approach is seen in other areas of sentencing, as the next section illustrates.

Three Strikes and You're Out

> ▶ **Three strikes and you're out** Legislation enacted in recent years and designed to impose long sentences on persons who commit three or more serious crimes.

The emphasis on reducing sentence disparity has been manifested most clearly in the national focus on the habitual offender, summarized in the 1994 political slogan **three strikes and you're out**. The phrase figured prominently at the state as well as the national level after 12-year-old Polly Klaas was kidnapped from her home in 1993 while her parents and her friends—who were attending her slumber party—were sleeping. Polly was sexually assaulted and murdered. Richard Allen Davis, who had two prior kidnap convictions, was convicted and sentenced to death for the crimes against Polly. California led in the enactment of three strikes legislation and was quickly followed by most states and the federal government. But California's legislation is one of the toughest. It provides for a mandatory sentence for all persons convicted of a third felony, and that third strike may be any felony. The first two felonies, however, must be serious or violent ones. California also provides harsher penalties for two strikes.

The alleged lack of justice in the California statute has been evidenced in many sentences, but one in particular should be noted. A defendant received a sentence of 25-years-to-life after his conviction for stealing a $20 bottle of vitamins, his third strike. The U.S. Supreme Court refused to review the case, but a written opinion signed by associate justices John Paul Stevens, David Souter, and Ruth Bader Ginsberg raised issues concerning the legality of such a long sentence and urged inmates with similar sentences to challenge their sentences.[45]

In 2003, the U.S. Supreme Court decided two three strikes cases and upheld the legislation in question. These cases are critical ones in sentencing, as illustrated by the following excerpts from *Ewing v. California*. Read carefully the detailed recounting of the facts of Ewing's crime, as well as the history and rationale for three strikes legislation. Note the U.S. Supreme Court's discussion of the discretion that still remains within the sentencing structure of this strict law, as the Court explains what is meant by a *wobbler*.[46]

Ewing v. California

In this case we decide whether the Eighth Amendment prohibits the State of California from sentencing a repeat felon to a prison term of 25 years to life under the State's "Three Strikes and You're Out" law.

California's three strikes law reflects a shift in the State's sentencing policies toward incapacitating and deterring repeat offenders who threaten the public safety. The law was designed "to ensure longer prison sentences and greater punishment for those who commit a felony and have been previously convicted of serious and/or violent felony offenses."…

Under California law, certain offenses may be classified as either felonies or misdemeanors. These crimes are known as "wobblers." Some crimes that would otherwise be misdemeanors become "wobblers" because of the defendant's prior record. Both types of "wobblers" are triggering offenses under the three strikes law only when they are treated as felonies.…

In California, prosecutors may exercise their discretion to charge a "wobbler" as either a felony or a misdemeanor. Likewise, California trial courts have discretion to reduce a "wobbler" charged as a felony to a misdemeanor either before preliminary examination or at sentencing to avoid imposing a three strikes sentence. In exercising this discretion, the court may consider "those factors that direct similar sentencing decisions," such as "the nature and circumstances of the offense, the defendant's appreciation of and attitude toward the offense,…[and] the general objectives of sentencing."

California trial courts can also vacate allegations of prior "serious" or "violent" felony convictions.…

[The U.S. Supreme Court then stated the facts of this case.]

On parole from a nine-year term, petitioner Gary Ewing walked into the pro shop…. He walked out with three golf clubs, priced at $399 apiece, concealed in his pants leg. A shop employee, whose suspicions were aroused when he observed Ewing limp out of the pro shop, telephoned the police. The police apprehended Ewing in the parking lot.

Ewing is no stranger to the criminal justice system. In 1984, at the age of 22, he pleaded guilty to theft. The court sentenced him to six months in jail, three years' probation, and a $300 fine. In 1988, he was convicted of felony grand theft auto and sentenced to one year in jail and three years' probation. After Ewing completed probation, however, the sentencing court reduced the crime to a misdemeanor, permitted Ewing to withdraw his guilty plea, and dismissed the case. In 1990, he was convicted of petty theft with a prior and sentenced to 60 days in the county jail and three years' probation. In 1992 Ewing was convicted of battery and sentenced to 30 days in the county jail and two years' summary probation. One month later, he was convicted of theft and sentenced to 10 days in the county jail and 12 months' probation. In January 1993, Ewing was convicted of burglary and sentenced to 60 days in the county jail and one year's summary probation. In July 1993, he was convicted of appropriating lost property and sentenced to 10 days in the county jail and two years' summary probation. In September 1993, he was convicted of unlawfully possessing a firearm and trespassing and sentenced to 30 days in the county jail and one year's probation.

In October and November 1993, Ewing committed three burglaries and one robbery at a Long Beach, California, apartment complex over a five-week period. He awakened one of his victims, asleep on her living room sofa, as he tried to disconnect her video cassette recorder from the television in that room. When she screamed, Ewing ran out the front door. On another occasion, Ewing accosted a victim in the mailroom of the apartment complex. Ewing claimed to have a gun and ordered the victim to hand over his wallet. When the victim resisted, Ewing produced a knife and forced the victim back to the apartment itself. While Ewing rifled through the bedroom, the victim fled the apartment screaming for help. Ewing absconded with the victim's money and credit cards.

On December 9, 1993, Ewing was arrested on the premises of the apartment complex for trespassing and lying to a police officer. The knife used in the robbery and a glass cocaine pipe were later found in the back seat of the patrol car used to transport Ewing to the police station. A jury convicted Ewing of first-degree robbery and three counts of residential burglary. Sentenced to nine years and eight months in prison, Ewing was paroled in 1999.

Only 10 months later, Ewing stole the golf clubs at issue in this case. He was charged with, and ultimately convicted of, one count of felony grand theft of personal property in excess of $400. As required by the three strikes law, the prosecutor formally alleged, and the trial court later found, that Ewing had been convicted previously of four serious or violent felonies for the three burglaries and the robbery in the Long Beach apartment complex.

At the sentencing hearing, Ewing asked the court to reduce the conviction for grand theft, a "wobbler" under California law, to a misdemeanor so as to avoid a three strikes sentence. Ewing also asked the trial court to exercise its discretion to dismiss the allegations of some or all of his prior serious or violent felony convictions, again for purposes of avoiding a three strikes sentence. Before sentencing Ewing, the trial court took note of his entire criminal history, including the fact that he was on parole when he committed his latest offense. The court also heard arguments from defense counsel and a plea from Ewing himself.

In the end, the trial judge determined that the grand theft should remain a felony. The court also ruled that the four prior strikes for the three burglaries and the robbery in Long Beach should stand. As a newly convicted felon with two or more "serious" or "violent" felony convictions in his past, Ewing was sentenced under the three strikes law to 25 years to life....

[The U.S. Supreme Court then began its lengthy analysis of the legal issues in the case, reviewing the relevant case law concerning the proportionality of sentences before continuing with the following statement of the history and rationale of three strikes legislation.]

For many years, most States have had laws providing for enhanced sentencing of repeat offenders...[but between 1993 and 1995 the current three strikes legislation approach began]. These laws responded to widespread public concerns about crime by targeting the class of offenders who pose the greatest threat to public safety: career criminals.... Throughout the States, legislatures enacting three strikes laws made a deliberate policy choice that individuals who have repeatedly engaged in serious or violent criminal behavior, and whose conduct has not been deterred by more conventional approaches to punishment, must be isolated from society in order to protect the public safety....

Our traditional deference to legislative policy choices finds a corollary in the principle that the Constitution "does not mandate adoption of any one penological theory." A sentence can have a variety of justifications, such as incapacitation, deterrence, retribution, or rehabilitation. Some or all of these justifications may play a role in a State's sentencing scheme. Selecting the sentencing rationales is generally a policy choice to be made by state legislatures, not federal courts.

When the California Legislature enacted the three strikes laws, it made a judgment that protecting the public safety requires incapacitating criminals who have already been convicted of at least one serious or violent crime. Nothing in the Eighth Amendment prohibits California from making that choice....

California's justification is no pretext. Recidivism is a serious public safety concern in California and throughout the Nation. According to a recent report, approximately 67 percent of former inmates released from state prisons were charged with at least one "serious" new crime within three years of their release. In particular, released property offenders like Ewing had higher recidivism rates than those released after committing violent, drug, or public-order offenses. Approximately 73 percent of the property offenders released in 1994 were arrested again within three years, compared to approximately 61 percent of the violent offenders, 62 percent of the public-order offenders, and 66 percent of the drug offenders....

[The U.S. Supreme Court then cited other studies of recidivism before discussing deterrence theory.]

The State's interest in deterring crime also lends some support to the three strikes law. We have long viewed both incapacitation and deterrence as rationales for recidivism statutes....

[The U.S. Supreme Court emphasized that after the passage of three strikes legislation there was a dramatic decrease in the number of parolees who committed additional crimes and, further, that many of those paroled in California left the state. The Court discussed some of the criticisms of the legislation and noted that those should be directed at the legislature, which is free to enact such legislation as long as it has a reasonable basis for doing so.]

Against this backdrop, we consider Ewing's claim that his three strikes sentence of 25 years to life is unconstitutional.... [The U.S. Supreme Court pointed out that it was not only the current crime of shoplifting golf clubs—although that is a serious crime—but also Ewing's entire history that was at issue. The Court concluded as follows.]

Ewing's sentence is justified by the State's public-safety interest in incapacitating and deterring recidivist felons, and amply supported by his own long, serious criminal record. Ewing has been convicted of numerous misdemeanor and felony offenses, served nine separate terms of incarceration, and committed most of his crimes while on probation or parole. His prior "strikes" were serious felonies including robbery and three residential burglaries. To be sure, Ewing's sentence is a long one. But it reflects a rational legislative judgment, entitled to deference, that offenders who have committed serious or violent felonies and who continue to commit felonies must be incapacitated. The State of California "was entitled to place upon [Ewing] the onus of one who is simply unable to bring his conduct within the social norms prescribed by the criminal law of the State." Ewing's is not "the rare case in which a threshold comparison of the crime committed and the sentence imposed leads to an inference of gross disproportionality."

We hold that Ewing's sentence of 25 years to life in prison, imposed for the offense of felony grand theft under the three strikes law, is not grossly disproportionate and therefore does not violate the Eighth Amendment's prohibition on cruel and unusual punishments.

In 2004, even though the state was facing a budget crisis and with prisons overflowing with inmates, California voters rejected Proposition 66. The result of this proposal would have been the release of many nonviolent inmates and a change in the state's three strikes law to require that the third felony be a serious or violent one. At the time, California was spending 6 percent of its total budget on corrections, housing 164,000 inmates at an average cost of approximately $33,470 each.[47]

Truth in Sentencing

> **Truth in sentencing**   The concept requiring that actual time served by offenders is closer to the time allocated for the sentence. Many jurisdictions are establishing 85 percent as their goal, meaning that offenders may not be released for any reason until they have served 85 percent of their sentences.

Another current trend in sentencing is illustrated by California's statutory provision for **truth in sentencing**, which requires that anyone in California convicted of a violent or serious crime serve at least 80 percent of the imposed sentence. This provision applies to all crimes and is designed to negate the previous policy, by which inmates could earn good time credits and reduce their sentences by 50 percent.[48]

Truth in sentencing laws require that inmates serve a specified percentage of their sentences before they are released from prison. Most states have such laws, which are encouraged by federal government grants. The Violent Offender Incarceration and Truth in Sentencing Incentive Grants Act of 1995 offers states some grants for prison construction and operation but provides that those states require violent offenders to serve 85 percent of their sentences.[49] Some states require that murderers (or other specified types of offenders) must serve all of their time before they are released. For example, an Illinois law provides that "a prisoner who is serving a term of imprisonment for first-degree murder shall receive no good conduct credit and shall serve the entire sentence imposed by the court." The statute then specifies that inmates serving sentences for certain crimes (such as aggravated kidnapping and attempted first-degree murder) may receive only 4.5 days of good conduct credit (toward early release) per month. Those serving time for crimes that are not enumerated may receive one day of good conduct credit for each day they serve.[50]

Treatment and Sentencing

The final sentencing issue to which we give attention is a relatively new one. After years of "locking them up and throwing away the key," some jurisdictions are beginning to review that approach and back away. The recent changes have come about because of the increased costs of incarceration at a time when government budgets have been cut significantly. There has also been some concern that the punitive approach, at least in some cases, such as drug offenses, is less effective than a treatment approach.

By 2003, with most states facing severe budget cuts, many state legislatures had begun changing sentencing policies to reduce the number of inmates on the states' payrolls. According to one professional organization, "With the third straight year of budget shortfalls looming and most of the easy cuts already enacted, services once considered untouchable were falling prey to legislators desperate for additional savings."[51] More attention is given in Chapter 11 to the issue of treatment rather than punishment.

8-4   Appeals and Writs

Defendants who have been convicted may have grounds for appealing that conviction or sentence. But appeals are limited to *issues of law*, not fact. Thus, a defendant cannot appeal a guilty verdict per se but, rather, must have a legal issue, such as a violation of state or federal constitutional rights. For example, an appealable issue might be that evidence was excluded in violation of existing laws or that evidence that should have been admitted was excluded.

A successful appeal does not necessarily mean that the case is over and the defendant is released from the criminal justice system. Generally, a successful appeal means that the case is retried (or resentenced), and in most of those retrials, the defendant is again convicted. A successful appeal on a sentence—for example, the death penalty—may result in another death sentence. The difference is that, in the retrial (or resentencing), the state must not commit the errors made in the previous trial (or sentencing). On appeal, a defendant may be successful on some issues but not on others. Appendix B explains how to read an appellate court citation and defines such terms as *reversed*, *affirmed*, and *remanded*.

In addition to appeals, defendants may petition for a **writ**, which is an order from the court. A writ gives permission to do whatever was requested or orders someone to do something specific. A common writ filed by offenders is a writ of *habeas corpus*, which means "you have the body." Originally, a writ of *habeas corpus* was an order from the court to someone, such as a sheriff or a jailer, to have the person in court at a specified time and to state the legal theory under which the person was being held. Today, it is more extensive, and its use is governed by statutes, which differ from jurisdiction to jurisdiction. Often, it is used by inmates who are questioning the legality of their confinement. It does not question the issue of guilt or innocence but asserts that some due process rights of offenders are being violated or have been violated.

▶ **Writ** An order from the court. *See also* **Writ of certiorari** and *Habeas corpus*.

Under some circumstances, sentences may be appealed. Occasionally, a sentence is reversed, and the case is sent back for resentencing. In practice, this rarely occurs. Appellate courts have given judges wide discretion in sentencing. As long as the sentence is within the statutory provisions and the sentencing judge has not abused his or her discretion or shown undue prejudice, it is difficult for defendants to challenge a judicial sentence successfully. In rare cases, courts may declare a legislatively determined sentence to be in violation of the defendant's rights.

One final word on appeals and writs relates to the inability of some defendants to file them. A federal commission has requested that prosecutors as well as defense attorneys and other criminal justice system personnel assist inmates who need help in filing appeals for new trials, especially when DNA testing might reveal that they could not have committed the crimes for which they have been convicted. Attorney General Janet Reno directed the National Institute of Justice to establish the commission in 1998, and it issued a report the following year. Reno acted after she was presented with documentation of 28 cases in which DNA evidence had exonerated inmates. Other cases have subsequently been identified. According to Reno, the justice systems are not perfect, and those who are "charged with the administration of justice have a responsibility to seek its continued improvement."[52] Recall that Figure 8-1 contains information concerning the exoneration of death row inmates in recent years.

Chapter Wrap-Up

This chapter focused on the criminal processes during the stages of trial, sentencing, and appeal. The procedures and issues surrounding these aspects of U.S. criminal justice systems are extensive and complicated, and are governed by numerous statutes and court decisions. It is not possible to state "the law" in many of these areas because the judges of state courts and lower federal courts often differ in their analyses of how statutes and constitutions apply to the facts before them.

Even when the U.S. Supreme Court agrees to hear and decide some of the controversies, we often do not know how these decisions will be applied in similar cases. Some of the Court's decisions are close, with many of them decided by a 5-to-4 vote. Thus, a change of one member of the Court may alter the direction of what has been called the revolution in criminal procedure of the past several decades.

It is possible, however, to state generally what happens in the trial of a criminal case and how the constitutional guarantees apply to any or all of the stages of a trial. This chapter began with a brief overview of those constitutional rights and gave closer attention to the rights that are more specific to the trial and appellate stages. The right to a speedy trial, the right to a public trial by an impartial jury, and the right to the confrontation and cross-examination of witnesses, along with defendants' right to remain silent and not be forced to testify against themselves, are crucial to understanding the implementation of the various stages of the trial. Although states have considerable freedom in establishing the procedures by which they will conduct criminal trials, they may not violate federal (or state) constitutional provisions.

In that sense, every stage of the trial must be understood and analyzed in light of the federal constitutional rights to which all criminal defendants are entitled. The right to a public trial by an impartial jury precludes selection of the jury in secret. It prohibits implicit or explicit exclusion of people because of their race, gender, religion, or ethnic origin. However, understanding the right to a jury of one's peers may seem elusive, for most juries are not representative of young adults, and courts have held that lack of representation to be permissible in most cases.

The importance of constitutional rights that apply to the trial is underscored by the fact that, when those rights are violated, with only a few exceptions, the demonstrative or testimonial evidence secured as a result of those violations should be excluded from the trial. In some cases, it is not possible to prove guilt beyond a reasonable doubt without this tainted evidence; thus, the case must be dismissed.

This use of the exclusionary rule has led to considerable controversy concerning U.S. criminal justice systems. Its implications are extensive. Police may become discouraged and refuse to arrest in certain situations, thinking the case will not result in a conviction. Society may become critical of a system that appears to let the guilty go free. Potential criminals may decide to commit crimes, thinking they will not be convicted even if arrested. But those protections are to ensure that, when people are convicted of crimes, their convictions occur only after proper procedures have been followed and constitutional safeguards have been observed.

In this chapter, each stage of the criminal trial was explained and discussed, beginning with the opening of the court session in which charges against the defendant are read, through jury selection, the presentation of evidence, the final arguments, and the verdict. In all of these stages, the defense, the prosecution, and the judge are primary figures in assuring that proper procedures are followed. But following proper procedures does not end the matter. It is important to consider and reconsider the issues involved in U.S. criminal justice systems.

Some of those important issues were raised in this chapter. The right of the public to know and of the media to tell may conflict with the right of the defendant to be tried fairly and impartially. Which right should give way? The right of the defendant to a trial by jury creates enormous expenses and consumes considerable time of all participants in the criminal trial. At what point, if ever, should that right give way to cost?

The criminal trial has an enormous effect on the rest of the criminal justice system. Long criminal trials increase the backlog in civil and criminal courts and result in a greater likelihood that defendants are denied their right to a speedy trial and that society must spend more money to keep the system operating. Mistrials increase the amount of time and money devoted to trials. Failure to convict in numerous cases might lead the public to question the effectiveness of the system. Conviction of the innocent undermines the entire system, but acquittal of those whom most believe guilty has led to rioting. Repeated appeals lead many to question whether there is any finality in the law.

Throughout this discussion of the procedures and issues of the trial, however, it should be remembered that the vast majority of defendants do not go to trial. Therefore, it is important not to let the issues of the trial overshadow the need to give attention to the pretrial stages of criminal justice systems. In addition, it is important to understand and analyze what happens after defendants plead guilty or are found guilty at trial. Sentencing is a critical stage of the system and was the focus of the next major section of the chapter.

The sentencing process, ranging from the sentencing hearing to the formal stage of imposing the sentence on the convicted defendant, involves numerous issues and problems. The major ones were discussed in this chapter, beginning with an overview of the various sentencing strategies. The sentencing hearing was noted, along with some of the processes and issues involved in the decision-making process of sentencing.

The various types of sentences, ranging from probation to the most severe—capital punishment—were noted, followed by a discussion of the current issues and trends in sentencing. The concern with alleged sentence disparity led to a return to determinate sentences, many of which are longer than previously. The current concepts of truth in sentencing and three strikes and you're out embody this return to longer and more determinate sentences. More recently, however, some jurisdictions have turned to treatment rather than punishment in an attempt to balance budgets and reduce crime.

The final section of the chapter focused on appeals and writs, both means by which individuals may challenge the legality of their incarceration, their sentences, or even their convictions.

This chapter concluded our study of what happens in adult criminal court systems. As we have seen, most people accused of crimes do not go through the entire system. But for the small percentage who do, and for a society that needs and deserves protection for property as well as from violent offenders, confinement and incarceration have become the solutions. Whether they are adequate solutions is the underlying issue in the next section of the text, which includes three chapters.

Key Terms

aggravating circumstances (p. 242)	consecutive sentence (p. 245)	directed verdict (p. 238)
beyond a reasonable doubt (p. 239)	contempt of court (p. 233)	direct evidence (p. 237)
capital punishment (p. 247)	corporal punishment (p. 247)	direct examination (p. 237)
circumstantial evidence (p. 237)	cross-examination (p. 237)	fine (p. 246)
community work service (p. 246)	demonstrative evidence (p. 236)	good time credit (p. 242)
concurrent sentence (p. 245)	determinate sentence (p. 242)	hearsay evidence (p. 237)

Apply It

1. Explain the importance of constitutional rights in a criminal trial.
2. What is the purpose of the Speedy Trial Act of 1974? What kinds of delays does it permit?
3. Why is the right to a public trial important to defendants? What are the legal problems and issues with public trials as far as the media are concerned?
4. Why is the jury system considered important in the United States? Should it be abolished? Why or why not? Do you think a fair and impartial jury can be selected in high-publicity trials?
5. What are the requirements for jury size and the selection of names for the jury pool? What is meant by an *impartial jury*? A *jury of peers*?
6. What is the role of the judge in controlling the conduct of defendants at trial?
7. Should people who are chosen for the jury pool be permitted to be excused from jury duty at their own request, or should all persons called be required to serve? Which, if any, requests should be honored? Which reasons should not be considered?
8. What is the significance of *Batson v. Kentucky*? Does the case apply to gender?
9. How do opening statements differ from closing statements? Are both required for the prosecution and the defense?
10. Define *demonstrative evidence*. How does it differ from witness testimony as evidence?
11. What is the *hearsay rule*?
12. What is the difference between direct and circumstantial evidence?
13. What is meant by *direct examination, cross-examination*, and *redirect examination*?
14. Contrast the prosecution's case with that of the defense.
15. Describe the role of the judge in presenting the case to the jury.
16. Describe and evaluate the role of the jury in a criminal trial.
17. Discuss the importance of sentencing, and explain sentencing strategies.
18. Is a sentencing hearing necessary? Is it required? What occurs in a sentencing hearing? What is the value of a presentence investigation? Should the presentence investigation be available to the prosecution and the defense, as well as the judge? Why or why not?
19. What are the legal issues concerning the role of victims in the sentencing process? What is your opinion regarding the role victims should be permitted to play?
20. Should capital punishment be abolished? Why or why not?
21. What is meant by *sentence disparity*? Discuss the issues of gender and racial discrimination in sentencing.
22. What problems have arisen with federal sentencing guidelines?
23. What is the difference between *determinate* and *indeterminate sentences*?
24. What do you think will be the effect of three strikes and you're out legislation? Evaluate the U.S. Supreme Court's recent decision on this concept. What is the effect of truth in sentencing?
25. What is a *wobbler*, and what is its significance? Should we treat rather than punish? Discuss.
26. Explain the meaning of *appeals* and *writs*.

Endnotes

1. Marc Galanter, *The Vanishing Trial: An Examination of Trials: Matters in Federal and State Court*, American Bar Association, http://www.abanet.org/litigation/litnews/press/vanishing.html, accessed 13 July 2006. See also, "U.S. Suits Multiply, but Fewer Ever Get to Trial, Study Says," *New York Times* (14 December 2003), p. 1.
2. Klopfer v. North Carolina, 386 U.S. 213 (1967).
3. U.S. Code, Title 18, Sections 3161–3174 (2007).
4. N.Y. Civil Rights Law, Section 12 (2007).
5. Tex. Code Crim. Proc. Art. 32A.02, Section 1 (2006).
6. Tex. Code Crim. Proc., Art. 32A.01 (2006).
7. Sheppard v. Maxwell, 384 U.S. 333, 356 (1966), quoting 135 N.E.2d 340, 342 (1956).
8. Globe Newspaper Co. v. Superior Court, 457 U.S. 596 (1982).
9. United States v. McVeigh, 955 F.Supp. 1281 (1997), *cert. denied sub nom.*, 522 U.S. 1142 (1998).
10. Duncan v. Louisiana, 391 U.S. 145, 149 (1968).
11. N.Y. Penal Code, Section 310.10 (2007).
12. Taylor v. Louisiana, 419 U.S. 522, 523 (1975), footnotes and citations omitted.
13. Swain v. Alabama, 380 U.S. 202 (1965).
14. Batson v. Kentucky, 476 U.S. 79 (1986).
15. Miller-El v. Dretke, 545 U.S. 231 (2005), *and on remand, remanded*, 2005 U.S. App. LEXIS 15206 (5th Cir. 2005).
16. See Johnson v. California, 545 U.S. 162 (2005).
17. J.E.B. v. Alabama *ex rel.* T.B., 511 U.S. 127 (1994).
18. Barber v. Ponte, 772 F.2d 982 (1st Cir. 1985), *cert. denied*, 475 U.S. 1050 (1986).
19. Illinois v. Allen, 397 U.S. 337 (1970).

20. Illinois v. Allen, 397 U.S. 337 (1970).

21. For a discussion of defenses, see Sue Titus Reid, *Criminal Law*, 7th ed. (Los Angeles: Roxbury Publishing, 2007), pp. 93–162.

22. "ABA Creates Kennedy Commission on Sentencing and Prison Policies," *Criminal Justice Newsletter* (3 November 2003), p. 6.

23. Ibid.

24. "ABA Passes Resolutions Dealing with Sentencing Guidelines," *Wisconsin Law Journal* (18 August 2004), n.p.

25. "Texas Governor Pardons 35 Arrested in Tainted Sting," *New York Times* (23 August 2003), p. 7; "Tulia, Texas: Narcotics Officer Accused of Targeting the Black Community of Tulia, Texas, in a Drug Sting," *Show: 60 Minutes* (7:00 P.M. ET), CBS (28 September 2003); "Inadmissible," *Texas Lawyer* 20, no. 47 (24 January 2005): 3.

26. Ring v. Arizona, 534 U.S. 1103 (2002).

27. Blakely v. Washington, 542 U.S. 296 (2004); United States v. Apprendi, 530 U.S. 466 (2000).

28. United States v. Booker, 543 U.S. 220 (2005); Rita v. United States, 177 Fed. Appx. 356 (4th Cir. 2006), *cert. granted, mot. granted*, 127 S.Ct. 551 (2006); Claiborne v. United States, 439 F.3d 479 (8th Cir. 2006), *cert. granted, in part, mot. granted*, 127 S.Ct. 551 (2006).

29. Shepard v. United States, 544 U.S. 13 (2005).

30. Booth v. Maryland, 482 U.S. 496 (1987), *overruled in part*, Payne v. Tennessee, 501 U.S. 808 (1991).

31. Payne v. Tennessee, 501 U.S. 808 (1991). The other case that was overruled is South Carolina v. Gathers, 490 U.S. 805 (1989).

32. State v. Gentry, 888 P.2d 1105 (Wash. 1995), *cert. denied*, 516 U.S. 843 (1995).

33. Michael J. Lynch and W. Byron Groves, *A Primer in Radical Criminology*, 2d ed. (New York: Harper and Heston, 1989), pp. 106–107, citations omitted.

34. Michael Tonry, "Racial Politics, Racial Disparities, and the War on Crime," *Crime & Delinquency* 40 (October 1994): 475, 483–488.

35. United States v. Armstrong, 517 U.S. 456 (1996).

36. For an analysis of gender and sentencing, see Marian R. Williams, "Gender and Sentencing: An Analysis of Indicators," *Criminal Justice Policy Review* 10, no. 4 (1999): 471–490.

37. Darrell J. Steffensmeier, "Assessing the Impact of the Women's Movement on Sex-Based Differences in the Handling of Adult Criminal Defendants," *Crime & Delinquency* 26 (July 1980): 344–57.

38. Darrell Steffensmeier et al., "Gender and Imprisonment Decisions," *Criminology* 31 (August 1993): 411–446; quotation is on p. 435.

39. Ronald L. Akers and Christine S. Sellers, *Criminological Theories: Introduction, Evaluation, and Application*, 4th ed. (Los Angeles: Roxbury Publishing, 2004), p. 213.

40. "Justice Dept. to Monitor Judges for Sentences Shorter Than Guidelines Suggest," *New York Times* (8 August 2003), p. 12.

41. "In Angry Outbursts, New York's U.S. Judges Protest New Sentencing Procedures," *New York Times* (8 December 2003), p. 25; "Judges Seek Repeal of Law on Sentencing," *New York Times* (24 September 2003), p. 17. The Protect Act is codified as Public Law 108-21 (2007).

42. "Chief Justice Attacks a Law As Infringing on Judges," *New York Times* (1 January 2004), p. 10.

43. Cal. Penal Code, Section 1170 *et seq.* (2007).

44. Cummingham v. California, 127 S.Ct. 856 (2007).

45. Riggs v. California, *cert. denied*, 525 U.S. 1114 (1999), footnotes and citations omitted.

46. Ewing v. California, 538 U.S. 11 (2003), footnotes and case citations omitted. See also Lockyer v. Andrade, 538 U.S. 63 (2003). The statute in question is Cal. Penal Code, Section 667(b) (2007).

47. "California Prison System Struggling to Find Balance in Upheaval," *Corrections Professional* 10, no. 17 (27 May 2005): n.p.; "Three-Strikes Reform in California," *Corrections Professional* 10, no. 6 (19 November 2004): n.p.

48. Cal. Penal Code, Title 16, Section 667 (2007).

49. Violent Offender Incarceration and Truth in Sentencing Incentive Grants, U.S. Code, Title 42, Section 13701 *et seq.* (2007).

50. Ill. Crim. Stat., Chapter 730, Section 5/3-6-3 (2007).

51. "Budget Deficits Forcing Changes in Sentencing, Lawmakers Say," *Criminal Justice Newsletter* (1 October 2003), p. 8, referring to the report *Dollars and Sentences: Legislators' Views on Prisons, Punishment, and Budget Crisis*, available from the Vera Institute of Justice, 233 Broadway, 12th Floor, New York, N.Y. 10279, (212) 334-1300.

52. *Postconviction DNA Testing: Recommendations for Handling Requests*, 1999, available from the National Criminal Justice Reference Services, Box 6000, Rockville, Md. 20849-6000, (800)851-3420.

Confinement and Corrections

After the processes of convicting and sentencing, society is faced with the issue of what to do with offenders. Historically, convicted offenders were treated informally by means of various psychological and physical punishments. Physical, or corporal, punishments became severe, however, and for humanitarian and other reasons, reformers decided corporal punishment should be replaced with confinement.

Confinement facilities—formerly used primarily for detaining the accused temporarily while they awaited trial or the convicted while they awaited corporal or other forms of punishment—were viewed as places for punishment and reformation. Although many reformers saw confinement facilities as a replacement for corporal punishment, others saw them as an environment in which offenders would be reformed through work, would have time for reflection, and in some cases, would be subjected to corporal punishment.

The history of the emergence of prisons and jails as places of punishment is a fascinating study, but it is laced with controversy, idealism, and unfulfilled promises. Part 4 traces that development from its beginning through modern times. Chapter 9 focuses on the history and structure of confinement, pointing out the differences between state and federal systems, the different levels of security that characterize confinement, and the emergence of prisons as places for punishment. The nature of private corrections is discussed, along with the problems of prison and jail overcrowding. This chapter provides the background needed for an analysis of some of the issues surrounding modern correctional practices.

Chapter 10 examines the administration and inmate life of modern prisons, looking particularly at the ways in which the internal structure of the prison may be used to control inmates. That control is not always successful, however, as illustrated by the discussions on prison violence and the lawsuits filed as a result of alleged violations of inmates' constitutional rights. Part 4 closes with a chapter on community corrections, probation, and parole.

The History and Structure of Confinement

9

In the past, when the confinement of offenders was necessary, it was not for long periods. Lengthy confinements would have been impractical in a less-populated world, where formal police protection did not exist and conditions were so unstable that populations moved from one place to another in search of food and shelter. Under those conditions, the punishment of persons who violated society's norms was usually carried out by quick methods, such as corporal punishment, or in extreme cases, capital punishment. Generally, confinement was for very short periods while defendants awaited corporal punishment, trial, or sentencing.

Places of confinement for suspects or convicted defendants should reflect the purposes for which they are intended. If confinement is for holding a person until trial or corporal punishment, little attention need be paid to that confinement facility except to keep it secure. The architecture, conditions, and administration should reflect the security goal. If humanitarian concerns are not important, the conditions of confinement are relatively unimportant. Likewise, if the reason for confinement is to remove offenders from society and punish them for their criminal acts, then programming, treatment personnel, and prison conditions are unimportant. Prison is a place of custody and punishment; being there is the punishment. The rationale is that offenders are getting what they deserve as a result of their criminal acts.

If the purpose of confinement is to rehabilitate offenders, more attention should be given to the total confinement program. The location of confinement facilities is important; facilities should be close enough to inmates' homes to enable family members to visit. Confinement conditions are important because they are related to inmates' rehabilitation. Treatment programs, educational and work opportunities, fairness in discipline, and many other activities behind prison walls are relevant. Administration and management must reflect a treatment-rehabilitation orientation and, at the same time, maintain security within the institution.

This chapter looks at the historical development of the incarceration of persons in prisons and jails for the purposes of detention and punishment,

OBJECTIVES

After reading this chapter, you should be able to do the following:

*   **Explain the reasons for the emergence of institutions for confining offenders.**
*   **Explain the significance of the Walnut Street Jail.**
*   **Distinguish the Pennsylvania system from the Auburn system, and evaluate the contributions of each.**
*   **Recall the contributions of Europeans to the emergence and development of prisons.**
*   **Explain the relevance of the Elmira Reformatory.**
*   **Summarize the development of modern U.S. prison systems.**
*   **Distinguish among jails, prisons, and community corrections.**
*   **List and describe the purposes of prison security levels.**
*   **Analyze the differences between prisons for men and women.**
*   **Describe state and federal prison systems, and evaluate the differences between them.**
*   **Discuss the implications of the growth in jail and prison populations, with particular attention to the negative effects of overcrowding.**
*   **Discuss the distinguishing features of jails, and analyze the role of the federal government in local jails.**
*   **Evaluate boot camps and work ethic camps.**
*   **Analyze the role of privatization in correctional facilities.**

along with an analysis of newer types of facilities: boot camps and work camps. Throughout the discussion, the purposes of confinement—retribution, incapacitation, deterrence, and rehabilitation—should be kept in mind (see again the discussion on these philosophies in Chapter 1, Spotlight 1-2). The focus on one or more of these purposes is not necessarily chronological in the history of prisons, but the purpose is tied to the type of prison that emerges.

9-1   The Emergence of Prisons for Punishment

The use of secure facilities for *confinement* is an ancient practice, but the use of secure facilities, such as prisons or jails, for *punishment* is a relatively recent practice. This transition took place in the 18th century. In 1704, Pope Clement XI erected the papal prison of San Michele in Rome. In 1773, the prison in Ghent, Belgium, was established by Hippolyte Vilain XIII. In 1776, England was faced with a rising crime rate, the elimination of the need for galley slaves, and decreasing opportunities for **transportation** of criminals to its colonies. England legalized the use of hulks, usually broken-down war vessels. By 1828, at least 4,000 **offenders** were being confined in English prison hulks. The ships were unsanitary, poorly ventilated, and vermin-infested. Contagious diseases killed many inmates, and punishments were brutal. There was little work for inmates, and idleness was demoralizing. Moral degeneration set in because of the "promiscuous association of prisoners of all ages and degrees of criminality."[1] This system of penal confinement in England lasted until the middle of the 19th century.

The spirit of **humanitarianism** that arose during the Enlightenment was among the reasons for the substitution of imprisonment for transportation and corporal and capital punishment. People began to realize the horrors inherent in the treatment of

Transportation   Historically, the practice of punishing criminals by exiling them to another country.

Offenders   Persons who have committed a criminal offense.

Humanitarianism   In penal philosophy, the doctrine advocating the removal of harsh, severe, and painful conditions in penal institutions.

incarcerated offenders. The French prison built in Paris in the 14th century, the Bastille, became a symbol of such treatment, as well as of tyrannical prison administration. French philosophers, shocked by what they called *judicial murders*, sought changes in criminal justice systems.[2]

Another important philosophical development in France during the French Revolution was the emphasis on rationalism. This approach was important in the history of prisons because of its influence on social and political philosophy. The philosophers believed that social progress and the greatest happiness for the greatest number would only occur through revolutionary social reform, which could be brought about only by applying reason.

These reform ideas flourished in the United States because many French people lived here during the French Revolution and many influential Americans had been to France. In fact, the Constitutional Convention was influenced significantly by the political philosophy of French philosophers.

There are other important reasons for the rise of the prison system in the United States. The increasing emphasis on personal liberty meant that the deprivation of liberty could be seen as punishment. In addition, after the Industrial Revolution, there was an increasing need for labor, which inmates could supply. It has been argued, too, that prisons were developed by those in power for the purpose of suppressing persons who were not in power.

Although these general conditions are important in explaining the rise of prisons, attention must also be given to one individual who was highly influential in the process: John Howard (1726–1790), known as the great European prison reformer. Howard, an Englishman, was credited with the beginning of the **penitentiary** system. Howard traveled throughout Europe and brought to the world's attention the sordid conditions under which inmates were confined.

Howard's classic work, *State of Prisons*, published in 1777, was extremely influential in prison reform in Europe and the United States. Among his other ideas, Howard suggested that inmates should be housed individually in sanitary facilities and provided clean clothing; that men, women, and children should be housed separately; and that jailers should be trained and well paid.[3]

> ▶ **Penitentiary** Historically, an institution intended to isolate convicted offenders from one another, giving them time to reflect on their bad acts and become penitent. Later, the term became synonymous with prison.

9-1a The Emergence of American Penitentiaries

The history of correctional institutions can be traced back to Roman, French, and English systems. An early English gaol (jail) is featured in Spotlight 9-1. The unique contribution of the United States was the substitution of imprisonment for corporal punishment, an innovation of the Quakers of West Jersey and Pennsylvania in the 18th century. They combined the prison and the **workhouse** to achieve a system of confinement at hard labor.

In 1787, Pennsylvania enacted a statute reducing the number of capital crimes, substituting imprisonment for many felonies, and abolishing most corporal punishments. A 1794 statute abolished capital punishment except for first-degree murder and substituted fines and imprisonment for corporal punishment in the case of all other crimes. The Pennsylvania criminal code reform set the stage for similar developments in other states. The main feature of early Pennsylvania reform was the Walnut Street Jail.

The Walnut Street Jail

In 1787 in Pennsylvania, Benjamin Rush, Benjamin Franklin, and others met to discuss punishment. Rush proposed a new system for the treatment of offenders. This system included classification, individualized treatment, and prison labor to provide jobs for inmates and to make prisons self-supporting. A 1790 statute codified the principle of solitary confinement and established the Walnut Street Jail, in which individual cells were provided for serious felons. Inmates were separated by gender and by whether they had been sentenced after being convicted of a crime or were being detained awaiting a

> ▶ **Workhouse** An English institution used to confine offenders who were forced to work at unpleasant tasks. Offenders were punished physically as well. The term is used in some places today to refer to institutions that emphasize reformation or rehabilitation through work.

Spotlight 9-1   The First London Gaol

Built shortly after the Norman Conquest in 1066, the Fleet Prison was the first London facility constructed solely for the purpose of holding prisoners. It was called the Gaol of London until 1188, when that name was taken over by the Newgate Prison and the original gaol became known as the Fleet Prison. The early gaol was built of stone and surrounded by a moat, typical of many structures in those days, serving the dual purpose of keeping the inmates in and outsiders out.

The primary purpose of this first London jail was the detention of suspects awaiting trial, after which they were punished elsewhere. One exception was debtors, who were held until their debts were paid. On occasion, jail inmates were permitted to leave the institution for limited periods, although a fee generally was charged for this privilege. Early physical conditions in the Fleet Prison were better than those in most English institutions, which is "not saying much since the state of the early English prisons was generally quite deplorable." Over time, conditions deteriorated, and "soon the Fleet had the reputation of being one of the worst in all the country."

The Fleet was burned in 1666, soon rebuilt, destroyed over 100 years later, rebuilt again, and closed in 1842. "The Fleet Prison was demolished some four years later, thus ending the career of one of the oldest English institutions, the original Gaol of London."

Source: Paraphrased from J. M. Moynahan, "The Original Gaol of London," *American Jails* 1 (Winter 1988): 88.

---

trial or punishment. This law was the beginning of the modern prison system in the United States, and the Walnut Street Jail is often cited as the first U.S. prison.

Some scholars have argued that the Walnut Street Jail was not the first American prison. Alexis M. Durham III has written extensively about the development of early prisons. According to Durham, Connecticut's Newgate Prison was the "first true colonial prison for the long-term punishment of serious offenders."[4] That prison was used for the incarceration and punishment of offenders who committed the following crimes: robbery, burglary, forgery, counterfeiting, and horse thievery. Unlike the Walnut Street Jail, Newgate was much more like the English houses of corrections and other early penal facilities, with an emphasis on punishment rather than rehabilitation.[5]

Offenders in the Walnut Street Jail worked an 8- to 10-hour day and received religious instruction. They labored in their cells and were paid for their efforts. Guards were not permitted to use weapons, and corporal punishment was forbidden. Inmates were allowed to talk only in the common rooms at night before retiring. With some variations, this plan was followed in other states. By 1800, problems with the system had become obvious. Crowded facilities made work within individual cells impossible; there was not enough productive work for the large number of inmates, and vice flourished. Ultimately, the Walnut Street Jail failed as a result of politics, finances, lack of personnel, and overcrowding, but not before it had gained recognition throughout the world.

The Walnut Street Jail and other early prisons faced serious problems. Despite the thick walls and high security, **inmates** escaped. To combat that problem, some **wardens** required inmates to wear uniforms; in some prisons, the color of the uniform reflected whether the convict was a first-, second-, or third-time offender. Discipline was a major issue; some wardens reinstituted corporal punishment, whereas others used solitary confinement.

Funding was a challenge in these early prisons, and facilities were needed for exercise. To alleviate these problems, work programs (such as gardening) were begun, but they were not effective. Inmates were neither reliable nor efficient, and administrators were not skilled in managing prison labor. The result was that most prisons operated at a loss. In 1820, the viability of the entire prison system was in doubt, and its most dedicated supporters conceded a nearly total failure. Institutionalization had failed to pay its own way and had encouraged and educated the criminal even more extensively to a life of crime.[6]

▶ **Inmates**   Convicted persons whose freedom has been replaced by confinement in a prison, mental ward, or similar institution.

▶ **Warden**   Historically, the chief administrative officer in a correctional facility.

In response to these problems, two types of prison systems developed: the Pennsylvania, or separate, system, based on solitary confinement; and the New York, or Auburn, system, known as the **silent system**. These two systems were the subject of intense debate. Tourists flocked to see the prisons; foreign nations sent delegates to examine the two systems. By the 1830s, the two American penitentiary systems were famous around the world.

▶ **Silent system** In penitentiaries, the historical practice of not allowing offenders to speak with one another.

The Pennsylvania System

With the demise of the Walnut Street Jail, solitary confinement at hard labor appeared to be a failure. Consideration was given to a return to corporal punishment. But in 1817, the Philadelphia Society for the Alleviation of the Miseries of Prisons began a reform movement, which led to a law providing for the establishment of the separate system of confining inmates in solitary cells without labor.

The first separate system prison was opened in Pittsburgh in 1826 and subsequently was known as the Western Penitentiary. Due to the problems resulting from inmate idleness in this prison, the law was changed to permit work in solitary confinement. The design of the Western Penitentiary became the basic architectural model for the Pennsylvania system.

The Eastern Penitentiary—or Cherry Hill as it was called because of its location in a cherry orchard—was established in 1829. It was the first large-scale attempt to implement the philosophy of solitary confinement at all times, with work provided for inmates in their cells. The law that authorized construction of this prison specified that, although the commissioners could make some alterations and improvements in the plan used for the Western Penitentiary, the principle of solitary confinement must be incorporated.

John Haviland, the architect of Cherry Hill, was faced with the problem of creating a structure that would permit solitary confinement but would not injure inmates' health or permit their escape. His solution was seven wings, each connected to a central hub by covered passageways. Each inmate had a single inside cell with an outside exercise yard. Inmates were blindfolded when taken to the prison and were not permitted to see other inmates. They were not assembled even for religious worship. The chaplain spoke from the rotunda, with inmates remaining in their cells.

Before Cherry Hill was completed, it became the focus of discussion among prison reformers around the world. Although it was the architectural model for most of the new prisons in Europe, South America, and later Asia, the design was not popular in the United States. Despite that fact, John Haviland's contributions to American prison architecture should not be minimized, as one criminologist stated:

> Compared with the penitentiaries of their day, Haviland's prisons were overwhelmingly superior, both technically and stylistically....Haviland's great service to penology would seem to be in establishing high standards of construction, standards which were to have an influence on almost all of the prison construction of the 19th century.[7]

Haviland should also be remembered for the fact that his prison architecture embodied a treatment philosophy.

The Auburn System

The prison system that became the architectural model for the United States was the Auburn system. In 1796, New York enacted a statute that provided for the building of two prisons. Newgate in New York City was first occupied in 1797. That prison soon became so crowded that, to make room for new inmates, as many inmates had to be released as were admitted.

The second prison, Auburn, was similar to Newgate, with workshop groups during the day and several inmates to a cell at night. Discipline was a problem, however, so a new system, which became known as the *Auburn system*, developed. The Auburn system featured congregate work during the day, with an enforced silent system. Inmates were housed in individual cells at night. The architecture created a fortresslike appearance, with a series of tiers set in a hollow frame, a much more economical system than that of Cherry Hill.

The silent system was strictly enforced at Auburn. The inmates ate face to back. They stood with arms folded and eyes down, so that they could not communicate with their hands. They walked in lockstep with a downward gaze. Strict regulation of letters and visits with outsiders and few or no newspapers further isolated the inmates. Inmates were brought together for religious services, but each sat in a boothlike pew, which prevented their seeing anyone other than the speaker.

Discipline was strictly enforced at Auburn. The warden, Captain Elam Lynds, thought that the spirit of a person must be broken before reformation could occur. He was credited with the Auburn punishment philosophy. It is said that he changed discipline rules without legislative authority, instituted the silent system, fed inmates in their cells, and required lockstep in marching. A committee from the legislature visited the prison, approved of the way it was being run, and persuaded the legislature to legalize the new system.

In 1821, a system of **classification** was instituted. It placed dangerous offenders in solitary confinement, which led to mental illness, inmates' pleadings for work, and sometimes even death. A commission established to study prisons recommended abolishing solitary confinement and putting all inmates to work.

> **Classification** The assignment of new inmates to the housing, security status, and treatment programs that best fit their individual needs.

Comparison of the Pennsylvania and Auburn Systems

Architecture is important in distinguishing the Pennsylvania system from the Auburn system. The latter emphasized the congregate but silent system; the former, solitary confinement. Both emphasized the importance of a disciplined routine and isolation from bad influences. Both reflected the belief that, because the inmate was not inherently bad but, rather, the product of defective social organization, he or she could be reformed under proper circumstances. Scholars, practitioners, and politicians debated the advantages and disadvantages of these two systems, but few questioned the premise on which both rested: incarceration is the best way to handle criminals.[8]

The architecture of the two systems resulted in cost differentials. The Auburn system was more economical to build, although the Pennsylvania system was less expensive to administer. It was argued that the Auburn system was more conducive to productive inmate labor and less likely to cause mental illness. The silent system continued into the 20th century, not for the original purpose of preventing cross-infection, but because it was easier to run an institution if the inmates were not allowed to speak to each other.

Both the Pennsylvania and the Auburn systems sound harsh today, but they must be viewed in historical perspective, as noted by one authority:

> The most that can be said for this period of American prison history is that, despite all its stupidities and cruelties, it was better than a return to the barbarities of capital and corporal punishment for crime. In the face of public indignation at the chaos existing in early American prisons in 1820, it maintained the penitentiary system.[9]

The Pennsylvania and Auburn systems were also important in that both were based on treatment philosophies, with architecture designed to accommodate those philosophies.

9-1b   The Emergence of the Reformatory Model

The disagreement over the Pennsylvania and Auburn systems led to an emphasis on reformation, along with a prison system characterized by indeterminate sentences, parole, work training, and education. Before looking at the emergence of that system in the United States, it is important to look briefly at the European developments that influenced U.S. prison systems.

We look to the works of Captain Alexander Maconochie, an Englishman, and Sir Walter Crofton, an Irishman, for the beginnings of a reformatory movement. Maconochie began the movement in 1840, when he was placed in charge of the British penal colony on Norfolk Island, off the coast of Australia. England used Norfolk Island for the worst offenders, who had been transported from England to mainland Australia, where they committed further crimes. Previously, England had transported its offenders to the American colonies. After the American Revolution, that was no longer an option, so many offenders were sent to Australia.

Maconochie was critical of the transportation conditions offenders faced. Offenders were chained together and in some cases had only standing room on the ships. Fevers and diseases were rampant, food was meager, sanitary conditions were nonexistent, and homosexual rape and other forms of violence were common.

Upon his arrival at Norfolk, Maconochie began to implement his reformation philosophy. He emphasized that he was not lenient and that society had a right to punish those who broke its laws, but

> We have no right to cast them away altogether. Even their physical suffering should be in moderation, and the moral pain framed so as, if possible, to reform, and not necessarily to pervert them. The iron should enter both soul and body, but not so utterly to sear and harden them.[10]

Maconochie's reform program was characterized by his advocacy of the indeterminate sentence and his belief that inmates should work, improve their conduct, and learn frugality of living before they were released. While in prison, inmates should work for everything they received. Their work earned them the required number of "marks." When they were qualified by discipline to do so, they should work in small groups of about six or seven, with all of the offenders answerable for the behavior of the entire group, as well as of each member. Before they were released, while still required to earn their daily tally of marks, offenders should be given a proprietary interest in their labor. They should be subjected to less rigorous discipline in order to be prepared to live in society without the supervision of prison officials.

Maconochie was never given the authority that he thought he would have when he went to Norfolk. His ideas were controversial and not greatly appreciated by the British authorities, but he made many changes in the penal colony, and it was a more humane place when he left.

Maconochie described his accomplishments as follows: "I found a turbulent, brutal hell, and left it a peaceful, well-ordered community." Evidence proved him right. But the controversy over his methods and philosophies led to his recall in 1844:

> He was replaced by Major Childs, an incompetent who sought to carry out instructions to restore the previous evil methods in place of Maconochie's reforms. This led, on 1 July 1846, to a revolt by some of the convicts, and four of the penal staff were murdered.[11]

Sir Walter Crofton, a disciple of Maconochie, applied Maconochie's reform ideas to the Irish prisons, where he served as chair of the board of directors. The Irish system was recognized for its emphasis on the following:

1. A reward system—all advantages, including release, were based on rewards for good behavior
2. Individual influence of the prison administrators on the inmates—prison populations were to be kept small (300 in ordinary prisons, 100 in intermediate prisons) to permit this influence
3. Gradual release from restrictions—restrictions were gradually removed until during the last stage, the intermediate prison, one-half of the restrictions were removed
4. A parole system involving strict supervision after release and revocation for infractions of the rules[12]

American reformers visited the Irish prison system in the 1860s and returned with great enthusiasm for their reformation philosophy. On 12 October 1870, a meeting led by penologist Enoch C. Wines was held in Cincinnati, Ohio, to settle the dispute between the Pennsylvania and Auburn systems. This meeting led to the organization of the American Correctional Association, then called the *National Prison Association*. The group drafted 37 principles calling for indeterminate sentences, cultivation of inmates' self-respect, inmate classification, and advancement of the philosophy of reformation rather than punishment.

The Elmira Reformatory, established in 1876, emerged from this meeting. It became the model for a **reformatory**, which was designed for young offenders. The architecture was similar to that of the Auburn system, but greater emphasis was placed on educational and vocational training. Indeterminate sentences with maximum terms, opportunities for parole, and the classification of inmates according to conduct and achievement were the greatest advances of this new institution.

Elmira was established at the same time that other reforms, such as the juvenile court, probation, parole, and indeterminate sentences, were emerging. It was predicted that Elmira would dominate U.S. prison systems.[13]

The significant contribution of the Elmira reformatory system was its emphasis on rehabilitation through education, which led to greater prison discipline, indeterminate sentences, and parole. The system declined eventually, mainly as a result of the lack of trained personnel to conduct the educational programs and to carry on the classification system adequately. Some scholars argue that the Elmira system was never intended to be a real reform but rather, was developed for the purpose of controlling the lower classes, women, and minorities. The system promised benevolent reform but delivered only repression.[14]

An increase in the prison population in the late 1800s resulted in severe overcrowding. Eventually, new prisons were built, including Attica (New York) in 1931, and Stateville (Illinois) in 1925. Most of these prisons followed the Auburn architectural plan and were characterized by increasing costs per inmate, Sunday services, a chaplain on duty most of the time, and insufficient educational and vocational training programs. The training programs were based on the needs of institutions, not the interests or needs of inmates. Insufficient funds were available to hire and retain adequate personnel.

Those institutions provided work for some inmates, and the prison products were sold on the open market. This industrial period of prison history irritated those in private industries, who complained that competition from prisons was unfair because of the low wages. In 1929, the Hawes-Cooper Act was passed, followed in 1935 by the Ashurst-Summers Act to restrict the sale of prison goods:

> These [federal statutes] in turn were followed by state laws designed to do the same. With the passage of these laws, the Industrial Prison was eliminated. In 1935 for the great majority of prisoners the penitentiary system had again reverted to its original status: punishment and custody.[15]

> **Reformatory** An early corrections facility that was less physically secure and that emphasized changing or reforming the offender. Usually used to refer to an institution.

9-2   Modern Prisons: An Overview

When they emerged, U.S. prisons were viewed as a substitute for corporal punishment, but corporal punishment continued. Supposedly, prisons were places in which inmates could be reformed.[16] However, the early reform approach was eventually abandoned in favor of a custody philosophy. According to David Rothman, this occurred for several reasons. The change was not inherent in prison designs. Some disappointment was inevitable because of the great expectations the founders had for the success of the prison movement. Change also came about as a result of the resources drained from prisons during the Civil War. Additionally, the rehabilitation goal promoted but also disguised the shift from reformation to custody. Too often, prison administrators assumed that incarceration was reformation, and no one recognized that reformation programs were lacking. The administrators relaxed their reformative efforts, and abuses of power arose within the prisons.

Custody Legal control over a person or property. Physical responsibility for a person or thing.

The nature of inmates' offenses was also related to the change from a reformation to a custodial emphasis. The silent, segregated systems were not designed for hardened offenders serving long-term or life sentences. The founders who envisaged reformation of the offender had not contemplated what to do with the hardened adult offender or the juvenile already committed to a life of crime. When the situation arose, **custody** seemed the best answer. The public accepted that approach because of the need for safety and security.[17]

The custodial institution seemed the best way to handle changes in the composition of inmate populations. As cities became larger and their populations became more heterogeneous, including an influx of immigrants as well as distinct social classes, traditional methods of social control became ineffective. When those persons entered prison, an emphasis on custody seemed appropriate.

By the late 1800s, it had become clear that reformation was no longer a major punishment goal. Later studies reported corruption between correctional officers and inmates, cruel punishment of inmates, overcrowded prisons with financial problems, and severe criticism of both the Pennsylvania and Auburn systems. As hardened offenders were held for long periods of time, prisons turned into holding operations, where wardens were content if they could prevent riots and escapes.

Some reformers began to express dissatisfaction with incarceration per se, criticizing long sentences as counterproductive and large expenditures on prisons as foolish and unnecessary. Probation and parole were advocated but slow to be adopted. Most reformers and the public seemed content to incarcerate for the sake of security.

Why did the public stand for the decline of the original prison philosophy? David Rothman suggests that part of the explanation is that usually it is easier to capture public interest "with predictions of success than with the descriptions of corruption." Some may have believed that incarceration was synonymous with rehabilitation. But, says Rothman, the reasons went deeper. Many persons saw the prison as performing an important social function, for they noted that the majority of inmates were from the lower social class and many were immigrants. Few upper-class or upper-middle-class persons were incarcerated.[18]

In recent years, reformation and rehabilitation were dealt a severe blow by researchers who claimed that empirical evidence showed that rehabilitation had failed. Some evidence of the rehabilitative ideal remained, but it was no longer the dominant reason for punishment. It was replaced by an emphasis on deterrence and retribution. In those jurisdictions in which reformation or rehabilitation was emphasized, the focus was usually on diversion from prison rather than on prison programs designed to reform. As we shall see, just within the past decade or so, a reemphasis on rehabilitation and treatment has emerged.

Many aspects of modern U.S. prisons are examined in this chapter and in Chapter 10, and they demonstrate that some modern prisons are characterized by disruption, violence, monotonous daily routine, lack of work opportunities, and unconstitutional living conditions. Some jails and prisons are under federal court orders to improve inmates' living conditions and to reduce inmate populations or be closed. Are these modern prisons an improvement over the earlier ones? Some may say the question is not relevant; offenders should be punished, which is just what the system is doing.

Jail A local, regional, or federal facility used to confine persons awaiting a legal proceeding, as well as those serving short sentences.

9-3 Confinement Institutions

Offenders are confined in various types of institutions. These institutions are classified most commonly as jails, prisons, and community-based correctional facilities.

Although the terms **jail** and **prison** are used interchangeably and the two types of institutions have many common characteristics, they can be distinguished by their purposes. Jails and detention centers confine persons awaiting trial. They are also used for the short-term detention of persons in need of care when no other facilities are available immediately. For example, a public drunk might be detained until sober or until

Prison A federal or state penal facility for detaining adult offenders (although juvenile offenders are also incarcerated in adult facilities on occasion) sentenced to a year or longer after conviction of crimes.

arrangements are made for admittance to a treatment facility. Occasionally, jails are used to detain witnesses to a crime if it is thought that otherwise they might not be available for trial. Finally, jails are used to incarcerate convicted offenders who are sentenced to short terms, usually less than one year. Prisons are used for the incarceration of offenders who have been convicted of serious offenses, usually felonies, and who have been sentenced for lengthy terms (usually over one year).

Another type of facility that is used for confinement is a **community-based correctional facility**, which houses offenders but permits them to leave during part of the day to work, attend school, or engage in treatment programs. Offenders may also be confined in special-purpose facilities, such as treatment centers for abusers of alcohol or other drugs, for sex offenders, or for the mentally ill.

> **Community-based correctional facility** A facility in which the punishment emphasizes assimilation into the community. Instead of imprisonment, the offender may be put on probation or placed in programs such as work release, foster homes, halfway houses, parole, and furlough.

9-3a   Prison Security Levels

Prison security levels may be divided into three main categories: maximum, medium, and minimum custody. The federal government and most states have all three types. Characteristics of the levels differ from one jurisdiction to another.

Many of the maximum-security prisons currently in use were built before 1925, when most inmates were housed in maximum-security prisons, although for many of them, that security level was excessive. Unfortunately, this also occurs in some jurisdictions today. Maintenance of these old maximum-security facilities is difficult and costly; many of the complaints about prison conditions are related to the problems of maintaining these old facilities. An example is that of San Quentin.

San Quentin, located in San Quentin Village, California (close to Oakland and San Francisco), was built in the 1850s on land purchased for $10,000. In 1934, its death row was constructed to handle 68 inmates, but today, the number of condemned persons is often over 600. Most of these inmates live in two overcrowded buildings that were originally built to house regular inmates. In 1984, a federal court ruled that the San Quentin facility was unfit because of needed repairs. Approximately $35 million was spent on renovation and, for the first time, inmates had hot running water in their cells. A study completed in 2001 recommended closing San Quentin because of the cost of repairs needed to make the facility more secure as well as more accommodating to its inmates. It appears, however, that this plan will not be implemented. California's governor, Gray Davis (who was recalled in the fall of 2003 and Arnold Schwarzenegger was then elected), had proposed building a new death row facility at San Quentin. This unit would have cost approximately $220 million, and the need to get approval for that expenditure came at a time (in 2003) when the state faced a multibillion-dollar shortfall in its budget, resulting in cuts in many state programs and institutions. San Quentin is the third oldest prison in the United States, following the New York prisons at Auburn and Sing Sing.[19]

The issue of what to do with San Quentin arose again in late 2004, with the *New York Times* featuring the prison on its front page. With a color photo of the prison in the background, the paper related that California's death row had grown sufficiently that the state was preparing to spend $220 million to build a new one next door. The article noted, however, that the prison is on an expensive piece of property with a spectacular view. Opponents were increasing their attempts to block the expansion, based on the value of the real estate and the views, urging that the new death row be built elsewhere. But by April 2005, the environmental impact statements, along with the legal analysis of the issue of moving death row, were complete. The conclusion was that San Quentin is the only place to build the new death row facility because that state's law requires that all male death row inmates be confined at San Quentin and that all executions occur at San Quentin. "The California Department of Corrections has no authority to change this law." Construction was to begin in the fall of 2005 on the planned $220 million facility, but as of March 2007, authorities were still arguing over the cost and even whether the project should be done. California has the largest death row population in the United States but does not conduct many executions.[20]

Maximum-, medium-, and minimum-security prisons differ in the emphasis on treatment and related programs and in the freedom permitted inmates. In maximum-security prisons, inmates are detained in their cells for longer periods of time and are given less freedom of movement within the cell blocks than are those in the other security levels.

Another type of prison is the **open prison**. Open prisons make use of the natural environment for security. An example was Alcatraz Island, located in San Francisco Bay. Called "the Rock" because the island is mainly rock, Alcatraz has been used for numerous purposes, including a military prison and a maximum-security federal prison. Officially, it became a federal prison on 1 January 1934, and its purpose was to incarcerate the most dangerous federal offenders. A former U.S. attorney general described Alcatraz as a prison that would make no pretense at rehabilitation. Rather, it was a place for "the ultimate punishment society could inflict upon men short of killing them; the point of no return for multiple losers." Alcatraz was described by one writer as "the great garbage can of San Francisco Bay, into which every federal prison dumped its most rotten apples."[21]

> **Open prison**   A prison that makes use of the natural environment for security. For example, the prison might be located on an island surrounded by treacherous waters, as in the case of Alcatraz, located in San Francisco Bay and once used as a maximum security federal prison.

Alcatraz incarcerated some of the most notorious federal offenders, men such as George "Machine Gun" Kelly, a college-educated man from a prosperous family, convicted of bootlegging, and Robert F. Stroud, a young pimp who killed a customer after he had attacked one of Stroud's prostitutes. Stroud became known as the "Birdman of Alcatraz" because of his knowledge of bird diseases. Men such as Kelly and Stroud were sent to Alcatraz because it was considered the most secure U.S. prison at the time. It was assumed that no one could survive in the icy waters and current long enough to swim to San Francisco. There are no records of successful escapes, although on 11 June 1962 three inmates escaped, and their bodies were never found.

The cost of keeping an offender at Alcatraz was three times as high as it was at any other federal prison, and costly capital improvements were needed. On 21 March 1963, the prison was closed as a federal penitentiary. Inmates were transferred to other federal prisons. After a period of occupation by Native Americans between 1969 and 1971, Alcatraz became a tourist attraction and currently is the most frequently visited one in the San Francisco area. In recent years, Alcatraz has been renovated, and in 1991, a museum filled with "Alcatrivia" was opened on the island. By the summer of 2003, tourists were able to buy a piece of one of the concrete buildings, as the administrators decided it would be less expensive to sell the concrete than to have it hauled off the premises. And a British travel agency was offering couples a package, including a wedding at Alcatraz. Numerous books have been written about the prison and the island, some by former inmates and others by prison staff or their families.[22]

Alcatraz illustrated some of the problems with open prisons. They may be more secure, but they are costly and inconvenient. Land is scarce, and finding appropriate places for prison colonies is difficult. It is unlikely, therefore, that the open prison system will be used extensively in the future. The former federal penitentiary on McNeil Island off the coast of Washington State remains in use, although it is now part of the Washington State prison system.

In recent years, special prisons for high security needs have been built. These secure facilities are referred to as *maxi-maxi prisons* or *supermaximum-security prisons*. The author of a federal correctional report urged a conservative approach toward classifying inmates for supermax prisons and implored states not to use them to confine mentally ill inmates, those who need protective custody from other inmates, or those who are merely a nuisance. Supermax prisons are expensive to build and to operate, but they are popular with politicians. It is argued that the presence of these institutions—and thus the threat of being incarcerated in them—serves as a deterrent to inmates who might otherwise become disruptive within less secure facilities.[23]

A federal maxi-maxi, or supermax, prison opened in 1994 in Colorado. It is a state-of-the-art prison designed and built specifically for predator inmates—those who

Spotlight 9-2 Supermax Prisons: A Look at the Federal System

The federal supermax prison in Florence, Colorado, is the most secure in the federal system, having surpassed Marion, Illinois, which held that position for many years. One of its newest occupants is Eric Rudolph, who in April 2005, pleaded guilty to multiple terrorist acts in the 1990s, including the 1996 bombings at Atlanta's Olympic games. Another inmate at the Colorado supermax prison is Richard Reid, the shoe bomber terrorist who attempted to blow up a flight from Paris, France, to Miami, Florida. The Colorado supermax prison also houses other terrorists, such as Theodore "Ted" Kaczynski, the Unabomber (who used the mails to kill three people and injure 22 over a period of 17 years, serving four life sentences plus 30 years); Ramzi Ahmed Yousef (convicted of masterminding the 1993 bombing of the World Trade Center, which killed six and injured more than 1,000 people, serving a life sentence); and Khalfan Khamis Mohamed, also serving life, who, along with three others, was convicted of bombing the U.S. embassies in Kenya and Tanzania in 1998, killing 224 people. Timothy McVeigh, who bombed the federal building in Oklahoma City in 1995, was incarcerated in this prison before he was flown to the federal death row facility at Terre Haute, Indiana, where he was executed. McVeigh's accomplice, Terry L. Nichols, was also housed in Florence until he was transferred to Oklahoma to stand trial for state murder charges. Nichols was convicted of 168 murders and sentenced to life in prison without parole.

The inmates at the Florence prison spend most of their days and nights in their cells in isolation. As one behavioral therapist said, Florence is the only U.S. prison "specifically designed to keep every occupant in near-total solitary confinement....The worst-behaved men could serve an entire sentence—decades—in isolation." The isolation is brutal but, said the therapist, so are the inmates. "This is it. The end of

the line."[1] Some of the inmates are under court orders that severely restrict their communications with the outside world—for example, Yousef is not permitted to communicate by mail, telephone, or visits without court permission. Inmates are constantly monitored by surveillance cameras. The prison cost $150 million to build, and it costs approximately $100 a day to provide services for each inmate. No one has ever escaped from the institution.[2]

The model of a supermax prison emerged in the 1970s and 1980s after inmates murdered numerous correctional officials. Various security measures were taken, including locking down an entire prison population. Soon, the idea of building special facilities for the "worst of the worst" emerged, with the philosophy of almost total lockdown for these inmates.

Supporters claim that the supermax prisons have resulted in fewer inmate and staff deaths; critics warn that locking inmates down in almost total isolation for years may have serious repercussions. Further, there is evidence that in some states the guidelines for supermax eligibility are ignored, resulting in the incarceration of some inmates who do not need or deserve such intense security and isolation. As one news article concluded, "[T]he available numbers suggest that casual overuse of these facilities is common. For in tough-on-crime America, imposing grim conditions on prisoners is all too often seen as a good in itself, regardless of the long-term costs."[3]

1. "Monsters Doomed to Rot in a Hellish Dungeon," *New York Post* (19 October 2001), p. 6.
2. Ibid.
3. Sasha Abramsky, "Return of the Madhouse: Supermax Prisons Are Becoming the High-Tech Equivalent of the Nineteenth-Century Snake Pit," *The American Prospect* (11 February 2002), p. 26.

have demonstrated that they cannot live in other prisons without causing trouble for inmates as well as staff and administration. The facility, located at the foot of the Rockies, was built for 400 inmates. The inmates live in a "super-controlled environment that enforces a hard-edged solitude to contain the risk of social mixing and violence. Even the cell windows deny them all views of the outside except the sky above."[24] A British newspaper described this prison as looking "more like a chemical weapons installation than anything else" because of the obvious security measures, including 14-foot-high razor wire bundles and a "triangular ring of mirrored-glass towers guarding the new tomblike highest security prison," which "can be seen from six miles across the prairie wastelands of Colorado's Rockies."[25] Spotlight 9-2 presents more information on this secure federal prison.

In a case involving the Ohio supermax prison (OSP), the U.S. Supreme Court held that conditions there are so severe that inmates have a right to due process before they are assigned to such institutions. In that particular case, however, the Court found that the state had given the inmate adequate due process. The unanimous Supreme Court made the following observations, among others, about life in the Ohio supermax prison in its 2005 decision in *Wilkinson v. Austin*.[26]

Wilkinson v. Austin

Conditions at OSP are more restrictive than any other form of incarceration in Ohio, including conditions on its death row or in its administrative control units. The latter are themselves a highly restrictive form of solitary confinement. In the OSP almost every aspect of an inmate's life is controlled and monitored. Inmates must remain in their cells, which measure 7 by 14 feet, for 23 hours per day. A light remains on in the cell at all times, though it is sometimes dimmed, and an inmate who attempts to shield the light to sleep is subject to further discipline. During the one hour per day that an inmate may leave his cell, access is limited to one of two indoor recreation cells.

Incarceration at OSP is synonymous with extreme isolation. In contrast to any other Ohio prison, including any segregation unit, OSP cells have solid metal doors with metal strips along their sides and bottoms which prevent conversation or communication with other inmates. All meals are taken alone in the inmate's cell instead of in a common eating area. Opportunities for visitation are rare and in all events are conducted through glass walls. It is fair to say OSP inmates are deprived of almost any environmental or sensory stimuli and of almost all human contact.

Aside from the severity of the conditions, placement at OSP is for an indefinite period of time, limited only by an inmate's sentence. For an inmate serving a life sentence, there is no indication of how long he may be incarcerated at OSP once assigned there. Inmates otherwise eligible for parole lose their eligibility while incarcerated at OSP.

Although the U.S. Supreme Court did not detail all of the elements of due process that it considers required before a decision is made to assign an inmate to a maximum security prison, the Court did emphasize that one of the most important of the acceptable policies in Ohio is the requirement that the inmate who is being considered for assignment to the OSP be given the reasons and a chance for rebuttal of those reasons. The Court also spoke with favor about the requirement that three decision-makers—the warden, the classification committee, and the Bureau of Classification—must agree to the proposed assignment, and the assignment can be negated by any one of those three.

9-3b   Women's Prisons

Until the late 19th century, women, men, and children occupied the same dungeons, almshouses, and jails. The institutions were plagued with physical and sexual abuses. Prison reform led to segregated areas for women within the existing institutions. There were few female inmates, and that fact was used to justify not providing separate facilities. Some women's sections did not have a female matron. Vocational training and educational programs were not considered important.

In 1873, the first separate prison for women, the Indiana Women's Prison, was opened. Its emphases were rehabilitation, obedience, and religious education. Other institutions followed: in 1877 in Framingham, Massachusetts; a reformatory for women in 1891 in New York; the Westfield Farm (New York) in 1901; and in 1913 an institution in Clinton, New Jersey.

In contrast to institutions for adult men, most institutions for women are more aesthetic and less secure. Most female inmates are not considered high security risks and are not as violent as male inmates. There are some exceptions, but on the whole, the institutions are built and maintained to reflect the assumption that the occupants are not great risks to themselves or to others. Usually, female inmates are permitted greater privacy than incarcerated men.

Historically, female inmates have had fewer educational, vocational, and treatment programs than their counterparts in all-male penal institutions. The movement toward inmates' rights that began in the 1970s led to a recognition of these discrepancies, as we will see in the next chapter, along with a discussion of the special needs of female inmates. But here it is important to look at the issue of classification of female inmates. In a 2000 study, the National Institute of Corrections (NIC) surveyed all state correctional departments to determine which had systems for identifying and accommodating the differences in the risks and needs of male and female inmates. The study found that only four states (Idaho, New York, Massachusetts, and Ohio) had separate custody classification systems for women and that "only eight states used a system [of classification] that identified needs in a gender-responsible manner." Most classification models were developed for male inmates or for both genders but not specifically for women. The study found that female inmates respond more positively when classification is geared toward the variables that are most important to women upon release: "children, relationships, abuse, early trauma, mental illness and job skill."[27]

Construction of women's prisons has also become a high-priority item in some state budgets despite budget cutbacks. The reason for this is the increase in female inmates.

9-4   Federal and State Prisons

Most U.S. prisons are state institutions, but the federal government has a large prison system as well. This section examines both of these systems.

9-4a   The Federal System

The chapter's earlier discussion of the emergence of U.S. prisons referred to state-supported prisons. The federal government, which did not have prisons until the 1900s, contracted with states to incarcerate federal inmates. One of the first acts of Congress was to pass a statute encouraging states to permit the incarceration of federal inmates, at the federal government's expense, in state prisons. Most federal inmates with less than a year to serve or those awaiting trial were kept in local jails.[28]

In 1870, Congress established the Department of Justice (DOJ), which had a general agent in charge of the federal inmates in local jails and state prisons. Later, that position was called the *superintendent of prisons*. The superintendent was in charge of the care and custody of federal inmates and reported to an assistant attorney general in the DOJ.

Overcrowding in state prisons after the Civil War made some state officials reluctant to house federal offenders; other states accepted only federal offenders from within their borders. Transporting federal offenders to other states was expensive. In 1891, Congress authorized the purchase of land for three federal prisons.

The first federal prison was taken over from the War Department at Fort Leavenworth, Kansas. The facility had been used to house military offenders. It was found to be inadequate for the federal prison system, and Congress authorized the building of a prison on the Fort Leavenworth military reservation. Federal offenders housed at Fort Leavenworth built the prison. On 1 February 1906, inmates were moved to the new prison, and Fort Leavenworth was returned to the War Department. Final work on Leavenworth was not completed until 1928.

Leavenworth was followed by the construction of federal prisons—all for men—in Atlanta, Georgia, and McNeil Island, Washington (which, as noted earlier, is now a state prison). These prisons followed the architecture and philosophy of the Auburn system.

Prison overcrowding, poor conditions, and inconsistent administration of prisons, which were run primarily by local wardens, led to the need for more organization in the federal system. On 14 May 1930, President Herbert Hoover signed the law that created the federal Bureau of Prisons (BOP). Today, that bureau is a complex system, consisting of a main office in Washington, D.C., six regional offices, two staff training centers, 28 community corrections offices, and more than 106 institutions. The BOP is headed by a director, Harley Lappin (who took office in 2003, becoming the seventh director since the bureau was established, and replacing Kathleen Hawk Sawyer, who

Professions 9-1

Federal Bureau of Prisons: Career Opportunities

Welcome to the Federal Bureau of Prisons' (BOP) career opportunities web pages, where you can learn about BOP careers, the employment process, and current vacancies.

We recognize that the Bureau's real strength is derived from our staff. The BOP "family" is a diverse, well-trained, and career-oriented team with the finest corrections professionals in the country. The Bureau has approximately 35,000 highly motivated individuals working in more than 105 correctional institutions across the country...and in a wide range of occupations. We encourage you to explore our web pages and consider a career in corrections with the Federal Bureau of Prisons.

We are always accepting applications for the following positions:

Chaplain
Correctional Officer
Clinical Psychologist
Medical Officer
Nurse Practitioner
Physician Assistant
Registered Nurse

Source: Federal Bureau of Prisons, http://www.bop.gov/jobs/index.jsp, retrieved 16 July 2006.

retired). Lappin, who was the warden at the federal prison in Terre Haute, Indiana, when Timothy McVeigh was executed in June 2001, reports to the U.S. DOJ. The BOP has a prison industries division as well as a research arm, the National Institute of Corrections (NIC). The regional offices of the BOP facilitate the supervision and administration of all federal correctional institutions, inmates, and staff. The bureau has an extensive legal department, as well as divisions overseeing programming, medical services, and administration.

On 14 May 2003, Lappin testified before the House Judiciary's subcommittee on crime, terrorism, and homeland security. Among other information supplied by Lappin was the following:

- The BOP continues to meet its mission to "protect society by confining offenders in facilities that are safe, humane, cost-efficient, and appropriately secure, and that provide work and other self-improvement opportunities to assist offenders in becoming law-abiding citizens."
- Earlier in 2003, the BOP added to its strategic plan the goal "to enhance our efforts regarding the prevention, disruption, and response to terrorist activities."...
- The bureau's primary mission is to incarcerate federal inmates, but it also houses some pretrial detainees and unsentenced convicted offenders under the jurisdiction of the U.S. Marshals Service (USMS). It also houses...detainees of the Bureau of Immigration and Customs Enforcement, now located within the Department of Homeland Security.
- The BOP has four levels of security for its prisons, along with detention centers and medical facilities.
- New technology and changes in staff training (and drug testing) have been implemented to improve the safety and security of federal prisons.[29]

In 2006, the BOP reported that approximately 185,000 individuals were under its jurisdiction, with 85 percent of those in federal facilities and the rest in state or local facilities through contract. Approximately 35,000 persons were employed by the BOP.[30] Professions 9-1 contains general information about career opportunities in the federal BOP, from the BOP website.

9-4b   State Systems

All states have correctional systems; most are centralized and headed by a director, who reports to the governor. The director is responsible for overseeing all correctional facilities.

Most states have all levels of security for male offenders, in addition to separate institutions for juveniles and women and treatment centers in the communities. Not all levels of security are available for women because of the smaller number of female inmates.

States may contract with other states for the incarceration of some inmates. After a riot, it is not uncommon for inmates to be transferred to another state until the riot-damaged facilities are remodeled, repaired, or replaced. Such transfers may be made to remove the riot's leaders. States may also contract with other states to house inmates whose lives are in danger in their own states. Such arrangements might be made between a state and the federal system as well.

State prison systems differ considerably from each other in size and complexity, as well as in prison conditions, administrative problems, and the cost of maintaining inmates. Most incarcerated persons are in local jails, rather than in state or federal prisons.

9-5   Local Systems: The Jail

Jails are local facilities that are used to confine persons awaiting trial, persons for whom no alternative facilities are immediately available (such as persons arrested for driving while intoxicated who do not have a responsible driving adult to whom they may be released), and persons serving short sentences, usually less than a year. Most jails are operated by counties. Jails may be the most important facilities in criminal justice systems because they affect more people than do any other criminal justice facilities. The "jail is [not only] a major intake center…for the entire criminal justice system, but also a place of first or last resort for a host of disguised health, welfare, and social problem cases."[31] Spotlight 9-3 examines other functions of local jails.

Jails may be traced far back into history, when they made their debut "in the form of murky dungeons, abysmal pits, unscaleable precipices, strong poles or trees, and suspended cages in which hapless prisoners were kept."[32] The primary purpose of those jails, also called *gaols* (see again Spotlight 9-1), was to detain people awaiting trial, transportation, the death penalty, or corporal punishment. The old jails were not escape-proof, and frequently, the person in charge received additional fees for shackling inmates. Inmates were not separated according to classification, physical conditions were terrible, food was inadequate, and no treatment or rehabilitation programs existed.

These early detention centers were followed in the 15th and 16th centuries in Europe by facilities characterized by work and punishment, called workhouses, or houses of correction. After the breakup of the feudal system, all of western Europe experienced a significant increase in pauperism and public begging. To combat this problem, a workhouse called the Bridewell was established in London in 1557. The dominant philosophy at the Bridewell was a belief that, if people had to work at hard and unpleasant tasks, they would abandon their wantonness and begging.

The sordid conditions of jails and workhouses in Europe were brought to the attention of the world by John Howard, the prison reformer mentioned earlier. After his tour of European institutions, Howard said in 1773 that more inmates died of jail fever than of execution.[33]

The first jails in the American colonies were places of confinement used primarily to hold suspects awaiting trial, persons who could not pay their debts, and convicted offenders waiting to be taken to prison. Jails were rarely used for punishment. Most of the offenses for which people may be sentenced to jail or prison today were handled in other ways then: by corporal punishment, capital punishment, fines, or publicly humiliating activities, such as sitting in the stocks or pillory, where people could jeer at the offenders. In the stocks, the victim's ankles were chained to holes in a wooden frame. The pillory was a device of varying shapes and sizes, to which the offender was secured in several ways, one of which was to be nailed to boards. The pillory was driven through town so that people could throw rotten eggs or vegetables at the offenders.

In the 1600s, to replace such severe punishments, Pennsylvania Quakers suggested what they considered to be a more humane form of treatment, the use of jails as

Spotlight 9-3   The Function of Jails

Jails are locally operated correctional facilities that confine persons before or after adjudication. Inmates sentenced to jail usually have a sentence of one year or less. Jails also:

- Receive individuals pending arraignment and hold them awaiting trial, conviction, or sentencing
- Readmit probation, parole, and bailbond violators and absconders
- Temporarily detain juveniles pending transfer to juvenile authorities
- Hold mentally ill persons pending their movement to appropriate mental health facilities

- Hold individuals for the military, for protective custody, for contempt, and for the courts as witnesses
- Release convicted inmates to the community upon completion of sentence
- Transfer inmates to federal, state, or other authorities
- House inmates for federal, state, or other authorities because of crowding of their facilities
- Sometimes operate community-based programs as alternatives to incarceration.

Source: Peter M. Harrison and Allen J. Beck, Bureau of Justice Statistics Bulletin, *Prison and Jail Inmates at Midyear 2005* (Washington, D.C.: U.S. Department of Justice, May 2006), p. 7.

punishment. U.S. jails came to be used not only for the detention of those awaiting trial but also as confinement for those serving short-term sentences.

The horrible conditions of American jails continued over the years. In 1923, Joseph Fishman, a federal prison inspector, investigator, and consultant, wrote a book, *Crucible of Crime*, in which he described U.S. jails. He based his descriptions and evaluations on visits to 1,500 jails. He said that some of the convicted would ask for a year in prison in preference to six months in jail because of the inhumane jail conditions.

According to Fishman, most jails were characterized by a lack of space; inadequate amenities, such as meals, bathing facilities, and hospitals; and no separate facilities for juveniles. Although Fishman said jail conditions were terrible nationwide, the facilities were worse in the South. Fishman's conclusion might be summarized by his definition of a U.S. jail as

> an unbelievably filthy institution....Usually swarming with bedbugs, roaches, lice, and other vermin; has an odor of disinfectant and filth which is appalling; supports in complete idleness thousands of able-bodied men and women, and generally affords ample time and opportunity to assure inmates a complete course in every kind of viciousness and crime. A melting pot in which the worst elements of the raw material in the criminal world are brought forth, blended and turned out in absolute perfection.[34]

Today, the typical U.S. jail is small, at least 30 years old, and in need of renovation. It is located in a small town, usually the county seat of a predominantly rural county. These small, rural jails constitute the majority of jails but house a minority of the total U.S. jail population. Some are used infrequently, and many are not crowded, in contrast to jails in urban areas. The typical jail is locally financed and administered.

Some states have assumed partial control of their jails and have established statewide minimum standards. Professional organizations have also been involved with jail standards. In the 1980s, the American Correctional Association sponsored the Commission on Accreditation for Corrections. That commission develops jail standards and certifies jails that meet those standards, but supervision or evaluation by states or professional organizations may not be sufficient to raise jail standards to an acceptable level. Federal courts have become involved, and their actions are discussed in Chapter 10 in conjunction with court orders concerning jail and prison conditions.

The influence of the federal government on jails is also seen in other areas, such as federal technical assistance, financial assistance, and the imposing of standards. In addition, the federal government has provided states and local governments with assistance to build new correctional facilities and to remodel existing ones.

9-6 Short Incarceration with Intensive Training

The jail is used for short-term detention, but generally, little effort is made to provide intensive training or education. Prisons are for long-term incarceration, and many do provide educational and vocational programs as well as work, but treatment and behavior modification is not a primary goal of most prisons. Perhaps something in-between might work better. In this section, we look at two approaches: the boot camp and the work camp.

9-6a The Boot Camp Approach

A recent approach to incarceration is the use of military-style boot camps, which have been utilized for the shock incarceration of some offenders, usually young ones with their first prison term for nonviolent offenses such as drug possession. Although there was some initial criticism of boot camps, the concept spread quickly in the 1990s. For example, in 1991, a private association that had been critical of the correctional system in New York praised the boot camp program and called for its expansion. According to the Correctional Association of New York, "In contrast to many other prisons, shock camps are safe, drug-free, and well-run institutions."[35]

Not everyone agreed. Some scholars noted that the boot camp model is conducive to abuses of power, as well as to aggressive behavior by both inmates and staff. Further, as criminologists found, "Research does not provide indications that there will be beneficial effects."[36] A 1994 National Institute of Justice (NIJ) study of boot camps concluded that "the boot camp experience in itself does not successfully reduce recidivism." But graduates of boot camps were more likely than those released from prison to state that the experience had been a positive one. It is important, however, to control for the supervision factor, for there is evidence that close supervision within the community after release from boot camp is important to the success of the shock incarceration experience.[37]

A 1995 research article reporting on the NIJ data from eight state boot camp programs noted the variation in the programs and the difficulty of measuring all the variables that might influence results. The authors suggested that programs should be evaluated on a state-by-state basis and concluded that "those who complete boot camp do not inevitably perform either better or worse than their comparison group counterparts."[38]

Some jurisdictions have found, however, that boot camps worked only until youths left. Researchers who evaluated boot camp programs for the NIJ reported in 1996 that "what appeared to be a promising prognosis at the conclusion of boot camp disintegrated during aftercare."[39]

A study published in 2003 by Abt Associates, a research firm, questioned the effectiveness of boot camps in reducing **recidivism**. The scholar who conducted the study pointed out that boot camps have had difficulty meeting their goals of reducing prison populations, prison costs, and recidivism. There were some positives, however, such as the reduction of impulsive behavior, anxiety, and depression and an improvement in the social attitudes of boot camp participants. In the study, reading and math skills, along with self-esteem, improved among some. The study suggested that the time spent in boot camps (90 to 120 days in most) might have been too low to result in marked reductions in recidivism.[40]

Other jurisdictions experienced sufficient problems with boot camps that the programs were eliminated. Two examples stand out. First, in 2001, Tony Haynes, age 14, died in a privately owned and operated Arizona boot camp, the Buffalo Soldiers' Camp. It was alleged that Haynes was forced to stand for five hours in 116-degree heat and that he was dehydrated; he was then taken to a motel and put in a bathtub to cool off. In February 2002, the director of the camp, Charles F. Long II, age 56, was arrested on second-degree murder and child abuse charges. Several staffers were also charged in the

> ▶ **Recidivism** The process of committing additional crimes.

boy's death. Troy A. Hutty, 29, a former corporal at the camp, who was charged with manslaughter, pleaded guilty to negligent homicide and was promised probation as he agreed to testify against Long.[41]

Long's trial began in October 2004. Just before the trial recessed for the Thanksgiving holidays, Long's wife, Carmelina, was called to testify. She blurted out that the alleged victim's mother, upon hearing that her son died, had said, "I can't believe he did it." According to Carmelina, who worked with her husband, the mother "said he [her son] had been trying to kill himself for three years and he finally did it." Prosecutors objected to the comment, but the judge overruled that objection and downgraded some of the child abuse counts against Long to lesser felonies.[42] In January 2005, Long was convicted of reckless manslaughter and sentenced to six years in prison.

The second example is from Florida. On 6 January 2006, Martin Lee Anderson, 14, who was detained at a boot camp in Panama City, died. Anderson, who had been at the camp only a day, was admitted on a charge of grand theft after he was accused of stealing his grandmother's car. He had also violated the terms of his probation. It was alleged that Anderson died as the result of being kicked by correctional officials after he stopped running during a drill, all of which was videotaped. The Anderson case led to the enactment of a statute, the Martin Lee Anderson Act of 2006, that eliminated boot camps and replaced them with juvenile detention centers that focus on education.[43]

In January 2005, the federal BOP gave notice that its three boot camp programs would be closed and recommissioned as minimum security prison camps. The three facilities are located in Lompoc, California; Lewisburg, Pennsylvania; and Bryan, Texas (a facility for women).[44]

9-6b   The Work Ethic Camp

The work camp has been used for some time, but recently, a modification of the traditional work camp has been in use in Nebraska. It is called the *work ethic camp*, and it is not a prison or a boot camp but, rather, a detention facility that focuses on changing offenders' thinking patterns that enable them to violate laws and replace those patterns with thinking patterns that are conducive to law-abiding actions. The program includes educational and vocational training, as well as substance abuse treatment, cognitive restructuring, family dynamics, physical training, and group involvement. The program's objectives for offenders are as follows:

- Develop and enhance job-readiness skills to prepare them to obtain and maintain employment
- Develop life skills that will help them with money management, time management, family, daily living, relationships, leisure, education, and independent living
- Identify patterns of thinking and behavior that have resulted in past failures
- Develop a positive view of themselves, and consider the harm they have caused their victims
- Become more responsible, improve their decision-making skills in the face of challenging situations, and enhance problem-solving abilities when faced with conflicts
- Be able to identify possible high-risk circumstances and strategies of how to avoid, cope with, or escape from trouble in the future.[45]

The Nebraska work ethic camp was designed to detain offenders for 120 days, but some may stay longer (up to 180 days total). Only nonviolent, first-time felony offenders are admitted. Sex offenders are excluded. Offenders must be mentally and medically fit, have been sentenced to no more than 10 years, and be between 17 and 35 years of age. Many of the offenders are drug abusers, with 39 percent of the first group assigned having convictions for drug-related offenses and 23 percent of the remaining inmates having records of prior drug offenses. In an evaluation of the Nebraska program, it was stated that a review of the literature suggested that "the most successful correctional programs are believed to be those that address the cognitive functioning of offenders." Programs such as Vermont's Cognitive Self-Change Program were cited as having a 20 percent reduction in recidivism, compared to the repeat offense rates of inmates who were released without participating in a short-term program with intensive training and supervision.[46]

The initial evaluation of the Nebraska program notes the difficulty of accurate comparisons between the cost and the success rates of this approach, compared to traditional incarceration, and emphasizes that a long-term study will be necessary. But the preliminary conclusion was that "there is the potential for considerable cost savings without a significant increase of risk to the community when clientele are assessed and screened for appropriate characteristics, a program is operated effectively, and an effort is made to provide continuity between the program and transition back to the community." Offenders who are released from the program are then placed on intensive probation supervision.[47]

The following section considers some of the effects of jail and prison overcrowding and the efforts to combat them. The legal issues surrounding overcrowding are discussed in Chapter 10.

9-7 Prison and Jail Overcrowding

During the last two decades of the 20th century, federal and state prisons experienced dramatic population growth, as well as continued expansion, even as crime rates were going down. Figure 9-1 diagrams the growth of the U.S. incarceration rate between 1980 and 2005. This increased incarceration rate was due in part to the three strikes and truth in sentencing policies, discussed in Chapter 8, as well as to stricter laws and enforcement.

Spotlight 9-4 contains information about jail and prison populations at midyear 2005. In 2002, for the first time in history, U.S. prisons and jails held more than 2 million people, and that figure had reached 2,186,230 by midyear 2005. State and federal prisons incarcerated 1,438,701 inmates; local municipal and county jails held or supervised 747,529 inmates. That figure does not include persons under supervision in community-based programs. Between 2004 and 2005, the numbers under state jurisdiction increased by 1.2 percent, while those under federal supervision rose by 2.9 percent. The total number of women under the jurisdiction of state and federal prison authorities increased by 3.4 percent, compared with a 1.3 percent increase for men.[48]

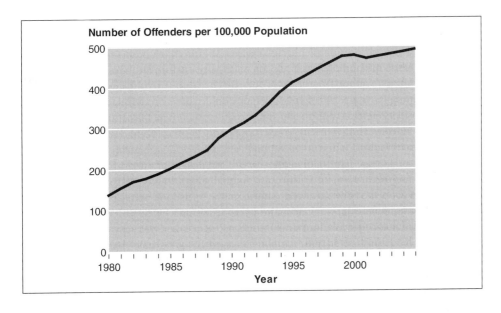

Figure 9-1
U.S. Incarceration Rate, 1980–2005
Source: Bureau of Justice Statistics, "After Sharp Increases in the 1980s and 1990s, the Incarceration Rate Has Recently Grown at a Slower Pace," http://www.ojp.usdoj.gov/bjs/glance/incrt.htm, accessed 12 May 2007.

| *Spotlight 9-4* | Highlights of Jail and Prison Populations, Midyear 2005 |

From midyear 2004 to midyear 2005:

- The number of inmates in custody in local jails rose by 33,539; in State prison by 15,858; and in Federal prison by 6,584.
- The smaller State prison systems had the greatest percentage increase: Montana (up 7.9 percent) and South Dakota (up 7.8 percent).

On June 30, 2006:

- A total of 2,266 State prisoners were under age 18. Adult jails held a total of 6,759 persons under age 18.
- State and Federal correctional authorities held 91,117 noncitizens (6.4 percent of all prisoners), down from 91,815 at midyear 2004.
- There were 129 female prison and jail inmates per 100,000 women in the United States, compared to 1,366 male prison and jail inmates per 100,000 men.
- An estimated 12 percent of black males, 3.7 percent of Hispanic males, and 1.7 percent of white males in their late twenties were in prison or jail.

- In three States—Iowa, South Dakota, and Wisconsin—black prison and jail inmates represented 4 percent of the black State population. Pennsylvania (with 1,714 Hispanic inmates per 100,000 Hispanic residents) and Idaho (1,654) had the highest Hispanic incarceration rates.
- Local jails were operating 5 percent below their rated capacity. In contrast, at year-end 2004, State prison systems were between 1 percent below capacity and 15 percent above; the Federal prison system was operating at 40 percent above rated capacity.
- Privately operated prison facilities held 101,228 inmates (up 2.7 percent since midyear 2004). The Federal system reported the largest increase among inmates in private prisons (up 2,038).

Source: Paige M. Harrison and Allen J. Beck, Bureau of Justice Statistics, *Prison and Jail Inmates at Midyear 2005* (Washington, D.C.: U.S. Department of Justice, May 2006), p. 1, http://www.ojp.usdoj.gov/bjs, accessed 31 March 2007.

In 2005, 23 states and the federal prison system were operating at or above their highest capacity,[49] and such overcrowding has significant negative effects.

9-7a The Effects of Overcrowding

Social scientists and federal judges have noted the negative impact of jail and prison overcrowding on inmates. In a Texas prison case, which was in the federal courts for almost two decades, an appellate court concluded during the initial stage, that inmates were "routinely subjected to brutality, extortion, and rape....The overcrowding...exercises a malignant effect on all aspects of inmate life." The court noted that inmates were in the presence of other persons almost constantly, sleeping only with the knowledge that they might be attacked by cellmates. "There is little respite from these conditions, for...inmates have wholly inadequate opportunities to escape the overcrowding in their living quarters."[50]

The problems in the California prison system are also illustrative. In 2004, officials predicted that some California prisons would be closed, but by 2005, despite its budget crisis, the state opened a new prison and reopened a correctional facility that had been managed privately. Still, inmates were jammed into cells and dormitory facilities, with little space for personal movement or exercise; tensions were high. The crowded conditions made it more difficult for correctional authorities to see inmates in some areas, thus reducing security. Approximately 10,000 inmates were housed in what officials called *ugly beds*, which referred to beds that were located in areas that were not designed for housing, such as recreation rooms and hallways. A nonpartisan legislative committee reported that between 1997 and 2003, when the California prison system experienced significant growth, the rate of inmate altercations rose 18 percent. A corrections consultant stated it this way: "The problem with overcrowding is that you lose flexibility in how you house inmates." The overcrowding is thwarting the governor's promise to overhaul California prisons and restore that state to its prior position as a leader in corrections.[51]

The harmful effects of prison overcrowding have led to numerous lawsuits. In 2002, five Alabama female inmates filed a lawsuit alleging that the "outrageously over-crowded and dangerous conditions" in which women were serving time were causing physical assaults by inmates who were slashing each other with razors. In the spring of 2003, in the case of *Laube v. Haley*, a district court admonished state prison officials for their failure to submit an acceptable plan for alleviating the unconstitutional conditions under which Alabama's female inmates were confined in the Julia Tutwiler Prison for Women and two other institutions. The court stated that a lack of money was not an acceptable reason for failure to submit the plan. On 2 December 2002, the court had ordered prison officials to submit a plan to correct the unconstitutional conditions; in the spring of 2003, the court decided, after hearing oral arguments, that the submitted plan was not sufficient. The court ordered state officials to devise a new plan to solve the unconstitutional conditions under which Alabama female inmates were being held.[52]

During several months in 2004, both parties to this suit negotiated and reached settlements, which the court accepted. The terms range from safety and security to medical issues and are quite extensive. Numerous inmates participated in giving their comments when they had the opportunity to do so, and the judge, in accepting the settlement agreements, commended them and the other parties to the litigation, noting that, as recently as December 2002, this court had described the conditions at Tutwiler as "essentially a time bomb ready to explode facility-wide at any unexpected moment." When he accepted the agreements in the summer of 2004, the judge noted the improvements in conditions at the prison, attributed those to the work of the warden, and emphasized that the "court has full confidence that, in accordance with the provisions of the settlement agreements, [the warden] will build on her notable success." To ensure that occurs, the court appointed a special master—an expert, (often an attorney or a prison official), who oversees the implementation of the court orders.[53]

A review published in 2003 by the Justice Policy Institute (JPI), which conducts research and promotes alternatives to incarceration, reported that 10 states (representing one-third of the U.S. population) had seen reductions in their prison populations, but most states were facing budget cuts that severely affected corrections. Some were reducing their prison populations solely for budgetary reasons. Michigan's outgoing governor signed legislation repealing mandatory minimum sentences for drug offenders. Kentucky's governor granted early release to 567 nonviolent offenders for a reported savings of $5 million. That state saved over $20 million by postponing construction on three proposed prison projects, cutting correctional staff positions, and reducing spending on private correctional facilities. According to Kentucky's governor, "Kentucky and most other states simply don't have the revenue it takes to house increasing prisoners." JPI cited other states with proposals to reduce the number of inmates, along with three public opinion polls showing that the public supported policies that deemphasize incarceration. One poll revealed that two-thirds of its respondents favored treatment rather than incarceration for nonviolent drug offenders.[54]

9-7b Prison and Jail Expansion

Some jurisdictions have responded to overcrowding by building new facilities, an extremely costly measure. Others have remodeled existing facilities, resulting in a corrections business that is one of the fastest-growing industries in the United States.

Construction costs are not the only expenses to be considered in the expansion of facilities or building of new ones. Operational costs of jails and prisons are high, and they continue to increase, outstripping the ability of many jurisdictions to cover them. Construction time is a factor as well. Because many jurisdictions are under federal court orders to reduce their prison and jail populations, they need available space quickly. As a result, some have sought faster construction plans and methods, which may result in construction problems.

9-7c Private Correctional Facilities

One solution to prison problems has been to hire private firms to build and operate prisons or to provide special services, such as medical care or food. Privatization of correctional facilities, thought by many to be a modern movement, was actually used in the 1800s, in many cases for the same reasons as today, such as prison overcrowding.

The latest trend is different from previous privatization of prisons in several ways. For a long time, correctional facilities, particularly jails and juvenile and adult community-based correctional facilities, relied on outside agencies to provide certain goods and services. Studies showed this practice to be more cost-effective than each institution's providing every service and product that it needed. Medical service contracts were mentioned most frequently as more cost-effective than in-house services.[55]

The private sector is involved in corrections in three main areas: (1) prison work programs, (2) the financing of construction, and (3) the management of facilities. A state or the federal government might contract for one, two, or all of these.

Many states and the federal government use some private contractors for the management and operation of correctional institutions. In April 2003, Corrections Corporation of America (CCA) celebrated its 20th anniversary of providing private services to government correctional facilities. CCA is the sixth largest correctional system in the United States, behind the federal system and the state systems in California, Texas, New York, and Florida. CCA controls more than 50 percent of the private correctional sector.[56]

In January 2005, a corrections journal reported that the three largest private prison companies look "like solid investments." Due to state and federal budget cuts, increasing prison populations, and resulting prison overcrowding, states and the federal government were turning to private corporations to solve the problems of the "chronic scarcity" of jail and prison beds. Over one-half of state facilities were over capacity, along with 33 percent of federal institutions.[57]

By the end of 2005, 6 percent of state inmates and 14.4 percent of federal inmates were being held in private prisons, representing a 7.2 percent increase in state systems and a 74.2 percent increase in the federal system when compared to the year 2000. In New Mexico, Wyoming, Hawaii, Alaska, and Montana, at least 25 percent of the state's inmates were housed in private prisons. The largest prison populations in private facilities were in Texas (17,517) and Florida (6,261).[58]

Several advantages to the use of private correctional facilities have been cited. A study released in April 2003 and conducted by two Vanderbilt University professors concluded that states with private prisons had more success in keeping public spending for corrections under control than did states that did not have private prisons. Even states that had small levels of private prison use saved significant amounts in their correctional budgets.[59]

Although we do not know whether private prisons can exist successfully with traditional government programs, some believe there are definite advantages. The private sector can concentrate on special offenders. This includes women, juveniles, illegal aliens, and inmates who are at risk in the general prison population, such as child molesters, former law enforcement officials, and prison informants.

The private sector may also provide an invaluable service simply by showing jail and prison officials that efficient and flexible management is possible in corrections. In most government facilities, competitive business principles, creative use of staff, adaptation of existing buildings and programs to meet changing needs, and experimentation with new ideas all seem to lag behind the private sector. Private involvement in corrections may encourage correctional administrators to modernize management styles, staff relations, and inmate care.

The private sector's involvement in corrections, however, raises many questions. First is the issue of whether private companies can deliver what they promise, such as "high-tech prisons that offer a full-range of rehabilitative programs, including college courses and job training,…pristine facilities that are efficiently managed without crowding problems" and at a lower cost than current facilities. These types of promises are made by companies such as Wackenhut Corrections Corporation and Corrections Corporation of America.[60] The issue is whether the companies can deliver.

Another issue regarding private correctional facilities is whether they are effective. A recent study by Florida scholars concerning private prisons in that state concluded that there was no evidence that inmates released from private prisons (including those for adult males, adult females, and juveniles) were less likely to become recidivists once they were released. The authors did, however, acknowledge that there is limited empirical information on this subject and that studies should be conducted in other states as well.[61]

In reacting to the Florida study, a scholar at the National Institute of Justice stated:

> The original promise was that prison privatization would increase service quality. The premise was that the free market would introduce efficiency previously unknown.…The resulting performance suggests that neither promise nor premise was correct. The research results are clear.[62]

Another scholar, however, pointed out that both the Florida study and the earlier ones by other scholars that suggested that private prison releasees were less likely to recidivate than those released from public facilities have methodological problems, resulting in limitations on their conclusions.[63]

There are also allegations that privatization of correctional facilities may be dangerous. Specifically, it is argued that private security firms cut security short to save money. One labor economist stated that "the daily pressures that these [private] companies face to satisfy Wall Street [cause] them to pay employees low wages, and to under-staff facilities, under-train employees and hire unqualified staff." The labor economist concluded that, if the government thinks airport security is so critical that it requires government rather than private regulation, it does not make sense to contract out the security of our prisons. A noted criminal justice policy analyst also believes that government prisons are better managed than private ones and that "inmate assaults on other inmates and guards, drug use and escapes occur at higher rates in private prisons."[64]

There are other issues concerning private prisons. Politically, it is argued that corrections is a government function that should never be delegated. To do so increases problems, leading to lobbying for programs that might not be in the best interests of the public or corrections. The profit motive reduces the incentive to decrease the number of incarcerated people. The profit incentive encourages larger and larger private prisons. To make a profit, those facilities must be occupied. When the incentive for full prisons is combined with the public's call for longer and harsher sentences, the result may be more inmates serving more time.

Another issue concerns what happens if an inmate in a private correctional facility sues for damages and wins. Are both the government and the private company legally liable? Still other concerns are as follows:

- Should the government be involved in internal discipline or staff training?
- Will the short-term relief offered by private prisons turn into long-term, costly government obligations?
- Will public employees accept the presence of private staff?
- Will corrections administrators allow the transfer of inmate control to private business?
- Will the public lose its voice in determining the location of private prisons?[65]

Private security is utilized in law enforcement beyond prisons and jails, as noted on 1 May 2007, by Joseph Ricci, the executive director of the National Association of Security Companies (NASCO), as he addressed the Committee on House Homeland Security of the U.S. Congress. Ricci pointed out that almost 2 million persons work in private security in the United States, compared to fewer than 700,000 in public law enforcement. NASCO employs almost 450,000 trained security officers who work in government and in the commercial sector. According to Ricci, at present, private security officers

> are guarding federal facilities, critical infrastructure, business and public areas, working with the armed forces in Iraq and at DoD installations, supporting the operations of the Customs and Border Patrol, and providing screening at airports for TSA. Private security guards are often the "first" responder on the scene of any security or terrorism related incident, and private security protects 85 percent of the nation's critical infrastructure.[66]

According to Ricci, we must improve the standards for private security and the recruitment, hiring, and training of persons who serve in this critical area. NASCO is working on legislation in several states that currently do not regulate private security. Ricci also stressed that government and private security must work together "to develop and access the best solutions and capabilities."[67]

Chapter Wrap-Up

This chapter set the stage for the next two chapters, which discuss life in prison and community corrections. It is important to understand the history of jails and prisons in order to evaluate what is happening today. The chapter began with the European background of incarceration, emphasizing the reform efforts of John Howard. Howard was influential in America, but the Quakers led the movement toward incarceration, intended as a milder sanction to replace the death penalty and the inhuman methods of corporal punishment that prevailed in U.S. criminal justice systems.

Two systems that emerged in the United States—the Pennsylvania system, with its emphasis on solitary confinement, and the Auburn system, with its emphasis on the silent system—competed for recognition in the United States and in Europe. The influence of the systems is still seen today; many U.S. maximum-security prisons, built in the late 1800s and early 1900s, reflect an architecture typical of the Auburn system. In Europe, many prisons built on the architectural model of the Pennsylvania system remain in use.

The Elmira Reformatory did not survive long as a place of reformation, but it set the stage for the movement toward rehabilitation and established the reformatory model that became characteristic of institutions for juveniles.

It is impossible to talk about a prison system in the United States because states have their own unique systems, the jail systems of local communities differ widely, and the federal government has a separate system. The federal system has traditionally been considered the most efficient and effective, but it is also the fastest growing. State prisons have been the sites of most of the riots and overcrowded conditions that are discussed in subsequent chapters. But many local jails also face problems of overcrowding and inadequate facilities, leading to the establishment of jail standards by the federal government, the American Correctional Association, and some states. Overcrowding has also led to inmate lawsuits, some resulting in federal court orders to reduce prison and jail populations or make changes in prison conditions.

The use of military-style boot camps, once popular in recent years, has resulted in numerous problems, including inmate deaths. In many jurisdictions, boot camps have been abolished. The concept has some support remaining, however, for it gives the appearance of punishment as well as some semblance of preparing inmates to live more productive lives. The chapter also discussed the Nebraska work ethic camp as an alternative to prison and to boot camps.

Many of the problems of incarceration are related to overcrowding. There are two basic ways to solve this problem. First, we can build more facilities. The costs, however, are overwhelming. Perhaps even more important, if we build them, we fill them, and the problem of a lack of prison space remains. The second solution is to reduce prison populations. This has been done in some states by enacting statutes that permit governors to declare an emergency and authorize early release of some inmates when prison populations reach 95 percent (or some other figure) of legal capacity. Problems occur, however, when the releasees commit new crimes.

The cost of building new facilities to handle the overcrowding of jails and prisons, coming at a time when many government budgets are being cut, has led to the involvement of the private sector in the financing and management of jails and prisons. This is a controversial innovation, as the chapter discussion demonstrated, and the increased number of illegal immigrant detainees in particular means that the controversy will continue.

Inadequate conditions, overcrowding, and management problems in jails and prisons increase the problems of living behind the walls, as we will see in Chapter 10.

Key Terms

classification (p. 267)
community-based correctional facility (p. 271)
custody (p. 270)
humanitarianism (p. 263)
inmates (p. 265)

jail (p. 270)
offenders (p. 263)
open prison (p. 272)
penitentiary (p. 264)
prison (p. 270)
recidivism (p. 279)

reformatory (p. 269)
silent system (p. 266)
transportation (p. 263)
wardens (p. 265)
workhouse (p. 264)

Apply It

1. Explain why prisons emerged in Europe, and relate your discussion to the contributions of John Howard.
2. What characterized the emergence of prisons in the United States, and how did the Walnut Street Jail contribute to this development?
3. Compare and contrast the Pennsylvania and the Auburn systems.
4. What is a reformatory? Why were reformatories developed? Explain the importance of European reformers to this development. How did European reform programs influence the emergence of the Elmira Reformatory?
5. How do jails differ from prisons? From community-based correctional facilities?
6. What is the difference between prisons centered on a philosophy of custody and those that focus on rehabilitation?
7. Distinguish among the levels of prison security. What is meant by a *supermax* or a *maxi-maxi* prison? Evaluate.
8. Explore the general and unique features of prisons for women, and compare them with the features of those for men.
9. Distinguish between the state and federal prison systems, and analyze population growth in each.
10. How does the present-day purpose of jails compare with their historical purpose? What are the problems of administering jails? What role, if any, should the federal government play in the administration of local jails?
11. What are boot camps? How effective are they?
12. How does the Nebraska work ethic camp compare to traditional incarceration? To boot camp?
13. What are the effects of prison and jail overcrowding?
14. What is the place of the private sector in jails and prisons? In other security areas?

Endnotes

1. Harry Elmer Barnes, *The Story of Punishment* (Boston: Stratford, 1930), pp. 117, 122. The introductory material on the history of prisons is based on this source unless otherwise noted.
2. Stephen Schaefer, *Theories in Criminology* (New York: Random House, 1969), pp. 104–105.
3. John Howard, *State of Prisons*, 2d ed. (Warrington, England: Patterson Smith, 1792).
4. Alexis M. Durham III, "Social Control and Imprisonment during the American Revolution: Newgate of Connecticut," *Justice Quarterly* 7 (June 1990): 293.
5. Alexis M. Durham III, "Newgate of Connecticut: Origins and Early Days of an Early American Prison," *Justice Quarterly* 6 (March 1989): 89–116.
6. David J. Rothman, *The Discovery of the Asylum: Social Order and Disorder in the New Republic* (Boston: Little, Brown, 1971), pp. 92–93.
7. Norman B. Johnston, "John Haviland," in *Pioneers in Criminology*, ed. Herman Mannheim (Montclair, N.J.: Patterson Smith, 1960), p. 122.
8. Rothman, *The Discovery of the Asylum*, p. 83.
9. Howard Gill, "State Prisons in America 1787–1937," in *Penology*, ed. George C. Killinger and Paul F. Cromwell (St. Paul, Minn.: West, 1973), p. 41.
10. Quoted in John Vincent Barry, "Alexander Maconochie," in *Pioneers in Criminology*, 2d enlarged ed., ed. Hermann Mannheim (Montclair, N.J.: Patterson Smith, 1972), p. 90.
11. Ibid., pp. 91, 95–97. For a more recent account of Maconochie's contributions, see Norval Morris, *Maconochie's Gentlemen: The Story of Norfolk Island and the Roots of Modern Prison Reform* (New York: Oxford University Press, 2002).
12. Barry, "Alexander Maconochie," pp. 99–100.
13. Orlando G. Lewis, *The Development of American Prisons and Prison Customs* (1922; reprint, Montclair, N.J.: Patterson Smith, 1967), p. 7.
14. See Alexander W. Pisciotta, *Benevolent Repression* (New York: New York University Press, 1994).

15. Gill, "State Prisons in America," p. 53.
16. See Michael Foucault, *Discipline and Punish: The Birth of the Prison*, trans. Alan Sheridan (New York: Pantheon, 1977).
17. Rothman, *The Discovery of the Asylum*, pp. 238–239.
18. Ibid., pp. 243–253.
19. "Fabled Prison's Uncertain Fate," *New York Post* (12 August 2001), p. 26; "San Quentin Village Fights to Save Neighborhood Prison," *Corrections Professional* 6, no. 21 (27 July 2001): n.p.; "New Life for Death Row in Marin," *San Francisco Chronicle* (26 April 2002), p. 1; "California's Death Row Opened for Governor," *Corrections Professional* 8, no. 11 (3 March 2003): n.p.
20. "San Quentin Debate: Death Row vs. Bay Views," *New York Times* (18 December 2004), p. 1; "Death Row Can't Be Moved, Report Says," *Marin (California) Independent Journal* (15 April 2005), n.p; "All about Marin; Midgen Scoffs at Cost of New Death Row," *Marin (California) Independent Journal* (29 March 2007), n.p.
21. Francis J. Clauss, *Alcatraz: Island of Many Mistakes* (Menlo Park, Calif.: Briarcliff, 1981), p. 35. The brief history of Alcatraz comes from this source.
22. See, for example, Jolene Babyak, *Eyewitness on Alcatraz: Life on THE ROCK as Told by the Guards, Families & Prisoners* (Berkeley, Calif.: Ariel Vamp Press, 1988, revised 1996); Darwin E. Coon (former inmate), *Alcatraz: The True End of the Line* (Sacramento, Calif.: New Desmas Press, 2002); Pierre Odier, *Alcatraz: The Rock: A History of Alcatraz: The Fort/The Prison* (Eagle Rock, Calif.: L'Image Odier, 1982).
23. National Institute of Corrections, *Supermax Prisons: Overview and General Considerations*, summarized in "Supermax Prisons Established in Most States, Study Finds," *Criminal Justice Newsletter* 29 (15 December 1999): 4–5.
24. "A Futuristic Prison Awaits the Hard-Core 400," *New York Times* (17 October 1994), p. 1.
25. "There Are Jails …," *The Daily Telegraph* (10 August 1996), p. 22.
26. Wilkinson v. Austin, 545 U.S. 209 (2005), footnotes and citations omitted.

27. "Classification Systems Adapted for Women Offenders," *Corrections Professional* 8, no. 4 (18 October 2002): n.p.

28. This history of the federal prison system comes from a publication by Gregory L. Hershberger, *The Development of the Federal Prison System* (Washington, D.C.: U.S. Department of Justice/Federal Prison System, 1979). See also the Federal Bureau of Prisons, http://www.bop.gov/about/index.jsp, accessed 16 July 2006.

29. Harley G. Lappin, Testimony before the House Subcommittee on Crime, Terrorism, and Homeland Security (14 May 2003); Lappin, Testimony before the House Appropriations Committee (17 March 2005).

30. Federal Bureau of Prisons, "About the Bureau of Prisons," http://www.bop.gov/about/index.jsp, accessed 16 July 2006.

31. Hans Mattick, "The Contemporary Jails of the United States: An Unknown and Neglected Area of Justice," in *Handbook of Criminology*, ed. Daniel Glaser (Skokie, Ill.: Rand McNally, 1974), p. 781.

32. Edith Elisabeth Flynn, "Jails and Criminal Justice," in *Prisoners in America*, ed. Lloyd E. Ohlin (Englewood Cliffs, N.J.: Prentice Hall, 1973), p. 49.

33. Jerome Hall, *Theft, Law and Society* (Boston: Little, Brown, 1935), p. 108.

34. Joseph F. Fishman, *Crucible of Crime: The Shocking Story of the American Jail* (New York: Cosmopolis Press, 1923), pp. 13–14.

35. "New York Correctional Group Praises Boot Camp Programs," *Criminal Justice Newsletter* 22 (1 April 1991): 4.

36. Merry Morash and Lila Rucker, "A Critical Look at the Idea of Boot Camp as a Correctional Reform," *Crime & Delinquency* 36 (April 1990): 204.

37. National Institute of Justice Update, *Researchers Evaluate Eight Shock Incarceration Programs* (Washington, D.C.: U.S. Department of Justice, October 1994), p. 2.

38. Doris Layton Mackenzie et al., "Boot Camp Prisons and Recidivism in Eight States," *Criminology* 33 (August 1995): 327–358; quotation is on p. 327.

39. "Boot Camps Seem to Work—Until Youths Leave, Study Finds," *Criminal Justice Newsletter* 27 (3 June 1996): 3.

40. "Boot Camps Found Ineffective in Reducing Offender Recidivism," *Criminal Justice Newsletter* (1 October 2003), p. 1, summarizing the report by Dale G. Parent, *Correctional Boot Camps: Lessons from a Decade of Research* (NCJ-197018), available from the National Criminal Justice Reference Service, Box 6000, Rockville, MD 20849-6000, http://www.ncjrs.org/pdffiles1/nij197018.pdf, accessed 16 June 2005.

41. "Ex-Camp Worker Pleads Guilty," *Arizona Republic* (21 February 2002), p. 1B.

42. "Wife of Man Accused in Camp Death Shocks Courtroom," *Arizona Republic* (19 November 2004), p. 6B; "New Tough-Love Trial Possible: Jury Saw News Clippings," *Arizona Republic* (5 March 2005), p. 1B.

43. Martin Lee Anderson Act of 2006, 2006 Fl. ALS 62 (2006).

44. "Federal Boot Camps Closing," *Corrections Professional* 10, no. 11 (25 February 2005): n.p.

45. "Costs and Outcomes of a Work Ethic Camp: How Do They Compare to a Traditional Prison Facility?" *Corrections Compendium* 30, no. 6 (1 November 2005): n.p.

46. Ibid.

47. Ibid.

48. Paige M. Harrison and Allen J. Beck, Bureau of Justice Statistics, *Prison and Jail Inmates at Midyear 2005* (Washington, D.C.: U.S. Department of Justice, May 2006), pp. 1, 5.

49. Paige M. Harrison and Allen J. Beck, Bureau of Justice Statistics, *Prisoners in 2005* (Washington, D.C.: U.S. Department of Justice, November 2006), p. 7.

50. Ruiz v. Estelle, 503 F.Supp. 1265, 1281-1282 (S.D. Texas, 1980), *aff'd. in part, vacated in part, modified, in part, appeal dismissed in part*, 679 F.2d 1115 (5th Cir. 1983), cert. denied, 460 U.S. 1042 (1982). Other proceedings occurred, resulting in the most recent ones, later proceeding sub. nom., 981 F.2d 1256 (5th Cir. 1992), *dismissed without opinion*, 114 F.3d 1180 (5th Cir. 1997).

51. "Crowding at Prisons Has State in a Jam," *Los Angeles Times* (13 March 2005), Metro Desk, Part A, p. 1.

52. Laube v. Campbell, 255 F.Supp. 2d 1301 (M.D. Ala. 2003), *settlement, judgment entered*, 333 F.Supp. 2d 1234 (M.D. Ala. 2004).

53. Laube v. Campbell, 333 F.Supp. 2d 1234 (M.D. Ala. 2004). The 2002 statement is from Laube v. Haley, 234 F.Supp. 2d 1227 (M.D. Ala. 2002).

54. "Detroit Jails May Be Forced to Release Inmates," *Corrections Professional* 8, no. 14 (11 April 2003): n.p.

55. See Camille G. Camp and George M. Camp, *Private Sector Involvement in Prison Services and Operations*, Criminal Justice Institute for the National Institute of Corrections (Washington, D.C.: U.S. Government Printing Office, February 1984), cited in *Corrections and the Private Sector*, Joan Mullen, National Institute of Justice (Washington, D.C.: U.S. Government Printing Office, March 1985), p. 2.

56. "CCA Marks 20th Anniversary," *Corrections Professional* 8, no. 15 (25 April 2003): n.p.

57. "Private Prison Stocks Poised to Break Out," *Corrections Professional* 10, no. 9 (21 January 2005): n.p.

58. Harrison and Beck, *Prisoners in 2005*, pp. 5–6.

59. "Details of the Study," *Corrections Professional* 8, no. 16 (9 May 2003): n.p.

60. "Prisons Turn Profit for Private Firms: Lawmakers Seek OK to Buy Services," *St. Louis Post-Dispatch* (30 March 1995), p. 1, Illinois Section.

61. William D. Bales et al., "Recidivism of Public and Private State Prison Inmates in Florida," *Criminology and Public Policy* 4, no. 1 (February 2005): 57–82.

62. Gerald G. Gaes, "Prison Privatization in Florida: Promise, Premise, and Performance," *Criminology and Public Policy* 4, no. 1 (February 2005): 83–88.

63. Charles W. Thomas, "Recidivism of Public and Private State Prison Inmates in Florida: Issues and Unanswered Questions," *Criminology and Public Policy* 4, no. 1 (February 2005): 89–100.

64. "Experts Argue against Prison Privatization," *Federal Human Resources Week* 9, no. 3 (29 April 2002): n.p.

65. Mullen, *Corrections and the Private Sector*, pp. 2–8.

66. Joseph Ricci, executive director, National Association of Security Companies, testifying on Capitol Hill before the Committee on House Homeland Security, 1 May 2007 *CQ Congressional Quarterly, Inc.*

67. Ibid.

Life in Prison

From inmates' points of view, imprisonment is a series of status degradation ceremonies intended to destroy their identities and to assign them new identities of a lower order.[1] The way offenders are treated when they enter prison exemplifies society's rejection; they are stripped of most of their personal belongings, given a number, searched, examined, inspected, weighed, and documented. To the inmates, these acts represent deprivation of their personal identities. The actions may be conducted in a degrading way that emphasizes their diminished status. They face the correctional officers, who have contacts and families in the outside world but who are there to ensure that the inmates conform to institutional rules.

Gresham M. Sykes referred to the psychological and social problems that result from the worst punishment, deprivation of liberty, as the "pains of imprisonment." In his classic study of male inmates in a maximum-security prison, Sykes discussed the moral rejection by the community, which is a constant threat to the inmate's self-concept; the deprivation of goods and services in a society that emphasizes material possessions; the deprivation of heterosexual relationships and the resulting threat to the inmate's masculinity; and the deprivation of security in a population in which the inmate faces threats to his safety and sometimes to his health and life.[2]

In their attempts to adjust to the pains of imprisonment, inmates devise ways of manipulating the prison environment. Sometimes, this manipulation creates serious control problems for the correctional officers, staff, and administrators charged with the ultimate responsibility of maintaining safety and order within the prison and keeping inmates from escaping. This is not an easy task, and the problems are becoming more serious. But at the same time, federal courts have interpreted various constitutional amendments as providing standards for the treatment of inmates, along with reasonable accommodations while they are incarcerated.

This chapter examines life in prison for inmates, as well as for the prison administrators and correctional officers charged with the responsibility of maintaining prisons. The chapter begins with an overview of life in prison and then looks at some of the major issues connected with incarceration. The traditional approach to inmates' rights is contrasted with the modern approach as we analyze substantive and procedural issues raised by the U.S. Constitution and the modern cases interpreting that document. The roles of the primary persons charged with administering prisons—administrators and correctional

OBJECTIVES

After reading this chapter, you should be able to do the following:

- **Relate the historical to the more recent position of federal courts on the issue of inmates' rights.**
- **State the general criteria the U.S. Supreme Court uses to determine whether inmates' rights, such as to be free of cruel and unusual punishment, have been violated.**
- **Trace the evolution of prison management styles, and compare them with today's needs.**
- **Explain the functions of correctional officers, exploring ways in which they controlled inmates historically and how that has changed recently.**
- **Analyze correctional officer recruitment and training.**
- **Discuss gender and racial issues concerning correctional administrators.**
- **Identify some of the issues that new inmates face, and give a brief overview of inmate prison life.**
- **Explain the inmate subculture, discuss its origin, and explore how it affects the adjustment of male and female inmates.**
- **Analyze the social control role of the inmate system.**
- **Discuss the influence of prison gangs in men's prisons.**
- **Analyze the needs of female inmates and of those requiring special care and programs, and discuss how those needs are or are not accommodated.**
- **Discuss the nature and analyze the impact of the Prison Rape Elimination Act of 2003.**
- **Contrast same-gender sexual behavior of female and male inmates.**
- **Discuss the impact of AIDS in a prison setting.**
- **Comment on the problems of inmates who are elderly, or physically or mentally challenged, and discuss the latest developments in these areas.**
- **Discuss briefly the nature and availability of prison programs.**
- **Analyze the impact of prison violence.**

officers—are explored historically and in light of recent developments, along with issues such as recruitment, training, and the importance of diversity.

The chapter then focuses on how inmates adapt to prison life. A general discussion of inmate subcultures is followed by a look at the inmate social system as a method of social control. The special needs of female inmates, such as the ways in which they provide for their children and their unique health needs, are noted. Inmate sexual behavior is also examined, with a comparison of male and female inmates. Among other critical issues associated with prison life are the subjects of AIDS (and ways to deal with those who are infected) and the growing concerns regarding inmates who are elderly, or physically or mentally challenged. Prison programs, such as education and work, are highlighted before the chapter closes with a discussion of prison violence, a growing concern in many institutions.

10-1   The Incarceration of Offenders

After offenders have been sentenced, official papers are prepared to turn them over to the custody of the state's department of corrections (or the Federal Bureau of Prisons in the federal system). They may be transported to prison immediately or retained in jail for a short period. In some states they are sent to a diagnostic center for a physical examination, psychological testing, and orientation, and they are assigned to a particular institution after an evaluation of the test results. In other states, the placement decision may be made according to the seriousness of the offense, the age and gender of the offender, and whether the offender has a prior record (and if so, the extent and nature of that record). In the case of female offenders there may be no choice; the state may have only one institution, which must accommodate all security levels, unless the state contracts with another state or the federal system.

If the state has a central diagnostic unit, inmates must be transported from that unit to their individual assignments for incarceration. Upon arrival at the assigned institution, usually they are isolated from the general population for several days or even a week or longer. During that period, they are told the rules or given a rule book to read. Physical exams are given. In most institutions, they are strip searched for drugs and weapons. They may be required to take a bath with a disinfectant soap and shampoo. Urine samples are collected to determine whether they are on drugs, and laxatives may be given to determine whether they are smuggling drugs.

The inmates' clothing may be taken and special prison clothing issued. In lower-security institutions, especially in some women's prisons, inmates are permitted to wear their own clothing, although there may be restrictions concerning the type of clothing. The rules differ from state to state and even within states, depending on the institution's security level and other factors. When inmates are not allowed to keep personal clothing, they may be required to pay to have the clothing shipped home or may find upon release that it has been donated to a charity. When the inmate is released, many prisons issue only one new set of clothing.

During the orientation period, inmates are required to complete numerous forms concerning their backgrounds, medical histories, and potential visitors. They may be asked whether they fear any persons in the prison; some inmates may need to be placed in protective custody for protection from the general population. Other inmates and correctional officials may test the inmate during the orientation period; seasoned inmates suggest that it is wise to be respectful to the officers and to be careful about making friends among other inmates. Generally inmates are not permitted to have visitors during this orientation period. Phone calls are prohibited or limited. Thus, it is a lonely, frustrating, and stressful time. Inmates may be interviewed for job assignments or educational programs in an effort to determine placement within the institution.

Inmates are permitted to buy personal items from the **commissary**, but times for purchases and frequency of purchases are limited. Inmates cannot keep money inmates in most institutions; it is placed in a trust fund against which they may draw for purchases. Money that may be received from the outside is limited. Any or all of the rules in effect during the orientation period may also apply to the inmate's life in the general population.

Eventually, inmates are relocated in the facility to which they are assigned, and normal prison life begins. Before we look at the details of adaptation to prison life, it is important to discuss the legal implications of incarceration.

> **Commissary** The prison store, as well as the incidental items sold to inmates. Also, an inmate's account, which is debited when an item is purchased.

10-2   Legal Implications of Incarceration

The recognition of inmates' legal rights has had a short history. The earlier judicial position on rights was expressed in an 1872 case, in which a federal court declared bluntly that by committing a crime the convicted felon forfeits his or her liberty and "all his personal rights except those which the law in its humanity accords to him. He is for the time being the slave of the state."[3]

From 1872 until the 1960s, the federal courts generally observed a **hands off doctrine** toward inmates and prisons, reasoning that prison administration is a part of the executive, not the judicial, branch of government. In 1974, however, the U.S. Supreme

> **Hands off doctrine** A policy that courts use to justify nonintervention in the daily administration of corrections agencies.

Court held that, although an incarcerated person loses some rights because of institutional needs, "a prisoner is not wholly stripped of constitutional protections when he is imprisoned for crime. There is no iron curtain drawn between the Constitution and the prisons of this country."[4]

Even before the 1974 decision, however, lower federal courts had begun looking into inmates' claims that they were being denied basic constitutional rights. By the 1980s, inmates had filed numerous lawsuits, and federal courts had scrutinized prison conditions, particularly regarding overcrowding. Entire prison systems were placed under federal court orders to reduce populations and to make other changes in prison conditions. By the 1990s, jail and prison overcrowding had resulted in an explosion of federal lawsuits concerning incarceration conditions. Recently, however, many jurisdictions have been taking steps to remove their prison systems from federal court oversight, and some have succeeded in doing so.

What was responsible for the increasing recognition of inmates' rights in federal courts? Among other issues, the **civil rights** activism of the 1960s included the treatment of inmates, and during that period, federal courts began to look at what was happening inside prisons. Many of the earlier cases involved allegations of physical brutality, as well as questionable living conditions. For example, in 1970, a federal district court heard evidence on the prison conditions in Arkansas, concluded that inmates were living under degrading and disgusting conditions, and found the prison system unconstitutional. The need for judicial intervention into the administration of prisons was stated emphatically by the federal court: "If Arkansas is going to operate a Penitentiary System, it is going to have to be a system that is countenanced by the Constitution of the United States."[5]

The dilemma that courts face regarding the hands off policy is illustrated by the following comments, which were made in 1985 by a federal court:

> In the great majority of cases, it would be sheer folly for society to deny prison officials the discretion to act in accordance with their professional judgment. At the same time, it would be an abrogation of our responsibility as judges to assume (or, more precisely, to reassume) a "hands off" posture, requiring categorical acquiescence in such judgments. Where an inmate alleges that precious constitutional rights are being abridged, the judiciary has the power, and indeed the duty, to intervene in the internal affairs of a prison. Balancing the wisdom of judicial deference against the need for courts to involve themselves in preserving precious liberties is a task of inordinate difficulty. But face it we must if we are to discharge our arduous and delicate duty as protectors and defenders of the Constitution.[6]

Since the 1970s, federal courts have heard many cases on prison conditions. Federal intervention has also been extended to jails. Some prison officials have been ordered to close facilities until conditions are corrected; others have been ordered to change specific conditions. Some officials who have defied these orders have been held in contempt of court. Judges continue to defer to prison authorities concerning day-to-day prison operations, but they intervene when federal constitutional rights are violated. It is important to look at those rights more closely, considering the differences between rights and privileges. It is also important to consider how actions are brought by inmates who seek legal remedies to alleged conditions.

Historically, prison officials spoke of the difference between *rights* and *privileges.* Rights require constitutional protection; privileges are there by the grace of prison officials and may be withdrawn at their discretion. In 1971, the U.S. Supreme Court rejected the position that "constitutional rights turn upon whether a governmental benefit is characterized as a 'right' or a 'privilege.'"[7]

It is clear, however, that a hierarchy of rights is recognized. Some rights are considered more important than others and therefore require more extensive due process before they may be infringed upon. For example, an inmate's right to be released from illegal confinement is more important than the right to canteen privileges. Some of the

Civil rights Sometimes called *civil liberties.* All the natural rights guaranteed by the U.S. Constitution (or by individual state constitutions), such as free speech and the right to religious beliefs and practices. Also the body of law concerning natural rights.

other rights high in the hierarchy are the right to protection against willful injury, access to courts, freedom of religious belief, freedom of communication, and freedom from cruel and unusual punishment. If an inmate succeeds in a lawsuit against prison officials, he or she may be entitled to civil damages, as noted in Spotlight 10-1.

Spotlight 10-1   Enforcing Inmate Rights through Civil Cases

In September 1971, the bloodiest prison uprising in U.S. history to date took place in New York State's Attica prison (approximately 30 miles from Buffalo). Inmates were angry about their living conditions and the food they were served. They were asking for better educational programs, higher pay for prison work, and more minority correctional officers (COs). The inmates took control of the prison for four days, after which COs, armed with pistols and shotguns, ascended the prison's roofs and towers and fired 2,000 rounds of ammunition. When the riot ended, 32 inmates and 11 COs were dead; many more were wounded. Inmates who survived claimed that COs had tortured and brutalized them. Finally, in February 2000, some of the surviving victims had an opportunity to tell a judge what had happened to them. The inmates testified regarding the issue of whether the $8 million the state had offered to settle the remaining claims was a reasonable and fair provision.[1] The money was distributed in December 2000.

This was not the first civil suit in the Attica case. In 1989, a New York court awarded a total of $1.3 million in seven lawsuits brought by inmates or their estates for damages caused in the Attica prison riots and their aftermath. These awards were granted to inmates who did not take part in the riots but were subjected to excessive force by authorities attempting to regain control of the prison. Police efforts (the governor had sent in 500 members of the National Guard) during that uprising were described by a state investigating committee as constituting the "bloodiest encounter between Americans since the Civil War." Individual damage awards ranged from $35,000 to $473,000.[2]

In 1997, a federal judge awarded one former Attica inmate $4 million for damages sustained when he was beaten and tortured by COs during the 1971 Attica riot. The suit, first filed in 1974, alleged that Frank Smith was "forced to walk over broken glass, beaten with batons, locked in his cell for four days,...[and] made to lie on a picnic table [naked] for hours with a football under his chin." During that time, officers "struck his testicles with batons" and burned his body with cigarettes while threatening to kill him or castrate him if he allowed the ball to roll away. Mr. Smith commented after the verdict: "The jury has sent a message that people everywhere need to be treated like humans, not animals." The principal attorney for Mr. Smith, Elizabeth Fink, had spent her entire career representing inmates who were incarcerated at Attica at the time of the uprising.[3] In observance of the 30th anniversary of the Attica riot, Court TV produced a documentary, "Ghosts of Attica," which featured Elizabeth Fink and her paralegal, former inmate Frank Smith.

Also, in September 2001, Fink alleged that the conditions that precipitated the Attica riot still existed in many U.S. prisons.[4]

In a 2003 case, a Texas jury awarded $4 million to a former inmate who alleged that a CO at the prison camp in which she was incarcerated had slammed her up against a wall in a supply room (where she was summoned for a drug test) and raped her. The jury took only 30 minutes to reach its verdict. The victim kept the clothing she was wearing at the time of the attack, and the semen stains provided incriminating evidence when she turned them over to authorities after she was released from the camp. She testified that, as she was being raped, the officer, Michael Miller, asked, "Do you think you're the first? This happens all the time."[5]

Allegations of brutality, even sexual abuse, are not limited to charges by female inmates against male officers. In January 2003, a male inmate of a Las Vegas correctional center filed a lawsuit asking $3 million in damages and alleging that a female officer forced him to become a sex slave. Ryan Layman claimed that between November 2000 and January 2001 he was forced to submit to sexual relations with CO Jennifer Burkley on numerous occasions. Burkley and another officer pleaded guilty to having sex with an inmate, a misdemeanor. Both were accused of performing oral sex on jailed teens. They were each sentenced to two years probation. When she was sentenced, Burkley said, "It was wrong....It should never have happened."[6]

The result of the sexual harassment of inmates by COs may be a return to same-gender COs. For example, in January 2006, Michigan state correctional officials became the "latest among 15 other states that have replaced male corrections officers with female COs in corrections facilities for women." Between 2000 and 2003, the most recent data, female inmates filed 169 complaints against male correctional officers. The change in personnel is designed to eliminate this problem.[7]

1. "Ex-Inmates Hurt at Attica Tell the Judge Their Tales," *New York Times* (15 February 2000), p. 27.
2. "Court Awards $1.3 Million to Inmates Injured at Attica," *New York Times* (26 October 1989), p. 14.
3. "Ex-Attica Inmate Wins $4 Million in Suit over Reprisals after 1971 Uprising," *New York Times* (6 June 1997), p. 20.
4. UPI news release (7 September 2001).
5. "Rape Victim Wins Suit against CO," *Corrections Professional* 8, no. 19 (20 June 2003): n.p.
6. "Lawsuits Increasingly Allege Sexual Assault by Female COs," *Corrections Professional* 8, no. 14 (11 April 2003): n.p.
7. "States Grapple with Rising Female Inmate Populations," *Corrections Professional* 11, no. 8 (13 January 2006): n.p.

The recognition of inmates' rights and of the hierarchy of rights does not mean that the government (or prison officials acting as government agents) may not restrict those rights. Rights may be restricted if prison officials can show that the restriction is necessary for security or for other recognized penological purposes, such as discipline and order.

Another important issue concerns the tests used for determining whether an inmate's constitutional rights have been violated. One right is illustrative—the Eighth Amendment's ban against *cruel and unusual punishment* (see Appendix A). Generally, the U.S. Supreme Court's tests regarding this ban are stated broadly and thus are open to interpretation. In 1976, in examining allegations of cruel and unusual punishment with regard to prison conditions, the Court held that an inmate may bring a successful action against prison officials who deny him or her adequate medical care for a serious medical problem only if it can be shown that the officials acted with *deliberate indifference* to the inmate's needs. In *Estelle v. Gamble*, the Court stated that allegations of "inadvertent failure to provide adequate medical care" or of a "negligent…diagnos[is]" do not establish the requisite state of mind for a violation of the cruel and unusual punishment clause.[8]

In subsequent years, the U.S. Supreme Court has construed the cruel and unusual punishment issue further. In 1991 in *Wilson v. Seiter*, the Court held that, "[I]f the pain inflicted is not formally meted out *as punishment* by the statute or the sentencing judge, some mental element must be attributed to the inflicting officer before it can qualify." The Court interpreted the Constitution to require that, when inmates question prison conditions, they must show a negative state of mind of officials in order to win their cases. Specifically, they must prove that prison officials harbor *deliberate indifference*. Dissenters noted correctly that in many cases this standard will be difficult if not impossible to prove.[9]

In 1994, the U.S. Supreme Court applied a subjective rather than an objective standard to determine whether prison officials have the required state of mind to constitute deliberate indifference. *Farmer v. Brennan* involved an inmate who was biologically male but had some characteristics of a woman. He alleged that he was raped by another inmate after he was incarcerated in an all-male prison. He argued that placing a transsexual in an all-male population constituted deliberate indifference to his safety. Officials should have known of the risks involved because a reasonable person (the objective standard) would have known that. The Supreme Court rejected the objective standard, stating that prison officials may be held liable for unsafe prison conditions only if they "know that inmates face a substantial risk of serious harm and disregard that risk by failing to take reasonable measures to abate it."[10]

In 1992 in *Hudson v. McMillian*, the U.S. Supreme Court held that inmates may bring actions for cruel and unusual punishment against prison officials who engage in physical force that results in injuries, even if those injuries are not significant. Justice Sandra Day O'Connor wrote the majority opinion, in which she stated, "When prison officials maliciously and sadistically use force to cause harm, contemporary standards of decency always are violated."[11]

Finally, at the end of its 2005–2006 term, the U.S. Supreme Court decided a Pennsylvania case in which inmates alleged that their First Amendment rights were violated by a prison regulation prohibiting their access to newspapers, magazines, and personal photographs. The prohibition applied to inmates who were in the most restrictive level of the long-term segregation unit, which housed 40 inmates classified as dangerous or disruptive. Inmates housed in this unit began in the most restrictive level, Level 2, but they could progress to Level 1 with good behavior, and in that level, inmates were permitted some papers and magazines. Ronald Banks, a Level 2 inmate, had a subscription to the *Christian Science Monitor*, and he brought this action after one of his copies of the paper was seized. Prison officials claimed that the deprivation was necessary to promote better behavior among inmates whose behavior was so disruptive that they had already been denied most privileges. By a 6-to-2 vote, the Court determined that the reasons presented for the prohibition were sufficient and that Banks had not success-fully refuted them. Justice Samuel Alito did not participate in the decision due to his involvement with the case at a lower level before he was confirmed as a justice on the U.S. Supreme Court.[12]

10-3   Prison Administration

State prison systems have a director, who reports to the governor or a corrections board. In the federal system, the director of the U.S. Bureau of Prisons (BOP), who reports to the U.S. attorney general's office in the Department of Justice (DOJ), also serves as commissioner of the Federal Prison Industries (FPI). In the spring of 2003, Harley G. Lappin became the director of the BOP, replacing retiring Kathleen Hawk Sawyer, who is featured in Professions 10-1 as an example of a woman who rose to a position of power within the correctional field. Serving as the chief prison administrator in a state or in the federal system is a high-pressure job, and turnover is high.

Corruption and other problems may exist at the top of a system's correctional divi-sion. In 2006, the secretary of corrections for the state of Florida, James Crosby, submit-ted his resignation at the request of the state's governor, Jeb Bush. Subsequently, the interim secretary, James McDonough, dismissed two regional directors, four wardens, and three assistant wardens. The following day, a deputy assistant secretary resigned. The firings and resignations came as the result of an ongoing investigation of wrong-doing in the Florida Department of Corrections (DOC). A task force investigated and made recommendations, emphasizing that although an average of 274 employee arrests had been made per year for three years, with 26,000 employees, the problems were "not systemic." The task force was chaired by Laura Bedard, Deputy DOC Secretary, who stated that probably the most important of the recommendations from the study was to "identify early warning signs of employee emotional or psychological problems and de-velop a list of red flags, such as stress-related symptoms or acts of aggression, on or off the job."[13]

Professions 10-1

Women in Corrections

During an internship at the Federal Correctional Institution in Morgantown, West Virginia, Kathleen M. Hawk decided on a career in corrections. When she retired in 2003, Kathleen Hawk Sawyer, who holds a bachelor's degree in psychology and master's and doctoral degrees in counseling and rehabil-itation, was the director of the Federal Bureau of Prisons. Prior to assuming the highest position in the bureau, Sawyer had served as its assistant director. She had also been a staff psychologist, the chief of psychology services, an associate warden, and a warden. In her earlier years, she served in training administration in the federal system. While she served as assistant director, she made the following state-ment:

> I feel strongly that as women we should take full positive advantage of the marvelous career opportunities available to us today and pursue them not as our given right, but rather as occasions to demonstrate our talents and abilities so that many more doors will be open for generations of women after us.[1]

Kathleen Hawk Sawyer's elevation to the highest position in the Federal Bureau of Prisons demonstrates that women are assuming administrative positions in the criminal justice field.

Women have made contributions to corrections as well as to other criminal justice functions. "Beginning in the mid-1800s, they chaired, as well as served on, governing boards and citizen committees overseeing correctional agencies." They served as volunteers and later as correctional officers, assistant and associate wardens, and more recently as war-dens.[2] Today, they serve as correctional officers in men's as well as women's prisons, and they have been appointed to some of the higher administrative positions as well, as Hawk's appointment illustrated.

1. Karen Carlo Ruhren, "Kathleen M. Hawk: Profile: BOP Programming Administrator Sees Opportunities for Women," *Corrections Today* 54 (August 1992): 132.
2. Ibid.

10-3a   Wardens or Superintendents

Prison directors hire and fire wardens or superintendents of the institutions within their respective jurisdictions and manage the correctional agency's central staff. Preparing and managing a budget is one of the director's most important functions. Directors must justify to the legislature the need for additional funds for operating the prisons, a difficult problem today with so many jurisdictions facing budget cuts while prison populations increase. Despite the importance of the director's position, the day-to-day administration of adult prisons is the responsibility of the warden or superintendent of each institution.

In early prisons, wardens had great power. Although some exercised control as a result of strong personalities, most controlled their institutions with the authority that came from their positions. The strict chain of command from the warden down to the inmates was emphasized by the military atmosphere of most institutions: the wearing of uniforms, the use of job titles, lockstep marching, and total deference to the warden and his staff. Strict discipline, and in some cases corporal punishment, were part of that traditional, authoritarian management style.

The earlier prison wardens also exercised authoritarian management styles in their interactions with the staff. The wardens had total authority to hire and fire the staff, and they required undivided loyalty, which in staff selection was a more important factor than competence. The warden controlled the institution's resources as well. Most wardens lived on the grounds of the institutions, and the warden's household budget was included in that of the prison. The authoritarian style dominated prison management until the middle of the 20th century.[14]

During the 1970s, significant changes took place in many American prisons. First, there were demographic changes. Harsh drug laws led to the incarceration of more young people with drug problems. The percentage of the prison population that was poor, minority, and urban increased. Attempts to suppress gang activity resulted in the incarceration of greater numbers of gang members, many of whom maintained close ties to their colleagues outside prison. Increased politicalization within prisons occurred as the younger, more radical prison population viewed incarceration as a political process. They looked with disdain on the traditional rewards the officers might offer in exchange for their cooperation.

A second factor that precipitated change during the 1970s was the warden's decreased power. Many inmates and COs were unwilling to accept the authoritarian governance style, and their rejection of that style has been supported by federal court orders. Court decisions that require changes in prison physical conditions as well as provisions for due process in some correctional proceedings have reduced the traditional power of prison administrators and COs.

There are numerous obstacles to significant changes in prison management. First, the values of each social group within the prison may clash. Second, the conflict between the goals of custody and rehabilitation remains. Third, there are insufficient facts on which to base decisions. Part of this results from limited research, a lack of evaluation of treatment programs, and insufficient knowledge of the applicability of new management techniques to prison settings. With a lack of knowledge of treatment and management, the prison administrator tends to fall back on rule books and manuals, which are likely to produce a more rigid and authoritarian type of organization.

Finally, prisons continue to be faced with serious financial problems, which have reduced expenditures for management training programs and have resulted in difficulties in recruiting trained persons at competitive salaries. Budget cuts have reduced the degree to which prison managers can provide the resources that are needed for many prison programs, as well as hire sufficient staff and COs.

Some signs of progress are evident in the area of corrections management. First, more institutions are implementing research techniques to measure the success of programs and evaluation strategies for personnel. Therefore, an increasing amount of information is available to correctional managers. Second, professional organizations are developing standards for criminal justice administration, including correctional administration. These standards reflect a general concern with effective management. More important, the standards being developed by correctional managers in the field may be more responsive to problems and more acceptable to administrators.

The third, and the most important, reform in prison administration is the increased attention to professionalism. More attention has been given to attracting highly educated people to the correctional field. Management has sought to improve correctional training and to introduce new management techniques. An issue arises, however, when professionalism is viewed as the *solution* to organizational problems, which may result in a better image of the organization without sufficient attention to underlying problems.

Some research suggests, for example, that more highly educated correctional officers do not have more positive and humane attitudes toward inmates than do less educated officers. Furthermore, the more highly educated officer may be more frustrated in the job. Thus, the appearance of professionalism may be only that, unless adequate prior and on-the-job training programs are implemented to prepare correctional officers for the difficulties they will face. Important organizational changes must be made, too.

10-3b   Correctional Officers

The goals of the correctional institution and the management style of the warden or superintendent are very important in determining the institution's success or failure. However, the individuals with the most extensive contact and perhaps the greatest effect on inmates are the **correctional officers (COs),** or **guards.**

> **Correctional officer (guard)** A corrections employee with supervisory power over a suspect or convicted offender in custody.

Correctional officers in maximum-security prisons spend almost all of their workdays behind bars in close contact with inmates. It is impossible to generalize the working conditions or the reactions of COs, but the job is often monotonous and boring. Salaries are low, fringe benefits are limited, and the stress and risk are tremendous. Recruiting is difficult, and the turnover among officers is high in most institutions.

Attempts are being made, however, to assist officers in adjusting to the stress caused by violence and other problems within prisons. Stress management is becoming an important element of officer training. The American Correctional Association (ACA) provides numerous publications and correspondence courses to assist officers in dealing with the daily problems they face. Criminal justice institutes provide continuing education programs. Some prison systems are giving correctional officers a taste of life as an inmate by sending them to prison to be treated as inmates for a short period of time, but these programs are expensive and not widely used.

The initial formal training of COs is also critical. Usually, training is conducted at a central place within the prison system, and the nature of the training varies from one system to another. Of necessity, it covers institutional security; however, in addition, COs must learn how to protect themselves from inmates who attack them physically and how to react when inmates curse at, spit at, or urinate on them. Recruits are taught the rules and regulations that govern inmate behavior in prisons, and they must learn the rules and constitutional provisions that govern the behavior of COs in relation to inmates.

The fact is, however, that the primary function of COs is to maintain internal security and discipline. In the past, when corporal punishment was allowed, COs controlled inmates by physical force and, if necessary, brutality. Although courts have held that excessive force is not permitted constitutionally, recent evidence suggests that some COs have brutalized inmates, as noted in Spotlight 10-2.

In 2006, New York City officials agreed to a long list of changes aimed at controlling the use of force against inmates by city COs. The New York Legal Aid Society brought the lawsuit that resulted in the settlement, giving the 22 inmate-plaintiffs a

Spotlight 10-2   Correctional Officers and Allegations of Inmate Brutality

In February 2000, eight Florida correctional officers were indicted in the beating death of inmate Frank Valdes in the summer of 1999. An autopsy of Valdes revealed that all of his ribs were broken; the upper part of his body contained boot marks; and his testicles were swollen. The officers were part of the cell extraction team that had removed Valdes from his cell prior to his death. Valdes, age 36, was on death row for killing a correctional officer in 1987. He had been in the prison system since he was 17 years old.[1]

Three officers were tried and acquitted. Florida's attorney general decided not to prosecute the other five officers accused in the death, stating that he had no reason to believe he could get a conviction after losing the case against the officers who were tried.

In January 2000, two correctional officers at the Nassau County Jail in Uniondale, New York, pleaded guilty to beating an unarmed inmate who was serving a 90-day sentence for violating traffic ordinances. The officers admitted that the inmate, Thomas Pizzuto, age 38, had done nothing to provoke them, although the former heroin addict was noisy and demanding methadone. The officers, Edward Velazquez and Patrick Regnier, faced a maximum sentence of 30 years to life in prison for murder; after a guilty plea, they were each sentenced to 11 years in prison. Joseph Bergen, also a correctional officer at the jail, was sentenced to 5 years and 10 months for altering paperwork in an attempt to cover up the crime.[2]

Seven county jail correctional officers in Charleston, West Virginia, were fired in 1990 after investigators concluded that, without any provocation, they had beaten a handcuffed inmate who had been arrested for public intoxication and resisting arrest. At the time of the beating, the suspect was so drunk that he could not even give his name to authorities.[3]

In the fall of 1992, 14 former employees of the women's prison in Georgia at Hardwick were indicted on charges of sexually abusing female inmates. It was labeled the worst case of such abuse in prison history, with alleged offenders charged with trading sex for coerced abortions, prostitution rings, rape, and sodomy. The accused included men and women. One of the accused was a former deputy warden. The indictments stemmed from a 1984 lawsuit against the institution's officials. The recently appointed female warden, Mary Esposito, said the charges reflected the change in attitudes toward women's rights in prison.[4]

In March 1993, after a state prison employee was killed at the Hardwick prison, ABC News reported that the killing occurred to prevent the victim from testifying in the case of alleged sexual abuse. By that time, almost 200 female inmates at the Georgia Women's Correctional Institution and two from other Georgia prisons had accused officers and other staff and former staff of sexual and other forms of abuse.[5] By July 1994, a former deputy warden accused of sexual molestation in the Georgia case had been rehired, and all charges against him had been dismissed. Cornelius Stanley was rehired as a lieutenant at the same salary he had held formerly at the rank of captain. Stanley received more than $58,000 in back pay plus another $50,000 from the state. It was the second time Stanley had been rehired after a firing involving alleged misconduct. He may not, however, work at a prison that houses female inmates. Of the 15 men and women indicted in the Georgia prison sex case, charges against three were dropped because the statute of limitations had expired. Two entered guilty pleas and received probationary sentences. One officer was acquitted.[6]

In 1999 and 2000, a total of 51 prison correctional officers and staff members were fired for improper behavior toward inmates in South Carolina. The investigation was begun after reports that one or two correctional officers had sex with Susan Smith, who is serving a life sentence for driving her two little boys into the lake and leaving them to drown while she escaped. By January 2003, 20 former prison employees had entered guilty pleas or been convicted of drugs, sex, or other misconduct offenses within South Carolina prisons, and 29 more cases were pending. Houston Cagle, who had sex with Smith, was sentenced to 10 years in prison but the sentence was suspended upon service of 90 days.[7]

In November 2002 seven guards at the federal supermax prison in Florence, Colorado, were indicted for alleged abuse of inmates. Those allegations were described as follows:

> According to court documents, those guards were a renegade group called "The Cowboys" who roamed the maximum-security penitentiary in 1995 and 1996 administering punishment ranging from smashing inmates' heads into walls to mixing human waste into prisoners' food.[8]

In June 2003, three of the former officers were convicted of beating handcuffed or shackled inmates; four were acquitted.[9]

1. "Guards Indicted in Slaying," *St. Petersburg Times* (3 February 2000), p. 1.
2. "Two Guards Plead Guilty and Describe Fatal Beatings of a Prisoner," *New York Times* (13 January 2000), p. 26.
3. "Guards Fired Over Beating of Prisoner," *Tallahassee Democrat* (31 May 1990), p. 1B.
4. "Fourteen Are Charged with Sex Abuse in Women's Jail," *New York Times* (14 November 1992), p. 1.
5. "ABC: Prison Worker's Death May Be Part of Sex Scandal," *Orlando Sentinel* (16 March 1993), p. 6.
6. "Prison Guard Accused of Abusing Female Inmates Is Rehired," *Atlanta Journal and Constitution* (12 July 1994), p. 1.
7. "Prison Vice Probe Over," *Greenville News* (20 January 2003), p. 1.
8. "Guards Accused of Sex at Prison: Women Indicted on Federal Counts," *Denver Post* (12 July 2002), p. 1B.
9. "U.S. Prison Guards Guilty of Brutality," *Morning Star* (26 June 2003), p. 2.

total of $2.2 million in damages (ranging from $15,000 to $575,000) for their injuries. One inmate even lost the sight in one eye after a CO kicked him in the face. The lawsuit claimed that COs were not adequately trained—for example, beginning with blows to the face or head instead of less violent approaches. It alleged that COs altered records to cover up their actions. Without admitting fault, the city agreed to revise its training policies for COs and improve training.[15]

In June 2006, the Commission on Safety and Abuse in America's Prisons published its conclusions and recommendations after a year's study involving the testimonies of over 1,000 people in four major cities throughout the United States. Seven of the thirty reforms that commission suggested are reproduced in Spotlight 10-3.

Another method COs have used to control inmates is to manipulate the inmates' **social system**. COs permit selected inmates to have positions of authority and control over other inmates. In recent years, however, federal courts have prohibited the practice of elevating certain inmates to positions of power over other inmates. In some cases, the changes resulting from the removal of inmate power over other inmates have occurred quickly without the addition of more COs to fill the power void. In other cases, inmates have gained control of institutions for temporary periods, leading to devastating riots.

In some institutions, COs' use of inmates to help control other inmates has led to corruption, including officers' acceptance of bribes from inmates. Some COs have taken *contraband* (any forbidden items, such as alcohol, other drugs, weapons, and pornograph) into prisons.

More recently, some institutions have permitted COs to use force—such as mace, pepper spray, or stun devices—to reduce or eliminate prison violence. For example, the *stun belt* is a device attached to a person's waist. From a distance as far away as 300 feet, the device can be activated to send an eight-second, 50,000-volt electric stun. Some judges permit the use of the device for the purpose of keeping defendants in order; others do not approve its use.

One suggestion for improving the control COs have over inmates is increased professionalism and training of officers. In many jurisdictions, a high school diploma is sufficient for the entry-level officer, although it would be difficult today for someone without college experience to advance to an administrative position. Good physical health is also required, for the duties of a CO may involve strenuous physical work, particularly during a riot or other prison disturbance. Mental and emotional health are

> **Social system** The interrelationship of roles, acts, and statuses of people who make up the social structure. A social group or set of interacting persons or groups considered a unitary whole because it reflects the common values, social norms, and objectives of the individuals whom it comprises, even though the group is considered distinct from those individuals.

| *Spotlight 10-3* | The Commission on Safety and Abuse in America's Prisons: Final Report: Findings and Recommendations |

Highlights

Among 30 practical reforms, the Commission recommends:

- A re-investment in programming for prisoners to prevent violence inside facilities and reduce recidivism after release.
- Changing federal law to extend Medicaid and Medicare reimbursement to correctional facilities and ending prisoner co-pays for medical care, reforms necessary to protect the public health.
- Reducing the use of high-security segregation and ending the release of prisoners directly from these units to the streets, which contributes to recidivism.
- Increased investment at state and local levels to recruit, train, and retain skilled, capable workers at all levels.

- Expanding the capacity of the National Institute of Corrections to help states and localities foster a positive institutional culture in corrections facilities.
- Creating an independent agency in every state to oversee prisons and jails and changing federal law to narrow the scope of the Prison Litigation Reform Act [litigation aimed at reducing inmate lawsuits].
- Developing standardized reporting nationwide on violence and abuse behind bars so that corrections officials, lawmakers, and the public can have reliable measures of violence and monitor efforts to make facilities safer.

Source: Commission on Safety and Abuse in America's Prisons, http://www.prisoncommission.org/report.asp, retrieved 18 July 2006.

important, too, although many jurisdictions provide inadequate testing and training in this area.

In 2006, COs in several states began to protest conditions of their work environments. For example, in Nevada, COs in Carson City left pamphlets at homes near the facility in which they work, stating that they could not guarantee that the community was not threatened by the prison facility. "As correctional officers at the Nevada State Prison, it is our obligation to inform you, the public, that we feel that we can no longer assure your safety." The reason, stated the pamphlet, was that the administration was not communicating effectively and efficiently with the COs. One hundred COs signed a petition asking for another change in administration (they had recently had a change). According to the COs, the new administration had eliminated most of the prison programs, leading to morale problems. COs in Pennsylvania alleged that their administration was endangering the security of the public by the way in which inmates were housed in the city jail. COs in several facilities have complained that their administrations do not talk to or listen to them. In short, according to one corrections journal published in 2006, in the

> past two years, unions and corrections officers in at least 12 states have called for the ouster of the head of the corrections departments, staged strikes and sick-outs, or demanded strong reviews of policies that dictate such things as overtime, overcrowding and understaffing.[16]

Despite these issues, along with problems of high turnover, corruption and brutality, difficulties in recruiting, and stress, some correctional officers see themselves as correctional agents (not just as officers primarily responsible for maintaining security and order), with a belief that the system can have positive effects on inmates.

10-3c Female and Minority Officers

It is important that women and minorities have opportunities to participate fully in all professions, and their perspectives are vital in corrections, which has a high representation of minorities and an increasing number of women. Despite the small number of female inmates in corrections overall, women have unique problems in the correctional setting, and those problems might best be understood by female COs. In addition, female COs allege that, to gain parity with male officers, they must be able to work in prisons that incarcerate male inmates.

Several court cases have established the right of women to work in correctional institutions for men and have affected their hiring and promotion, but these changes have occurred only within the past decade or so. In 1997, for example, in order to settle a lawsuit, Arkansas hired 400 more female COs to work in the state's prisons for men.[17] In 1995, a federal court held that the U.S. Constitution does not prohibit the viewing of a male inmate by a female CO. Thus, women may work in men's prisons even when those jobs involve monitoring nude male inmates. The court stated,

> How odd it would be to find in the Eighth Amendment a right not to be seen by the other sex. Physicians and nurses of one sex routinely examine the other. In exotic places such as California people regularly sit in saunas and hot tubs with unclothed strangers....Women reporters routinely enter locker rooms after games. How could an imposition that male athletes tolerate be deemed cruel and unusual punishment?[18]

There have been problems, however, between male and female COs in some institutions, with women reporting acts of sexual harassment or a hostile work environment. In 2003, a federal judge in Boston, Massachusetts, awarded damages to two female COs who alleged that male officers in their work environment (the jail and house of correction operated by the Franklin County Sheriff's Office) had created a hostile working environment. The women also alleged that they were retaliated against after they made complaints about the sexually harassing situation. The judge awarded each of the two women $150,000 in compensatory damages and $20,000 in punitive damages; one was awarded $10,000 and the other $5,000 for the reimbursement of medical fees associated with their damages. They were also entitled to compensation for their respective attorney fees.[19]

In spite of potential problems and some negative attitudes in their work environments, female COs seem able to establish and maintain personal authority in a prison setting; they are not manipulated by inmates any more often than male officers. One study reported that "the authority of women correctional officers is as legitimate as that of their male colleagues."[20]

Many women find the position of CO to be rewarding and challenging. And there is evidence that female officers contribute to a reduction of violence in prisons. A Minnesota corrections consulting firm that secured data from one maximum-security prison in each of the contiguous 48 states, the District of Columbia, and the federal prison system, reported that "over the course of a year, 12.3 percent of the male officers were assaulted by inmates, compared to 3.4 percent of female officers." The differences did not appear to be caused by female officers being too lenient with male inmates. The president of the firm concluded that "other facilities should consider employing more female officers....It appears that if a greater percentage of women were employed, an overall reduction in assaults on officers might result."[21]

10-4   Adaptation to Prison Life

Adapting to prison is difficult for both male and female inmates, and much of the information in this section applies to both genders. However, the initial studies of inmate prison life were conducted solely on male inmates. With the increasing number of women and their special needs, female inmates have also become a focus of research. We begin by looking at the traditional approaches; the next major section focuses primarily on female inmates.

10-4a   Daily Routine

Life in prison is monotonous and routine. In maximum-security prisons, inmates are regulated for most of each day, beginning with the time for rising in the morning. Meal schedules may be unusual; for example, in some prisons, inmates eat breakfast at 3 or 4 A.M. and then go back to bed for naps before beginning the regular workday. This is done because of the long time period required to feed a large population in a secure facility. Dinner may be served as early as 3 P.M. Some inmates are fed in their cells. During lockdown, when there has been internal trouble among inmates and particularly after riots, inmates may be confined to their cells most of the day, with all meals served there.

Most prisons do not have sufficient jobs for all inmates to work an eight-hour day, so many inmates must find ways to fill their time. The security needs of the institution, along with inmates' classification status, determine how free they are to do so, but in some prisons, they are permitted to move about rather freely within certain areas of the prison. Inmates may be out of their cells (or rooms) and permitted to mingle with other inmates.

Recreational facilities may be available in the prison's common areas. Ping-Pong and board games are examples. Some prisons have gyms; others have weight rooms or a provision for outdoor recreation, such as baseball or basketball, but hours of use are limited. Some books are available for inmates to take to their cells or rooms. In large prisons, particularly maximum-security institutions, inmates are limited to a specified number of showers per week (e.g., three) and they are marched to and from and are supervised during their showers. Privacy is nonexistent in most prisons. During the hours of the regular workweek, inmates may be assigned to jobs or be permitted to attend educational or vocational classes. Others may have no organized activities.

After dinner, inmates may be permitted to socialize informally in the common areas. The institution may provide activities such as movies, Alcoholics Anonymous meetings, drug-abuse seminars, or other self-help programs. Many institutions make television available; some permit inmates to have a television and radio in their cells, provided the equipment is purchased from the commissary to avoid the problem of contraband being brought into the institution by this means. However, as prisons have become crowded and more expensive in a society that has become more punitive, some prison officials have eliminated television and other amenities for inmates.

Part of the inmate's day may be spent writing letters to friends and family, although there may be limits on the number of letters that may be sent and received. Gifts from the outside are limited or excluded. Inmates may spend time taking care of their personal or prison-issued clothing and working at institutional assignments.

In minimum-security institutions, some inmates may be permitted to leave the institution from time to time for various purposes. For the most part, however, inmates are confined day and night for the duration of their sentences. During confinement, particularly in maximum-security prisons for men, inmates may be subjected to violence by other inmates; some are raped. Prison life is bleak for most inmates.

10-4b   Prisonization

How do inmates adapt to the prison environment? In earlier prisons, they were not allowed to interact with other inmates. With the end of the segregated and silent systems discussed in Chapter 9 came the opportunity for inmates to interact. One result of this interaction has been the opportunity for inmates to form a prison subculture, or community. The new inmate encounters this subculture through the process of socialization or **prisonization**.

> **Prisonization**   The process of an inmate becoming accustomed to the subculture of prison life.

In 1940, Donald Clemmer reported his study of the male prison community at the Illinois maximum-security prison at Menard. Many of the more recent studies of prisons have been conducted as tests of Clemmer's theories, the most important of which was his concept of prisonization. Clemmer defined *prisonization* as "the taking on, in greater or lesser degree, of the folkways, mores, customs, and general culture of the penitentiary." The process begins as the newcomer learns his or her status as an inmate. The most important aspects of prisonization are "the influences which breed or deepen criminality and antisociality and make the inmate characteristic of the ideology in the prison community."[22]

The degree to which prisonization is effective in a given inmate depends on several factors: (1) the inmate's susceptibility and personality; (2) the inmate's relationships outside the prison; (3) the inmate's membership in a primary group in prison; (4) the inmate's placement in the prison, such as which cell and cellmate; and (5) the degree to which the inmate accepts the dogmas and codes of the prison culture. Clemmer contended that the most important of these factors is the primary group in prison.

Clemmer saw prisonization as the process by which new inmates become familiar with and internalize prison **norms** and values. He argued that, once inmates become prisonized, they are, for the most part, immune to the influences of conventional value systems.

> **Norms**   The rules or standards of behavior, shared by members of a social group, that define appropriate behavior.

Other scholars have tested Clemmer's conclusions. Stanton Wheeler found strong support for Clemmer's position on prisonization in his study at the Washington State Reformatory. Wheeler found that the degree to which inmates became involved in prisonization varied by the length of time the inmate was in prison. Inmates were more receptive to the larger, institutional values during the first and the last six months of incarceration, but during their middle period of incarceration, they were more receptive to the values of the inmate subculture.[23]

In comparing the prisonization of male and female inmates, researchers have questioned the Wheeler hypothesis. Geoffrey P. Alpert and others have found that, although time spent in prison is related significantly to prisonization among female inmates, this is not the case among male inmates. In their study of inmates in the Washington State prison system, these researchers found that other variables were predictive of prisonization, too. Among the women, attitudes toward race and the police were significant.

Among the men, age was a significant variable, as were attitudes toward law and the judicial system.[24]

10-4c   The Inmate Subculture: Models for Analysis

In earlier studies, scholars analyzed the emergence and development of the inmate subculture and created two models for explaining the phenomenon: deprivation and importation. In the **deprivation model**, the inmate's pattern of behavior is an adaptation to the deprivations of his or her environment. The inmate social system is functional for inmates; it enables them to minimize the pains of imprisonment through cooperation. For example, inmate cooperation in the exchange of favors not only removes the opportunity for some to exploit others but also enables inmates to accept material deprivation more easily. Their social system redefines the meaning of material possessions. Inmates come to believe that material possessions, so highly valued on the outside, result from connections instead of hard work and skill, which enables them to insulate their self-concepts from failures in work and skill.

In addition, those goods and services that are available may be distributed and shared if the inmates have a cooperative social system. Because of the pains of imprisonment and the degradation of inmates, which result in a threat to their self-esteem, inmates repudiate the norms of the staff, administration, and society and join forces with each other, developing a social system that enables them to preserve their self-esteem. By rejecting their rejecters, they avoid having to reject themselves.[25]

The more traditional approach to an understanding of the inmate subculture, according to John Irwin and Donald R. Cressey, is that inmates take patterns of behavior with them to prison. This constitutes the **importation model**. Irwin and Cressey argued that social scientists have overemphasized inside influences as explanations for the prison inmate culture. In reality, the prison subculture is a combination of several types of subcultures that inmates import from past experiences and use within prison to adjust to the deprivations of prison life.[26]

Charles W. Thomas conducted research on the deprivation and importation models at a maximum-security prison for men. Thomas's research was designed to show the importance of both importation and deprivation variables. When an inmate arrives at prison, both the formal organization and the inmate society compete for his allegiance; these two represent conflicting processes of socialization. Thomas calls the efforts of the formal organization *resocialization* and those of the inmate society *prisonization*. The success of one requires the failure of the other. The prison is not a closed system.

In explaining the inmate culture, one must examine all of the following factors: preprison experiences, both criminal and noncriminal; expectations of prison staff and fellow inmates; quality of the inmate's contacts with persons or groups outside the walls; postprison expectations; and the immediate problems of adjustment that the inmate faces. Thomas found that, the greater the degree of similarity between preprison activities and prison subculture values and attitudes, "the greater the receptivity to the influences of prisonization." Thomas also found that inmates from the lower social class are more likely to become highly prisonized, as compared with those from the upper social class. Those who have the highest degree of contact with the outside world have the lowest degree of prisonization, and those having a higher degree of prisonization are among inmates who have the bleakest postprison expectations.[27]

Other researchers have concurred with one or the other of the models. In his study of race relations in a maximum-security prison for men, Leo Carroll found support for the importation model, although he concluded that it needed refinement. Carroll criticized the deprivation model as diverting attention from important factors within prison, such as racial violence.[28] Support for both the importation and the deprivation models has been found in studies of prisons in other countries.[29]

Studies of jail inmates are also important in determining whether the inmate subculture is imported into the institution or results from adaptations to the institutional

> **Deprivation model**   A model of prisonization based on the belief that the prison subculture stems from the way inmates adapt to the severe psychological and physical losses imposed by imprisonment. *See also* **Importation model**.

> **Importation model**   A model based on the assumption that the inmate subculture arises not only from internal prison experiences but also from the external patterns of behavior the inmates bring into prison. *See also* **Deprivation model**.

setting. Findings from these studies support both the importation and the deprivation theories.[30]

10-4d The Inmate System as a Social Control Agency

The inmate social system may create problems for correctional officers and other prison personnel, for inmates upon release, and for society. The inmate social system serves as a social control agency within the prison, wielding a powerful influence over inmates because it is the only reference group available. It is powerful because inmates need status. In addition, they may be more susceptible than usual to peer-group pressure and more prone to look to the peer group than to authority figures for social support. This form of social control is functional to the prison when it maintains order within the institution. To understand it, we must look more carefully at the control problems that penal institutions face.

Within the prison, two powerful groups seek to control one another: the correctional officers, whose primary responsibilities are custody and security, and the inmates, who are interested in escaping as much as possible from the pains of imprisonment. Richard A. Cloward studied the power struggle between these two groups. Cloward noted that in most institutions inmates reject the legitimacy of those who seek to control them. A serious social control problem may result. In many ways, the job of the custodian in prison is an impossible one. He or she is expected to maintain control and security within the institution but may not use the traditional method of doing this—force. The new, more liberal philosophy of recognizing due process and other inmates' rights has increased problems of social control for correctional officers.[31]

Under the authoritarian regime of prison administration and management, inmate cooperation was necessary to maintain peace within institutions. The few COs could not have kept a disorganized body of inmates under control. Inmates ran the institutions, and the COs cooperated. For example, COs permitted inmate leaders to take the supplies they needed. When a "surprise" search was conducted, they told the inmate leaders in advance. The leaders spread the word as a form of patronage. The COs were aiding certain inmates in maintaining their positions of prestige within the inmate system; in return, inmate leaders maintained order. The system was a fairly stable one, with little disorder.

Federal court orders to abolish inmate power positions changed the traditional system of inmate-officer interaction and altered the role of the inmate social system in social control. The results are illustrated by the Texas prison system, which has been plagued with administrative attempts to maintain order. After a disturbance in 1985, during which eight inmates were killed in eight days, Texas prison officials announced that they were declaring war on the prison system. They locked down 17,000 inmates in 13 prisons. Sociologists studying the Texas prison system had reported earlier that the elevation of inmates to positions of power had kept racial tension in check, and little violence existed.[32]

10-4e Prison Gangs

In the Texas prison system, inmates were removed from positions of power over other inmates as the result of a federal court order. The consequence was a power vacuum, which was then filled by gangs, beginning with one in 1983 (the Texas Syndicate, 56 members) and increasing to eight gangs with a total of 1,400 members less than two years later. Violence increased, with gang warfare occurring between the Texas Syndicate and the Mexican Mafia, two of the largest prison gangs. In his analysis of the organizational structure of these two gangs, one scholar described them as similar. Among other characteristics, each follows a code of rules, called the *constitution*. The penalty for violating any of these rules is death.[33]

Gangs exist in many, if not all, prisons and may be very influential in prison social control, with activities ranging from sex to murder. Effective control of gang influence demands knowledge of the gang members and their activities. Gangs are difficult to control, and one administrator emphasized that prisons do not create the gangs, "and they will not be eliminated no matter how successful our programs." The public needs to keep in mind that prisons are small societies, "temporary places of custody and control for individuals that society has chosen to reject from its membership."[34]

The collection of data on gang crime and the analysis of gang activities and memberships have increased in recent years. Some of these studies include prison settings; others do not. Some of the research focuses on gangs and drugs. The research leaves many questions unanswered. Despite this fact, it is clear that gangs have affected prison life. Inmates cite gang formation as one of the reasons for the increased turmoil within prisons. The presence of gangs, along with administrative policies concerning them, adds to the increasingly unpredictable world in which inmates live.

One corrections journal referred to prison gangs as creating a reign of terror, using assaults, murder, fear, and intimidation to control life within prison and make it a place of horror for many inmates. The journal suggested that prison gangs are controlling every major street gang and that many of these gangs "control and direct organized criminal enterprises that have tentacles reaching" into many areas of society outside of prisons.[35]

The best way to control prison gangs may be to be familiar with their expected activities, so intelligence gathering is critical. In California, where prison gangs are a constant threat,

> intelligence gathering is the method and the cornerstone of all efforts to curb, suppress and prevent gang activity that is both criminal and disruptive to public safety and the safety and security of penal institutions.[36]

Some progress has been made in the prosecution of prison gangs. In March 2006, the federal government began its prosecution of the Aryan Brotherhood prison gang, which, it claimed, was one of the most violent and controlling gangs in the country. This gang, thought to number around 100, emerged in the 1960s at the California prison in San Quentin. The gang was accused of using terror, including murder, to control inmates nationwide. In this first of several planned trials, the prosecution presented witnesses who testified of horrendous murders and assaults, with the allegations as high as 15 murders over 25 years. Some of the accused entered guilty pleas; four were tried. The defense admitted that the defendants were members of the Aryan Brotherhood but claimed that it was only a group for self-protection, which is necessary to survive prison life. One defense lawyer characterized the government's case as "a fantasy fed by informants."[37]

In July 2006, guilty verdicts were returned against the defendants, who included the gang's top leaders: Barry "The Baron" Mills and Tyler "The Hulk" Bingham. The defendants are eligible for the death penalty under California law.[38]

From this focus on male inmates, we turn to a look at female inmates.

10-5   Female Inmates

Characteristics of the female offender may help explain the nature of her adaptation to prison life and the differences between her methods of adapting and those of the typical male offender. Women constituted 7 percent of state and federal prison inmates in 2005, and their numbers have increased more rapidly than those of male inmates in recent years, as noted in Spotlight 10-4. Women are more likely than men to be serving time for drug offenses and to have used crack cocaine. More than three-fourths of female inmates are mothers, with two-thirds having children under the age of 18. In comparison with male inmates, women are more likely to be married and unemployed at the time of their incarceration.

Women are also serving longer sentences than they did in the past. Between 1977 and 2004, the number of women sentenced to more than a year in prison increased by

Spotlight 10-4 — The Growth of the Population of Female Inmates

Female Prisoners Increased 2.6 Percent during 2005; Male Prisoners, 1.9 Percent

During 2005 the number of females under the jurisdiction of State or Federal prison authorities increased by 2.6 percent. The number of males in prison rose 1.9 percent. At yearend 2005, 107,518 females and 1,418,406 males were in prison. Since 1995 the annual rate of growth in female prisoners averaged 4.6 percent, which was higher than the 3.0 percent increase in male prisoners. By yearend 2005 females accounted for 7.0 percent of all prisoners, up from 6.1 percent in 1995 and 5.7 percent in 1990.

Relative to their number in the U.S. resident population, males were over 14 times more likely than females to be incarcerated in a State or Federal prison. At yearend 2005 there were 65 sentenced female inmates per 100,000 females in the resident population, compared to 929 sentenced male inmates per 100,000 males.

Since 1995 the total number of male prisoners has grown 34 percent; the number of female prisoners, 57 percent. At yearend 2005, 1 in every 1,538 women and 1 in every 108 men were incarcerated in a State or Federal prison.

Over a Third of Female Prisoners Held in the Three Largest Jurisdictions

Texas (13,506), the Federal system (12,422), and California (11,667) held more than a third of all female inmates at yearend. Oklahoma (129 sentenced female inmates per 100,000 female residents), Idaho (110), and Mississippi (107) had the highest female incarceration rates. States with the lowest female incarceration rates were concentrated in the Northeast, led by Rhode Island (with 10 sentenced female prisoners per 100,000 female residents), Massachusetts (12), and Maine (17).

Thirteen States had an average annual increase in the female prison population of more than 10 percent between 1995 and 2005, led by North Dakota (18.2 percent), Idaho (14.1 percent), and West Virginia (14.0 percent). During this period the State female prison population increased an average of 4.5 percent per year; the Federal female prison population increased 5.3 percent per year.

Source: Paige M. Harrison and Allen J. Beck, Bureau of Justice Statistics, *Prisoners in 2005* (Washington, D.C.: U.S. Department of Justice, November 2006), pp. 4–5.

---

757 percent, compared to a 388 percent increase in the number of men serving more than a year. The nature of the offenses for which women are serving time has also changed. In 1979, approximately 49 percent of state female prison inmates had been convicted of a violent crime, compared to 33 percent of state female inmates serving time in 2002. In 1979, approximately 10 percent of female inmates had been convicted of drug offenses; in 2002, that percentage was 33 percent. The professor who reported this information, based on her study of state prison inmates over the previous 27 years, concluded as follows:

> Incarcerating women does not solve the problems that underlie their involvement in the criminal justice system. Their imprisonment creates enormous turmoil and suffering for their children and society. What makes far more sense is sensible sentencing reforms and public investment in effective drug treatment, and gender-responsive services to aid women who seek to live law-abiding lives and provide a healthy and stable home for their children.[39]

10-5a   The Female Inmate Subculture

In her earlier and classic study of the Federal Reformatory for Women, Rose Giallombardo considered the issue of whether the female inmate subculture is an adaptation to the pains of imprisonment or is imported from outside experiences. Giallombardo concluded that the prison inmate culture, or social system, cannot be explained solely as a response to prison deprivations, although they may precipitate its development. She illustrated her point primarily by looking at gender roles within correctional institutions for women and girls. Those gender roles reflected the roles women play in society. Her point was that attitudes and values, as well as roles and statuses, are imported into the prison system. Prison deprivations provide the structure in which these roles are performed.[40]

The evidence seems to suggest that, although roles within the inmate systems of men and women differ, they reflect the differences in the attitudes, values, and roles that have distinguished men and women traditionally. For example, in his study of a men's prison, Sykes suggested that loss of security was the greatest problem the male inmate faced. For the female inmate, however, it appears that the loss of liberty and autonomy is the major deprivation. Women miss the freedom to come and go, and resent the restrictions on communications with family and friends. In the institutions, everything is planned for them. Furthermore, female inmates may be frustrated because they have no control over events that occur in the outside world: their children may be neglected, a loved one may become sick or die, and husbands or boyfriends may be unfaithful.

For some female inmates, prison life is a deprivation of the goods and services to which they are accustomed. As soon as they enter the institution, female inmates, like male inmates, are stripped of most of their worldly possessions, a "kind of symbolic death." They must endure supervised baths and bodily examinations for drugs and contraband. They may have to give up their personal clothing and wear prison uniforms, although in some institutions, female inmates are permitted to wear their own clothes. Generally, personal items such as jewelry, pictures, cosmetics, and other beauty products are banned or limited.[41]

10-5b   Children of Inmates

Although some male inmates have children, the issue of child care is usually a more critical factor with female inmates. Not only do most female inmates have children, but they were living with those children when they were incarcerated. Care for their children is a primary concern of many inmate mothers, and separation from them is one of the greatest pains of their incarceration.

An inmate mother must face her inability to care for her children, along with the loss of self-esteem that may come with incarceration. She must cope with the readjustment she and her children face when she is released from prison. She must deal with the lack of visitation opportunities for children and the difficulty of telling her children what is happening. Some may face lawsuits over the legal custody of their children. All of these factors may affect the ways in which incarcerated mothers adapt to prison life.

Children suffer when one or both parents are incarcerated. Young children may suffer separation anxiety, which appears to be magnified when it is the mother who is incarcerated. The reason may be that when women are incarcerated their children usually live with grandparents (53 percent of the cases) or other relatives, or even in foster homes (almost 10 percent), rather than with their fathers. But when men are incarcerated, the children of 90 percent of them live with their mothers. Women are incarcerated in institutions that are, on the average, 160 miles from their homes, compared to men, only 100 miles. Most incarcerated parents do not have any visits from their children while they are in prison.[42]

Some jurisdictions have developed programs to encourage interaction between incarcerated parents and their children. For example, in 2000, Florida began its program Reading Family Ties: Face-to-Face. This program permits women at the Lowell and Hernando Correctional Institutions to have live video visits with their children each week. The children go to a special center where they may interact with their mothers for one hour weekly, while the incarcerated mothers are in a room with a video camera, a computer, and a speaker phone. Officials claimed that the program had improved the conduct of the mothers and of the children.[43]

The Tennessee Prison for Women opened a child visitation unit, dedicated to the memory of a former warden, Penny A. Bernhardt, who was instrumental in the success of the program. The unit permits children from three months to six years to spend the weekends with their parents in relative privacy. Activities oriented toward child development are also provided.[44]

Some states—for example, Ohio, Nebraska, New York, and Washington—have made provisions for inmates who give birth to keep their babies with them while they are incarcerated. Although, historically, mothers were permitted to keep their children in prison, the practice was abandoned in most jurisdictions in the 1970s and 1980s because of legal liability issues.[45]

Some provisions have also been made for incarcerated fathers to interact with their children. The first program was developed in the early 1990s in Fort Worth, Texas, at the all-male federal correctional facility. According to one psychologist, "The one concern I hear the most often from inmates is not about legal battles, but concerns about their families....Family communication and support is extremely important to the inmate."[46]

10-5c Medical and Other Needs

Inmates are entitled to basic health care needs, but the issue of whether special medical care for women should be available in prisons, along with legal issues surrounding the differences in programs that are available to male as compared to female inmates, has led to numerous court cases. In a 1996 case, *Women Prisoners of the District of Columbia Department of Corrections v. District of Columbia*, a federal court of appeals held that the district court had gone too far in its orders for the plaintiffs in a class action suit. The court noted that, if all prisons were required to provide *identical* programs for men and women, prison administrators might not provide programs at all, especially with current budget problems in most prisons. The court held that using physical restraints on women during the third trimester of pregnancy, sexual harassment by correctional officers, lack of adequate fire safety provisions, and the quality of the general living conditions at the institution in question constituted cruel and unusual punishment and thus must be changed. However, with regard to programs and work opportunities, the court emphasized that there is no constitutional right to these programs; some are available only for women, some for men. This is not unconstitutional, especially given the differences in the sizes of the institutions involved. A specific program provided for men but not for women does not in and of itself violate equal protection. But on remand, numerous orders were made concerning the medical and other treatment of female inmates.[47]

In 1995 in the California correctional system, female inmates filed a suit concerning special health care and other needs. Subsequently, the parties entered into a stipulated agreement that the California Department of Corrections would provide or exceed the minimum Eighth Amendment requirements for health care for inmates. The women had originally alleged inadequate health care, including delays and disruptions in receiving medications, as well as inadequate sick call, triage (determining priorities for help in an emergency), emergency care, nurses, urgent care, chronic care, care for AIDS/HIV, and many other areas.[48] Prior to the final settlement in 2000, the attorneys for the inmates, referring to their allegations that the state had not complied with all of the earlier agreements, did recognize some success but warned as follows:

> [These plaintiffs] have endured too much suffering and taken too many risks by coming forward for us to consider that this case is over....We hope that the Department of Corrections will implement the settlement in good faith, but in case they do not, we are prepared to return to the court to protect the women's constitutional rights....
>
> The women who brought this suit aren't asking for "Cadillac care" and they aren't out for money or fame....They've stuck their necks out and stood up to the state for one simple reason—to hold the state of California responsible for meeting their basic medical needs.[49]

A professor who studied the special conditions encountered by female inmates by interviewing them and correctional officers in two Texas prisons concluded that the system has not kept up with the changing female populations; in short, the special needs of female inmates have been neglected. According to Denise Huggins of the University of Arkansas, the prison system "delivers secondhand services and offers inadequate or inappropriate training, treatment and educational programs." Huggins continued, claiming that the "daily lives of female inmates is mind-numbing time punctuated by inadequate educational programs and humiliating treatment."[50] As humiliating treatment, Huggins cited strip searches, conducted as frequently as five times daily. Job training programs often train women for work in primarily male-dominated fields (such as plumbing or auto repair) in which they are not likely to get jobs. The few educational programs may be reserved for younger inmates or for those with five years or less to serve and thus not be available to most inmates. Huggins concluded, "It is clear that we need to take a good look at the way we treat female inmates and come up with solutions that are more appropriate and more realistic for their needs."[51]

The Federal Bureau of Prisons (BOP) is addressing some of these issues. The BOP director testified in May 2003 before a congressional committee, stating that "female offenders have different social, psychological, educational, family, and health care needs." As a result of recognizing these differences, the BOP "continues to design and implement special programs for female offenders." Several BOP facilities "operate intensive programs that focus on helping women who have histories of chronic sexual, emotional, or physical abuse by addressing their victimization and enabling positive change."[52]

10-6   Prison Issues

This section focuses on only a few of the more important issues regarding prison life, including visitation policies, sexual behavior, medical and aging issues, prison education and work programs, and prison violence.

10-6a   Visitation Policies

As noted earlier, some provision for parental/child interaction is important for inmates with children. But it is also important for inmates to have visits from other family members and friends. Some inmates do not have anyone to visit; others have families who cannot visit at all due to cost and distance. But for those who have family and friends who wish to visit them, prisons establish strict rules. Some of these rules are necessary for security reasons; others might be questionable.

In 2003, in *Overton v. Bazzetta*, the U.S. Supreme Court approved the Michigan corrections policies that limit the number of visitors inmates may receive. Michigan authorities argued that as their prison populations grew, which resulted in increased visitors, their problems with discipline, including the use of alcohol and other drugs as well as maintaining order, also increased. It was necessary, they argued, to limit visits, especially from children, who required additional supervision.[53]

Under the Michigan policy in question, inmates may receive visits only from persons on their approved lists (excluding clergy and attorneys). Each inmate may list an unlimited number of members of his or her immediate family plus 10 other individuals (with some restrictions). Children under 18 may not be listed unless they "are the children, stepchildren, grandchildren, or siblings of the inmate." Children of inmates for whom parental rights have been terminated may not visit. Further, "[a] child authorized to visit must be accompanied by an adult who is an immediate family member of the child or of the inmate or who is the legal guardian of the child."[54] The policies also provide that inmates who are cited for multiple substance abuse violations may not have any visitors except clergy and attorneys.

These regulations pertain to those inmates who are permitted only noncontact visits, meaning that they visit with a wall in between them and their visitors and they may not touch each other. This practice was not at issue in the lawsuit, which was confined only to the policies concerning which inmates were permitted noncontact visits.

The U.S. Supreme Court reviewed its history of cases concerning inmate rights, especially the right of association, but concluded that the Michigan policies did not violate those holdings. In particular, the Court noted, "freedom of association is among the rights least compatible with incarceration....Some curtailment of that freedom must be expected in the prison context." The Court concluded that the prison authorities had presented rational reasons for the prohibition and the goal of security, and that was all they were required to do.

With regard to the curtailing of visits for inmates with multiple substance abuse violations, the Court emphasized that this restriction was subject to removal in two years. The restriction, however, "serves the legitimate goal of deterring the use of drugs and alcohol within the prisons. Drug smuggling and drug use in prison are intractable problems."[55]

10-6b   Inmate Sexual Behavior

Inmates face sexual harassment and abuse from other inmates, and this occurs more frequently among male than among female inmates. The issue of same-gender sex, and especially rape, has been a topic of research in male prisons for years.

Isolation from the opposite gender implies abstinence from the satisfaction of heterosexual relationships at a time when the sex drive is strong. Some inmates turn to same-gender behavior not by preference but because they need an outlet for sexual expression. Earlier studies reported that between 30 and 40 percent of male inmates had some same-gender experiences while in prison. These estimates were discussed at a conference on prison homosexuality in the early 1970s. Peter C. Buffum wrote a synthesis of the five working papers presented at that conference. Buffum contended that the belief that we can eliminate same-gender sex in prisons by establishing other outlets for sexual drives is a myth.[56] Others have not agreed, however, and the subject deserves further attention.

Same-gender sexual behavior among male inmates seldom involves a close relationship. In some cases, a man who is vulnerable to sexual attacks enters into a sexual relationship with another man, who agrees to protect him from abuse by other inmates. Earlier studies found that sexual acts between male inmates seemed to be a response to their sexual needs coupled with their socialization. Men are taught to be aggressive, and playing the male role (the wolf) in a sexual act with another man might enable the inmate to retain this self-concept. Further, male inmates may see a prison sexual relationship as little more than a search for a casual, mechanical act of physical release.[57]

Same-gender sexual behavior among men and the forms it takes in prison should be viewed in light of the importation and deprivation models discussed earlier in this chapter. Prison presents the inmate with a problem of sexual deprivation, but "the meaning, amount, and character of these adjustments will be strongly dependent on the meaning that these same behaviors had for the inmate before he or she was incarcerated."[58]

Some researchers have found prostitution to be the most frequent type of same-gender sexual behavior among male inmates. Usually, the behavior is not the result of violence; however, when violence occurs, it often has racial implications.[59] It is a power play, which may be compared to the rape of a woman by a man. It represents the need to dominate, to control, to conquer.

Daniel Lockwood, who reported on his study of male inmates in New York prisons, interviewed men designated as targets of sexual propositions or sexual abuse, as well as those who were identified as sexual aggressors. He found that many verbal threats of sexual aggression did not result in actual aggression.[60]

Most inmate same-gender rape victims do not report the acts, primarily because of the fear of reprisal from other inmates. Some fear for their lives if they cooperate with officials in trying to solve violent acts. These fears may not be unreasonable.

Other inmates have filed lawsuits after being victimized by same-gender rape. The standard courts use in analyzing these claims is whether officials were *deliberately indifferent* to the needs of inmates and the situations in which they were placed. This standard was illustrated by a 1991 case, in which a heterosexual jail detainee alleged that he was raped by a gay male with whom he was assigned a cell. An appellate court held that the inmate had stated a sufficient claim that his due process rights were violated when he showed that prison officials engaged in a custom or policy of placing aggressive gay males in the general population while isolating passive ones. This action permits aggressive gays to prey on other inmates, especially in an overcrowded facility. Defendants in the case argued unsuccessfully that inmates should have to prove that prison officials showed a *reckless indifference* to their welfare or that officials acted with *callous disregard*.

The appellate court rejected those standards and held that the same standard required for cases involving a lack of medical treatment should be used: that of deliberate indifference. According to the court, this standard is an appropriate balance between the responsibility of jail officials to manage the facility and maintain security and the right of pretrial detainees to personal security. Although the case involves pretrial detainees (who have not been convicted and thus cannot be punished), it is reasonable to expect the same standard to be applied in prisons.[61]

In a more recent case, heard by the U.S. Supreme Court and sent back to the lower court for reconsideration, an inmate who considered herself a woman, but whom prison officials classified as a man, sued for rape by a male inmate in a men's prison. Dee Farmer alleged that on 1 April in 1989 she was raped in her cell in a high-security federal prison in Terre Haute, Indiana, where she was incarcerated for credit card fraud. Subsequently, Farmer was transferred to a low- and medium-security prison in North Carolina. Farmer claimed that federal officials purposely put her at risk. Her suit for $200,000 and placement in a facility that housed both genders was dismissed by a federal court in Wisconsin and by a federal appeals court. Farmer, who has a penis, had enhanced her female appearance through silicone breast implants and hormone injections.

In deciding Farmer's case, the U.S. Supreme Court focused on the meaning of *deliberate indifference*, defining the term for the first time. The concept is similar to criminal negligence and calls for subjective rather than objective knowledge. "The officials must both be aware of facts from which the inference could be drawn that a substantial risk of serious harm exists, and he must also draw the inference." The case was sent back to determine more facts.[62]

In contrast to the sexual behavior of gay male inmates, same-gender sexual behavior among female inmates may develop out of mutual interest to alleviate the depersonalization of the prison and to gain status.[63] For a female inmate, a lesbian relationship may take the place of the primary group relationship for some male inmates. Talk of loyalty, sharing, trust, and friendship among female inmates may refer to the same-gender relationship, not to primary groups per se. Lesbian relationships represent an attempt to simulate the family found outside the prison and are not primarily for sexual gratification. One study reports that same-gender relationships are the most important relationships among female inmates.[64]

For female inmates, pseudofamilies may compensate for the lack of the close family environment on the outside. They permit the exercise of dominant and submissive roles, which the women learned outside of prison. Within these pseudofamilies is an opportunity for sexual behavior, but sexual behavior does not appear to be the primary reason for forming family relationships.[65]

Another characteristic of the sexual behavior of female inmates distinguishes their behavior from that of male inmates' sexual involvement. Whereas in most cases male sexual behavior, especially rape, is manifested in actual physical sexual contact (oral or anal sex), for female inmates, sexual relationships may involve only a strong emotional relationship, with some bodily contact that would be acceptable outside prison (e.g., embracing upon seeing one another). However, some women may hold hands or fondle breasts, whereas others engage in more serious forms of sexual contact, such as oral-genital contact and bodily contact that attempts to simulate heterosexual intercourse.[66]

Another issue regarding sexual behavior in women's prisons is that of relationships (including rape) between inmates and correctional officers. Allegations that male COs have sexually abused female inmates have been substantiated in several recent studies; some are noted in Spotlight 10-1. The General Accounting Office (GAO) conducted a study of the correctional facilities in the District of Columbia, along with the three largest systems: California, Texas, and the federal system, which house more than one-third of all female inmates in the United States. The GAO study revealed that the three largest correctional systems had 506 allegations of sexual misconduct from 1995 to 1998. Of those allegations, 18 percent were substantiated. During the same period, women in the District of Columbia made 111 allegations of sexual misconduct, of which 11 percent were substantiated. The investigators concluded that the actual number of incidents is not known because "many female inmates may be reluctant or unwilling to report staff sexual misconduct, and jurisdictions lack systematic data collection and analysis of reported allegations." Sexual misconduct includes "consensual" sexual activities, due to the inherently coercive nature of the prison environment. Most of the reported incidents involved "verbal harassment, improper visual surveillance, improper touching, and/or consensual sex," with allegations of rape and related forms of sexual violence noted only rarely.[67]

More recent studies, however, have shown that more than half of the sexual assaults committed against female inmates are perpetrated by other female inmates, not male staffers. Two researchers from the University of South Dakota studied sexual abuse in three midwestern medium- and maximum-security prisons that house women. The researchers included sexual activity by coercion as well as by force. They found greater coercion (about double) in the larger prison, which was more racially diverse and housed women who had committed the more serious crimes. In that institution, approximately 25 percent of the interviewed women said they had been sexually coerced while in prison, over 33 percent of them by one assailant and 40 percent by two or three persons together. Less than one-third of these victims reported the attacks to prison officials. The two researchers concluded as follows:

> Overall the female situation is not as violent and serious as what happens typically in a male prison....There are some women's prisons that are so well-managed that this problem is kept to a very low level. That's good. But we need to recognize that women in prison are sexually coercing other women. It's not just male corrections officers.[68]

Female inmates are not the only targets of sexual activity in prisons. In summer 2002, two female former correctional officers at the supermax federal prison in Florence, Colorado, Kellee S. Kissinger, 34, and Christine Achenbach, 42, were accused of having had oral sex or sexual intercourse with inmates. Achenbach, who held the fourth highest position at the prison, that of executive assistant to the warden, was convicted in December 2002. In May 2003, she was sentenced to five years' probation and four months' home detention, and fined $3,000. The sentencing judge, commenting that she had no option but to require the defendant to register as a sex offender, stated, "Even though I personally would not want to see this kind of conviction treated as a sex-offender conviction, I must apply the law as it is written, not as I wish it were written." Of the inmates, the judge said, "I don't think they felt victimized at all....They probably enjoyed it." Kissinger, who accepted a plea bargain that Achenbach refused, was sentenced to four years' probation and a $2,400 fine. She was given the option of serving 100 hours of community service in lieu of the fine.[69]

One solution to sexual assaults on inmates, particularly on women, has been offered by Alanco Technologies, which developed a belt alarm system. The component called PSD-II, a belt equipped with a transmitter, could be worn by all prison staff. When that belt is removed, the system records the event and can be used to verify where the staffer was at a particular time and how long the person was in that area.[70]

Legislation is another way to attempt to reduce or eradicate sexual assaults against both female and male inmates. In July 2003, the U.S. Senate unanimously passed Senate Bill 1435, the Prison Rape Elimination Act of 2003. Lara Stemple is the executive director of Stop Prisoner Rape (SPR), a national organization devoted to stopping prison rape, which Stemple refers to as "dehumanizing and sometimes deadly....Victims have been left beaten and bloodied, they have suffered long-term psychological harm, they have been impregnated against their will, and they have contracted HIV. It's time to take this important step to address the problem." According to SPR, one in five inmates has been sexually abused; among female inmates, the number is one in four. Stemple emphasizes that frightened inmates do not report many of the abuse incidents; if the incidents are reported, the administration may ignore them. She concluded, "We hope federal legislation will not only create incentives for states to take this problem seriously, but also give facilities the tools and information they need to prevent it."[71]

The U.S. House of Representatives also passed the Prison Rape Elimination Act, and it was signed by President George W. Bush in 2003. This new law pertains not only to sexual assaults but also to other prison issues, such as AIDS, mental illness, general violence, and psychological problems, discussed in the sections that follow. Portions of the law are presented in Spotlight 10-5.

10-6c   AIDS and Other Medical Issues

As mentioned earlier, female inmates have special medical needs. But medical issues are important for both male and female inmates. The first major issue is that of AIDS.

Acquired immune deficiency syndrome (AIDS) has become a household word in the United States, as educational efforts to alert people to the deadly and rapidly spreading disease have had some success. Human immunodeficiency virus (HIV) causes AIDS. Evidence indicates that HIV is spread primarily through sexual contact and intravenous drug use. Thousands of people have died of AIDS, and there is no known cure.

HIV and AIDS are major concerns in correctional facilities, as well as in other areas of criminal justice systems. The number of AIDS cases among prison inmates has dropped recently, and the number of AIDS-related deaths in prison decreased 82 percent between 1995 and 2004. However, the number of confirmed cases of AIDS has remained significantly higher in prison than in the general population (more than three times higher in 2004).

More female (2.4 percent) than male (1.7 percent) inmates are HIV positive. The highest rates of HIV-positive inmates are in the Northeast.[72] As Spotlight 10-5 notes, AIDS is one focus of the Prison Rape Elimination Act of 2003.

One issue of concern is whether inmates contract the HIV virus before or after they enter prison. A study by the Centers for Disease Control (CDC) found that although there is a high rate of HIV-positive male inmates in the Georgia prison system (1.9 percent of total inmates), only about 10 percent of them contracted the virus while in prison. Of that 10 percent, 9 percent said they were raped in prison; most reported that they had consensual sex in prison.[73]

The most common disease among inmates is hepatitis C, with approximately 29 percent of inmates in a recent study in Maryland testing positive (compared to about 2 percent of the general population). The analysis reported that approximately 65 percent of the prison inmates with HIV were also infected with hepatitis C. An American Civil Liberties Union study in Virginia reported that 39 percent of inmates were infected with hepatitis C.[74] And in addition to the problem of spreading the disease within the prison is that of infecting others upon release. In 2003, the CDC held a conference of prison medical personnel to discuss the public health issues associated with released inmates infected with contagious diseases. The CDC expressed concern that inmates were not being treated for contagious diseases, while the American Civil Liberties Union and 24 other organizations concerned with health issues within prisons called for Congress to investigate the state of medical care within U.S. prisons and jails.[75]

Inmates in one study estimated that 44 percent of inmates engage in unprotected sex while in prison. Approximately 15 percent of all persons in the United States who are HIV positive and one-third who have hepatitis C are in prison in any given year. It

Spotlight 10-5   Prison Rape Elimination Act of 2003

[I]n 2003, the U.S. Congress passed and President George W. Bush signed the Prison Rape Elimination Act, which is designed to reduce the extensive problems resulting from prison rape. This Spotlight relates some of the major findings as well as the provisions of the new law, the purpose of which is to] provide for the analysis of the incidence and effects of prison rape in Federal, State, and local institutions and to provide information, resources, recommendations, and funding to protect individuals from prison rape.[1]

Section 15601. Findings

Congress makes the following findings:...

(2) Insufficient research has been conducted and insufficient data reported on the extent of prison rape....[The estimates are that over one million inmates have been assaulted during the past 20 years.]

(3) Inmates with mental illnesses are at increased risk of sexual victimization. America's jails and prisons house more mentally ill individuals than all of the Nation's psychiatric hospitals combined. As many as 16 percent of inmates in State prisons and jails and 7 percent of Federal inmates suffer from mental illness.

(4) Young first-time offenders are at increased risk of sexual victimization. Juveniles are five times more likely to be sexually assaulted in adult rather than juvenile facilities—often within the first 48 hours of incarceration.

(5) Most prison staff are not adequately trained or prepared to prevent, report, or treat inmate sexual assaults.

(6) Prison rape often goes unreported, and inmate victims often receive inadequate treatment for the severe physical and psychological effects of sexual assault—if they receive treatment at all.

(7) HIV and AIDS are major public health problems within America's correctional facilities....Prison rape undermines the public health by contributing to the spread of these diseases, and often giving a potential death sentence to its victims.

(8) Prison rape endangers the public safety by making brutalized inmates more likely to commit crimes when they are released....

(9) The frequently interracial character of prison sexual assaults significantly exacerbates interracial tensions....

(10) Prison rape increases the level of homicides and other violence against inmates and staff, and the risk of insurrections and riots.

(11) Victims of prison rape suffer severe physical and psychological effects that hinder their ability to integrate into the community and maintain stable employment upon their release from prison. They are thus more likely to become homeless and/or require government assistance....

(13) The high incidence of sexual assault within prisons involves actual and potential violations of the United States Constitution....

(14) The high incidence of prison rape undermines the effectiveness and efficiency of United States Government expenditures through grant programs such as those dealing with health care; mental health care; disease prevention; crime prevention; investigation, and prosecution; prison construction, maintenance, and operation; race relations; poverty; unemployment and homelessness. The effectiveness and efficiency of these federally funded grant programs are compromised by the failure of State officials to adopt policies and procedures that reduce the incidence of prison rape.

Section 15602. Purposes

The purposes of this Act are to—

(1) establish a zero-tolerance standard for the incidence of prison rape in prisons in the United States;

(2) make the prevention of prison rape a top priority in each prison system;

(3) develop and implement national standards for the detention, prevention, reduction, and punishment of prison rape;

(4) increase the available data and information on the incidence of prison rape, consequently improving the management and administration of correctional facilities;

(5) standardize the definitions used for collecting data on the incidence of prison rape;

(6) increase the accountability of prison officials who fail to detect, prevent, reduce, and punish prison rape;

(7) protect the Eighth Amendment rights of Federal, State, and local prisoners;

(8) increase the efficiency and effectiveness of Federal expenditures through grant programs such as those dealing with health care; mental health care; disease prevention; crime prevention, investigation, and prosecution; prison construction, maintenance, and operation; race relations; poverty; unemployment; and homelessness; and

(9) reduce the costs that prison rape imposes on interstate commerce.

[The statute provides for the collection of data on prison rape, the reporting of such data, the establishment of a Review Panel on Prison Rape within the U.S. Department of Justice, and many other provisions.]

---

1. The Elimination of Prison Rape Act of 2003 is codified at U.S. Code, Title 42, Sections 15601 *et seq.* (2007).

is argued that prisons should provide condoms to prevent the spread of contagious diseases by inmates, many of whom will eventually leave the prisons and perhaps spread those diseases to others outside of prison. In a 2005 news release, a group of medical doctors noted that prison officials have a duty to provide condoms but that condoms are not available in 95 percent of U.S. prisons.[76]

Some progress is being made. In 2004, Michigan prisons began an inmate testing and treatment program for hepatitis C.[77] Also, effective 1 January 2006, a California statute provides that all prisons must offer to incoming inmates information about hepatitis C and offer free, voluntary testing and treatment for that disease, HIV virus, and other contagious diseases.[78]

The most extensive study of prison health issues was conducted by the National Commission on Correctional Health Care, a nonprofit group that focuses on prison health. The study was funded by the U.S. Department of Justice (DOJ) and the CDC. The research, which focused on a three-year period during the mid-1990s, was presented to Congress in May 2002. Some of the findings were as follows:

- An estimated 34,800 to 46,000 inmates as of 1997 were infected with HIV, with an estimated 9,000 with full-blown AIDS.
- An estimated 98,500 to 145,500 HIV-positive inmates were released from prisons and jails during that time.
- As much as one-fifth of the nationwide jail and prison population of two million could be infected with hepatitis C.
- There were an estimated 1,400 cases of tuberculosis in jails and prisons across the country as of 1997, and as many as 12,000 inmates carrying the disease were released that same year.[79]

Many states do not have adequate medical facilities or staff to handle contagious diseases. In the case of HIV inmates, two states—Mississippi and Alabama—isolate the inmates from the general population, which means those inmates are unable to participate in most prison programs. Prison officials argue that it would be too expensive to establish programs just for isolated inmates and that to be forced to do so would go beyond the reasonable accommodations required by federal legislation for inmates with disabilities. Under the Americans with Disabilities Act (ADA) of 1990, individuals who pose a "direct threat to the health and safety of others" may be excluded from prison programs. The ADA defines *direct threat* as "a significant risk to the health or safety of others that cannot be eliminated by reasonable accommodation" or through the modification of existing programs. Alabama inmates filed a lawsuit against the prison system in 1985 under the federal Rehabilitation Act, which is similar to the ADA. In April 1999, the Eleventh Circuit Court of Appeals upheld the prison policy because of the risk of death for those infected with HIV and because of security problems in prisons. In January 2000, the U.S. Supreme Court refused (without comment) to accept the case for review, thus allowing the lower appellate court ruling to stand.[80]

Other lawsuits have been more successful for inmates or their estates. For example, Washington settled a wrongful death suit for $1 million after the death of Phillip Montgomery, age 32, who died a few hours after he was turned away from a prison health clinic. Montgomery had contracted hepatitis C. Class-action lawsuits concerning the lack of diagnosis and treatment for hepatitis C within prisons have been filed in several states.[81]

One final point concerning AIDS in prisons is the issue of contact visits between inmates and their families. In 1987, New York's highest court upheld the decision of prison officials to prohibit **conjugal visits** between an inmate infected with AIDS and his wife. The court held that this refusal was not an unreasonable interference with the rights of the inmate or of his spouse.[82] This is not an issue in most institutions, as they do not permit conjugal visits for any inmates.[83]

In 2006, the DOJ began efforts to educate state and local law enforcement officers regarding the requirements of the ADA. In particular, the DOJ stated that it receives

Conjugal visits Visits that permit inmates to engage in sexual and other social contacts with their spouses in an unsupervised, private setting.

complaints about the inability of law enforcement to communicate with persons who are hard of hearing or deaf. These materials are available on the Internet.[84]

10-6d   Inmates Who Are Elderly, or Physically or Mentally Challenged

Another characteristic of changing prison life is the increase in the number of inmates who are elderly, or physically or mentally challenged. Physically and mentally challenged persons have been incarcerated for years, but recently, some courts have held that the Americans with Disabilities Act (ADA) and its predecessor, the 1973 federal Rehabilitation Act, apply to inmates in some circumstances. The Ninth Circuit Court of Appeals has held that in its administration of programs, prison officials may not discriminate against inmates with disabilities who are "otherwise qualified" (a requirement of the statute).[85] It has been held, however, that the statutes do not apply to inmate employment.[86]

The aging of the prison population also presents new challenges. In some states, such as Florida, the increased costs of a large aging inmate population are leading officials to question how the costs will be financed. In 2000, the Florida legislature enacted a law requiring an annual report on the status of the elderly inmate population.[87] Florida has five correctional facilities with special units for the elderly. Approximately 10 percent (projected to be 14 percent by 2009) of Florida's inmate population is elderly (defined by that state as 50 or older); the national average is approximately 8 percent. These numbers are straining Florida's correctional system, as inmates over 50 use three times the medical care resources as those under 50.[88]

A geriatrician at the San Francisco Veterans Administration Medical Center, after conducting a study of elderly inmates in California, concluded: "Prison is not a safe place for vulnerable older people....Prisons are not geared to the needs of older people." The study focused on the responses of 120 California female inmates, age 55 or older. Approximately 69 percent of the women had difficulty in one or more of the following daily activities: standing in line, listening to orders, climbing into a top bunk, dropping to the floor rapidly when the alarm sounds, or walking to and from the dining hall. Fifty-one percent of the women had fallen within the previous year, and 16 percent (twice the national average for 65 or older persons in the general population) could not perform at least one daily function without assistance. Some of the recommendations are obvious: assign these inmates to lower bunks; install grab bars in showers and tubs and on toilets; and house the inmates closer to the dining hall.[89]

The special needs of mentally challenged inmates should also be addressed. In its 2006 report (based on data through midyear 2005), the Bureau of Justice Statistics (BJS) reported that over one-half of all jail and prison inmates have a mental health problem. Approximately 15 percent of state prison inmates and 24 percent of jail inmates met the criteria for a psychotic disorder. Nearly one-fourth of the mentally challenged prison and jail population have served three or more sentences for previous convictions, and approximately three-fourths meet the criteria for substance abuse or dependency. More female inmates than male inmates are mentally challenged. Mentally challenged inmates are more likely than other inmates to report being physically or sexually abused in the past.[90]

A study published in 2001 and conducted by the U.S. Public Health Service focused on the mental health problems of minorities and noted several significant problems that they had in getting adequate treatment both outside and inside prisons. Their difficulties outside prison may make minorities more likely to be drawn into the criminal justice system through inappropriate behavior. In general, society does not know how to react to people who act out problems because of a lack of medication or treatment—other than to lock them up. They are arrested rather than diverted to medical care. In analyzing these issues, one commentator noted that Texas was paying approximately $22,000 a year to incarcerate each inmate and that some mentally ill offenders could be treated less expensively in group homes or other diversion facilities. He concluded that there is a "clear correlation with mental illness, the state's minority populations, poverty and prisons."[91]

Concerned persons and organizations have called for investigations into the way mentally ill inmates are treated. Many are kept in isolation 23 to 24 hours a day in tiny rooms with little ventilation or light, conditions that, according to mental health experts, may lead to deterioration, depression, and even suicide. After judges found that a disproportionate number of mentally ill inmates were being housed in isolation in Wisconsin and Ohio prisons in 2002, those states agreed to be monitored. The American Civil Liberties Union (ACLU) filed suit in 2002 after eight mentally ill inmates died in Colorado's El Paso County Jail.[92]

There are some encouraging signs. In 2002, a plan submitted by Texas prison officials concerning the care of mentally ill inmates in solitary confinement (called *administrative segregation* in Texas) received a guarded endorsement from attorneys who have been involved in the general prison lawsuit that has gone on in that state since 1972.[93]

Minnesota prison systems stand out in the mental health field. For example, the Linda Berglin Mental Health Center at the Minnesota Correctional Facility—Red Wing, is one of the newest correctional health facilities. The center provides treatment for inmates are seriously mentally challenged.[94]

In New York City, officials agreed in principle to a settlement that would end a three-year lawsuit and provide help—such as transition medications, assistance in finding housing, transportation from incarceration to their homes, and help in getting Medicaid and welfare benefits—for mentally challenged inmates after they are released from jail. A lawyer representing the inmates called the plan one that requires sweeping changes and is, as far as he knows, the only lawsuit of its kind in the country. Another lawyer involved in the case said, "New York City has developed a program unique in the country in its content and scope which we believe will provide significant assistance to mentally ill inmates with the hope that these inmates will be able to successfully reintegrate into the community."[95]

In 2003, a federal appeals court upheld the decision of a U.S. district judge in Portland, Oregon, who ruled that the state violated the rights of mentally ill persons by keeping them in county jails for weeks or months before they were sent to the state hospital, where they could receive psychiatric care. According to the Ninth Circuit Court of Appeals, mentally ill persons who are awaiting trial have a higher rate of suicide and "are often locked in their cells for 22 to 23 hours a day, which further exacerbates their mental illness." Only the state hospital is charged with their psychiatric care; thus, if they are held in jail and not transferred to that facility, they will not get the psychiatric care they need to become competent to stand trial.[96]

A mental health program in New York has gained recognition. The Albany County Correctional Facility was the scene of the tragic death of a mentally ill inmate in 1995. After that incident, the superintendent and the president and chief executive officer of the Mental Health Association in New York met to discuss what they could do to prevent another such occurrence. With the assistance of grants, they began a program to divert mentally ill offenders from prisons. In their efforts, the officials engaged housing officials, support groups, mental health experts, legislators, and corrections officials, forming the Options Committee to develop diversion plans. Between January and June 2003, the committee diverted 11 inmates, with plans to have 25 by September and 75 by 2004. The diversion program saves money, as mental health inmates are usually incarcerated 30 percent longer than other inmates and cost approximately 30 percent more to incarcerate. The Options Committee needs additional funding, and that comes at a time when city, county, and state budgets are being cut (they received some funding from United Way), but if the program can get adequate funding, it may be able to divert 50 percent of the mentally challenged persons from jails.[97]

Despite these efforts, the treatment of mentally ill offenders remains a problem, as noted by the congressional findings in the Prison Rape Elimination Act of 2003, discussed in Spotlight 10-5. And in 2003, a major study by Human Rights Watch concluded that although significant progress has been made in the treatment of mentally ill offenders in prisons, much remains to be done. The 215-page report concluded that prisons were "never intended as facilities for the mentally ill, yet that is one of their primary roles today." Other conclusions are as follows:

- On any given day 70,000 inmates are psychotic.
- Between 200,000 and 300,000 inmates are mentally ill.
- Correctional officers who are not trained to recognize mental illness often punish these offenders for their illnesses (for e.g., citing an offender for "creating a disturbance" when the inmate is screaming because he or she "hears voices").
- Mentally ill offenders who do not receive proper treatment are "afflicted with delusions and hallucinations, debilitating fears, and extreme and uncontrollable mood swings....They huddle silently in their cells, mumble incoherently, or yell incessantly. They refuse to obey orders or lash out without apparent provocation. They beat their heads against cell walls, smear themselves with feces, self-mutilate, and commit suicide."
- Untrained correctional officers may escalate the problems when they use excessive force to discipline mentally ill offenders. "Several mentally ill prisoners have died from asphyxiation after struggling with guards who used improper methods to control them."[98]

One encouraging development is to divert some mentally offenders from criminal justice systems to treatment programs by processing their cases through mental health courts, which are discussed in Chapter 11. In the fall of 2004, Congress enacted the Mentally Ill Offender Treatment and Crime Reduction Act of 2004, which is to divert mentally ill persons to special courts for treatment. The bill provides up to $100 million a year in grants for states and localities. According to Senator Mike DeWine, who introduced the bill: "Unfortunately, the reality of our criminal justice system is that jails and prisons do not provide a therapeutic environment for the mentally ill, and are unlikely to do so any time soon....Indeed the mentally ill inmate often is preyed upon by other inmates or becomes even sicker in jail. Once released from jail or prison, many mentally ill people end up on the streets. With limited personal resources and little or no ability to handle their illnesses alone, they often commit further offenses resulting in their rearrest and reincarceration. This "revolving door" is costly and disruptive for all involved." Portions of this legislation are featured in Spotlight 10-6.[99]

Finally, brief attention should be given to the 2003 U.S. Supreme Court decision holding that it is permissible to medicate defendants so they will be competent to stand trial. That decision, *Sell v. United States*, which was decided by a 6-to-3 vote, did not, however, answer the question of whether it is constitutional to forcibly medicate mentally ill death row inmates so that they are legally competent for execution. In *Sell*, the justices stated that it should be a rare case in which involuntary medication is used. It is appropriate "only if the treatment is medically appropriate, is substantially unlikely to have side effects that may undermine the fairness of the trial, and, taking account of less intrusive alternatives, is necessary significantly to further important governmental trial-related interests." The defendant in this case, Charles Sell, had a long history of mental illness. He was charged with numerous crimes, including mail fraud, Medicaid fraud, and attempted murder. Since 1999, Sell, a former dentist, has been held in the U.S. Medical Center for Federal Prisoners in Missouri. He refused antipsychotic medications. The Eighth Circuit Court of Appeals found that Sell was not dangerous and held that he could be medicated against his will to make him competent to stand trial. The U.S. Supreme Court upheld that decision.[100]

10-6e Prison Programs

The special needs of female inmates, as well as of inmates who are HIV positive or have already contracted AIDS, elderly inmates, and those who are physically or mentally

| **Spotlight 10-6** | **Mentally Ill Offender Treatment and Crime Reduction Act of 2004** |

[T he Mentally Ill Offender Treatment and Crime Reduction Act of 2004 became law in the fall 2004 and is designed to improve the correctional systems' work with mentally ill inmates. Some of its provisions are reprinted here.][1]

(1) According to the Bureau of Justice Statistics, over 16 percent of adults incarcerated in United States jails and prisons have a mental illness.

(2) According to the Office of Juvenile Justice and Delinquency Prevention, approximately 20 percent of youth in the juvenile justice system have serious mental health problems, and a significant number have co-occurring mental health and substance abuse disorders.

(3) According to the National Alliance for the Mentally Ill, up to 40 percent of adults who suffer from a serious mental illness will come into contact with the American criminal justice system at some point in their lives.

(4) According to the Office of Juvenile Justice and Delinquency Prevention, over 150,000 juveniles who come into contact with the juvenile justice system each year meet the diagnostic criteria for at least one mental or emotional disorder.

(5) A significant proportion of adults with a serious mental illness who are involved with the criminal justice system are homeless or at imminent risk of homelessness; and many of these individuals are arrested and jailed for minor, nonviolent offenses.

(6) The majority of individuals with a mental illness or emotional disorder who are involved in the criminal or juvenile justice systems are responsive to medical and psychological interventions that integrate treatment, rehabilitation, and support services.

(7) Collaborative programs between mental health, substance abuse, and criminal or juvenile justice systems that ensure the provision of services for those with mental illness or co-occurring mental illness and substance abuse disorders can reduce the number of such individuals in adult and juvenile corrections facilities, while providing improved public safety.

Section 3. Purpose.
The purpose of this Act is to increase public safety by facilitating collaboration among the criminal justice, juvenile justice, mental health treatment, and substance abuse systems. Such collaboration is needed to–

(1) protect public safety by intervening with adult and juvenile offenders with mental illness or co-occurring mental illness and substance abuse disorders;

(2) provide courts, including existing and new mental health courts, with appropriate mental health and substance abuse treatment options;

(3) maximize the use of alternatives to prosecution through graduated sanctions in appropriate cases involving nonviolent offenders with mental illness;

(4) promote adequate training for criminal justice system personnel about mental illness and substance abuse disorders and the appropriate responses to people with such illnesses;

(5) promote adequate training for mental health and substance abuse treatment personnel about criminal offenders with mental illness or co-occurring substance abuse disorders and the appropriate response to such offenders in the criminal justice system;

(6) promote communication among adult or juvenile justice personnel, mental health and co-occurring mental illness and substance abuse disorders treatment personnel, nonviolent offenders with mental illness or co-occurring mental illness and substance abuse disorders, and support services such as housing, job placement, community, faith-based, and crime victims organizations; and

(7) promote communication, collaboration, and intergovernmental partnerships among municipal, county, and State elected officials with respect to mentally ill offenders.

1. The Mentally Ill Offender Treatment and Crime Reduction Act of 2004, 118 Stat. 2327 (2007).

challenged, should not be ignored. But neither should the mental, social, and physical needs of the inmates who do not fall into these categories. This section delves into the programs that might be implemented for the well-being of all inmates. In particular, education and work are examined.

Education

Despite the importance of education, insufficient attention is given to educational opportunities in correctional institutions. It is estimated that as many as 50 to 75 percent of American adult inmates are illiterate. The latest data available from the Bureau of Justice Statistics indicate that inmates have considerably less education than the general public. Approximately 18 percent of the general public have not completed high school, compared to 40 percent of state prison inmates, 27 percent of local jail inmates, and 31 percent of probationers. In terms of college-level or postsecondary vocational classes, which are taken by approximately 48 percent of the general population, the corresponding figures for correctional populations are as follows: 11 percent of state prison inmates, 24 percent of federal inmates, 14 percent of jail inmates, and 24 percent of probationers.[101]

If inmates are to return to society as law-abiding individuals, they must have skills, many of which are gained primarily through formal education. Most prisons provide some educational opportunities; some have college courses. Jails lag far behind prisons in this, as well as in many other areas.

Despite the evidence of the beneficial effects of education, those who argue that prisons should be for punishment and that state or federal government money should not be used for educating inmates may be winning in some jurisdictions. For example, the 1994 revision of the federal criminal code eliminated grants that were used to provide college courses in prisons. Further, courts have not ruled that inmates have a *right* to any educational opportunities they may choose, and some courts have held that inmates do not have a right to a free college education.[102]

In recent years, several states, in cutting their overall budgets, have cut funding for prison education. In California, however, the governor announced in June 2006 that due to a tax windfall gain, the state would be able to increase its funding for education, including programs within prisons.[103] And a California jail has a leading program in education, both short-term and long-term, for its inmates. According to the California Department of Education, the Santa Ana jail facility "is a leader in inmate programming, and it may be the only city jail in America that provides inmates with the opportunity for long-term growth through formal education."[104]

The Utah State Prison boasts a new facility for housing, along with vocational and educational training. According to one of the prison officials, "By putting them [the inmates] through these training programs, we're giving them the thinking skills, practical skills, and the ability to actually make a living and stay out of prison."[105]

Finally, the Arizona prison system's educational program has been revamped by the new director, who was appointed in 2004. In her first year of office, the number of inmates who received their GEDs (high school equivalency) increased fourfold. The director has also increased the educational opportunities for staff and revised training policies.[106]

Work

Work programs are a second area of important focus. A noted criminologist has said that "the most difficult prison to administer is the one in which prisoners languish in idleness. Absence of work leads to moral and physical degradation and corrupts institutional order."[107] Work has been an important part of U.S. prisons historically, and some of the early prison industries were profitable economically. State laws prohibiting the sale of prison-made goods to the general public, along with federal laws prohibiting shipping prison-made goods across state lines into states with these statutes, changed the nature of prison labor. Prisons were confined primarily to making goods for state (or federal) use.

In recent years, additional attempts have been made to introduce meaningful vocational opportunities into prisons, along with "just plain work" to keep inmates busy and provide needed services for state and federal institutions. The federal Bureau of Prisons (BOP) led the way, announcing in 1994 the need to expand the Federal Prison Industries (FPI). All federal inmates are required to work, but the increase in the inmate population was outstripping available jobs. Further, most of the inmates work in jobs that maintain the institution and thus may not prepare them for the marketable skills they need when they are released from prison. Federal prisons are limited to producing goods for federal institutions in order to avoid competition, but some have suggested a change in that policy.[108]

Inmates may but do not have to be paid for their work. A 1990 federal court ruling held that "compelling an inmate to work without pay is not unconstitutional."[109]

Inmates' wages are very low (some as low as 25 cents an hour), although it has been suggested that inmates should be paid the minimum wage but required to pay for room and board.

Inmates may also work outside the prisons. In Louisiana, which has the highest incarceration rate in the country, the "men in orange," as they are called, are permitted to work for private citizens. "They do anything you ask them to do," said one employer. Some of the work is free; some is just low paid (the lowest that locals can get). In areas hard-hit by hurricane Katrina in 2005, there is a lot of work to be done.[110]

In 1995, the BOP finalized its regulations concerning requiring inmates to pay for the cost of incarceration. The regulations apply to all inmates convicted after 1 January 1995.[111] Legal issues have been raised concerning imposing on inmates the requirement of paying the costs of their incarceration, and courts are not uniform in their reactions to these issues.

10-6f Prison Violence

Prison officials are warning that one of the results of reducing or eliminating prison programs may be increased violence, manifested in the murders of other inmates or prison officials, escapes, or riots that may result in serious property damage, injuries, or deaths. For example, on 13 December 2000, seven dangerous inmates escaped from a Texas maximum-security prison. They were not captured until January, when four of the seven were arrested in Colorado, where a fifth inmate killed himself after officers arrived. The other two were captured later. The inmates were charged with, among other crimes, killing a law enforcement officer. Four were convicted and sentenced to death. In June 2003, the fifth inmate, Randy Halprin, 25, was convicted and sentenced to death. In November 2003, Patrick Murphy, Jr. was convicted and also sentenced to death.

Prison violence also involves injuries and deaths to other inmates, as illustrated by the killing of defrocked priest John J. Geoghan in August 2003 in a Massachusetts state prison. Geoghan, who was accused of molesting children for decades, admitted to engaging in sexual acts with three boys. The inmate accused of Geoghan's murder allegedly wrote a letter to a newspaper, in which he stated that he had been sexually abused when he was a child, and apologized to Geoghan's sister for murdering her brother. The letter was signed, "Regretfully but sincerely, Joseph L. Druce." Subsequently Druce, entered a plea of not guilty to beating and strangling Geoghan.[112] In March 2006, Druce was convicted and given a life sentence without parole.

Other types of prison violence involve riots. Although few in number, prison riots are serious in their injuries to humans—injuries that in some cases result in death— and in their destruction of property.

Two of the most destructive and highly publicized U.S. prison riots occurred in 1971 in Attica, New York, and in 1980 in Santa Fe, New Mexico. The Attica riot is summarized in a 1985 opinion of a federal judge whose court heard allegations of violations of constitutional rights in that facility. The judge noted that 43 persons (32 inmates and 11 correctional employees) were killed during the riot, the "bloodiest one-day encounter between Americans since the Civil War." Prior to the riot, the prison was overcrowded, with 2,200 inmates in a facility built for 1,700. Although 54 percent of the inmates were African American and 9 percent were Puerto Rican, all officers were white. The institution had no meaningful programs for inmates. As was noted in Spotlight 10-1, the civil suits regarding this riot continued for years.[113]

On 2 February 1980, a riot as devastating as the Attica riot occurred at the state prison in Santa Fe, New Mexico. Estimates of damage ranged from $20 million to repair to $80 million to replace the prison. At least 90 persons required hospitalization, and 33 inmates were killed. Characteristic of the violence was the torture and incredible brutality of inmates toward inmates, which led National Guardsmen to regurgitate on the scene and firefighters who had fought in Vietnam to proclaim that they had not seen such atrocities as those that were committed during this riot.[114]

Spotlight 10-7 Selected Disturbances or Riots in American Prisons, 1985–2003

Calico Rock, Arkansas: June 2003

Twelve inmates were injured and sent to the infirmary and sixteen more were transferred to the isolation unit of the medium-security prison of the North Central Unit of the Arkansas Prison System. The fighting broke out in three cell-blocks after one inmate was sent to isolation for refusing to leave the shower during a fire drill. Other inmates, especially the cousin of the isolated prisoner, began protesting, with comments such as, "We are not going to take this." No prison personnel were injured, and the unit's emergency response team brought the fighting under control quickly. Prison officials, who refused to characterize the incident as a riot, stated that such events seldom occur at that prison.

Lamesa, Texas: April 2000

One inmate was killed and thirty-one were injured, some critically, in a minimum to medium-security prison after approximately 300 African American and Hispanic inmates became involved in a riot, which lasted only a few hours before prison officials brought the institution under control by using pepper spray. The riot began after two inmates started fighting in the dining hall.

Crescent City, California: February 2000

One inmate was killed and eight were injured, one critically, after approximately 200 African American and Hispanic inmates began fighting with handmade weapons. The incident occurred on the day that a federal grand jury indicted two former correctional officers for violating the civil rights of inmates by the use of brutality, which resulted in the death of one victim. This prison at Pelican Bay, located on

the coast about 20 miles south of the California/Oregon border, houses the state's most violent inmates. It was designed for 2,280 inmates but contained 3,400 at the time of the 2000 riot. In a 1997 riot at the institution, six inmates were killed.[1]

Lucasville, Ohio—Southern Ohio Correctional Facility: April 1993

In March 1995, Jason Robb, an inmate accused of helping lead the 1993 riot that resulted in the deaths of nine inmates and one correctional officer, was convicted of killing the officer and one inmate. Robb was convicted of six of the seven charges against him, including aggravated murder and kidnapping. The riot began on Easter Sunday, when a fight broke out as inmates returned from the recreation yard to their cellblocks. It lasted 11 days. Inmates surrendered after they agreed with prison officials on 21 issues, including numerous improvements in prison conditions. Officials agreed that inmates would not be subjected to retaliations by correctional officers, although it was made clear that those who committed crimes, such as murder, would be subject to prosecution. It was not until 10 years later, however, in May 2003, that the last of four inmates charged in the death of officer Robert Vallendingham was convicted. For the second time, a jury found James Were, 46, guilty of kidnapping and two counts of aggravated murder, one for plotting the death of the officer and the second for killing him during the kidnapping. Were's first conviction was overturned by the Ohio Supreme Court. The prosecution was seeking the death penalty, but Were's mental condition was at issue and may preclude execution.

Although no major riots have occurred in U.S. prisons in recent years, some of the more recent U.S. prison riots or disturbances are featured in Spotlight 10-7.

One final form of violence is less obvious but very important, and that is inmate self-inflicted violence. This violence may not be reported in jails and prisons for a variety of reasons, but when such violence leads to suicide, the acts become known and may trigger investigations by public officials and lawsuits by survivors. Suicides are more common in jails than in prisons, and little is known about the reasons for inmate death by suicide. The issue gained national attention in 1993, when U.S. Attorney General Janet Reno ordered a federal investigation of the 46 hanging deaths that had occurred in Mississippi jails since 1987. Some argued that these deaths of young African Americans were lynchings, not suicides. After an eight-month investigation, federal officials ordered the state to correct "gross deficiencies" in Mississippi jails or face closure of the facilities. In 1995, after almost two years of additional investigation, the FBI reported that it found no evidence of misconduct on the part of jail officials. Not all agreed with that finding, with some alleging that the FBI had not talked to all of the witnesses.[115]

According to an American Bar Association publication, approximately one-third of all jail suicides occur in the South, which is characterized by more lax jail standards compared to other jails throughout the nation. For example, during the Mississippi suicides under investigation between 1993 and 1995, one-fourth of all of the jails in that

Maryland and New York Prisons: May 1991

Fourteen correctional officers and forty-four inmates were injured when Maryland inmates rioted in the Correctional Institution at Hagerstown on 25 May 1991. Of the 1,600 inmates at the institution, approximately 1,000 were involved in the riot, "which officials described as the most serious disturbance at the prison in decades." Inmates caused over $1 million of damage before the riot was quelled. The prison was approximately 60 percent overcrowded at the time of the riot.[2]

On 28 May 1991, a disturbance began at the Southport Correctional Facility at Pine City, New York. This facility is a maxi-maxi prison designed to house the state's most serious and dangerous offenders. Three correctional officers, taken hostage by approximately 50 inmates, were held for 26 hours before being released. Although there were no deaths in this riot, several officers were stabbed or beaten. Inmates were protesting the institution's lockdown policy, which kept them in their cells 23 hours a day with only 1 hour out for supervised exercise; poor living conditions and food; and some of the restrictions on visitation.[3]

Moundsville, West Virginia—West Virginia Penitentiary: January 1986

Inmates wielding homemade weapons took correctional officers hostage and seized control of the prison. Three inmates were killed, 16 hostages were taken, and the prison was held by inmates for 43 hours. Officers taken hostage were forced to watch inmates brutalize, torture, and then kill inmates thought to be snitches. The body of one inmate, a convicted murderer and child molester, was dragged up and down a cellblock as other inmates spat on him. The riot was triggered by inmate anger regarding restrictions on contact visits with family and friends and the cancellation of a Christmas open house.

State officials blamed each other for the problems. The current governor and the former governor "traded charges of accusing each other of cowardice and misguided policies." The current governor said that the killed inmates were accused of being informants for the administration and that the informant policy was started by the previous governor, who retorted that during the three-day crisis, the current governor was not available. On 16 January 1986, inmates began a work strike to protest continued restrictions of their activities since the riot. In February, 25 inmates who had been placed in isolation since the New Year's Day riot broke out of their cells. Correctional officers persuaded 23 of the inmates to surrender and then captured the other 2. Sixty-eight inmates were in isolation as a result of the riot.

The West Virginia Penitentiary had been placed under court order in 1983 after the court found unconstitutional conditions, including maggot-infested food and raw sewage in living areas. The prison at that time was overcrowded, and officials were ordered to reduce the population.

Source: Summarized from media sources unless otherwise noted.

1. "Inmate Dies and 8 Are Hurt in California Prison Riot," *New York Times* (24 February 2000), p. 21.
2. "Maryland and New York Prisons Suffer Serious Disturbances," *Criminal Justice Newsletter* 22 (3 June 1991): 5.
3. Ibid.

state were under federal court orders for failure to comply with national safety standards. Three southern states—Georgia, Mississippi, and Alabama—did not conduct jail inspections and had no state standards for jail conditions. An expert on jail suicides stated, "Jail officials in the South pay extremely low wages, hire unqualified jailers and offer no training in suicide recognition and prevention." A Mississippi medical examiner, who ruled that the deaths he investigated were all suicides, concluded that the suicide issue in that state was "much more of a public health issue…than it is a criminal justice issue.…There's nobody watching the inmates." But an independent pathologist from Chicago, who examined the autopsy of one of the dead inmates, concluded that inmate did not commit suicide but was murdered. The pathologist stated that it was "almost impossible to hang oneself" in the position in which that inmate was found. "This is a fairy tale." But the official federal investigation ruled that all of the inmate deaths under investigation were suicides.[116]

Official data from the Bureau of Justice Statistics indicate that from 1983 to 2002 the suicide rate fell in local jails. In 1983, suicides were the major cause of death among jail inmates; in 2002, that was not the case, as natural causes and illnesses had surpassed suicides. The suicide rate, defined as the number of suicides per 100,000 inmates, declined between 1980 and 2003, as shown in Figure 10-1.

The reasons for self-inflicted violence and suicide in jails and prisons are various. They have been linked to overcrowded institutions, mental illness, the extended use of

Figure 10-1
Suicide Rates in Prisons and Jails, 1980–2003
Source: Bureau of Justice Statistics, Office of Justice Programs, http://www.ojp.usdoj.gov/bjs/glance/shipj.htm, accessed 15 July 2005.

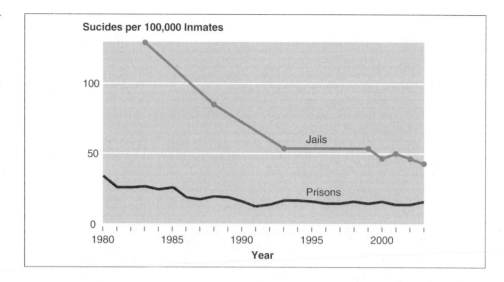

solitary confinement, and the psychological consequences of being victimized in jail or prison. Some inmates who are threatened with rape or other violence become depressed and desperate about their physical safety, because their only options are fight and flight. If they submit to violence, they are branded as weak and forced to face further violent attacks from aggressive inmates. If they seek help from the prison administration, they are branded as snitches or rats. Furthermore, the inmate social system rewards violence against weaker inmates.

What can be done to prevent jail and prison suicides? A jail that opened in South Bend, Indiana, in 2001 placed a psychiatrist on duty in an attempt to prevent suicides after two recent suicides occurred in the county jail. And after two jail inmates committed suicide within a six-month period in 2002, a new cellblock was opened in early 2003 at the Madison County Jail (Missouri). The facility houses male inmates who may be suicide risks because of depression or mental illness. The sheriff commented, "We want to see the inmates who walk into this jail walk out, and not be carried out."[117]

The belief that jail suicides, at least in many cases, can be prevented, is implicit in the lawsuits for wrongful death won by the families of deceased inmates who committed suicide. In April 2003, a New Mexico mother whose daughter committed suicide in jail won a settlement consisting of attorney fees plus a $5,500 annuity for each of her daughter's three children. The lawsuit alleged that jail officials were negligent in their failure to provide adequate medical and psychiatric care. And a Maine family filed both state and federal lawsuits for the wrongful death of their loved one, a man who committed suicide in the Maine State Prison mental health unit. The family of Adam J. Dupuis alleged that prison officials were deliberately indifferent to Dupuis's medical needs and that correctional officials were playing cards when Dupuis hanged himself in his cell. Dupuis, who was in a mental health unit and had been diagnosed as bipolar, was on medication for severe anxiety and depression. The treatment was successful but had been changed. On the day in question, Dupuis had placed a sign in his window to block the correctional officers' view of him and was not seen for 45 minutes, during which time he committed suicide. He had made an unsuccessful suicide attempt a week prior.[118]

One final observation is that violence in prison is not always limited to inmate causes. In June 2006, in a Tallahassee, Florida, state prison, one correctional officer and one federal agent died in an altercation that began when federal law enforcement authorities arrived to arrest officers indicted for conspiracy and other crimes associated with allegedly providing contraband to female inmates in exchange for sexual favors and then bribing the inmates not to report them. They faced 20 years in prison. A jury convicted Alan F. Moore and Gregory Dixon, and the judge sentenced each to one year in prison, followed by three years of supervised release.[119]

Chapter Wrap-Up

In 1984, the U.S. Supreme Court said that the continuing guarantee of substantial rights to prison inmates "is testimony to a belief that the way a society treats those who have transgressed against it is evidence of the essential character of that society."[120] This chapter explored life in prison, historically and currently. It began with a brief look at the events that might accompany an inmate's arrival at prison and proceeded to an overview of the legal issues that govern incarceration today.

The U.S. Supreme Court has made it clear that inmates forfeit some rights and that prison security needs may justify the restriction of rights normally recognized in prison. This chapter surveyed the historical and current approaches to inmates' legal rights, beginning with a look at the traditional hands off doctrine, in which federal courts refused to become involved in daily prison administration and maintenance. As a result of the recognized abuse of inmates and the civil rights movement, which brought the nation's attention to the problems not only of minorities in society but also to the conditions under which inmates lived, courts began to abandon the hands off doctrine. Courts continue to defer to prison officials, but they no longer tolerate violations of basic rights. The concept of cruel and unusual punishment, along with ways of determining what that means, was discussed as an example.

The chapter focused next on prison administration and its relationship to security goals. In earlier days, authoritarian prison wardens or superintendents and correctional officers maintained security by keeping inmates separated and by not permitting them to talk to each other, or by using fear and force, often involving corporal punishment. Those methods are not permitted today; new management techniques are necessary.

Correctional officers are crucial to prison management. They have primary responsibility for maintaining internal discipline, order, and security. Their jobs are difficult and at times boring, but the position can also be challenging and rewarding. The chapter emphasized the importance of selecting and training officers carefully and of including women and minorities within their ranks. It also noted examples of brutality by prison correctional officers.

When we think of life behind bars, however, we think mainly of inmates serving time within those facilities. This chapter noted how inmates adjust to prison life through the prisonization process. The resulting subculture was discussed in view of its origin: whether inmates develop the subculture as a method of adapting to the deprivations of prison or whether they acquired the values of the subculture and then imported them into prisons.

The male inmate subculture is characterized by social roles that assist inmates in maintaining some self-esteem and positive self-concepts. Some accomplish these goals at the expense of other inmates: social control through economics, through racial and gang violence, and through homosexual attacks. Prison gangs play a critical role in these interactions.

Female inmates develop patterns of adaptation to prison life, too, but normally, their adaptations are less violent than those of male inmates. Their social roles mirror the roles they have played in society. Women face many of the same deprivations as male inmates, but they face the additional problems of adjusting to daily life without their children. Mothers behind bars have become a subject of research only recently, and even today, few provisions are made for female inmates to interact with their children. Women also have special medical needs, and institutions are attempting to accommodate those needs, although some are doing so only under court orders or the threat of such orders.

The sexual behavior of male and female inmates is contrasted and discussed in the context of a relatively recent issue of prison life: AIDS. The complications are increasing, too, as officials must determine how to cope with AIDS without violating inmates' constitutional rights. The incidences of violent sex in both institutions for females and males were discussed, with particular attention given to the Prison Rape Elimination Act of 2003 and its implications. The chapter also discussed the existence and implications of contagious diseases, such as hepatitis C and tuberculosis, in prisons. Attention was also given to the special needs of inmates who are elderly, or physically or mentally challenged.

Adaptation to prison is made more difficult by the lack of activities, including education and work. Recent attention to the need for such programs, along with budget cuts that have reduced prison programs, was discussed.

The final chapter section looked at the impact of prison violence, with particular attention given to the major prison riots of recent times. The Attica riot of 1971 and subsequent studies of the riot illustrate the devastation of riots in terms of personal injury, death, and property damage, as well as the slowness with which meaningful changes are made. The New Mexico and West Virginia riots illustrate the torture and brutality of which inmates are capable. The more recent riots remind us that serious prison disturbances still occur.

Another type of violence in prison is self-inflicted violence, apparently the only way some inmates find to adjust. In some cases, suicide results.

This chapter's discussion of the problems of controlling inmates within prison looked at the issues historically and in terms of recent events. But eventually, most inmates are released from prison. The meaning that has for them and for society is the topic of Chapter 11.

Key Terms

civil rights (p. 292)
commissary (p. 291)
conjugal visits (p. 315)

correctional officers (COs), or guards (p. 297)
deprivation model (p. 303)
hands-off doctrine (p. 291)

importation model (p. 303)
norms (p. 302)
prisonization (p. 302)
social system (p. 299)

Apply It

1. What is the *hands off doctrine*, and to what extent (and why) has it been abandoned?
2. What is meant by a *hierarchy of rights*?
3. What were the characteristics of the authoritarian warden? What do you think should be the characteristics of the ideal warden or prison superintendent?
4. What events have occurred within prisons during the past three decades and forced changes in prison administration?
5. How did early correctional officers control inmates? If permitted, would those techniques be effective today?
6. Discuss recruitment and training issues with regard to correctional officers. Note the issues regarding gender and race.
7. Describe some of the daily aspects of inmate prison life.
8. Define *prisonization* and *subculture*, and explain the development and importance of each in a prison setting. Would the importance be different in prisons for female as compared to male inmates?
9. Distinguish the importation and deprivation models, and explain the social control role of inmate social systems.
10. What is the significance of prison gangs? What could be done to lessen their influence?
11. What provisions do you think should be made for incarcerated women who have children at home or for women who give birth during incarceration? What

provisions should be made for incarcerated fathers to visit with their children? Do female inmates have special problems other than child care, and if so, how should they be handled? Should inmate fathers have the same access to visitation arrangements that inmate mothers have?
12. Explain the Prison Rape Elimination Act of 2003, and discuss what you think its impact will be on prison life.
13. Distinguish the sexual behavior in prison of gay males from that of lesbians.
14. What has been the impact of AIDS on prisons? How should the problems be handled? What about the spread of other contagious diseases, such as tuberculosis and hepatitis C?
15. Discuss the situations that prison officials face as the result of aging inmate populations. What are the special needs of physically and mentally challenged inmates?
16. If most inmates are relatively poorly educated, why do we not make a greater effort to provide education classes in prisons?
17. Should inmates be required to work within the prisons? If there is a lack of jobs, how should that problem be solved?
18. What policies would you recommend to prison administrators if they were to ask you how to prevent prison riots? What policies might prevent jail or prison suicides?

Endnotes

1. See Harold Garfinkel, "Conditions of Successful Degradation Ceremonies," *American Journal of Sociology* 61 (March 1956): 420–424.
2. Gresham M. Sykes, *The Society of Captives* (Princeton, N.J.: Princeton University Press, 1958), pp. 63–83.
3. Ruffin v. Commonwealth, 62 Va. 790, 796 (1872).
4. Wolff v. McDonnell, 418 U.S. 539 (1974).
5. Holt v. Sarver, 309 F.Supp. 362 (E.D.Ark. 1970). This case has a long history of remands and reversals leading to the U.S. Supreme Court case, Hutto v. Finney, 437 U.S. 678 (1978).
6. Abdul Wali v. Coughlin, 754 F.2d 1015 (2d Cir. 1985).
7. Graham v. Richardson, 313 F.Supp. 34 (D.Ariz 1970), *aff'd.*, 403 U.S. 365, 375 (1971).
8. Estelle v. Gamble, 429 U.S. 97, 106 (1976).
9. Wilson v. Seiter, 501 U.S. 294 (1991).
10. Farmer v. Brennan, 511 U.S. 895 (1994).
11. Hudson v. McMillian, 503 U.S. 1 (1992).
12. Beard v. Banks, 126 S.Ct. 2572 (2006).
13. "Florida Corrections Secretary Steps Down Following Scandals," *Criminal Justice Newsletter* (1 March 2006), p. 3.
14. Norman Holt, "Prison Management in the Next Decade," *Prison Journal* 57 (Autumn/Winter 1977): 17–19. Unless otherwise noted, this discussion of prison management comes from this source.
15. "New York City Accepts Limits on Use of Force against Jail Inmates," *Criminal Justice Newsletter* (15 March 2006), p. 6.
16. "Unions, COs Become Activists for Reform in U.S. Prisons," *Corrections Professional* 11, no. 18 (23 June 2006): n.p.
17. "Female Guards at Men's Prisons," *Orlando Sentinel* (20 June 1997), p. 10.
18. Johnson v. Phelan, 69 F.3d 144 (7th Cir. 1995), *cert. denied*, 519 U.S. 1006 (1996).
19. Brissette v. Franklin County Sheriff's Office, 235 F.Supp. 2d 63 (D. Mass. 2003).
20. Rita J. Simon and Judith D. Simon, "Female COs: Legitimate Authority," *Corrections* 50 (August 1988): 132.
21. "Female Correctional Officers Said to Reduce Prison Violence," *Criminal Justice Newsletter* 27 (1 April 1996): 2.
22. This discussion of Clemmer's concept of prisonization comes from his book, *The Prison Community* (New York: Holt, Rinehart and Winston, 1958), pp. 298–301.
23. Stanton Wheeler, "Socialization in Correctional Communities," *American Sociological Review* 26 (October 1961): 697–712.
24. Geoffrey P. Alpert et al., "A Comparative Look at Prisonization: Sex and Prison Culture," *Quarterly Journal of Corrections* 1 (Summer 1977): 29–34.
25. See Sykes, *Society of Captives*; and Gresham M. Sykes and Sheldon L. Messinger, "The Inmate Social System," in *Theoretical Studies in Social Organization of the Prison*, ed. Richard A. Cloward et al. (New York: Social Science Research Council, 1960).
26. See John Irwin and Donald R. Cressey, "Thieves, Convicts and the Inmate Culture," *Social Problems* 10 (Fall 1962): 142–155.
27. Charles W. Thomas, "Prisonization or Resocialization: A Study of External Factors Associated with the Impact of Imprisonment," *Journal of Research in Crime and Delinquency* 10 (January 1975): 13–21.

28. Leo Carroll, "Race and Three Forms of Prisoner Power Confrontation, Censoriousness, and the Corruption of Authority," in *Contemporary Corrections: Social Control and Conflict*, ed. C. Ronald Huff (Beverly Hills, Calif.: Sage Publications, 1977), pp. 40–41, 50–51.

29. Ronald L. Akers et al., "Prisonization in Five Countries: Type of Prison and Inmate Characteristics," *Criminology* 14 (February 1977): 538.

30. See James Garofalo and Richard D. Clark, "The Inmate Subculture in Jails," *Criminal Justice and Behavior* 12 (December 1985): 431.

31. Richard A. Cloward, "Social Control in the Prison," in *Theoretical Studies*, ed. Cloward et al.

32. James W. Marquart and Ben M. Crouch, "Coopting the Kept: Using Inmates for Social Control in a Southern Prison," *Justice Quarterly* 1, no. 4 (1984): 491–509.

33. Robert S. Fong, "The Organizational Structure of Prison Gangs," *Federal Probation* 54 (March 1990): 36–43.

34. Michael P. Lane, "Inmate Gangs," *Corrections Today* 51 (July 1989): 98–102.

35. "Intelligence: The Key to Gang Suppression," *Corrections Today* 68, no. 2 (1 April 2006): 42.

36. Ibid.

37. "Trial Begins for Members of Aryan Prison Gang," *New York Times* (15 March 2006), p. 17.

38. "4 Leaders of Aryan Brotherhood Prison Gang Found Guilty in O.C.," *Los Angeles Times* (30 July 2006), p. 3B.

39. Dr. Natasha Frost, assistant professor at Northeastern University College of Criminal Justice, quoted in "National Study Examines Rise in Female Inmate Populations," *Corrections Professional* 11, no. 18 (23 June 2006): n.p.

40. Rose Giallombardo, *The Social World of Imprisoned Girls: A Comparative Study of Institutions for Juvenile Delinquents* (New York: John Wiley, 1974).

41. David A. Ward and Gene G. Kassebaum, "Women in Prison," in *Correctional Institutions*, ed. Robert M. Carter et al. (Philadelphia: J. B. Lippincott, 1972), p. 215.

42. Justice Policy Center, *Families Left Behind: The Hidden Costs of Incarceration and Reentry*, a 12-page report, summarized in "Incarceration of Parents Causes Enormous Problems, Report Says," *Criminal Justice Newsletter* (17 November 2003), p. 5.

43. "DOC Program Strengthens Family Ties," *Corrections Professional* 8, no. 4 (18 October 2002): n.p.

44. "Child Visitation Unit Added to Female Prison," *Corrections Professional* 7, no. 15 (19 April 2002): n.p.

45. "Mothering Behind Bars," *State Legislatures* 28, no. 10 (1 December 2002): 11.

46. "Prison Systems Slowly Implementing Parent Training Programs for Males," *Correctional Educational Bulletin* 6, no. 3 (26 November 2002): n.p.

47. Women Prisoners of the District of Columbia Department of Corrections v. District of Columbia, 899 F.Supp. 659 (D.D.C. 1995), *vacated, in part, remanded*, 93 F.3d 910 (D.C.Cir. 1996), *cert. denied*, 520 U.S. 1196 (1997), *on remand*, 968 F.Supp. 744 (D.D.C. 1997).

48. The case is Shumate v. Wilson, filed in the U.S. District Court, Eastern District of California, in 1995; "Plaintiff Class," *AIDS Policy and Law* 18, no. 12 (20 June 2003): n.p.

49. "Lawyers to Get $1.2M in Prison Settlement," *The Recorder* (American Lawyer Media, L.P.) (14 August 1997), p. 1.

50. "Services for Women Inadequate," *Correctional Educational Bulletin* 6, no. 4 (24 December 2002): n.p.

51. "Study: Programs Could Help Humiliated, Bored Female Inmates: Researchers Say More Education Is Needed," *Corrections Professional* 8, no. 8 (20 January 2003): n.p.

52. Capitol Hill Hearing Testimony of Harley Lappin, Director, Federal Bureau of Prisons, before the House Judiciary Committee on Crime, Terrorism and Homeland Security, FDCH Political Transcripts (14 May 2003), n.p.

53. Overton v. Bazzetta, 539 U.S. 126 (2003).

54. Rule 791.6609(5); Michigan Department of Corrections Procedure OP-SLF/STF-05.

55. Overton v. Bazzetta, 539 U.S. 126 (2003).

56. Peter C. Buffum, *Homosexuality in Prisons* (U.S. Department of Justice et al., Washington, D.C.: U.S. Government Printing Office, 1972), p. 13.

57. Sykes, *Society of Captives*, p. 97.

58. Buffum, *Homosexuality in Prisons*, p. 9.

59. Leo Carroll, *Hacks, Blacks, and Cons: Race Relations in a Maximum Security Prison* (Lexington, Mass.: D.C. Heath, 1974), p. 194.

60. Daniel Lockwood, *Prison Sexual Violence* (New York: Elsevier Science Publishing, 1980), p. 21.

61. Redman v. San Diego County, California, 942 F.2d 1435 (9th Cir. 1991), *cert. denied*, 502 U.S. 1074 (1992).

62. Farmer v. Brennan, 511 U.S. 825 (1994).

63. Ward and Kassebaum, "Women in Prison," pp. 217–219.

64. Rose Giallombardo, *Society of Women: A Study of a Woman's Prison* (New York: John Wiley, 1966).

65. John Gagnon and William Simon, "The Social Meaning of Prison Homosexuality," *Federal Probation* 32 (March 1968): 27–28.

66. David Ward and Gene Kassebaum, "Sexual Tensions in a Women's Prison," in *Crime and Justice: The Criminal in Confinement*, ed. Leon Radzinowicz and Marvin E. Wolfgang (New York: Basic Books, 1971), pp. 146–155.

67. "Study Describes Extent of Staff-on-Inmate Sex Misconduct," *Criminal Justice Newsletter* 30 (2 March 1999): 5–6. The full report, *Women in Prison: Sexual Misconduct by Correctional Staff*, is available without charge from the General Accounting Office, Box 37050, Washington, D.C. 20013 (202)512-6000. Fax: (202)512-6061, http://www.gao.gov.

68. "Inmates Commit Most Sexual Assaults in Women's Prisons," *Corrections Professional* 8, no. 8 (20 January 2003): n.p.

69. "Official Gets Probation for Inmate Sex," *Denver Post* (16 May 2003), p. 4B.

70. "Belt Alarm Could Curb Sexual Abuse in Women's Prisons," *Corrections Professional* 8, no. 14 (11 April 2003): n.p.

71. "U.S. Senate Passes Legislation to Curb Prisoner Rape; House to Vote Wednesday," *Business Wire* (22 July 2003), n.p.

72. Laura M. Maruschak, Bureau of Justice Statistics Bulletin, *HIV in Prisons, 2004* (Washington, D.C.: U.S. Department of Justice, November 2006), pp. 1–5.

73. *HIV Transmission among Male Inmates in a State Prison System—Georgia, 1992–2005*, http://www.cdc.gov, accessed 19 July 2006.

74. "Maryland Prison System Has High HIV Rate," *Corrections Professional* 8, no. 17 (23 May 2003): n.p.

75. "Infections in Newly Released Inmates Are Rising Concern," *New York Times* (28 January 2003), p. 14.

76. "Doctors Encourage Inmate Condom Access," *Corrections Professional* 10, no. 16 (13 May 2005): n.p.

77. "Michigan Prisons Test Inmates for Hepatitis C," *Corrections Professional* 10, no. 7 (7 December 2004): n.p.

78. Cal. Health & Safety Code, Section 122415(a)(2) (2007).

79. "When Prison Cells Breed Disease," *Legal Times* (9 December 2002), p. 1.

80. Davis v. Hopper, 171 F.3d 1289 (11th Cir. 1999), *cert. denied*, 528 U. S. 1114 (2000).

81. "When Prison Cells Breed Disease," p. 1.

82. Doe v. Coughlin, 523 N.Y.S.2d 782 (N.Y.Ct.App. 1987), *cert. denied*, 488 U.S. 879 (1988).

83. For an analysis of conjugal visiting as it may be related to inmate violence, see Christopher Hensley et al., "Does Participating in Conjugal Visitations Reduce Prison Violence in Mississippi? An Exploratory Study," *Criminal Justice Review* 27, no. 1 (Spring 2002): 52–65.

84. These resources may be secured from http://www.ada.gov, accessed 19 July 2006.

85. Bonner v. Lewis, 857 F.2d 559 (9th Cir. 1988), *cert. denied*, 498 U.S. 1074 (1991). The ADA is the Americans with Disabilities Act of 1990, Public Law 101-336, U.S. Code, Title 42, Section 12101 *et seq.* (2007).

86. See Torcasio v. Murray, 57 F.3d 1340 (4th Cir. 1995), *cert. denied*, 516 U.S. 1071 (1996).

87. Fla. Stat. Ann., Section 944.8041 (2007).

88. National Commission on Correctional Health Care, "The Graying of America's Prisons: Seeking Solutions in Florida," http://www.ncchc.org/pubs/CC/aging_inmates_florida.html, accessed 19 July 2006.

89. "Study: U.S. Prisons Fall Short in Caring for Elderly Inmates," *Corrections Professional* 11, no. 14 (7 April 2006): n.p.

90. Doris J. James and Lauren E. Glaze, Bureau of Justice Statistics Special Report, *Mental Health Problems of Prison and Jail Inmates* (Washington, D.C.: U.S. Department of Justice, September 2006), p. 1. Online at http://www.ojp.usdoj.gov/bjs/abstract/mhtsp00.htm.

91. James C. Harrington, "Criminal Justice System Fails Those with Mental Disabilities," *Texas Lawyer* 17, no. 31 (8 October 2001): 47.

92. "Courts Review Solitary Confinement for Mentally Ill Inmates: Several States are under Fire from Civil Rights Groups," *Corrections Professional* 8, no. 5 (8 November 2002): n.p.

93. "Inmates' Lawyers Support Care for Mentally Ill," *Corrections Professional* 7, no. 10 (12 February 2002): n.p.

94. "Minnesota DOC," *Corrections Professional* 7, no. 21 (9 August 2002): n.p.

95. Tom Perrotta, "City Settles Class Action, Agrees to Provide Health Care to Released Mentally Ill Inmates," *New York Law Journal* 229 (9 January 2003): 1. The case is Brad H. v. City of New York, 185 Misc. 2d 420 (Sup.Ct. 2000), *aff'd., mot. denied, mot. granted*, 716 N.Y.S.2d 852 (1st Dep't. 2000).

96. "Court Orders Swifter Review of Mentally Ill Defendants," *Metropolitan News Enterprise* (Los Angeles, California) (7 March 2003), p. 3. The case is Oregon Advocacy Ctr. v. Mink, 322 F.3d. 1101 (9th Cir. 2003).

97. "Funding the Program," *Corrections Professional* 8, no. 19 (20 June 2003): n.p.

98. Ill-Equipped: U.S. Prisons and Offenders with Mental Illness, summarized in "Report Cites Limited Progress in Prison Mental Health Programs," *Criminal Justice Newsletter* (3 November 2003), p. 2.

99. "Bill Would Fund Treatment of Mentally Ill Criminal Offenders," *Criminal Justice Newsletter* (16 June 2003), p. 2; quotation is on p. 3. The bill is the Mentally Ill Offender Treatment and Crime Reduction Act of 2004, Public Law 108-414 (2004), 118 Stat. 2327 (2007).

100. Sell v. United States, 539 U.S. 166 (2003).

101. Caroline Wold Harlow, Bureau of Justice Statistics, *Education and Correctional Populations* (Washington, D.C.: U.S. Department of Justice, January 2003), pp. 1–2, http://www.ojp.usdoj.gov/bjs/abstract/ecp.htm, accessed 19 July 2006.

102. See Hernandez v. Johnston, 833 F.2d 1316 (9th Cir. 1987).

103. "California Tax Windfall Boosts Prison Education Funding," *Corrections Professional* 11, no. 17 (26 May 2006): n.p.

104. "California Jail Garners Accolades for Inmate Education," *Corrections Professional* 11, no. 14 (7 April 2006): n.p.

105. "Utah Prison Gets Facilities to Improve Inmate Education," *Corrections Professional* 11, no. 17 (26 May 2006): n.p.

106. "Arizona Director Directs Educational, Training Policies," *Corrections Professional* 11, no. 14 (7 April 2006): n.p.

107. Elmer H. Johnson, *Crime, Correction, and Society*, rev. ed., (Homewood, Ill.: Dorsey, 1968), p. 559.

108. "Bureau of Prisons Cites Need to Expand Prison Industries," *Criminal Justice Newsletter* 25 (16 May 1994): 4.

109. Murray v. Mississippi Department of Corrections, 911 F.2d 1167 (5th Cir. 1990), *cert. denied*, 498 U.S. 1050 (1991).

110. "With Jobs to Do, Louisiana Parish Turns to Inmates," *New York Times* (5 January 2006), p. 1.

111. The statute providing for such fees is Public Law 102-395, Section 111, enacted in 1992.

112. "Embattled Prisons Chief Takes Leave," *Chicago Tribune* (3 December 2003), p. 20.

113. Abdul Wali v. Coughlin, 754 F.2d 1015 (2d Cir. 1985).

114. Cited in Joseph W. Rogers, "Postscripts to a Prison Riot" (paper presented at the annual meeting of the Academy of Criminal Justice Sciences, Louisville, Ky., 25 March 1982).

115. See, for example, "After Mississippi Hangings, Feds Order Jails to Shape Up," *Atlanta Journal and Constitution* (31 December 1993), p. 1; "Around the South: Mississippi Jail Deaths Probe Ends; FBI Finds No Evidence of Civil Rights Violated," *Atlanta Journal and Constitution* (26 January 1995), p. 3.

116. Mark Curriden, "Suicide or Lynching? Human Rights Commissions Holds Hearings on Jail Hangings," *American Bar Association Journal* 79, no. 14 (June 1993): n.p.

117. "Jail Changes to Target Inmate Suicide," *South Bend Tribune* (Indiana) (22 May 2003), p. 4D; "Jail Adds Unit for Suicidal Inmates," *St. Louis Post-Dispatch* (25 February 2003), p. 1B.

118. "Inmate Suicide Lawsuit Settled," *Albuquerque Journal* (N. Mex) (21 April 2003), p. 8B; "Family to Sue State over Prison Inmate's Suicide," *Portland Press Herald* (5 December 2002), p. 1B.

119. "Judge Denies Bail to Three Charged in Prison Scandal," *New York Times* (23 June 2006), p. 17; "Two Ex-FCI Guards Get One Year," *Tallahassee Democrat* (11 January 2007), p. 1B.

120. Hudson v. Palmer, 468 U.S. 517, 523, 525 (1984).

Community Corrections, Probation, and Parole

11

Supervision of offenders within the community is a frequent alternative to imprisonment, although the conditions placed on offenders may be severe. This chapter focuses on community treatment of offenders, probation, and parole. It begins with an overview of community-based corrections, noting the historical development and discussing problems offenders face when they enter these programs. It focuses on diversionary programs, such as drug courts, and the general treatment approach characteristic of some jurisdictions today. It examines how problems might be minimized through programs that prepare inmates for their release from prison back into the community.

Probation, the most frequently imposed sentence, and parole, until recently a major form of release from prison, are discussed in their historical contexts and with their modern changes. Both have been the focus of considerable attention in recent years. Frequently, crimes committed by probationers and parolees receive widespread publicity, leading to public pressure to reduce the use of probation and parole. In some cases, these pressures have been successful.

Like other changes in criminal justice systems, however, changes in the use of probation and parole must be viewed in terms of their effects on the rest of the system. A significant reduction in the use of one or both of them places severe strain on correctional systems, increasing prison overcrowding and all of its consequences. In addition, it may result in the incarceration of offenders who do not need such severe restraints. But crimes committed by probationers and parolees reduce the safety and security of society. It is not possible to predict with great accuracy who will harm society while on probation or parole.

The chapter considers some of the major federal constitutional issues that govern community corrections, probation, and parole. Finally, it focuses on Megan's Laws, which evolved in an effort to protect the community from released sexual predators.

11-1 Supervision of Offenders in the Community

Discussions in earlier chapters described some methods used in the past to permit the accused or the convicted offender to remain in the community. Family members, friends, or attorneys served as sureties to guarantee the presence of the accused at trial. Later, sureties were replaced by a variety of methods of posting bond.

OBJECTIVES

After reading this chapter, you should be able to do the following:

- Explain the meaning of *community corrections*, and state the advantages of using this approach.
- Discuss the development and impact of drug courts and other diversionary programs.
- Comment on mental health issues regarding community corrections.
- Assess the contributions of California to the modern treatment approach toward minor, nonviolent drug offenders.
- Explain furlough, work release, and prerelease programs.
- Distinguish probation from parole, and analyze recent data on each.
- Explain felony probation, and analyze recent approaches to its use.
- Analyze the use of electronic monitoring and house arrest.
- Discuss the legal limitations on probation and parole conditions.
- Recognize the advantages and disadvantages of intensive probation supervision.
- Analyze the process of searching and seizing of parolees.
- Identify three organizational models of parole systems.
- Explain the parole process, with particular attention to due process.
- Explain the legal controls on parole and probation revocation.
- Analyze the future of probation and parole.
- List and discuss the major constitutional issues relating to community corrections, probation, and parole. Note in particular the impact of the Americans with Disabilities Act.
- Discuss the issues surrounding probation or parole revocation.
- Assess the impact of Megan's Laws, and analyze the constitutional issues raised by these statutes.

Early reformers, such as John Augustus, were successful in their efforts to have convicted persons placed on probation in the community. In the late 1880s in New York City, halfway houses were used to permit inmates a gradual readjustment to the community.

11-1a Overview

The major impetus for the modern movement toward supervision of the offender within the community grew out of the Federal Prisoner's Rehabilitation Act of 1965 and the President's Commission on Law Enforcement and the Administration of Justice. The latter stated in its 1967 report that the new direction in corrections recognized that crime and delinquency are community as well as individual failures. The commission saw the task of corrections as one of reintegrating offenders into the community, restoring family ties, assisting offenders to get an education or employment, and securing for them a place in the normal functioning of society. That required changes in the community and in offenders. The commission described the traditional methods of institutionalizing offenders as fundamentally deficient. It concluded that **reintegration** was likely to be more successful if we worked with offenders in the community rather than confining them in prisons.[1]

▶ **Reintegration**
A punishment philosophy emphasizing the return of the offender to the community, so that employment, family ties, and education can be restored.

In 1973, the National Advisory Commission on Criminal Justice Standards and Goals called for an increased emphasis on probation. The commission concluded, "The most hopeful move toward effective corrections is to continue to strengthen the trend away from confining people in institutions and toward supervising them in the community."[2]

Reintegration of the offender into the community is not a one-way process, however. The community must take an active role in treating offenders. It might not be sufficient to try to reintegrate the offender into the community; the latter may need to change along with the offender. For example, if resources for reintegration, such as work opportunities, are not available, they must be provided.

Some punishments that do not involve incarceration do not fall within the definition of *community-based corrections.* Fines and restitution are alternatives to incarceration, but they are not community-based corrections. The important factor in community-based corrections is the relationship between those involved in the program, both clients and staff, and the community. Community-based programs involve an element of supervision aimed at assisting offenders to reintegrate into the community. In some programs, supervision may not be adequate, but it is the effort to supervise and improve that distinguishes community-based programs from fines and restitution, both of which could be combined with community-based corrections.

Community-based corrections should be distinguished from *diversion* (defined and discussed in Chapter 12), a process of directing the offender away from the criminal (or juvenile) systems and into other programs. Diversion usually occurs instead of, not in addition to, criminal (or juvenile) court processing. Diversion has been used primarily in the processing of juveniles, but it can be used for adult offenders as well. The alcoholic or drug addict who is apprehended for petty theft might be counseled to enter a drug and alcohol treatment program in the community and told that successful completion of that program will result in the dropping of criminal charges. That program could be a community-based treatment program. Because of the importance of the recently enacted approach of diverting minor adult drug offenders, attention is given to that subject in this chapter.

Supervised programs may be offered within prisons to prepare offenders for release. They may also be offered outside of prisons, with inmates reporting back to their prisons on a part-time basis before their release. Or the programs may be provided for convicted offenders who are placed on probation or released on parole.

Community-based programs and supervision may be provided in residential facilities, such as community treatment centers, group homes, foster homes, or halfway houses. Foster homes and group homes may be used for juveniles who do not need specialized treatment programs but who have experienced difficulties living in their own homes. They may house juveniles who need specialized programs, which may be provided in nonresidential community treatment centers, schools, or other institutions.

Halfway houses are places for offenders nearing the end of their terms to live during a period of gradual reentry into society. The offender lives in a supervised environment but may leave that facility during the day to work or to participate in vocational, treatment, or educational programs.

Residential facilities may be used for more than halfway programs. Some are viewed as long-term housing for offenders, usually juveniles, who need intensive treatment and supervision. They may be designed for offenders with particular needs. For example, some are limited to first offenders; others are limited to repeat offenders who do not function effectively without intensive supervision. Residential facilities may include community treatment centers that provide housing and supervision for persons who have not been to prison, such as those who are on probation and need more supervision than may be provided in a nonresidential environment.

Some community treatment facilities are nonresidential. Offenders live in their own homes or with relatives or friends but go to the treatment centers for individual or group therapy and for participation in seminars and other programs designed to assist them with adjustment problems.

California illustrates one state's recent emphasis on community corrections. In the summer of 2006, the governor called a special legislative session to discuss the extensive problems in that state's correctional facilities which were faced with an all-time-high population of 171,000. Inmates were double-bunked, with over 16,000 of them being housed in gyms, dayrooms, and television rooms. The prediction was that by June 2007 the prison system would be without beds for new inmates. In addition to suggesting building more prisons, the governor proposed to remove from the prisons those inmates who were close to their release dates and place them in transitional local facilities. He suggested that 4,500 nonviolent female inmates from the prisons be placed instead in community correctional facilities.[3]

Before offenders are placed in community corrections following time in prison, attention should be given to the problems they will face after release. But first, we will look at to a recent focus in community treatment: diverting nonviolent drug offenders from incarceration.

11-1b   Diversion of Nonviolent Drug Offenders

Prison overcrowding and the expenses that entails, dissatisfaction with severe sentencing, and humane concern have led in some states to recently enacted statutes providing for the diversion from incarceration of minor, nonviolent drug offenders. This is accomplished primarily in two ways: by processing those offenders through special drug courts and by making statutory provisions for the treatment rather than the incarceration of offenders processed through the adult criminal courts.

Drug Courts

Discussions in earlier chapters have noted that many prisons and jails are overcrowded. In November 2006, the Bureau of Justice Statistics (BJS) reported that in 2003, inmates who were sentenced for drug violations constituted the largest group of federal inmates. Although that percentage of total federal inmates was down from 60 percent in 1995,[4] a 2003 BJS publication noted the increase in federal drug prosecutions: "Drug prosecutions have comprised an increasing proportion of the federal criminal caseload—from 21 percent of defendants in cases terminating in U.S. district court during 1982 to 37 percent during 2001."[5]

This increase in drug prosecutions has led to an attempt to process some of these offenders through special drug courts. Drug courts may focus on particular types of offenses or problems, such as those that occur in families when parents are accused of drug violations and their children are removed from the families for their own protection. Reintegrating those children back into the family is important. Drug courts may also focus on types of offenders—for example, first- or second-time minor offender—or they may focus on types of drug offenses, such as possession of small amounts of illegal drugs.

Drug courts began in Miami, Florida, in 1989 and have spread to all states. According to a December 2003 speech by a Massachusetts judge, in 2000 all of the chief justices and court administrators in the 50 states signed a statement supporting drug courts. The judge explained drug courts as follows:

> The typical drug court combines substance abuse treatment in the community, strict
> case management with direct judicial involvement, regular drug testing, and graduated
> incentives and sanctions based on performance in treatment. The ultimate reward is
> avoidance of a jail sentence or the expunging of criminal charges. The ultimate sanction
> is imprisonment.[6]

The judge maintained that mandatory treatment within drug courts is more effective than voluntary treatment or imprisonment "if the goal is to keep addicts from relapsing into drug habits and crime." He alleged that the war on drugs is not only expensive but also ineffective, both in reducing drug addiction and crime. He also stated that the sentences for drug offenders are too harsh And that decriminalization, which offers treatment with little threat of punishment, "diverts scarce resources from those who can most benefit: addicted offenders. Drug courts deal with the shortcomings of both approaches, favoring treatment over jail but constructing a system that allows treatment to stick."[7]

The judge contended that in his 13 years on the bench, he had learned the following:

- "Substance abuse is a significant factor in the majority of criminal cases that enter the judicial system each year....
- Almost all substance abusers and addicts need treatment to become clean and sober. The vast majority of them will not do it on their own.
- The longer someone remains in treatment, the more successful he or she generally is in maintaining sobriety and law-abiding behavior....
- Coerced treatment works. Most addicts and substance abusers will not enter treatment or stay very long if treatment is voluntary....
- Treatment that is not only coerced but coordinated has an even higher success rate....
- Success in treatment should be rewarded. Treatment is hard work. Most addicts have zero self-esteem and no track record of accomplishment in life. Rewarding offenders is a strange concept to most judges and court officials, but it is essential in substance abuse cases."[8]

New York's chief judge agreed. Referring to what she called a "startling fact"—that almost one-half of New York's inmates were serving sentences for drug-related offenses—she emphasized that courts cannot ignore drug offenses. Because of the serious impact of drug offenses on the state's courts, New York instituted drug courts less than a decade ago, and "their effectiveness in halting the destructive cycle of addition and criminality is indisputable." To support her conclusions, the judge referred to the study of the U.S. Department of Justice (DOJ) and the Center for Court Innovation. That report, one of the most comprehensive about state drug courts, was published in 2003. It concluded that the New York drug courts reduced recidivism by almost 32 percent. Over 18,000 offenders had participated in the state's drug courts, resulting in an estimated savings to the state of over $254 million in incarceration costs alone.[9]

A variation of the drug court is the family drug court. A Kentucky court, for example, is designed to help mothers who are addicted to drugs, and who as a result have lost custody of their children, to come clean and recover the custody of their children. A recent publication, citing a successful mother who just regained custody of her children, said of the woman, "She's a great mother. She may have made mistakes but that's why they put erasers on pencils, because everyone makes mistakes."[10]

The federal government has been supportive of drug courts. In May 2002, the government announced through the Substance Abuse and Mental Health Services Administration (SAMHSA) that it was appropriating an additional $10 million for drug courts. And when the U.S. drug czar, John P. Walters, testified before a congressional committee in February 2003, he announced that the White House would be supporting more funding for drug courts.[11]

In February 2005, in his announcement of the new White House National Drug Control Strategy, Walters stated, "Drug treatment courts...are an effective way of reducing the drug problem in America. By giving judges the power to refer people to treatment, we reduce criminal recidivism, save taxpayer money, and heal those who have become enslaved by drug addiction."[12]

The cost savings of drug courts was underscored by a representative of a California state agency, who reported in 2005 that the state had saved over $42 million in incarceration costs by greater use of drug courts. However, a study by the Rand Corporation reported that increased plea bargaining by defendants charged with drug offenses might have contributed to that cost savings.[13]

Spotlight 11-1   **Treatment of Minor Drug Offenders: The California Approach**

One of the boldest treatment approaches for substance abuse is found in California, which provides treatment rather than punishment for minor first and second offenders. The California statute is as follows:[1]

(a) Notwithstanding any other provision of law, and except as provided in subdivision (b), any person convicted of a nonviolent drug possession offense shall receive probation. As a condition of probation the court shall require participation in and completion of an appropriate drug treatment program. The court may also impose, as a condition of probation, participation in vocational training, family counseling, literacy training and/or community service. A court may not impose incarceration as an additional condition of probation.

Aside from the limitations imposed in this subdivision, the trial court is not otherwise limited in the type of probation conditions it may impose. Probation shall be imposed by suspending the imposition of sentence.

In addition to any fine assessed under other provisions of law, the trial judge may require any person convicted of a nonviolent drug possession offense who is reasonably able to do so to contribute to the cost of his or her own placement in a drug treatment program. [The statute then specifies the types of offenders who are excluded from this statute.]

1. Possession of Controlled Substances; Probation; Exceptions, California Penal Code, Section 1210.1 (2007).

Statutory Provisions for Treatment

A second approach to the treatment rather than punishment of selected categories of drug offenders is illustrated by the California state statute reproduced in Spotlight 11-1. California led the way in this most recent emphasis on the treatment rather than the punishment of minor nonviolent first or second drug offenders. Under the California system, once a drug offender completes the treatment program successfully, that person's conviction is removed from the records. The California statute does not apply to those who *sell* drugs.

Idaho also has legislation providing for the treatment of drug addicts. In addition to providing for additional research on addiction, the statute states, "It is the policy of this state that alcoholics, intoxicated persons or drug addicts … should be afforded treatment in order that they may lead normal lives as productive members of society."[14]

11-1c Diversion of Mentally Challenged Persons

Chapter 10 noted that many offenders are mentally challenged. Spotlight 10-6 reproduces portions of the Mentally Ill Offender Treatment and Crime Reduction Act of 2004, which went into effect in late 2004. That act emphasizes that the majority of mentally challenged persons who come into contact with criminal justice agencies can benefit from treatment. One suggestion for diverting these offenders is to process them through mental health courts rather than juvenile or adult criminal courts.

Mental health courts were started in Broward County, Florida, in 1997; other states have followed. The Center for Court Innovation (the research and development arm of the New York state court system) studied the mental health courts in Florida, California, Washington, and other states. These courts were established specifically for handling mentally ill offenders. They are similar to drug courts in that they are geared toward the treatment rather than punishment of offenders. The courts are optional; treatment is not available unless the offender is willing to participate. The targets for these courts—which have their own special judges and some support staff, such as clinical persons—have serious mental illnesses and face nonviolent misdemeanor charges. According to the Center for Court Innovation report, these special courts aim "to move beyond standard case processing to address the underlying problems that bring people to court. In the process, they seek to shift the focus of the courtroom from weighing past facts to changing the future behavior of defendants."[15]

In 2000, Congress enacted a provision for federal mental health courts. The bill, passed unanimously by the Senate and by a voice vote in the House, provides for federal grants for up to 100 programs to establish special mental health courts, which target offenders who are charged with nonviolent offenses or misdemeanors. The statute provides for training law enforcement and judicial personnel to identify persons who should qualify for the special programs. There is a provision for "voluntary outpatient or inpatient mental health treatment, in the least restrictive manner appropriate, as determined by the court, that carries with it the possibility of dismissal of charges or reduced sentencing upon successful completion of treatment." It also provides for the centralized management of all charges against a defendant. Finally, the statute provides for "continuing supervision of treatment plan compliance for a term not to exceed the maximum allowable sentence or probation for the charged or relevant offense and, to the extent practicable, continuity of psychiatric care at the end of the supervised period.[16]

For those offenders who are incarcerated, however, assistance is needed for their transition back into society.

11-2   Problems of Offenders on Release

The most important concern with the release of offenders is that they will commit additional crimes and thus become **recidivists**. Consider Spotlight 11-2, which includes Figure 1, reproducing the data on the recidivism of inmates who were released in 1983 and 1994, the latest compilations published by the Bureau of Justice Statistics.

> ▶ **Recidivists** Offenders who commit crimes repeatedly.

Clearly, efforts should be made to assist inmates in their transitions back into society. In that regard, in 2006, the National Institute of Corrections (NIC) announced its new program, Transition from Prison to the Community Initiative. According to the NIC, 97 percent of inmates will eventually be released back into society, and many of them will not be prepared. The transition initiative "is intended to help states improve their transition processes, thereby increasing public safety, reducing recidivism, reducing new victimization, and making better use of resources in correctional facilities and communities." One of the key components in assisting an inmate to transition from prison to society is individual mentoring once the inmate is back in society.[17]

Many of these released inmates will be apprehended again, some rather quickly. All will face problems. Some problems will be individualized; others will be difficulties that most if not all releasees face. For example, releasees need street and work clothing. Although most prisons provide clothing or permit inmates to receive it from home, this is usually insufficient. The prison may allow only one set, and the inmate may not have family or friends who provide additional clothing. Even a prearranged job may not be much help, for the inmate will not get a paycheck for a week or longer.

Many prison systems give inmates a small amount of money upon release. The amount varies from state to state but may be as low as $50. With these funds, inmates must buy a bus ticket to their immediate destinations; pay for additional clothing and room and board; and in many cases, repay debts incurred before incarceration and restitution. They may also have families to support.

Employment is another problem the released offender must face. Institutions may or may not provide offenders assistance in seeking employment. Inmates also must deal with social adjustments upon release. The day of release may be characterized by a sense of optimism, the belief that life will be different and more pleasant. Release from prison has been called a positive life change, but people experience uncertainty, loneliness, depression, and disorganization as well.

For many ex-offenders, release from prison means frustration and anxiety over how to act and what to say in social situations and on the job. Feelings of helplessness, insecurity, fear, indecision, and depression may result in physical problems, such as loss of appetite, chronic exhaustion, sleeping problems, or sexual difficulties. Fear of the unknown may be particularly acute for inmates who have not been able to maintain close ties with their families during incarceration.

Relationships with family members may create problems for ex-offenders. Spouses and children suffer as a result of the offender's incarceration; anger and hostility may

Spotlight 11-2   Recidivism of Prisoners Released in 1994

Figure 1

1994 Recidivism Data by Offense

Among nearly 300,000 prisoners released in 15 states in 1994, 67.5 percent were rearrested within three years. A study of 1983 releases estimated a 62.5 percent rate of recidivism.

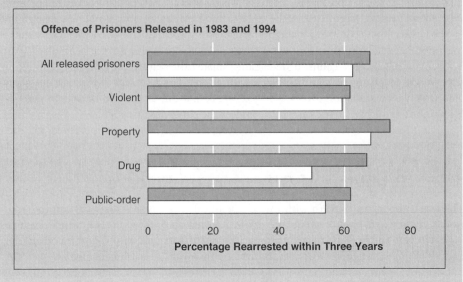

Offence of Prisoners Released in 1983 and 1994

Percentage Rearrested within Three Years

Highlights

- Within three years from their release in 1994:
  - 67.5 percent of the prisoners were rearrested for a new offense (almost exclusively a felony or a serious misdemeanor),
  - 46.9 percent were reconvicted for a new crime,
  - 25.4 percent were resentenced to prison for a new crime, and
  - 51.8 percent were back in prison, serving time for a new prison sentence or for a technical violation of their release, like failing a drug test, missing an appointment with their parole officer, or being arrested for a new crime.
- Released prisoners with the highest rearrest rates were robbers (70.2 percent), burglars (74.0 percent), larcenists (74.6 percent), motor vehicle thieves (78.8 percent), those in prison for possessing or selling stolen property

(77.4 percent), and those in prison for possessing, using, or selling illegal weapons (70.2 percent).
- Released prisoners with the lowest rearrest rates were those in prison for homicide (40.7%), rape (46.0 percent), other sexual assault (41.4 percent), and driving under the influence (51.5 percent).
- Within three years, 2.5 percent of released rapists were arrested for another rape, and 1.2 percent of those who had served time for homicide were arrested for homicide.
- The 272,111 offenders discharged in 1994 had accumulated 4.1 million arrest charges before their most recent imprisonment and another 744,000 charges within three years of release.

Source: Patrick A. Langan and David J. Levin, Bureau of Justice Statistics, *Recidivism of Prisoners Released in 1994* (Washington, D.C.: U.S. Department of Justice, June 2002), p. 1.

greet the offender who returns home. Years of absence, with few opportunities for family members to visit their loved ones in prison, may create interpersonal problems that are beyond repair. Financial hardships caused by the offender's absence may compound the interpersonal tensions.

Financial, economic, social, and other difficulties that inmates encounter on release from prison may be eased if the community provides adequate services for ex-offenders, but preparation for release is also important.

11-2a   Furlough and Work Release Programs

A **furlough** involves permitting the inmate to leave the institution once or occasionally for a specified purpose other than work or study. The offender may be given a furlough to visit a sick relative, to attend a family funeral, or to look for a job. The leave is temporary and is granted for a short period of time.

▶ **Furlough**   An authorized, temporary leave from a prison or other penal facility in order to attend a funeral, visit the family, attempt to secure employment, or engage in any other approved activity.

In **work release** programs, inmates are released from incarceration to work or to attend school. They may participate in work study, take courses at an educational institution, or work at jobs in the community. Work release is referred to by other names as well: day parole, outmate program, day work, daylight parole, free labor, intermittent jailing, and work furlough.

The first work release law, the Huber Law, was enacted in Wisconsin in 1913. The next statute, in North Carolina, was not enacted until 1957. The first furlough program was introduced by legislation in Mississippi in 1918. A few states passed laws providing for work release or furloughs before 1965, but most of the programs in existence today were established by state laws after the passage of the 1965 federal law, the Prisoner Rehabilitation Act.

State legislation varies regarding who decides which inmates are placed on work release and whether inmates may retain any or all of the money they earn. Most legislation permits states to contract with other political subdivisions for housing of inmates who cannot find work near their institutions of incarceration. Some provide halfway houses or work release centers, and some use county jails. Generally, inmates may not work in areas where there is a surplus of labor. They must be paid the same as others doing the same jobs. If a union is involved, it must be consulted, and the releasee may not work during a labor dispute.

Furlough and work release programs are important for several reasons. Work release programs enable offenders to engage in positive contacts with the community, assuming, of course, that the work placement is satisfactory. The programs permit offenders to provide some support for themselves and their families. This can eliminate the self-concept of failure that may be the result of the loss of the supporter role, which is so important in American society. Through work release, the offender may obtain more satisfying jobs than the prison could provide.

Work release and furlough programs provide a transition for the incarcerated inmate from a closely supervised way of life in prison to a more independent life within society. These programs give the community a transition period to accept offenders back into society, and they have permitted some states to close one or more correctional facilities, thus decreasing the cost to taxpayers.

Problems with work release involve the process of selecting the participants, finding sufficient jobs for them, gaining community acceptance, and ensuring that inmates do not commit crimes while they are on release. There is no guarantee, of course, that offenders placed on furlough or work release will not commit crimes: in fact, the possibility that they will do so has led to community action to eliminate these methods of early release in some jurisdictions. However, many U.S. correctional systems have retained work release and educational release programs. In some of these programs, inmates are required to pay room and board, to help support their families, to pay fines and costs, or to contribute to victims' compensation funds.

> ▶ **Work release** The release of an inmate to attend school or to work outside the institution but requiring that person to return to the institution at specified times.

11-2b Prerelease Programs

Before release, all inmates should have an opportunity to participate in prerelease programs. It is unreasonable to expect that the difficulties releasees face can be resolved without any assistance from counselors and other professionals.

Prerelease centers are one avenue for preparing inmates who have serious adjustment problems but who are being released because they have completed their terms. In a residential environment that provides more supervision than offenders would have under probation or parole but less than they experience in prison, releasees may be able to make the adjustment to freedom gradually enough to succeed upon final release. In these cases, for a specified period before their release, inmates are transferred to prerelease facilities to finish their terms. The housing facility alone, however, is not sufficient for most inmates. Ideally, those facilities would provide the full range of services needed to prepare inmates for release, including meaningful work opportunities.

Figure 11-1
Number of Persons under Correctional Supervision, by Type of Supervision, 1990–2005
Source: Lauren E. Glaze and Thomas P. Bonczar, Bureau of Justice Statistics, *Probation and Parole in the United States 2005* (Washington, D.C.: U.S. Department of Justice, November 2006), p. 2.

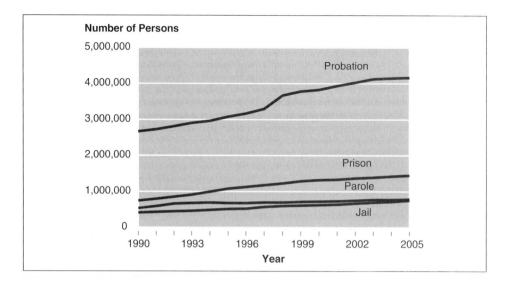

Above all, programs should be targeted to individual needs. Researchers who reviewed the recent literature in the reentry field and conducted research on their own, concluded that there is "substantial evidence that appropriate treatment does work when targeted to the specific needs of offenders."[18]

Consider the unusual case of an inmate who spent 35 years in prison for stealing a television. When he was released in 2006, 61-year-old Junior Allen could not even prove he existed. In an effort to get a birth certificate, he went to Georgia, where he was living with his sister, and was told he had to go to Alabama, where he was born. He went to Alabama and was told he should go to Georgia. Allen just wanted to get a driver's license, and after 35 years in prison, he probably had no concept of what had happened to bureaucracy since he entered prison after stealing a black-and-white television from inside a house with an unlocked door. He had left the television in the woods, and his footprints were traced by police, who quickly arrested him. State records claimed that he had assaulted the 87-year-old woman who lived in the house, but he was never charged with assault. His conviction for second-degree burglary carried a life sentence; today, it would only be three-and-one-half years in that jurisdiction.[19] Aftercare services for this former inmate might be rather simple—if you showed him how to cut through bureaucratic tape.

Finally, the preparation of inmates for release is not sufficient to ensure that they will make adequate adjustments when they leave prison. Families of inmates also need to be prepared for the adjustments that they must make when their loved ones are released from prison; thus, counseling should be provided for families.

11-3 Probation and Parole: An Overview

Probation and parole have been the most frequently used alternatives to prison (see Figure 11-1, graphing the use of probation, parole, prison, and jail) and probably the most controversial. Probation is a sentence that does not involve confinement but may involve conditions imposed by the court, usually under supervision.

The term **probation** refers to the status of a person placed on probation, to the subsystem of the criminal justice system that handles this disposition of offenders, and to a process that involves the activities of the probation system: preparing reports, supervising probationers, and providing or obtaining services for probationers.

Parole is the release of persons from correctional facilities after they have served part of their sentences. It is distinguished from unconditional release, which occurs when the full sentence (or the full sentence minus time reduced for good time credits) has been served.

▶ **Probation** A type of sentence that places the convicted offender under the supervision of a probation officer within the community instead of in prison. Also, the part of the criminal justice system that is in charge of all aspects of probation.

▶ **Parole** The status of an offender who is released before the completion of a prison sentence. Usually, the parolee must be supervised in the community by a parole officer.

TABLE 11-1	Persons under Adult Correctional Supervision in the United States, 1995, 2000–2005				
Year	Total Estimated Correctional Population^a	Community Supervision		Incarceration	
		Probation	Parole	Jail	Prison
1995	5,342,900	3,077,861	679,421	507,044	1,078,542
2000	6,445,100	3,826,209	723,898	621,149	1,316,333
2001	6,581,700	3,931,731	732,333	631,240	1,330,007
2002	6,758,800	4,024,067	750,934	665,475	1,367,547
2003	6,883,200	4,073,987	774,588	691,301	1,390,279
2003 (revised)^b	6,924,500	4,120,012	769,925	691,301	1,390,279
2004	6,995,300	4,143,466	771,852	713,990	1,421,911
2005	7,056,000	4,162,536	784,408	747,529	1,446,269
Percentage change, 2004–2005	0.9%	0.5%	1.6%	4.7%	1.7%
Average annual percentage change, 1995–2005^c	2.5%	2.5%	1.4%	3.9%	3.0%

Note: Counts of probationers, parolees, and prisoners are for December 31. All jail counts are for June 30. Jail and prison counts include inmates held in private facilities. Totals in 2000 through 2005 exclude probationers held in jail or prison.

^aBecause some offenders may have multiple statuses, totals were rounded to the nearest 100.

^bDue to changes in reporting, total probation and parole counts include estimated counts for Massachusetts and Pennsylvania based on reporting methods comparable to 2004.

^cPercentage change based on comparable reporting agencies, excluding 219,195 probationers from agencies added since 1995.

Source: Lauren E. Glaze and Thomas P. Bonczar, Bureau of Justice Statistics, *Probation and Parole in the United States 2005* (Washington, D.C.: U.S. Department of Justice, November 2006), p. 1.

Probation and parole permit convicted persons to live in the community, with conditions imposed on their behavior and, in some cases, under supervision. Both are based on the philosophy that the rehabilitation of some individuals might be hindered by imprisonment (or further imprisonment) and could be aided by supervised freedom. The processes differ in that parole is granted after a portion of the prison term has been served, whereas probation is granted in lieu of incarceration. Probation is granted by the judge. Usually, parole is granted by a **parole board** appointed or elected specifically for that purpose.

In recent years, probation and parole have come under severe attack, and attempts have been made to reduce the number of people who are permitted to participate. However, the programs have not been cut back as severely as some had hoped, primarily because of overcrowded prisons and jails. Problems arise; security of the community and supervision cost are the two biggest.

Despite these problems, probation and parole are important elements of criminal justice systems, with probation the most widely used sentence overall. Table 11-1 reports the numbers of adult correctional populations in 1995, and in 2000–2005, showing the differences in the numbers confined in jail or prison compared to those on probation or parole. Spotlight 11-3 highlights information on probation and parole from the Bureau of Justcie Statistics data for 2005.

▶ **Parole board** A panel at the state or federal level that decides whether an inmate is released on parole from a correctional institution before the expiration of his or her sentence.

11-4 Probation

In the United States, probation is traced to John Augustus, a prosperous Boston shoemaker. He asked that offenders be given their freedom within the community under his supervision, and Massachusetts responded with a statute in 1878. By 1900, six states had probation statutes; by 1915, thirty-three states had statutes providing for adult

Spotlight 11-3 **Probation and Parole in the United States, 2005 Highlights**

Probation

- The adult probation population grew 0.5 percent in 2005. This was an increase of 19,070 probationers, or the smallest increase in the last 26 years.
- About 50 percent of all probationers had been convicted of a felony, 49 percent of a misdemeanor, and 1 percent of other infractions. Twenty-eight percent were on probation for a drug law violation, and 15 percent for driving while intoxicated.
- One State, Mississippi (up 17 percent), had an increase of 10 percent or more in its probation population in 2005.
- The adult probation population decreased in 15 States, led by Maine (down 9 percent) and Vermont (down 8 percent).

Parole

- In 2005, the Nation's parole population grew 1.6 percent. This was an increase of 12,556 parolees during the year.
- Mandatory releases from prison as a result of a sentencing statute or good-time provision comprised 51 percent of those entering parole in 2005, up from 45 percent in 1995.
- Eleven States had double-digit increases in their parole population in 2005, led by Arkansas (up 23 percent), North Dakota (up 17 percent), and West Virginia (up 16 percent).
- Fourteen States had a decrease in their parole population. Nebraska (down 17 percent) was the only State with a decrease of more than 10 percent.

Source: Lauren E. Glaze and Thomas P. Bonczar, Bureau of Justice Statistics, *Probation and Parole in the United States 2005* (Washington, D.C.: U.S. Department of Justice, November 2006), p. 1.

probation; and by 1957, all states had probation statutes. In 1925, a statute authorizing probation in federal courts was enacted.[20]

11-4a Types of Probation

Probation may be administered in several ways. In some cases, it is reserved for only minor offenses; supervision may or may not be imposed. But there are several other types of probation that deserve attention: felony probation, house arrest, and shock probation combined with periodic sentencing.

The use of probation for offenders convicted of *serious* offenses is referred to as *felony probation*. Studies by the Rand Corporation disclosed that many felony probationers committed additional crimes while they were on probation. Thus, they were *recidivists*. In 1985, the Rand Corporation published the results of its study of 16,000 felons on probation. Over a 40-month period, the research team tracked 1,671 felons; a total of 2,608 criminal charges had been filed against them. Of the felony probationers, 65 percent were arrested, 51 percent were convicted, and 34 percent were returned to jail or prison. Most of the offenses committed by the probationers were serious. The director of the Rand research warned that this information should not be used to abolish probation, but rather, should be used to assess the problems created by increasing the use of probation rapidly without adequate increases in funds and staff. As the lead investigator noted, "No single human can adequately evaluate, report on, and supervise 300 criminals at a given time."[21]

The Rand Corporation study concluded that probation in its current form was not successful, but the researchers emphasized that sending felons to overcrowded prisons would not solve the problem, either. They suggested alternatives:

> The answer may be intensive surveillance programs that include intense monitoring and supervision, real constraints on movement and action, requirement of employment, mechanisms to immediately punish infractions, and added requirements of community service, education, counseling, and therapy.[22]

Studies in other states suggested that some felony probation programs were more successful than those Rand evaluated. After reviewing the Rand research and studies of more successful programs, such as those in Kentucky and Missouri, one scholar used data from New Jersey to examine the effectiveness of felony probation programs.

He recommended that more attention be given to such problems of probationers as drug abuse and employment and that the studies of felony probation be scrutinized more carefully:

> The major conclusion is that probation is an acceptable sentencing alternative for some felony offenders in some states but that recidivism rates can be alarmingly high for particular categories of offenders.[23]

Probation may be combined with **house arrest** (or home detention or confinement), a relatively recent development in the United States, dating back only a couple of decades. Offenders who are confined by house arrest are placed under specific restrictions. They may live at home or in another designated facility, but they may leave only under specified conditions.

In some jurisdictions, house arrest is accompanied by *electronic monitoring*, in which monitors are attached to the offender, usually to the ankle or the wrist. The devices are monitored by probation officers or other personnel who can determine whether the probationer leaves home (or another area of confinement, such as the place of employment) during restricted hours.

Although electronic monitoring is not new to criminal justice systems, the technology has become increasingly sophisticated. An expert on electronic monitoring and tracking emphasized that global positioning systems (GPS) have been used effectively in tracking terrorists as well as offenders. "The U.S. military invented GPS during the Cold War to mobilize troops and missiles. These electronic products are so resourceful that they're also being implemented here at home for other 'enemies of the state': convicted criminals." Here is how the system works:

> Subjects under GPS tracing and monitoring wear a removable tracking unit (PTU) and a non-removable wireless ankle cuff. The ankle cuff is the size of a large wristwatch. The cuff communicates with the PTU to ensure that both items are always within a close and specific proximity of each other. If communication with the cuff is lost, the PTU assumes that the user has abandoned it and a violation is recorded. The PTU acquires its location from the Department of Defense's GPS satellites, and records this time and location into an Internet-based database system.
>
> This information is communicated back to probation, parole, bonding, and court officials using a Web browser; authorities are able to look at a detailed map to determine where the person has been. If a violation is detected, that is, if a person was in a forbidden area, authorities can take action.[24]

The use of government satellites gives local and state law enforcement officials extensive coverage. For example, child abductions often result in the child being taken to another state; this could be tracked with GPS. A spokesperson for a company that manufactures these monitoring devices described their security as second only to keeping inmates behind bars. In June 2003, about 1,000 persons in Los Angeles were wearing the device, for which they each paid approximately $40 a month. During 2002, Los Angeles County saved $18 million by using electronic monitoring over the detention of persons sentenced to 60 days or less. The offenders are required to pay for the monitoring services, however, and that raises a legal issue for those who cannot afford to pay. Further, approximately two offenders per month attempt to elude the system; most are back in jail within two days.[25]

GPS was proposed in 2005 in Hillsborough County (Florida) to alleviate jail overcrowding. In the county jail on some days, the population was 600 over the bed count. The sheriff estimated that the use of electronic monitoring would save about $2 million a year.[26] Also in 2005, the acting governor of New Jersey signed into law a controversial bill, the implementation of which will be very expensive, providing for the use of GPS to track the 12,000 released sex offenders, who are required to register in that state, along with the 3,600 incarcerated ones when they are released.[27]

In 2006, several counties in Nebraska began using GPS to monitor juveniles. GPS enables law enforcement to know exactly where juveniles go if they violate the terms of their probation.[28]

House arrest A form of confinement, usually on probation or parole, in which the offender is permitted to live at home (or some other approved place) but is restricted in his or her movements to and from the area. A curfew may be imposed, and the offender may be subject to unannounced visits from a probation or parole officer. In some cases, electronic devices are used to monitor the person's location.

Some empirical research is available on the use of electronically monitored home confinement. A 1985 study concluded that the operation of electronic equipment was successful, that most local criminal justice personnel accepted the program, that no serious legal problems appeared to develop when the plan was used as an alternative to detention, and that significant savings resulted when the cost of electronic monitoring was compared with that of detention.[29]

A more recent study of electronic monitoring, which compared types of supervision provided for those monitored, along with probationers and inmates, concluded that electronic monitoring "added little value to more traditional forms of community control." Although rates were high for program completion, the rates of recidivism were not reduced significantly by the use of electronic monitoring.[30]

An important factor in the success of monitoring releasees is that the programs be adequately staffed. As a Connecticut probation officer noted, "One of the critical issues we face in releasing individuals into the community so abruptly, is that funding has been cut for a reasonable number of trained probation and parole officers to effectively work with offenders." She continued by stating, "My ability to work successfully with offenders is compromised when large number [sic] of offenders are suddenly released into the community and I am forced to be held accountable to monitor probationers using the same policies, standards and guidelines as when I have an ideal caseload." Yet, in recent years, most states have faced the worst budget crises they have encountered since World War II. As a result, the executive director of the American Probation and Parole Association concluded as follows: "My concern is that at a time when probation and parole agencies could be more effectively utilized as a successful alternative to incarceration, they are being set-up for failure by being overburdened."[31] That comment also applies to the use of electronic monitoring with probation, parole, or diversion.

Electronic monitoring is used extensively with abusers of alcohol and other drugs. As substance abuse violations have increased in number and have swelled prison populations, as well as court dockets, many jurisdictions have turned from incarceration to alternative treatment programs combined with electronic monitoring. One problem with this approach, however, is that the dropout rate in drug treatment programs is high, especially when those programs are voluntary and unsupervised. As noted earlier, there is some evidence that drug treatment is more effective when it is mandatory and supervised.

Electronic monitoring may also be used with violent offenders, such as sexual predators. In Iowa, for example, authorities are using sophisticated systems to track sex offenders and other dangerous offenders placed on probation or released from prison on parole. The system notifies authorities when the offenders are near areas they are forbidden to visit, such as any place where children can be expected to play.[32] Some empirical evidence indicates that electronic monitoring is reasonably safe with sex offenders, although not with violent offenders in general.[33] Violent sex offenders, especially those who victimize children, are often required, in addition to wearing monitors, to register with law enforcement authorities at periodic intervals. Some of the more than half of states that have enacted Jessica's Laws (named after a Florida girl who was kidnapped, raped, and murdered) require that violent sexual predators be monitored. In April 2007, North Dakota joined those states, requiring lifetime monitoring, along with registration, of violent sexual predators.[34]

The escape of some sex offenders, however, is a reasonable and serious concern. In early 2003, Andrew Luster, a great grandson of Max Factor, the cosmetics mogul, was on trial in San Diego for multiple rape counts. It was alleged that Luster spiked the drinks of his dates and later raped the women. Luster, who was wearing an electronic bracelet, was permitted to be away from his home during the day. He fled in the morning, and the signal was not acknowledged until he missed his 8 P.M. curfew that night.[35] The trial was continued in his absence; he was convicted and sentenced in February 2003. In June 2003, he was captured in Mexico and returned to the United States to serve his prison sentence of 124 years.[36]

Another concern with the use of electronic monitoring (and also house arrest) is that the approach is too lenient. However, either or both may be accompanied by intensive probation supervision (IPS) (discussed later in the chapter), fines, restitution, or a combination of these. Electronic monitoring and house arrest may also be combined with brief jail or prison sentences. For example, some statutes permit sending offenders to prison for a short period of time and then placing them on probation. It is assumed that this procedure will shock offenders into appropriate behavior. This process is called *shock probation*, although technically, that term is incorrect because probation is an *alternative* to incarceration. The purpose of shock probation is to expose offenders to the shock of prison before placing them on probation and to release them before they are influenced negatively by the prison experience.

Probation may also be combined with a jail term, a procedure called *periodic sentencing*. The offender may be confined to jail during the night but be permitted to go to work or school during the day. The jail term might be served on weekends only, with the offender free to move about in the community during the week, although under some probation terms. The weekend alternative has been used frequently for offenders who have been convicted of driving while intoxicated, particularly in jurisdictions in which jails are crowded and the offender has a steady job.

11-4b   Probation Administration

In most jurisdictions, probation administration is a court function, meaning that it is located in the judicial branch of government. The trial judge, who presides over probation hearings, may reject a probation recommendation made by the attorneys.

Despite the role of the trial judge in making probation decisions, it is possible for various courts within a particular jurisdiction to have probation departments, resulting in an overlap of services and other administrative problems. Other jurisdictions may have a statewide probation system with branches at the city and county levels. Probation departments may be found in the executive branch, too, reporting to the governor in the case of statewide systems. Probation departments differ in size and complexity and in the extent and quality of services that they provide for clients.

One division of the probation department provides services to courts. Usually, the probation department prepares the *presentence investigation (PSI)* by interviewing clients and related parties, investigating and compiling materials relevant to each case, and developing recommendations for the sentencing body. In addition, the department provides the court with processing and reporting services for probation cases. This section keeps records of all persons on probation, the status of their probation, whether probation has been revoked, and other pertinent data.

Probation departments also provide services for probation clients, such as counseling, referral to other community sources, and supervision. Some probation departments counsel substance abusers and their families.

Usually, probation departments are headed by a chief probation officer, who has the primary responsibility for hiring, training, and firing **probation officers** and for managing all sections of the probation department. The chief probation officer has public relations functions as well, working with community leaders, attorneys, police officers, and court personnel.

If the probation department is large enough, it may have an assistant chief probation officer, who reports to the chief probation officer and may be assigned such responsibilities as coordinating volunteer efforts and administering the department. A supervisor might be in charge of coordinating the efforts of those who prepare the PSI, assign cases, and handle other administrative functions.

Probation officers work directly with probationers. These officers should have training in the various aspects of probation work, including skills in interpersonal relationships. They provide counseling for probationers and engage in surveillance to determine whether their clients are violating probation conditions.

▶ **Probation officer**
A government official responsible for writing the presentence reports on offenders, supervising probationers, reporting violations of probation conditions, and providing evidence of those violations.

Professions 11-1

Federal Probation Services

Most people in the United States who are under the supervision of criminal justice systems are on probation. Theoretically, probationers are supervised by probation officers, who perform a variety of functions. This Professions box features the federal probation system, but many state systems are similar. Reference is made to several specialties within the federal probation system.

Functions of Federal Probation Officers[1]

Probation officers have two basic duties: presentence investigations and the supervision of offenders. Both require written and oral skills; a broad understanding of criminal justice systems; knowledge of federal probation and parole systems, of the federal prison system, federal sentencing guidelines, and federal case law; and an ability to work with diverse populations.

Presentence investigations require a probation officer to prepare for the court a document that includes information on the offense in question, the offender's history and personal characteristics, sentencing options, and the application of federal sentencing guidelines. Collecting and analyzing the data may require extensive time by the officer, who must make recommendations regarding the potential risk of the offender as well as the need for restitution, treatment, or other options. Probation officers prepare these reports by interviewing the offender and other persons, reading available documents, and analyzing other evidence. Probation officers also supervise inmates. Such supervision may involve extensive visits or be limited to phone calls, depending on the officer, the offender, the offense, and available resources.

Functions of Federal Pretrial Services Officers[2]

Federal pretrial services officers have two main functions: investigation and supervision. They investigate each offender in order to recommend to the court whether the individual should be released pending trial. If the offender is released, they provide supervision for some but not all offenders. The

court may determine that some offenders do not pose a threat to themselves or to society and can be predicted to show up for trial; thus, they need no supervision.

Pretrial services officers also attend court sessions concerned with pretrial services and detention. They prepare release status reports for the courts. These reports summarize the offender's compliance with prerelease orders and make recommendations for release or detention if the offender is released after sentencing and pending an appeal. Supervision may include meeting with offenders to counsel them about the details of their release, the need to attend treatment programs for the abuse of alcohol or other drugs, other treatment programs, job opportunities, and so on.

To be eligible for the position, an applicant must have a bachelor's degree in an academic subject, such as sociology, criminology or criminal justice, psychology, or some other social science, although occasionally, those with majors in other disciplines, such as business, are hired. Many individuals working as pretrial services officers have graduate degrees, and many of the federal officers have experience at the local or state level.

Functions of Substance Abuse Specialists[3]

Most probation officers must deal with offenders who have abused alcohol or other drugs, but substance abuse specialists are senior-level officers whose job is to oversee and manage a substance abuse program. They are in charge of the budget for substance abuse, which includes the contracts for substance abuse treatment programs. They may provide in-service training for those who supervise offenders with drug problems and may or may not have their own caseloads.

1. Adapted from John P. Storm, "What United States Probation Officers Do," *Federal Probation* 61 (March 1997): 13–18.
2. Adapted from Thomas J. Wolf, "What United States Pretrial Services Officers Do," *Federal Probation* (March 1997): 19–24.
3. Adapted from Edward M. Read, "Challenging Addiction: The Substance-Abuse Specialist," *Federal Probation* 61 (March 1997): 25–26.

Probation officers do most of the investigative work in preparing the PSI and may be required to make a sentence recommendation to the judge before sentencing. This involvement in the sentencing decision and then in supervising the probationer may present problems. Probationers may resent the position the probation officer has in relationship to the judge. Furthermore, it is questionable whether probation officers can be effective counselors while also being responsible for surveillance.

Average beginning salaries for probation officers are not high enough to attract many well-qualified people, particularly if the goal is to attract people who have baccalaureate degrees, as the National Advisory Commission recommended. Efforts must be made to raise salaries and to improve working conditions for probation officers. Opportunities to work in the federal probation system are discussed in Professions 11-1.

One final point on the administration of probation systems is that some charge for their services. According to a 2003 report, in 2001, adult probationers in the state of Texas paid $237 million in court-ordered fines and probation fees and performed 8.5 million hours of unpaid community service, which otherwise would have cost the state approximately $45 million in pay to minimum-wage workers. These fees, fines, and work service accommodated approximately one-half of the probation supervision costs of the state.[37]

11-4c Probation Conditions

The purpose of probation is to assist offenders in making social adjustments and in reintegrating into society as law-abiding citizens. Thus, the policy is to impose restrictions on their freedom. Restrictions differ from jurisdiction to jurisdiction, but some are common to all.

It is customary to require probationers to report to an officer periodically at specified times and places; the officer may visit the client, too. Probationers may change residence only with the permission of the supervising officer. They must work (or attend school or some other approved activity); any changes must be reported. In some cases probationers, are not allowed to make changes without the prior permission of the supervising officer or the court.

Most probationers are required to submit periodic reports of their activities and progress. They are not permitted to use nonprescription drugs and may be restricted (or prohibited) in the use of alcoholic beverages and forbidden to frequent bars or other questionable places. They may be required to submit to periodic drug testing if the facts of their cases suggest drug violations. Substance abuse is a serious problem among probationers, as it is among inmates. The Bureau of Justice Statistics reported in its first national survey of adults on probation, published in 1995, that almost half of all probationers were using alcohol or illegal drugs when they committed their current offense. Sixty-four percent stated that they had driven a motor vehicle while under the influence of alcohol. Sixty-seven percent had used illegal drugs at some time in their lives.[38] Review Spotlight 11-3 (see Section 11-4), which notes that 28 percent of all probationers in 2005 were sentenced for violating a drug law and 15 percent had been convicted of driving while intoxicated.

Among other restrictions, probationers are not permitted to own, possess, use, sell, or have deadly weapons or firearms under their control. Their personal associations are restricted. In some jurisdictions, probationers are not permitted to drive an automobile; in others, driving is permitted only with prior permission of the supervising officer. Normally, probationers may not leave the county or state without permission, which is granted infrequently and only for extraordinary reasons. They are required to refrain from violating laws, and they must cooperate with their probation officers. In some cases, courts impose curfews or restrictions on where probationers may live. Their civil rights may be affected as well. Usually, they are not permitted to marry, engage in business, or sign contracts without permission.

Probation conditions must comply with certain court restrictions. Just as courts have been reluctant to interfere with daily prison administration, they traditionally have taken a hands-off policy toward the imposition of probation conditions as well. In recent years, however, courts have rejected some restrictions as constituting improper restraints on probationers' rights.

Several cases illustrate constitutional issues with regard to probation conditions. A federal court in Illinois held that it was reasonable for a court to order a probationer to get a paying job rather than become a missionary. The probationer had been ordered to pay restitution and fines after conviction of a series of religious scams. A federal court in New York held that it is unconstitutional to require a convicted drunk driver to attend Alcoholics Anonymous (AA) meetings while on probation. The court noted the spiritual and religious nature of AA meetings and held that requiring one to attend them violated the probationer's First Amendment rights (see Appendix A). The case was affirmed on appeal, and the U.S. Supreme Court refused to review it.[39]

In a Wisconsin case, the state supreme court held that the trial judge did not abuse discretion in his decision that, as a condition of probation, the father of nine children must agree not to father any more children unless he could prove that he could support them. The Wisconsin Supreme Court gave its reasons, along with the factual allegations, in the following brief excerpt. The state court twice denied a reconsideration, and the U.S. Supreme Court declined to hear the case.[40]

State v. Oakley

We conclude that in light of Oakley's ongoing victimization of his nine children and extraordinarily troubling record manifesting his disregard for the law, this anomalous condition—imposed on a convicted felon facing the far more restrictive and punitive sanction of prison—is not overly broad and is reasonably related to Oakley's rehabilitation. Simply put, because Oakley was convicted of intentionally refusing to pay child support—a felony in Wisconsin—and could have been imprisoned for six years, which would have eliminated his right to procreate altogether during those six years, this probation condition, which infringes on his right to procreate during his term of probation, is not invalid under these facts. Accordingly, we hold that the circuit court did not erroneously exercise its discretion.

A recent example of a case in which the appellate court did not approve of a probation condition is that of *United States v. Sofsky.* This case involved a defendant who entered a guilty plea to receiving more than 1,000 still and moving pictures of child pornography over the Internet. One of his probation conditions was that he could not access the Internet without the permission of his probation officer. The appellate court stated its position regarding the probation condition as follows: "We conclude that the [probation] condition exceeds even the broad discretion of the sentencing judge with respect to conditions of supervised release, and must be substantially modified." In a separate action, the court also rejected Sofsky's appeal of his conviction. The U.S. Supreme Court refused to review the decision.[41]

Other cases demonstrate varying probation conditions approved by courts. The key is whether the conditions are reasonably related to the offense for which the individual is on probation. For example, an order requiring that a probationer "make every attempt to avoid being in contact with children" was held reasonable in a case involving an offender who was convicted of a sex crime against a 12-year-old. The court held that the condition fell within the statutory provision "as the court, in its discretion, deems reasonably necessary to insure that the defendant will lead a law-abiding life or to assist him to do so." It also met the provision that the court has discretion to require a defendant to "[s]atisfy any other conditions reasonably related to his [or her] rehabilitation."[42]

A probation order designed solely to embarrass or humiliate an offender may not be upheld. A California judge "whose penchant for innovative sentencing has made him a media darling"[43] ordered an offender to wear a T-shirt proclaiming "I am on felony probation for theft." That condition was held to be a violation of the offender's right to privacy. The appellate court noted that the statute provides that a purpose of probation is rehabilitation, but the requirement in question was designed to expose the offender to public ridicule and humiliation. Further, the order would have made it impossible for the offender to fulfill another probation condition, which was to get a job. The court stated that the questionable probation order

> could adversely affect [the probationer's] ability to carry on activities having no possible relationship to the offense for which he was convicted or to future criminality.... The condition was unreasonably overbroad and as such was invalid.[44]

Likewise, requiring that one convicted of aggravated battery erect a large sign on his property stating, "WARNING! A violent felon lives here: Enter at your own risk," was held to be unreasonable. The condition might hinder the offender's rehabilitation as well as cause psychological problems for him and for the innocent members of his family. The sign was viewed as a "drastic departure" from the state's sentencing provisions.[45] Warnings might be appropriate, however, in some cases, such as those involving sex offenders, as noted later in this chapter.

An issue arises concerning prohibiting a probationer from engaging in an activity such as drinking alcohol, which is legal for other adults. In 1997, a California court upheld abstention from alcohol as a probation condition. The court noted that, when a probationer is required to abstain from conduct that is otherwise legal, the requirement must be "reasonably related to the underlying crime or to future criminality." The court cited data linking alcohol use and crime, concluding, "It is well-documented that the use of alcohol lessens self-control and thus may create a situation where the user has reduced ability to stay away from drugs." The probationer in this case had been placed on probation for three years after a guilty plea to simple possession of methamphetamine and possession of the substance for sale.[46]

Finally, in 2006, a judge upheld a contested probation condition: a juvenile was required to tell the parents of any female he dated that he had entered a guilty plea to endangering the welfare of his half-sister when she was six years old. The defense did not contest the probation requirement that the juvenile could not have unsupervised contact with any child age 10 or younger.[47]

11-4d   Probation Supervision

One of the primary functions of the probation officer is to supervise probationers. The type and degree of supervision vary. In some probation departments, the probation officer counsels probationers. In other departments, a probation officer is expected to supervise only the activities of probationers, and that supervision may be limited. The model that is chosen depends on the availability of resources, the caseloads of probation officers, their professional training, probationers' needs, and many other factors. Essentially, the officer's function is to assist the probationer in making important transitions—from law-abiding citizen to convicted offender, from free citizen to one under supervision, and finally, back to free citizen.

Some probation officers may prefer to have close interpersonal relationships with the clients they are assisting. The literature contains numerous articles discussing ways in which probation officers can improve their supervisory relationships with their clients. Many articles discuss the expectation that probation officers will go beyond supervision and serve as treatment agents for their clients. Treatment of probationers may be multidimensional. Many probationers need to learn the social skills involved in successful interpersonal relationships. Most offenders have long histories of personal failures, and probation officers are crucial in helping them increase their self-confidence and acquire the social skills and habits necessary for successful interpersonal relationships.

When probation officers go beyond supervising their clients and begin a treatment process, some problems may occur. Many officers lack sufficient training in treatment techniques. Even if probation officers are trained, skilled, and licensed in treatment techniques, the very nature of the position may preclude successful treatment. Because of the legal nature of probation work, probation officers cannot promise the confidentiality that an effective treatment relationship needs. In reality, probation officers have a conflict of interest. The officers not only represent the interests of the state in taking action against violations of probation agreements or of the law; they also represent the interests of clients in treatment and supervision.

The National Institute of Corrections (NIC) has suggested that probation, parole, and community corrections staff need more training to cope with their dual roles of treatment *and* surveillance. In the past, these workers were primarily social workers who focused on their clients' rehabilitation. While performing that role only, the staff rarely had to be concerned with personal safety. Now, however, the supervisors may be in danger of physical harm as they check on their clients to determine whether they are violating the terms of their releases, and even make arrests in some cases. In a recent study, the NIC emphasized that social workers need training in how to protect themselves from physical harm by their clients. The report cited examples in which probation and parole officers were injured or killed, while performing their jobs. Among other recommendations, the NIC listed appropriate training in the use of firearms and in recognizing and responding appropriately to the escalation of violence, or what the report called *continuum training*. In conclusion, the NIC stated as follows:

> Under stress, in a crisis, officers instinctively respond the way they have been trained. If trained only in verbal skills and then given a firearm, an officer will likely first try to control a situation verbally and then jump to the use of lethal force. In failing to provide defensive tactics training, the agency is failing to provide the officer with skills to deal with statistically the largest assailant population: offenders who use physical assault that requires a response of less-than-lethal force.[48]

Probation supervision has come under severe criticism, especially when persons on probation have committed additional crimes. In 1999, a panel of probation experts (including several from the American Parole and Probation Association), called the Reinventing Probation Council (RPC), suggested much stronger probation supervision, with such measures as no "free" violations—that is, any probation violation would carry sanctions. Probationers would not be told in advance that they might be subject to drug testing. Furthermore, probation supervisors should meet with probationers in the probationers' homes at all hours—not just regular probation office hours—a process the panel called *fortress probation*. The panel recommended lighter caseloads, noting the absurdity of expecting any meaningful supervision when an officer has a caseload of 500. The panel also noted that attitudes and policies of probation staff must be changed. For example, the policy of avoiding dangerous neighborhoods may increase the safety of officers, but it makes it essentially impossible to be a probation officer, as many probationers live in those areas. The RPC concluded, "We believe probation is at once the most troubled and the most promising part of America's criminal justice system." However, the members admitted, "[P]erhaps more candidly than leading members of our profession have ever admitted, that widespread political and public dissatisfaction with community corrections has often been totally justified."[49]

The subject of probation supervision needs to be explored in more detail. In the past, researchers debated the effect of the officer's caseload size on the success or failure of probationers. That issue is not settled, and many factors are important in determining what type of caseload is most efficient. Today, the focus of probation has shifted in many jurisdictions. No longer is rehabilitation the primary purpose of probation. The function of probation is to divert from prison persons who might not need that intensive security and supervision, and through that diversion process, reduce the populations that are swelling prisons. It is argued that many offenders can succeed on probation if they are under **intensive probation supervision (IPS)**.

IPS programs began developing in the 1960s. Two researchers who studied earlier programs suggested that three conclusions may be drawn from those analyses:

1. Intensive supervision is difficult to achieve.
2. Close contact does not guarantee greater success.
3. Intensive supervision produces an interactive effect.

The third conclusion refers to the evidence that, although IPS appears to assist some offenders, "[I]t is entirely reasonable that intensive supervision might interfere with the functionings of some clients who would otherwise be successful."[50]

In a comparison of IPS clients with regular probation clients, it was found that the former had more technical probation violations, but that probably resulted from their being watched more closely. The IPS probation clients were not more likely to be rearrested or incarcerated. However, if IPS does not result in lower recidivism, why continue with the program, given its higher costs over minimal-supervision probation?

Intensive probation supervision (IPS) Close and intensive supervision of probationers by probation officers, presumably with small caseloads.

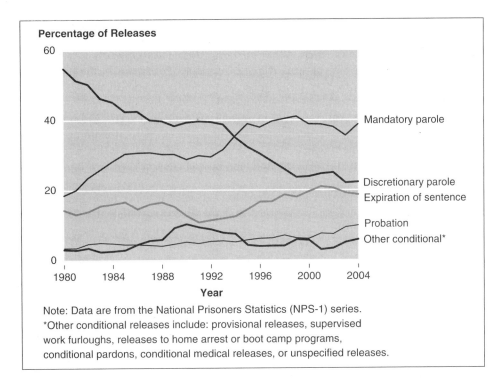

Figure 11-2
Releases from State Prison, by Method of Release, 1980–2004
Source: Lauren E. Glaze and Thomas P. Bonczar, Bureau of Justice Statistics, *Probation and Parole in the United States 2005* (Washington, D.C.: U.S. Department of Justice, November 2006), p. 8.

Further research needs to be conducted, but one consideration is that probation conditions for IPS may be too severe.[51]

A research monograph that contains several articles on IPS, including a review of several specific programs and the research findings concerning those and other programs, concluded that more research is needed on the effectiveness of IPS. Although there is some evidence that increased supervision decreases recidivism among some offenders, "[T]here is mounting evidence that increased supervision of low-risk offenders actually increases their rate of failure." The researchers stated that the "research issues are complex, but society can ill afford to let them go unanswered."[52]

11-5   Parole

Parole is an administrative decision to release an offender after he or she has served time on a sentence to a correctional facility. It may be distinguished from other methods of release from prison. Some inmates are released before serving their full sentences because they have accumulated credits given for good behavior during incarceration. The amount of prison time that may be reduced for good time credits is determined by prison policies or by legislation. Some offenders are not released from prison until they serve the full term imposed at sentencing; at the end of that term, they must be released. Figure 11-2 graphs the major reasons for release and the trend for each from 1980 through 2004. During that period, the number of inmates who were released from prison by discretionary parole decreased from 55 percent to 22 percent. In terms of gender distribution, by the end of 2005, one out of every eight adults on parole was female, with that proportion having increased since 1995. Approximately one in five of all parolees in 2005 were Hispanic, 41 percent were white, and 40 percent were black.[53]

Rehabilitation, justice, prison overcrowding: these are the three main reasons for parole in the United States. Ironically, the movement to abolish parole, a movement that paralleled the one toward determinate sentencing in the late 1970s and 1980s, was propelled by the cry for justice, disillusionment with rehabilitation, and the argument that the lack of justice in the parole decision process hindered rehabilitation. Parole was called the "never-knowing system" by many inmates who argued that it was granted for arbitrary and capricious reasons.

Parole has come under severe attack in the United States primarily as a result of violent crimes committed by persons released on parole. For example, the killing of a police officer in New York City in 1998 led to proposals to abolish parole. Anthony Mosomillo, age 36 and the father of two, was called a hero by New York City's mayor, who proclaimed the 14-year veteran "an exceptional police officer." Mosomillo was gunned down by a parolee whom he and his fellow officers were attempting to arrest for a parole violation. The offender, Jose Serrano, managed to get another officer's gun and shoot Mosomillo four times in the neck and body. Before he died, Mosomillo killed Serrano.

Serrano was on parole after serving time for a drug conviction, but he was wanted for a parole violation when he was arrested in April 1998 on a minor drug offense. At that time, he was released from custody after giving police an alias. He was ordered to return to court on 18 May. Serrano had been fingerprinted, but those prints were not available when he gave police the alias.

When Serrano failed to show up for his 18 May court date, a warrant was issued for his arrest. Mosomillo and his colleagues apprehended Serrano, who was hiding under a bed. Serrano's girlfriend, who was on probation until the year 2005 for her conviction for smuggling heroin, struggled with a female officer, whose gun was knocked away. Serrano then grabbed the gun and began shooting. Mosomillo was taken to a hospital, where he died, with his wife and children, one a toddler, by his side.

The killing of Officer Mosomillo by a parolee led to calls for the abolition of New York's parole system. In August 1998, the state enacted a statute that limits access to early release for first-time violent felons. The statute requires that these felons serve 85 percent of their maximum sentences before they are covered by mandatory release. Previously, these offenders were released after they had completed two-thirds of their maximum sentences unless they had been involved in disciplinary problems while in prison. The new law is the result of lobbying by the parents of Jenna Grieshaber, who was killed in her Albany, New York, apartment in 1997 by a parolee, and it is called "Jenna's Law," although it was Mosomillo's death that gave impetus to the law's passing. Spotlight 11-4 contains another example of reaction to the crimes of a parolee.

Such crimes give rise to cries for parole abolition. After a decade of attempts, the federal criminal code was revised when President Ronald Reagan signed the Comprehensive Crime Control Act of 1984. That act abolished early release by parole in the federal system and, over a five-year period, phased out the U.S. Parole Commission. Under the new statute, inmates in the federal system could receive only a maximum of 15 percent good time credit on their sentences. Under the former statute, they were eligible for parole after serving only half of their sentences.[54]

By January 1999, 15 states had abolished parole boards, although criminologists had warned that there was no significant evidence that abolishing parole reduces crime. Some of the states that had abolished parole boards later reinstituted them because of prison overcrowding that resulted in a need to release some inmates before they had completed their sentences. Some politicians argued that parole boards are such failures that their abolition would have no effect on criminal justice systems anyway. Others insisted that parole boards may actually result in some inmates serving longer terms than they would under some sentencing structures that allow for a reduction in sentences for good time and other reasons. For example, criminologist Joan Petersilia noted that Richard Allen Davis, who was convicted of killing Polly Klaas, was rejected for parole six times before California abolished its parole board. But Davis had to be released after he had served a specified period of time; shortly thereafter, he killed Klaas.[55]

California Governor Gray Davis (who was recalled in the fall of 2003) frequently refused (as permitted by state law) to grant parole to offenders recommended for parole by the State Board of Prison Terms, perhaps following the conclusions of state watchdog agency, the Little Hoover Commission. According to this commission, the parole system

---

Spotlight 11-4 **Paroled Murderer Convicted of Rape and Murder**

In December 1969, Reginald McFadden and three other men were accused of killing a 60-year-old woman during a burglary. McFadden was convicted and sentenced to life without parole. In 1992, McFadden's sentence was commuted by a four-to-one vote of the Pennsylvania Board of Parole, but the board required that he spend two years in a halfway-house program. Due to mistakes in paperwork and a long delay by the governor's office in signing the appropriate papers, McFadden did not enter a halfway house; nor did he receive any other type of supervised release.

By October 1994, McFadden was back in custody, charged with kidnapping, beating, and raping a 55-year-old woman. On 27 March 1995, he was indicted for the murder of Robert Silk, who was abducted from his home and killed. He was convicted of these crimes and sentenced to prison.

In 1997, McFadden sued the Department of Corrections for $1.05 million in damages, claiming that through "gross negligence" they had failed to rehabilitate him, thus causing the crimes he committed after his release. His case was dismissed, but later in the year, it led to the passage of Senate legislation limiting frivolous lawsuits filed by inmates. Pennsylvania's attorney general, in praising the bill, noted that the state is sued an average of 90 times a week, and many of those lawsuits are filed by inmates.[1]

After McFadden's rape conviction, the victim, Jeremy Brown, made a public statement. Brown described herself as the "only living victim" of the defendant. She promised to work to change the state's parole law. Brown spoke angrily about the trial in which McFadden served as his own attorney: "I think it is perfectly ludicrous that I was tortured by this man for five hours and then to have to sit there and answer his ridiculous questions....I think it's crazy."[2]

When he was sentenced in 1996, McFadden told the judge he was proud that he was the symbol of "everything that is wrong with society" and that he would take the life of the judge "as quick as you can blink your eye....Think about that." In a sentencing the previous year, McFadden told the judge not to give him any mercy. "If I was sitting where you are at, I wouldn't show you a bit of mercy."[3]

It is expected that McFadden will spend the rest of his life in prison.

Source: Summarized from media sources.

1. "Pennsylvania Attorney General Fisher Applauds Legislation Limiting Frivolous Lawsuits," *PR Newswire*, State and Regional News (4 June 1997).
2. "Rape Victim Takes Spotlight and Aims It at Parole System," *New York Times* (25 August 1995), p. 1.
3. "Why We Need the Death Penalty," *The Record* (Bergen Record Corp. 15 April 1996), p. 16.

---

in California was a "costly, colossal failure," resulting in the fact that 67 percent of the offenders incarcerated in the state each year are parolees who have violated one or more terms of their previous release. According to one California paper, "[T]his staggering return rate, double the national average, means that California is getting a miserable return on its $1.4 billion parole system."[56]

In 2004, it was reported that only 21 percent of California's parolees complete parole without being returned to prison, but it was also noted that many of those returned were the result of decisions by parole officers, not the courts. A study of the parole system emphasized that many parole officers have backgrounds as prison guards, unlike previous parole officers, who were usually trained as probation officers or social workers. The result is a tendency today to "nail and jail" parolees, sending them back to prison, rather than referring them to community treatment programs. In 2004, the California Department of Corrections announced that it was instituting a graduated sanctions policy, using such programs as halfway houses, electronic monitoring, and restitution, rather than sending so many parolees back to prison. The state was facing a $200 million budget deficit in its prison system at the end of 2004—compared to a $544 million deficit at the end of 2003.[57] As noted previously, however, in 2006 California began to restore some prison programs, such as education.

11-5a   The Organization of Parole Systems

The organization of parole is complex. One reason for this complexity is the variety of sentencing structures under which parole systems must operate. In jurisdictions where sentences are long, with little time off for good behavior, parole may involve a long supervision period. In jurisdictions where sentences are short, parole may be unimportant as a form of release, and supervision is for shorter periods.

Despite the wide variety of parole programs, there are three organizational models: institutional, independent authority, and consolidated. Under the *institutional model*, found mainly in the juvenile field, the decision to release is made by the correctional staff. The assumption is that those who work closely with the offender are in the best position to make a decision concerning his or her release. Arguments against this model are that institutions may make decisions in their own best interests, not in the best interests of the offender or the community. Decisions may be based on institutional overcrowding. Staff members may be less objective in the decisions because they are closely involved with the offender. Abuse of discretion may be a greater possibility under this model than in the independent authority model.

As a result of those problems, many parole boards for adult correctional facilities follow the *independent authority model,* in which the parole board is established as an agency independent of the institution. This model has been criticized severely. Frequently, the parole board is composed of people who know little or nothing about corrections. The board is removed from the institution and may not understand what is taking place there. Decisions may be made for inappropriate reasons, and as a result, parole boards may release those who should not be paroled and retain those who should be released.

A new model has emerged, a *consolidated model* of organization for parole boards, and there is a trend toward adopting it. This trend accompanies a move toward consolidating correctional facilities into one common administration—usually, a department of corrections. Under the consolidated model, the parole-granting board is within the administration of the department of corrections but possesses independent powers.

Parole board members should have an understanding of all correctional programs in the system. It is more likely that such understanding will occur under the consolidated model than under the other two models. However, the board should possess independence, so that it can act as a check on the rest of the system.

With the exception of the institutional model, most parole systems are located in the executive branch of government and are administered at the state level. Most systems have one parole board, whose members are appointed by the executive branch. In most states, that board has final authority to decide who is granted parole. In other states, the board makes recommendations to someone else, who has the final decision-making authority. That person might be the governor, as noted earlier.

Some parole board members serve full-time; others serve part-time. They may or may not have specific qualifications for the position. As political appointees, they may be appointed for reasons unrelated to expertise in the kind of decision making that is the board's function. The board may have the authority to revoke as well as to grant parole.

The parole system has a division responsible for parole services, which includes parole supervision. Parole services may be delegated to smaller divisions throughout the state. Generally, the parole system provides some parole services at the institutions in which inmates are incarcerated. Often, one person has the responsibility of interviewing all those eligible for parole and writing written recommendations to the parole board.

Parole officers should have the same qualifications as probation officers. Increasingly professional organizations and commissions are recommending that parole and probation officers hold a bachelor's degree, and some recommend that additional education be required. In-service training is very important as well and should be continued throughout the officer's period of work and evaluated periodically.

Finally, in some states, parole as such has been replaced with statutory provisions for early release when prison and jail populations reach a crisis stage. Even in those cases, however, parole *supervision* remains important.

11-5b The Parole Process

In those jurisdictions with a parole release system, the parole *process* is very important, and adequate preparation should be made for the parole hearing. The inmate's ability to convey an improved self-image and to demonstrate an ability to work with others and to stick with a job may influence the board's decision. Inmates who have maintained strong family ties may have an edge in the decision-making process. Inmates who have had successful experiences on work release, education release, or furlough may also have an advantage. And a good behavior record in the institution may be viewed favorably.

Inmates should be told what to expect regarding the timing of the decision and the kinds of questions to anticipate. Demeanor and behavior are important; some inmates are put through mock decision-making situations to prepare them for the parole board hearing. It is also important to prepare the inmate for the parole board's decision; a negative decision may have a disastrous effect on an inmate who has not been adequately prepared for that result.

Eligibility for Parole

The determination of eligibility for parole varies, but usually, there are statutory specifications, such as requiring that inmates serve a certain percentage of their sentences before they are eligible for parole. Good time credits may reduce that period. Many jurisdictions require that inmates have job commitments before parole is granted; others grant parole on the condition that the inmate has a job by the time he or she is released on parole.

The Parole Hearing

The parole candidate may appear before the entire parole board or only a committee of the board. Larger boards may split into smaller groups to process paroles faster. Usually, the parole hearing is held at the institution where the inmate is incarcerated. However, if only a few inmates at one institution are eligible, the state (or federal government) might transport them to a central location for the hearing.

Many parole systems allow inmates to participate in the hearings, although that participation might be very short. This gives inmates a greater sense of fairness in that they have an opportunity to express to the board members their perceptions of their chances for success.

Numerous factors may be considered in a parole decision. Those factors require information from the past, present, and future. They include statements made by the sentencing judge concerning the reasons for sentencing, as well as the inmate's future plans. They include disciplinary action, if any, that has occurred during the inmate's incarceration. Documentation on changes in attitude and ability is also important. The crime for which the inmate is serving time, along with any prior experience on parole or probation, is considered as well as are family relationships, the ability to get along with others, and jobs.

Parole Board Discretion

Historically, parole boards have had almost total discretionary power in determining parole. Parole was viewed as a privilege, not a right. Because parole was not a right, no reasons had to be given for denial. Elements of due process were not required at the time the decision was made. Courts reasoned that due process is not required at the determination of parole because parole granting is not an adversary proceeding. Parole granting is a complicated decision, and the parole board must be able to use evidence that would not be admissible in an adversary proceeding, such as a trial. The general lack of due process at the parole decision stage has resulted in bitter complaints from inmates. Perhaps the late Justice Hugo Black of the U.S. Supreme Court best summarized the view of many inmates toward the parole board:

> In the course of my reading—by no means confined to law—I have reviewed many of the world's religions. The tenets of many faiths hold the deity to be a trinity. Seemingly,

the parole boards by whatever names designated in the various states have in too many instances sought to enlarge this to include themselves as members.[58]

Due Process and the Parole Hearing

The Fourteenth Amendment (see Appendix A) prohibits the denial of life, liberty, or property without due process of law. Claims by inmates for due process at the parole decision are based on the argument that they have a liberty interest in parole. The U.S. Supreme Court has held that, although there is no constitutional right to parole, statutes may create a protected liberty interest. When that is the case, parole may not be denied if the conditions of those statutes are met.

How do we know whether a protected liberty interest has been created and therefore due process is required? According to the U.S. Supreme Court, if a state creates a parole system and provides that if inmates meet certain conditions, they are entitled to parole, a liberty interest has been created. Under those circumstances, the state has created a presumption that inmates who meet certain requirements will be granted parole. If the statute is general, however, giving broad discretion to the parole board, no liberty interest is created.

In *Greenholtz v. Nebraska*, decided in 1979, the U.S. Supreme Court examined the Nebraska statute, which provided for two hearings before a final parole decision. At the first hearing, an informal one, the inmate is interviewed, and all relevant information in the files is considered. If the board decides the inmate is not ready for parole, parole is denied, and the inmate is given reasons. If the board finds evidence that the inmate might be ready for parole, it notifies the inmate of a formal hearing, at which time the inmate may present evidence, call witnesses, and be represented by retained counsel.

In *Greenholtz*, the Supreme Court found that a liberty interest was created by the Nebraska statute but that the procedures required by the statute met due process requirements. "The Nebraska procedure affords an opportunity to be heard and when parole is denied it informs the inmate in what respects he falls short of qualifying for parole; this affords the process that is due under these circumstances. The Constitution does not require more."[59]

In 1987, while analyzing the Montana parole statute, the U.S. Supreme Court reaffirmed its holding in *Greenholtz* that, although the existence of a parole system does not by itself give rise to an expectation of parole, states may create that expectation or presumption by the wording of their statutes. In *Board of Pardons v. Allen*, the Supreme Court held that the Montana statute, like the Nebraska statute examined in *Greenholtz*, creates an expectation of parole, provided certain conditions are met. Thus, if those conditions are met, parole must be granted.[60]

In both of these cases, the U.S. Supreme Court emphasized that the language—the use of the word *shall* rather than *may*—creates the presumption that parole will be granted if certain specified conditions are met. Thus, the Supreme Court injected some procedural requirements into the parole granting process in the states that use mandatory language in their parole statutes.

Control of Parole Decisions

Inmates criticize parole boards, and many scholars find some parole decisions to be arbitrary and capricious. Criticism of parole decisions has led to the suggestion that some restrictions be placed on this important decision-making process.

In the 1920s, sociologists developed scales to be used in situations such as predicting success in marriage. Some of those scales were adapted to the parole decision. Charts involved factors such as age, education, and prior criminal record to predict whether most inmates with certain characteristics would be successful if paroled. The application of prediction scales yielded conflicting results, although the various approaches are difficult to compare. The only general conclusion that might be drawn from statistical prediction studies is that it may be easier to predict nonviolent than violent crime.

Social scientists have used the clinical approach to prediction as well, looking at the specific characteristics of a particular inmate and trying to predict whether that person would be successful on parole. Generally, this approach has led to an overprediction of dangerousness, which means that fewer inmates who are thought to be dangerous actually are.

Another method of control over parole is to require written reasons for denying parole. In the past, most parole boards did not give reasons for denial, and courts did not require them to do so. Today, some jurisdictions that have retained parole require that reasons be given for its denial. Although the result may be only a checklist given to the inmate, this information lets the inmate know what is required for a successful parole hearing in the future.

Parole guidelines are used as a method of control over parole decision making. Not only has the use of systemwide guidelines given inmates a feeling of greater fairness in the parole process, but also, in some states, guidelines have had the advantage of being used to reduce prison overcrowding. Critics of objective guidelines for parole decision making argue that they do not result in greater fairness and may actually increase prison overcrowding.

Parole Conditions

Parole conditions are an essential element of the release process. The U.S. Supreme Court has stated,

> The essence of parole is release from prison, before the completion of sentence, on the condition that the prisoner abide by certain rules during the balance of the sentence....
> [T]he conditions of parole...prohibit, either absolutely or conditionally, behavior that is deemed dangerous to the restoration of the individual into normal society.[61]

Parole conditions vary from jurisdiction to jurisdiction and are similar to probation conditions. Many parole conditions have been challenged in court. They are valid, however, if they are reasonably related to the crimes in question, if they are not against public policy, and if it is reasonably possible for the parolee to comply with them.

11-5c   Parole Supervision

When inmates are released from prison on parole, they must report to a parole supervisor or **parole officer**. They are told the circumstances under which they are to report, how often, when and where to file reports, and what to expect regarding visits from parole officers.

Parole supervision has come under attack. The surveillance function of parole officers may be undermined by large caseloads; officers may not have time for anything more than brief contacts with their parolees. Because of this, some argue that home visits and monthly reports are costly and useless devices for the control of parolee behavior and that this function would be better performed by police. Changing the conditions of parole supervision is another suggested reform. Conditions that have only slight relevance to criminal behavior could be eliminated. This change would leave parole officers free to concentrate on the service aspect of supervision: helping with employment, housing, and other adjustments to the community.[62]

11-6   Constitutional Issues

Some of the constitutional issues that govern probation and parole are the same as those that govern other aspects of criminal justice systems and were discussed earlier in the text. Examples are the rights to privacy, due process, equal protection, and to be free of cruel and unusual punishment. Other constitutional issues are discussed in this section.

> **Parole officer**
> A government employee who supervises and counsels inmates paroled to the community.

11-6a Search and Seizure

In general, law enforcement officials may not search and seize without probable cause. There are exceptions, however, and particularly with regard to probationers and parolees.

In 1987, in *Griffin v. Wisconsin*, the U.S. Supreme Court held that probation officers who suspect their clients of probation violations may search their homes (without a warrant) for evidence of such.[63]

In 1998, the California Supreme Court ruled that law enforcement officers may search the person or property of a parolee without reasonable suspicion and that any evidence of a crime may be used against the parolee at a subsequent trial for that crime. In this case, *People v. Reyes*, an anonymous phone call tipped Rudolph Reyes's parole officer that Reyes (1) was using methamphetamine, (2) had lost his job because his employer suspected that he was stealing, (3) had made a false report to police that his home had been burglarized, and (4) had threatened his wife with a gun. The parole officer asked police to visit Reyes's home. When they did so, they saw Reyes exiting a shed on his property. Reyes did not appear to be under the influence of drugs; however, after the police conversed with the parole officer by phone, they conducted a search of the shed and found methamphetamine. After Reyes was charged with illegal possession, he moved to suppress the drugs because, he argued, they had been seized illegally. His motion was denied; the evidence was admitted, and Reyes was convicted. On appeal, he argued that the drug evidence should have been suppressed because the police did not have reasonable suspicion to search his shed, as required by previous cases. The court of appeals agreed that the drug evidence should have been suppressed. The California Supreme Court reversed the lower court and held that reasonable suspicion is no longer required for a search and seizure of the property of a parolee. The court concluded, "Because of society's interest both in assuring the parolee corrects his behavior and in protecting its citizens against dangerous criminals, a search pursuant to a parole condition, without reasonable suspicion, does not intrude on a reasonable expectation of privacy, that is, an expectation that society is willing to recognize as legitimate." The court emphasized that its decision does not mean that all searches are reasonable. For example, a search might be unreasonable if it were "made too often, or at an unreasonable hour, or if unreasonably prolonged, or for other reasons establishing arbitrary or oppressive conduct by the searching officer." In addition, a search that is made at the "whim or caprice" of an officer or one that is motivated by "personal animosity toward the parolee" is not reasonable; such a search would constitute a "form of harassment." The U.S. Supreme Court refused to review the case.[64]

In 2001, in *United States v. Knights*, the U.S. Supreme Court held that the Fourth Amendment's protection against unreasonable searches and seizures is limited in the case of probationers and that the warrantless search of a probationer's home by law enforcement officers in this case was constitutional because it was based on reasonable suspicion. The probationer (Knights) had signed a statement that he understood that he could be subjected to a search "at anytime *[sic]*, with or without a search warrant, warrant of arrest or reasonable cause by any probation officer or law enforcement officer." Right above Knights's signature was a capitalized statement that the undersigned had received a copy of the document. In the brief excerpts that follow, the U.S. Supreme Court explains its reasoning.[65]

United States v. Knights

[W]e conclude that the search of Knights was reasonable under our general Fourth Amendment approach of "examining the totality of the circumstances."

The touchstone of the Fourth Amendment is reasonableness, and the reasonableness of a search is determined "by assessing, on the one hand, the degree to which it intrudes upon an individual's privacy and, on the other, the degree to which it is needed for the promotion of legitimate governmental interests...."

The judge who sentenced Knights to probation determined that it was necessary to condition the probation on Knights's acceptance of the search provision. It was reasonable to conclude that the search condition would further the two primary goals of probation—rehabilitation and protecting society from future criminal violations. The probation order clearly expressed the search condition and Knights was unambiguously informed of it. The probation condition thus significantly diminished Knights's reasonable expectation of privacy....

The State has a dual concern with a probationer. On the one hand is the hope that he will successfully complete probation and be reintegrated back into the community. On the other is the concern, quite justified, that he will be more likely to engage in criminal conduct than an ordinary member of the community. The view of the Court of Appeals in this case would require the State to shut its eyes to the latter concern and concentrate only on the former. But we hold that the Fourth Amendment does not put the State to such a choice. Its interest in apprehending violators of the criminal law, thereby protecting potential victims of criminal enterprise, may therefore justifiably focus on probationers in a way that it does not on the ordinary citizen.

We hold that the balance of these considerations requires no more than reasonable suspicion to conduct a search of this probationer's house. The degree of individualized suspicion required of a search is a determination of when there is a sufficiently high probability that criminal conduct is occurring to make the intrusion on the individual's privacy interest reasonable. Although the Fourth Amendment ordinarily requires the degree of probability embodied in the term "probable cause," a lesser degree satisfies the Constitution when the balance of governmental and private interests makes such a standard reasonable....

The District Court found, and Knights concedes, that the search in this case was supported by reasonable suspicion. We therefore hold that the warrantless search of Knights, supported by reasonable suspicion and authorized by a condition of probation, was reasonable within the meaning of the Fourth Amendment.

The *Knights* case is included here not only to demonstrate the reduced privacy rights of probationers but to emphasize the U.S. Supreme Court's reasoning regarding balancing those rights against public safety. Some lawyers argue that this case has broad implications for the war on terrorism. As an attorney for the Criminal Justice Legal Foundation in Sacramento, California, stated, "This decision is important because it recognizes that public safety, rather than the privacy rights of criminals, should be the government's chief concern when it comes to conditions of probation." And, according to a publication of the American Bar Association, "Although the case had nothing to do with the war on terrorism, some lawyers say the Sept. 11 attacks made it unlikely that any justice would champion the rights of a criminal who appeared intent on bombing a local utility."[66]

The Ninth Circuit was not to be significantly deterred by the U.S. Supreme Court's reversal of its decision in *Knights*. In March 2003, the Ninth Circuit held unconstitutional the search of a parolee's home without a warrant and without reasonable suspicion. The case involved a parolee who had signed a "Fourth waiver," which gave permission for parole officers to search his home. The FBI agent who conducted the parole search admitted that he did not expect to find any evidence of criminal activity and nothing to connect the parolee to an unsolved robbery that occurred two years previously. But he thought the pressure might entice the parolee to confess to that robbery. In less than two hours, the parolee confessed. In the case of *United States v. Crawford*, a panel of the Ninth Circuit stated as follows:

> We hold that the search of Crawford's home without any reasonable suspicion, although pursuant to a parole condition authorizing such searches, violated the Fourth Amendment. Because Crawford's confession resulted from the suspicionless search of his residence, we reverse the district court's decision denying his motion to suppress and remand to allow him to withdraw his guilty plea.

The entire court of the Ninth Circuit agreed to hear this case and reached a different decision. The full court affirmed Crawford's conviction but remanded the case for resentencing. The U.S. Supreme Court declined to hear the case.[67]

Finally, in June 2006, the U.S. Supreme Court upheld the search of a California parolee in a case in which the parole officer had no reason to suspect the parolee of committing a parole violation or a crime but decided to search him under a California statute that permitted this search based solely on the person's status as a parolee. In *People v. Samson*, the parolee had, in accordance with the California law, signed a waiver to "agree…to be subject to search or seizure by a parole officer or other peace officer…, with or without a search warrant and with or without cause." Donald Curtis Samson was searched without cause, resulting in the finding of illegal drugs. Samson was charged with drug possession, and the trial judge refused his motion to suppress the evidence. He was convicted and sentenced to seven years in prison. The U.S. Supreme Court upheld the search by a 6-to-3 vote, with extensive references to *Knights*, excerpted earlier. According to Justice Clarence Thomas, who wrote the opinion for the Court in *Samson*, in reference to prior cases, the state has a substantial interest in supervising persons on parole because those individuals "are more likely to commit future criminal offenses" and the Fourth Amendment "does not render the States powerless to address these concerns effectively." Justice John Paul Stevens also wrote a dissenting opinion, in which Justices David Souter and Stephen Bryer joined.[68]

11-6b   The Americans with Disabilities Act (ADA)

A second area of constitutional issues concerning probation and parole is that of the Americans with Disabilities Act (ADA). In 2002 in a California case, the Ninth Circuit Court of Appeals ruled that the ADA applies to parole decisions. The case of *Thompson v. Davis* involved two inmates incarcerated in Vacaville, California, and serving terms of 15 years to life for second-degree murder. The appellants argued that the Board of Prison Terms had not recommended them for parole because they were drug addicts. Past drug addiction is considered a disability under the ADA. The federal court found that the appellants, who had received substance abuse treatment while in prison, had been drug-free for many years, one since 1984 and the other since 1990. Both had been eligible for parole release since 1993. The Ninth Circuit ruled that the appellants met the conditions of the ADA and concluded:

> Since a parole board may not deny African-Americans consideration for parole because of their race, and since Congress thinks that discriminating against a disabled person is like discriminating against an African-American, the parole board may not deny a disabled person parole because of his disability.[69]

The case was sent back to the district court to determine whether the paroles were denied because of the inmates' former drug addition or for some other reason. The U.S. Supreme Court refused to review the case, thus permitting the Ninth Circuit decision to stand.

11-6c   Probation and Parole Revocation

▶ **Parole revocation** The process of returning a released offender to an institution for technical violations of parole conditions or for committing a new crime.

Historically, probation and **parole revocation** occurred without due process hearings. In probation cases in which the offender had been sentenced to prison but the judge

| Spotlight 11-5 | Due Process and Parole and Probation Revocation: The Supreme Court Responds |

Mempa v. Rhay, 389 U.S. 128 (1967)

A probationer is entitled to be represented by appointed counsel at a combined revocation and sentencing hearing. This is because sentencing is a stage of the actual criminal proceeding, "where substantial rights of a criminal accused may be affected."

Morrissey v. Brewer, 408 U.S. 471 (1972)

Before parole can be revoked, the parolee is entitled to two hearings. The first is a preliminary hearing at the time of arrest and detention, and is for the purpose of determining whether there is probable cause to believe that parole has been violated. The second hearing is a more comprehensive hearing, which must occur before making a decision to revoke parole.

Minimum due process requirements at that second hearing are

1. Written notice of the alleged violations of parole
2. Disclosure to the parolee of the evidence of violation
3. Opportunity to be heard in person to present evidence as well as witnesses
4. Right to confront and cross-examine adverse witnesses unless good cause can be shown for not allowing this confrontation
5. Right to judgment by a detached and neutral hearing body
6. Written statement of the reason for revoking parole and of the evidence used in arriving at that decision.

The Court did not decide whether retained or appointed counsel is required at a parole revocation hearing.

Gagnon v. Scarpelli, 411 U.S. 778 (1973)

The minimum due process requirements enumerated in *Morrissey v. Brewer* apply to revocation of probation. A probationer is entitled to the two hearings before revocation.

The Court considered the issue of whether counsel is required and held that there is no constitutional right to counsel at revocation hearings and that the right to counsel should be determined on a case-by-case basis. The Court left the matter of counsel to the discretion of parole and probation authorities and indicated in part that an attorney should be present when required for fundamental fairness. An example is a situation in which the parolee or probationer is unable to communicate effectively.

Bearden v. Georgia, 461 U.S. 660 (1983)

The state may not revoke probation in the case of an indigent who has failed to pay a fine and restitution, unless there is a determination that the probationer has not made a bona fide effort to pay or that there were not adequate alternative forms of punishment. "Only if alternative measures are not adequate to meet the state's interests in punishment and deterrence may the court imprison a probationer who has made sufficient bona fide efforts to pay."

Black v. Romano, 471 U.S. 606 (1985)

The due process clause generally does not require a sentencing court to indicate that it considered alternatives to incarceration before revoking probation. This case did not involve the indigency issue regarding failure to pay a fine and restitution, as did the *Bearden* case.

suspended the sentence and placed the offender on probation, a violation of probation conditions could, without a due process hearing, result in incarceration to serve the original sentence.

In 1967 in *Mempa v. Rhay*, the U.S. Supreme Court held that, when sentencing has been deferred and the offender placed on probation, the revocation of that probation and the determination of a sentence of incarceration require the presence of counsel. The Court reasoned that this situation, in which in reality the offender is being sentenced, invokes the requirement that "at every stage of a criminal proceeding where substantial rights of a criminal accused may be affected," counsel is required. This case and others pertinent to probation and parole revocation are noted in Spotlight 11-5. **Probation revocation** that does not involve deciding a sentence, however, does not always require counsel, although there are some due process requirements.

Like probation, parole revocation historically was conducted with little concern for due process. Lack of due process was justified on the basis that parole was a privilege, not a right, or that it involved a contract. The inmate contracted to behave in exchange for freedom from incarceration. If that contract were broken, the inmate could be returned to prison. Others argued that parole is a status of continuing custody, during which the offender is subject to prison rules and regulations; thus, revocation requires no greater due process than that required for any action against the inmate while incarcerated.

> **Probation revocation** The process of declaring that a sentenced offender violated the terms of probation and that probation will, as a result, be revoked or cancelled. If probation involved a suspended prison or jail sentence, the revocation may mean that the original sentence is invoked and the individual is sent to a prison or jail.

In 1972 in *Morrissey v. Brewer*, the Supreme Court looked at parole revocation in the case of two offenders, Morrissey and Booher. Morrissey's parole was revoked for these allegations:

1. He had bought a car under an assumed name and operated it without permission.
2. He had given false statements to police concerning his address and insurance company after a minor accident.
3. He had obtained credit under an assumed name.
4. He had failed to report his place of residence to his parole officer.

Booher's parole was revoked because allegedly

1. He had violated the territorial restriction of his parole without consent.
2. He had obtained a driver's license under an assumed name.
3. He had operated a motor vehicle without permission.
4. He had violated the employment condition of his parole by failing to keep himself in gainful employment.[70]

No hearing was held before parole was revoked in these two cases. In its discussion of the cases, the U.S. Supreme Court made several findings. According to the Court, the purpose of parole is rehabilitation. Until parole rules are violated, an individual may remain on parole, and parole should not be revoked unless those rules are violated. Parole revocation does not require all the due process rights of a criminal trial, but some due process elements must be observed. Informal parole revocation hearings are proper, and the requirements of due process for parole revocation change with particular cases.

In *Morrissey*, the U.S. Supreme Court enumerated the minimum requirements for revocation; they are reproduced in Spotlight 11-5. The Court also ruled that there should be two hearings before the final decision is made. The first is to determine whether there is probable cause to support a parole violation. At the second and more formal hearing, the final decision is made whether to revoke parole.

One year after *Morrissey*, the U.S. Supreme Court extended these minimum due process requirements to probation revocation, but in *Gagnon v. Scarpelli*, the Supreme Court also discussed whether counsel is required at probation and parole revocation; the Supreme Court had not decided that issue in *Morrissey*. In *Gagnon*, the Court held that there might be some cases in which counsel is necessary in order for the offender to have a fair hearing, but counsel is not constitutionally required in all revocation cases.[71]

Two other cases of significance to revocation hearings are summarized in Spotlight 11-5. Taken together, *Bearden v. Georgia* and *Black v. Romano* demonstrate that there are some restrictions on probation revocation. In *Bearden*, the U.S. Supreme Court held that it is improper to revoke the probation of an indigent who has not paid a fine and restitution unless there is a finding that the indigent has not made a sufficient effort to pay. Even then, the court must look at other alternatives before revoking probation and incarcerating the offender. But in *Romano*, when the offender's probation was revoked because he was charged with leaving the scene of an automobile accident (a felony), the U.S. Supreme Court held that due process does not require that, before incarcerating the offender on the original sentence, other sentencing alternatives be considered.[72]

It is clear from these decisions, read in conjunction with those involving the decision whether to grant parole, that the U.S. Supreme Court sees a significant difference between granting parole and revoking parole. The Court stated it this way:

> The Court has fashioned a constitutional distinction between the decision to revoke
> parole and the decision to grant or to deny parole. Arbitrary revocation is prohibited by
> *Morrissey v. Brewer*…whereas arbitrary denial is permitted by *Greenholtz v. Nebraska*.[73]

The courts have also considered other issues regarding parole and probation revocation. In a 1998, decision a divided U.S. Supreme Court held that the exclusionary rule, which bars the use at trial of illegally seized evidence, would not bar the use of the same material at a parole revocation hearing. In *Pennsylvania Board of Probation and Parole v. Scott*, Justice Clarence Thomas, writing for the majority, emphasized, "The costs of allowing a parolee to avoid the consequences of his violation are compounded by the fact that parolees (particularly those who have already committed parole violations) are more likely to commit future criminal offenses than are average citizens." Thus, the U.S. Supreme Court held that a weapon found during a home search of a parolee, who was forbidden to have weapons, was admissible at his parole revocation hearing. The four dissenting justices argued unsuccessfully that if the exclusionary rule is necessary to deter police from making unreasonable searches and seizures, it is also necessary to deter parole officers from doing so.[74]

11-7 Megan's Laws

Another measure taken in some jurisdictions to avoid recidivism by offenders released from prison or parole is to require registration and notice, especially of sex offenders. In 1994, New Jersey enacted a community notification statute, commonly called *Megan's Laws*, after Megan Kanka, who had been sexually assaulted and murdered earlier that year. Jesse K. Timmendequas, a neighbor with two sex offender convictions, was charged, convicted, and sentenced to death for her murder.[75]

Megan's parents turned the tragedy into a national effort to enact legislation requiring that, when sex offenders are released from prison, notification must be given to the law enforcement officers in the areas in which the offenders plan to live. New Jersey's statute was followed by statutes in most other states and the District of Columbia as well as the federal system.[76] The statutes vary in their provisions, but many require that residents be notified of the presence of a sex offender in the neighborhood.

Megan's Laws may also require that schools, community organizations, and entire neighborhoods be notified when sex offenders move into the area. Notification includes the offender's name, address, description, picture, license plate number, and place of employment, depending on the assessment assigned to the offender by the prosecutor's office. That office is required to assess whether the released sex offender is a low, moderate, or high risk for subsequent sex crimes, a difficult task that is requiring much prosecutorial time.

There are problems with registration, however, and a lack of resources to check on registered sex offenders has resulted in offices "losing" them. For example, in 2003 it was announced that California had lost track of more than 33,000 sex offenders, representing 44 percent of the 76,350 who had registered at least once. This information was reported by the Associated Press, which stated that it had made repeated requests over a nine-month period to get this information. The AP release noted that, although no one knows how many of those sex offenders had committed additional sex crimes, Department of Justice (DOJ) data showed that over 52 percent of sex offenders in the nation are recidivists.[77] The AP release prompted a child advocacy group, Parents for Megan's Law, to contact all 50 states by telephone and request information about their sex offender registrations. This group reported in February 2003 that on the average, states were unable to account for 24 percent of their registered sex offenders. The executive director of this nonprofit agency said that states are "implementing Megan's Law, then turning their back on them."[78]

The California picture regarding the registration of sex offenders was even bleaker later in 2003, when a study conducted by the Bureau of State Audits reported that in California the Megan's Law database contained "thousands of errors, inconsistencies, and out-of-date information" and that these mistakes placed the public at risk. On the one hand, the public could be misled in checking the database and finding no sexual offenders in their neighborhoods when they, in fact, do reside there. On the other hand, the public could become unreasonably alarmed by the erroneous reporting that 1,142 convicted sex offenders are in the community. In addition, the state violated the privacy of 42 juvenile sex offenders by including their names within the registry, thus making public the names of juvenile offenders. And although the failure of a sex offender to register is a crime, the state rarely knows who is avoiding the registry unless those offenders, most of whom move often, are arrested for other crimes.[79]

On 15 December 2004, California began posting the names of registered sex offenders on its website. By evening of that day, the site was too busy to navigate; in only four days, it had 14 million hits. But the site was criticized as inadequate. Approximately 22,000 names were omitted, and of the 63,000 included, there was insufficient information on many. And for the 63,000 registered sex offenders on whom data were available online, exact addresses could be retrieved for only the 33,500 who had been convicted of the most serious sex crimes. Further, it was not possible to search any of the names by physical characteristics or vehicle registration information.[80]

Important legal developments with regard to Megan's Laws have also occurred in courts, with some upholding state statutes but others declaring the statutes (or parts of them) unconstitutional. But the important point is that in 2003 the U.S. Supreme Court upheld sex offender registration laws in two states: Alaska and Connecticut. The Alaska case raised the issue of whether the law violated the *ex post facto* clause of the U.S. Constitution, while the Connecticut case raised the due process issue. The Alaska case was challenged by two men, each having served eight years for sexually molesting their own daughters. After the Alaska Megan's Law was enacted in 1994, the men (both of whom had been released from prison in 1990) were required to register as sex offenders. They argued on appeal that since the law was not in effect when they committed their crimes, it could not be imposed on them. To do so would constitute additional punishment, which is prohibited by the *ex post facto* clause. The Connecticut statute was challenged by appellants who argued that the lack of a requirement to determine whether a released sex offender was dangerous before requiring registration violated due process. The U.S. Supreme Court rejected both challenges. By a 6-to-3 vote in *Smith v. Doe*, the Court held that the Alaska statute does not violate the *ex post facto* clause. According to the majority, sex offender registration requirements do *not* constitute punishment. The *purpose* of required registration is to protect society, not to punish defendants.[81]

In *Connecticut Department of Public Safety v. Doe*, by a unanimous vote, the U.S. Supreme Court upheld the Connecticut statute, which, the Court stated, does not violate due process of law. No hearing on the issue of whether a sex offender is dangerous is necessary prior to requiring that offender to register. About one-half of the state Megan's Laws do not require a hearing.[82]

The legal challenges to Megan's Laws may be expected to continue, along with local and state efforts to publicize information on sex offenders. In addition to the legal challenges to sex offender registration laws, treatment-oriented persons have noted the burden the laws place on sex offenders who committed their crimes many years ago and have been rehabilitated. Since the laws generally apply to all sex offenders, they sweep within their coverage teenagers who have impregnated their underage lovers, whom they plan to marry; gay males or lesbians convicted of engaging in oral sex before such laws were declared unconstitutional by the U.S. Supreme Court; and so on. Opponents of the sex registration statutes refer to them as the swift reaction to a high-profile case and criticize lack of attention to the details by which the statutes are implemented.[83]

Supporters argue that, by making the public more aware of the location of sexual predators in their neighborhoods, sex offender registration statutes will deter additional sexual offenses. The only other alternative, they argue, is to confine sex offenders for longer periods of time. They cite the Kansas Sexually Violent Predator Act, which was enacted in 1994 and upheld by the U.S. Supreme Court in 1997. This act permits the potentially indefinite confinement of "sexually violent predators." But the act reaches only those offenders who have "been convicted of or charged with a sexually violent offense" and who suffer from a "mental abnormality or personality disorder which makes the person likely to engage in predatory acts of sexual violence."[84]

Finally, on 27 July 2006, the U.S. Congress passed, and President George W. Bush signed, the Adam Walsh Child Protection and Safety Act of 2006. This act is named for a young Florida boy, Adam Walsh, age 8, who was kidnapped and murdered 25 years previously. His father, John Walsh, hosts the media program "America's Most Wanted," and in that capacity, has assisted law enforcement officers in apprehending persons wanted for sexually assaulting and murdering young children. This new act is expected to increase the effectiveness of law enforcement attempts to apprehend sexual pedophiles by permitting officers to share information across state lines. Federally recognized tribal lands are also included. The act tightens and broadens sex offender registration requirements. For example, the act precludes the right to use the Internet to ensnare children for sexual purposes. Registration is required prior to, not after, release, along with registering any subsequent address changes. Sex offenders must report to offices within their jurisdictions to update their information; the frequency of reporting depends upon their sex offender level of dangerousness. The act also requires that offenders wear tracking devices, that states maintain statewide registries (in addition to local ones), and that states adopt felony penalties for offenders who do not comply with the requirements, along with many other requirements.[85]

Chapter Wrap-Up

This chapter covered some critical areas of criminal justice. Despite the current public demand for stricter reactions to criminals, overcrowded jails and prisons force most jurisdictions to use some types of community corrections. And even though many jurisdictions have retreated from rehabilitation as a purpose for punishment and corrections, offenders are (and will continue to be) in the community, usually with limited or no supervision. The issue is not whether we wish to have community corrections; the issue is how much attention and funding we will provide to make sure the use of community corrections does not impair the goal of security.

In recent years, there has been somewhat of a return to a rehabilitation philosophy, especially in the processing of substance abuse offenders. The chapter discussed the use of drug courts, as well as statutory provisions for the treatment, rather than punishment, of first-or-second time drug offenders, as illustrated by the California approach. The chapter also discussed the diversion and treatment of mentally challenged persons.

The chapter began, however, with an overview of community-based corrections: it considered the history of this approach to corrections, along with the cost. Financing is a problem, particularly with the cutbacks in federal and state budgets. However, the costs for community corrections are far less than the costs of incarceration, and that is true even when intensive supervision is provided for offenders residing in the community. The problems that offenders face when they live in the community were discussed, along with the need for services in assisting them to cope with these adjustments. In particular, attention was given to furlough, work release, and prerelease programs.

Probation and parole were discussed in greater depth in this chapter than were other community corrections because they are the methods used most frequently. Probation is the sentence imposed most often and is used today for serious as well as minor offenders. The prognosis for success is not great, although it is thought that with intensive probation supervision the probability for success improves. Special attention was given in the chapter to felony probation, house arrest, and shock probation, as well as to electronic monitoring.

Brief attention was given to the administration of probation systems before focusing on probation conditions. Courts uphold most restrictions on the daily lives of probationers, provided the imposed conditions are reasonably related to the offenses in question and do not interfere with constitutional rights. The chapter's final section on probation focused on the supervision of probationers and, in particular, on the process of search and seizure.

Parole has been the most frequently used method of release from prison, but its use for early release has been restricted in recent years. The various methods of organizing parole systems were discussed in the chapter, along with the parole process, including eligibility for parole and the parole hearing. The due process requirements for the parole decision-making hearings were discussed as well. Attempts to decrease the perceived arbitrariness of parole decisions have involved the use of parole guidelines. Due process in the revocation of probation and parole has helped remove the arbitrariness and unfairness of those important processes.

The movement away from rehabilitation has resulted in problems for community corrections. Perhaps the most bitter criticisms have been hurled at parole, resulting in action in many states to abolish or at least curtail its use. Despite the call for parole abolition, it has become obvious that some form of discretion in the release of offenders must be retained, especially if sentences are long.

No one can say which is the real problem: the failure of parole per se or the abuse of discretion by parole-granting authorities. In 1975, Maurice H. Sigler, chairman of the U.S. Board of Parole, argued that parole "has now become the scapegoat of all of corrections' ills." He suggested that the system deserves the same objective, dispassionate analysis that its critics demand of parole decisions:

To those who say "let's abolish parole," I say that as long as we use imprisonment in this country we will have to have someone, somewhere, with the authority to release people from imprisonment. Call it parole—call it what you will. It's one of those jobs that has to be done.[86]

The abolition of parole may result only in shifting discretion to another area, such as prosecution. Prosecutors may refuse to prosecute; juries may refuse to convict in cases involving long, mandatory sentences with no chance of parole. Efforts to control discretion within the parole system may be a more reasonable approach than the total abolition of the system.

The final section of the chapter analyzed Megan's Laws, now enacted in most states and in the federal system and upheld by the U.S. Supreme Court. The discussion detailed the types of no-tification that are required and looked at the constitutional issues raised by these statutes, which were passed after the 1994 rape and murder of Megan Kanka, age seven, of New Jersey. The discussion included the recently enacted federal legislation, named after sex crime and murder victim Adam Walsh and designed to enhance law enforcement efforts to apprehend sexual predators.

We can expect continued controversy over these sex offender registration laws as courts balance society's rights against those of ex-offenders.

Key Terms

furlough (p. 336)

house arrest (p. 341)

intensive probation supervision (IPS) (p. 348)

parole (p. 338)

parole board (p. 339)

parole officer (p. 355)

parole revocation (p. 358)

probation (p. 338)

probation officer (p. 343)

probation revocation (p. 359)

recidivists (p. 335)

reintegration (p. 330)

work release (p. 337)

Apply It

1. Define *community-based corrections*, and give reasons why some argue that it is to be preferred over incarceration of offenders.

2. Evaluate the role of drug courts and other diversionary processing and treatment of nonviolent drug offenders.

3. Do we need mental health courts? Why or why not?

4. What problems do offenders face when they return to the community from incarceration? What is being done to assist them in coping with those problems? Evaluate furlough, work release, and prerelease programs.

5. What is the difference between probation and parole? Which is used more frequently and why? What are the trends in the use of probation and parole?

6. What are the arguments for and against the use of house arrest?

7. What is electronic monitoring? What are global positioning systems?

8. Discuss and evaluate shock probation.

9. What typical restrictions or conditions are placed on probationers? What should be the guidelines, legally or practically, for such restrictions?

10. What is meant by *intensive probation supervision*? How does it compare in effectiveness with traditional methods of supervision?

11. Describe and analyze recent trends in parole systems.

12. What effect do due process requirements have on parole granting? On parole revocation?

13. What are the search and seizure issues in probation and parole, and how have they been resolved?

14. Explain and discuss the implications of Megan's Laws. Comment on the constitutionality of these laws.

Endnotes

1. President's Commission on Law Enforcement and Administration of Justice, *The Challenge of Crime in a Free Society* (Washington, D.C.: U.S. Government Printing Office, 1967), p. 121.

2. National Advisory Commission on Criminal Justice Standards and Goals, *A National Strategy to Reduce Crime* (Washington, D.C.: U.S. Government Printing Office, 1973), p. 121.

3. "California's Prison Issues: State Eyes Bonds to Reduce Overcrowding," *The Bond Buyer* 357, no. 32423 (14 July 2006): n.p.

4. Paige M. Harrison and Allen J. Beck, Bureau of Justice Statistics, *Prisoners in 2005* (Washington, D.C.: U.S. Department of Justice, November 2006), p. 10.

5. Bureau of Justice Statistics, *Federal Criminal Case Processing, with Trends 1982–2001* (Washington, D.C.: U.S. Department of Justice, January 2003), p. 14.

6. "Treatment with Teeth: A Judge Explains Why Drug Courts That Mandate and Supervise Treatment Are an Effective Middle Ground to Help Addicts Stay Clean and Reduce Crime," *The American Prospect* (December 2003): 45.

7. Ibid.

8. Ibid.

9. Quoted in "Drug Courts Reduce Recidivism by 32 Percent," *The Daily Record of Rochester* (Rochester, N.Y.) (14 November 2003), n.p.

10. "Drug Court Is All about Family," *The Courier-Journal* (Louisville, Ky.) (24 December 2003), p. 1B.

11. The testimony of Walters may be found in the *Federal News Service* (27 February 2003), n.p. The enactment statute for drug courts may be found in Sections 50001–50002 of the Violent Crime Control and Law Enforcement Act of 1994, Public Law 103-322 (13 September 1994).

12. "White House Drug Czar Calls for Dramatic Increase in Number of Drug Treatment Courts Nationwide," Office of National Drug Control Policy, http://www.whitehousedrugpolicy.gov/news/press05/022305, accessed 7 March 2005.

13. "Diversions Saving California Millions in Prison Costs," *Corrections Professional* 11, no. 1 (5 August 2005): n.p.

14. Idaho Code, Section 39-301 (2007).

15. "Mental Health Courts Offer Detention Alternatives," *Legal Intelligencer* 231, no. 12 (19 July 2004): 4.

16. The statute is codified at U.S. Code, Title 41, Section 379611 (2007).

17. "NIC Aids Corrections with Inmate Transition Program," *Corrections Professional* 11, no. 13 (24 March 2006): n.p.

18. James A. Wilson and Robert C. Davis, "Good Intentions Meet Hard Realities: An Evaluation of the Project Greenlight Reentry Program," *Criminology and Public Policy* 5, no. 2 (May 2006): 303–338, quotation is on p. 331.

19. "Man Who Spent 35 Years in Prison for Stealing TV Finds Freedom Frustrating," *Conway Daily* (New Hampshire) (2 July 2005), p. 4.

20. See Sanford Bates, "The Establishment and Early Years of the Federal Probation System," *Federal Probation* 51 (June 1987): 4–9.

21. Joan Petersilia, "Rand's Research: A Closer Look," *Corrections Today* 47 (June 1985): 37.

22. *Criminal Justice Research at Rand* (Santa Monica, Calif.: Rand Corp., January 1985), p. 11.

23. John T. Whitehead, "The Effectiveness of Felony Probation: Results from an Eastern State," *Justice Quarterly* 8 (December 1991): 525–543.

24. "GPS Tracking Is the Wave of the Future for Law Enforcement Authorities," *Journal of Counterterrorism & Homeland Security International* 9, no. 1 (2003 Winter): n.p.

25. "Long Arm of the Law Has Them by the Anklet," *Los Angeles Times* (27 June 2003), Part 2, p. 2.

26. "GPS to Ease Crowding in Florida Jails," *Corrections Professional* 11, no. 2 (19 August 2005): n.p.

27. "Tracking Sex Offenders: GPS Bill Signed into Law," *New Jersey Lawyer* 14, no. 33 (15 August 2005): 2.

28. "Nebraska Tracks Offenders with GPS," *Corrections Professional* 11, no. 8 (13 January 2006): n.p.

29. Daniel Ford and Annesley K. Schmidt, *Electronically Monitored Home Confinement*, National Institute of Justice Report (Washington, D.C.: U.S. Department of Justice, November 1985), p. 2.

30. James Bonta et al., "Can Electronic Monitoring Make a Difference? An Evaluation of Three Canadian Programs," *Crime & Delinquency* 46 (January 2000): 61–75; quotation is on p. 61.

31. "Community-Based Supervision Dilemma: Corrections Programs Targeted for Cuts as Prison Populations Rise," *State Government News* 46, no. 5 (1 May 2003): 15.

32. "Officials Hail Novel Tracking System," *Corrections Professional* 8, no. 4 (18 October 2002): n.p.

33. See the study by Mary A. Finn and Suzanne Muirhead-Steves, "The Effectiveness of Electronic Monitoring with Violent Male Parolees," *Justice Quarterly* 19, no. 2 (June 2002): 293–312.

34. "Sex Offender Bills Signed," *Bismarck Tribune* (4 April 2007), p. 1B.

35. "Long Arm of the Law Has Them by the Anklet."

36. United States v. Luster, 2000 U.S. App. LEXIS 15987 (8th Cir. 2000).

37. "Probationer Fees Cover Half of Supervision Costs in Texas," *Criminal Justice Newsletter* (2 January 2003): p. 7.

38. Bureau of Justice Statistics, *Substance Abuse and Treatment of Adults on Probation*, 1995 (Washington, D.C.: U.S. Department of Justice, March 1998), p. 1.

39. United States v. Myers, 864 F.Supp. 794 (N.D.Ill. 1994); Warner v. Orange County Department of Probation, 870 F.Supp. 69 (S.D.N.Y. 1994), aff'd., 115 F.3d 1068 (2d Cir. 1996), cert. denied, 528 U.S. 1003 (1999).

40. State v. Oakley, 629 N.W.2d 200 (Wis. 2001), cert. denied, Oakley v. Wisconsin, 537 U.S. 813 (2002).

41. United States v. Sofsky, 287 F.3d 122 (2d Cir. 2002), supplemental opinion, 2002 U.S. App. LEXIS 5296 (2d Cir. 2002), cert. denied, Sofsky v. United States, 537 U.S. 1167 (2003).

42. People v. Griffith, 657 N.Y.S.2d 823 (App.Div.3d Dept. 1997).

43. Stephanie B. Goldberg, "No Baby, No Jail: Creative Sentencing Has Gone Overboard, California Court Rules," *American Bar Association Journal* 78 (October 1992): 90.

44. People v. Hackler, 13 Cal.App.4th 1049 (5th Dist. 1993).

45. People v. Meyer, 680 N.E.2d 315 (Ill. 1997).

46. People (California) v. Beal, 70 Cal.Rptr.2d 80 (Cal.App.4th Dist. 1997), review denied, 1998 Cal. LEXIS 2172 (Cal. 1998).

47. State of New Jersey ex rel. D.A., 897 A.2d 425 (N.J.App.Div., 2006).

48. National Institute of Corrections, *New Approaches to Staff Safety*, http://www.nicic.org, summarized in "New Enforcement Duties Require Safety Training, Report Says," *Criminal Justice Newsletter* (1 May 2003), pp. 7–8; quotation is on p. 8.

49. *"Broken Windows" Probation: The Next Step in Fighting Crime*, available from the Manhattan Institute, 52 Vanderbilt Avenue, New York, NY 10017, (202) 599-7000, http://www.manhattan-institute.org. The publication is summarized in "Leading Officials Issue Plan for 'Reinventing' Probation," *Criminal Justice Newsletter* 30 (1 April 1999): 1–2.

50. Todd R. Clear and Patricia L. Hardyman, "The New Intensive Supervision Movement," *Crime & Delinquency* 36 (January 1990): 42–44. The entire journal is devoted to issues on intensive probation supervision.

51. Referred to in *Criminal Justice Newsletter* 24 (1 July 1993): 1.

52. James M. Byrne et al., "The Effectiveness of the New Intensive Supervision Programs," *Research in Corrections* 2 (September 1989): 42.

53. Lauren E. Glaze and Thomas P. Bonczar, Bureau of Justice Statistics, *Probation and Parole in the United States, 2005* (Washington, D.C.: U.S. Department of Justice, November 2006), pp. 8–9.

54. The Sentencing Reform Act was passed as part of the Comprehensive Crime Control Act of 1984, Pub.L.No. 98-473, 98 Stat. 1837, 1976 (1984), and is codified with its subsequent amendments in U.S. Code, Title 18, Sections 3551 et seq. (2007) and U.S. Code, Title 28, Sections 991-998 (2007).

55. "Eliminating Parole Boards Isn't a Cure-All, Experts Say," *New York Times* (10 January 1999), p. 11.

56. "Revolving Door: Parole System Is Expensive Failure," *San Diego Union-Tribune* (24 November 2003), p. 6B.

57. "Must Reduce Inmate Numbers," *San Gabriel Valley Tribune* (13 May 2004), n.p.; "California's Prison Deficit Soars Past $200 Million," *Scripps Howard News Service* (16 December 2004), n.p.

58. Quoted in Jessica Mitford, *Kind and Usual Punishment: The Prison Business* (New York: Alfred A. Knopf, 1973), p. 216.

59. Greenholtz v. Nebraska, 442 U.S. 1 (1979).

60. Board of Pardons v. Allen, 482 U.S. 369 (1987).

61. Morrissey v. Brewer, 408 U.S. 471, 478 (1972).

62. Andrew von Hirsch and Kathleen J. Hanrahan, *Abolish Parole?* (Washington, D.C.: U.S. Government Printing Office, 1978), p. 21.

63. Griffin v. Wisconsin, 483 U.S. 868 (1987).

64. People v. Reyes, 968 P.2d 445 (Cal. 1998), *cert. denied*, 526 U.S. 1092 (1999.)

65. United States v. Knights, 534 U.S. 112 (2001).

66. David G. Savage, "Searches at Stake: New Limits on Probationers' Privacy Rights May Have Post-Sept. 11 Implications," *American Bar Association Journal* 88 (February 2002): 30.

67. United States v. Crawford, 323 F.3d 700 (9th Cir. 2003), *and vacated, reh'g., en banc, granted*, 2003 U.S. App. LEXIS 18402 (9th Cir. 2003), *and different results reached on rehearing, remanded*, 372 F.3d 1048 (9th Cir. 2004), *cert. denied*, 543 U.S. 1057 (2005).

68. People v. Samson, 126 S.Ct. 2193 (2006), case citations omitted. The California statute in question is Cal. Penal Code, Section 3067(a) (2007).

69. Thompson v. Davis, 295 F.3d 890 (9th Cir. 2002), *cert. denied*, 538 U.S. 921 (2003).

70. Morrissey v. Brewer, 408 U.S. 471 (1972).

71. Gagnon v. Scarpelli, 411 U.S. 778 (1973).

72. Black v. Romano, 471 U.S. 606 (1985); and Bearden v. Georgia, 461 U.S. 660 (1983).

73. Jago v. Van Curen, 454 U.S. 14 (1981).

74. Pennsylvania Board of Probation and Parole v. Scott, 524 U.S. 357 (1998).

75. The statute is codified in N.J. Stat., Section 2C:7-1 *et seq.* (2007).

76. The federal statute is part of the Violent Crime Control and Law Enforcement Act of 1994, Public Law 103-323 (13 September 1994), Section 20417.

77. "Nearly Half of Calif. Sex Offenders Not Tracked," *St. Petersburg Times* (8 January 2003), p. 5.

78. "States Losing Track of Sex Offenders, Survey Says," *Tallahassee Democrat* (7 February 2003), p. 1.

79. *California Law Enforcement and Correctional Agencies: With Increased Efforts, They Could Improve the Accuracy and Completeness of Public Information on Sex Offenders*, http://www.bsa.ca.gov/pdfs/reports/2003-105.pdf, accessed 07 April 2007.

80. "Sex-Offender List Draws Quick Criticism," *New York Times* (26 December 2004), p. 27.

81. Smith v. Doe, 538 U.S. 84 (2003).

82. Connecticut Department of Public Safety v. Doe, 538 U.S. 1 (2003).

83. "Registry Laws Tar Sex-Crime Convicts with Broad Brush," *New York Times* (1 July 1997), p. 11.

84. Kan. Stat. Ann., Section 59-29aO1 *et seq.* (2006). The case is Kansas v. Hendricks, 521 U.S. 346 (1997).

85. Adam Walsh Child Protection and Safety Act of 2006, HR 4472 (2007).

86. Maurice H. Sigler, "Abolish Parole?" *Federal Probation* 39 (June 1975): 48.

Juvenile Justice:
A Special Case

Juvenile court systems emerged as separate systems for processing juveniles who engage in criminal and delinquent activities or who are dependent or neglected. Historically, these special courts and systems were viewed as being concerned with the welfare of children who did not need the procedural safeguards characteristic of adult criminal court systems.

In recent years, that orientation has changed. Some but not all procedural safeguards recognized in adult criminal courts have been extended to juvenile court systems, leaving the two systems far less distinguishable than was originally the case. Whether these are positive or negative changes is debatable, but clearly, the increased attention given to the involvement of juveniles in violent crimes has resulted in efforts to change juvenile justice systems or process violent juveniles in adult criminal court systems.

Chapter 12 discusses the early development and recent changes that have been made in juvenile court systems, along with the development and changes that have occurred in juvenile correctional systems.

Juvenile Justice Systems

CHAPTER OUTLINE

Criminal responsibility in adversary systems is based on the premise that the accused has the ability to understand and control his or her behavior. Most people are presumed to have this ability, but among the exceptions have been persons of tender years. Separate systems for them emerged in the late 1800s in the United States. In recent years, these systems have gone through significant changes, which led criminologist Alida V. Merlo to state in her 2000 presidential address before the members of the Academy of Criminal Justice Sciences (ACJS) the following:

> We are at a unique point in our history, a crossroads. First, there is a paradox: on the one hand, official crime statistics demonstrate that juvenile violent crime is decreasing. On the other, punitiveness toward juvenile offenders continues to increase
>
> Second,...evidence suggests that public attitudes are softening. Support for early intervention efforts may even be growing.[1]

This chapter looks at some of the changes Merlo discussed in her presidential address. It begins with a brief historical overview of the background of U.S. juvenile justice systems. The origin of juvenile courts is discussed, along with the dispute over the purposes of juvenile justice systems. Data on delinquency are analyzed, with particular emphasis on violent crimes by and against juveniles, as well as the impact of youth gangs. The chapter examines how U.S. Supreme Court decisions have changed traditional juvenile justice systems before looking more closely at how those systems operate today. The constitutionality of juvenile curfews is noted, along with a look at race and gender issues relating to juveniles.

Juvenile court organization and procedures are examined, followed by an analysis of juveniles in adult criminal courts, including the role of attorneys. Megan's Laws, discussed in Chapter 11 with reference to adults, are analyzed here as they apply to juveniles. The chapter gives attention to juveniles in corrections, as well as to the issue of capital punishment. A final section contains a brief assessment of adult criminal and juvenile justice systems.

OBJECTIVES

After reading this chapter, you should be able to do the following:

- **List and explain the basic procedural and philosophical differences between juvenile and adult criminal courts historically and currently.**
- **Discuss current data on delinquency, especially data on violent crimes.**
- **Analyze the impact of youth gangs on our society.**
- **List and explain the major U.S. Supreme Court cases regarding juveniles' constitutional rights, and assess the impact of the right to counsel.**
- **Enumerate and explain the purpose and practice of juvenile curfews, and discuss the legal issues involved.**
- **Explore the racial and gender issues of juvenile justice systems.**
- **Discuss the general procedures of juvenile courts.**
- **Analyze the role of attorneys in juvenile courts.**
- **Explain the processing of juvenile offenders in adult criminal courts, and relate your discussion to persistently violent juvenile offenders.**
- **Discuss the application of Megan's Laws to juveniles.**
- **Assess the importance of drug courts to juvenile justice systems, and compare them to those in adult criminal court systems.**
- **Summarize recent changes in juvenile corrections.**
- **Evaluate the current legal status of the capital punishment of juveniles.**
- **Assess the future of juvenile court systems.**

12-1 Juvenile Justice Systems: An Overview

Special justice systems for children rest on the belief that a **juvenile delinquent** should be treated separately from and different than adults. Juveniles need special handling and processing when they engage in delinquent or criminal acts. They are considered amenable to treatment, to change, and to rehabilitation.

Although the first discussion of **juvenile** problems of which we have records dates back 4,000 years to the Code of Hammurabi, the treatment of children in the United States can be traced to the philosophy of the English, who in the 11th and 12th centuries developed the practice of treating children differently than adults. A child under the age of 7 was considered incapable of forming the intent required for criminal prosecutions. A child between the ages of 7 and 14 years was presumed to be incapable of forming the intent, but that presumption could be refuted. A child over 14 was treated as an adult.

During this earlier period of English history, when the death penalty was provided for many crimes, children were not exempted, although few children were executed. Later in England the *chancery*, or equity courts, were established for the purpose of avoiding the harshness of the strict technicalities of the English common law. Equity courts were to decide cases on the principles of justice and fairness. These courts were called *chancery courts* because they were under the jurisdiction of the king's chancellor. Equity courts had jurisdiction over many types of cases, including those involving children.

The English king could exercise the power of a parent over children and others, a concept called ***parens patriae***, literally meaning the "parent of the country." In time, this concept became so important that England enacted statutes permitting the legal rights of parents and other family members to be terminated in the cases of persons who needed the legal guardianship of the king.

> ▶ **Juvenile delinquent**
> A person under legal age (the maximum age varies among the states from 16 to 21, but 18 is the most common) whom a juvenile court has determined to be incorrigible or in violation of a criminal statute.

> ▶ **Juvenile** A young person under age for certain privileges, such as voting or drinking alcoholic beverages. If accused of a criminal or juvenile offense, a juvenile usually is not tried by an adult criminal court but is processed in the juvenile court.

> ▶ ***Parens patriae*** Literally, "parent of the country." The doctrine from English common law that was the basis for allowing the state to take over guardianship of a child. In the United States, the doctrine forms the basis for juvenile court jurisdiction. The doctrine presumes that the state acts in the best interests of the child.

Status offense A class of crime that does not consist of proscribed action or inaction but, rather, of the personal condition or characteristic of the accused--for example, being a vagrant. In juvenile law, a variety of acts that would not be considered criminal if committed by an adult--for example, being insubordinate or truant or running away from home.

Detention centers Facilities for the temporary confinement of persons (such as juveniles) in custody who are awaiting court disposition.

Juvenile court The court having jurisdiction over juveniles who are accused of delinquent acts or offenses or criminal acts or who are in need of supervision because they are being neglected or mistreated by their parents or guardians.

Petition A formal document for filing an action in juvenile court, in contrast to a grand jury indictment or a prosecutor's presentment in the criminal court.

Detention *See* **Pretrial detention**.

Adjudication The process of decision making by a court. Normally used to refer to juvenile proceedings. The term is also used to refer to rule enforcement by administrative agencies.

Disposition In a juvenile court, the final decision regarding the legal status of a child or a juvenile under that court's jurisdiction.

Parens patriae was interpreted in England to mean that the sovereign had the responsibility to oversee any children in the kingdom who might be neglected or abused. The court exercised this duty only when it was thought necessary for the welfare of the child, and that rarely occurred. The protection of society and the punishment of parents were not considered to be sufficient reasons to invoke the responsibility. In the English system and in the system as adopted during the early period of American history, the *parens patriae* doctrine applied only to children who were in need of supervision or help because of the actions of their parents or guardians, not to children who were delinquent. These children had various names, such as *children in need of supervision, persons in need of supervision,* or *dependent or neglected children.* The extension of juvenile court jurisdiction over delinquent children was an innovation adopted in Illinois in 1899.[2]

In the United States, juvenile court jurisdiction was extended to children considered incorrigible because they would not obey their parents or other adults. Even if they were not violating the law, these juveniles could be accused of committing a **status offense**. The trend in recent years has been to remove status offenses from juvenile court jurisdiction; however, where jurisdiction remains, the status offender generally is included within the definition of juvenile delinquent. Some states have a minimum age for juvenile court jurisdiction, but as a practical matter most courts do not decide cases involving very young children.

Prior to the emergence of the juvenile court, children in the United States were treated as adults. Capital punishment was permitted but seldom used; however, many children were deprived of adequate food, were incarcerated with adults, or were subjected to corporal punishment. Some institutions were established to separate incarcerated juveniles from adults. The New York House of Refuge, established in 1824, was the first and served as a model. These early institutions eliminated some of the evils of imprisoning children with adult criminals, although some scholars have questioned whether they provided much improvement in the treatment of juveniles.[3]

By the middle 1800s in the United States, probation for juveniles had been established, and separate **detention centers** had been built. The 1800s saw the evolution of progressive ideas in the care and treatment of dependent and neglected children. Protective societies, such as the Society for the Prevention of Cruelty to Children (developed in New York in 1875), paved the way for the first **juvenile court**, established in 1899 in Illinois. Other states quickly followed.

Spotlight 12-1 lists some of the historical differences between U.S. adult criminal courts and juvenile courts. The juvenile court, with its emphasis on individualized treatment, was visualized as a social agency or clinic rather than a court of law, a vision that has encountered much criticism in recent years. The court was to be a social institution designed to protect and rehabilitate the child, rather than to determine the child's guilt or innocence. Juvenile courts were to be treatment-oriented, not punishment-oriented. The purpose of juvenile courts was to prevent children from becoming criminals by catching them in the budding stages and giving them the protection and concern that a parent would be expected to provide.

The vocabulary of juvenile and criminal courts differed, too. Children would not be arrested but, rather, summoned or apprehended; they would not be indicted, but a **petition** would be filed on their behalf. If **detention** were necessary, the children would be placed in special facilities separate from adults, not in jails. They would not have a public trial but a private hearing, in which juries and prosecuting attorneys would rarely, if ever, be used. In most cases, they would not have an attorney.

The juvenile hearing would be informal, for the ordinary trappings of the courtroom would be out of place. Judges would not act as impartial observers, as was their function in criminal courts. Rather, they would act as wise parents, disciplining their children with love and tenderness and deciding in an informal way what was best for those children. Juveniles would not be sentenced as the concept is used in adult criminal courts. Instead, after the hearing, there would be an **adjudication**. A **disposition**

Spotlight 12-1 — U.S. Adult Criminal and Juvenile Courts: Some Historically Important Contrasts

Adult Criminal Court	Juvenile Court
Court of law	Social institution, agency, clinic
Constitutional rights	*Parens patriae* approach—supra constitutional rights
Purpose to punish, deter	Purpose to salvage, rehabilitate
Begins with arrest	Begins with apprehension, summons; process of intake
Indictment or presentment	Petition filed on behalf of child
Detained in jails or released on bail	Detained in detention centers or released to family or others
Public trial	Private hearing
Strict rules of evidence	Informal procedures
Right to trial by jury	No right to trial by jury
Right to counsel	No right to (or need for) counsel
Prosecuted by state	Allegations brought by state
Plea bargaining	No plea bargaining; state acting in child's best interests
Impartial judge	Judge acting as a wise parent
Pleads guilty, innocent, or *nolo contendere*	Admits or denies petition
Found guilty or innocent	Adjudicated
Sentenced	Disposition of the case
Probation	Probation
Incarcerated in jail or prison	Placed in reformatory, training school, foster home, etc.
Released on parole	Released to aftercare

would be made only after a careful study of the juvenile's background and potential, and the decision would be made in the best interests of the child.

The juvenile court hearing differed from that of the adult criminal court in procedure as well as in philosophy. Rules of evidence required in criminal courts were not applied to juvenile courts. Adult criminal court procedural safeguards were set aside in the interest of treatment and the welfare of children. Because the state, in recognizing its duty as parent, was helping, not punishing, children, no constitutional rights were violated. The emphasis in juvenile court was not on what the *child did* but who the child *was*. Juvenile courts were to be concerned with the children as individuals, and this enabled judges to save children from criminal careers through proper treatment. In contrast, the adult criminal court was concerned at trial with the narrow issue of the guilt or innocence of the accused.

Early advocates of juvenile courts believed that law and humanitarianism were not sufficient for the treatment of juveniles. They expected juvenile courts to rely heavily on the findings of the physical and social sciences. It was anticipated that these research findings would be applied scientifically in the adjudication and disposition of juveniles. The failure of the social sciences to develop sufficient research to implement this philosophy adequately, the failure of the legal profession to recognize and accept those findings that would be of assistance, and the abuse of discretion by correctional officials all contributed to the tensions that developed over the lack of procedural safeguards in juvenile courts.

The rehabilitative ideal of the founders of juvenile courts has not been realized. In actuality, many juveniles receive punishment, not treatment, and being processed through juvenile rather than adult criminal courts does not remove the stigma of *criminal*.

Not only may a juvenile suffer the worst of both the adult criminal and the juvenile court worlds, but some scholars take the position that this was the intent. Disputing the benevolent motives of the founders of the juvenile court system, some scholars have argued that juvenile courts diminish the civil liberties and privacy of juveniles, and that the child-saving movement was promoted by the middle class to support its own interests.[4]

Professions 12-1

Careers in Juvenile Justice

The increase in juvenile crime, especially violent crime, has led officials to pay greater attention to research into juvenile crime. Research provides numerous job opportunities for those who are trained in research methodology. The opportunities exist in all areas of criminal justice, but juvenile justice is one area that often appeals to young people. The desire to find out why crime happens and what to do—how to treat—may lead to intriguing days at the office.

Those who prefer the hands-on approach will also find numerous chances to become involved in juvenile justice. Jobs are available in juvenile detention and correctional facilities, juvenile probation and parole, school service, community treatment programs, court services, and many other

areas. Others may be interested in teaching positions that focus on children with behavior problems, as well as on those who have already committed juvenile or criminal offenses.

Another area of service to juveniles is in victimization, as larger numbers of children, some very young, become crime victims, often at the hands of other children or juveniles.

A variety of agencies offer employment in working with juveniles. One is the Office of Juvenile Justice and Delinquency Prevention (OJJDP) of the U.S. Department of Justice, http://www.ojjdp.ncjrs.org. States also have juvenile justice offices that offer positions in research, data analysis, and other areas.

Others have contended that the development of juvenile courts represented neither a great social reform nor an attempt to diminish juveniles' civil liberties and to control them arbitrarily. Rather, it represented another example of the trend toward bureaucratization and an institutional compromise between social welfare and the law. The juvenile court "was primarily a shell of legal ritual within which states renewed and enacted their commitment to discretionary social control over children."[5]

Changes have occurred in the juvenile court philosophy and procedures. However, before discussing those, we take a brief look at delinquency data, an area of research that provides interesting job opportunities, as noted in Professions 12-1

12-2   Juvenile Delinquency Data

▶ **Delinquency**   *See* **Juvenile delinquent**.

It is impossible to get accurate data on the amount of **delinquency**, since jurisdictions differ in their definitions of the term. Theoretically, *delinquency* does not refer to children processed through juvenile courts because they are in need of supervision, because they are dependent or neglected, or because they are abused. Nevertheless, some jurisdictions include in delinquency data all categories of juveniles over which juvenile courts have jurisdiction.

Methods of collecting delinquency data vary, too, and in most cases, juvenile records are confidential; some states require that the records be destroyed or sealed. How, then, do we know about juvenile offenses? Chapter 2 discusses the use of self-report studies, in which respondents are asked to state the types of offenses they have committed and how often they have committed them. From carefully selected samples of the population, predictions may be made on the overall extent of delinquency.

Official arrest rates recorded by age brackets and published by the FBI are another source of data. The official data reveal that in 2005, persons under age 18 accounted for 15.3 percent of all arrests, 15.8 percent of arrests for violent crimes, and 26 percent of all arrests for property crimes. Figure 12-1 graphs the percentage of total arrests in 2005 of persons under age 18 for all serious offenses and several other crimes. The figure demonstrates that, according to official data, juveniles under age 18 do *not* commit most of the violent crimes. If the age is extended from 18 to 25, however, the picture is different. In 2005, those under age 25 constituted 44.3 percent of all arrests, 44.5 percent of all arrests for violent crimes, and 53.9 percent of all arrests for property offenses.[6]

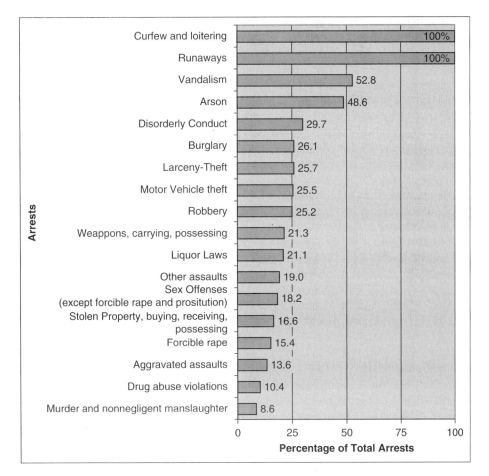

Figure 12-1
Percentage of Total Arrests in 2005 Involving Youths under 18 Years of Age
Source: Federal Bureau of Investigation, *Uniform Crime Reports, 2005* (Washington, D.C.: U.S. Government Printing Office, 2006), http://www.fbi.gov/ucr/05cius/data/table_41.html, accessed 12 December 2006.

In recent years, some states have changed their approach to juvenile justice. For example, 62 percent of California voters endorsed Proposition 21, which became effective 8 March 2000. Proposition 21 provides that an individual age 14 or over who is accused of committing one of a list of crimes (such as murder, rape, lewd and lascivious acts on a child under age 14) "shall be prosecuted under the general law in a court of criminal jurisdiction."[7] Other juveniles are under the jurisdiction of the juvenile court. The statute contains language stating that serious crimes by juveniles had increased and were expected to continue doing so. According to the findings and declarations of the statute, while overall crime had declined, "juvenile crime had become a larger and more ominous threat."[8] Other states have also become more punitive toward violent juveniles, and the issue of juvenile violence deserves closer attention.

12-2a Violence by and Against Juveniles

It is the violence by juveniles, often with juvenile victims, that raises great concern, along with the types of violent crimes that are being committed. Consider the following, most of which captured national attention. Perhaps the most publicized and shocking was the violence at Columbine High School in Littleton, Colorado. On 20 April 1999, two students, Eric Harris and Dylan Klebold, went on a shooting spree that resulted in the deaths of 12 students and a teacher and injuries to two dozen others. In December of that year, tapes made by Harris and Klebold were released, revealing their anger and their plans to kill up to 250 people. The "tapes are a macabre documentary of the meticulous planning for the attack, which the two youths called retaliation for years of taunting that they said friends and relatives had inflicted on them because of an unwillingness to dress and act as others wanted." Their anger had built to the point that they could no longer cope.[9]

In December 2003, an 11-year-old boy was sentenced to 18 years in the custody of the New Jersey juvenile justice system after he admitted that he kidnapped Amir Beeks, a 3-year-old boy, from a library and then beat the child to death with a baseball bat, apparently because the child kept bothering him about his scooter. The offender, whose name was not released, is one of the youngest persons in the custody of the New Jersey juvenile system. Under the New Jersey system, the boy will be under the control of authorities (either in custody or under supervision on parole) until he is 35.[10]

Sixteen-year-old Antonio Nunez, who was 14 when he kidnapped a businessman and shot at police in California, was sentenced to life without parole and four additional life terms plus 121 years in prison for the crimes of attempting to murder a police officer, assault, evading a police officer, street terrorism, and committing crimes for the benefit of a street gang. Nunez is one of the youngest persons in California history to be sentenced to life in prison without parole.[11]

In addition to murder, youths are also committing sex crimes, frequently against other youths or children. Many of these incidents are publicized in the national media. Some are processed through juvenile court systems, while others are transferred to adult criminal courts. And in many cases, the violence occurs in gangs, a subject that has received increased research attention in recent years.

12-2b   Youth Gangs

Gang membership is not limited to juveniles, but juvenile gangs are a major focus in today's efforts to combat crime, especially violent crimes. Research on gangs and delinquency is not a new phenomenon, but the nature of gang activities has changed in recent years. Although violence might have been characteristic of some early gangs, it appears to be the focal point of today's gangs. Whereas the gangs that were the focus of early sociological research may have fought over turf, today's gangs go to war over drug trafficking, even killing their own members if they become informers.

The violent nature of gangs was emphasized by the president of the California Gang Investigators Association when he testified before a U.S. Senate committee in 2003. Wesley D. McBride reported that the Los Angeles-based gangs had spread throughout the country and that the "most important weapon in the gang's arsenal is fear." McBride continued:

> Gangs are the master predators of the urban landscape. Their ability to instill fear into the people of a community knows no bounds. This fear percolates through the community [and becomes] part of the atmosphere. After a time, physical threats are not needed; the threat is unspoken but part of the community culture.[12]

The Nature and Extent of Gangs

In 2006, the Office of Juvenile Justice and Delinquency Prevention (OJJDP) published the results of its analyses of gang violence. The first publication resulted from a compilation of the agency's 1999, 2000, and 2001 surveys of gangs. The OJJDP estimated that an estimated 731,500 gang members and 21,600 gangs were active in 2002, down from 846,000 gang members and 30,800 gangs in 1996, with gangs and gang members existing in all major cities. The OJJDP concluded that despite the decreased data, gangs remain a serious problem in the United States, particularly with regard to homicides. Overall, 43 percent of the identified gangs had female as well as male members.[13]

The OJJDP also published the results of its analysis of the 2004 survey of youth gangs, estimating that 760,000 gang members and 24,000 gangs were active in that year. The 2004 data revealed an 11 percent increase in gang participation in homicides that year, compared to the average of the previous eight years. Of the agencies responding to the 2004 survey, 47 percent indicated that their gang situation was getting worse, while

53 percent said their gang problems were getting better or staying about the same as compared to 2003.[14]

The importance of studying youth gangs is emphasized by a study of juvenile violence and gangs that disclosed that gang members commit most juvenile crime. The study tracked 808 children for seven years and found that 85 percent of robberies by youths were committed by the 15 percent of the youths who had joined gangs. These gang members committed 54 percent of the felony thefts, 58 percent of the juvenile crimes, and 62 percent of the drug sales committed by the sample youths. Data were obtained from self-report studies as well as from juvenile court records; both sources showed that most crimes committed by youths were by those who had joined gangs. Other conclusions were that, with the exception of drug involvement, youth crimes dropped when the teens left the gangs. The following factors were found to be associated with joining gangs: "poverty, unstable family living conditions, the availability of drugs and alcohol, parents who tolerate or commit violence, falling behind or failing in school, and 'hanging out' with delinquents."[15]

The impact of gangs is illustrated by a look at Los Angeles, where gang murders have played a significant role in that city's position as the murder capital of the United States. While crime remained relatively unchanged throughout the country in 2002 and murders were down in New York City, this serious crime in Los Angeles increased from 581 in 2001 to 654 in 2002. The New York City police chief during the decline in that city's murder rate was William J. Bratton, who is now the Los Angeles police chief. Bratton admitted that in Los Angeles he would need a new approach to lowering the crime rate, especially the murder rate, because that city has large and highly organized gangs, which are thriving. In June 2003, Bratton acknowledged that he did not yet have the solution to the Los Angeles gang problem.[16]

In November 2003, Chief Bratton called for a program similar to the one he instituted in New York City. Bratton declared that it was not possible to "just arrest your way out of the situation." Hiring more police for the streets will not solve the problems created by the estimated 96,000 gang members in Los Angeles County. In addition, said Bratton, it is necessary to provide after-school programs and jobs for youths in order to remove Los Angeles as the U.S. gang capital. Chief Bratton made significant changes in his administration and proclaimed that he was refocusing the department's crime-fighting efforts. The new focus is on gang members, ex-cons, and the rest of the 10 percent of the population responsible for 50 percent of the area's crimes. Bratton was described as wanting to "build on efforts that saw homicides drop 24 percent during his first year in office...and violent crimes decrease 5.4 percent." According to Bratton, "We have started some momentum that I don't want to lose."[17]

Los Angeles city officials increased efforts to combat the city's gang members, whom Chief Bratton referred to as *violent sociopaths*. Bratton also referred to gang issues as a "domestic-terrorist problem."[18] By 2006, the murder rate in the city had declined, but of the homicides that were committed, almost 50 percent were attributed to gang violence, which was associated with 84 percent of all homicides of victims who were 35 or older.[19]

Although Los Angeles is the gang capital of the United States, gangs have also pushed up the murder rate in Chicago. In an earlier effort to curb gangs in Chicago, the city enacted an antiloitering ordinance that permitted police to disperse people gathered in a public place "with no apparent lawful purpose." In 2000, the U.S. Supreme Court decided the case of *City of Chicago v. Morales*, in which the Court held that the ordinance was unconstitutional because it was vague and gave police too much discretion to arrest people who might not be engaging in any illegal acts.[20] In February 2000, the city tried again, with an ordinance designed to inconvenience gangs by dispersing them so frequently that they could not keep a hold on a community or an area within one. Three Hispanic men, who were among the first to be arrested under the new ordinance, challenged its constitutionality. On 19 March 2002, a Cook County (Chicago) circuit judge ruled that the ordinance is constitutional.[21]

Officials in other cities have also taken measures to intervene in gang activities and to prosecute the extreme cases, but district attorneys report that their efforts are being met with serious problems. They complain about the leniency of the juvenile justice system and gang intimidation of victims and witnesses. Prosecutors allege that many gang members "pass through the system without serving any sentence." Prosecution efforts are hindered further by the changing roles of the persons involved. "In gang crime, today's victim may become tomorrow's perpetrator seeking revenge."[22]

Female Gang Members

Gangs and gang activities are not limited to male members. Earlier sociological researchers reported that female juveniles participated in gangs, too, and that they did so for some of the same reasons as their male counterparts: to find a sense of belonging that they had not found elsewhere. One researcher found that female gang members did not view themselves as criminals, even when they engaged in behavior that violated the law. They rationalized their behavior by saying that it was necessary in their society or by denying responsibility for what they did. Generally, female gang members were aggressive against other women but not against men.[23]

A 1999 report by the Chicago Crime Commission, based on a two-year study of female teen gangs, concluded the following:

> They are stepping to the forefront, selling their own drugs, making their own decisions, and avenging their own wrongs. Females are willing to participate in the full range of violent criminal activity at the same rate and the same level—and sometimes more—as their male counterparts.[24]

The National Youth Gang Center recently reported that although the number of females in youth gangs is still low, "women are taking more active roles, assisting the movement of drugs and weapons, and gathering intelligence from other groups."[25]

12-3   The Constitutional Rights of Juveniles

The U.S. Supreme Court has held that the U.S. Constitution extends some but not all of the rights of adult defendants to juveniles. In most situations, juveniles have a right to counsel (and to have counsel appointed if they cannot afford private defense counsel), the right not to be tried twice for the same offense, and the right to have the allegations against them proved by the same standard—beyond a reasonable doubt—that is used in an adult criminal trial. They do not have a federally recognized constitutional right to a trial by jury, although some state statutes provide for one.

The U.S. Supreme Court has not decided the issue of whether juveniles have the right to a public trial, but it has held that the media may not be punished criminally for publishing the name of a juvenile delinquent when they obtain the name by lawful means.[26] Some states have statutes permitting the media to attend juvenile hearings. Others leave the decision to the discretion of the judge or prohibit the media entirely. The issue of whether juveniles have a federal constitutional right to a speedy trial has not been decided, but many states have provided by statute for limitations on the period of time the state may take to process a juvenile case. Two recent cases illustrate.

In 1999, the Pennsylvania Superior Court held that the Sixth Amendment right to a speedy trial applies to juvenile delinquency proceedings. *Commonwealth v. Dallenbach* involved a juvenile who was accused of harassing and threatening a Spanish family. Dallenbach's hearing was not set until five months after the petition was filed, but shortly before the scheduled hearing, the state requested and obtained a continuance. The hearing was scheduled for 13 months later. The court noted that, although the U.S. Supreme Court had not ruled on this precise issue, it had ruled that juveniles are entitled to fundamental fairness. With that in mind, the Pennsylvania court said,

> To ensure successful rehabilitation, the reformation program (including punishment) must commence within a reasonable time of the child's delinquent act so that the child can comprehend the consequences of his act and the need for reform. As a result, the

concept of "fundamental fairness" in juvenile proceedings would seem to require that at least some time limit be placed on the length of time between the delinquent act and the case disposition, including any associated punishment.[27]

Also in 1999, the New York Court of Appeals ruled that, under that state's constitution, juveniles have a right to a speedy trial. In addition to the problems that delays may create for adults, juveniles are more likely than adults to suffer from a loss of memory and thus be even more disadvantaged in recalling the facts of the alleged incident. Furthermore, the court stated that delay hinders rehabilitation, which is still an important part of juvenile justice.[28]

12-3a   U.S. Supreme Court Cases

Juveniles' constitutional rights have been recognized in a limited number of cases decided by the U.S. Supreme Court, beginning with *Kent v. United States*, decided in 1966. Technically, this case does not apply to juvenile courts in other jurisdictions because it involved the interpretation of a District of Columbia statute. The case is important, however, because it signaled the beginning of the movement to infuse juvenile court proceedings with some due process elements.[29]

Morris A. Kent, Jr. a 16-year-old, was arrested and charged with rape, six counts of housebreaking, and robbery. In accordance with a Washington, D.C., statute, the juvenile court waived its jurisdiction over Kent, who was transferred to the adult criminal court for further proceedings. Kent requested a hearing on the issue of whether he should be transferred, and his attorney requested the social service file used by the court in the transfer decision. Both requests were denied.

Although the D.C. statute required a full investigation prior to the waiver of a juvenile from the jurisdiction of the juvenile court to that of the adult criminal court, the juvenile court judge did not state any findings of facts; nor did he give reasons for his decision to transfer Kent to the adult criminal court, which might lead one to think a full investigation did not occur.

Kent was indicted by a grand jury and tried in an adult criminal court. A jury found him not guilty by reason of insanity on the rape charge and guilty on the other charges. He was sentenced to serve from 5 to 15 years on each count, for a total of 30 to 90 years in prison. Kent appealed his case. The first appellate court affirmed; the U.S. Supreme Court reversed. The U.S. Supreme Court agreed that juvenile courts need great latitude; it affirmed the doctrine of *parens patriae* but concluded that this doctrine does not constitute "an invitation to procedural arbitrariness." The Court suggested that the "original laudable purpose of juvenile courts" had been eroded and that there "may be grounds for concern that the child receives the worst of both worlds; that he gets neither the protection accorded to adults nor the solicitous care and regenerative treatment postulated for children."[30]

The first juvenile case from a state court to be heard by the U.S. Supreme Court was *In re Gault*. On 8 June 1964, 15-year-old Gerald Gault and a friend were taken into custody in Arizona after a Mrs. Cook complained that two boys were making lewd phone calls to her. Gault's parents were not notified that their son was in police custody. When they returned home from work that evening and found that Gerald was not there, they sent his brother to look for him and were told that he was in police custody.

Gault's parents were not shown the petition that was filed the next day. At the first hearing, attended by Gerald and his mother, Mrs. Cook did not testify; no written record was made of the proceedings. At the second hearing, Mrs. Gault asked for Mrs. Cook, but the judge said that Mrs. Cook's presence was not necessary. The judge's decision was to commit Gerald to the state industrial school until his majority. When the judge was asked on what basis he adjudicated Gerald delinquent, he said he was not sure of the exact section of the code. The section of the Arizona Criminal Code that escaped his memory defined as a misdemeanant a person who "in the presence or hearing of any woman or child uses vulgar, abusive, or obscene language." For this offense, a 15-year-old boy was committed to a state institution until his majority. The maximum legal penalty for an adult was a fine of $5 to $50 or imprisonment for a maximum of two months. In contrast to an accused juvenile, an adult charged with this crime would be afforded due process at the trial.

The case was appealed to the U.S. Supreme Court, which reversed. Justice Abe Fortas delivered the opinion for the majority. Counsel had raised six basic rights: notice of the charges, right to counsel, right to confrontation and cross-examination, privilege against self-incrimination, right to a transcript, and right to appellate review. The Supreme Court ruled on the first four of these issues. The Court limited the extension of procedural safeguards in juvenile courts to those proceedings that might result in the commitment of juveniles to an institution in which their freedom would be curtailed. Justice Fortas excluded from the Supreme Court's decision the preadjudication and the postadjudication, or dispositional, stages. Justice Fortas reviewed the humanitarian philosophy of juvenile courts, but he said that the reality of juvenile courts is an unfulfilled dream. Courts that had been designed to act in the best interests of the child had become courts in which procedures frequently were arbitrary and unfair.[31]

The U.S. Supreme Court explained the importance of due process and of the procedural rules that protect it, especially the right to counsel. The Supreme Court compared procedure in law to the scientific method in science. The Court noted that Gault was "committed to an institution where he may be restrained of liberty for years." Calling the institution an industrial school made no difference. The fact was that the juvenile's world became "a building with whitewashed walls, regimented routine and institutional hours peopled by guards, custodians, state employees, and 'delinquents' confined with him for anything from waywardness to rape and homicide." In light of the seriousness of this confinement, it would be "extraordinary if our Constitution did not require the procedural regularity and the exercise of care implied in the phrase 'due process.' Under our Constitution, the condition of being a boy does not justify a kangaroo court."[32]

Despite the *Gault* ruling that juveniles have a right to counsel, a recent American Bar Association (ABA) study of the Maryland juvenile justice system concluded that "the spirit and promise" of the case "had been largely unfilled." Among other findings, the report stated the following:

- Many juveniles waive their right to counsel because no one has sufficiently explained the importance of that right to them.
- Most courts in the study did not even keep track of the number of juveniles who waive their right to counsel.
- Many juvenile court officials continue to believe that the juvenile proceedings should be adversarial.
- Those juveniles who are represented by counsel are often represented by less-than-ideal counsel, characterized by a lack of preparation and advocacy. "At least 90 percent of detained youth did not even know their public defender's name."
- Most public defenders who represent juveniles spend very little time with their clients.

This ABA study concluded that "the majority of youth in detention are incarcerated without effective representation" and that youth are routinely detained in secure facilities for the purpose of punishment. The ABA recommended that juveniles should not be permitted to waive their right to counsel until they spoke with counsel, and that there should be increased training and greater resources for defense counsel who represent juveniles; oversight and monitoring of juvenile court actions to avoid disparate treatment of minorities, youth with educational needs, and those who are mentally ill; and an end to the "misuse and abuse of secure detention."[33]

The U.S. Supreme Court has considered other constitutional rights for juveniles. In 1970, in *In re Winship*, the Supreme Court faced the issue of whether juvenile court proceedings require the same standard of proof as that of adult criminal courts or whether a lesser standard can be used. The Court applied the criminal court standard, concluding that "the observance of the standard of proof beyond a reasonable doubt will not compel the States to abandon or displace any of the substantive benefits of the juvenile process."[34]

In 1971, in *McKeiver v. Pennsylvania*, the U.S. Supreme Court refused to extend the right to a trial by jury to juvenile court proceedings. The Supreme Court emphasized that the underlying reason for its decisions in *Gault* and *Winship* was the principle of fundamental fairness. When the issue is one of fact finding, elements of due process must be present. But a jury is not a "necessary component of accurate fact-finding." The Supreme Court concluded that unlike adult criminal courts, juvenile courts should not become full adversary systems. The Court left open the possibility for state courts to experiment, *inviting* them to try trial by jury in juvenile proceedings but refusing to require them to do so.[35]

In 1975, in *Breed v. Jones*, the U.S. Supreme Court held that the constitutional provision that defendants may not be tried twice for the same offense applies to juveniles. Breed, 17, was apprehended for committing acts while armed with a deadly weapon. He was adjudicated in the juvenile court, which found the allegations to be true. At the hearing to determine disposition, the court indicated that it intended to find Breed "not...amenable to the care, treatment and training program available through the facilities of the juvenile court," as required by the statute. Breed was transferred to adult criminal court, where he was tried and found guilty of robbery in the first degree. Breed argued on appeal that the transfer after a hearing and decision on the facts in juvenile court subjected him to two trials on the same offense. The U.S. Supreme Court agreed.[36]

In 1984, in *Schall v. Martin*, the U.S. Supreme Court upheld the New York statute that permitted preventive detention of juveniles. The Supreme Court held that preventive detention fulfills the legitimate state interest of protecting society and juveniles by detaining those who might be dangerous to society or to themselves. The Court reiterated its belief in the doctrines of fundamental fairness and *parens patriae*, stating that it was trying to strike a balance between the juvenile's right to freedom pending trial and the right of society to be protected. The juveniles in this case were apprehended for serious crimes. According to the U.S. Supreme Court, the period of preventive detention was brief and followed proper procedural safeguards. Three justices disagreed with the Supreme Court's decision.[37]

In 1994, the California Supreme Court interpreted *Schall v. Martin* as not requiring that juveniles be granted a probable cause hearing within 48 hours after arrest, as is required for adults. The California court recognized significant differences in the detention of juveniles as compared with adults, noting that in many cases, it is in the juvenile's best interest that detention occur. The court cited specific sections in the California statute that provide adequate safeguards for detained juveniles. For example, a juvenile may not be detained for more than 24 hours without written review and approval. The U.S. Supreme Court refused to hear the case, thus leaving the California decision intact.[38]

In 1992, in *United States v. R.L.C.*, the U.S. Supreme Court held that juveniles may not be punished more harshly in sentencing than they would have been had they been charged and convicted of the same crime as an adult.[39] And in 2004, the U.S. Supreme Court considered whether juveniles must be given the Miranda warning before the police question them at the police station. In *Yarborough v. Alvarado*, the Los Angeles police questioned a 17-year-old suspect at police headquarters without giving him the Miranda warning. The police argued that the warning was not necessary because the suspect was free to leave. The Ninth Circuit Court of Appeals had ruled in the suspect's favor, holding that a person his age would not feel free to leave the police station. The U.S. Supreme Court reversed, holding that under the facts of the case, when the police questioned the appellant, he was not in police custody for purposes of the Miranda warning; he was free to leave. Michael Alvarado was suspected of being involved with a group of teens who were at a mall the night a murder occurred there. About a month after the shooting, the officer in charge of the investigation left word at Alvarado's house and called his mother at work, stating that she would like to talk with their son. The parents took Alvarado to the sheriff's office and waited in the lobby while the officers interviewed him for about two hours; the Miranda warning was not given.[40] This case is to be distinguished from the issue of whether juveniles have a constitutional right to the Miranda warning, a subject that is discussed later in this chapter. The issue in this case was whether the juvenile had come within the Miranda warning embrace— that is, was he at the time free to go and thus the Miranda warning was not required?

12-3b   Juvenile Curfews

Constitutional issues have arisen in recent years with the imposition of curfews in an attempt to reduce crime by keeping juveniles who are not accompanied by an adult off the streets after specified hours. One example of this trend, which more and more cities are adopting, is the Dallas, Texas, ordinance. This ordinance provides that youths under 17 must be off the streets from 11 P.M. to 6 A.M. During those hours, juveniles may not be in public places or establishments. There are some exceptions: youths who are running errands for their parents or other adults; returning from school, civic, or religious functions; passing time on sidewalks in front of their homes; or exercising First Amendment rights (see Appendix A). Violations may result in a fine not to exceed $500 for each offense.

In 1993, the U.S. Court of Appeals for the Fifth Circuit upheld the Dallas ordinance, emphasizing that the ordinance was narrowly tailored to further the city's compelling interest in reducing and preventing juvenile crime and victimization. The U.S. Supreme Court refused to hear the case, thus allowing the decision of the Fifth Circuit to stand.[41]

The U.S. Supreme Court took a similar position in 1999, when it refused to review a challenge to a Charlottesville, Virginia, midnight weekday curfew for teens. Parents had challenged the curfew as an infringement on their parental discretion and their children's freedom, claiming that the ordinance puts their children under "house arrest." The ordinance covers teens under 17 and provides that from midnight to 5 A.M. on weekdays and 1 to 5 A.M. on Saturdays and Sundays, they may not be on the streets. Some exceptions are permitted, such as a teen who is running an errand for a parent and is carrying a note from a parent.[42]

Some curfews are more restrictive on times, and some extend beyond the streets, for example, including malls. Some curfews have been held unconstitutional. In 1997, for example, a federal appellate court in California held that the San Diego ordinance, which made it illegal for minors to "loiter, idle, wander, stroll or play" after 10 P.M., was unconstitutional.[43]

What distinguishes these cases? Why are some curfew ordinances constitutional and others are not? Portions of the decision involving the Charlottesville, Virginia, ordinance are included here to help us understand. The opinion is lengthy and involves numerous constitutional issues. Only a few are included here.[44]

Schleifer v. City of Charlottesville

This appeal involves a challenge to the constitutionality of a juvenile nocturnal curfew ordinance enacted by the City of Charlottesville. The district court held that the ordinance did not violate the constitutional rights of minors, their parents, or other affected parties and declined to enjoin its enforcement. We agree that the ordinance is constitutional and affirm the judgment of the district court.

On December 16, 1996, the Charlottesville City Council, after several months of study and deliberation, amended Section 17-7 of the City Code to enact a new juvenile nocturnal curfew ordinance. The City Council designed the curfew ordinance to:

(i) promote the general welfare and protect the general public through the reduction of juvenile violence and crime within the City;

(ii) promote the safety and well-being of the City's youngest citizens, persons under the age of seventeen (17), whose inexperience renders them particularly vulnerable to becoming participants in unlawful activities, particularly unlawful drug activities, and to being victimized by older perpetrators of crime; and

(iii) foster and strengthen parental responsibility for children.

Effective March 1, 1997, the ordinance generally prohibits minors, defined as unemancipated persons under seventeen, from remaining in any public place, motor vehicle, or establishment within city limits during curfew hours. The curfew takes effect at 12:01 A.M. on Monday through Friday, at 1:00 A.M. on Saturday and Sunday, and lifts at 5:00 A.M. each morning.

The ordinance does not restrict minors' activities that fall under one of its eight enumerated exceptions. Minors may participate in any activity during curfew hours if they are accompanied by a parent; they may run errands at a parent's direction provided that they possess a signed note. The ordinance allows minors to undertake employment, or attend supervised activities sponsored by school, civic, religious, or other public organizations. The ordinance exempts minors who are engaged in interstate travel, are on the sidewalk abutting their parents' residence, or are involved in an emergency. Finally, the ordinance does not affect minors who are "exercising First Amendment rights protected by the United States Constitution, such as the free exercise of religion, freedom of speech and the right of assembly."

The ordinance sets forth a scheme of warnings and penalties for minors who violate it. For a first violation, a minor receives a verbal warning, followed by a written warning to the minor and the minor's parents. For subsequent violations, the minor is charged with a Class 4 misdemeanor. The ordinance also makes it unlawful for certain other individuals, including parents, knowingly to encourage a minor to violate the ordinance....

Plaintiffs are five minors under age seventeen who are subject to the ordinance, one eighteen-year-old, and two parents of minor children. The minors allege that, with their parents' permission, they occasionally wish to engage in lawful activities which the curfew will not permit. These activities include attending late movies; getting a "bite to eat"; playing in a band; socializing with older siblings; and attending concerts in Richmond, which would bring them back through Charlottesville during curfew hours. The eighteen-year-old plaintiff alleges that he has been deprived of opportunities to associate with his younger friends by the ordinance. The parent plaintiffs allege that the ordinance interferes with their decisions on which activities, at what times, are appropriate for their children....

[The court discussed the constitutional tests that should be used to determine this case and contrasted the San Diego curfew ordinance, which was held unconstitutional.]

The San Diego curfew applied to all minors under the age of eighteen, began at 10:00 P.M., and extended until "daylight immediately following." It contained four exceptions: (1) when a minor is accompanied by a parent or other qualified adult; (2) when a minor is on an emergency errand for his parent; (3) when a minor is returning from a school-sponsored activity; and (4) when a minor is engaged in employment.

By contrast, Charlottesville's curfew applies only to minors less than seventeen years of age, does not begin until midnight on weekdays and 1:00 A.M. on weekends, lifts at 5:00 A.M., each morning, and contains no fewer than eight detailed exceptions....[Those are listed; see the same list earlier in the opinion].

The Charlottesville ordinance carefully mirrors the Dallas curfew ordinance....Like the Charlottesville ordinance, the Dallas curfew covered fewer hours than San Diego's and affected minors under the age of seventeen, not eighteen....[The court listed the exceptions in the Dallas curfew ordinance, which are similar to those in the Charlottesville one, and concluded that the Charlottesville curfew] with its narrow scope and comprehensive list of exceptions, represents the least restrictive means to advance Charlottesville's compelling interests....

[The court noted the stated purposes of the Charlottesville curfew ordinance, the arguments regarding whether those purposes were being met, and concluded as follows:]

The Charlottesville curfew serves not only to head off crimes before they occur, but also to protect a particularly vulnerable population from being lured into participating in such activity. Contrary to the dissent's protestation, we do not hold that every such curfew ordinance would pass constitutional muster. The means adopted by a municipality must bear a substantial relationship to significant governmental interests; the restrictiveness of those means remains the subject of judicial review. As the district court noted, however, the curfew law in Charlottesville is "among the most modest and lenient of the myriad curfew laws implemented nationwide." Charlottesville's curfew, compared to those in other cities, is indeed a mild regulation: it covers a limited age group during only a few hours of the night. Its various exceptions enable minors to participate in necessary or worthwhile activities during these times. We hold that Charlottesville's juvenile curfew ordinance comfortably satisfies constitutional standards.

Accordingly, we affirm the judgment of the district court. We do so in the belief that communities possess constitutional latitude in devising solutions to the persistent problem of juvenile crime.

Recall that the U.S. Supreme Court refused to hear this case; thus, the decision stands. The opinion gives some of the reasons why the Charlottesville and Dallas ordinances are constitutional, while that of San Diego was not.

A separate issue from the constitutionality of juvenile curfews is whether we *should* have them. One study of the effects of juvenile curfews led the researchers to conclude that the preventive effect of such ordinances "appeared to be small."[45]

12-3c   Race Issues

Both race and gender are important factors to consider in analyzing juvenile justice systems. A study sponsored by the National Council on Crime and Delinquency (NCCD) reported that at every stage of criminal justice systems, African American youths were overrepresented. Although they constituted only 15 percent of all youths under age 18, of those juvenile cases coming to the attention of the police, African American youths, as compared to whites, represented the following:

- 26 percent of all juvenile arrests
- 31 percent of those referred to juvenile courts (rather than processed informally outside the system)
- 44 percent of the youths who are detained pending adjudication
- 32 percent of those who are adjudicated delinquent
- 46 percent of those who are transferred to adult criminal courts
- 40 percent of the youths who are sent to residential juvenile facilities
- 58 percent of the youths who are sent to adult jails or prisons[46]

The NCCD report found that Latino youths are also overrepresented in the system, although it is difficult to assess the extent, since some Latinos are classified as white. But the data did indicate that when Latino and white youths were charged with the same offenses, Latinos were three times more likely than whites to be incarcerated

(African Americans were six times more likely). The NCCD referred to the juvenile justice system as having a "double standard of justice"—one for whites and one for minorities—and concluded that, "[K]ids of color are much more likely to spend their formative years behind bars." Officials warned that there is a danger in concluding that these differences are *caused* by racist police, prosecutors, and juvenile court officials. Rather, the evidence *suggests* that justice systems for juveniles are not racially neutral. Despite the warnings, the report concluded that, "Throughout the system, minority youth—especially African American youth—receive different and harsher treatment. This is true even when white youth and minority youth are charged with similar offenses. This report documents a juvenile justice system that is 'separate but unequal.'"[47]

A 2002 report comparing the treatment of white and Latino youths in criminal justice systems also concluded that Latinos were "significantly over-represented in the U.S. justice system and receive[d] harsher treatment than white youth, even when charged with the same types of offenses." When youths were charged with drug offenses, the Latinos were 13 times more likely than whites to be incarcerated.[48]

In contrast, a publication by two criminologists, supported by a grant from the Office of Juvenile Justice and Delinquency Prevention, concluded that police decisions to take juveniles into custody were not based on race. According to this report, the data

> offer no evidence to support the hypothesis that police are more likely to arrest non-white juvenile offenders than white juvenile offenders, once other incident attributes are taken into consideration....The data do indicate, however, an indirect bias effect in the arrest of nonwhite juveniles in that they are more likely to be arrested when the victim is white than when the victim is nonwhite.[49]

Earlier in the chapter, we noted that there is evidence that juveniles do not have adequate legal assistance. The same study, by the American Bar Association (ABA), reported that the situation may be worse for minorities:

> [T]oo many children, particularly of color, fall victim to conveyer-belt justice—with kids rushed through a system riddled with institutional flaws, without regard for their individual cases or needs.
> Collectively, the reports paint a disturbing picture [according to the ABA president, with the overall result being] a massive misdirection of resources that fails children and undermines public safety.[50]

There are some signs of successful efforts to reduce apparent racial disparity among juveniles in our justice systems. A study of the detention of juveniles in the Oregon county that contains Portland concluded as follows: "Multnomah County has shown the country that you can reduce racial disparities in juvenile justice, make more modest use of detention, and still uphold public safety." The study was conducted by the Justice Policy Institute, a criminal justice research group based in Washington, D.C. The successful efforts included hiring more minority personnel, seeking additional alternatives to detention, and establishing written criteria for selecting those youths who should be detained.[51]

12-3d   Gender Issues

Another issue crucial to an analysis of differential reactions within juvenile justice systems is that of gender. The 1974 Juvenile Justice and Delinquency Prevention Act (JJDPA) encouraged states to find means other than incarceration for juveniles who had committed nonserious offenses (status offenders, most of whom were girls) and for juveniles who were dependent or neglected but who had not committed any offenses. The statute called for an end to incarcerating juveniles with adults.[52]

Some jurisdictions have made reforms in the manner in which they treat status offenders. In New York State, for example, where such offenders are called *persons in need of supervision* or *PINS*, the legal age was extended to include 16- and 17-year-old juveniles in 2001 as the result of parents who looked to governmental agencies to assist them with problem teens. This statutory change meant that the number of PINS could increase by up to 105 percent, with a resulting cost of millions of dollars. A review of the state's PINS programs revealed that many status offenders were being placed in the court systems, after which court orders were violated, and the process escalated. The new approach was to increase diversionary programs and try to avoid placing status offenders in courts at all. One program, entitled *Family Keys,* involves dispatching counselors to families within two hours after teen problems are reported. Reports are that fewer juveniles are being processed through the courts, which are now considered a last resort. New York counties are also looking at alternatives to foster care for teens who defy their parents or engage in other status-type offenses without violating the law. Teens are kept within their homes but provided intensive supervision and services under a program entitled *Juvenile Release Under Supervision (JRUS).* The Vera Institute reported that these programs have resulted in cutting $1.5 million from the Albany County's $2.3 million detention budget.[53]

12-4 Juvenile Court Organization and Procedures

Juvenile courts differ somewhat from jurisdiction to jurisdiction, but our discussion in this section involves the organization and procedures that are found in most U.S. juvenile court systems. Figure 12-2 diagrams a typical organizational model and should be used as a reference for this discussion.

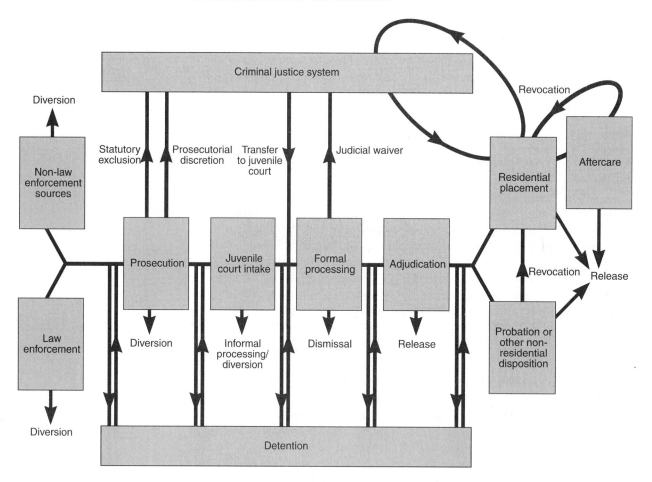

Figure 12-2
The Stages of Delinquent Case Processing in the Juvenile Justice System

Source: Melissa Sickmund, Bureau of Justice Statistics, *Juveniles in Court* (Washington, D.C.: U.S. Office of Juvenile Justice and Delinquency Prevention, U.S. Department of Justice, June, 2003), p. 3.

12-4a   Court Procedures

Juveniles may be referred to a juvenile justice system in various ways. Although most juvenile offenders are referred by law enforcement agencies, some referrals come from parents, relatives, schools, probation officers, other courts, and miscellaneous other sources. Juveniles may be counseled and released to their parents. Some may be diverted to social services or other programs. In juvenile systems, **diversion** historically was used to remove the juveniles from *official* juvenile or criminal proceedings before a hearing. If a decision was made not to divert the juvenile to some other agency or to his or her parents, other dispositions had to be made.

In some cases, after a referral has been made and the police have observed delinquent behavior, or an offense has been reported and juveniles are suspected, the police may begin surveillance and investigation. There is no way of knowing how many cases are handled by the police without any formal action being taken, but most juveniles are not taken into custody upon apprehension by police. Police are not the only people who may take children into custody. Officials in child protective services, probation offices, family services, and youth services may do so in many jurisdictions.

Historically, there were few guidelines for taking juveniles into custody. In the *Gault* case, discussed earlier in this chapter, the U.S. Supreme Court excluded prejudicial activities (such as police apprehension) that occur prior to a court appearance from the due process requirements of that case. Some lower courts have held that taking a juvenile into custody is not an arrest, and therefore, the due process requirements that must be observed in the arrest of an adult are not applicable. But most courts appear to consider the process an arrest, which should be accompanied by due process requirements.[54]

If a juvenile is taken into custody, the issues of search and seizure may arise. Most state courts have interpreted *Gault's* fundamental fairness test to mean that the constitutional prohibition against unreasonable searches and seizures applies to juvenile proceedings. Some states have incorporated exclusionary rules into their statutes; thus, evidence seized illegally in juvenile cases may not be admitted as evidence against the accused.

Whether or not a search is conducted, there may be a decision to detain the juvenile. Most often, juveniles are taken into custody without a summons or a warrant. Police must then decide what to do with the juveniles in their custody. Most are released to their parents. When that is not possible or reasonable, most jurisdictions require that juveniles be placed in special juvenile detention centers. As noted earlier in this chapter, in *Schall v. Martin*, the U.S. Supreme Court upheld preventive detention for juveniles. After noting that juveniles have a substantial interest in liberty, the Supreme Court said, "But that interest must be qualified by the recognition that juveniles, unlike adults, are always in some form of custody." The Supreme Court reiterated its belief that courts have special powers over children, as compared with adults. "[C]hildren, by definition, are not assumed to have the capacity to take care of themselves," and therefore, they need additional protection. Preventive detention of juveniles may be appropriate to protect the juveniles themselves, not just to protect society, as in the case of preventive detention of adults, which the U.S. Supreme Court upheld in 1987.[55]

The power to detain juveniles does not mean the power to detain them in jails rather than in special juvenile detention facilities. The Juvenile Justice and Delinquency Prevention Act, passed by Congress in 1974 and amended in subsequent years, provides that funds be made available for juvenile justice and delinquency projects and programs to those states that comply with the statute's mandates. Among other provisions is the phasing out of juvenile detention in *adult* jails, but a 1999 publication of the Department of Justice (DOJ) reported that, between 1994 and 1997, the number of youths under 18 who were held in jails increased by 35 percent, and in 1997, they constituted approximately 2 percent of the total jail population.[56]

> **Diversion**   The removal of the offender from the criminal proceeding before or after guilt is determined and disposition through other procedures, such as work release, drug treatment, or community service.

A 2001 publication by the Institute of Crime, Justice, and Corrections, along with the National Council on Crime and Delinquency, described the "phenomenon of youth offender incarceration in adult correctional facilities" as a "burgeoning issue in many correctional systems" and recommended changes such as better classification systems to take into consideration the "special needs or the maturation issues presented by youthful offenders."[57] However, the number of juveniles held in adult correctional facilities peaked in 1995 and decreased every year thereafter to 2005.[58]

One study concluded that when juveniles are detained in adult facilities, as compared to youth facilities, they are:

- Eight times as likely to commit suicide
- Five times as likely to be sexually assaulted
- Two times as likely to be assaulted by staff
- 50 percent more likely to be attacked with a weapon"[59]

Placing juveniles in adult prisons is a serious and controversial measure, but some courts have upheld the practice. In 1997, the Washington Supreme Court upheld that state's provision that juveniles deemed to constitute a "continuing and serious threat to the safety of others at the institution" may be transferred administratively from a juvenile facility to an adult prison. The juvenile who appealed the case argued that, since his juvenile court hearing did not provide him with all of the procedural protections of an adult court, he was denied his constitutional rights. The court responded that changing the location of detention did not alter the system: the youth offender remained under the juvenile system and retained the benefits of that system.[60]

The issue of incarcerating juveniles in adult prisons was raised in the case of *Ratliff v. Cohn*, decided by the Indiana Supreme Court in 1998. Donna Ratliff was 14 when she set fire to her home, killing her mother and 16-year-old sister. Ratliff claimed that she had been beaten repeatedly by her mother and sexually molested by another older sister and an uncle. Ratliff was charged in an adult criminal court and entered guilty pleas to arson and two counts of reckless homicide. Although the trial court recommended that Ratliff be placed in an alternative facility, the Indiana Department of Corrections sent her to the Indiana Adult Women's Prison, where she was confined in a special needs unit away from the general population. On appeal, Ratliff raised several issues, most of which were denied. The state supreme court held that the state constitution and laws did not require that all juveniles be incarcerated in facilities designed especially for them but only that such facilities must exist. The court upheld the decision to incarcerate Ratliff in the women's prison and rejected most of her claims concerning her incarceration there. But the court did state that Ratliff had a due process claim with regard to her allegation that she was "subjected to hostility and threats by adult inmates…and fears for her safety" and that older inmates sexually propositioned her. The court expressed no view with regard to the accuracy of these claims but sent the case back to the trial court for consideration. Subsequently, Ratliff was transferred to a private juvenile facility. In 1999, she was removed to a special dorm for youthful offenders at the Indiana Women's Prison.[61]

One final issue with regard to juvenile detention or incarceration is that of bail. Some states have granted juveniles the right to release on bail; others have denied that right; and still others have decided that it is not an issue because of the provision of special facilities for juvenile detention.

Consider also the question of whether juveniles should be interrogated by police. Originally, it was assumed that it would be therapeutic for children to confess; thus, juveniles had few procedural protections concerning police interrogation. Today, the rule is that juvenile confessions may be used against them in court, provided those confessions are made voluntarily.

Certain police procedures, however, may not be applicable in juvenile cases. Most statutes covering juvenile proceedings attempt to protect juveniles from some of the harshness of adult criminal courts and therefore prohibit publication of the pictures of suspects and the taking of fingerprints. The use of lineups and showups, however, has been left to the courts, most of which have held that the same standards applicable to adults must also be applied in juvenile proceedings.

If a decision is made to detain a juvenile, that individual will be taken to intake screening, which is designed to remove the juveniles who should be diverted if that decision was not made earlier. A decision could be made at this stage to refer the juvenile to another agency or to his or her parents to await a hearing. A third alternative is to detain (or continue to detain) the juvenile before the hearing.

The **intake decision** is made by an intake officer, who may also be a probation officer. Theoretically, these officers conduct an investigation before making the intake decision; however, with heavy caseloads, this may not be done thoroughly, if at all. Some states have placed statutory requirements on the intake officer regarding referrals out of the system or dismissals. For example, in some jurisdictions, the intake officer may not dismiss a case without the prosecutor's written permission. In others, the case may not be dismissed or diverted if the complaining witness insists that formal action proceed beyond this stage.

If the juvenile is detained with the intent that a petition will be filed to bring formal procedures, a hearing usually is held to determine whether there is reason to continue with the case. This is true whether the juvenile is being held as a dependent and neglected child or for alleged delinquency. The hearing must be held within a reasonable period after detention begins, but it does not involve all of the specific procedural safeguards.

After the preliminary inquiry or hearing, the juvenile may be released from detention, or the case may be dismissed. If the case is not dismissed, it may proceed only with the filing of a petition, the formal document for initiating a case in the juvenile system. This petition is in contrast to a grand jury indictment or a prosecutor's presentment in adult criminal courts.

The *Gault* case requires that juveniles and their parents be given adequate notice of the charges and of the proceedings to follow. Most states require that the adjudicatory hearing be held within a specified period after the petition is filed. In some jurisdictions, if this does not occur the case must be dismissed.

Juveniles may admit or deny guilt; most admit that they committed the acts of which they are accused. This plea must be a knowing and voluntary one, and juveniles have the right to counsel if they are involved in proceedings that could lead to confinement in an institution.

Since the *Kent* case, discussed earlier, some jurisdictions have enacted statutes to permit juveniles some discovery procedures. *Discovery* involves the right to find out what the opposing side is going to use in the case. This information is necessary for the juvenile and his or her attorney to know how best to proceed with the case, and it might affect the juvenile's decision to admit or deny the allegations.

> **Intake decision** In prosecution, the first review of a case by an official in the prosecutor's office. Weak cases may be weeded out at this stage. In juvenile courts, the reception of a juvenile against whom complaints have been made. The decision to dismiss or proceed with a case is made at this stage.

12-4b   The Role of Attorneys

In traditional juvenile court systems, there was no place for attorneys. The proceedings were not considered adversarial; all parties were thought to be acting in the child's best interests, and no need was seen for attorneys.

Prosecutors were not needed because the decision to proceed was made by intake officers. In reality, however, whether the individual is called an intake officer or a prosecutor, the person permitted to decide who will or will not be processed in the system has considerable power. The question is not whether prosecutors have power but how much power they have. Some jurisdictions restrict their power to dismiss the case after the petition is filed, but even in those cases, prosecutors retain considerable discretion over determining whether to proceed with cases referred by the police or others.

The defense attorney's primary function in a juvenile case is to ensure that the juvenile's constitutional rights are protected during all of the proceedings. The attorney should be familiar with all the facts of the case and be prepared to present the defense at the hearing. The lack of formality in the hearing does not mean that the defense is any less important in a juvenile than in an adult criminal court hearing.

An important issue in juvenile court cases is whether the *Miranda* case applies to juveniles. In 1971, when the U.S. Supreme Court considered the question, the Court stated in a footnote that, although it had not ruled that *Miranda* applies to juveniles, it was assuming that its principles were applicable to the proceedings despite the Court's holding that the juvenile is not entitled to all procedures applicable to criminal trials. Most courts ruling on the question have held that *Miranda* applies to juvenile cases.[62]

The issue also arises over whether juveniles may waive their *Miranda* rights. Some courts have refused to accept a juvenile waiver without parental guidance. Others have held that children may not waive complicated legal rights. As mentioned earlier in the chapter, in the discussion of the quality of legal assistance provided for juveniles, the American Bar Association recommends that courts should not recognize a juvenile's waiver of the right to counsel unless that juvenile had the assistance of counsel in making the waiver decision.

The interaction between those who serve as prosecutors and those who serve as defense attorneys is as important in juvenile as in adult criminal court systems. The relationship between prosecutors and defense attorneys in juvenile systems is similar to the relationship they share in adult criminal court systems. They may serve as checks on the potential abuse of power, or they may cooperate to the point of violating juveniles' rights. They may serve diligently and competently, with the best interests of juveniles as their goals. But in some cases, those who take that perspective find their goals thwarted by a system that has inadequate resources and insufficient personnel.

Another interaction that occurs between prosecutors and defense attorneys in criminal court proceedings is also applicable to juvenile proceedings. Plea bargaining does occur, and some have argued that this process often is in the best interests of the child and of society.

The juvenile hearing is less formal than that of the adult criminal court, but the same general procedures occur. The prosecutor presents the evidence against the juvenile, the defense has an opportunity to cross-examine the witnesses, and some rules of evidence apply. Hearsay evidence may be presented in a juvenile hearing, in contrast to an adult criminal court trial. Evidence is presented to a judge and not to a jury unless the jurisdiction provides for a trial by jury and the juvenile has not waived that right.

At the end of the presentation of evidence, there is an adjudication of whether the juvenile did what he or she is accused of doing. Technically, the terms *guilty* and *not guilty* are not used in juvenile proceedings, although the obvious purpose is to determine whether the alleged acts were committed. To support a finding of responsibility, the evidence must be sufficient to convince the judge beyond a reasonable doubt.

In traditional language, juveniles are not sentenced; dispositions are made. Dispositions tend to be indeterminate, although the court loses jurisdiction over the child when he or she reaches the age of majority. Several types of dispositions are available. Figure 12-2 illustrates that the court may take one of three routes. Nominal dispositions, such as warnings and reprimands, may be made. Conditional dispositions in juvenile courts are similar to those in adult criminal courts: restitution, fine, community service, suspended disposition, or community supervision (probation). A final method of disposition is to place juveniles in secure or nonsecure facilities.

What procedures must be followed at the disposition hearing? In *Gault*, the U.S. Supreme Court stated that it was not answering the question of which federal constitutional due process rights apply to the pre- or postadjudicatory hearing stages of the juvenile process. Therefore, the required procedures are established by state statutes or by state court decisions, and they vary from state to state. Because most juvenile cases do not involve a dispute over the facts, the disposition hearing becomes the most significant part of the process, and the right to counsel is important. Normally, disposition of a juvenile case involves a separate hearing from that of adjudication, and it is preceded by an investigative report, or social report, on which the decision may be based.

Source: Howard N. Snyder and Melissa Sickmund, *Juvenile Offenders and Victims: 1999 National Report* (Washington, D.C.: Office of Juvenile Justice and Delinquency Prevention, U.S. Department of Justice, September 1999), p. 103.

Spotlight 12-2 Juveniles in Criminal Courts

Many States Have Changed the Boundaries of Juvenile Court Jurisdiction

Traditionally, discretionary judicial waiver was the transfer mechanism on which most states relied. Beginning in the 1970s and continuing through the present, however, state legislatures have increasingly moved juvenile offenders into criminal court based on age and/or offense seriousness, without the case-specific consideration offered by the discretionary juvenile court judicial waiver process.

State transfer provisions changed extensively in the 1990s. From 1992 through 1997, all but six states enacted or expanded transfer provisions. An increasing number of state legislatures have enacted mandatory waiver or exclusion statutes. Less common, then and now, are concurrent jurisdiction provisions.

In Most States, Juveniles Convicted in Criminal Court Cannot Be Tried in Juvenile Court for Subsequent Offenses

In thirty-one states, juveniles who have been tried as adults must be prosecuted in criminal court for any subsequent offenses. Nearly all of these "once an adult/always an adult" provisions require that the youth must have been convicted of the offenses that triggered the initial criminal prosecution.

Judicial Waiver Is the Most Common Transfer Provision

In all states except Nebraska, New Mexico, and New York, juvenile court judges may waive jurisdiction over certain cases and transfer them to criminal court. Such action is usually in response to a request by the prosecutor; in several states, however, juveniles or their parents may request judicial waiver. In most states, statutes limit waiver by age and offense.

Waiver provisions vary in terms of the degree of decision-making flexibility allowed. Under some waiver provisions, the decision is entirely *discretionary*. Under the others, there is a rebuttable *presumption* in favor of waiver. Under others, waiver is *mandatory* once the juvenile court judge determines that certain statutory criteria have been met. Mandatory waiver provisions are distinguished from statutory exclusion provisions in that the case originates in juvenile rather than criminal court.

Statutes Establish Waiver Criteria Other Than Age and Offense

In some states, waiver provisions target youth charged with offenses involving firearms or other weapons. Most state statutes also limit judicial waiver to juveniles who are "no longer amenable to treatment." The specific factors that determine lack of amenability vary but typically include the juvenile's offense history and previous dispositional outcomes. Such amenability criteria are generally not included in statutory exclusion or concurrent jurisdiction provisions.

Many statutes instruct juvenile courts to consider other factors when making waiver decisions, such as the availability of dispositional alternatives for treating the juvenile, the time available for sanctions, public safety, and the best interests of the child. The waiver process must also adhere to certain constitutional principles of fairness.

The social report is crucial to the philosophy that juveniles are to be treated individually and that it is possible to rehabilitate them. The social report should include any information that might have a bearing on assessing the needs of the particular child. The types of evidence that may be admitted at the dispositional stage are much broader than those permitted at the adjudicatory hearing.

After the disposition, the juvenile may have grounds for an appeal. In *Gault*, the U.S. Supreme Court refused to rule that there is a constitutional right to appeal from a juvenile court decision, but since *Gault*, all jurisdictions have made some statutory provisions for appeals.

12-5   Juveniles in Adult Criminal Courts

Concern with what appears to be an increasing number of juveniles involved in violent crimes has resulted in a push for more stringent treatment of these offenders. As Spotlight 12-2 reports, most states provide that, in certain cases, juveniles may be tried in adult criminal courts. This may be permitted because both the adult criminal and the juvenile courts have jurisdiction, the offenses are excluded from the jurisdiction of juvenile courts, or there is a *waiver* from the juvenile to the adult criminal court. This last procedure, also called *transfer* or **certification**, means that the juvenile court waives jurisdiction, the case is transferred from the juvenile court to the adult criminal court,

Certification The process used to remove juveniles from the jurisdiction of the juvenile court to that of the adult criminal court. Also called *transfer* or *waiver*.

or the juvenile court certifies that the juvenile should be tried as an adult. When certification occurs, the juvenile goes through the same procedures as those required in adult criminal courts and has the same constitutional rights as others who are tried in those courts.

Certification to an adult criminal court may result in more severe consequences for the juvenile, although this is not always the case. The certification process that must be followed differs from state to state. In some states, the prosecutor makes the decision; in others, the decision is made by the juvenile court judge.

The procedural requirements for waiver were articulated by the U.S. Supreme Court in the *Kent* case, discussed earlier. Although that case applied only to a statute at issue in Washington, D.C., most courts have interpreted it as stating the minimum due process requirements for transfer from a juvenile court to an adult criminal court. The juvenile is entitled to a hearing on the issue of transfer, and the right to counsel attaches to that hearing. Upon request, the defense counsel must be given access to the social record that the court has compiled on the juvenile. If jurisdiction is waived from the juvenile court to the adult criminal court, the juvenile must be given a statement of the reasons for the waiver.

Some statutes give adult criminal courts jurisdiction over juveniles who commit specified serious crimes, such as murder, but permit the adult criminal court to transfer the case to a juvenile court. New York is an example. Under the New York statute, children age 13 or older who are charged with second-degree murder and children age 14 or older who are charged with any one of a number of serious crimes (including burglary, sodomy in the first degree, aggravated sexual abuse, manslaughter in the first degree, murder, rape, and robbery) are under the *exclusive* original jurisdiction of adult criminal courts. But those courts may transfer the cases to juvenile courts by a process known as *reverse certification*.[63]

The Colorado Court of Appeals has held that, when a juvenile is transferred to an adult criminal court, due process does not require that the evidence supporting transfer be clear and convincing. Under the Colorado statute, a juvenile who is 14 or older and is accused of an act that would be a felony if committed by an adult, may be transferred to an adult criminal court at the request of the prosecutor, provided the juvenile court conducts an investigation. The purpose of that investigation is to determine whether there is probable cause to believe that the juvenile committed the act and, if so, whether it is in the interests of society and of the accused juvenile that the case be transferred. The Colorado appellate court noted that the decision of whether or not to transfer is more analogous to a sentencing hearing than to a trial to determine guilt. The court emphasized that there is no constitutional right to be tried as a juvenile and that the risk to society of not trying the juvenile as an adult may outweigh any reasons for leaving the case in the juvenile court.[64]

The transfer of juveniles to adult criminal courts has been severely criticized by some juvenile court judges. According to the National Council of Juvenile and Family Court Judges, the "assumption is that…[adult] criminal courts will be tougher and can serve as a more effective deterrent for juvenile crime.…This assumption is not borne out by the facts."[65]

Two scholars who tested the results of Idaho's statutory automatic waiver to adult criminal courts of juveniles who are accused of violent crimes found that the process did not result in a reduction of violent juvenile crime. The authors concluded that their results were similar to those of a study of New York's automatic waiver statute: "There does not appear to be a deterrent effect of legislative waiver on rates of juvenile violent crimes." The researchers noted that the finding is particularly interesting in light of the vast differences between the two states—one a highly urbanized state with high crime rates and the other a much more rural state with low crime rates.[66]

In his dissertation at the University of Maryland, David L. Myers reported that juveniles processed through adult criminal courts, in comparison with those in juvenile courts, were more likely to be released prior to trial but that their recidivism rates were higher. If they went to trial they were more likely than juveniles in the juvenile court system to be convicted and incarcerated, and their sentences were longer. Myers concluded, "This suggests that the price of any short-term public safety achieved through prosecuting juveniles as adults might be an increase in long-term criminal offenses.... Although the transferred offenders received harsher punishment than did their counterparts retained in juvenile courts, public safety did not appear to be enhanced." Dr. Larry Sherman, chair of the University of Maryland's Department of Criminology and Criminal Justice, where Myers was a student when he conducted this study, described this as an unintended result of the "get-tough" laws: "It shows the bankruptcy of the legislative process where such crucial decisions are made in the absence of scientific evidence....If the Food and Drug Administration had been asked to approve this policy, they would have rejected it for lack of evidence that the policy was safe and effective."[67]

According to data released by the U.S. Bureau of Justice Statistics (BJS), of the juveniles in the 75 largest U.S. counties who were transferred to adult criminal courts, two-thirds had been charged with violent offenses. Those who were convicted were sentenced to an average 10-year term. Most juveniles who are transferred to adult criminal courts are convicted, and if convicted, they are more likely than those in juvenile courts to be incarcerated. This is true even for the crime of murder. For example, 100 percent of the juveniles convicted of murder in adult criminal courts during this study were sentenced to prison, compared with only 77 percent of the juveniles adjudicated of murder in juvenile court proceedings. The remaining 23 percent were given probation or other forms of sentences.[68]

Florida leads the nation, with about 7,000 juveniles per year tried as adults. Florida houses approximately 10 percent of the 16,000 juveniles who are incarcerated in U.S. prisons.[69] Two recent cases—those of Lionel Tate and Nathaniel Brazill— caught the nation's attention. Tate's case was discussed in Chapter 7 in the context of plea bargaining.

Brazill, like Tate, was also 14 when he was tried in a Florida adult criminal court, but unlike Tate, who was convicted of first-degree murder, Brazill was convicted of second-degree murder and thus escaped the mandatory sentence of life without parole specified by Florida law for first-degree murder convictions. Brazill, who was 13 when he shot and killed his favorite teacher, faced a possible 25-years-to-life sentence. He received 28 years. In May 2003, Brazill's conviction and sentence were upheld by a Florida court of appeals; the state's supreme court refused to review the case, but subsequently Brazill, representing himself, won the right to challenge the effectiveness of his defense counsel at his original trial. Brazill's prosecutor, Marc Shiner, described the defendant as a killer whose "demeanor sends chills up my spine." But he also said that it was very difficult for him to prosecute a young man who was not much older than his own son. Shiner subsequently became a defense attorney, and one of his first clients was a 16-year-old girl accused of killing her newborn son.[70]

Not all juveniles who commit serious crimes are tried in adult criminal courts, and not all who are tried in those courts receive such harsh punishments as Tate and Brazill. (Recall from Chapter 7 that Tate's case was reversed on appeal, and he was released, but after subsequent allegations of criminal conduct, he was sentenced to 30 years in prison.) For example, the youngest child ever tried for murder in an adult court was convicted and sentenced to only seven years in a maximum-security juvenile facility. Nathaniel Abraham, age 13 at sentencing and age 11 when he murdered Ronnie Greene Jr., age 18, could have been sentenced to life in prison. Abraham was tried under a three-year-old Michigan statute that permitted trying juveniles of any age in adult courts. The judge criticized the law as "fundamentally flawed" and assailed the criminal justice system for failing young people such as Abraham, stating that, "The Legislature has responded to juvenile criminal activity not by helping to prevent and rehabilitate, but rather by treating juveniles more like adults....The real solution is to prevent an adult criminal population ever coming into existence."[71]

Some constitutional challenges to automatic waivers from juvenile to criminal courts have been successful. For example, the Delaware provision that a juvenile who turns 18 before trial should be transferred to an adult criminal court automatically if one or more enumerated crimes were charged was held to violate the state and federal constitutions because it removed from the judiciary the authority to make the transfer decision. In essence, the decision was made by the prosecutor, who had the power to effect a transfer by bringing charges of an enumerated offense.[72]

There are a number of reasons for and against certification or waiver. One of the strongest arguments in favor of waiver is that it sends a message to juveniles and thus serves as a deterrent. It serves as notice to society that we are getting tough on juvenile crime. But it can also be argued that this "get-tough" approach does not work but, rather, gives only the *appearance* of toughness and deterrence. If the system is too severe, police may not arrest; prosecutors may not prosecute or will charge lesser offenses; juries may not convict. In addition, there is evidence that many juveniles who are tried in adult courts are not legally competent. A study published in 2003 by the MacArthur Foundation and conducted by a nine-member team led by a physician at the University of Massachusetts Medical School concluded that juveniles who are tried in adult criminal courts are far more likely than adult defendants to have serious impairment of their competency. They are less likely to understand that it may be to their advantage not to talk freely to the police during interrogation. The report concluded that "States should consider implementing policies and practices designed to ensure that young defendants' rights to a fair trial are protected." That might mean requiring competency evaluations before a juvenile is transferred to an adult court.[73]

12-6 Megan's Laws and Juveniles

Recall Chapter 11's discussion of Megan's Laws. In some jurisdictions, Megan's Laws extend to juvenile sex offenders, who may be required to register for life. In 2003, the Illinois Supreme Court upheld the sentencing of a 12-year-old who is required to register as a sex offender for the remainder of his life. In a 5-to-1 decision the court rejected the argument that life-time registration conflicts with the rehabilitative purposes of juvenile systems. The defendant in *People v. J.W.* pleaded guilty to two counts of aggravated sexual assault on two seven year-old boys (in exchange for the state dropping other charges). The acts included oral and anal sex as well as bestiality (in this case, sex with a dog). The defendant was placed on probation for five years and required to register as a sex offender for life. He appealed the registration requirement, but the appellate court held that because of the nature of his sex acts, he is a sexual predator under Illinois law and thus required to register as a sex offender for the rest of his life. In 1999, the Illinois legislature amended the juvenile statutes to include not only rehabilitation of juveniles but protection of the public as goals; thus, said the judge, the sentence is rational in light of that purpose. Another term of the defendant's probation was that he could not live in or even return to the village in which the incidents took place. The defendant's parents said that they would move; until that occurred, the boy was to live with his aunt. He was eventually placed in a treatment center.[74]

The Illinois Sex Offender Registration Act provides for two registries: one, which is public, applies to persons age 17 and over. The other, which is available only to law enforcement and schools, applies to offenders under age 17. In 2006, the Illinois legislature passed a bill to ease the requirement for registration of juvenile sex offenders when they reach age 17. Under the current law, they are treated as adults at that age; under the proposed law, the decision whether to treat them as adults for purposes of registration would be left to the judge, who would be required to consider 10 specified factors (e.g., age, relationship between the victim and the offender, and nature of the sex offense). However, the governor vetoed the bill.[75]

In 2006, the Illinois Supreme Court agreed to reconsider the issue of whether juvenile sex offenders may be required to register for life. The most recent case involves the issue of whether juveniles are denied due process when they are assessed with what is essentially an adult penalty, but have been processed through the juvenile court, in which they do not have a right to a jury trial. The case arose after a DuPage County judge ruled in several cases that juvenile offenders did not have to register. The state attorney then asked the court to order the judge to require that they do register, in accordance with the Illinois Sex Offender Registration Act. The Illinois Supreme Court has previously upheld the constitutionality of the state's sex offender act as it applies to juveniles (and the U.S. Supreme Court refused to review the case); the current case raises the issue of imposing an adult penalty on someone who did not have the constitutional protection of a jury trial, as provided in adult criminal courts.[76]

Not all applications of Megan's Laws to juveniles have been upheld. In 1999, the Alabama Court of Criminal Appeals held that Alabama's Megan's Law was unconstitutional as applied to juveniles. The statute was applied to juveniles by a 1998 amendment, which required that juveniles who are adjudicated on the basis of certain enumerated acts must declare their intention to reside in a specific location before they can be released from custody. The juvenile's offense history, fingerprints, and a photograph are provided to law enforcement officials in the designated area. In larger cities, this information is distributed on fliers, which are sent to residences within a specified distance of schools, day-care centers, and other places that care for children, and all schools within three miles of the offender's declared residence. The court ruled that the statute's provision that an adult may return to a home that has a minor, but a juvenile may not do so (although an exception may be made for a juvenile offender who is the parent of the minor in the designated home), violates the juvenile's right to equal protection. Further, the court ruled that the statute violated the *ex post facto* rights of all juveniles who had committed their acts before the statute was amended to include them.[77]

12-7   Juvenile Drug Courts

Chapter 11 discussed drug courts, which are designed primarily for treatment rather than punishment. Because of that emphasis, drug courts are particularly applicable to juveniles. A comprehensive study by the National Drug Court Institute (NDCI) and the National Council of Juvenile and Family Court Judges (NCJFCJ) published in 2003 emphasized, however, that drug courts for juveniles should not mirror those for adults. The NDCI and the NCJFCJ created a council to develop a plan for juvenile drug courts.

The first main difference between juvenile and adult drug courts is that the former are dealing primarily with individuals who are usually not yet addicted to alcohol or other drugs. Thus, it is important for the drug courts to assess the level of juvenile involvement in drugs, ranging from abuse to dependency, and in some cases, to addiction. But substance abuse is a serious problem among juveniles, as Spotlight 12-3 notes.

A second contrast between juveniles and adults who might benefit from drug courts is that most juveniles are living with their families; so the court must focus on the entire family, not just the individual in trouble. The NDCI report emphasized the need to focus on positive rather than negative aspects of the juvenile's family. Juvenile drug courts must focus on "the idea that youth and their families—even though they have problems—have innate resources that can positively change their lives." Further, the court should treat juveniles and their families as "experts on their own case. As youth and families become more aware of their strengths, they begin to feel more capable. This in itself is a powerful intervention tool."[78]

A third difference is that most juveniles are in school—or at least are required by law to be there. Thus, school systems should be involved in the drug court treatment plans. Fourth, juvenile drug courts must comply with the privacy and confidentiality requirements of juvenile court systems—which are not part of adult criminal court systems. Finally, although drug testing is important in both juvenile and adult drug courts, it should be utilized frequently with juveniles, but the youth's behavior should be watched carefully, as another measure of drug involvement.[79]

Spotlight 12-3 **Substance Abuse and Juveniles: A Report**

[I n 2004, the National Center on Addiction and Substance Abuse at Columbia University (CASA) published a groundbreaking report on substance abuse among juveniles. Some of the findings were as follows:]

- At least 30 percent of adults in prison for felony crimes were incarcerated as juveniles.
- Ninety-two percent of arrested juveniles who tested positive for drugs, tested positive for marijuana; 14.4 percent, for cocaine.
- Up to three-quarters of incarcerated 10- to 17-year-olds have a diagnosable mental health disorder.
- As many as eight out of ten incarcerated juveniles suffer from learning disabilities.
- Compared to juveniles who have not been arrested, those who have been arrested once in the past year are: more than twice as likely to have used alcohol; more than 3.5 times likelier to have used marijuana; more than three times likelier to have used prescription drugs for nonmedical purposes; more than seven times likelier to have used Ecstasy; more than nine times likelier to have used cocaine; and more than 20 times likelier to have used heroin....
- The arrest rate for black juveniles is more than 1.5 times the rate for white juveniles.

[As a result of its findings, CASA] is calling for a complete overhaul of the juvenile justice system [including some of the following recommendations]:

- Creating a model juvenile justice code to set practice standards and accountability for states in handling juvenile offenders.
- Training all juvenile justice system staff, including juvenile judges, law enforcement and other court personnel, how to recognize and deal with substance-involved offenders.
- Extending to juveniles diversion programs such as juvenile drug courts and comprehensive home-based services.
- Making available treatment, healthcare, education, and job training programs to children in juvenile justice systems.
- Expanding grant programs through the U.S. Office of Juvenile Justice and Delinquency Prevention and conditioning such grants on providing appropriate services to juvenile offenders....
- Ensuring that each child receives a comprehensive assessment to determine needs...

Source: "Report Indicts Juvenile Justice System for Lack of Treatment: CASA Calls for Overhaul of State Systems" in *Alcoholism & Drug Abuse Weekly* 16, no. 40, October 18, 2004, p. 1. Copyright © 2004 Wiley Periodicals, Inc., A Wiley Company.

12-8   Juveniles in Corrections

The placement of juveniles in closed institutions is a relatively new practice. In the 1700s and early 1800s, it was thought that the family, the church, and other social institutions should handle juvenile delinquents. Jail was the only form of incarceration, and it was used primarily for detention pending trial. From 1790 to 1830, the traditional forms of social control began to break down as mobility and town sizes increased. Belief in sin as the cause of delinquency was replaced by a belief in community disorganization. A method was needed whereby juveniles could be put back into orderly lives. It was decided that the institution—the house of refuge, the well-ordered asylum patterned after the family structure—was the answer.

The institutional model was used for juveniles, adult criminals, elderly persons, the mentally ill, orphans, unwed mothers, and vagrants. It was thought that by institutionalizing these persons their lives could become ordered as they were removed from the corruption of society. Life in the total institution was characterized by routine, head counts, and bells signaling the beginning and end of activities.[80]

By the 1850s, many people were admitting that custody was all the institutions offered. Problems such as overcrowding, lack of adequate staff, and heterogeneous populations led to the realization that institutionalization was not accomplishing its goal. The next concept for juveniles was the **training school**, typically built around a cottage system. It was thought that cottage parents would create a homelike atmosphere. Hard work, especially farmwork, was emphasized.

In recent years, overcrowding, shortage of staff, and a lack of resources, along with due process violations, have characterized juvenile corrections. The first nationwide investigation of juvenile institutions, published in 1993, disclosed that 75 percent of

Training school   A secure corrections facility to which juveniles are confined by court order.

juveniles were housed in institutions that violated at least one standard relating to living space. Forty-seven percent lived in overcrowded institutions, up from 36 percent in 1987. Overcrowding was described as a "pervasive and serious problem across the nation."[81]

The study, mandated by Congress in 1988, found that only 27 percent of juvenile facilities met security standards. Only 25 percent of juveniles were in facilities that met standards for controlling suicidal behavior, and 11,000 youths committed more than 17,000 suicidal acts in a year, although only 10 were completed in 1990. The study disclosed that between 1987 and 1991 the proportion of confined juveniles who were minorities increased from 53 percent to 63 percent, with Hispanics increasing from 13 percent to 17 percent and African Americans from 37 percent to 44 percent.[82] The results of this congressionally mandated study led then-U.S. Attorney General Janet Reno to declare, "This study puts an exclamation point on the obvious conclusion that America must take better care of its children before they get into trouble and not abandon them once they are in trouble."[83]

In 1999, the results of the first Census of Juveniles in Residential Placement (CJRP) was published. This census provided the most detailed information available on juveniles in corrections. According to the CJRP, on 29 October 1997, 106,000 juveniles were being held in juvenile residential placement facilities. Most (95 percent) had been committed by juvenile courts, with the remaining 5 percent there on orders from adult criminal courts. Twenty-six percent of the juveniles were being detained awaiting adjudication, disposition, or placement. Twenty-five percent of all juveniles in residential facilities had been charged with violent offenses, and seven of ten of those were minorities. Custody rates for African American juveniles were substantially higher than rates for other groups. Female juveniles represented only a small proportion of the juveniles in residential facilities (1 in 17), and they tended to be younger than male juveniles.[84]

Later studies of juvenile facilities also reported findings of overcrowded facilities. In a 2002 publication, the Office of Juvenile Justice and Delinquency Prevention (OJJDP) stated that approximately 40 percent of the juvenile facilities in its study were overcrowded. The OJJDP concluded that while its census "cannot establish a causal relationship, these crowded facilities were more likely than other facilities to report that they had transported youth to an emergency room in the last month because of injuries resulting from a conflict with another resident or individual."[85]

In its 2006 report, the OJJDP reported that although some juvenile facilities were still overcrowded, there had been some improvement; that most juveniles were being held in facilities that screened for mental health needs; and that "between 1997 and 2004, while prison populations grew, the number of prisoners under age 18 fell 54 percent."[86]

12-8a   Types of Institutions for Juveniles

Despite the movement toward diverting juveniles from closed institutions, today most juveniles who are under the care and custody of the state are confined in public institutions or in traditional training schools. Detention centers and shelters are used to confine those who have been referred to juvenile courts and are awaiting disposition by those courts. These facilities are used for detaining juveniles who cannot be confined in their own homes. A child who is to be placed in a correctional institution may be held temporarily in a reception or diagnostic center, pending a decision concerning which institution would be the best placement for the child. Our primary concern in this section is with the facilities in which the juveniles are placed for their more lengthy confinement, and those are of three basic types: training schools, boot camps, and group homes.

Generally, the *training school*, which houses most confined juveniles, is the largest of the facilities. It was the first type of facility that was widely accepted for the confinement of juveniles, and it is the most secure. Some jurisdictions operate other types of facilities that are less secure, such as ranches, forestry camps, or farms. Most of these facilities are located in rural areas and permit greater contact with the community than the training school provides.

Boot camps, discussed in greater detail in Chapter 9, are also used to incarcerate juveniles. In the boot camp atmosphere, the offender must participate in a strongly regimented daily routine of physical exercise, work, and discipline, which resembles military training. Many of the programs include rehabilitative measures, such as drug treatment and educational programs, but this method of incarcerating offenders has its critics, and some programs have been abolished.

The least physically secure facilities are *group homes*. Unlike *foster homes*, which are community-based facilities in which juveniles live with families, many group homes are small institutions. Most are operated by a staff, not a family. The cost per juvenile resident is twice as high for staff-operated group homes as for foster care. Group homes may be a poor substitute for foster care homes because they remove the positive influence of the family atmosphere.

The staff of many juvenile institutions attempt to make the facilities as homelike as possible. A campuslike environment or cottage setting, with a small number of juveniles housed in each building along with cottage or house parents, is typical. Despite these efforts, the architecture of many juvenile facilities reflects the premise that all who are confined there must face the same type of security as those few who need the more secure environment. Security is very important, but the facilities should not preclude opportunities for rehabilitation.

Institutions for detaining juveniles have come under criticism. After complaints about how incarcerated juveniles were being treated in Georgia, the Civil Rights Division of the U.S. Department of Justice (DOJ) began investigating some of the institutions that house juveniles. In 2003, the DOJ cited abuses in the Mississippi correctional system, charging the system with violating the constitutional rights of juveniles and failing to provide general and special education services at two institutions: the Oakley Training School (which confines serious male offenders) and the Columbia Training School in Clarion (which confines both female and male juveniles). Among the findings were the following:

- The schools violated the juveniles' First Amendment rights by forcing them to engage in religious activities.
- The juveniles were subjected to unsafe living conditions and received inadequate treatment and care.
- Disciplinary practices included pole-shackling, the improper use and overuse of restraints and isolation, pepper spray and staff assaults on juveniles.[87]

The report documented the following specific abuse cases:

- "A 13-year-old boy under suicide watch at Columbia was hog-tied face down with his hands and feet shackled together.
- Suicidal girls at Columbia were forced to undress and then were placed naked in a dark room for three days to a week, with only a hole in the floor as a bathroom.
- A girl at Columbia was sprayed with pepper spray for yelling at an employee during an exercise drill.
- Several girls at Columbia were forced to eat their own vomit if they threw up during an exercise."[88]

In February 2006, the DOJ announced that it had reached agreements with juvenile systems in several states, including Indiana and Hawaii. In Indiana, the agreement filed in court requires officials to implement programs to provide juveniles with mental health care and special education and to ensure that inmates are safe and secure. The DOJ spent 18 months investigating two facilities: Logansport Juvenile Intake/Diagnostic Facility and the South Bend Juvenile Correctional Facility. They found numerous civil rights violations; all must be corrected. The assistant attorney general for the Civil Rights Division of DOJ stated, "Juveniles in the care of the state have a right to be safe. They also have a right to adequate services to promote their rehabilitation."[89]

Similar problems and requirements resulted from the DOJ's investigation of the Hawaii Youth Correctional Facility in Kailua. According to a DOJ attorney, "When a state places juveniles under its care, the state must protect those juveniles from harm."[90]

12-8b   Treatment and Juvenile Corrections

Originally, special facilities were established to isolate juveniles from the harmful effects of society and from incarcerated adults. Later, with the development of juvenile courts, the treatment philosophy prevailed. During the past century, however, various commissions have pointed out the failure of juvenile corrections to provide adequate services and programs to enable the successful implementation of a treatment philosophy. In more recent years, courts have entered the picture, requiring some elements of due process in the adjudication of juveniles, changes in the disciplinary handling of institutionalized juveniles, and changes in the degree and kinds of services provided in those institutions.

The assignment of juveniles to special facilities for the purpose of treatment after they have been through proceedings that do not involve all elements of due process raises the critical issue of whether juveniles have a constitutional right to treatment. Recall that the original reason for not infusing the juvenile court with due process requirements was that, unlike adult offenders, juveniles were not being punished. They were being treated; juvenile court judges acted in the best interests of the children. Thus, juveniles did not need due process requirements to protect them from governmental action.

The U.S. Supreme Court has discredited the practice of using the philosophy of rehabilitation to deny juveniles their basic constitutional rights, and it has acknowledged that rehabilitation has failed. However, the Supreme Court has also articulated its support for the retention of at least part of the *parens patriae* philosophy in juvenile proceedings while applying some but not all due process requirements. This has had a somewhat confusing result.

Scholars and many courts have taken the position that, under the doctrine of *parens patriae*, juveniles have given up some of their constitutional rights in order to be processed through a system that is based on treatment rather than punishment. Therefore, the state must provide that treatment or relinquish custody of the child. A juvenile's right to treatment is based on cases involving the legal rights of the confined mentally ill.

The U.S. Supreme Court has not decided a case on the constitutional right to treatment for juveniles, although in *O'Connor v. Donaldson*, a case involving confinement of the mentally ill, the opinion of the Court *implied* that the justices might not hold that juveniles have a constitutional right to treatment.[91] However, recall the discussions in the previous section, regarding DOJ requirements concerning mental health treatment and special education in Indiana and Hawaii juvenile facilities. States may provide treatment for juveniles even though the U.S. Supreme Court has not ruled that juveniles have a *constitutional right* to treatment. States may also be required to provide treatment programs in order to meet DOJ standards.

Some lower courts have ruled that specific constitutional rights of adults must be extended to incarcerated juveniles. For example, the Sixth Circuit Court of Appeals has held that the right to counsel applies to incarcerated juveniles when they raise claims involving other constitutional rights as well as for civil rights actions that relate to their incarceration. If the juveniles cannot afford counsel, the state must provide it for them in these cases. The issue arose in a class action suit in Tennessee and involved incarcerated youths who claimed that they were being denied access to courts.[92]

There is little question, however, that some forms of treatment should be provided for juveniles. Like adults, juveniles are entitled to reasonable medical care, and some medical problems might be even more critical for them than for adults. For example, the U.S. Centers for Disease Control and Prevention (CDC) state that juveniles are at a particularly high risk for contracting viral hepatitis. Incarcerated juveniles are more likely than their nonincarcerated counterparts to practice unsafe sex and to use injection drugs, both of which are highly associated with the spread of hepatitis. Since most juveniles are released from incarceration and from 50 to 75 percent of them will at some time be incarcerated in an adult facility, they have maximum opportunities to spread the disease to others.[93]

Juvenile offenders also have a higher rate of mental and emotional problems than their nonincarcerated counterparts. Yet, most do not receive adequate treatment (if at all) while they are confined. A representative of the U.S. Department of Education has alleged that the juvenile justice system "has largely become a warehouse for children suffering from mental illness....Somewhere between 50 and 75 percent of incarcerated young offenders are estimated to have a diagnosable mental health disorder, yet the U.S. juvenile justice system is unprepared to adequately identify or treat them."[94] But again, as discussed earlier, the DOJ has recently required that Indiana and Hawaii provide mental health treatment in their juvenile facilities.

12-8c   Juveniles in the Community

Juveniles may be released from institutions and placed on parole, usually called **aftercare**. Historically, juveniles have had no right to early release, but most do not remain in confinement for long periods of time. Usually, they are released to aftercare, but if they violate the terms of that release, they may be returned to confinement. Many of the rules that the U.S. Supreme Court has applied to adult parole and probation revocation have been applied to juveniles.

The type of aftercare of juveniles is important. Aftercare should begin with a prerelease program while the juvenile is in confinement. There are two kinds of prerelease programs in juvenile institutions. In the first type, juveniles may be given furloughs or weekend passes to visit their families, a practice that permits gradual reentry into society. In the second type, juveniles may be moved to special cottages within the institution, where they live for a period of time with other inmates who are almost ready to be released and where special programs are provided to prepare them for that release. The length of the aftercare period depends on the needs of each juvenile.

Another procedure for keeping the juvenile in the community is probation. Recall that probation is the most frequently used sanction for adults; the same is true for juveniles. And the same issues are raised. As with adults, the key issue with juveniles is whether serious offenders may be placed in the community without causing unreasonable harm to others. There is some evidence that intensive probation supervision (IPS) of serious juvenile offenders is an effective alternative to incarceration but that the cost-effectiveness of IPS is difficult to achieve without the widespread use of diversion.[95]

Another type of community care of juveniles is called *respite care*. Respite care programs, which exist in various jurisdictions throughout the country, are designed for runaways and their families. Under respite care, the children are given a break from their families and vice versa. A report on these programs states that some families actually lock their children out, practically begging the county or the state to take charge of children they have found to be incorrigible. Many of these children are not a threat to society, but they need a place to stay while problems with their families can, hopefully, be worked out. Respite care gives juvenile court judges an option other than the potentially detrimental detention centers and jails. These programs provide a cooling-off period, followed by counseling for all involved parties. The goal is to reunite the child with his or her family as quickly as possible.[96]

Finally, several juvenile justice systems have developed aftercare programs that focus on the juvenile as soon as he or she is sentenced and continue through incarceration and the return of the juvenile to the community. The Intensive Aftercare Programs

Aftercare The continued supervision of juveniles after they are released from a correctional facility. Similar to the term *parole* in adult criminal court systems.

(IAP) are sponsored by grants from the DOJ's Office of Juvenile Justice and Delinquency Prevention (OJJDP). The model programs are in Denver, Colorado; Las Vegas, Nevada; and Norfolk, Virginia. The central component of the IAP is an "overarching case management system," which begins with risk-assessment and classification programs designed to target the juveniles who are most likely to commit additional delinquent or criminal acts. The programs are individualized to each participant, considering family and school problems the participant faces, drug abuse, and other issues. Random urinalysis and electronic monitoring of juveniles after their release from institutions is important in the maintenance of close supervision and control. Other features are a graduated set of sanctions for those who need to be punished and a reward system for those who show progress in their treatment plans. The goal of the current research on these model programs is to determine "whether a well-conceived and strongly implemented IPA model will have the desired effect of reducing recidivism and recommitments among high-risk parolees."[97]

12-8d   The Effect of Institutionalization on Juveniles

The National Advisory Commission on Criminal Justice Standards and Goals advocated that, when possible, juvenile delinquents should be diverted from institutionalization. The commission concluded as follows:

> The failure of major juvenile and youth institutions to reduce crime is incontestable. Recidivism rates, imprecise as they may be, are notoriously high. The younger the person when entering an institution, the longer he is institutionalized, and the farther he progresses into the criminal justice system, the greater his chance of failure.[98]

The advisory commission emphasized that these institutions are places of punishment, and they do not have a significant effect on deterrence. They remove juveniles from society temporarily. In that sense, society is protected, but the changes in the offender during that incarceration are negative, not positive. The institutions are isolated geographically, which hinders delivery of services from outside the institution, decreases visits from families and friends, reduces opportunities for home furloughs, and limits the availability of staff. Many of these institutions have outlasted their functions. Because of their architecture, the institutions are inflexible at a time when flexibility is needed. They were built to house too many people for maximum treatment success. The large numbers have resulted in an excessive emphasis on security and control. The advisory commission maintained that these institutions are dehumanizing and that they create an unhealthy need for dependence.

According to the advisory commission, the traditional juvenile correctional institution must change. It should not continue to warehouse failures and release them back into society without improvement. It must share a major responsibility for the successful reintegration of those juveniles into society; however, as institutions change their goals, the public must be involved in the planning, goals, and the programs, as well as in the efforts toward reintegration into the community. Most important, the public must give full acceptance to these institutional and community programs for juveniles. The advisory commission concluded its discussion of juvenile corrections by saying, "It is no surprise that institutions have not been successful in reducing crime. The mystery is that they have not contributed even more to increasing crime."[99]

12-8e   Deinstitutionalization

Dissatisfaction with closed institutions has led to several movements. One is diversion. Another is community corrections. A third movement, related to diversion and community corrections, is deinstitutionalization. This movement began with an emphasis on probation, foster homes, and community treatment centers for juveniles. The establishment of the California Youth Authority in the early 1960s and the closing of juvenile institutions in Massachusetts in 1970 and 1971 gave impetus to the movement.

What caused this movement toward deinstitutionalization for juveniles? Some say it started in the early 1960s, when the government began granting money to localities to improve conditions in the processing and treatment of delinquency. Others say it emerged when social scientists began to assume the role of clinicians and became involved in policy decision making at local and federal levels. Still others point to the interest of lawyers in the 1960s and 1970s in reforming juvenile courts. Some scholars take the position that the movement came primarily from a desire to save the costs of constructing new facilities and repairing existing ones.

Whatever the reasons, it is clear that this movement is unlike most others in the field. It involves a major change: abandoning the large institution and replacing it with a different concept of corrections. The era of the large institution may be over, with some jurisdictions abolishing them. An example is that of Massachusetts.

In 1969, Jerome G. Miller took charge of the Department of Youth Services in Massachusetts. At first, he attempted to reform the system; however, "after fifteen months of bureaucratic blockades, open warfare with state legislators, and sabotage by entrenched employees, Miller abandoned reform and elected revolution."[100] Between 1969 and 1973, Miller closed the state's juvenile institutions, placing juveniles in community-based facilities.

A team of social scientists from Harvard University evaluated The Massachusetts experiment with deinstitutionalization. In the early stages of evaluation, the researchers guardedly concluded that the experiment was a success. In 1977, the tentative conclusions were questioned. The recidivism rates of the youth had not increased or decreased; therefore, it might be concluded that deinstitutionalization, though no better, was no worse than institutionalization and was certainly more humane. However, the evaluators reported a crisis in the reaction of the public, the courts, and the police.[101]

Empirical studies of the Massachusetts system conducted in the 1980s to determine the success of deinstitutionalization were contradictory, but in 1998, a researcher who looked at the Massachusetts situation concluded,

> Twenty-five years later, the fight remains a good one, and the cause remains just. Our strategies did not go far enough, but they went farther than anyone thought. Their failure was largely not a failure of will but rather a failure of our own political naiveté, the general community's faith in its own compassion, and everyone's readiness to assume responsibility for our young people. Let us hope we have learned these lessons well.[102]

In evaluating deinstitutionalization, we must raise the issue of whether the negative effects of institutionalization, at least to some extent, will crop up in community treatment centers or other forms of handling juveniles as well. In responding to the argument that large juvenile institutions should be abolished because they are schools for crime, one researcher points out that in many cases those large institutions are confining juveniles who previously were in the smaller institutions. Thus, the smaller institutions must take responsibility for part of the failure of the correctional system to rehabilitate juveniles. Furthermore, replacing the large institutions with smaller facilities "may not really change the amount of teaching and learning that takes place among offenders."[103] If juveniles who already have a strong orientation toward crime are confined together, they may continue to infect and teach each other.

12-9 Juveniles and Capital Punishment

According to the Death Penalty Information Center, as of December 2004, there were 71 persons (all men) on death row in 12 states for murders they committed when they were ages 16 (19 percent of the 71) or 17 (81 percent), out of a total death row population of 3,471 (as of 1 October 2004). Texas had the largest number, with 40 percent of the total of juveniles on death row. Two-thirds of the men who were juveniles when they committed the murders for which they are on death row were persons of color; over two-thirds of their victims were white; over one-half of the victims were female;

81 percent were adults. As noted later in this section, it is no longer permissible to execute these persons, but between 1976 and 2005, when the U.S. Supreme Court upheld executing persons for crimes committed when the persons were juveniles, 22 persons in that category were executed.[104] A review of cases leading up to the 2005 decision is important for historical purposes.

The 1986 execution of James Terry Roach, then 25 but executed for a crime he committed when he was 16, raised the issue of whether capital punishment should be imposed on juveniles. In an earlier case, Monty Lee Eddings, who was 15 when he murdered an Oklahoma highway patrol officer who stopped him for a traffic violation, was successful in the appeal of his death sentence to the U.S. Supreme Court. Eddings's attorney argued that capital punishment for a crime committed while the offender was a juvenile constituted cruel and unusual punishment. The Supreme Court did not decide that issue but sent the case back for resentencing on the grounds that at the sentencing hearing the lower court did not consider mitigating circumstances. The trial court considered the mitigating circumstances and resentenced Eddings to death. Before his case reached the U.S. Supreme Court a second time, however, Oklahoma's Court of Criminal Appeals changed the sentence from death to life imprisonment.[105]

In 1985, the U.S. Supreme Court upheld the death sentence of a defendant who was 18 at the time he committed his atrocious capital crime.[106] But in 1988, the Supreme Court decided *Thompson v. Oklahoma*, in which it reversed the capital sentence of William Wayne Thompson, who was 15 when he committed the crime for which he was given the death penalty. In *Thompson*, a majority of the Supreme Court agreed that the execution of an individual who was 15 at the time he committed a capital crime is cruel and unusual punishment even though the crime was heinous. In deciding the issue, the Supreme Court used the standard established in *Trop v. Dulles*, decided in 1958. The standard is "the evolving standards of decency that mark the progress of a maturing society."[107]

The U.S. Supreme Court's decision in *Thompson* banned capital punishment for youths who are under 16 when they commit a capital offense; however, it did not answer the question of whether capital punishment is cruel and unusual when imposed on youths between the ages of 16 and 18 at the time the capital murder is committed. The Supreme Court made this very clear in its opinion, noting that it had been asked to declare capital punishment unconstitutional for all youths under age 18:

> Our task today, however, is to decide the case before us; we do so by concluding that the Eighth and Fourteenth Amendments prohibit the execution of a person who was under sixteen years of age at the time of his or her offense.[108]

In 1989, the U.S. Supreme Court decided the cases of two other death row inmates who had committed murders while they were juveniles. One was approximately 17 years and 4 months old when he raped and sodomized a 20-year-old woman repeatedly, before he killed her with a bullet in the front and another in the back of her head. The second juvenile was 16 years and 6 months of age when he killed a 26-year-old mother of two by multiple stab wounds in her chest. The U.S. Supreme Court held that capital punishment for these youths did not constitute cruel and unusual punishment.[109]

In June 2002, the U.S. Supreme Court held that a national consensus had emerged that executing mentally retarded persons constitutes cruel and unusual punishment. Some legal scholars thought the reasoning might be extended to executing persons who committed murders when they were 16 or 17 years old. The U.S. Supreme Court declined to make that extension, as demonstrated by its refusal in October 2002 to review the case of Kevin Stanford, who has been on Kentucky's death row since 1982 for raping and murdering a 20-year-old gas station attendant when Stanford was 17. Stanford argued that there is an emerging consensus that juveniles under 18 should not be executed. When the U.S. Supreme Court refused to review Stanford's case, the dissenting justices issued an opinion, stating that, "The practice of executing such offenders is a relic of the past and is inconsistent with evolving

| *Spotlight 12-4* | **Capital Punishment for Crimes Committed as a Juvenile** |

During its 2004–2005 term, the U.S. Supreme Court decided the case of Christopher Simmons, 27, who was 17 when he committed murder. In 1993, Simmons solicited friends to assist him in committing a robbery, tying up the victim, and throwing her off a bridge. He boasted that they would get away with the crime because they were juveniles. One of his friends (age 15 and thus not eligible for the death penalty) agreed. The two broke into the home of Shirley Crook to commit burglary. Crook was home and recognized Simmons from an automobile accident in which both had been involved. Crook, age 46 and scantily clad, was bound, gagged, and her arms were taped behind her back. She was driven around in a minivan and, when she tried to escape, beaten before she was pushed off a railroad trestle, still conscious. Her body was later found in the river by fishermen.

Simmons was convicted of murder and sentenced to death. The Missouri Supreme Court initially upheld the conviction and the sentence but subsequently held that imposing the death penalty on a person who was 17 when the murder was committed constitutes cruel and unusual punishment. The court imposed a life sentence. The state of Missouri asked the U.S. Supreme Court to reverse. Eight states and numerous individuals, including former U.S. president Jimmy Carter and Soviet president Mikhail S. Gorbachev, along with organizations such as the American Bar Association and the American Medical Association (arguing that the brains of 16- and 17-year-olds are not fully developed in the areas that regulate decision making) and over 30 religious organizations, filed briefs with the U.S. Supreme Court, asking the Court to declare that executing a person for a murder committed as a juvenile is unconstitutional.[1]

The U.S. Supreme Court decided *Roper v. Simmons* in March 2005, holding that the execution of persons who committed their capital crimes when they were 16 or 17 is unconstitutional. Portions of the opinion follows:[2]

> The State sought the death penalty. As aggravating factors, the State submitted that the murder was committed for the purpose of receiving money; was committed for the purpose of avoiding, interfering with,

or preventing lawful arrest of the defendant; and involved depravity of mind and was outrageously and wantonly vile, horrible, and inhuman. The State called Shirley Crook's husband, daughter, and two sisters, who presented moving evidence of the devastation her death had brought to their lives.

> In mitigation Simmons' attorneys first called an officer of the Missouri juvenile justice system, who testified that Simmons had no prior convictions and that no previous charges had been filed against him. Simmons' mother, father, two younger half brothers, a neighbor, and a friend took the stand to tell the jurors of the close relationships they had formed with Simmons and to plead for mercy on his behalf. Simmons' mother, in particular, testified to the responsibility Simmons demonstrated in taking care of his two younger half brothers and of his grandmother and to his capacity to show love for them.

> During closing arguments, both the prosecutor and defense counsel addressed Simmons' age, which the trial judge had instructed the jurors they could consider as a mitigating factor. Defense counsel reminded the jurors that juveniles of Simmons' age cannot drink, serve on juries, or even see certain movies, because "the legislatures have wisely decided that individuals of a certain age aren't responsible enough."

> Defense counsel argued that Simmons' age should make "a huge difference to [the jurors] in deciding just exactly what sort of punishment to make."

> The jury recommended the death penalty after finding the State had proved each of the three aggravating factors submitted to it. Accepting the jury's recommendation, the trial judge imposed the death penalty....

> The prohibition against "cruel and unusual punishments," like other expansive language in the Constitution, must be interpreted according to its text, by considering history, tradition, and precedent, and with due regard for its purpose and function in the constitutional design. To implement this framework we have established the propriety and affirmed the necessity of referring to "the evolving standards of decency that mark the progress of a maturing society" to determine

standards of decency in a civilized society. We should put an end to this shameful practice." The dissent noted that since its 1989 decision five states had banned the execution of juveniles under age 18.[110]

In August 2002, when the U.S. Supreme Court declined to stay the execution of Toronto M. Patterson, who was 17 when he committed murder, three justices urged their colleagues to reconsider their decision regarding the execution of offenders who were 16 or 17 when they committed capital murder. Patterson was executed.[111]

In January 2003, the U.S. Supreme Court rejected the appeal of Scott A. Hain, 32, an Oklahoma death row inmate who committed murder when he was 17. Hain was executed in April 2003.[112] In October 2003, the U.S. Supreme Court refused to review the case of Nanon McKewn Williams, a Texas inmate who was on death row which punishments are so disproportionate as to be cruel and unusual....

[The Supreme Court reviewed its precedent cases involving capital punishment of juveniles, along with those involving executing the mentally challenged. The Court then distinguished between the maturity levels of adults and juveniles and continued]

Three general differences between juveniles under 18 and adults demonstrate that juvenile offenders cannot with reliability be classified among the worst offenders. First, as any parent knows and as the scientific and sociological studies respondent and his *amici* (friends of the court briefs) cite tend to confirm, "[a] lack of maturity and an underdeveloped sense of responsibility are found in youth more often than in adults and are more understandable among the young. These qualities often result in impetuous and ill-considered actions and decisions."...

It has been noted that "adolescents are overrepresented statistically in virtually every category of reckless behavior." In recognition of the comparative immaturity and irresponsibility of juveniles, almost every State prohibits those under 18 years of age from voting, serving on juries, or marrying without parental consent.

The second area of difference is that juveniles are more vulnerable or susceptible to negative influences and outside pressures, including peer pressure. This is explained in part by the prevailing circumstance that juveniles have less control, or less experience with control, over their own environment.

The third broad difference is that the character of a juvenile is not as well formed as that of an adult. The personality traits of juveniles are more transitory, less fixed.

These differences render suspect any conclusion that a juvenile falls among the worst offenders. The susceptibility of juveniles to immature and irresponsible behavior means "their irresponsible conduct is not as morally reprehensible as that of an adult." Their own vulnerability and comparative lack of control over their immediate surroundings mean juveniles have a greater claim than adults to be forgiven for failing to escape negative influences in their whole environment. The

reality that juveniles still struggle to define their identity means it is less supportable to conclude that even a heinous crime committed by a juvenile is evidence of irretrievably depraved character. From a moral standpoint it would be misguided to equate the failings of a minor with those of an adult, for a greater possibility exists that a minor's character deficiencies will be reformed....

Our determination that the death penalty is disproportionate punishment for offenders under 18 finds confirmation in the stark reality that the United States is the only country in the world that continues to give official sanction to the juvenile death penalty....

Over time, from one generation to the next, the Constitution has come to earn the high respect and even the veneration of the American people. The document sets forth, and rests upon, innovative principles original to the American experience, such as federalism; a proven balance in political mechanisms through separation of powers; specific guarantees for the accused in criminal cases; and broad provisions to secure individual freedom and preserve human dignity. These doctrines and guarantees are central to the American experience and remain essential to our present-day self-definition and national identity. Not the least of the reasons we honor the Constitution, then, is because we know it to be our own. It does not lessen our fidelity to the Constitution or our pride in its origins to acknowledge that the express affirmation of certain fundamental rights by other nations and peoples simply underscores the centrality of those same rights within our own heritage of freedom.

The Eighth and Fourteenth Amendments forbid imposition of the death penalty on offenders who were under the age of 18 when their crimes were committed. The judgment of the Missouri Supreme Court setting aside the sentence of death imposed upon Christopher Simmons is affirmed.

It is so ordered.

1. "Dozens of Nations Weigh in on Death Penalty Case," *New York Times* (20 July 2004), p. 1.
2. Roper v. Simmons, 543 U.S. 551 (2005).

for a murder he committed when he was 17. Williams's attorney said that, had the case been reviewed, he had planned to argue by analogy to the Supreme Court's 2002 decision that capital punishment is unconstitutional in the case of the mentally retarded.[113]

In October 2004, the U.S. Supreme Court heard the case of Christopher Simmons, 27, who killed at age 17. The state of Missouri had overturned his death sentence in the summer of 2003. Despite the Court's decision to hear the case of *Roper v. Simmons*, Texas scheduled (between March and June 2004) the executions of four persons who were juveniles when they committed capital murder.[114] Subsequently, the state agreed to stay those executions pending the U.S. Supreme Court's decision. The facts and the holding of the *Simmons* case are featured in Spotlight 12-4.

12-10   Juvenile and Adult Criminal Justice Systems: An Assessment

She appeared to be a perfect candidate for Harvard University, which granted her early admission for the fall class of 1995. Gina Grant, an orphan, had top grades in a highly rated high school, an IQ of 150, excellent references, and a high score on entrance exams. She was co-captain of the tennis team and tutored underprivileged kids. However, after a published article about her and other orphans, an anonymous source sent Harvard information about her previous life in South Carolina. When she was 14, Grant entered a plea of no contest to manslaughter in the death of her mother, whose skull was smashed by at least 13 blows from a candlestick. Harvard revoked her early admission letter after notification of her act.

The case of Gina Grant is an excellent one to note in closing this text's study of adult criminal and juvenile justice systems. Although she was accused of a violent crime, Grant was processed through the juvenile justice system. She was given only a short term of incarceration and placed on probation. Her records were sealed, and she was given a chance at rehabilitation. Many argued that she was successful. She had served her time and deserved a chance for a new life; that is the purpose of the juvenile system.

Others argued that the case illustrated that juveniles are becoming more violent and that juvenile justice systems are soft on crime. They said that Grant should have been processed through the adult criminal justice system and sentenced to a long term, and that Harvard officials acted appropriately in revoking their admissions offer.

Grant's case and others like it focus on many of the issues facing justice systems today. Should we continue to preserve juvenile justice systems or should all serious crimes be processed through adult criminal justice systems? If we retain juvenile systems, how closely should they mirror criminal systems in structure and in procedure? Most important, will crime rates be affected by changing the current systems?

We began the chapter with a reference to the 2000 presidential address at the annual meeting of the Academy of Criminal Justice Sciences. President Alida V. Merlo focused her address on juvenile justice, which she described as being at a crossroads between the "get-tough" punitive legislative approaches and the recent reductions in juvenile violence and the apparent softening of public attitudes toward juveniles. In her summary Merlo stated the following:

> We can either continue to move toward more punitive juvenile justice policies, greater intolerance for adolescents, growing racism, more costly and more inhumane policies, and an ever-widening gulf between poor children and the rest of us, or we can blaze a new path. As teachers, scholars, researchers, students, and practitioners, we have the opportunity to infuse the system with a new kind of thinking—thinking that is informed by research, by the evaluation of programs, and by an understanding of the complex societal conditions that cannot be eliminated without substantial long-term investments.[115]

Chapter Wrap-Up

Juvenile justice systems held the highest hopes for success in rehabilitation, reformation, and reintegration, but they contained some of the greatest deprivations of constitutional rights. In the name of "the best interests of the child," the state took away liberty without due process of law. Under the guise of treatment and rehabilitation, not punishment, juvenile court systems swept into their clutches many who otherwise would not have been processed by court systems.

There is a need to treat juveniles differently than adults. There is a need to segregate them from adults in confinement. There is a need to offer them opportunities for improvement so that they can succeed in a competitive world. Those needs may not be met by violating their rights.

After an overview of juvenile justice systems, this chapter looked at the current data on juveniles as offenders and as victims. In particular, it considered violent acts by and against juveniles before looking closely at the impact of youth gangs on our society. Efforts to combat gang crimes were noted, with a special look at Los Angeles.

The constitutional rights of juveniles were considered in some detail, with the chapter focusing first on the critical U.S. Supreme Court cases and looking in particular at the right to counsel (noting that it is often not effective counsel). Juvenile curfews were explored, followed by legal issues concerning race and gender.

The chapter then turned to an analysis of the juvenile court, beginning with a look at court procedures. The discussion showed that, although not all procedural requirements of criminal courts have been applied to juveniles, many due process rights have been extended to them in juvenile courts. No longer is it sufficient to say that juveniles are not arrested; they are apprehended. They are not found guilty; they are adjudicated. They are not sentenced, but dispositions are made of their cases. The change in wording does not compensate for a lack of due process. In many respects, present-day adult criminal and juvenile court systems are similar, but states have some room to experiment in their juvenile systems. For example, trial by jury is not required by the U.S. Constitution but has been extended by statute to juvenile courts in some states.

Violent crimes appear to be committed by a few juveniles, but those violent few are responsible for a large percentage of the total crimes that juveniles commit. Concern with this violence and with recidivism has led some states to pass statutes giving criminal courts jurisdiction over juveniles who commit serious crimes. In other states, after a proper hearing, juvenile courts may waive jurisdiction over juveniles who have committed serious crimes.

All reforms have problems, and one problem with the "get-tough" laws concerning juveniles has been the unwillingness of courts and juries to convict if they know there will be an automatic penalty that they consider too severe. Thus, in some cases, the "get-tough" policy results in less, not more, protection for the community. It is important to evaluate changes carefully for that reason. Insufficient attention has been given to evaluating legislative changes in juvenile systems.

Two major areas discussed earlier in the text with regard to adult criminal courts were also explored in this chapter as they relate to juveniles. The application of Megan's Laws concerning the registration of released sex offenders and the use of drug courts were noted.

The next major focus of the chapter was on juveniles in corrections. Juveniles have received differential treatment in corrections, too, although it is not at all clear that those differences are positive. Indefinite detention of juveniles under the guise that they are being treated when they are being detained without treatment has been held by courts to be inappropriate. Unfortunately, disillusionment with treatment and rehabilitation in many jurisdictions has resulted in a decreased emphasis on treatment, even in the case of juveniles. At the other extreme has been the position that institutionalization is bad for juveniles and therefore should be abandoned, with juveniles being cared for in community treatment facilities.

The execution of juveniles is one of the most controversial areas in juvenile court systems. This chapter noted the recent changes in the legal aspects of executing juveniles, including an excerpt from the U.S. Supreme Court's analysis of the issue.

In conclusion, some scholars are questioning the wisdom and efficiency of retaining juvenile court systems if most of the procedures of adult court systems become a part of juvenile systems. Others note the unfairness of a system that is moving toward criminal court sentences without all of the elements of due process provided in those courts. One law professor stated the issue as follows:

> As juvenile courts' sentencing practices resemble increasingly those of their criminal counterparts, does any reason remain to maintain a separate court whose sole distinguishing characteristic is its persisting procedural deficiencies?[116]

Another scholar commented that juvenile court systems are old enough that we should consider whether it is time for them to die; however, after considering carefully the pros and cons of abolishing juvenile courts, he decided that, on balance, we should keep them.[117]

It may be that the future of criminal justice is related to what we do with juvenile court systems. Certainly, this is an area to follow closely as the U.S. Supreme Court ponders and decides whether to continue the march toward greater due process and equal protection or to retract from that path to a more conservative interpretation of the U.S. Constitution.

Key Terms

adjudication (p. 370)
aftercare (p. 398)
certification (p. 389)
delinquency (p. 372)
detention (p. 370)
detention centers (p. 370)

disposition (p. 370)
diversion (p. 385)
intake decision (p. 387)
juvenile (p. 369)
juvenile court (p. 370)
juvenile delinquent (p. 369)

parens patriae (p. 369)
petition (p. 370)
status offense (p. 370)
training school (p. 394)

Apply It

1. How were juveniles treated historically?
2. What events led to the emergence of juvenile courts in the United States?

3. What are the basic ways in which juvenile courts and adult criminal courts differ?
4. Analyze current data on juveniles as offenders and as victims.

5. Briefly describe what the Supreme Court held in each of the following cases: *Kent, Gault, Winship, McKeiver, Breed, Schall,* and *R.L.C.*

6. What are the legal issues involved in juvenile curfews? What are the practical implications of curfews?

7. What are the major race and gender issues regarding juvenile offenders?

8. What is the relationship of the police to juveniles?

9. Define and discuss intake proceedings in juvenile systems.

10. Describe the role of the prosecutor and of the defense attorney in juvenile proceedings.

11. Discuss the disposition of a juvenile case and the appeal process.

12. Why are some juveniles tried in adult criminal courts, and how is this accomplished?

13. Should Megan's Laws be applied to juveniles? Why or why not? What do the courts hold?

14. Should drug courts be extended to juvenile offenders? Why or why not?

15. Why did separate institutions for juveniles develop? Are they successful? Should they be continued? What is meant by deinstitutionalization?

16. Discuss some of the recent findings about juvenile institutions.

17. What is the current legal status of the capital punishment of juveniles?

Endnotes

1. Alida V. Merlo, "Juvenile Justice at the Crossroads: Presidential Address to the Academy of Criminal Justice Sciences," *Justice Quarterly* 17, no. 4 (December 2000): 639–661; quotation is on pp. 640, 641.

2. Orman Ketcham, "The Unfulfilled Promise of the American Juvenile Courts," in *Justice for the Child*, ed. Margaret Keeney Rosenheim (New York: Free Press, 1962), p. 24.

3. See Alexander W. Pisciotta, "*Parens Patriae*, Treatment and Reform: The Case of the Western House of Refuge, 1849–1907," *New England Journal of Criminal and Civil Confinement* 10 (Winter 1984): 65–86.

4. See Anthony Platt, *The Child Savers* (Chicago: University of Chicago Press, 1969).

5. John R. Sutton, "The Juvenile Court and Social Welfare: Dynamics of Progressive Reform," *Law and Society Review* 19, no. 1 (1985): 142.

6. Federal Bureau of Investigation, *Crime in the United States: Uniform Crime Reports, 2005,* http://www.fbi.gov/ucr/05cius/data/table_41.html, and http://www.fbi.gov/ucr/05cius/arrests/index.html, accessed 12 December 2006.

7. Cal. Wel. & Inst. Code, Section 602 (2007).

8. Proposition 21, the Gang Violence and Juvenile Crime Prevention Act of 1998, Section 2(a) (2007).

9. "Student Killers' Tapes Filled with Rage," *New York Times* (14 December 1999), p. 19.

10. "Boy, 11, Gets 18 Years in the Juvenile System for Murder of 3-Year-Old," *New York Times* (13 December 2003), p. 14.

11. "California Teenager Given Life Sentence," *New York Times* (15 June 2003), p. 19.

12. Quoted in "California Law Enforcement Praises School Anti-Gang Program," *Criminal Justice Newsletter* (3 November 2003), p. 4; quotation is on p. 5.

13. Arlen Egley Jr. et al., Office of Juvenile Justice and Delinquency Prevention, *National Youth Gang Survey, 1999–2001,* http://www.ncjrs.gov, accessed 8 August 2006.

14. Arlen Egley Jr. and Christina E. Ritz, Office of Juvenile Justice and Delinquency Prevention, *Highlights of the 2004 National Youth Gang Survey,* www.ojp.usdoj.gov, accessed 8 August 2006.

15. "Most Juvenile Crime Committed by Gang Members, Study Finds," *Criminal Justice Newsletter* 28 (2 January 1997): 5.

16. "Bratton's Challenge," *New York Times* (22 June 2003), Section 4, p. 2.

17. "Cops Seek Allies: Public Called Key to Beating Gangs," *Daily News of Los Angeles* (14 November 2003), p. 1N; "Bratton Shuffles LAPD Brass: Department to Focus on Top 10 Percent," *Daily News of Los Angeles* (18 November 2003), p. 3N.

18. "The Gang Buster: Bratton Cut Crime in New York, and Now He's Doing It in L.A. His Secret: Giving Cops More Power," *Time Magazine* (19 January 2004), p. 56.

19. "Killings Drop 11% As Crime Totals Decline," *Los Angeles Times* (10 June 2006), p. 1B.

20. City of Chicago v. Morales, 527 U.S. 41 (2000).

21. "Urban Law," *American Bar Association Journal* 88, no. 54 (December 2002), n.p.

22. "Prosecutors Cite Difficulties in Prosecuting Gang Members," *Criminal Justice Newsletter* 26 (3 April 1995): 3, referring to *Prosecuting Gangs: A National Assessment* (Rockville, Md.: National Criminal Justice Reference Service).

23. Anne Campbell, "Self-Definitions by Rejection: The Case of Gang Girls," *Social Problems* 34 (December 1987): 451–466.

24. Terry Carter, "'Equality with a Vengeance': Violent Crimes and Gang Activity by Girls Skyrocket," *American Bar Association Journal* 85 (November 1999): 22. See also Karen Heimer and Stacy DeCoster, "The Gendering of Violent Delinquency," *Criminology* 37 (May 1999): 277–318.

25. "New Report Shows Gang Problems Continue to Plague Communities Nationwide," *PR Newswire US* (7 August 2006), p. 1.

26. Smith v. Daily Mail Publishing Co. 443 U.S. 97 (1979).

27. Commonwealth v. Dallenbach, 729 A.2d 1218 (Pa. Super. 1999).

28. *In re* Benjamin L., 708 N.E.2d 156 (N.Y. App. 1999).

29. Kent v. United States, 383 U.S. 541 (1966).

30. Kent v. United States, 383 U.S. 541, 554–555 (1966).

31. *In re* Gault, 387 U.S. 1 (1967).

32. *In re* Gault, 387 U.S. 1, 19–21, 26–28 (1967).

33. American Bar Association, *Maryland: An Assessment of Access to Counsel and Quality of Representation in Delinquency,* an 81-page report summarized in, "ABA Finds Right to Lawyer Is 'An Unfilled Promise,'" *Criminal Justice Newsletter* (17 November 2003), p. 2.

34. *In re* Winship, 397 U.S. 358 (1970), quoting *In re* Gault.

35. McKeiver v. Pennsylvania, 403 U.S. 528 (1971).

36. Breed v. Jones, 421 U.S. 519 (1975).

37. Schall v. Martin, 467 U.S. 253 (1984).

38. Alfredo A. v. Superior Court, 849 P.2d 1330 (Cal. 1994), *subsequent opinion on reh'g.*, 865 P.2d 56 (Cal. 1994), *cert. denied*, 513 U.S. 822 (1994).

39. United States v. R.L.C., 503 U.S. 291 (1992).

40. Yarborough v. Alvarado, 541 U.S. 652 (2004).

41. Qutb v. Strauss, 11 F.3d 488 (5th Cir. 1993), *cert. denied*, 511 U.S. 1127 (1994).

42. Schleifer v. City of Charlottesville, 159 F.3d 843 (4th Cir. 1998), *cert. denied*, 562 U.S. 1018 (1999).

43. Nunez by Nunez v. City of San Diego, 114 F.3d 935 (9th Cir. 1997).

44. Schleifer v. City of Charlottesville, 159 F.3d 843 (4th Cir. 1998), *cert. denied*, 562 U.S. 1018 (1999), case names and citations omitted. The ordinance is codified at Charlottesville, Va., Code Section 17-7.

45. David McDowall et al., "The Impact of Youth Curfew Laws on Juvenile Crime Rates," *Crime & Delinquency* 46 (January 2000): 76–92; quotation is on p. 76.

46. Cited in "Race Disparity Seen throughout Juvenile Justice System," *Criminal Justice Newsletter* 30, no. 20 (25 April 2000): 6–7.

47. Ibid.

48. "Donde Está la Justicia?" News release by Building Blocks for Youth, http://www.buildingblocksforyouth.org/latino_rpt/pr_english.html (18 July 2002), accessed 26 July 2007.

49. Carl E. Pope and Howard N. Snyder, Office of Juvenile Justice and Delinquency Prevention *Race As a Factor in Juvenile Arrests*, (Washington, D.C.: U.S. Department of Justice, April 2003), pp. 1, 6.

50. "ABA Finds Right to Lawyer Is 'An Unfulfilled Promise'," quoting *Maryland: An Assessment of Access to Counsel*, pp. 2–3.

51. Justice Policy Institute, *Reducing Disproportionate Minority Confinement: The Multnomah County, Oregon, Success Story and Its Implications*, http://www.justicepolicy.org, accessed 26 July 2006.

52. Juvenile Justice and Delinquency Prevention Act, U.S. Code, Title 42, Section 5633 (2007).

53. *Changing the Status Quo for Status Offenders: New York State's Efforts to Support Troubled Teens*, Vera Institute, http://www.vera.org, accessed 26 July 2006.

54. See Lanes v. State, 767 S.W.2d 789 (Tex.Crim.App. 1989), requiring probable cause to arrest a juvenile.

55. Schall v. Martin, 467 U.S. 253, 265 (1984). The adult preventive detention case is United States v. Salerno, 481 U.S. 739 (1987).

56. Howard N. Snyder and Melissa Sickmund, Office of Juvenile Justice and Delinquency Prevention, *Juvenile Offenders and Victims: 1999 National Report* (Washington, D.C.: U.S. Department of Justice, September 1999), p. 208. The statute is codified at U.S. Code, Title 18, Section 5031 *et seq.* (2007).

57. *Juveniles in Adult Prisons and Jails: A National Assessment*, cited in "Juveniles in Adult Prisons 'A Burgeoning Issue,' Study Finds," *Criminal Justice Newsletter* 31, no. 5 (10 January 2001): 6.

58. Paige M. Harrison and Allen J. Beck, *Prison and Jail Inmates at Midyear 2005*, Bureau of Justice Statistics (Washington,

D.C.: U.S. Department of Justice, May 2006), p. 5, http://www.ojp.usdoj.gov/bjs, accessed 15 July 2006.

59. "Donde Está la Justicia?"

60. Monroe v. Soliz, 939 P.2d 205 (Wash. 1997).

61. "Girls' Needs Addressed in Prison's Special Unit; Younger Convicts Have Their Own Dorm, Along with Special Classes and Training," *Indianapolis Star* (12 September 1999), p. 4B; Ratliff v. Cohn, 693 N.E.2d 530 (Ind. 1998).

62. For the U.S. Supreme Court's decision, see McKiever v. Pennsylvania, 403 U.S. 528 (1971). For a state example, see State v. Whatley, 320 So.2d 123 (La. 1975).

63. New York CLS Family Court Act, Section 301.2 (2006).

64. *In re A.D.G.*, 895 P.2d 1067 (Colo.Ct.App. 1994), *cert. denied sub nom.*, 1995 Colo. App. LEXIS 423 (Colo. 5 June 1995).

65. "Judges' Group Criticizes Trend toward Waiver to Adult Court," *Criminal Justice Newsletter* 25 (1 March 1994): 1.

66. Eric L. Jensen and Linda K. Mitsger, "A Test of the Deterrent Effect of Legislative Waiver on Violent Juvenile Crime," *Crime & Delinquency* 40 (January 1994): 102.

67. "Adult Court Is Stricter, but Recidivism Higher, Study Finds," *Criminal Justice Newsletter* 30 (4 January 1999): 3–4.

68. "Criminal Courts Give 10-Year Terms to Violent Juveniles, Study Finds," *Criminal Justice Newsletter* 29 (17 August 1998): 4. See also Carol J. DeFrances and Kevin Strom, Bureau of Justice Statistics, *Juveniles Prosecuted in State Criminal Courts*, March 1997, http://www.ojp.usdoj.gov/bjs, accessed 26 July 2006.

69. "Florida Leads Nation in Trying Kids as Adults," *Tallahassee Democrat* (31 August 1999), p. 1; "Juveniles in Adult Courts: Editorials," *The Ledger* (Lakeland, Fla.,) (17 December 2003), p. 12.

70. "After Conviction of Boy, Prosecutor Switches Sides," *New York Times* (18 November 2002), p. 14; Brazill v. State, 845 So.2d 282 (Fla.Dist.Ct.App. 4th Dist. 2003), *petition denied*, 876 So.2d 561 (Fla. 2004), and post conviction proceeding, remanded, 937 So. 2d 272 (Fla. Dist.Ct.App. 4th Dist. 2006).

71. "Boy Who Killed Gets 7 Years, Judge Says Law Too Harsh," *New York Times* (14 January 2000), p. 1.

72. Hughes v. State, 653 A.2d 241 (Del. 1994), *clarified, reh'g. denied*, 1995 Del. LEXIS 36 (Del. 1995).

73. *Juveniles' Competence to Stand Trial: A Comparison of Adolescents' and Adults' Capacities As Trial Defendants* (Philadelphia Pa: MacArthur Foundation Research Network on Adolescent Development and Juvenile Justice, 2003), as cited in "Many Juveniles Lack Competence for Adult Court, Study Finds," *Criminal Justice Newsletter* (18 March 2003), p. 5.

74. People v. J.W., 787 N.E.2d 747 (Ill. 2003), *cert. denied*, 540 U.S. 873 (2003).

75. "Governor Vetoes Bill on Registration Duty of Juvenile Sex Offenders," *Chicago Daily Law Bulletin* (7 July 2006): 1003. The Illinois Sex Offender Registration Act is codified at ILCS (Illinois Compiled Statutes Annotated), Chapter 730, Section 150/1 *et seq.* (2006).

76. "Juveniles: Sex Offender List—Again," *Chicago Daily Law Bulletin* (21 July 2006), n.p. The precedent case is *In re J.W.*, 204 Ill. 2d 50 (2003), *cert. denied*, 540 U.S. 873 (2003).

77. State v. C. M., 746 So.2d 410 (Ala.Crim.App. 1999).

78. National Criminal Justice Reference Service (NCJRS), *Juvenile Drug Courts: Strategies in Practice*, http://www.ncjrs.gov, accessed 26 July 2006.

79. Ibid.

80. See David J. Rothman, *The Discovery of the Asylum* (South Salem, N.Y.: Criminal Justice Institute, 1988), pp. 50, 51.

81. "Crowding of Juvenile Facilities Is 'Pervasive,' Study Finds," *Criminal Justice Newsletter* 24 (15 April 1993): 4.

82. Dale G. Parent et al., *Conditions of Confinement: Juvenile Detention and Corrections Facilities. Research Summary* (Washington, D.C.: U.S. Department of Justice, February 1994), p. 1. This publication is a summary of the congressionally mandated study, and it was prepared by Abt Associates, Inc., under a grant from the Office of Juvenile Justice and Delinquency, Office of Justice Programs, U.S. Department of Justice.

83. "Crowding of Juvenile Facilities," p. 5.

84. Snyder and Sickmund, *Juvenile Offenders and Victims*, pp. 186–198.

85. Melissa Sickmund, Office of Juvenile Justice and Delinquency Prevention, *Juvenile Residential Facility Census, 2000: Selected Findings* (Washington, D.C.: U.S. Department of Justice, December 2002), p. 1.

86. *Juvenile Offenders and Victims: 2006 National Report*, Office of Juvenile Justice and Delinquency Prevention, http://www.ojp.usdoj.gov/bjs, accessed 15 July 2006.

87. "Abuse Cited at Mississippi Youth Correctional Education Centers," *Correctional Educational Bulletin* 6, no. 12 (19 August 2003): n.p.

88. Ibid.

89. "Justice Department Reaches Settlement Regarding Conditions at Two Indiana Juvenile Justice Facilities," *Justice Department Documents and Publications* (8 February 2006), n.p.

90. "Justice Department Reaches Settlement Regarding Conditions at the Hawaii Youth Correctional Facility," *Justice Department Documents and Publications* (8 February 2006), n.p.

91. O'Connor v. Donaldson, 422 U.S. 563 (1975).

92. Shookoff v. Adams, 750 F.Supp. 288 (M.D.Tenn. 1990), *aff'd. sub nom.*, 969 F.2d 228 (6th Cir. 1992). The U.S. Supreme Court case on which the decision relies concerns the right of adult offenders to access to courts. See Bounds v. Smith, 430 U.S. 817 (1977).

93. "Imprisoned Youth at High Risk for Viral Hepatitis," *Hepatitis Weekly* (14 May 2001), n.p.

94. "Teachers Must Handle Mental Health Students with Care," *Correctional Educational Bulletin* 4, no. 11 (30 July 2001): n.p.

95. See, for example, Richard G. Wiebush, "Juvenile Intensive Supervision: The Impact on Felony Offenders Diverted from Institutional Placement," *Crime & Delinquency* 39 (January 1993): 68–89.

96. *Respite Care: A Promising Response to Status Offenders at Risk of Court-Ordered Placements* (New York: The Vera Institute of Justice, 2003), as cited in "'Respite Care' Helping Runaways and Other Status Offenders," *Criminal Justice Newsletter* (16 January 2003), p. 3.

97. "Researchers Conducting Review of Juvenile Aftercare Programs," *Criminal Justice Newsletter* (15 October 2003): 6–7, referring to the OJJDP publication, *Aftercare Services*

(NCJ-201800), available from the Juvenile Justice Clearinghouse, Box 6000, Rockville MD 20849-6000.

98. The National Advisory Commission on Criminal Justice Standards and Goals, *Corrections* (Washington, D.C.: U.S. Government Printing Office, 1973), p. 350.

99. Ibid., pp. 350–352.

100. *Time* (30 August 1976), p. 63.

101. Alden D. Miller et al., "The Aftermath of Extreme Tactics in Juvenile Justice Reform: A Crisis Four Years Later," in *Corrections and Punishment*, ed. David F. Greenberg, *Sage Criminal Justice System Annuals* (Beverly Hills, Calif.: Sage Publications, 1977), p. 245.

102. Yitzhak Bakal, "Reflections: A Quarter Century of Reform in Massachusetts Youth Corrections," *Crime & Delinquency* 44 (January 1998): 110–116; quotation is on p. 116.

103. Maynard L. Erickson, "Schools for Crime?" *Journal of Research in Crime and Delinquency* 15 (January 1978): 32–33; Death Penalty Information Center, "Fact Sheet," http://www.deathpenaltyinfo.org/FactSheet.pdf, accessed 8 April 2007.

104. "Overview of Those Under Juvenile Death Sentences," Death Penalty Information Center, referring to Victor L. Streib, "The Juvenile Death Penalty Today," http://www.deathpenaltyinfo.org/article.php?did=2048scid=27#streibstats, accessed 25 July 2006.

105. Eddings v. Oklahoma, 455 U.S. 104 (1982).

106. Baldwin v. Alabama, 472 U.S. 372 (1985).

107. Thompson v. Oklahoma, 487 U.S. 815 (1988); Trop v. Dulles, 356 U.S. 86, 101 (1958) (plurality opinion).

108. Thompson v. Oklahoma, 487 U.S. 815 (1988).

109. Stanford v. Kentucky, 492 U.S. 361 (1989).

110. Stanford v. Parker, 2001 U.S. App. LEXIS 26419 (6th Cir. 2001), *cert. denied*, 537 U.S. 831 (2002).

111. "3 Justices Call for Reviewing Death Sentences for Juveniles," *New York Times* (30 August 2002), p. 1; Patterson v. Cockrell, 2002 U.S. App. LEXIS 6396 (5th Cir. 2002), *cert. denied*, 536 U.S. 967 (2002).

112. Hain v. Mullin, 852 P.2d 744 (Okla. Crim. App. 1993), *cert. denied*, 537 U.S. 1173 (2003).

113. "High Court Passes on Local Case: Activists Sought Ruling on Killers Younger than 18," *Houston Chronicle* (21 October 2003), p. 17. The case is Williams v. Texas, 540 U.S. 969 (2003).

114. "Despite Upcoming Supreme Court Argument, Texas Schedules Execution Dates for Four Juvenile Offenders," Death Penalty Information Center (13 February 2004), http://www.deathpenaltyinfo.org/article.php?did=878&scid=64. The case is Roper v. Simmons, 543 U.S. 551 (2005).

115. Merlo, "Juvenile Justice at the Crossroads," p. 657.

116. Barry C. Feld, "The Punitive Juvenile Court and the Quality of Procedural Justice: Disjunctions between Rhetoric and Reality," *Crime & Delinquency* 36 (October 1989): 443.

117. Robert O. Dawson, "The Future of Juvenile Justice: Is It Time to Abolish the System?" *Journal of Criminal Law and Criminology* 81 (Spring 1990): 136–155.

Selected Amendments to the U.S. Constitution

Amendment I (1791)

Congress shall make no law respecting an establishment of religion, or prohibiting the free exercise thereof; or abridging the freedom of speech, or of the press; or the right of the people peaceably to assemble, and to petition the Government for a redress of grievances.

Amendment IV (1791)

The right of the people to be secure in their persons, houses, papers, and effects, against unreasonable searches and seizures, shall not be violated, and no Warrants shall issue, but upon probable cause, supported by Oath or affirmation, and particularly describing the place to be searched, and the persons or things to be seized.

Amendment V (1791)

No person shall be held to answer for a capital, or otherwise infamous crime, unless on a presentment or indictment of a Grand Jury, except in cases arising in the land or naval forces, or in the Militia, when in actual service in time of War or public danger; nor shall any person be subject for the same offence to be twice put in jeopardy of life or limb; nor shall be compelled in any criminal case to be a witness against himself, nor be deprived of life, liberty, or property, without due process of law; nor shall private property be taken for public use, without just compensation.

Amendment VI (1791)

In all criminal prosecutions, the accused shall enjoy the right to a speedy and public trial, by an impartial jury of the State and district wherein the crime shall have been committed, which district shall have been previously ascertained by law, and to be informed of the nature and cause of the accusation; to be confronted with the witnesses against him; to have compulsory process for obtaining witnesses in his favor, and to have the Assistance of Counsel for his defence.

Amendment VIII (1791)

Excessive bail shall not be required, nor excessive fines imposed, nor cruel and unusual punishments inflicted.

Amendment X (1791)

The powers not delegated to the United States by the Constitution, nor prohibited by it to the States, are reserved to the States respectively, or to the people.

Amendment XIV (1868)

Section 1. All persons born or naturalized in the United States, and subject to the jurisdiction thereof, are citizens of the United States and of the State wherein they reside. No State shall make or enforce any law which shall abridge the privileges or immunities of citizens of the United States; nor shall any State deprive any person of life, liberty, or property, without due process of law; nor deny to any person within its jurisdiction the equal protection of the laws.

   Section 5. The Congress shall have power to enforce, by appropriate legislation, the provisions of this article.

How to Read a Court Citation

Pugh v. Locke, 406 F.Supp. 318 (M.D.Ala. 1976), *aff'd., remanded,* Newman v. Alabama, 559 F.2d 283 (5th Cir. 1977), *reh'g. denied,* 564 F.2d 97 (5th Cir. 1977), *and rev'd. in part sub nom.,* 438 U.S. 781 (1978), *later proceeding sub nom.,* 466 F.Supp. 628 (M.D.Ala. 1979), *later proceeding,* 688 F.2d 1312 (11th Cir. 1982), *cert. denied,* 460 U.S. 1083 (1983), *later proceeding sub nom.,* 740 F.2d 1513 (11th Cir. 1984), *dismissed,* 1988 U.S.Dist LEXIS 18634 (M.D.Ala., 28 December 1988).

The preceding case has a number of citations, and that is not common among all cases but is common among cases involving unconstitutional conditions in prisons and jails. The case is used here because it illustrates so many elements of case citations, some of which are omitted because of their length.

Original Citation

[Pugh v. Locke][1] [406][2] [F.Supp.][3] [318][4] [M.D.Ala.][5] [1976][6].

1. Name of case.
2. Volume number of reporter in which case is published.
3. Name of reporter; see "Abbreviations for Commonly Used Reporters for Court Cases."
4. Page in the reporter where the decision begins.
5. Court deciding the case.
6. Year decided.

Additional Case History

[*aff'd., remanded*][7] [Newman v. Alabama][8] [559][9] [F.2d][10] [283][11] [(5th Cir. 1977)][12] [*and rev'd., in part*][13] [438][14] [U.S.][15] [781][16] [1978][17] [*later proceeding*] or [*later proceeding*][18] [*cert. denied*][19] [*dismissed*][20]

7. Affirmed and remanded (sent back for further proceedings). The appellate court told the lower court that it agreed with part of its decision but that some aspect of the decision needed to be reconsidered.
8. The name under which the case was affirmed and remanded. In some cases, the name will be omitted, and the citation will carry the notation *sub nom.,* which means "by another name." That occurs in this case several times, but they are omitted here.
9. Volume number of the reporter in which case is published.

10. Abbreviated name of reporter (Federal Reporter Second Series).
11. Page number on which the opinion begins.
12. The court deciding the case and the date the decision was given.
13. Additional history—appeal to U.S. Supreme Court, which reversed the lower court in part, under another name.
14. Volume number of reporter in which Supreme Court decision is published.
15. Abbreviated name of reporter.
16. Page number on which Supreme Court decision begins.
17. Year in which Supreme Court decided the case.
18. The case had a later proceeding under a different name before the Middle District of Alabama court (in 1979) and another before the Eleventh Circuit in 1982.
19. The U.S. Supreme Court refused to grant *certiorari;* thus, the case was not heard by that Court.
20. The case was dismissed by the Middle District of Alabama court in 1988.

Abbreviations for Commonly Used Reporters for Court Cases

Decisions of the U.S. Supreme Court

> S.Ct.: Supreme Court Reporter
> U.S.: United States Reports

Decisions from Other Courts: A Selected List

> A., A.2d: Atlantic Reporter, Atlantic Reporter Second Series
> Cal.Rptr: California Reporter
> F.2d: Federal Reporter Second Series
> F.3d: Federal Reporter Third Series
> F.Supp: Federal Supplement
> N.Y.S.2d: New York Supplement Second Series
> N.W., N.W.2d: North Western Reporter, North Western Reporter Second Series
> N.E., N.E.2d: North Eastern Reporter, North Eastern Reporter Second Series
> P., P.2d: Pacific Reporter, Pacific Reporter Second Series
> S.E., S.E.2d: South Eastern Reporter, South Eastern Reporter Second Series

Definitions

Aff'd. Affirmed. The appellate court agrees with the decision of the lower court.

Aff'd. per curium Affirmed by the courts. The opinion is written by the court instead of by one of the judges. A decision affirmed but without a written opinion.

Aff'd. sub nom Affirmed under a different name. The case at the appellate level has a different name from that of the trial court level.

Cert. denied *Certiorari* denied. The U.S. Supreme Court refuses to hear and decide the case. Some state supreme courts use this terminology; others use review denied.

Concurring opinion An opinion agreeing with the court's decision but offering different reasons.

Dismissed The court dismissing the case from legal proceedings, thus refusing to give further consideration to any of its issues.

Dissenting opinion An opinion disagreeing with the reasoning and result of the majority opinion.

Later proceeding Any number of issues could be decided in a subsequent proceeding.

Reh'g. denied Rehearing denied. The court's refusal to rehear a case.

Remanded The appellate court sending a case back to the lower court for further action.

Rev'd. Reversed, overthrown, set aside, made void. The appellate court reverses the decision of the lower court.

Rev'd. and remanded Reversed and remanded. The appellate court reverses the decision and sends the case back for further action.

Vacated Abandoned, set aside, made void. The appellate court sets aside the decision of the lower court.

Glossary

A

Acquittal   Legal verification of the innocence of a person in a criminal trial.

Adjudication   The process of decision making by a court. Normally used to refer to juvenile proceedings. The term is also used to refer to rule enforcement by administrative agencies.

Administrative law   Rules and regulations made by agencies to which power has been delegated by a state legislature or by the U.S. Congress. Administrative agencies investigate and decide cases concerning potential violations of these rules.

Adversary system   One of two primary systems for settling disputes in court. The accused is presumed to be innocent. A defense attorney and a prosecuting attorney attempt to convince a judge or a jury of their versions of the case. *See also* **Inquisitory system**.

Aftercare   The continued supervision of juveniles after they are released from a correctional facility. Similar to the term *parole* in adult criminal court systems.

Aggravated assault   Technically, an assault is a threat to commit a battery, but often, the term is used to refer to a battery. Aggravated assault involves a battery inflicted by use of a deadly weapon.

Aggravating circumstances   Circumstances that are above and beyond those required for the crime but that make the crime more serious. May be used in reference to many crimes, but the concept is critical particularly in capital punishment cases, where it is required.

AIDS (acquired immune deficiency syndrome)   A deadly disease that attacks the immune system. It is communicated through exchange of body fluids, especially during sexual activity and blood transfusions, but it can also be transmitted in other ways.

Anticipatory search warrant   A warrant that is issued for a search at a particular place at a particular time *in the future*. It is based on evidence of a *triggering* event that gives probable cause to believe that the evidence, contraband, or fugitive will be at that place at that time.

Appeal   The stage in a judicial proceeding in which a higher court is asked to review a decision of a lower court.

Appellant   The losing party in a lower court, who seeks a review of the decision by a higher appellate court.

Appellee   The winning party in a lower court, who argues on appeal against reversing the lower court's decision.

Arraignment   A hearing before a judge, during which the defendant is identified, hears the formal reading of the charges, is read his or her legal rights, and enters a plea to the charges.

Arrest   The act of taking an individual into custody in order to make a criminal charge against that person.

Arson   The willful and malicious burning of the structure of another with or without the intent to defraud. Burning of one's own property with the intent to defraud is included in some definitions. Many modern statutes carry a more severe penalty for the burning of a dwelling than of other real property.

Assigned counsel   An attorney appointed by and paid for by the court to represent a defendant who does not have funds to retain a private attorney.

Attempt   In criminal law, refers to a crime that may be defined as involving a *substantial* step toward the commission of a crime, combined with the *intent* to commit that crime.

Attendant circumstances   Facts surrounding a crime that are considered to be a part of that crime and that must be proved along with the elements of the crime.

B

Baby Moses laws   Provisions for protecting mothers (or fathers) who abandon their newborn children in ways that will protect those infants. These laws are becoming more common in the United States as well as some other countries. Normally, the laws permit new parents to leave the babies in designated *safe places* and avoid prosecution.

Bail   Money or property posted to guarantee that the defendant will appear for a legal proceeding, such as a trial, sentencing, or imprisonment. If the defendant does not appear, the court may require that the money or property be forfeited.

Beyond a reasonable doubt   The standard for evidence required for a conviction in an adult criminal court or a juvenile court. A lack of uncertainty. The facts presented to the judge or jury are sufficient to lead a reasonable person to conclude without question that the defendant committed the act for which he or she is charged.

Bond   A written document indicating that the defendant or his or her sureties assure the presence of that defendant at a criminal proceeding and that, if the defendant is not present, the court may require that the security posted for the bond be forfeited.

Booking   The official recording of the name, photograph, and fingerprints of a suspect, along with the offense charged and the name of the officer who made the arrest.

Bow Street Runners   The mid-18th-century London system that gave the police powers of investigation and arrest to constables who were given some training and paid a portion of the fines in successfully prosecuted cases.

Bureau of Justice Statistics (BJS)   A federal agency authorized by Congress to collect and analyze crime data based on surveys of the general population, who are questioned about crime victimizations.

Burglary   The illegal or forcible entering of any enclosed structure in order to commit a crime, usually theft. Some jurisdictions require that the intent be to commit a felony rather than a less serious crime.

C

Capital punishment Punishment by death for those convicted of capital crimes.

Case law Legally binding court interpretations of written laws or rules made by the courts. *See also* **Common law**.

Castration Removal of the testes in the male or the ovaries in the female. In earlier times, castration was used as a punishment for male rape offenders. In recent times, some courts have ordered chemical castration of sex offenders. This process involves using female hormones to alter the male's chemical balance to reduce his sex drive and potency.

Causation In criminal law, the requirement that the act be the *cause* of the harmful consequence.

Certification The process used to remove juveniles from the jurisdiction of the juvenile court to that of the adult criminal court. Also called *transfer* or *waiver*.

Circumstantial evidence Evidence that may be inferred from a fact or a series of facts. *See also* **Direct evidence**.

Civil law Distinguished from criminal law as that law pertaining to private rights.

Civil rights Sometimes called *civil liberties*. All the natural rights guaranteed by the U.S. Constitution (or by individual state constitutions), such as free speech and the right to religious beliefs and practices. Also the body of law concerning natural rights.

Classification The assignment of new inmates to the housing, security status, and treatment programs that best fit their individual needs.

Commissary The prison store, as well as the incidental items sold to inmates. Also, an inmate's account, which is debited when an item is purchased.

Common law Broadly defined, the legal theory and law that originated in England and is also common in the United States. More specifically, common law consists of the guidelines, customs, traditions, and judicial decisions that courts use in decision making. It is contrasted with *constitutions* and *written laws*.

Community-based correctional facility A facility in which the punishment emphasizes assimilation into the community. Instead of imprisonment, the offender may be put on probation or placed in programs such as work release, foster homes, halfway houses, parole, and furlough.

Community-oriented prosecution Similar to community-oriented policing, utilizes a more integrated, solution-based approach to crime, going beyond traditional criminal justice systems to look at such issues as quality of life.

Community work service Punishment assigning the offender to community service or work projects. Sometimes, it is combined with restitution or probation.

COMPSTAT A strategic management process acclaimed by numerous organizations today as effective in crime reduction. Utilizes computer technology and other modern management techniques to devise methods of fighting crime.

Concurrent sentence A sentence for more than one offense served at the same time. For example, if an offender receives a three-year prison term for robbery and a five-year prison term for assault, these sentences to be served concurrently, the total prison sentence is five years.

Concurring opinion A judge's written opinion agreeing with the result in a case but presenting other reasons for the decision or emphasizing some of the reasons stated by the majority opinion.

Conjugal visits Visits that permit inmates to engage in sexual and other social contacts with their spouses in an unsupervised, private setting.

Consecutive sentence A term of imprisonment for more than one offense that must be served one following the other. If an offender

receives a three-year term for robbery and a five-year term for assault, the defendant has an eight-year term.

Constable An officer of a municipal corporation who has duties similar to those of a sheriff, such as preserving the public peace, executing papers from the court, and maintaining the custody of juries.

Contempt of court An act (usually committed in violation of a court order or rule) considered as embarrassing, humiliating, or as undermining the power of the court. May be civil or criminal.

Continuance The adjournment of a trial or another legal proceeding until a later date.

Contraband Any item (such as weapons, alcohol, or other drugs), possession of which is illegal or violates prison rules.

Contract system System for providing defense attorneys in which a governmental agency contracts with a local bar association, a private law firm, or a private attorney to provide legal services for indigent defendants.

Corporal punishment Physical punishment, such as beatings or whippings.

Correctional officer (guard) A corrections employee with supervisory power over a suspect or convicted offender in custody.

Crime An illegal act of omission or commission that is punishable by criminal law.

Crime rate The number of crimes per 100,000 population.

Crimes known to the police All serious criminal offenses that have been reported to the police and for which the police have sufficient evidence to believe the crimes were committed.

Criminal A person found guilty of an act that violates criminal law.

Criminal justice system The entire system of criminal prevention, detection, apprehension, trial, sentencing, punishment, parole, probation, or other forms of supervision within the community.

Criminal law Statutes defining acts so offensive that they threaten the well-being of society and require that the government prosecute the accused. Criminal laws prescribe punishments that may be imposed on offenders.

Cross-examination The questioning of a court witness by adversary counsel after one attorney concludes the direct examination.

Cruel and unusual punishment The punishments prohibited by the Eighth Amendment to the U.S. Constitution, as interpreted by the courts. Some examples are torture, prison conditions that "shock the conscience," excessively long sentences, and the death penalty for rape but not murder of an adult woman.

Curtilage The enclosed ground and buildings immediately around a dwelling.

Custody Legal control over a person or property. Physical responsibility for a person or thing.

D

Date rape Forced sexual acts that occur during a social occasion. The alleged victim may have agreed to some intimacy but not to the activities defined in that jurisdiction as constituting the elements of rape.

Deadly force Force likely to cause serious bodily injury or death.

Defendant The person charged with a crime and against whom a criminal proceeding has begun or is pending.

Defense attorney The counsel for the defendant in a criminal proceeding, whose main function is to protect the legal rights of the accused.

Defenses Responses by the defendant in a criminal or civil case. They may consist only of a denial of the factual allegations of the prosecution (in a criminal case) or of the plaintiff (in a civil case). If the defense offers new factual allegations in an effort to negate the charges, there is an *affirmative defense*.

Delinquency *See* **Juvenile delinquent**.

Demonstrative evidence Real evidence. The kind of evidence that is apparent to the senses, in contrast to evidence presented by the testimony of other people.

De novo Literally, anew or *fresh*. A trial *de novo* is a case that is tried again, as if no decision had been previously rendered. In some jurisdictions, the first appeal from a lower court may be a trial *de novo*. The term may be used to refer to other proceedings, such as hearings.

Department of Homeland Security (DHS) The cabinet-level department created after the 9/11 terrorist attacks. Its creation constituted the most extensive federal government reorganization in 50 years. It combines 22 federal agencies and constitutes the third largest federal agency.

Deposition Oral testimony taken from the opposing party or a witness for the opposing party. Depositions are taken out of court but under oath. They are recorded verbatim, usually by a court reporter. Attorneys for both sides are present. Depositions may be used when the deposed is not able to appear in court. They may also be used to impeach the testimony of a witness in court.

Deprivation model A model of prisonization based on the belief that the prison subculture stems from the way inmates adapt to the severe psychological and physical losses imposed by imprisonment. *See also* **Importation model**.

Detention *See* **Pretrial detention**.

Detention centers Facilities for the temporary confinement of persons (such as juveniles) in custody who are awaiting court disposition.

Determinate sentence A sentence for a specific crime and determined by the legislature. The parole board, correctional officials, or a judge cannot make changes in the sentence length. In some jurisdictions, the trial judge may have the power to suspend the sentence or to impose probation rather than the legislatively specified prison term.

Deterrence A punishment philosophy based on the assumption that the acts of potential offenders can be prevented. *Individual deterrence* refers to the prevention of additional criminal acts by the specific individual being punished. *General deterrence* refers to the presumed effect that punishing one offender will have on other potential offenders.

Dicta The written portions of a judge's opinion that are not part of the actual ruling of the court and are not legally binding precedents for future court decisions.

Directed verdict Upon a finding of insufficient evidence to convict a defendant, the judge may direct the jury to return a verdict of not guilty. The judge may not direct a verdict of guilty.

Direct evidence Evidence offered by an eyewitness who testifies to what he or she saw, heard, tasted, smelled, or touched.

Direct examination The examination of a witness, which is conducted by the attorney who called the witness to testify.

Discovery A legal motion requesting the disclosure of information held by the opposing counsel and intended for use in the forthcoming trial.

Discretion In the criminal justice system, authority to make decisions based on one's own judgment rather than on specified rules. The result may be inconsistent handling of offenders, as well as positive actions tailored to individual circumstances.

Disposition The final decision of a court in a criminal proceeding to accept a guilty plea, to find the defendant guilty or not guilty, or to terminate the proceedings against the defendant.

Diversion The final decision of a court in a criminal or juvenile proceeding to accept a guilty plea, to find the accused guilty or not guilty, or to terminate the proceedings against the accused.

Domestic violence The causing of serious physical harm or the threatening of such harm to a member of one's family or household, including spouses, ex-spouses, parents, children, persons otherwise related by blood, persons living in the household, or persons who lived there formerly. May include relationships of persons who do not live together but who have had or currently have intimate relationships, such as courtship.

Due process The constitutional principle that a person should not be deprived of life, liberty, or property without reasonable and lawful procedures that must be made available in any criminal proceeding, including postconviction procedures, such as prison disciplinary hearings or parole revocations.

E

Equal protection All persons under like circumstances must receive essentially the same treatment in the criminal justice system; they may not be discriminated against because of race or ethnicity, gender, minority status, disability, or religion.

Exclusionary rule Evidence secured as the result of illegal actions by law enforcement officers should be excluded from a legal proceeding, such as a trial.

Expert witness A person with extensive training or education in a particular field, such as medicine, who testifies at depositions or at trials concerning a critical issue of that case, such as what caused the death of the deceased.

F

Federal Bureau of Investigation (FBI) A federal agency established in 1908 and delegated the power to investigate all federal laws (unless they are otherwise assigned to another agency). The FBI investigates alleged civil, criminal, and securities violations. Although the agency is a federal one, it can, when invited, assist local and state law enforcement agencies.

Felony A serious offense, such as murder, armed robbery, or rape. Punishment ranges from execution to imprisonment in a state or federal institution but also includes probation, community work service, fines, and other less punitive sanctions, as well as a combination of these measures.

Fetal abuse The abusing of a fetus, which may or may not lead to its death. In some jurisdictions, any resulting injury may lead to legal culpability. In a few states, killing a fetus may result in murder charges.

Fine The payment of a sum of money to a court by the convicted defendant in addition to or instead of other punishment(s).

Fleeing felon rule The common law rule that permitted police to shoot at any fleeing felon. The rule has been modified to require circumstances involving (1) the threat of serious injury to or death of an officer or others, (2) the prevention of an escape if the suspect threatens the officer with a gun, or (3) the officer having probable cause to believe that the suspect has committed or has threatened to commit serious bodily harm.

Frankpledge system In old English law, a system whereby the members of a tithing had corporate responsibility for the behavior of all members over 14 years old. Ten tithings formed a hundred, and hundreds were later combined to form shires, similar to counties, over which a sheriff had jurisdiction.

Frisk An action by a law enforcement officer or a correctional officer consisting of patting down or running one's hands quickly over a person's body to determine whether the suspect or inmate has a weapon or other contraband. This is in contrast to a body search, which is a more careful and thorough examination of the person.

Furlough An authorized, temporary leave from a prison or other penal facility in order to attend a funeral, visit the family, attempt to secure employment, or engage in any other approved activity.

G

General deterrence *See* **deterrence**.

Good faith exception The provision that illegally obtained evidence will not be excluded from a subsequent trial if it can be shown that police officers secured the evidence in good faith, meaning that they had a reasonable belief that they were acting in accordance with the law.

Good time credit Credit resulting in a reduction of prison time. Awarded for satisfactory behavior in prison.

Grand jury A group of citizens, convened by legal authority, who evaluate evidence to ascertain whether a crime has been committed and whether there is sufficient evidence against the accused to justify prosecution. If so, the grand jury may return an indictment. In some jurisdictions, grand juries are empowered to conduct investigations into alleged criminal activities.

H

Habeas corpus Technically, a written court order requiring that the accused be taken to court to determine the legality of custody and confinement. Also refers to writs that inmates file regarding the alleged illegality of their confinement or the conditions of that confinement.

Hands off doctrine A policy that courts use to justify nonintervention in the daily administration of corrections agencies.

Harmless error A minor or trivial error not deemed sufficient to harm the rights of the parties who assert the errors. Cases are not reversed on the basis of harmless errors.

Hate crime As defined in the federal criminal code, a crime "that manifests evidence of prejudice based on race, religion, disability, sexual orientation, or ethnicity, including where appropriate the crimes of murder, nonnegligent manslaughter, forcible rape, aggravated assault, simple assault, intimidation, arson, and destruction, damage or vandalism of property."

Hearsay evidence Secondhand evidence of which the witness does not have personal knowledge but merely repeats what the witness says he or she heard another person say. Hearsay evidence must be excluded from a trial unless it meets one of the exceptions to the hearsay rule.

House arrest A form of confinement, usually on probation or parole, in which the offender is permitted to live at home (or some other approved place) but is restricted in his or her movements to and from the area. A curfew may be imposed, and the offender may be subject to unannounced visits from a probation or parole officer. In some cases, electronic devices are used to monitor the person's location.

Humanitarianism In penal philosophy, the doctrine advocating the removal of harsh, severe, and painful conditions in penal institutions.

Hundred In English law, a combination of 10 tithings as part of the frankpledge system. *See also* **Tithing** and **Frankpledge system.**

I

Identity theft The stealing of an individual's Social Security number or other important information about his or her identity and using that information to commit crimes, such as removing funds from the victim's bank account.

Importation model A model based on the assumption that the inmate subculture arises not only from internal prison experiences but also from the external patterns of behavior the inmates bring into prison. *See also* **Deprivation model.**

Incapacitation A punishment theory usually implemented by imprisoning an offender to prevent the commission of any other crimes by that person. In some countries (and in earlier days in the United States), incapacitation involved mutilation, such as removing the hands of thieves and castrating sex offenders.

Incarceration Imprisonment in a jail, a prison, or another type of penal institution.

Indeterminate sentence A sentence to confinement without a definite term. Parole boards or professionals determine when the offender should be released.

Index offenses The FBI's *Uniform Crime Reports* of the occurrences of the eight crimes considered most serious: murder and nonnegligent manslaughter, forcible rape, robbery, aggravated assault, burglary, larceny-theft, motor vehicle theft, and arson. In June 2004, the FBI discontinued publishing data according to index offenses because of the misrepresentation of crime in an area that can be caused by a very high (or low) volume or rate of only one of these serious crimes in that area.

Indictment The written accusation of a grand jury, formally stating that probable cause exists to believe that the suspect committed a specified felony.

Individual deterrence *See* **Deterrence.**

Inevitable discovery rule Evidence secured illegally by police will not be excluded from the suspect's trial, provided it can be shown that the evidence would have been discovered anyway under legal means.

Informant A person who gives information to law enforcement officials about a crime or planned criminal activity.

Information A formal written document used to charge a person with a specific offense. Prosecutors issue informations, in contrast to *indictments*, which are issued by grand juries.

Initial appearance The first appearance of the accused before a magistrate. If the accused is detained in jail immediately after arrest, he or she must be taken quickly to a magistrate for the initial appearance. At that point, the magistrate decides whether there is probable cause to detain the suspect and, if so, tells the suspect of the charges and of his or her constitutional rights, including the right to an attorney.

Injunction A prohibitive remedy issued by a court and ordering someone or an agency to do something or stop doing something; based on a request by a party who petitions the court for the relief. There are several kinds of injunctions, including those that are preliminary (effective until a further decision), partial, temporary, or permanent.

Inmates Convicted persons whose freedom has been replaced by confinement in a prison, mental ward, or similar institution.

Inquisitory system One of two primary systems for settling disputes in court, in which defendants must prove their innocence, in contrast to the adversary system, which has a presumption of innocence, requiring the state (or federal prosecutors in federal cases) to prove a defendant's guilt beyond a reasonable doubt.

Intake decision In prosecution, the first review of a case by an official in the prosecutor's office. Weak cases may be weeded out at this stage. In juvenile courts, the reception of a juvenile against whom complaints have been made. The decision to dismiss or proceed with a case is made at this stage.

Intensive probation supervision (IPS) Close and intensive supervision of probationers by probation officers, presumably with small caseloads.

INTERPOL A world police organization that was established for the purpose of cooperation among nations in common policing problems.

Interrogatories A set of questions given to a party thought to have pertinent information that may be used at a trial or other legal proceeding. The party completing the interrogatories must sign an oath that the statements are correct.

Intimate partner violence Violence toward a current or former spouse, girlfriend, or boyfriend.

J

Jail A local, regional, or federal facility used to confine persons awaiting a legal proceeding, as well as those serving short sentences.

Judge An elected or appointed officer of the court who presides over a court of law. The final and neutral arbiter of law who is responsible for all activities within that court system.

Judicial review The authority of an appellate court to check the decisions of lower courts as well as those within the executive and legislative branches of government within its jurisdiction to determine whether any of those acts are in violation of statutes or constitutions. Also, the power of an appellate court to review the actions of a trial court or a lower appellate court.

Jurisdiction The lawful exercise of authority. The area within which authority may be exercised, such as the geographical area within which a particular police force has authority. Courts may have *original jurisdiction* to hear a case. If more than one court has authority to hear the same case, those courts have *concurrent jurisdiction*. *Exclusive jurisdiction* means that only one court may hear the case. *Appellate jurisdiction* is the power of a court to hear a case on appeal.

Jury In a criminal case, a group of people who have been sworn in to listen to the evidence during a trial and to decide whether the defendant is guilty or not guilty. In some jurisdictions, a jury may recommend or even determine the sentence.

Just deserts The belief that those who commit crimes should suffer for those crimes. Also, the amount or type of punishment a particular offender deserves to receive.

Juvenile A young person under age for certain privileges, such as voting or drinking alcoholic beverages. If accused of a criminal or juvenile offense, a juvenile usually is not tried by an adult criminal court but is processed in the juvenile court.

Juvenile court The court having jurisdiction over juveniles who are accused of delinquent acts or offenses or criminal acts or who are in need of supervision because they are being neglected or mistreated by their parents or guardians.

Juvenile delinquent A person under legal age (the maximum age varies among the states from 16 to 21, but 18 is the most common) whom a juvenile court has determined to be incorrigible or in violation of a criminal statute.

L

Larceny-theft The unlawful removal and taking away of someone else's property with the intention of keeping it permanently. Historically, small thefts were categorized as *petit larceny* and large thefts as *grand larceny*. The latter was punished by the death penalty, a punishment no longer permitted for larceny-theft in the United States. Some modern theft laws do not distinguish between the two types of larceny-theft.

Law Enforcement Assistance Administration (LEAA) The agency, established by Congress in 1965, that provided funding for the development of police departments, police techniques, police education, and police training. It was abolished in 1982. Money for education was provided through the Law Enforcement Education Program (LEEP).

Law Enforcement Education Program (LEEP) *See* **Law Enforcement Assistance Administration (LEAA)**.

Legal duty An obligation to another that is imposed by law, such as the duty of a parent to go to the rescue of his or her child.

Lineup A procedure in which a group of people are placed together in a line to allow the complainant or an eyewitness to identify the alleged offender.

M

Magistrate A judge from the lower courts of the state or federal court system. Usually, magistrates preside over arraignments, preliminary hearings, bail hearings, and minor offenses.

Mala in se Actions that are intrinsically immoral, such as murder, forcible rape, and robbery.

Mala prohibita Actions that are wrong because legislation prohibits them, although there may not be general agreement that they are wrong in themselves, such as the possession of small amounts of marijuana.

Mandatory sentence A sentence having a length imposed by the legislature, with no discretion given to the trial judge. If the defendant is convicted, the specified sentence must be imposed.

Manslaughter The unlawful killing of a human being by a person who lacks malice. Manslaughter may be *involuntary* (or *negligent*), the result of recklessness while committing an unlawful act (such as driving while intoxicated), or *voluntary*, an intentional killing committed in the heat of passion.

Marshal A sworn law enforcement officer who performs the civil duties of the courts, such as the delivery of papers to begin civil proceedings. In some jurisdictions, marshals serve papers for the arrest of criminal suspects and escort inmates from jail to court or into the community when they are permitted to leave the jail or prison temporarily. Marshals may also transport offenders from one jurisdiction to another, escort fugitives from their places of capture to the jurisdictions in which they will be tried, provide security for designated persons, or fly on planes as an added security measure.

Mens rea The criminal intent of the accused at the time the criminal act is committed.

Miranda warning The rule, stemming from *Miranda v. Arizona*, that stipulates that anyone in custody for an offense that might result in a jail or prison term must be warned of certain rights before being questioned by law enforcement officials. These rights include the right to remain silent, to be told that anything said can and will be held against the suspect, the right to counsel (which will be appointed if the suspect cannot afford to retain private counsel), and the right to cease talking at any time. If the warning is not given or is given and violated, any information obtained from the suspect may be inadmissible as evidence at trial. The rights may be waived if done so willingly and knowingly by one who has the legal capacity to waive them.

Misdemeanor A less serious offense, punishable by a fine, probation, or a short jail term, in contrast to a felony, a more serious crime.

Mistrial A trial that cannot stand, that is invalid. Judges may call a mistrial for such reasons as an error on the part of the prosecution or the defense, the illness or death of any of the parties participating in the legal proceedings, jury tampering, or the jury's inability to reach a verdict.

Mitigating circumstances Circumstances that do not justify or excuse a crime but that, because of justice and fairness, make the crime less reprehensible. They may be used to reduce a crime to a lesser offense, such as to reduce murder to manslaughter. Mitigating circumstances must be considered before the death penalty can be imposed. *See also* **Aggravating circumstances**.

Model Penal Code (MPC) A systematized statement of criminal law by the American Law Institute. This code is often used as the model for state criminal codes.

Molly Maguires A powerful secret police organization in the 1870s in Pennsylvania.

Moot The term used to describe a controversy that has ended or evolved to the stage at which a court decision is no longer relevant or necessary.

Motion A document submitted to the court, asking for an order or a ruling.

Motor vehicle theft The stealing of an automobile, in contrast to the stealing of an automobile part or larceny-theft *from* an automobile.

Murder The unlawful killing of another person with either express or implied malice aforethought.

N

National Crime Victimization Survey (NCVS)   Crime data collected by the Bureau of Justice Statistics (BJS) and based on surveys of people to determine who has been victimized by crime.

National Incident-Based Reporting System (NIBRS)   A reporting system used by the FBI in collecting crime data. In this system, a crime is viewed along with all of its components, including the type of victim, type of weapon, location of the crime, alcohol/drug influence, type of criminal activity, relationship of victim to offender, and residence of victims and arrestees, as well as a description of the property and its value. This system includes 22 crimes, rather than the 8 that constitute the FBI's Part I Offenses, or serious crimes.

Negligence   In law, an act that a reasonable person would not do, or would not fail to do under similar circumstances. Negligence does not require a criminal intent.

Nolo contendere   Literally, "I will not contest it." In a criminal case, this plea has the legal effect of a guilty plea, but the plea cannot be used against the defendant in a civil action based on the same act. The plea might be used in a case involving a felony charge of driving while intoxicated. A guilty plea could be used as evidence of liability in a civil action of wrongful death filed by the family of the victim who died in the accident, whereas a *nolo* plea requires that the plaintiff in the civil action *prove* liability.

Norms   The rules or standards of behavior, shared by members of a social group, that define appropriate behavior.

O

Offenders   Persons who have committed a criminal offense.

Open prison   A prison that makes use of the natural environment for security. For example, the prison might be located on an island surrounded by treacherous waters, as in the case of Alcatraz, located in San Francisco Bay and once used as a maximum-security federal prison.

P

Pardon   An act by a state governor or the U.S. president (in federal cases) that exempts a convicted offender from punishment or, in the case of those already serving terms, further punishment and removes the legal consequences of the conviction. Pardons may also be granted after a person is released from prison. They may be absolute or conditional; individual or granted to a group, or class, of offenders; and may be full or partial, in which case the pardon remits only part of the punishment or removes some of the legal disabilities resulting from the conviction.

Parens patriae   Literally, "parent of the country." The doctrine from English common law that was the basis for allowing the state to take over guardianship of a child. In the United States, the doctrine forms the basis for juvenile court jurisdiction. The doctrine presumes that the state acts in the best interests of the child.

Parole   The status of an offender who is released before the completion of a prison sentence. Usually, the parolee must be supervised in the community by a parole officer.

Parole board   A panel at the state or federal level that decides whether an inmate is released on parole from a correctional institution before the expiration of his or her sentence.

Parole officer   A government employee who supervises and counsels inmates paroled to the community.

Parole revocation   The process of returning a released offender to an institution for technical violations of parole conditions or for committing a new crime.

Penitentiary   Historically, an institution intended to isolate convicted offenders from one another, giving them time to reflect on their bad acts and become penitent. Later, the term became synonymous with prison.

Peremptory challenge   A challenge that may be used by the prosecution or the defense to excuse a potential juror from the jury panel. No reason is required. Each attorney gets a specified number of peremptory challenges. Peremptory challenges are distinguished from *challenges for cause*, which are unlimited and based on a reason for disqualification, such as a conflict of interest with the case.

Petition   A formal document for filing an action in juvenile court, in contrast to a grand jury indictment or a prosecutor's presentment in the criminal court.

Petit jury   *Petit* literally means "small, minor, or inconsiderate." A trial jury, in contrast to a grand jury. *See also* **Jury**.

Plain view doctrine   The legal doctrine that permits a law enforcement officer who is legally searching a place for particular items to seize those that are in plain view but not listed on a search warrant.

Plea bargaining   The process of negotiation between the defense and the prosecution before or during the trial of a defendant. The process may involve reducing or dropping some charges or a recommendation for leniency in exchange for a plea of guilty on another charge(s). Plea bargaining may also result in no changes in the charges or sentence recommendation.

Police   A government official authorized to enforce the law, provide services, and maintain order, using physical (including deadly) force if necessary.

Posse   The rural police system in which the sheriff may call into action any number of citizens over a certain age if they are needed to assist in law enforcement.

Prejudicial errors   Errors made during legal proceedings that affect the rights of parties substantially and thus may result in the reversal of a case.

Preliminary hearing   An appearance before a lower court judge to determine whether there is sufficient evidence to submit the case to the grand jury or to the trial court. Preliminary hearings may include the bail decision.

Presentence investigation (PSI)   An investigation of the background and characteristics of the defendant. It may include information that would not be admissible at the trial. It is presented to the judge to be used in determining sentence.

Presentment   A document issued by a grand jury that states that probable cause exists to believe that the suspect committed the crime. Presentments are issued without the participation of the prosecutor. *See also* **Indictment**.

Presumption of innocence   A cornerstone of the adversary system. It provides that a defendant is innocent unless and until the prosecution proves guilt beyond a reasonable doubt.

Presumptive sentence   The normal sentence is specified by statute for each offense. Judges are permitted to deviate from that sentence but usually may do so only under specified circumstances or must give reasons for the deviation.

Pretextual stop   A stop allegedly for a minor traffic offense but actually conducted as a pretense to look for a more serious offense, such as the possession of illegal drugs.

Pretrial detention   The detention of a defendant in jail between arrest and trial, either because the judge has refused bail or the defendant cannot meet the requirements of bail. Generally the purpose is to assure the presence of the accused at trial. Also, *preventive detention* involves defendants who are detained because they are thought to present a danger to themselves, to others, or to both if released pending trial.

Preventive detention   *See* **Pretrial detention**.

Prima facie **evidence**   Evidence that, on its face, is sufficient to constitute a fact unless it is sufficiently refuted.

Prison   A federal or state penal facility for detaining adult offenders (although juvenile offenders are also incarcerated in adult facilities on occasion) sentenced to a year or longer after conviction of crimes.

Prisonization   The process of an inmate becoming accustomed to the subculture of prison life.

Private security forces   Persons employed by private agencies instead of governmental ones to provide security from criminal activity.

Proactive   In policing, preparing for, intervening in, or taking the initiative in finding criminals, rather than depending on the reports of citizens.

Probable cause   In search warrant cases, a set of facts and circumstances that leads to the reasonable belief that the items sought are located in a particular place. In arrest cases, the facts and circumstances lead to the reasonable belief that the suspect has committed a crime.

Probation   A type of sentence that places the convicted offender under the supervision of a probation officer within the community instead of in prison. Also, the part of the criminal justice system that is in charge of all aspects of probation.

Probation officer   A government official responsible for writing the presentence reports on offenders, supervising probationers, reporting violations of probation conditions, and providing evidence of those violations.

Probation revocation   The process of declaring that a sentenced offender violated the terms of probation and that probation will, as a result, be revoked or cancelled. If probation involved a suspended prison or jail sentence, the revocation may mean that the original sentence is invoked and the individual is sent to a prison or jail.

Property crimes   Crimes aimed at the property of another person rather than at the person. Serious property crimes include larceny-theft, burglary, motor vehicle theft, and arson.

Pro se   Literally, "on behalf of self." Acting as one's own attorney.

Prosecuting attorney   A government official responsible for representing the state (or federal government) against an offender in criminal proceedings.

Prosecution   The process that occurs when the state (or federal government) begins the formal process in a criminal case. The action is taken by a prosecuting attorney.

Public defender   An attorney retained and paid by the government to represent indigent defendants in criminal proceedings.

R

Racial profiling   The reaction by law enforcement officers to potential suspects based solely on their race or ethnicity.

Rape   Historically, unlawful vaginal intercourse with a woman. It is called *forcible rape* if engaged in against the will of the woman by the use of threats or force. It is called *statutory rape* if the sexual intercourse was consensual between a man and a woman who was under the age of consent. More recently, some rape statutes have been rewritten to include male victims and female perpetrators, as well as penetration of any body opening by any instrument, including but not limited to the male sexual organ.

Reactive   In policing, depending on the reports of citizens to find criminal suspects, rather than working independently. It is important because police are not in a position to observe most criminal behavior.

Recidivism   The process of committing additional crimes.

Recidivists   Offenders who commit crimes repeatedly.

Recusal   The removal of oneself from a proceeding, such as done by a judge who has a conflict of interest in a case.

Reformatory   An early corrections facility that was less physically secure and that emphasized changing or reforming the offender. Usually used to refer to an institution.

Rehabilitation   A punishment philosophy based on the belief that the offender can and will change into a law-abiding citizen through treatment programs and facilities. Rehabilitation may be most likely to occur in community-based programs rather than during incarceration in penal institutions. The *rehabilitative ideal* is embodied in probation, parole, the indeterminate sentence, and the juvenile court.

Reintegration   A punishment philosophy emphasizing the return of the offender to the community, so that employment, family ties, and education can be restored.

Restitution   Punishment that requires an offender to repay the victim with services or money. This punishment may be imposed instead of or in addition to other punishment or fines and may be a requirement of parole.

Retribution   *See* **Just deserts**.

Reversible error   An error in a legal proceeding, such as a trial, that is considered sufficient to require the reversal of a conviction or a sentence.

Right to counsel   The right to be represented by an attorney at crucial stages in the criminal justice system. Indigent defendants have the right to counsel provided by the state.

Robbery   The use of force or fear to take personal property belonging to another against that person's will.

S

Sanction   A penalty or punishment that is imposed on a person in order to enforce the law.

Search and seizure   The examination of a person or a person's property and the taking of items that may be evidence of criminal activity. It generally requires a search warrant. Unreasonable searches and seizures are prohibited.

Search warrant   *See* **Warrant**.

Self-report data (SRD)   The process of collecting crime data by asking people about their criminal activity, usually by use of anonymous questionnaires.

Sentence   The punishment that the court imposes on a convicted offender.

Sentence disparity   Inequalities and differences in sentencing as, for example, when people found guilty of the same crime receive sentences varying in length and type, without reasonable justification for those differences.

Sheriff   The chief law enforcement officer in a county, usually chosen by popular election.

Shires   *See* **Frankpledge system**.

Showup   An identification procedure during a police investigation. It involves showing the alleged victim only one person rather than several, as in a *lineup*. It is permitted only in extraordinary circumstances.

Silent system   In penitentiaries, the historical practice of not allowing offenders to speak with one another.

Social system   The interrelationship of roles, acts, and statuses of people who make up the social structure. A social group or set of interacting persons or groups considered a unitary whole because it reflects the common values, social norms, and objectives of the individuals whom it comprises, even though the group is considered distinct from those individuals.

Specific deterrence   *See* **Deterrence**.

Stare decisis   Literally, "let the decision stand." The doctrine that courts will abide by or adhere to the rulings of previous court decisions when deciding cases having substantially the same facts.

Status offense   A class of crime that does not consist of proscribed action or inaction but, rather, of the personal condition or characteristic of the accused—for example, being a vagrant. In juvenile law, a variety of acts that would not be considered criminal if committed by an adult—for example, being insubordinate or truant or running away from home.

Statute of limitations   The time limit in which to bring a charge for a crime. The statute of limitations may differ from jurisdiction to jurisdiction, but most have no limitations on filing murder charges.

Statutory law   Law that the legislature has originated and passed by a written enactment.

Statutory rape   *See* **Rape**.

Subculture   A group of significant size whose behavior differs significantly from the behavior of the dominant groups of society.

Subpoena   A command, issued by a court, ordering a person to appear in court (or at another designated place) at a specified time and place for the purpose of giving testimony on a specified issue. Persons may be ordered to bring documents pertinent to the case. That order is called a subpoena *duces tecum*.

Summons   A formal document issued by the court to notify a person that his or her presence is required in court for a particular reason at a specified time and date.

T

Theft   See **Larceny-theft**.

Three strikes and you're out   Legislation enacted in recent years and designed to impose long sentences on persons who commit three or more serious crimes.

Tithing   In English history, a system of 10 families who had responsibility for the behavior of members over the age of 14. Tithings were also important in protecting the group from outsiders.

Training school   A secure corrections facility to which juveniles are confined by court order.

Transportation   Historically, the practice of punishing criminals by exiling them to another country.

Transportation Security Administration (TSA)   A federal agency created by the Aviation and Transportation Security Act (ATSA), enacted two months after the 9/11 terrorist attacks. The TSA was developed to take over the security screening functions for all commercial flights in the United States.

Trial   In criminal law, court proceedings during which a judge, a jury, or both listen to the evidence as presented by the defense and the prosecution, and determine whether the defendant is guilty beyond a reasonable doubt or should be acquitted. *See also* **Mistrial**.

True bill   The prosecutor's indictment returned with the approval of the grand jury. After hearing the prosecutor's evidence, the grand jury determines that the indictment is accurate—that is, it is a *true bill*.

Truth in sentencing   The concept requiring that actual time served by offenders is close to the time allocated for the sentence. Many jurisdictions are establishing 85 percent as their goal, meaning that offenders may not be released for any reason until they have served 85 percent of their sentences.

U

Uniform Crime Reports (UCR)   Official crime data, collected and published by the Federal Bureau of Investigation (FBI) and based on "crimes known to the police"—crimes that are reported to or observed by the police and that the police have reason to believe were committed.

USA Patriot Act   The Uniting and Strengthening America by Providing Appropriate Tools Required to Intercept and Obstruct Terrorism Act of 2001, enacted in fall 2001 in response to the 9/11 terrorist attacks. The act expands the powers of the federal government to deal with terrorism. Some of those powers involve using wiretaps on terrorist suspects' email, telephone conversations, and use of the Internet.

V

Venue   The location of a trial. A *change of venue* is the removal of a trial from the location where it normally would be held to another location, either to avoid public pressure or to obtain an impartial jury.

Victim compensation programs   Plans for assisting crime victims in making social, emotional, and economic adjustments.

Victimology   The discipline that studies the nature and causes of victimization, as well as programs for aiding victims and preventing victimization.

Victim precipitation   The concept that a criminal act may have been brought on by the alleged victim's actions.

Vigilantism   Literally, "watchman." Action by a person who is alert and on guard, cautious, suspicious, and ready to take action to maintain and preserve peace. Actions of citizens who take the law into their own hands in an effort to catch and punish criminals.

Violent crimes   Crimes defined by the FBI's *Uniform Crime Reports* as serious crimes against a person. They include murder and nonnegligent manslaughter, robbery, forcible rape, and aggravated assault.

Voir dire   To speak the truth. The process of questioning prospective jurors to determine their qualifications and desirability for serving on a jury.

W

Waiver   The giving up of one's rights, such as the right to counsel or to a jury trial. Waivers must be made knowingly and intelligently; that is, the defendant must understand what is being relinquished. Some rights may not be waived.

Warden   Historically, the chief administrative officer in a correctional facility.

Warrant   A court-issued *writ* authorizing an officer to arrest a suspect or to search a person, personal property, or a place.

Watch system   A system charged with the duties of overseeing, patrolling, or guarding an area or a person. Watchmen were prominent in the early watch system of policing.

White-collar crime   The illegal actions of corporations or individuals, committed while pursuing their legitimate occupations. Examples are consumer fraud, bribery, and embezzlement.

Workhouse   An English institution used to confine offenders who were forced to work at unpleasant tasks. Offenders were punished physically as well. The term is used in some places today to refer to institutions that emphasize reformation or rehabilitation through work.

Work release   The release of an inmate to attend school or to work outside the institution but requiring that person to return to the institution at specified times.

Writ   An order from the court. *See also* **Writ of *certiorari*** and ***Habeas corpus***.

Writ of *certiorari*   *Certiorari* literally means "to be informed of." A *writ* is an order from a court giving authority for an act to be done or ordering that it be done. A writ of *certiorari* is used by courts that have discretion to determine which cases they will hear. Today, this writ is most commonly associated with the U.S. Supreme Court.

Case Index

Name Index

Subject Index